PHYSICIAN'S HANDBOOK

SIXTEENTH EDITION

PHYSICIAN'S HANDBOOK

MARCUS A. KRUPP, MD

Clinical Professor of Medicine
Stanford University School of Medicine, Palo Alto
Director, Palo Alto Medical Research Foundation
Palo Alto

NORMAN J. SWEET, MD

Associate Professor of Medicine
University of California School of Medicine
San Francisco

ERNEST JAWETZ, PhD, MD

Professor of Microbiology and Chairman
Department of Microbiology
Professor of Medicine, Lecturer in Pediatrics
University of California School of Medicine
San Francisco

EDWARD G. BIGLIERI, MD

Associate Professor of Medicine
University of California School of Medicine
San Francisco

Lange Medical Publications
Los Altos, California

1970

A Concise Medical Library for Practitioner and Student

Current Diagnosis & Treatment, 1970 H. Brainerd, M.A. Krupp, M.J. Chatton, S. Margen, Editors	$11.00
Review of Physiological Chemistry, 12th Edition, 1969 H.A. Harper	$7.00
Review of Medical Physiology, 4th Edition, 1969 W.F. Ganong	$7.50
Review of Medical Microbiology, 9th Edition, 1970 E. Jawetz, J.L. Melnick, E.A. Adelberg	$7.50
Review of Medical Pharmacology, 2nd Edition, 1970 F.H. Meyers, E. Jawetz, A. Goldfien	$8.50
General Urology, 6th Edition, 1969 D.R. Smith	$8.00
General Ophthalmology, 5th Edition, 1968 D. Vaughan, R. Cook, T. Asbury	$6.50
Correlative Neuroanatomy & Functional Neurology, 14th Edition, 1970 J.G. Chusid	$7.50
Principles of Clinical Electrocardiography, 7th Edition, 1970 M.J. Goldman	$7.00
Handbook of Psychiatry, 1969 P. Solomon, V.D. Patch, Editors	$7.00
Handbook of Surgery, 4th Edition, 1969 J.L. Wilson, Editor	$6.00
Handbook of Obstetrics & Gynecology, 3rd Edition, 1968 R.C. Benson	$5.50
Physician's Handbook, 16th Edition, 1970 M.A. Krupp, N.J. Sweet, E. Jawetz, E.G. Biglieri	$6.00
Handbook of Medical Treatment, 12th Edition, 1970 M.J. Chatton, S. Margen, H. Brainerd, Editors	$6.50
Handbook of Pediatrics, 8th Edition, 1969 H.K. Silver, C.H. Kempe, H.B. Bruyn	$6.00
Handbook of Poisoning: Diagnosis & Treatment, 6th Edition, 1969 R.H. Dreisbach	$6.00
Current Medical References, 6th Edition, 1970 M.J. Chatton, P.J. Sanazaro, Editors	$12.00

Preface

The Physician's Handbook is a compilation in convenient pocket-size format of diagnostic and therapeutic information and procedures that the authors feel to be of greatest daily interest and value to the student and practitioner of medicine. The Sixteenth Edition has been extensively reviewed, revised, and brought up to date.

In preparing this revision, the authors have drawn freely upon the advice and criticism of many colleagues. Though space does not permit individual acknowledgement, let each of them accept our sincere appreciation for helping us in the effort to maintain the usefulness of this volume.

Marcus A. Krupp
Norman J. Sweet
Ernest Jawetz
Edward G. Biglieri

May, 1970

Table of Contents

NOTICE

In describing medications, the authors have been careful to recommend those drug dosages that are in agreement with current official pharmacologic standards and responsible medical literature. However, all clinicians are strongly advised to refer to the drug manufacturers' product information (e.g., package inserts), especially in the case of new or infrequently prescribed medications.

THE CLINICAL EXAMINATION

The medical history is of first importance in the clinical examination. Symptoms not only stimulate the patient to see the physician but also provide information and clues which are likely to suggest or establish a diagnosis. Next in importance is observation of the patient in the course of a careful physical examination. The laboratory examination, although important, is merely an extension of the clinical examination. All components of the clinical examination must be carefully performed and correctly interpreted and correlated.

ROUTINE LABORATORY EXAMINATION*

Urine.
A freshly voided sample should be used for examination. Observe for color and appearance (see p. 109); test for reaction (pH) (see p. 111), specific gravity (see p. 112, and glucose (see p. 116). Examine unstained sediment after centrifuging urine sample for five minutes (see p. 125). If bacteria are present, note motility and check staining characteristics with Gram's stain.

Blood.
RBC (see p. 147) or hematocrit (see p. 152), WBC (see p. 155), Hgb. (see p. 146), differential smear (see p. 156), and sedimentation rate (see p. 178). Hematocrit should be taken on patients with anemia.

Serologic Tests for Syphilis.
Flocculation and complement fixation tests (according to local practice) (see p. 306).

Feces.
Observe gross appearance (see p. 277); test for occult blood (see p. 279). Examine microscopically if indicated (see p. 280).

Chest X-rays.
These should be included as part of a complete physical examination. Both anteroposterior and lateral views should be taken. In routine screenings a "minifilm" may suffice.

Pregnancy Routine.
Laboratory examination should include complete blood count, urinalysis, serologic test for syphilis, and Rh typing (see p. 174). Diagnostic tests may be performed (see p. 253).

---

*A chapter on Simplified Laboratory Procedures may be found on pp. 100 to 108.

1...

Emergency Medical Examination

The examination of the injured or unconscious patient or the patient suffering from shock, hemorrhage, or acute respiratory distress must proceed simultaneously with life-saving treatment. Detailed histories are often not available; diagnosis depends principally upon physical examination and to a lesser extent on laboratory procedures or radiologic examination.

All patients with a history or findings of trauma must be examined for internal and external injuries.

INITIAL EMERGENCY EXAMINATION AND MANAGEMENT

Ask for help. Pride may be fatal.

Initial Management.
Maintain adequate circulation and respiration.
A. Emergency Measures:
  1. Stop hemorrhage with pressure or tourniquet.
  2. Relieve asphyxia -
    a. Clear the upper air passages -
      (1) Pull the tongue forward; insert an airway.
      (2) Draw the chin forward with the patient supine by inserting the second and third fingers behind the angles of the mandibles (see p. 7).
      (3) Suction mucus or blood.
      (4) If indicated, insert an endotracheal tube or perform tracheostomy.
    b. Close sucking wounds of thorax.
    c. Institute artificial respiration or use a mechanical respirator if necessary to ensure proper ventilation.
    d. Administer oxygen if necessary.
  3. Avoid spinal cord damage in any patient suspected of back injury. Maintain normal alignment of the vertebrae both in examination and transportation. Use sand bags to immobilize cervical vertebrae.
  4. Monitor electrocardiogram, central venous pressure, and BP if indicated.

B. Follow-up Measures:
1. Examine for concealed hemorrhage into the thorax, abdomen, gastrointestinal tract, or soft tissues.
2. If indicated, arrange for administration of plasma, plasma substitutes, or blood.
3. Splint fractures before moving patient.
4. Relieve pain - Narcotics and sedatives may mask pain of diagnostic importance. Use narcotics cautiously in the presence of shock because of the danger of sudden absorption of multiple doses on recovery.
5. Insert a 14 gauge plastic intravenous catheter at once. Meticulously cleanse the site of insertion; insert the needle; take measures to prevent catheter embolus; and apply antibiotic ointment. Change to the other arm at least every 48 hours (see p. 596).
6. Draw blood for laboratory analysis.
7. Catheterize if bladder is distended or if patient is in shock.
8. Prevent aspiration.
9. Remove false teeth.
10. Protect the eyes.
11. Hyperventilate every 4 hours.
12. Turn patient frequently.

Initial Rapid Survey Examination.

A. History: (From the patient himself or from relatives, friends, bystanders, police, ambulance drivers, previous charts, other patients, other physicians.)
1. Present illness - Prodromes, onset, recent illness, progression of symptoms, environment, medicines, syringes, etc. In case of injury, elicit exact details.
2. Past history - Previous attacks, chronic illness, habits, medications, occupation. Examine patient's personal effects (diabetic or epileptic identification card, prescription labels, etc.).

B. Physical Examination:
1. Note position of body and extremities, evidence of external or internal bleeding, skin color, rate and quality of pulse and respiration, temperature, BP (both arms), state of consciousness, and unusual odors. Note neck vein distention; check pulsation in major arteries, paradoxic pulse. Look for needle marks or insect bites on skin, drugs in the mouth.
2. Head and neck - Injuries of skull and face, neck rigidity, breath aroma, appearance of pupils and reaction to light, ophthalmoscopic examination in coma, fluid or blood from ears or nose, mucous membranes of mouth, position of trachea, crepitation in the neck.
3. Chest - External evidence of injury, sucking wounds, **gentle** compression for rib fractures, flail chest, per-

cussion and auscultation for evidence of fluid, quality of breath sounds, loud murmurs, cardiac arrhythmias, increase in area of cardiac dullness.

4. Abdomen - External evidence of injury, distention, presence of rigidity or tenderness, bowel sounds. Percuss bladder and other palpable or percussable organs.

5. Back - Examine for injuries. Maintain normal alignment of vertebrae.

6. Extremities - Note position and color of extremities; ask patient to move extremities, or move passively and palpate gently for evidence of fracture. Compress the wings of the ileum, and palpate the symphysis pubis. Examine the perineum.

7. Neurologic - Deep and superficial reflexes, flaccidity or rigidity; response to pinprick or noxious stimuli. Elicit cranial nerve abnormalities when possible.

C. **Record initial and serial findings. Diagnosis often depends on changing signs.**

D. Record fluid intake and urinary output.

E. Explain to and reassure friends or family.

F. Do not neglect tetanus prophylaxis.

HEART-LUNG RESUSCITATION*
(For treatment of asphyxia or cardiac arrest.)

Phase I: First Aid (Emergency Oxygenation of the Brain). Must be instituted within 3 to 4 minutes for optimal effectiveness and to minimize permanent brain damage. **Do not wait for confirmation of suspected cardiac arrest.**

Step 1: Place patient in a supine position on a firm surface (not a bed). (A 4 × 6 foot sheet of plywood should be available at emergency care centers.)

Step 2: Tilt head backward and maintain in this hyperextended position. Keep mandible displaced forward by pulling strongly at the angle of the jaw.

If Victim Is Not Breathing:

Step 3: Clear mouth and pharynx of mucus, blood, vomitus, or foreign material.

Step 4: Separate lips and teeth to open oral airway.

Step 5: If steps 2 to 4 fail to open airway, forcibly blow air through mouth (keeping nose closed) or nose (keeping mouth closed) and inflate the lungs 3 to 5 times. Watch for chest movement. If chest movement does not occur immediately and if pharyngeal or tracheal tubes are available, use them without delay. Tracheostomy may be necessary.

---

*Modified after Safar.

Step 6:   Feel the carotid artery for pulsations.

a. If Carotid Pulsations Are Present:

Give lung inflation by mouth to mouth breathing
(keeping patient's nostrils closed) or mouth to
nose breathing (keeping patient's mouth closed)
12 to 15 times per minute - allowing about 2 seconds for inspiration and 3 seconds for expiration -
until spontaneous respirations return. Continue
as long as the pulses remain palpable and previously dilated pupils remain constricted. Bag-
mask technics for lung inflation should be reserved for experts. If pulsations cease, follow
directions as in 6b, below.

b. If Carotid Pulsations Are Absent:

Alternate cardiac compression (closed chest
cardiac massage) and pulmonary ventilation as
in 6a, above. Place the heel of one hand on the
sternum just above the xiphoid. With the heel
of the other hand on top of it, apply firm vertical
pressure sufficient to force the sternum about
2 inches downward (less in children) about once
every second. After 15 sternal compressions,
alternate with 3 to 5 deep lung inflations. Repeat
and continue this alternating procedure until it
is possible to obtain additional assistance and
more definitive care. Resuscitation must be
continuous during transportation to the hospital.
Open heart massage should be attempted only in
a hospital. When possible, obtain an Ecg., but
do not interrupt resuscitation to do so.

Phase II: Restoration of Spontaneous Circulation.

Until spontaneous respiration and circulation are restored,
there must be no interruption of artificial ventilation and
cardiac massage while steps 7 to 13 (below) are being carried out. Three basic questions must be considered at
this point:

(1) What is the underlying cause, and is it correctable?
(2) What is the nature of the cardiac arrest?
(3) What further measures will be necessary? The
physician must make plans for the assistance of
trained hospital personnel, an Ecg., a defibrillator,
and emergency drugs.

Step 7:   If a spontaneous effective heart beat is not restored after 1 to 2 minutes of cardiac compres-

sion, have an assistant give epinephrine (adrenaline), 1 mg. (1 ml. of 1:1000 or 10 ml. of 1:10,000 aqueous solution) I.V. **or** 0.5 mg. (0.5 ml. of 1:1000 aqueous solution) by the intracardiac route. Repeat dose at five- to ten-minute intervals if necessary. The intracardiac method is not without hazard.

Step 8: Promote venous return and combat shock by elevating legs, and give I.V. fluids as available and indicated. The use of firmly applied tourniquets on the extremities to occlude arteries in order to reduce the circulating bed may be of value.

Step 9: If the victim is pulseless for more than 5 minutes, give sodium bicarbonate solution, 3 to 4 Gm. per 50 ml. (1.5 to 2 Gm. per 50 ml. in children) I.V. to combat impending metabolic acidosis. Repeat every 5 to 10 minutes as indicated.

Step 10: If pulsations still do not return, suspect ventricular fibrillation. Obtain Ecg.

Step 11: If Ecg. demonstrates ventricular fibrillation, maintain cardiac massage until just before giving an external defibrillating shock of 440 to 1000 volts AC for 0.25 second with one electrode firmly applied to the skin over the apex of the heart and the other over the sternal notch. Monitor with Ecg. (A 2.5 msec., 50 to 400 watt-second DC shock is superior if a DC defibrillator is available.) If cardiac action is not restored, resume massage and repeat 3 shocks at intervals of 1 to 3 minutes. If cardiac action is reestablished but remains weak, give calcium chloride or calcium gluconate, 5 to 10 ml. (0.5 to 1 Gm.) of 10% solution I.V.; it probably should not be used in patients who have been taking digitalis.

Step 12: Thoracotomy and open heart massage may be considered (but only in a hospital) if cardiac function fails to return after all of the above measures have been used.

Step 13: If cardiac, pulmonary, and C.N.S. functions are restored, the patient should be carefully observed for shock and complications of the precipitating cause.

Phase III: Follow-up Measures.

When cardiac and pulmonary function have been reestablished and satisfactorily maintained, evaluation of C.N.S. function deserves careful consideration. Decision as to the nature and duration of subsequent treatment must be individualized. The physician must decide if he is "prolonging life" or simply "prolonging dying." Apparent C.N.S. recovery has been reported in a few patients unconscious up to a week after appropriate treatment.

Step 14: Support ventilation and circulation. Treat any other complications which might arise. Do not overlook the possibility of complications of external cardiac massage (e.g., broken ribs, ruptured viscera).

Step 15: If circulation and respiration are restored but there are no signs of C.N.S. recovery within 30 minutes, hypothermia at 30°C. for 2 to 3 days may lessen the degree of brain damage.

Step 16: Meticulous post-resuscitation care is required, particularly for the first 48 hours after recovery. Observe carefully for possible multiple cardiac arrhythmias, especially recurrent fibrillation or cardiac standstill.

TECHNIC OF CLOSED CHEST CARDIAC MASSAGE
(Heavy circle in heart drawing shows area of application of force. Circles on supine figure show points of application of electrodes for defibrillation.)

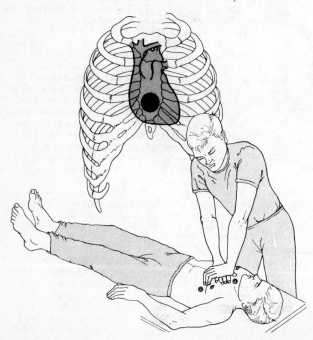

TECHNIC OF MOUTH-TO-MOUTH INSUFFLATION

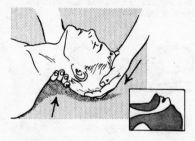

(1)

The operator takes his position at the patient's head.

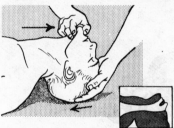

(2)

With the right thumb and index finger he displaces the mandible forward by pressing at its central portion, at the same time lifting the neck and tilting the head as far back as possible.

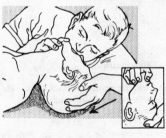

(3)

After taking a deep breath, the operator immediately seals his mouth around the mouth (or nose) of the victim and exhales until the chest of the victim rises.

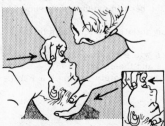

(4)

The victim's mouth is opened by downward and forward traction on the lower jaw or by pulling down the lower lip.

AIRWAY FOR USE IN MOUTH-TO-MOUTH INSUFFLATION

(The larger airway is for adults. The guard is flexible and
may be inverted from the position shown for use with infants and children.)

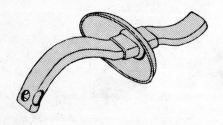

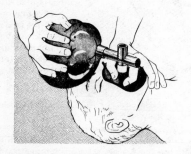

Instructions for Use of Manual Resuscitator.

1. Lift the victim's neck with one hand.
2. Tilt head backward into maximum neck extension. Remove secretions and debris from mouth and throat,
   and pull the tongue and mandible forward as required
   to clear the airway.
3. Hold the mask snugly over the nose and mouth, holding
   the chin forward and the neck in extension as shown in
   diagram.
4. Squeeze the bag, noting inflation of the lungs by the
   rise of the chest wall.
5. Release the bag, which will expand spontaneously.
   The patient will exhale and the chest will fall.
6. Repeat steps 4 and 5 approximately 12 times per minute.

COMMON CAUSES OF UNCONSCIOUSNESS

Rule out shock, hemorrhage, or cardiopulmonary arrest at once.

Brain Disease.

A. Cerebral Thrombosis: Older age group; develops slowly, commonly occurs at night; localizing neurologic signs; occasionally fever with leukocytosis; spinal fluid findings are rare; check serology for C.N.S. syphilis; moderate glycosuria may occur in either thrombosis or hemorrhage.

B. Intracerebral Hemorrhage: Hemiplegia; develops more rapidly than thrombosis and is more apt to cause unconsciousness. Hypertension, fever, and leukocytosis are often present; spinal fluid under increased pressure, and frequently contains blood.

C. Subarachnoid Hemorrhage: Sudden occipital pain followed by unconsciousness, stiff neck, and bloody spinal fluid; hypertension common; localizing neurologic signs may be absent.

D. Meningitis: Severe headache, fever, stiff neck, facial flush, rapid pulse and respiration, purpuric rash (with meningococcemia), leukocytosis, abnormal spinal fluid findings, positive blood and spinal fluid culture (see chart on p. 262).

E. Epilepsy: History of epilepsy, "epileptic identification card"; tonic and clonic convulsions followed by marked muscular relaxation, incontinence, and spontaneous recovery; signs of injury due to falling; bitten tongue. Rule out other causes of epileptiform seizures.

Systemic Diseases.

A. Diabetic Coma: History of diabetes, "diabetic identification card"; gradual onset, blurring of vision, thirst, air hunger (Kussmaul breathing), fever, rapid pulse, dehydration, soft eyeballs, retinopathy, acetone breath, red reduction (sugar) in the urine, elevated blood sugar, low serum CO_2 combining power, ketonuria and ketonemia, infection or other precipitating cause. If unable to differentiate from insulin shock, give 50% glucose I.V.

B. Hypoglycemic Shock: History of diabetes mellitus and use of insulin; "diabetic identification card"; weakness, nervousness, trembling, confusion, seizures, coma, rapid pulse, elevated BP. Blood glucose invariably below 50 mg./100 ml. No reducing substances (sugar) in the urine. Relieved by oral sweets or I.V. glucose (50 ml. of 50%).

C. Renal Azotemia (Uremia): History of nephritis; pallor; hardened arteries in a young person; deep, rapid respirations with urinous breath; hypertension; muscle twitching and convulsions; retinal hemorrhages and exudates, papilledema; anemia; low fixed specific gravity of urine, with protein and casts; serum N. P. N. usually over 100 mg./ 100 ml.

D. Hepatic Coma: History of alcoholism and malnutrition, gastrointestinal hemorrhage, use of thiazides; wasted appearance, jaundiced scleras, grayish hue to the skin, sickening sweet odor of the breath, deep and rapid respiration, spider angiomas, enlarged liver (sometimes small), abdominal collateral circulation, ascites, flapping tremor, edema.

Drug Intoxication.

A. Alcoholic Intoxication: Rule out other causes of coma. Alcohol breath, facial flushing, ocular injection, slow pulse and respiration; patients occasionally violent, may lose deep reflexes and develop positive Babinski. See p. 461 for differentiation of intoxication from alcoholic withdrawal syndrome.

B. Barbiturates: History or evidence of barbiturate ingestion, facial flushing, shallow or deep respirations; fever common; pupils usually moderately or markedly dilated; corneal and deep reflexes may be absent, with positive Babinski. Quantitative or qualitative serum or urine barbiturate tests are difficult (see p. 124), but are important for diagnosis and prognosis and in determining treatment.

C. Narcotics: Pinpoint pupils, very slow respiration, slow pulse, powder-blue spots along course of veins at sites of self-injection. Other sites of injection should be sought. Patients with cirrhosis and myxedema are very sensitive to very small doses of narcotics.

D. Bromides: Diagnosis fundamentally depends on thinking of the possibility and demonstration of high blood level. Toxic delirium common; striking cyanosis in chronic users of proprietary bromides because of combination with acetanilid; striking neurologic abnormalities with no localizing pattern occasionally occur; blood bromide level (see p. 124) usually 175 mg./100 ml. or more. Look for other causes of coma if blood level is under 100 mg./100 ml.

E. Carbon Monoxide Poisoning: History of exposure, scarlet lips and flushed cheeks, fever, 30 to 60% concentration of carboxyhemoglobin in the blood.

Other Causes.

A. Toxemia from systemic infection.

B. Drug poisoning (other than above).

C. Brain tumor or abscess.

D. Hypertensive encephalopathy.

E. Fainting (simple syncope).

F. Asphyxia.

G. Eclampsia.

H. Electrolyte imbalance syndromes.

I. Electric shock.

J. Myocardial infarction.

K. Cardiac or respiratory
   arrest.
L. Severe heart failure.
M. C. N. S. syphilis.
N. Senile cachexia.
O. Malaria.
P. Heat stroke and pros-
   tration.

Q. Encephalitis.
R. Adrenocortical insuffi-
   ciency or hypoglycemic
   shock.
S. Myxedema coma.
T. Hysteria or catatonia.
U. Status epilepticus.
V. Postictal states.

HEMORRHAGE AND SHOCK

Manifestations of Hemorrhage.

Hemorrhage may be superficial and obvious or may occur within body cavities or visceral organs, in which case diagnosis may be difficult. Arterial bleeding may lead to rapid exsanguination, and calls for immediate control and blood replacement. Blood loss in venous oozing from large surfaces may be extensive, but is slower than arterial bleeding. The general picture of severe hemorrhage is that of weakness, pallor, cold sweat, apprehension, and thirst. The pulse rate is rapid; at first full, but progressively more feeble. The BP may fall rapidly or may remain at normal levels for hours and then fall gradually or suddenly as a manifestation of hypovolemic shock. Confusion and disorientation eventually occur, and progress to coma in irreversible states. Serial hematocrits, pulse rates, and blood pressure determinations are essential for prompt diagnosis of inapparent hemorrhages following trauma. Determination of blood volume is probably the most accurate and earliest objective manifestation.

A. Intracranial Bleeding Following Trauma: Progressive increase in intracranial pressure; progressive disorientation leading to coma; focal neurologic findings, papilledema, ipsilateral pupil dilatation and fixation, elevated spinal fluid pressure (with xanthochromia or red cells), and eventually Cheyne-Stokes respiration. Fracture may be demonstrated on skull films.

B. Intrathoracic Bleeding Following Trauma: Signs of accumulation of intrapleural fluid (see p. 15).

C. Gastrointestinal Bleeding: Hematemesis, tarry stool, or a positive stool test for occult blood. (See pp. 105 and 277.)

D. Intraperitoneal Bleeding: Progressive abdominal tenderness, muscle spasm, abdominal distention, shifting dullness upon percussion, appearance of blood with four-quadrant aspiration of abdomen. (A plastic catheter of the "Jelco" or "Argyle Medicutt" type, $2^{1/2}$ in. long, is preferable.)

Shock. (See also p. 439.)
  A. Definition: "Shock" may be defined as a variable clinical
     syndrome resulting from transient or progressive dimi-
     nution of tissue perfusion due to impairment of the com-
     pensatory mechanisms of the cardiovascular system. If
     the cardiovascular system cannot compensate for criti-
     cal diminution of cardiac output, blood volume, and ve-
     nous return, inadequate tissue perfusion follows. If it
     progresses to the point of irreversible cellular changes,
     other mechanisms are activated which may progress in-
     tractably, even though the initiating cause is corrected.
  B. Classification of Shock: Although any classification of
     shock is artificial because of multiple changing mechani-
     nisms which may occur in each type, the following may
     be of value as a guide.
     1. Hypovolemic shock most commonly follows hemor-
        rhage, trauma, and dehydration, and is characterized
        by an absolute or relative diminution in blood volume.
     2. Burn shock is a form of hypovolemic shock in which
        plasma, electrolyte, and fluid loss is complicated by
        trauma and often by infection.
     3. Cardiogenic shock may follow any acute diminution of
        cardiac output and usually is associated with varying
        degrees of vasoconstriction. Examples include myo-
        cardial infarction, paroxysmal tachycardia, and shock
        due to myocardial depressant drugs including some
        anesthetic agents.
     4. Endotoxin ("gram-negative") shock - Although shock
        may complicate any significant infection, that follow-
        ing bacteremia due to gram-negative organisms and
        their endotoxins is being frequently described and
        recognized as a distinct clinical entity. Gram-negative
        endotoxins initially produce vasoconstriction followed
        by peripheral pooling of blood and reduction in venous
        return, leading to decreased cardiac output.
     5. Neurogenic shock, as seen in simple fainting, spinal
        shock, and C.N.S. injury, is usually associated with
        peripheral vasodilatation.
     6. Metabolic shock may occur in a wide variety of dis-
        eases including many of those listed above. Diabetic
        acidosis, hepatic insufficiency, renal insufficiency,
        and pulmonary insufficiency may all lead to fluid and
        electrolyte abnormalities resulting in impairment of
        cardiovascular mechanisms leading to shock.
     7. Allergic or anaphylactic shock is characterized by
        marked vasodilatation with relative hypovolemia.
        This may be induced by acute sensitivity to penicillin
        or horse serum, among other causes.
     8. Adrenal shock is seen in Addison's disease due to idio-
        pathic, malignant, or tuberculous adrenocortical in-

sufficiency. Characteristically, it is also seen with meningococcemia complicated by adrenocortical hemorrhage.

9. Vascular obstructive shock with impaired tissue perfusion is seen in major pulmonary or systemic arterial embolism. It may also result from intravascular thrombotic phenomena as part of irreversible shock.

10. Drug shock may result from excessive administration of vasodilator or vasoconstrictor agents. It may also follow poisoning. Barbiturate intoxication is usually associated with hypovolemia due to venous pooling.

C. Clinical Manifestations of Shock: The manifestations of shock vary with the initiating cause, the compensatory mechanisms impaired, previous therapy, the age of the patient, and his over-all physical status before onset. Most forms of shock, however, have in common certain recognizable features. These include venous collapse, pallor due to vasoconstriction, falling blood pressure, cold perspiration, tachycardia, narrowing pulse pressures, impaired mental acuity, and oliguria.

D. Treatment: The management of shock must be aimed at simultaneous correction of the initial cause and support of the compensatory mechanisms necessary to restore adequate cellular perfusion. Excessive use of vasopressors may raise blood pressure to normal levels, but the vasoconstriction may result in diminished cellular perfusion with eventual irreversible shock. Vasodilators are now being evaluated. In general, a peak systolic pressure of 85 mm. Hg is now considered the optimal endpoint.

Measurement of central venous pressure variations is used as a valuable guide to the amount of fluid administered. Attention must be paid to blood electrolyte abnormalities and fluid shifts and their correction. Respiration must be monitored and, if necessary, mechanical ventilators, tracheostomy, oxygen administration, and suction of the airways employed. Ideally, periodic blood volume determinations and the fractions thereof should be determined. In some instances, mean brachial artery pressure and cardiac output are monitored.

Above all, the knowledge, good judgment, and constant availability of an experienced physician together with the necessary diagnostic and therapeutic resources and agents are most important in the ever-changing clinical course of the patient in shock.

COMMON INJURIES FOLLOWING TRAUMA

Head Injury.
　　Skull films are mandatory for demonstration of possible
skull fracture or pineal shift.
　A. Cerebral Concussion: A functional disturbance without
　　gross brain damage. Consciousness varies from slight
　　daze to unconsciousness. Post-traumatic and occasionally
　　retrograde amnesia may be present. Headache is almost
　　always present. Dilated fixed pupils, areflexia, and
　　shock may be present. Delirium and vomiting may occur
　　on recovery of consciousness. The prognosis is good.
　B. Cerebral Contusion: Diffuse brain damage occurs, char-
　　acterized by edema and capillary hemorrhages. Uncon-
　　sciousness is usual and is followed by a state of drowsiness
　　or confusion lasting days or weeks. Headache, mental
　　symptoms, and light-headedness are a characteristic
　　triad which may persist indefinitely. Other symptoms
　　depend upon the damage done and include convulsions,
　　aphasia, cranial nerve palsies, and (rarely) hemiparesis.
　　Focal lesions are not usual. Spinal fluid usually shows
　　elevated pressure, xanthochromia, red blood cells, and
　　increased protein.
　C. Cerebral Compression: (Subdural or epidural hematoma.)
　　History of head injury followed in hours, days, or months
　　by fluctuating drowsiness and confusion progressing slow-
　　ly to coma. Increased intracranial pressure is evidenced
　　by coma, slowing of pulse and respiration, irregular
　　breathing, and rising BP. Choked disks are infrequent.
　　Localizing neurologic signs occur, including ipsilateral
　　dilatation of the pupil. Spinal fluid pressure is increased,
　　and fluid may be xanthochromic or blood-tinged. X-ray
　　evidence of skull fracture and pineal shift is common.
　　Avoid aspiration of spinal fluid in the presence of choked
　　disks.
　D. Skull Fracture: History of head injury, usually associ-
　　ated with evidence of external trauma. Fracture may
　　occur with minimal brain injury or symptoms related
　　thereto. Obvious depressed skull fractures require sur-
　　gical management. Skull films are the most reliable
　　diagnostic aid.
　E. Penetrating Wounds: Minute point of entry may conceal
　　extensive brain damage. Surgical exploration may be
　　indicated.

Chest Injury.
　　External evidence of injury may not be present.
　A. Rib Fracture: Localized pleuritic pain (sharp pain with
　　breathing), localized severe pain with pressure at frac-
　　ture site, or pain with compression of sternum or lateral

chest. Pleural friction rub may be present. Examine
for fluid (hemothorax) and pneumothorax.

B. Flail Chest: Crushing injury to the chest with multiple
rib fractures results in separation of an area of chest
wall which then functions independently of the rib cage
proper. With inspiration, the segment is sucked in,
which limits expansion of the lung on the involved side.
Flail chest is characterized by pain, dyspnea, cyanosis,
and paradoxic motion of the involved segment. Immediate
immobilization is required.

C. Pneumothorax: Pneumothorax is classically characterized by dyspnea and cyanosis, chest lag, absence of
fremitus, hyperresonance, and absence of breath and
voice sounds on the involved side. X-ray will confirm the
diagnosis. The classical picture varies greatly with the
amount of air. If fluid is also present, findings of pneumothorax predominate. There are three types: spontaneous, tension, and open.

  1. Spontaneous pneumothorax - Rupture of bleb with leakage of air into the pleural cavity; source of leak seals
spontaneously. Characterized by sudden onset of
dyspnea, pleuritic pain, or both; respiratory lag, hyperresonance, and absent breath and voice sounds on the
involved side. Symptoms and signs do not progress.

  2. Tension pneumothorax - Failure of the lung leak to
seal results in increasing amount of air in the pleural
space with each breath. This causes rapidly progressive dyspnea, cyanosis, and physical findings
as noted above. Marked intrathoracic pressure may
prevent hyperresonance. Tension pneumothorax may
result from lung trauma (penetrating wounds) or may
occur with spontaneous pneumothorax. Immediate
measures must be taken to aspirate air and to allow
continued egress of trapped air.

  3. Open pneumothorax - Characterized by presence of an
open wound, severe respiratory distress with cyanosis,
audible sucking sounds, and ingress or egress of
frothy, blood-tinged fluid with each breath. Opening
must be closed **at once** with an emergency airtight
bandage and the patient placed on the injured side.

D. Hemothorax: Signs of pleural fluid as evidenced by absent
fremitus, loss of resonance, absent breath and voice
sounds, and tracheal shift to the opposite side, together
with general symptoms of hemorrhage following chest
injury; may be associated with pneumothorax. Physical
findings of pneumothorax may obscure those of hemothorax. Confirm by needle aspiration.

E. Penetrating Wounds of Chest: May be closed or open.

  1. Closed wounds - A minute point of entry may be
associated with extensive intrathoracic damage.

Check for rib fracture, pneumothorax, hemothorax, subcutaneous (palpation) or mediastinal emphysema (crunching sound with each heartbeat), and cardiac contusion.

2. Open wounds inevitably produce critical pneumothorax; see above.

F. Cardiac Injury: May consist of simple contusion, a penetrating wound, valve rupture, or cardiac tamponade. Contusion may be associated with arrhythmia or non-specific electrocardiographic findings. Rupture occurs most commonly in the aortic valve and is manifested by a loud, ''cooing'' diastolic murmur; signs of acute left heart failure may be present.

Cardiac tamponade due to blood in the pericardial sac progresses to limitation of diastolic filling of the heart with resultant progressive narrowing of pulse pressure, increase in pulse rate, paradoxic pulse, engorged neck veins, and eventually critically low cardiac output. Pericardial paracentesis may be life-saving (see p. 611).

Nonpenetrating Abdominal Injuries.

May be accompanied by varying degrees of shock, hemorrhage, or peritonitis. The nature and direction of injury should be ascertained. Serial examinations are imperative.

A. Liver Rupture: Manifestations are due to hemorrhage, shock, and possible bile peritonitis. Liver rupture is characterized by a history of injury followed immediately or after a few hours by right upper quadrant pain, tenderness, and signs of hemorrhage. Shock and rapid exsanguination may occur.

B. Splenic Rupture: Manifestations are due to hemorrhage and shock. Splenic rupture is characterized by a history of injury followed immediately or after days (subcapsular hemorrhage) by left upper quadrant and shoulder pain, rebound tenderness, muscle rigidity, signs of bleeding (including shifting dullness), a mass in the left upper quadrant, and shock. Spontaneous rupture may occur with malaria or infectious mononucleosis.

C. Intestinal Rupture: Manifestations are due to localized peritonitis or to gangrene of the bowel following a mesenteric tear with impairment of blood supply. Characterized by history of injury followed by symptoms due to peritonitis, anemia, or gangrene of bowel.

D. Kidney Rupture: Manifestations are due to perirenal bleeding and urinary extravasation or intrarenal bleeding. Characterized by history of injury followed by flank pain, hematuria, local costovertebral angle tenderness, swelling, muscle spasm, a palpable mass, non-shifting flank dullness, shock, and ecchymosis. An intravenous urogram is valuable for confirmation and to determine the extent of injury.

E. Bladder Rupture: Manifestations are due to local injury with intra- or extraperitoneal extravasation of urine or blood, which may become infected. Rupture is caused by trauma to a full bladder. Characterized by history of injury to the lower abdomen, followed by persistent pain, suprapubic tenderness, muscle spasm, and hematuria. Signs of free fluid in peritoneal cavity may occur. A boggy suprapubic mass may be felt or percussed. X-rays of the pelvis should be taken to determine if fracture has occurred. A simple procedure is to empty the bladder, instill 300 ml. of sterile saline solution, and measure the return. A cystogram is the most dependable test for bladder injury: instill 350 ml. of sterile 5% sodium iodide and take anteroposterior and oblique views.

F. Urethral Rupture: Manifestations depend upon the segment of urethra involved; extravasation of urine or blood may be around the bladder, in the anterior abdominal wall, periprostatic, or perineal. An abdominal or perineal injury is followed by pain, blood at the urethral meatus, difficulty in voiding, and signs of extravasation (see above). Urethrograms (25 ml. radiopaque material instilled into urethra by catheter) should be taken to confirm and localize the site of rupture.

Penetrating Abdominal Injuries.

A minute entry wound may mask extensive internal damage. Penetrating abdominal wounds always require exploratory laparotomy. The patient should be stripped and carefully examined for entry and exit wounds and for evidence of associated injuries or bleeding contributing to shock. Symptoms, signs, and laboratory evidence of severe hemorrhage must be evaluated promptly so that life-saving surgery may be done - in spite of shock, if necessary.

The status of the patient depends upon (1) the organs involved, as suggested by the type and direction of the injury and specific symptoms and signs; (2) the severity of hemorrhage, shock, and peritonitis; (3) the time elapsed since injury; and (4) treatment already administered.

Symptoms and signs of specific organ involvement are reviewed above. Manifestations of hemorrhage and shock are reviewed on pp. 11-13.

Fractures.

A. General Features: Clinical manifestations of fracture include pain, local tenderness, ecchymosis, deformity due to swelling and bone displacement, impaired function, abnormal motion, and crepitus at the site of fracture. In some instances only pain is present. Simple inspection is often diagnostic. X-ray confirmation is mandatory. Evaluate sensory changes and voluntary

motion of joints distal to the fracture for evidence of
nerve damage. Check distal portion of extremity for
evidence of impaired blood supply.
B. Spinal Injuries: Vertebral fractures and spinal cord injuries are suggested by the nature of the injury, back
pain, and abnormal position or mobility of the neck, back,
or extremities. All unconscious patients or those who
complain of back pain should be treated as potential spinal
cord injury cases. Every effort should be made to maintain the normal alignment of the spine both in examination and transportation. Never transport such patients
in a sitting or semi-reclining position; use a flat
stretcher without a pillow. By asking the patient to move
his toes, legs, and hands, one can roughly determine the
presence of significant cord injury and its approximate
location. Loss of sensation to pain will further identify
the level of the cord injury.

COMMON CAUSES
OF ACUTE RESPIRATORY DISTRESS

Heart Failure.
A. Left Heart Failure: Symptoms depend upon the degree of
failure. Paroxysmal nocturnal dyspnea and pulmonary
edema may both occur as the result of acute left ventricular failure of varying degree. Acute left heart failure
may occur with hypertensive cardiovascular disease,
coronary artery insufficiency, mitral incompetence,
aortic insufficiency, and aortic stenosis.
   1. Paroxysmal nocturnal dyspnea - Manifested by a
      sudden sense of suffocation, usually during the night,
      whereupon the patient sits upright acutely short of
      breath. Cough is usually present, and wheezing on
      auscultation. Cold sweat and cyanosis are common.
      BP is usually elevated. The attack ceases spontan-
      eously in 10-20 minutes.
   2. Acute pulmonary edema - Manifestations are the same
      as those of paroxysmal dyspnea except that rales are
      heard throughout the lung fields; frothy pink or white
      sputum is coughed up; and the episode may last for
      hours or until relieved by appropriate medications.
B. Right Heart Failure: Pure right heart failure is not
accompanied by pulmonary congestion, and the respiratory
distress is not as marked. In its pure form right failure
results from pulmonary hypertension, pulmonary embolism,
pulmonary stenosis, or left to right shunt. It is characterized by elevated venous pressure, enlargement and tenderness of the liver, and peripheral edema.

C. Congestive Heart Failure: Combined right and left heart failure. The clinical pictures of both are combined; pleural effusion is common.

Acute Pulmonary Edema (Noncardiac).

The clinical picture described above for pulmonary edema may occur without heart failure. Common causes are infectious pneumonitis, shock, and aspiration pneumonitis. Pulmonary embolism and irritant gases may also produce this clinical picture. Pulmonary edema due to these causes is not necessarily nocturnal and is not precipitated by the horizontal position. Duration and treatment depend upon the precipitating disease.

Bronchospasm.

A. Allergic (Bronchial Asthma): Usually begins in childhood. There may be a history of other allergic manifestations, and occurrence may be seasonal. Characterized by acute respiratory distress, use of accessory muscles of respiration, pinched facies, and bouts of nonproductive coughing. Auscultation reveals inspiratory and expiratory wheezing and rhonchi throughout, with forced, prolonged expiratory effort. Pulmonary emphysema may be present.

B. Nonallergic (Asthmatic Bronchitis): Usually occurs in elderly adults who have pulmonary emphysema, barrel chest, and a chronic cough. Scattered wheezes and rhonchi may be heard in the nonacute phase. The acute phase, usually precipitated by respiratory infection, is characterized by acute respiratory distress, spasms of dry cough, cyanosis, inspiratory and expiratory rhonchi and wheezing, and tachycardia.

Pulmonary Embolism. (See p. 453.)

Originates from a free-floating clot in the deep veins of the lower extremities or pelvis, or in the right heart. Factors contributing to clot formation are slowing of the circulation due to any cause, inflammatory changes in the vein wall, or increased coagulability of blood. Emboli may or may not produce infarction. Acute, severe respiratory distress usually occurs only with large emboli but may occur with smaller emboli if other causes of pulmonary or cardiac dyspnea are present also.

A. Large emboli are manifested by sudden severe dyspnea, severe substernal or generalized chest pain, sweating, pallor, cyanosis, abdominal discomfort, mental symptoms, and occasionally convulsions. Hypotension, a loud pulmonary second sound with a systolic murmur, and distended neck veins may be present. Death usually occurs in minutes or hours and before infarction occurs.

The Ecg. occasionally shows a pattern of right ventricular
strain. This clinical picture occurs most commonly in
association with a major operative procedure, thrombophlebitis or phlebothrombosis, or with congestive heart
failure (especially with atrial fibrillation).

B. A smaller embolus in a patient with congestive failure
or pulmonary hypertension may produce a similar picture,
a lesser degree of shock, tachycardia, development of infarct with pleuritic pain and rub, hemoptysis, and pulmonary effusion. The prognosis is better than in the case
of the larger emboli.

Pneumothorax.
   See p. 15.

Atelectasis. (See p. 457.)
   Atelectasis with acute respiratory distress usually occurs
postoperatively and with acute pulmonary infections due to an
inspissated plug of mucus in a bronchus, or bronchial spasm.
It is characterized by progressive dyspnea, dry cough, and
fever. The involved side may reveal chest lag on inspiration,
increased fremitus, dullness to percussion, and increased or
diminished breath and voice sounds. Radiologic confirmation
is important if the patient's condition does not contraindicate
the necessary manipulation. Bedside films are of little value.

2 . . .

Outlines for History Taking and Physical Examination

GENERAL HISTORY OUTLINE

Accurate diagnosis rests firmly upon the foundation of a thoughtful and inclusive history and a competently performed physical examination. A multitude of exceedingly valuable laboratory and technical aids are available to help in diagnosis, and more and better ones will come in the future. However, no matter what the future brings, it will remain true that in the study of a patient, unless we formulate first a tentative diagnosis or conclusion by means of a history and physical examination, we will be in a poor position to select, or even properly interpret, the very aids that may help us arrive at a correct decision. These two approaches to the study of illness are complementary and not separate. — (H. P. Lewis & P. H. Selling: The History and Physical Examination, 4th Ed. University of Oregon Medical School, 1967, p. 1.)

Name, address, sex, age, race, marital status, occupation. Date of entry and hospital or case number.

Previous Entries: Dates, diagnoses, therapy, other significant data.

Chief Complaint (C. C.): Presenting complaints and duration.

Present Illness (P. I.): Give chronologic story of illness, beginning with date of onset and duration before present entry. Include description of onset with exciting causes and environmental influences. Where indicated, define symptoms in terms of quality, severity, duration, radiation, and continuity or intermission. Mention aggravating and alleviating factors. Mention positive or significant negative facts which are compatible with or rule out the various diseases to be considered in differential diagnosis. Include statements about loss of weight, appetite, and strength. Close with remark about the reliability of the informant.

[Cont'd. on p. 26.]

AREAS OF VISCERAL REFERRED PAIN
(Posterior Aspect)

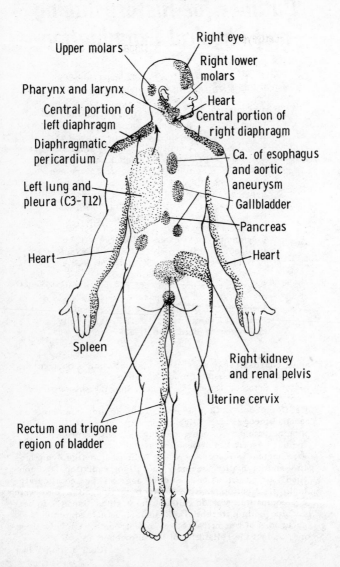

AREAS OF VISCERAL REFERRED PAIN
(Anterior Aspect)

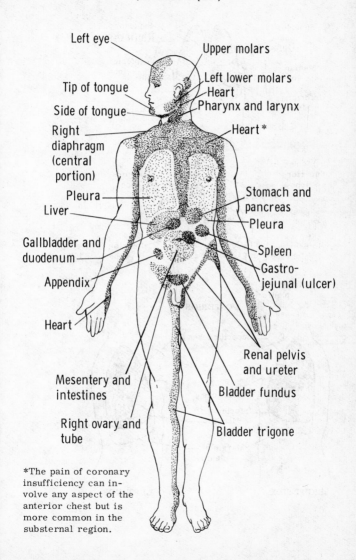

Left eye

Upper molars

Tip of tongue

Left lower molars
Heart
Pharynx and larynx

Side of tongue

Right diaphragm (central portion)

Heart *

Pleura

Stomach and pancreas

Liver

Pleura

Gallbladder and duodenum

Spleen

Gastro-jejunal (ulcer)

Appendix

Heart

Renal pelvis and ureter

Mesentery and intestines

Bladder fundus

Right ovary and tube

Bladder trigone

*The pain of coronary insufficiency can involve any aspect of the anterior chest but is more common in the substernal region.

LUNG FIELDS

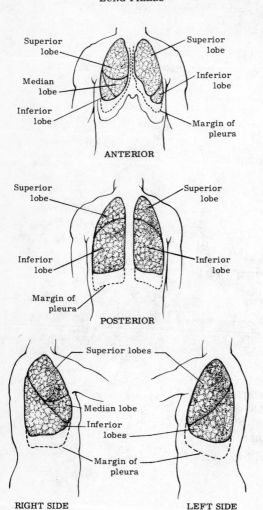

Superior lobe — Superior lobe
Median lobe — Inferior lobe
Inferior lobe — Margin of pleura

ANTERIOR

Superior lobe — Superior lobe
Inferior lobe — Inferior lobe
Margin of pleura

POSTERIOR

Superior lobes
Median lobe
Inferior lobes
Margin of pleura

RIGHT SIDE **LEFT SIDE**

LOCATION OF THE NORMAL LIVER*

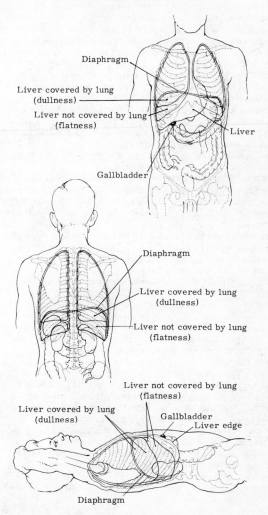

Diaphragm

Liver covered by lung
(dullness)

Liver not covered by lung
(flatness)

Liver

Gallbladder

Diaphragm

Liver covered by lung
(dullness)

Liver not covered by lung
(flatness)

Liver not covered by lung
(flatness)

Liver covered by lung
(dullness)

Gallbladder

Liver edge

Diaphragm

Note: A liver of normal size may be palpable in slender persons. Emphysema commonly causes marked downward displacement.

*Redrawn from Netter, in Popper, H.: Ciba Clinical Symposia 7:5:136. Reproduced with permission.

Family History: Present state of health or age at death and cause of death of parents and each brother and sister. Obtain statement of diseases among any relatives in which heredity or contact may play a role: infectious diseases, mental disease, neoplasms, metabolic diseases, endocrine diseases, cardiovascular or renal disease, allergy.

Marital History: Duration. Age and health of spouse and children, if living, or cause and age at time of death. Former marriage, pregnancies, miscarriages or still-births, degree of compatibility.

Residence and Occupation: Brief statement of localities in which patient has lived. Specify patient's various occupations, the possible physical or mental hazards thereof, and his occupational preference.

Social History: Education, home and environment, financial condition, number of dependents.

Diseases: Rheumatic fever, scarlet fever, tonsillitis, diphtheria, pleurisy, pneumonia, malaria, tuberculosis, measles, whooping cough, mumps, jaundice. Contact with diseased individuals; allergies. Record only significant entities.

Venereal Disease: In men, inquire about specific symptoms, signs, and the disease by name. Question women tactfully. Inquire about treatment. (Any treatment requiring injections may be significant.)

Accidents: Dates and any disabilities or other residua incurred.

Operations: Date, diagnosis, procedure, name and location of hospital and surgeon, complications, and results.

Military Service: Branch, time, station, rank on entry and discharge, diseases in service, service-connected disability and compensation therefor.

System History:

Head: Trauma, headaches, sinus pain.

Eyes: Vision, pain, inflammation, glasses, diplopia.

Ears: Pain, hearing, discharge, tinnitus, mastoid pain.

Nose: Olfaction, trauma, obstruction, discharge, epistaxis, postnasal drip, head colds, sneezing.

Mouth: Symptoms referable to teeth, lips, gums, and tongue; disturbance in taste.

Throat: Adenitis, goiter, B.M.R. determinations.

Cardiorespiratory: Chest pain, palpitation, dyspnea, cough, hemoptysis, orthopnea, edema, seasonal colds, asthma, expectoration, night sweats, choking on foreign body.

Gastrointestinal: Gas, nausea, vomiting, discomfort, pain, dysphagia, hematemesis, melena, colic, jaundice, hemorrhoids, constipation, diarrhea, use of antacids, belching, bloating. Relation of symptoms to eating, type and quantity of food.

Genitourinary: Dysuria, polyuria, frequency, hematuria, pyuria, nocturia and volume thereof, oliguria, anuria, dribbling, incontinence, colic.

Menses: Age at first appearance, date of last period, regularity, duration and amount, menstrual pain, associated headache, leukorrhea, other abnormalities, edema, menopausal symptoms.

Neuromuscular: Temperament, memory, worries, nervousness, emotional stresses, vertigo, fainting attacks, sensory disturbances, neuralgia, twitching, anesthesia, paresthesia, ataxia, convulsions, muscle or joint pains, muscular atrophies or dystrophies, deformities.

Endocrine: Undue hunger, loss of appetite, thirst, change of voice, speech, skin color or texture, sexual vigor or libido, weight, menses, vision, personality, mentality, loss of hair, hirsutism, growth abnormalities, somnolence, anomalies of sleep, temperature sensitivity, headaches, convulsions, coma, marked asthenia, lactation.

Blood: History of anemia and treatment given; blood disorders or bleeding tendencies.

Habits: Food and all details thereof, sleep, tobacco, tea, coffee, alcohol, drugs, patent medicines.

Weight: Average; amount and date of best weight, present weight; loss of weight over how long a period.

PHYSICAL EXAMINATION - GENERAL

General: Apparent age, nutrition, weight and height, frame, stature; temperature, pulse, and respiration (T.P.R.); mental status. (May give BP here.)

Skin: Color, texture, eruptions and petechiae, scars, sensitivity, hair distribution, striae, turgor, myxedema, sweating, pigmentation, nail abnormalities.

Lymph Nodes: Size, sensitivity, mobility, consistency.

Face: Expression, symmetry, sinus tenderness, color.

Head: Scalp, temporal vessels, tenderness, deformities, bruit.

Eyes: Expression, exophthalmos or enophthalmos, tension, movements, lids, pupils and pupillary reflexes, conjunctiva, cornea, sclera, extraocular movements, fundi (see p. 55), vision, visual fields.

Ears: Canals, tympanic membranes, tophi, hearing (air and bone conduction).

Nose: Exterior, mucosa, septum, patency, discharge, bleeding.

Mouth: Lips, mucosa, gums, teeth, tongue, tonsils, palate, pharynx, odor of breath, pigmentation, macroglossia.

Neck: Mobility, pulsations, nodes; thyroid size, contour, and bruit; position of trachea.

Chest: Skin, breasts (nipples, masses), thorax (shape and symmetry), anteroposterior and lateral diameters, abnormal pulsations, costal angle, rib or sternum tenderness, rib compression.

Lungs: Expansion, fremitus, resonance, excursion of diaphragms, breath and voice sounds, rales, friction rub.

Heart: Inspection - Abnormal pulsations. Palpation - Intensity of left or right ventricular thrust, intensity of sounds, thrill, point of maximal impulse, pericardial rub. Percussion - Cardiac contour. Auscultation - Rate, rhythm, and intensity of first sound (S_1); intensity and splitting of second sound (S_2); extra heart sounds (click, gallop, opening snap, friction rub); location, timing, duration, transmission, intensity, and quality of murmurs; effect of inspiration and expiration on heart sounds.

Peripheral Vessels: Venous distention, arteriosclerosis; presence, absence, or diminution of expected arterial pulsation; synchronicity and character of pulses, capillary pulsation, to-and-fro murmur over femoral artery with pressure (Duroziez's sign), BP in popliteal arteries if BP with diastolic hypertension in the arms.

Abdomen: Contour, skin, hair, and scars; intestinal activity, visible and audible; rigidity and tenderness; percuss for dullness; tympany, distention; organs and masses which can be palpated; shifting dullness, reflexes, hernias; size, contour, tenderness, pulsation, and motility of any organ or mass.

Back: Curvatures, symmetry, mobility; tenderness over spine, pelvis, and kidneys (costovertebral angle tenderness).

Rectal Examination: Sphincter tone, prostate (size, consistency, tenderness), seminal vesicles, masses, hemorrhoids and bleeding, color of feces; proctoscopy or sigmoidoscopy.

Genitals: Tumors, sores, scars, tenderness, discharge, penis, prepuce (retract and examine), testes, epididymides, varicocele, hydrocele. Note absence or presence of secondary sex characteristics.

Vaginal: External genitalia, Skene's and Bartholin's glands, vagina (hymen, discharge, rectocele, cystocele), cervix (color, consistency, outlet), uterus (size, position, and contour), adnexa (masses, tenderness); vaginoabdominal and rectovaginal examination; vaginoscopic examination.

Extremities: Size and shape of arms, legs, hands and feet in relation to torso; scars, wounds, swelling, redness, tenderness, pitting edema, temperature, color of skin and nails, varicosities, clubbing; Achilles tendon sensitivity, vibration sense; joints.

Reflexes: Biceps, triceps, patellar, Achilles, abdominal, cremasteric, Babinski. Note degree of activity (+ to ++++); compare right and left.

Cranial Nerves: See p. 36.

SUMMARY: Outline significant findings.

IMPRESSIONS: Tentative diagnosis and differential diagnosis.
A properly written diagnosis should be a succinct summary.
   A. Major Diagnosis:
      1. Anatomic characteristics.
      2. Physiologic characteristics.
      3. Other complications.
   B. Minor Diagnoses.
   C. Old Surgical Procedures.
   D. Rule Out:
      (Itemize possibilities.)

SUGGESTIONS FOR WORK-UP AND MANAGEMENT: Additional laboratory tests, x-rays, special procedures, and consultations.

UROLOGIC EXAMINATION

History.
   Perform a complete history and physical examination (as on p. 27) if there is any possibility that urologic abnormality may be due to systemic disease.
   A. Pain: Back, abdomen, kidneys, bladder, prostate and seminal vesicles, urethra, testes, epididymides.
   B. Urination: Difficulty, frequency, dribbling, retention, dysuria (pain, burning, urgency), hematuria, nocturia (volume), polyuria and oliguria, incontinence.
   C. Sexual:
      1. Women - Pregnancies, number and complications, children, intercourse, vaginal discharge, venereal disease.
      2. Men - Erection, ejaculation (premature, pain, blood), nocturnal emissions, libido, masturbation, children.
   D. Past Illness: Instrumentation and operations; stones, colic; venereal disease (symptoms, dates, duration, treatment).
   E. Family History: Tuberculosis, stones, gout, cancer, lues, prostatic or renal disease.

Physical Examination.
   A. General: Note color, conspicuous weight loss, regional lymph nodes.
   B. Abdomen: Complete examination. Inspection, palpation, percussion, auscultation, bimanual palpation of the kidneys.
   C. Back: Especially costovertebral angle for bulging, heat, redness or tenderness.

D. Male Genitalia: Tumors, congenital abnormalities, sores, scars, tenderness, discharge; palpate urethra, scrotum, testes, epididymides, and vasa.

E. Rectal: Sphincter tone, prostate (size, consistency, secretion), seminal vesicles, masses.

F. Female Genitalia: Examine externally; complete vaginal examination.

G. Urine: Two- or three-glass test as indicated (see p. 131). Check for residual urine, if indicated. Microscopic examination (see p. 125).

H. Special Diagnostic Procedures if Indicated: Urinalysis, stained smear of urine sediment, two- or three-glass test (see p. 125), serum N. P. N. or urea nitrogen kidney function tests, plain film of abdomen, I. V. pyelogram, cystoscopy, retrograde pyelogram; check for reflux, transillumination, concentration of follicle-stimulating hormone and 17-ketosteroids in the urine; Sulkowitch test, presacral air studies, kidney biopsy, perineal prostatic punch biopsy, and retrograde femoral arteriograms.

GYNECOLOGIC EXAMINATION

History.

Perform a complete history and physical examination (as on pp. 21 and 27) if there is any possibility gynecologic abnormality may be due to systemic disease.

A. Past History: Illnesses and operations; dates, duration, and complications. Previous diagnoses.

B. Menstruation: Onset, pain, duration, amount, date of last and preceding period, number of pads, clots, intermenstrual or contact bleeding, change in character of menses.

C. Vaginal Discharge: Character and duration.

D. Bladder: Frequency, urgency, nocturia, incontinence, pain.

E. Bowels: Regularity, catharsis, pain, bleeding.

F. Births: Dates, labor, complications. How are children now?

G. Miscarriages: Dates, gestation, spontaneous or induced, complications.

H. Menopause: Age, date, natural or induced, manner of onset, flushes, libido, mental changes, postmenopausal bleeding.

Physical Examination.

A. Complete abdominal, vaginal, and rectal examination (see p. 28).

B. Special Diagnostic Procedures as Indicated: Urinalysis, stained smear of cervix, hanging drop preparation for

Trichomonas vaginalis, **cytologic study for malignant cells**
(see p. 393), cervical biopsy, diagnostic curettage, pneu-
mosalpynx, concentration of follicle-stimulating hormone
and 17-ketosteroids in the urine, presacral air study,
culdoscopy.

ACCIDENTS - EMERGENCY ROOM EXAMINATIONS

The physician may be answerable in court for what he
records in an accident case (see p. 1 for examination of
unconscious patients).

Statistical Data.
1. Name and address of patient.
2. Brought, referred, or sent by (give name and address).
3. Name, address, and phone number of nearest relative.
4. Age, sex, color, height and weight, nutritional status,
   development, deformities, civil status.
5. Employment - Type of work, years of service, em-
   ployer.
6. List diseases which were present prior to accident.
7. History of tetanus toxoid vaccination.

Symptoms.
List in order of importance; give duration.
1. Pain - Type, location, severity, and radiation.
2. Unconsciousness, dizziness, faintness, retrograde
   loss of memory.
3. Headache, nausea, vomiting, especially in head injuries.
4. Determine loss of motion in any part of body as due to:
   a. Pain.
   b. Bone injury or locking.
   c. Nerve or tendon injury.
5. Respiratory difficulty, if any, and cause.
6. Blood loss, if any, and amount and source of bleeding.
7. Duration of conscious suffering.
Have patient acknowledge, "That is all," and record in
quotes.

Chronologic Story of Accident.
1. Date, exact time, and site of accident.
2. Patient's activity at that time, and general circumstances.
3. Description of accident itself. If there was a blow or
   fall, determine the direction of the force and the
   structures involved.
4. Patient's condition immediately after accident.
5. Chronologic progression of symptoms.
6. How moved from site of injury, and any first aid given.
   Names of doctors or attendants who saw patient.

Physical Examination.

1. Note respiration, pulse, and BP. Does patient "look sick" or appear to be in pain?
2. If possible, remove all clothing from patient and drape with a sheet. If indicated, cut clothes from patient to avoid further injury.
3. Examine as completely as possible (see pp. 1, 27, 35 for outlines). Note especially sensory defects: speech, confusion, coordination, odor of breath. Is patient intoxicated? If so, qualify. Describe all skin injuries.
4. Estimate probable degree and duration of disability.

Disposition.

Condition on disposition.

(Signature of examiner, date, and hour.)

PSYCHIATRIC EXAMINATION

Name, age, sex, race, address of patient and relatives. History of enuresis, divorce, accidents; work, school, military experiences. How did patient come in?

Chief Complaint: Illustrate with significant quotations from patient and/or other informant.

Behavior, Appearance, Attitude: Untidy? Tense? Tremulous? Comfortable? Apathetic? Preoccupied? Hesitant? Vague? Violent? Hostile? Listening? Irritable? Manneristic? Artificial? How does patient feel about his illness and the present interview? Does he "look sick"?

Relationship to Doctor: "Warm" or "frigid" feeling tone; aloof, clinging, etc. How do you feel toward patient?

Patient's insight into mechanisms relating to illness and personality, especially genetic factors (childhood background, insanity in family) vs. dynamic factors (present situation). How much hope does patient have?

Nonpsychotics. (Primarily neurotics; also social psychopaths.)

A. Mental Trend: Feelings about himself and others; superficial, inadequate, indecisive, cynical, guilty, doubtful; fearful of insanity and death (a universal fear); note sexual unhappiness, panic, pressure of speech, memory defects, confusion, blocking of thought, fear of own aggression against himself or others (suicidal?), dreams, daydreams, nightmares or night terrors, fear of failure, inability to concentrate.

B. Syndromes: Anxiety states (tension), chronic invalid reaction (neurasthenia), preoccupation with somatic complaints (hypochondriasis), phobias, obsessive-compulsive reactions, reactive depression (situational illness), hysteria (emotional stress converted into physical symptoms), fugues, emotional instability, psychopathic personality, mental deficiency, chronic and acute alcoholism. May include epilepsy, postencephalitis, mental deficiency.

Psychotics. (The mentally ill.)
   History from patient and his family.
   A. Mental Trend: Delusions, hallucinations, suspicions; ideas of unreality, reference, own importance, persecution, fear, and guilt; obsessions; stream of thought (coherent, relevant, circumstantial), thought content.
   B. Emotional Activity: Quantitative disturbances, including excessive lability or inadequate response (flatness). Qualitative disturbances, including depression, elation, inappropriate responses, silly behavior. Suicidal ideas?
   C. Sensorium: Orientation, memory (immediate: repeat numbers backwards; remote: childhood events); calculation (count from 20 to one, subtract seven from 100); retention and recall, writing, deterioration of memory, emotion, insight and judgement.
   D. Syndromes: Schizophrenia (simple, paranoid, catatonic, hebephrenic); manic-depressive state. Organic types: paresis, brain tumors. Toxic types: delirium, Korsakoff's psychosis, bromidism, etc.

Children.
   No routine examination is feasible. Get history, including relations with other children, and age at which child became dry; give opinion on the child's relationship to you and to his parents; note response to play overtures, symbolism, and observe behavior and feeling tone. Test hearing, vision, and intelligence as indicated.

SUMMARY: Outline significant findings and give tentative diagnosis and differential diagnosis.

IMPRESSION: Note your own response to patient, your impression of patient's intelligence and of the severity of his illness, his value to society, and degree of financial responsibility. What is the patient's own evaluation of the severity of his illness? Is he willing to undergo further psychiatric treatment?

SUGGESTIONS FOR WORK-UP AND MANAGEMENT: Rorschach test, intelligence test, other psychometric tests; consultation, referral, discharge, simple support.

DETENTION OF MENTAL PATIENTS

Detention of mental patients, even for an hour, is usually legal only on court order, e. g., a lunacy warrant. In actual practice, doctors authorize detention of intoxicated, drugged, suicidal, homicidal, and psychotic patients for a day or so until the court can decide the case. Long-term commitment requires a trial, proof of insanity, and a court order appointing a hospital as guardian. In most states, this hospital may release patient back to his own care as he improves, without further court action. However, such a patient has lost his civil rights until he is again declared sane by the court.

Commitment procedures should NOT be initiated by the physician, lest he be sued by the patient or family. After the family or district attorney initiates such procedures, the physician (in some states it must be a psychiatrist) may then safely give his professional opinion regarding the patient's mental state by signing the appropriate legal forms. He should have notes of his examination available for future reference.

3...

Neurologic Diagnosis

NEUROLOGIC EXAMINATION
(Supplementary to General History and Physical Examination)
(See also pp. 21 ff.)

History.
An attempt should be made to confirm significant historical findings when indicated.
A. Past History: Occupation, exposure to neurotoxins, handedness, nutrition, emotional disturbances, trauma, convulsions, venereal disease, meningitis, encephalitis, or alcoholism.
B. Family History: Mental or neurologic ailments.
C. Symptoms: Chronologic history of complaint. Symptoms of systemic disease with neurologic component; change in mental state, memory, personality, speech, comprehension, reading, writing, sleep, muscle strength or coordination, sphincter function, menstruation, sexual capacity. Appearance and progression of headache, pain, tremor, sensory disturbances.
D. Special Senses: See Cranial Nerves, below.

Physical Examination.
Complete general examination first (pp. 21 to 28).
A. General Observations:
 1. Position of body, extremities, and head; nutritional state.
 2. State of consciousness, drowsiness, promptness of response.
 3. Skin - Fine or coarse texture; pigmentation.
 4. Hair - Texture and distribution.
 5. Perspiration - General or localized; increased or decreased.
 6. Blood pressure, both arms.
 7. Palpation - Carotid arteries, pulsation and thrills; aorta.
 8. Audible bruits of skull and of carotid, subclavian, femoral, and renal arteries; aorta.
B. Head: Inspection (shape, size, veins), palpation (exostoses), percussion (tenderness, resonance), auscultation (bruit).

35

C. Neck: Involuntary rigidity, pain, deformity.
D. Cranial Nerves:
    I -
        a. Subjective - Impairment of smell; olfactory halluci-
           nations.
        b. Objective - Test sense of smell with coffee, pepper-
           mint, menthol.
    II -
        a. Subjective - Impairment of vision; field defects;
           hallucinations of light.
        b. Objective - Acuity (Snellen card, fingers, light
           changes); visual fields (finger test, perimeter,
           tangent screen); color blindness tests.
           Fundus: Disks (color, size and shape, distinct-
           ness of edges, presence of physiologic cup).
    III, IV, VI -
        a. Subjective - Diplopia.
        b. Objective - External ocular movements, nystagmus,
           palpebral fissures, ptosis, pupils (size, equality,
           regularity, reaction to light and accommodation).
           (III) Ptosis, divergent strabismus, diplopia, and
               loss of response to light and accommodation.
           (IV) Diplopia when looking down and to either
               side.
           (VI) Convergent strabismus, which may also be
               caused by increased intracranial pressure per
               se.
    V -
        a. Subjective - Sensation (pain, numbness, paresthesia).
        b. Objective -
           (1) Sensory - Facial sensation, corneal and sneeze
               reflex.
           (2) Motor - Deviation of jaw, weakness of masseter
               and temporal muscles.
    VII -
        a. Subjective - Taste disturbances, facial spasms,
           lacrimation, salivation, facial asymmetry.
        b. Objective -
           (1) Motor - Facial expression; nasolabial folds;
               forehead wrinkle (cannot be done in peripheral
               paralysis of VII, can be done in central paral-
               ysis of VII).
           (2) Sensory - Test anterior two-thirds of tongue
               with salt and sugar.
           (3) Secretory - Lacrimation, salivation.
    VIII -
        a. Cochlear -
           (1) Subjective - Hearing impairment, tinnitus
               (noises in the ear).
           (2) Objective - Tick of watch, whisper, Rinne test
               (tuning fork on mastoid, then to ear), Weber

test (tuning fork on vertex of skull), otoscopic examination.
  b. Vestibular -
      (1) Subjective - Unsteady gait, dizziness, nausea.
      (2) Objective - Nystagmus, swaying, Barany caloric test; test cerebellar functions.
IX -
  a. Subjective - Dysphagia.
  b. Objective - Gag reflex; test taste on posterior third of tongue.
X -
  a. Subjective - Regurgitation of fluids, speech difficulties, projectile vomiting.
  b. Objective - Deviation of soft palate, pulse rate, laryngeal paralysis.
XI - Inability to shrug shoulders (trapezius and sterno-cleidomastoid muscles).
XII - Deviation of protruded tongue toward affected side. Note atrophy, fine fibrillation.
E. Cerebrum: Localization (see p. 46).
  1. Frontal area - Cerebration, concentration, euphoria, personality and habit change, anosmia.
      a. Motor area - Convulsions, paresis, paralysis, motor aphasia.
      b. Premotor area - Forced grasping, clumsiness.
  2. Parietal area - Sensation intact but cannot tell shape.
  3. Occipital area - Hallucinations of light, field defects.
  4. Temporal area - Hallucinations of smell and taste, acuity of hearing impaired, slow voluntary movements, dream states, homonymous hemianopsia, sensory aphasia.
  5. Corpus striatum - Rigidity, tremors, mask facies.
F. Cerebellum: Hypotonicity, nystagmus, dysarthria, muscle incoordination (finger to nose, heel to knee, finger to finger), adiadochokinesia, Romberg test.
G. Spinal Cord: (See p. 47.)
  1. Subjective - Muscle weakness (local and general), difficulty in walking, sphincter disturbances, change in sensation (local or radiating).
  2. Objective -
      a. Motor - Muscle strength, all groups; atrophy, fibrillations.
      b. Sensation - Test with sharp and dull, hot and cold, cotton, tuning fork. Pinch Achilles tendons and testes, test position and vibratory sense, map any segmental defects.
  3. Reflexes -
      a. Superficial - Abdominal, cremasteric, Babinski, Chaddock, Oppenheimer, and Gordon.

b. Deep - Biceps, triceps, patellar, Achilles, clonus
(repeated rhythmic contraction when a single
muscle group is stretched).

SUMMARY: Subjective and objective.

IMPRESSION: Tentative diagnosis and differential diagnosis.

WORK-UP MAY INCLUDE THE FOLLOWING PROCEDURES
IF INDICATED: Lumbar puncture and cerebrospinal fluid
examination, x-rays, EEG, air encephalograms, psychometric tests, electromyographic studies, echoencephalo-
grams, skin temperatures; serum calcium determination,
glucose tolerance test, and electrocardiogram (in convulsive disorders); psychiatric consultation (if large functional
component is present), myelograms, cerebral angiograms,
and radioisotope localization of tumors.

THE ELECTROENCEPHALOGRAM (EEG)

Theory.

The EEG is a recording of the amplified electrical activity of the brain. The electroencephalograph is the instrument
with which the record is taken; it consists of an electronic
amplifying system activated by potentials taken from electrodes
attached to the scalp and activating in turn an ink-writing
oscillograph or other recording device. Normal patterns of
discharge are known for adults. There is very little electrical activity in infants. Gradual increase in activity occurs
with age, so that patterns are extremely variable in children.

Trauma, vascular disease, inflammatory processes and
neoplasms may all produce similar EEG abnormalities. Normal records may be present in spite of clinical evidence of
severe, organic brain disease. Therefore the chief value of
this technic is its use as an adjunct to other clinical diagnostic methods. If it is so employed it can be a most valuable
diagnostic tool.

When taken as a continuously running record for an hour
or more, the EEG is characterized by rhythmicity. The
record varies according to the frequency, amplitude, and
form of the waves. Frequency and amplitude are, in general,
inversely related. The most easily discernible rhythm has a
frequency of 8 to 13 cycles per second; waves of this frequency
are called alpha waves and are normally seen in adults in the
parieto-occipital area. The amplitude may vary considerably.
Characteristic alterations in discharge patterns occur with
sensory stimulation and with muscular activity. During sleep
the alpha waves disappear, to be replaced by intermittent

bursts of waves of low voltage and high frequency which have a spindle-shaped contour and are sometimes called "sleep spindles."

Technic.

Most modern electroencephalographs have eight channels, so that simultaneous recordings on the same time base and with matched amplification can be taken from several leads. The leads are fitted with small metal solder pellets or needles which are fastened to the scalp in standard locations and connected by small wires to the amplifiers. Leads are attached by parting the hair at the desired locations and fastening the pellets to the scalp with collodion. Good contact is secured by use of electrode paste on the pellets.

The record is taken with the patient in a chair or in bed, as quiet and comfortable as possible. In order to activate latent abnormal rhythms, records during and after hyperventilation are taken routinely. Other means of accomplishing this are photic stimuli (rhythmic flashes of light), sleep records (natural or induced), and the administration of pentylenetetrazol (Metrazol®).

Leads are usually placed bilaterally over the frontal, parietal, occipital, and temporal lobes of the brain. Leads can be placed in other positions for purposes of more accurate localization of small circumscribed areas of abnormal discharge, such as on the vertex of the skull, the ears, and tympanic membrane leads in conjunction with nasopharyngeal leads.

The two sides of the push-pull amplifier system can be connected to two of these leads (bipolar recording), or one side of the amplifier may be connected to one active lead and the other to an indifferent lead (monopolar recording) placed on the ear lobe or some other neutral position. In the first instance the record will represent the potential changes between the two active leads. In the second instance the record will represent the potential changes in the immediate vicinity of the active lead.

Uses.

The EEG may provide useful information in organic disease when used as an adjunct to other diagnostic methods. In epilepsy it may help to locate the focus or define the type and thus determine the feasibility of surgical excision or guide the type of anticonvulsant therapy. Fifteen per cent of patients with grand mal will have normal records. The EEG may also aid in the diagnosis and localization of brain tumor, brain abscess, traumatic lesions, and subdural hematoma. Abnormal records may be seen in meningitis, encephalitis, vascular abnormalities, measles, mumps, infectious mononucleosis, and idiopathic degenerative brain disease.

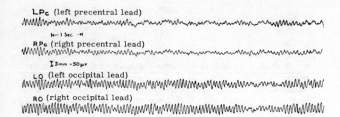

LPc (left precentral lead)

|← 1 sec →|

RPc (right precentral lead)

|5mm = 50μv

LO (left occipital lead)

RO (right occipital lead)

Normal Record

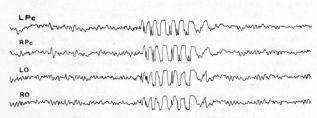

LPc

RPc

LO

RO

Epileptic Record with Paroxysmal Burst of Classical
"Spike and Dome" Formation

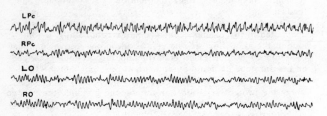

LPc

RPc

LO

RO

Record of Focal Damage in Left Precentral Area;
History of Right-sided Jacksonian Convulsions

Interpretation.

Interpretation of the EEG must be left to the expert in
electroencephalography. Samples of normal and abnormal
(arrhythmic) EEG patterns are shown above.

The EEG may vary widely with the skill of the technician,
the quality of the apparatus, the length of the record, the
number and location of the electrodes, and the clinical acumen
of the physician controlling these factors.

Examples of normal and abnormal EEG tracings are
shown above.

SUMMARY OF REFLEXES

Reflexes	Afferent Nerve	Center	Efferent Nerve
SUPERFICIAL REFLEXES			
Corneal	Cranial V	Pons	Cranial VII
Nasal (sneeze)	Cranial V	Brain stem and upper cord	Cranials V, VII, IX, X, and spinal nerves of expiration
Pharyngeal and uvular	Cranial IX	Medulla	Cranial X
Upper abdominal	T7, 8, 9, 10	T7, 8, 9, 10	T7, 8, 9, 10
Lower abdominal	T10, 11, 12	T10, 11, 12	T10, 11, 12
Cremasteric	Femoral	L1	Genitofemoral
Plantar	Tibial	S1, 2	Tibial
Anal	Pudendal	S4, 5	Pudendal
DEEP REFLEXES			
Jaw	Cranial V	Pons	Cranial V
Biceps	Musculo-cutaneous	C5, 6	Musculo-cutaneous
Triceps	Radial	C6, 7	Radial
Periosteo-radial	Radial	C6, 7, 8,	Radial
Wrist (flexion)	Median	C6, 7, 8	Median
Wrist (extension)	Radial	C7, 8	Radial
Patellar	Femoral	L2, 3, 4	Femoral
Achilles	Tibial	S1, 2	Tibial
VISCERAL REFLEXES			
Light	Cranial II	Midbrain	Cranial III
Accommodation	Cranial II	Occipital cortex	Cranial III
Ciliospinal	A sensory nerve	T1, 2	Cervical sympathetics
Oculocardiac	Cranial V	Medulla	Cranial X
Carotid sinus	Cranial IX	Medulla	Cranial X
Bulbocavernosus	Pudendal	S2, 3, 4	Pelvic autonomic
Bladder and rectal	Pudendal	S2, 3, 4	Pudendal and autonomics

DIAGRAM SHOWING MUSCLES USED IN CONJUGATE
OCULAR MOVEMENTS IN THE SIX CARDINAL
DIRECTIONS OF GAZE*

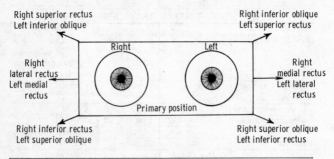

*Reproduced, with permission, from Chusid: Correlative
Neuroanatomy and Functional Neurology, 14th Ed. Lange,
1970.

CHART OF PARALYSES OF INDIVIDUAL
EYE MUSCLES*†

Muscle	Nerve	Deviation of Eyeball	Diplopia Present When Looking†	Direction of Image
Internal rectus	III	Outward (external squint)	Toward nose	Vertical
Superior rectus	III	Downward and inward	Upward and outward	Oblique
Inferior rectus	III	Upward and inward	Downward and outward	Oblique
Inferior oblique	III	Downward and outward	Upward and inward	Oblique
Superior oblique	IV	Upward and outward	Downward and inward	Oblique
External rectus	VI	Inward (internal squint)	Toward temple	Vertical

*Reproduced, with permission, from Chusid: Correlative
Neuroanatomy and Functional Neurology, 14th Ed. Lange,
1970.
†Diplopia is noted only when the affected eye attempts these
movements.

SCHEMATIC ILLUSTRATION OF A
TYPICAL SPINAL NERVE*

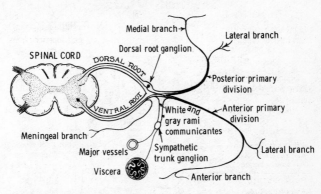

*Reproduced, with permission, from Chusid: Correlative Neuroanatomy and Functional Neurology, 14th Ed. Lange, 1970.

CUTANEOUS INNERVATION

PERIPHERAL
DISTRIBUTION

SEGMENTAL or RADICULAR
DISTRIBUTION

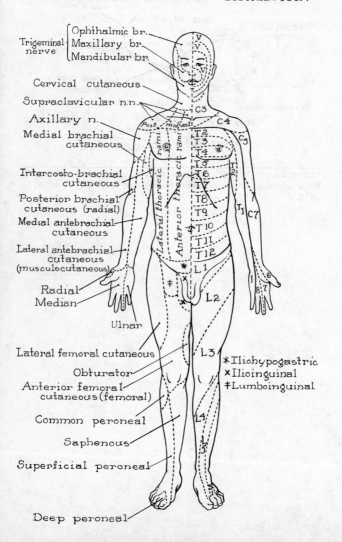

Trigeminal nerve
{ Ophthalmic br.
Maxillary br.
Mandibular br.

Cervical cutaneous

Supraclavicular n.n.

Axillary n.

Medial brachial cutaneous

Intercosto-brachial cutaneous

Posterior brachial cutaneous (radial)

Medial antebrachial cutaneous

Lateral antebrachial cutaneous (musculocutaneous)

Radial
Median

Ulnar

Lateral femoral cutaneous

Obturator

Anterior femoral cutaneous (femoral)

Common peroneal

Saphenous

Superficial peroneal

Deep peroneal

*Iliohypogastric
×Ilioinguinal
‡Lumboinguinal

CUTANEOUS INNERVATION

SEGMENTAL or RADICULAR DISTRIBUTION   PERIPHERAL DISTRIBUTION

‡Iliohypogastric (iliac branch)
*Obturator

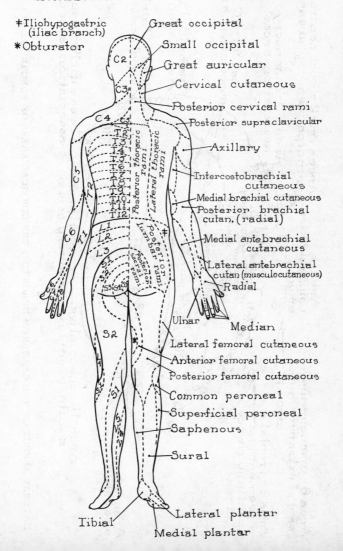

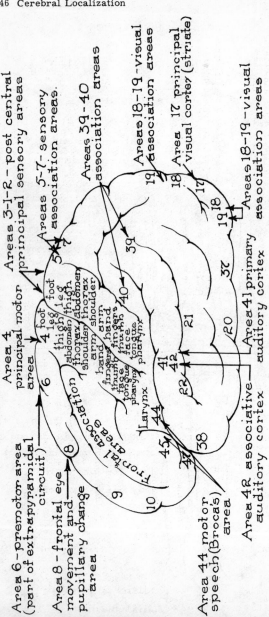

Area 6—premotor area (part of extrapyramidal circuit)

Area 8—frontal eye movement and pupillary change area

Area 44 motor speech (Broca's) area

Area 42 associative auditory cortex

Area 4 principal motor area

Areas 3-1-2 - post central principal sensory areas

Areas 5-7—sensory association areas.

Areas 39-40 association areas

Areas 18-19—visual association areas

Area 17 principal visual cortex (striate)

Areas 18-19—visual association areas

Area 41 primary auditory cortex

foot
leg   foot
thighs thigh
abdomen/thigh
thorax abdomen
shoulder thorax
arm shoulder
hand arm
fingers hand
thumb fingers
face thumb
tongue face
pharynx tongue
larynx pharynx

Frontal association area

Larynx

LATERAL ASPECT OF THE CEREBRUM INDICATING THE CORTICAL AREAS OF FUNCTIONAL LOCALIZATION

ASCENDING PATHWAYS

Posterior columns (conscious proprioception, deep touch and pressure, two-point discrimination, and vibration sense)

Dorsal spinocerebellar tract (reflex proprioception)

Lateral spinothalamic tract (pain and temperature)

Ventral spinocerebellar tract (reflex proprioception)

Spinotectal tract (reflex)

Spinoolivary tract (reflex proprioception)

Ventral spinothalamic tract (light touch)

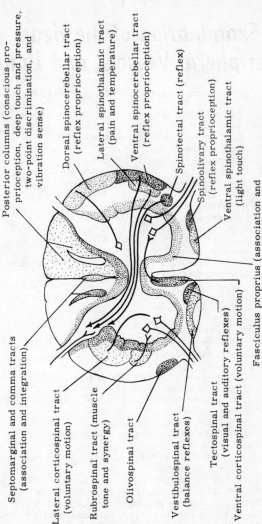

DESCENDING PATHWAYS

Septomarginal and comma tracts (association and integration)

Lateral corticospinal tract (voluntary motion)

Rubrospinal tract (muscle tone and synergy)

Olivospinal tract

Vestibulospinal tract (balance reflexes)

Tectospinal tract (visual and auditory reflexes)

Ventral corticospinal tract (voluntary motion)

Fasciculus proprius (association and integration) (both ascending and descending fibers)

NERVE PATHWAYS IN SPINAL CORD (Lower Cervical Region)

4...

Examination of the Heart, Peripheral Vessels, and Lungs

DIAGNOSTIC CRITERIA OF HEART DISEASE

The following five categories should be used whenever possible in diagnosis of diseases of the heart. (Criteria Committee, New York Heart Association, 1964.)

A. Etiologic Diagnosis:
   1. Acromegaly
   2. Anemia
   3. Atherosclerosis
   4. Carcinoid
   5. Congenital anomaly
   6. Hypertension
   7. Hyperthyroidism
   8. Hypothyroidism
   9. Infection
   10. Neoplasm
   11. Thiamine deficiency
   12. Pulmonary disease
   13. Rheumatic fever
   14. Systemic L. E.
   15. Toxic agent
   16. Trauma
   17. Unknown
   18. Uremia

B. Anatomic Diagnosis: Diseases of organ or part of organ -
   1. Acquired diseases -
      a. Aorta and pulmonary arteries
      b. Coronary arteries
      c. Endocardium and valves
      d. Myocardium (myocardopathy)
      e. Pericardium
   2. Congenital diseases -
      a. Noncyanotic group
      b. Potentially cyanotic group
      c. Cyanotic group

C. Physiologic Diagnosis:
   1. Disturbances in cardiac rhythm and conduction.
   2. Disturbances in myocardial contractility.
   3. Clinical syndromes, e.g., anginal syndrome. Adams-Stokes syndrome.

D. Functional Capacity: (Four classes.)
   I. Ordinary activity causes no discomfort.
   II. Ordinary activity causes discomfort.
   III. Less than ordinary activity causes discomfort.
   IV. Symptomatic at rest.

E. Therapeutic Classification: (Five classes.)
   Class A: Physical activity needs no restriction.
   Class B: Excessive physical efforts prohibited.
   Class C: Ordinary physical activity moderately restricted.
   Class D: Ordinary physical activity markedly restricted.
   Class E: Confined to bed or chair.

Example: (A) Rheumatic heart disease, inactive, with (B) mitral stenosis, (C) atrial fibrillation and congestive failure, (D) functional class IV, (E) therapeutic class E.

X-RAY SILHOUETTE OF THE HEART

The "normal" cardiac silhouette is quite variable; the illustrations on this and the following pages are intended to give only an approximate idea of its appearance.

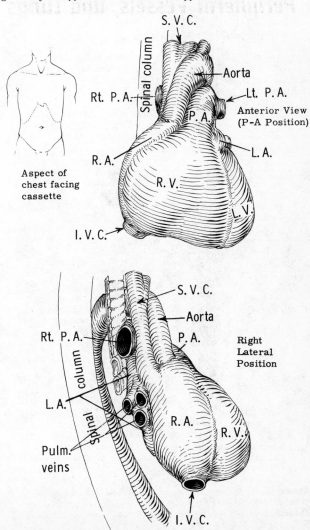

Aspect of chest facing cassette

S. V. C.

Aorta

Rt. P. A.

Spinal column

Lt. P. A.

Anterior View (P-A Position)

P. A.

L. A.

R. A.

R. V.

L. V.

I. V. C.

S. V. C.

Aorta

Rt. P. A.

column

P. A.

Right Lateral Position

L. A.

spinal

R. A.

R. V.

Pulm. veins

I. V. C.

X-RAY SILHOUETTE OF THE HEART

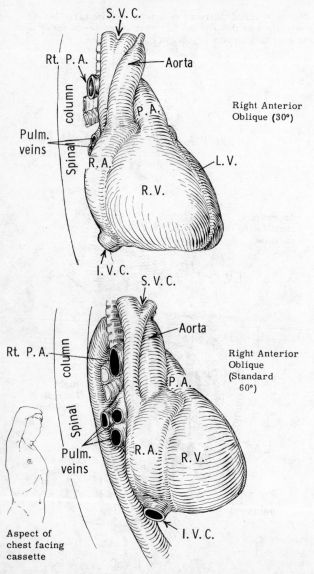

S.V.C.

Rt. P.A.

Aorta

column

P.A.

Spinal

Pulm.
veins

R.A.

L.V.

R.V.

I.V.C.

Right Anterior
Oblique (30°)

S.V.C.

Rt. P.A.

Aorta

column

P.A.

Spinal

Pulm.
veins

R.A.

R.V.

I.V.C.

Right Anterior
Oblique
(Standard
60°)

Aspect of
chest facing
cassette

X-RAY SILHOUETTE OF THE HEART

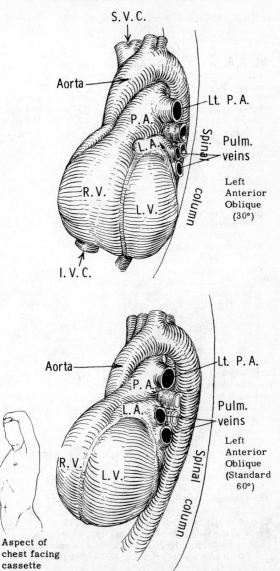

S.V.C.

Aorta

Lt. P.A.

P.A.

L.A.

Spinal

Pulm. veins

column

Left Anterior Oblique (30°)

R.V.

L.V.

I.V.C.

Aorta

Lt. P.A.

P.A.

L.A.

Pulm. veins

Spinal

column

Left Anterior Oblique (Standard 60°)

R.V.

L.V.

Aspect of chest facing cassette

THE ARTERIAL BLOOD PRESSURE

Standard Method of Blood Pressure Determination.
   (Amer. Heart Assoc., in Circulation 4:503, 1951.)
   Standard arm cuff for adults is 13 cm. wide; for thigh,
20 cm.; for children, 6 to 7 cm.
   Blood pressure in atrial fibrillation is not reliable.
   1. May use aneroid (calibrate yearly) or mercurial
      manometer.
   2. Have patient relaxed, sitting or supine, with the whole
      forearm supported at heart level. Record arm and
      position used.
   3. Use standard cuff; the hook-fastening type is preferred.
   4. Take palpatory systolic blood pressure (radial).
      Record it only if it is higher than auscultatory blood
      pressure.
   5. Auscultatory method - Place stethoscope snugly but not
      tightly over brachial artery. Inflate cuff rapidly to
      30 mm. Hg above where radial pulse disappears. De-
      flate at rate of **2 to 3 mm. Hg** per second. Systolic
      blood pressure is the highest point at which successive
      dull sounds are heard.
   6. The point of complete cessation of muffled sounds is
      the best index of diastolic pressure. Under hemody-
      namic conditions in which no cessation of sounds oc-
      curs, the point of muffling should be taken as diastolic
      pressure, if distinctly heard. If there is no clear de-
      marcation of muffling, indicate this with a question
      mark, e.g., ''150/30?''

Range of Normal Blood Pressure.
   There is no clear line of demarcation between normal
and abnormal blood pressure. The range of normal
blood pressure is a statistical definition based on the distribution of blood pressure readings around the mean or average
for each sex and for each age group. Pickering has aptly defined the situation as follows:

>   Arterial pressure rises with age and more in
>   some subjects than in others. At any age var-
>   iation is continuous. Expectation of life dimin-
>   ishes with rise in blood pressure; the relation-
>   ship is non-linear, mortality increasing faster
>   than arterial pressure. What is currently desig-
>   nated essential hypertension represents that sec-
>   tion of the population having arterial pressures
>   above an **arbitrarily** defined value, and having
>   no other disease to which the high pressure can

be attributed. If secondary hypertension is excluded, there is no evidence that high pressure is qualitatively different from normal pressure; the difference is not of kind but of degree. — (George W. Pickering: High Blood Pressure. Grune and Stratton, New York, 1955, p. 183.)

Insurance companies in the U.S.A. use the arbitrary figure of 140/90 as the upper limit of normal blood pressure, because actuarial statistics indicate that the mortality rate rises with pressures which persist above this level. The New York Heart Association considers hypertension to be present when the systolic pressure is persistently above 140 mm. Hg **and** the diastolic pressure is persistently above 90 mm. Hg.

The table on p. 54 still reflects present concepts of the range of normal blood pressure related to sex and age. It is of value as a guide, and not as a rigid criterion.

EVALUATION OF HYPERTENSION

Differential Diagnosis of Diastolic Hypertension.*

1. Essential hypertension
2. Diseases of the kidneys
   a. Pyelonephritis, chronic, rarely unilateral.
   b. Glomerulonephritis, chronic, acute.
   c. Obstructive uropathy
   d. Renal artery occlusive disease
   e. Polycystic kidney disease
3. Toxemias of pregnancy
4. Coarctation of the aorta
5. Pheochromocytoma
6. Cushing's syndrome
7. Primary aldosteronism
8. Polyarteritis nodosa
9. Lupus erythematosus
10. 17-Hydroxylation deficiency (Biglieri's syndrome)
11. Hyperthyroidism or hypothyroidism
12. Porphyria
13. Increased intracranial pressure

Diagnosis and Evaluation of Diastolic Hypertension.

A. Initial Evaluation:
1. Complete history and physical examination
2. BP in both arms and legs
3. BP and pulse rate supine and erect
4. Complete blood count
5. Urinalysis, complete, recently voided. Stain for bacteria.
6. X-ray of the chest
7. Electrocardiogram (see p. 89)
8. BUN or NPN

---

*Benign or malignant course may occur in all except coarctation of the aorta.

NORMAL RANGE, MEAN, AND LOWER LIMITS
OF HYPERTENSION*

Sex and Age	SYSTOLIC			DIASTOLIC		
	Normal Range	Mean	Hyper-tension Lower Limit	Normal Range	Mean	Hyper-tension Lower Limit
MEN						
16	105-135	118	145	60-86	73	90
17	105-135	121	145	60-86	74	90
18	105-135	120	145	60-86	74	90
19	105-140	122	150	60-88	75	95
20-24	105-140	123	150	62-88	76	95
25-29	108-140	125	150	65-90	78	96
30-34	110-145	126	155	67-92	79	98
35-39	110-145	127	160	68-92	80	100
40-44	110-150	129	165	70-94	81	100
45-49	110-155	130	170	70-96	82	104
50-54	115-160	135	175	70-98	83	106
55-59	115-165	138	180	70-98	84	108
60-64	115-170	142	190	70-100	85	110
WOMEN						
16	100-130	116	140	60-85	72	90
17	100-130	116	140	60-85	72	90
18	100-130	116	140	60-85	72	90
19	100-130	115	140	60-85	71	90
20-24	100-130	116	140	60-85	72	90
25-29	102-130	117	140	60-86	74	92
30-34	102-135	120	145	60-88	75	95
35-39	105-140	124	150	65-90	78	98
40-44	105-150	127	165	65-92	80	100
45-49	105-155	131	175	65-96	82	105
50-54	110-165	137	180	70-100	84	108
55-59	110-170	139	185	70-100	84	108
60-64	115-175	144	190	70-100	85	110

*From Master, Dublin, and Marks, JAMA **143**:1464, 1950.

B. Based on Initial Evaluation, Further Studies as Indicated:
   1. Mid-stream urine culture; colony count (see p. 289).
   2. Intravenous pyelograms (retrograde studies if necessary).
   3. Renal function tests -
      a. Twenty-four hour creatinine clearance (see p. 138).
      b. PSP test (see p. 136).
      c. Urea clearance (see p. 139).
   4. Serum Na^+, K^+, and CO_2.
   5. Phentolamine (Regitine®) test (see p. 251).
   6. Total serum protein and fractions (see p. 197).

7. Retrograde renal arteriogram.
8. Twenty-four hour urine for catecholamines or vanillylmandelic acid (see p. 250).
9. Twenty-four hour urine for total protein (see p. 115).
10. Lupus erythematosus cell preparations (see p. 158).
11. Twenty-four hour urinary steroids.

KEITH-WAGENER CLASSIFICATION OF HYPERTENSIVE RETINOPATHY

Class I: Essential hypertension, no obvious eye changes.
Class II: Essential hypertension with narrowing of arterioles, localized or generalized. A-V nicking is present. Exaggerated light reflex.
Class III: Essential hypertension with arteriolar changes of Class II plus exudate and hemorrhage in the retina.
Class IV: Essential hypertension with changes of Class III plus edema of the optic disk.

SPECIAL CIRCULATORY TESTS

Peripheral Venous Pressure Determination. (See p. 440 for Central Venous Pressure.)
Normal range: 6 to 11 cm. of water.
A. Direct Method: The patient is supine. Support his arm on pillows so that the antecubital vein is at a point approximately half the distance between the anterior and posterior surfaces of the trunk.

The venous pressure can be measured by an 18 gauge needle connected through a two-way stopcock to a vertical manometer and 2 ml. syringe. From the syringe, sterile saline is pushed into the manometer to a level above the possible venous pressure. The valve on the stopcock is then adjusted so that the vertical tube becomes continuous with the needle. The saline runs into the vein until the vertical height of the column of saline is in equilibrium with the venous pressure at the point of the needle.
B. Clinical Examination: With patient supine, lower arm to fill veins. Then slowly raise hand until veins collapse. Measure distance of antecubital or forearm veins above midpoint between anterior and posterior planes of the trunk to get venous pressure in cm. water.

The internal jugular venous pulse reflects the right atrial pressure. The reference point of measurement is the sternoclavicular angle with the patient propped up at 45 degrees. The distance between the top of the venous column and the sternal angle represents the central venous pressure. Normal jugular venous pressure should not exceed 3 cm. and is recorded in cm. of blood. This is a technic difficult to master but more than worth the effort.

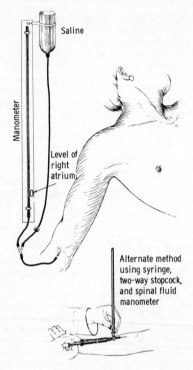

Two Technics of Measuring Peripheral Venous Pressure.
(Reproduced, with permission, from Ganong: Review of
Medical Physiology, 4th Ed. Lange, 1969.)

Circulation Time Determination.

In all circulation time tests, tell patient what he may experience and ask that he give a specific signal immediately.
Inject drug rapidly and take time from beginning injection.

A. Arm-to-tongue Time:

1. Sodium dehydrocholate (Decholin® Sodium) - Normal =
10 to 16 seconds. With elbow extended, enter antecubital vein with syringe needle. Note time, and rapidly
inject 5 ml. of a 20% solution of Decholin®. Note time
at which patient first notices a bitter taste. Severe,
protracted pain will follow extravasation of Decholin®
into the tissues. Bitter taste disappears in seconds,
at which time the test may be repeated without with-
drawing needle.

2. Calcium gluconate - Normal = 10 to 18 seconds. Inject 3 to 4 ml. of a 20% solution. Note time until patient has a sudden sensation of heat in pharynx (which spreads to face and trunk). Use cautiously if patients are receiving digitalis.

3. Magnesium sulfate - Normal = 9 to 16 seconds. Inject 5 ml. of a 10% solution of magnesium sulfate. Note the time until the patient experiences a sensation of warmth in the throat and tongue.

4. Saccharin - Normal = 9 to 16 seconds. Dissolve 2.5 Gm. (37$\frac{1}{2}$ gr.) of soluble saccharin in 3 ml. of water by boiling, allow to cool, and inject. A sweet taste appears in the throat, goes rapidly over the tongue to its tip, and then vanishes.

B. Arm-to-lung Time: Ether and saline are used for this determination. Normal = 3 to 8 seconds. With a tuberculin syringe inject a mixture of 0.66 ml. of saline and 0.33 ml. of ether. Note the time until the patient smells the ether. The patient also usually coughs and makes a wry face. Any queer sensations in the injected arm are transitory and harmless.

C. Lung-to-tongue Time: Normal = 4$\frac{1}{2}$ to 10 seconds. This is calculated by subtracting "arm-to-lung time" from "arm-to-tongue time."

D. Interpretation: In general, blood circulates more rapidly in hyperthyroidism, anemia, beri-beri, and Paget's disease; it circulates more slowly in myxedema, polycythemia vera, and cardiac failure. In isolated left heart failure, the arm-to-tongue time is usually 20 seconds or more. In isolated right heart failure the arm-to-lung time is usually prolonged, but not the lung-to-tongue time. Even in the absence of physical signs, circulation time is often prolonged in early heart failure.

Circulation time will be prolonged in a dilated heart without failure due to longer mixing time in a large reservoir of ventricular blood.

CARDIAC CATHETERIZATION
(See table on p. 58.)

Cardiac catheterization is a technic which may yield valuable information in the diagnosis and evaluation of congenital and acquired heart disease which cannot be precisely diagnosed by simpler methods.

In congenital heart disease cardiac catheterization is chiefly of value in the diagnosis of pulmonary stenosis, localization of left to right shunts, anomalous pulmonary veins, and the associated congenital anomalies which may be present. It is also of value in evaluating the severity of these anomalies

CARDIAC CATHETERIZATION DATA*

	Pressure (mm. Hg)			Percentage Oxygen Saturation					Significant Findings on Catheterization
	RA	RV	PA	VC	RA	RV	PA	A	
Normal Values	0-5	20-30/0-4	20-30/8-12	65-75	65-75	65-75	65-75	95-98	
Atrial septal defect	Normal	Normal or sl. incr.	Normal or sl. incr.	Normal	**> SVC**	Same as RA	Same as RA	Normal	Catheter may pass from RA to LA.
Ventricular septal defect	Normal or high	Normal or high	Normal or high	Normal	Normal	**> RA**	Same as RV	Normal	Catheter may pass into LV and aorta.
Patent ductus arteriosus	Normal or high	Normal or high	Normal or high	Normal	Normal	Normal	**> RV**	Normal	Catheter may pass from PA into aorta.
Pulmonary stenosis	Normal or high	**High**	**Normal or low**	Normal	Normal	Normal	Normal	**Normal**	Significant gradient of pressure across pulmonic valve.
Tetralogy of Fallot	Normal or high	**High**	**Normal or low**	Low	Same as SVC	Same as SVC	Same as SVC	**Low**	Catheter passes from RV into aorta; gradient across pulmonic valve.
Eisenmenger's syndrome	Normal or high	**High**	**High**	Low	Same as SVC	Same as SVC	Same as SVC	**Low**	Catheter passes into LV or aorta from RV; no gradient across pulmonic valve.

VC = vena cava   LA = left atrium   PA = pulmonary artery   > = greater than
RA = right atrium   RV = right ventricle   A = peripheral artery   SVC = superior vena cava

*Modified from T. G. Schnabel, Jr., & others, Pennsylvania M.J. **57**:363, 1954. The most significant findings are in bold type.

and in determining whether or not they are correctable. It is of value in determining the degree of pulmonary hypertension and the presence of reversal of flow across congenital shunts, with its poor prognosis.

In acquired heart disease cardiac catheterization is of value in determining the severity of valvular heart disease, constrictive pericarditis, and the myopathies.

The information obtained includes (1) the position of the tip of the catheter and its potential passage through an abnormal shunt under fluoroscopic visualization, (2) the pressures in vessels and chambers, (3) pressure gradients across valves, and (4) the oxygen content and capacity of the blood from various locations (as possible evidence of admixture of blood from the right side of the heart with that of the left). Volume of shunts can be determined by calculating pulmonary and peripheral blood flow and subtracting the latter from the former.

The chief complications of significance are cardiac arrhythmias. For this reason, cardiac catheterization should be performed under continuous ECG monitoring.

Right Heart Catheterization.

This is accomplished by passing the cardiac catheter into the right atrium, ventricle, pulmonary artery, and pulmonary capillary wedge position. The point of entry is most commonly the basilic vein.

Left Heart Catheterization (Retrograde Femoral Arteriography).

Another technic is the retrograde femoral arteriogram. The catheter is slipped into a femoral artery. Under fluoroscopic observation, it is passed up the aorta and through the aortic valve orifice during systole. The catheter may then be passed into the left atrium during diastole. The coronary arteries may also be visualized. Cineangiocardiographic recording is the optimal technic for interpretation of the dye injection. Right heart studies must of course be done separately as indicated above.

ANGIOCARDIOGRAPHY

Angiocardiography is a specialized x-ray method of outlining the chambers of the heart following the injection of a radiopaque material, meglumine diatrizoate (Renografin®). In adults, 1 ml./Kg. of a 76% solution of Renografin® is rapidly injected into an antecubital vein. In children, one-fourth to one-half this dose is used. Serial rapid x-rays of the chest are made in rapid succession to demonstrate contrast visualization of the various cardiac chambers. This technic is chiefly of use in the diagnosis of congenital heart disease, pulmonary arteriovenous fistula, and aneurysm of the aorta. In the latter, direct injection into an artery may give better delineation. Because of the hazards of this diagnostic method (primarily due to the high concentration of the radiopaque material), it should be reserved for those conditions which cannot be diagnosed by other means. Cineangiocardiography is the technic by which the entire procedure may be recorded on film for detailed study.

Left heart retrograde femoral catheterization now allows for specific angiograms of the left heart, aorta, and renal arteries.

EXAMINATION OF PERIPHERAL VESSELS

History.
Question patient about previous episodes of pain, claudication, weakness, numbness or paresthesia, temperature change, color change, edema, phlebitis.

Inspection.
Examine patient for visible pulsations, atrophy of muscles or skin, pigmentation, nail deformities, sweat, gangrene.

Auscultation.
Auscultate over great vessels for murmurs (aneurysm, atherosclerosis) or hums (veins).

By auscultation over the aorta, the common carotid, renal, common and external iliac, and femoral arteries, bruits may be heard which may be a manifestation of an obstructive process.

Palpation of Peripheral Pulses.
Palpate the following pulses: subclavian, carotid, temporal, axillary, brachial, radial, ulnar, digital, abdominal aortic, external iliac, femoral, popliteal, anterior tibial, dorsalis pedis, posterior tibial. Compare carotid and femoral.

The femoral pulse is best felt with the patient supine and fingertips over the artery at the inguinal ligament. Popliteal artery pulsation is best felt with the patient on his side with his knees flexed one in front of the other. Examiner faces the patient and places four fingers of each hand over the course of the artery with the thumbs on or at the edge of the patella.

Observations of Surface Temperature.
In the extremities the temperatures normally vary less than 1.5°C. at any given level bilaterally. However, there may be marked differences in temperature longitudinally.

Palpation with the back of the fingers will detect differences of 1°C. The patient should be exposed to the room temperature at least 15 minutes before comparing temperatures.

Special Examinations of Arteries of Legs.

A. Elevation Pallor and Dependent Rubor: The patient lies supine with his legs elevated 45° and with his heels supported on the examiner's outstretched hand or, more conveniently, on the back rest of the bed or examining table. The blood is stroked out of the sole of the foot, or the patient alternately flexes and extends the toes. At the end of three minutes, observation of the color is made. Only mild pallor should be present. If any part of the foot is dead white, arterial disease is present. The patient now returns to the sitting position with his feet dependent. A pink flush should return to the entire foot in ten seconds. With arterial disease it may be delayed up to two or three minutes and be replaced by a deep cyanotic rubor which is called dependent rubor.

B. Claudication Test: (Claudication occurs only in relation to muscular activity and ceases in minutes following cessation of activity. Claudication not uncommonly occurs in the low back, buttocks, thighs, and calves.) Have the patient, with shoes and socks on, walk at a rate of 120 steps per minute and record the time and point at which the pain appears and the time in which it disappears. Failure to claudicate after five minutes of rapid walking indicates that circulation is intact or collateralization is adequate.

Special Examinations of Arteries of Arms.

A. Allen Test (Modified): The patient's arm is abducted 90°, with his forearm at an angle of 90° to the upper arm and his palm facing the examiner. The examiner grasps the patient's elbow with his opposite hand, placing his thumb on the olecranon and his fingers on the lower brachial artery, which is tightly compressed against the humerus. The patient then quickly opens and closes his hand tightly ten times. The hand is then kept tightly closed. The examiner's free hand then grasps the patient's wrist firmly and the patient opens his hand, which should be almost devoid of blood. The hand occluding the brachial artery is released as the wrist is grasped. The examiner's free hand now massages any remaining color out of the hand. This position is maintained for three to five minutes. On release of the patient's wrist a hyperemic flush should sweep smoothly and rapidly through the palms and fingers. Occlusion of palmar or digital arteries is indicated by zones of pallor which fail to fill or fill slowly. If determination of the patency of the radial

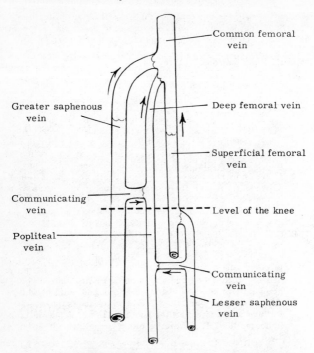

Common femoral vein

Greater saphenous vein

Deep femoral vein

Superficial femoral vein

Communicating vein

Level of the knee

Popliteal vein

Communicating vein

Lesser saphenous vein

Diagram Showing Veins of Legs, Their Valves, and Normal Direction of Blood Flow

or ulnar artery is desired, the radial or ulnar artery is occluded digitally by exerting pressure over the artery with counter-traction by the thumb against the radius or ulna before the occluding hand at the wrist is released. When the ulnar artery is occluded and the radial artery compressed, the hand should remain pallid and, on release, should fill the radial side first. In occluding the radial or ulnar arteries, care should be taken not to stretch the skin or fascia tightly over the vessel being tested.

B. Test for Scalenus Anticus Syndrome: The subclavian and radial arteries are identified. With his arm at his side and the examiner's hand on his radial pulse, the patient rotates his head to the examined side simultaneously with a deep inspiration and elevation of the chest wall. If there is compression, the radial pulse will disappear and a murmur may be heard over the subclavian artery just before total obliteration of the pulse. This test may be positive in some normal people.

Test for Varicose Veins (Modified Trendelenburg Test).

With the patient supine the limb is elevated and the superficial veins emptied. The greater saphenous vein is compressed proximal to the knee with a rubber tubing tourniquet. With simple varices due to sapheno-femoral valve incompetence, the varicosities distal to the tourniquet fill slowly in a central direction after 20 seconds. If the tourniquet is released, the simple varicosities will fill suddenly in a peripheral direction. If the varicosities fill rapidly from below with the tourniquet in place the test should be repeated with the tourniquet just below the knee. Nonfilling now indicates simple varices due to sapheno-popliteal valve incompetency. Rapid filling indicates postphlebitic varicosities with many incompetent perforating or communicating veins.

Other Methods of Examination.

Reflex vasodilatation test (Landis and Gibbon), arteriography, plethysmography, oscillometry, and skin temperature studies following peripheral nerve or sympathetic nerve block.

PULMONARY PHYSIOLOGY AND TESTS OF FUNCTION

The primary functions of the lung are to oxygenate pulmonary capillary mixed venous blood and, conversely, to eliminate excess CO_2. The lung thus acts as a gas exchange organ for the purpose of arterialization of venous blood. Three processes are involved in this gas exchange: (1) ventilation of the alveoli; (2) diffusion of O_2 and CO_2 across the alveolar-capillary membranes; and (3) perfusion of the alveoli by the pulmonary circulation.

Ventilation is the process by which environmental O_2 is delivered to the alveoli and CO_2 returned from the alveoli to the ambient atmosphere. The following factors are involved in the ventilatory process: (1) the bellows action of the thorax and diaphragm, which produces inspiratory and expiratory flow by creating cyclic pressure gradients between environmental air and intrapleural space; (2) airway resistance to flow; (3) lung compliance (stretch and recoil); and (4) uniformity of distribution of air to the alveoli.

Diffusion is the process by which O_2 passively crosses the alveolar—pulmonary capillary membranes; at the same time, CO_2 passes from pulmonary capillary blood into the alveolar sacs. This occurs because the pressure gradients of O_2 are higher in the alveoli than in the unoxygenated blood, whereas the reverse holds true for CO_2.

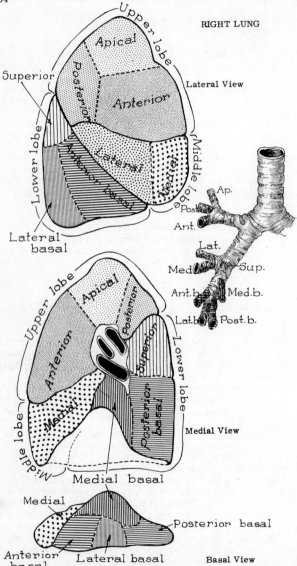

64

RIGHT LUNG

Lateral View

Medial View

Basal View

Redrawn and reproduced, with permission, from C.L. Jackson and
J.F. Huber, Dis. Chest 9:319, 1943.

LEFT LUNG

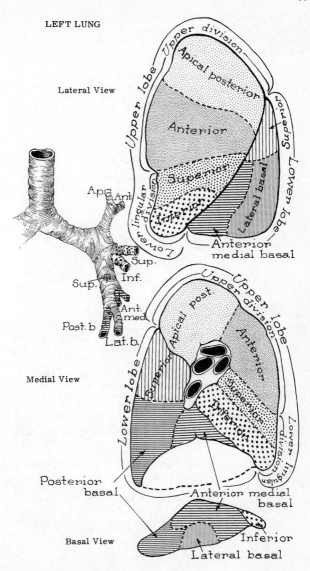

Lateral View

Medial View

Basal View

From Jackson and Huber, ibid.

Perfusion is the process by which mixed venous blood is carried to the alveolar capillaries in a volume and at a rate that allow effective exchange of O_2 and CO_2 across the alveolar-capillary membranes.

Ideally, optimal gas exchange would occur if all alveoli were effectively ventilated by air and perfused by alveolar capillary blood. This functional relationship is expressed by the ventilation-perfusion ratio $\dot{V}/\dot{Q}$, where $\dot{V}$ and $\dot{Q}$ represent, respectively, alveolar ventilation and pulmonary blood flow in liters per minute.

$$\text{Normal:} \quad \frac{\dot{V}}{\dot{Q}} = \frac{4 \text{ L./minute}}{5 \text{ L./minute}} = 0.8$$

Hypoxia can result from abnormalities of perfusion if blood is distributed to areas of the lung that are not ventilated. In this way unsaturated blood continuously mixes with blood effectively oxygenated by ventilated alveoli. This is comparable to a right-to-left shunt but does not necessarily presume an abnormal anatomic pathway, e.g., it may occur in early atelectasis or pulmonary edema.

PHYSIOLOGIC TESTS OF PULMONARY FUNCTION

Like all other tests of organ function, tests of pulmonary function should be interpreted in conjunction with the associated clinical picture. Some of the more sophisticated studies outlined below require special equipment in experienced hands; they are usually done in a general hospital or pulmonary function laboratory.

It must be emphasized that these tests only measure pulmonary function; their results do not identify the cause of impaired function nor the specific pathologic lesions responsible.

Tests of Ventilation. (There are significant variations with sex, age, height, position, and degree of activity.)
A. Lung Volumes:
   1. VT (tidal volume) - The volume of gas inspired or expired during each respiratory cycle. (Normal: ± 500 ml.)
   2. VE (minute ventilation) - Tidal volume times respiratory rate per minute. (Normal: ± 6000 ml./minute.)
   3. VC (vital capacity) - The maximal volume of gas that can be expired after maximal inspiration without regard to time elapsed. Predicted values in liters:
   VC = 0.133 × height in inches − 0.22 A (age in years) − 3.60. (Boren et al., Am. J. Med. **41**:96-114, 1966.) (Adult males.)

4. RV (residual volume) - The volume of gas in the lungs at the end of maximal expiration. (Normal: ± 1200 ml.)

5. TLC (total lung capacity) - The volume of gas in the lungs at the end of maximal inspiration. Predicted values in liters: TLC = 0.198 × height in inches − 7.3. (Boren et al., Am. J. Med. 41:96-114, 1966.) (Adult males.)

6. RV/TLC (ratio of residual volume to total lung capacity). (Normal: 0.2 to 0.4.)

7. VD (anatomic dead space) - Internal volume of conducting airway from nose and mouth to the alveoli. This volume dilutes the inspired and expired gas flow. (Normal: 100 to 200 ml.; roughly equal to body weight in pounds.)

8. Physiologic dead space - The anatomic dead space plus alveoli in which there is no gas exchange as a result of lack of perfusion. In good health, anatomic and physiologic dead space are identical; in disease states, the latter exceeds the former. Normally, in the standing position, upper lobe alveoli are not as well perfused as lower lobe alveoli.

B. Tests of Airway Resistance: (If abnormal, repeat after inhalation of bronchodilator, e. g., isoproterenol.)

1. FEV_1 (forced expiratory volume) - Volume of a maximally fast exhalation from a point of maximal inspiration in one second; usually expressed as percentage of actual vital capacity. (Normal: 84% ± 7%.)

2. MVV_F (maximal voluntary ventilation) or MBC (maximal breathing capacity) - Maximal volume expelled in 12 seconds of forced breathing. Predicted value in liters per minute: MVV = (3.39 × height in inches) − 1.26 A (age in years) − 21.4. (Boren et al., Am. J. Med. 41:96-114, 1966.) (Adult males.)

C. Test of Lung Compliance (CL): (Measurement of the elastic properties of the lung.) The change in lung volume per unit of intrapleural pressure change is expressed in liters/ml. H_2O. (Normal: 0.2 L./ml. H_2O.)

D. Test of Distribution of Inspired Air: A rapidly responding nitrogen analyzer is used to measure the change in nitrogen concentration during the plateau phase of an exhalation following a deep breath of oxygen. Patients with normal distribution of inspired air have less than 2% change in nitrogen concentration between 750 ml. and 1250 ml. of the exhalation (represents alveolar gas).

Test of Diffusion.

Diffusion is the passive process by which a gas moves from a region of high concentration to one of lower concentration. O_2 and CO_2 are thus exchanged across the alveolocapillary-erythrocyte membrane, providing a common meeting ground for the body's atmosphere and the ambient atmosphere. O_2 and CO_2 are technically difficult to use as testing gases. Therefore, CO, which is comparable to the physical characteristics of O_2, is used. The normal DL_{CO} (diffusing capacity of the lung for CO) is 25 to 35 ml./min./mm. Hg.

Test of Perfusion.

Several complicated tests are utilized to determine the $\dot{V}/\dot{Q}$ ratio. The test most commonly used specifically to determine perfusion abnormality caused by right-to-left shunt is the breathing of 100% oxygen for 10 to 20 minutes.

The individual without significant shunt will replace alveolar nitrogen with O_2 at increased tension in a sufficient number of alveoli to raise the arterial P_{O_2} from the normal 95 mm. Hg to 550 mm. Hg or more. The patient with hypoxia due to excessive shunt cannot achieve nearly such a rise in arterial P_{O_2}.

Other Normal Values.

Average alveolar ventilation (L./min.)	4
Average pulmonary blood flow (L./min.)	5
Ventilation-perfusion ratio	0.8
Mixed venous O_2 saturation (%)	75
Arterial O_2 saturation (%)	97
Venous P_{O_2} (mm. Hg)	40
Arterial P_{O_2} (mm. Hg)	95
Alveolar P_{O_2} (mm. Hg)	100
Venous P_{CO_2} (mm. Hg)	46
Arterial P_{CO_2} (mm. Hg)	40
Alveolar P_{CO_2} (mm. Hg)	40
pH of plasma, arterial blood	7.40
pH of plasma, venous blood	7.37

Bronchospirometry.

This technic allows separate measurement and recording of minute volume, vital capacity, exchanges of O_2, CO_2, and CO in each lung. This is achieved by inserting a double lumen catheter into the trachea. One catheter is passed into the left main stem bronchus. A balloon near the end of this catheter occludes the bronchus, and all air exchange in the left lung must occur through its catheter opening. The tip of the second catheter remains in the trachea, but a balloon just proximal to the opening occludes the trachea and all air from the right lung passes through the catheter.

Technics are also available for assessing lobar function.

5...

Electrocardiography

The electrocardiogram (Ecg. or EKG) is a graphic record of the voltage fluctuations produced by the myocardium during the cardiac cycle. It does not represent the mechanical events of the heart. The P, QRS, and T waves reflect the rhythmic electrical depolarization or repolarization of the myocardium which precedes or follows the contractions.

Damage to the myocardium or conduction system **may** show a change in point of origin, spread, and regression of electrical activity, and thus a change in the Ecg. pattern. A minute area of damage in the bundle of His may produce a more striking change than is produced by a larger area of damage in the ventricular wall. On the other hand, the electrical activity of some areas of the heart is not adequately reflected in the ordinary Ecg., and damage in those areas may not be demonstrable by Ecg. Normal variations of the position of the heart may influence the pattern markedly. Normal Ecg.'s may be found in severely damaged hearts and, infrequently, abnormal Ecg.'s may be found in normal hearts. The Ecg. should therefore be employed as a supplementary technic in the study of heart disease. It is a valuable diagnostic tool for a competent clinician who understands and can evaluate it in the context of the whole clinical situation.

The Ecg. is of particular value in recognition of the following cardiac disorders: (1) Arrhythmias, conduction defects, and ectopic foci. (2) Myocardial infarction. (3) Atrial and ventricular hypertrophy. (4) Drug effects, especially digitalis and quinidine. (5) Cardiac involvement in systemic diseases such as rheumatic fever, diphtheria, or viral diseases. (6) Hypokalemia or hyperkalemia. (7) Pericarditis. (8) Congenital heart disease.

NORMAL RANGES OF DEFLECTIONS
IN STANDARD LEADS

P Waves. (Deflection produced by atrial depolarization.)
1. Maximal normal amplitude = 2.5 mm.
2. Maximal normal duration = 0.10 sec.
3. Upright in leads I and II.

Q Waves. (Initial negative deflection of ventricular depolarization.)
1. Maximal normal amplitude = 25% of the height of the R wave, providing the R wave exceeds 5 mm. in amplitude. Some authorities use 50% as a criterion.

69

NORMAL RANGES OF DEFLECTIONS IN THE UNIPOLAR LIMB AND PRECORDIAL LEADS (ADULTS)

(Figures for range and mean in mm. from Sokolow and Friedlander, Amer. Heart J. 38:665, 1949.)

	P	Q	R	S	T	S-T Segment
V_1	Upright to inverted	Absent* 0	R < S 0-7 mm. (2.3)	S > R 2-25 mm. (8.6)	Upright or inverted -0.4 to +4.0 mm. (0.15)	†
V_2	Upright to diphasic	Absent* 0	R < S 0-16 mm. (5.9)	S > R 0-29 mm. (12.7)	Upright‡ -3 to +18 mm. (5.5)	†
V_3	Upright	Minute* 0-0.5 mm. (0.01)	Transition§ not < RV2 1.5-26 mm. (8.9)	Transition§ not > SV2 0-25 mm. (8.8)	Upright‡ -2 to +16 mm. (5.4)	†
V_4	Upright	Minute* 0-3 mm. (0.1)	Transition§ not < RV3 4-27 mm. (14.2)	Transition§ not > SV3 0-20 mm. (5.2)	Upright‡ 0-17 mm. (4.8)	†
V_5	Upright	Minute* 0-3 mm. (0.3)	> RV1-4 R > 1 4-24 mm. (12.1)	< SV4 S < R 0-6 mm. (1.5)	Upright 0-9 mm. (3.4)	†
V_6	Upright	Minute 0-2 mm. (0.4)	< RV5 R > 6 4-22 mm. (9.2)	Minute S < R 0-7 mm. (0.6)	Upright‡ -0.5 to +5 mm. (2.43)	†
aVL	**	** 0-3.5 mm. (0.2)	** 0-10 mm. (2.1)	** 0-18 mm. (0.4)	** -4 to +6 mm. (0.53)	
aVR	Inverted	** 0-8 mm. (2.0)	Small 0-5 mm. (0.8)	Prominent** 0-13 mm. (4.3)	Inverted** -5 to -1.5 mm. (-2.31)	
aVF	Upright	** 0-3 mm. (0.5)	** 0-20 mm. (1.3)	** 0-8 mm. (0.2)	** -0.5 to +5 mm. (1.86)	

*A QS complex may be present normally in V_1, at times in V_2, and even in V_3 with clockwise rotation. A normal Q wave should be less than 0.04 seconds in duration.

†Maximal normal ST elevation in V_{1-3} is 3 mm.; in V_{4-6} it is 1 mm. with contour being concave upwards. Maximal normal ST depression in V_{1-6} is 0.5 mm.

‡Usually inverted to age 16; juvenile pattern. Rarely persists to age 30.

§Marked variability in transition zone (see pp. 72-73).

**Marked variability depending on electrical position in the heart. Normal T inversion in aVL and aVF may occur if R < 5 mm.

2. Maximal normal duration = 0.04 sec.
   (A significant Q wave is one which meets both these criteria. As an isolated finding in lead III it may be normal.)

R Waves. (Initial positive deflection of ventricular depolarization.)
   1. Maximal normal amplitude = 16 mm. in lead I. $R_1 + S_3$
      should not exceed 23 mm.
   2. Maximal normal duration - The duration of the QRS com-
      plex is usually considered to be and should not exceed
      0.10 sec.

S Waves. (Initial negative deflection following the R wave.)
   1. Maximal normal amplitude - Deep S waves may occur in
      normal vertical hearts.
   2. Maximal normal duration = 0.04 sec.

T Waves. (Deflection of ventricular repolarization.)
   1. Appearance - Upright in leads I and II, variable in III.
   2. Minimal normal amplitude = 1 mm. if R wave is no less
      than 5 mm. With tall R waves, T:R ratio should be 1:10.
   3. Duration - No standard figure.

U Waves.
   A deflection (usually positive) seen following the T wave.
   Exact cause is not known. Usually a normal variant, but
   also appears with quinidine administration and hypokalemia.

P-R Interval, Q-T Interval: See below and p. 96.

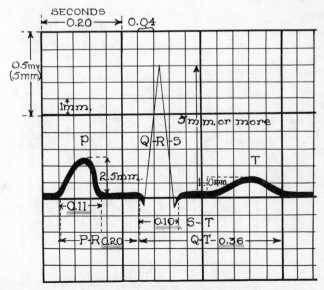

Waves of the Electrocardiogram

NORMAL ELECTROCARDIOGRAPHIC VARIATIONS
DUE TO VARIATIONS OF POSITIONS OF
THE HEART (ELECTRICAL AXIS)

(See p. 78.)

	Limb Leads		Precordial Leads	
	aVL (Left Arm)	aVF (Left Leg)	V₁* (Rt. Ventricle)	V₆* (Left Ventricle)
Vertical Heart	Resembles rt. ventricle (V₁)	Resembles left ventricle (V₆)		
Semi-vertical Heart	Small R	Resembles left ventricle (V₆)		
Inter-mediate Heart	Resembles aVF and left ventricle (V₆)	Resembles aVL and left ventricle (V₆)		
Semi-horizontal Heart	Resembles left ventricle (V₆)	Small R		
Horizontal Heart	Resembles left ventricle (V₆)	Resembles rt. ventricle (V₁)		

*Assuming no unusual rotation on long axis.

SIGNIFICANCE OF THE ELECTROCARDIOGRAPHIC LEADS

The electrical potentials produced by the heart are transmitted to all parts of the body. The electrical potential in the extremities depends on the portion of the heart directed to that extremity, either the thick left ventricle, the thin right ventricle, or the cavity of the heart.

Standard Leads.

The standard leads I, II, and III are bipolar indirect leads - bipolar because they represent the difference in electrical potential of two extremities, indirect because they are recorded at a point distant from the heart. The standard leads therefore reflect the algebraic sum of the electrical potentials at three pairs of points located at a distance from the heart. Abnormal potentials produced by a small infarct may be completely obscured by the normal electrical potentials generated by the remaining mass of normal heart.

Unipolar Leads.

The unipolar leads represent an attempt to record the electrical potential at any one point instead of the difference in potential between the two points of a bipolar lead by reducing the potential in one lead to almost zero (by the Wilson or Goldberger technic) and using the other lead as a semidirect exploring lead. It has been shown, however, that these leads do not record spot potential of a localized area of the heart, but record **all** the electrical events of the cardiac cycle as viewed from the point of lead application.

    A. Unipolar Precordial Leads: The unipolar precordial leads (V_1 to V_6) are semidirect leads approximately representing the variation of electrical potential from a single point of the heart. These leads are approximately comparable to direct leads placed on the epicardium of an exposed animal heart. This technic produces Ecg. complexes which are characteristic for each ventricle. Small lesions can be demonstrated which might be masked in the bipolar standard leads.

    B. Unipolar Limb Leads: The ventricular complexes of the unipolar limb leads show the variation of electrical potential at the right arm (aVR), the left arm (aVL), and the left foot (aVF). The potential variations and hence the ventricular complexes of aVL and aVF are similar to those of either the right or left ventricle, depending on the "electrocardiographic position" (electrical axis) of the heart. In the normal heart the appearance of the ventricular complexes of V_1 to V_6 remains relatively constant, varying chiefly with rotation around the longitudinal axis (see p. 78). The ventricular complexes of aVL and aVF will vary with the position of the heart. By comparing the unipolar precordial leads (V_1 to V_6) with the unipolar limb leads (aVL and aVF), the Ecg. position of the heart can be determined as follows: (See pp. 72, 73, 76.)

1. Vertical heart - Ventricular complexes of aVL resemble those of V_1 and V_2; ventricular complexes of aVF resemble those of V_5 and V_6.
2. Semivertical heart - Ventricular complexes of aVF resemble those of V_5 and V_6; those of aVL are small.
3. Intermediate heart - The ventricular complexes of aVL and aVF are similar to each other in size and form and resemble those of V_5 and V_6.
4. Semihorizontal heart - Ventricular complexes of aVL resemble those of V_5 and V_6; those of aVF are small.
5. Horizontal heart - Ventricular complexes of aVL resemble those of V_5 and V_6; ventricular complexes of aVF resemble those of V_1 and V_2.

Depending on the "electrocardiographic position" of the left and right ventricles in relation to aVL, aVF, and aVR, various characteristic abnormal patterns can be reflected in these leads. This is especially true in ventricular hypertrophy and myocardial infarction. These leads are also of value in detecting occasional normal variations in heart position.

CORRELATION OF EXCITATION WAVE AND QRS PATTERN

The concepts of intrinsic deflection and ventricular activation time (V.A.T.) have considerable practical significance in the Ecg. diagnosis of ventricular hypertrophy and bundle branch block.

Intrinsic deflection is synonymous with the downstroke of the R wave. The point at which it begins is the point of complete activation of the ventricular wall.

Ventricular activation time (V.A.T.) is the interval between the beginning of the QRS complex and the peak of the R wave. It represents the time elapsing from initial activation of the bundle of His to the point of complete activation of the muscle. The V.A.T. varies with the thickness of the ventricle. The upper limit of normal in V_1 and V_2 (right ventricle) is 0.03 sec. The upper limit in V_5 and V_6 (left ventricle) is 0.05 sec.

The excitation wave spreads through the Purkinje network parallel to the endocardium. It then turns at a right angle, passing through the myocardium from its endocardial to its epicardial surface; this produces the upstroke of the R wave. The peak of the R wave represents complete activation of the ventricular wall under the electrode. When the excitation wave reaches the epicardium, the electrical potential instantly drops to zero; this accounts for the downstroke of the R wave. Therefore, hypertrophy of either ventricle usually prolongs the time required by the excitation wave to pass from endocardium to epicardium and hence is reflected by a prolonged V.A.T.

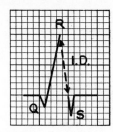

Intrinsic Deflection
(I.D.)

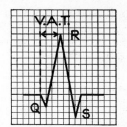

Ventricular Activation Time
(V.A.T.)

With bundle branch block, the V.A.T. of the involved chamber is markedly prolonged; this is due to the devious route through which the excitation wave must reach the wall of that ventricle. In this instance a bifid or notched R wave is produced and the V.A.T. is measured to the second peak, which is the beginning of the intrinsic deflection (see below).

VENTRICULAR ACTIVATION TIME ABNORMALITIES

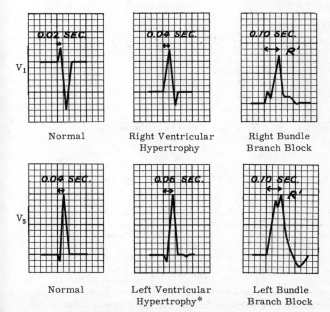

	Normal	Right Ventricular Hypertrophy	Right Bundle Branch Block
V_1	0.02 SEC.	0.04 SEC.	0.10 SEC.
V_5	0.04 SEC.	0.06 SEC.	0.10 SEC.
	Normal	Left Ventricular Hypertrophy*	Left Bundle Branch Block

*V.A.T. prolongation rarely seen.

NORMAL ELECTROCARDIOGRAPHIC PATTERNS

Intermediate Heart.

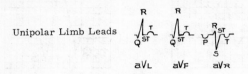

Unipolar Limb Leads

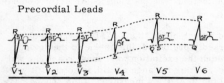

Precordial Leads

RT. VENT. COMPLEXES   LT. VENT. COMPLEXES

1. Position - Intermediate (R waves in aVL and aVF are upright and equal.
2. Transition zone - Between V_4 and V_5.
3. Rotation - None.
4. QRS interval - Maximum = 0.10 sec.
5. P wave - Inverted in aVR and sometimes in V_1.
6. Q wave - Minute in aVL, aVF, V_5, and V_6.
7. T wave - Inverted in aVR, sometimes in V_1. In children, T in V_{1-4} is normally inverted.
8. Ventricular activation time (V.A.T.) - Maximum V_1 = 0.03 sec.; $V_{5,6}$ = 0.05 sec.

Horizontal Heart With Counterclockwise Rotation.

Unipolar Limb Leads

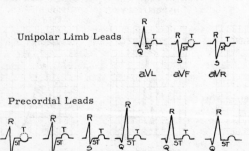

Precordial Leads

RT. VENT. COMPLEXES   LT. VENT. COMPLEXES

1. Position - Horizontal (AVL resembles V_6; aVF resembles V_1).
2. Transition zone - Between V_2 and V_3.
3. Rotation - Counterclockwise (see above).
4. Q wave - Minute in aVL, V_{4-6}.
5. QRS, T, and V.A.T. - As above.

Vertical Heart With Clockwise Rotation.

Unipolar Limb Leads

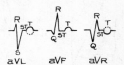

Precordial Leads

RT. VENT. COMPLEXES   LT. VENT. COMPLEXES

1. Position - Vertical (aVL resembles V_1; aVF resembles V_6).
2. Transition zone - Between V_5 and V_6.
3. Rotation - Clockwise (see p. 78).
4. Q wave - Minute in aVF and V_6.
5. QRS, T, and V.A.T. - As on p. 76.

ROTATION OF HEART

Precordial leads over the right ventricle present a small R with a prominent S wave; over the left ventricle, a minute Q wave, a tall R wave, and a minute S wave. Normally the heart may be rotated clockwise or counterclockwise on its longitudinal axis (viewed from the apex). With clockwise rotation, QRS complexes with a right ventricular pattern may be present even in V_5 or V_6. With counterclockwise rotation, left ventricular complexes may be found in V_2.

RELATIONSHIP OF UNIPOLAR TO STANDARD LIMB LEADS

$I = (aVL - aVR)\ 2/3$ aVR = reverse (mirror image) of $\dfrac{I + II}{2}$

$II = (aVF - aVR)\ 2/3$ $aVL = \dfrac{I - III}{2}$

$III = (aVF - aVL)\ 2/3$ $aVF = \dfrac{II + III}{2}$

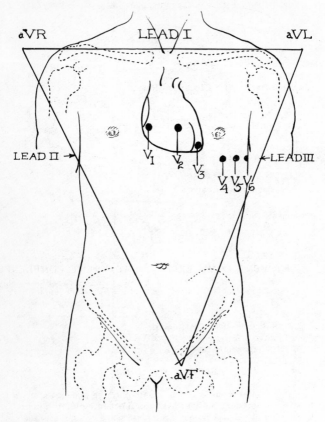

Graphic location of standard leads (I, II, III), unipolar limb leads (aVL, aVR, aVF), and unipolar precordial leads (V_{1-6}) with reference to the heart (see p. 79). The electrical potential of any extremity is the same anywhere from its point of attachment to the torso to its most distal end. Therefore, electrodes attached to wrists and ankles will give the same Ecg. pattern as those placed at the point of union of torso and extremity.

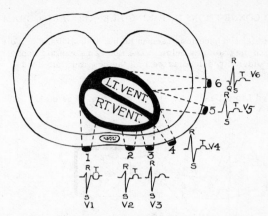

Precordial Leads in Relation to the Chambers of the Heart

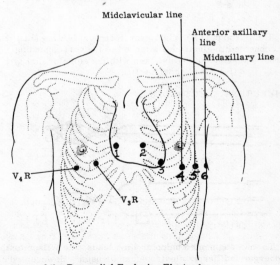

Locations of the Precordial Exploring Electrode.

    V_1 - Fourth interspace at right sternal border.
    V_2 - Fourth interspace at left sternal border.
    V_3 - Halfway between V_2 and V_4.
    V_4 - Fifth interspace at midclavicular line.
    V_5 - Anterior axillary line in same horizontal plane as V_4.
    V_6 - Midaxillary line in same horizontal plane as V_4.
    V_3R - Halfway between V_1 and V_4R.
    V_4R - Right fifth interspace at midclavicular line.

LEAD CONNECTIONS IN TAKING ELECTROCARDIOGRAM

The lead connections used in taking standard and unipolar leads are diagrammed below. The diagrams explain hookups for the older three-lead as well as the new multiple-lead Ecg.'s.

Standard Limb Leads. (I, II, III; 1, 2, 3 on Ecg. dial.)

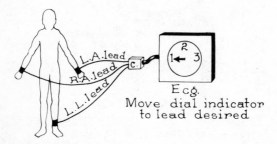

The left arm (LA), right arm (RA), and left leg (LL) leads are connected to electrodes attached to the corresponding limbs. The desired lead is taken with the selector dial at 1 (RA-LA), 2 (RA-LL), or 3 (LA-LL).

INDIFFERENT ELECTRODES

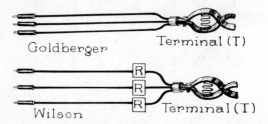

To take augmented unipolar limb leads, the Wilson or the Goldberger indifferent electrode can be used. However, the latter must be used in connecting the wires to the extremities. Both types of indifferent electrodes are composed basically of three separate lengths of insulated copper wire fastened together at one end by a battery clip (T; the central terminal). The Wilson electrode has a 5000-ohm resistor (R) connected to each wire between the tip and central terminal. These resistors eliminate the element of variation of skin resistances in the extremities.

Augmented Unipolar Limb Leads (aVR, aVL, aVF).

1. Central terminal is attached to RA lead from the Ecg.
2. LA lead is used as the exploring electrode.
3. LL lead from machine and any one of the 3 indifferent electrodes from central terminal (T) are left unattached.
4. The selector dial of the Ecg. is kept at lead 1.
5. Indifferent electrode lead is not attached to limb whose potential is being registered with the exploring LA lead.

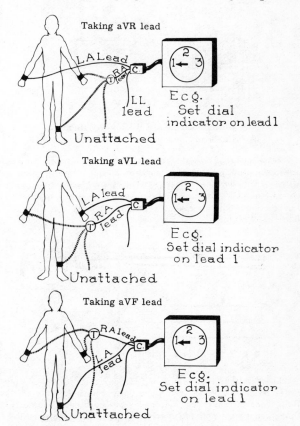

Taking aVR lead

LA Lead

RA lead

(T)

LL lead

Unattached

Ecg. Set dial indicator on lead 1

Taking aVL lead

LA lead

RA lead

(T)

Unattached

Ecg. Set dial indicator on lead 1

Taking aVF lead

RA lead

(T)

LA lead

Unattached

Ecg. Set dial indicator on lead 1

Unipolar Precordial Leads.

Either the Wilson or Goldberger indifferent electrode may be employed. The central terminal (T) remains attached to the RA lead of the Ecg.; the three wires of the terminal are

attached to the LA, RA, and LL. It makes no difference which
of the terminal wires is attached to a given extremity. The
LA lead of the Ecg. is used as the exploring chest electrode
at V_1 to V_6 (see p. 79). The selector dial is turned to lead 1
throughout as in the instance of the augmented limb leads.

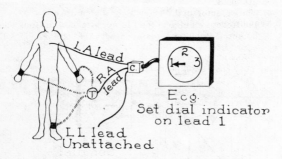

"Universal Lead Selector" (Wilson)
(Adaptable to Three-lead Electrocardiograph)

This compact unit may be attached to a three-lead Ecg.,
eliminating the need for wire changing (except for the various
position changes of the precordial leads). Circuit changes
are performed by rotating the selector dial. Any lead described above may be taken. A right leg wire is included to
serve as a ground.

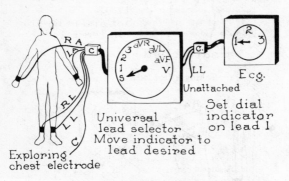

MODERN ELECTROCARDIOGRAPH MACHINES

Modern electrocardiographs are constructed so that augmented extremity leads can be taken with the same hook-up
used for standard leads by turning the dial to aVR, aVL, and
aVF. Unipolar chest leads are taken by applying the chest

lead to any position on the chest and turning the selector dial
to the V position.

TECHNIC OF READING THE ELECTROCARDIOGRAM

Interpretation of the Ecg. depends on the clinical acumen
of the interpreter. Although electrocardiography should be
considered a supplementary aid in the study of heart disease,
it may be the deciding factor in evaluating the clinical picture.
However, because various diseases and drugs may produce
similar patterns, objectivity is mandatory. Dogmatic statements regarding etiology, state of myocardial compensation,
and prognosis should not be based on Ecg. studies alone; when
Ecg. evidence is supported by adequate and accurate clinical
date, further inferences may be made.

A systematic approach to interpretation of the Ecg. is
essential to avoid errors. The following plan is suggested:

A. Routine Observations: (1) Detect any technical errors in
   preparations. (2) Observe rhythm. (3) Calculate rate
   (see p. 94). (4) Measure P-R interval (see p. 95). (5)
   Measure QRS interval. (6) Measure Q-T interval (see
   p. 95). (7) Determine axis in degrees and direction.
B. Observation of Abnormalities of Pattern:
   1. Standard leads (bipolar) - Significant P, QRS, ST, and
      T abnormalities.
   2. Unipolar extremity leads -
      a. Significant P, QRS, ST, and T abnormalities.
      b. Position of heart (horizontal, vertical, etc.).
   3. Unipolar precordial leads -
      a. Unusual rotation along the longitudinal axis.
      b. Significant P, QRS, ST, and T abnormalities.
      c. Abnormalities of V.A.T.
   4. Significant changes since previous record.
C. Ecg. Reports: Terminology varies. Unfortunately there
   is no standardized nomenclature. The following or various combinations thereof are suggested:
   1. "Within normal limits."
   2. "Borderline Ecg." (list questionable features).
   3. "Abnormal record characteristic of ...."
   4. "Abnormal record consistent with ...."
   5. "Abnormal record suggestive of ...."
   6. "Abnormal record of no characteristic pattern ...."
   7. "Abnormal record, evidence of myocardial disease."
   8. "Abnormal record suggestive of ... (drug) effect."
   9. "Serial Ecg.'s consistent with or characteristic of ...."
   10. "Abnormal Ecg. Suggest serial records or additional
       leads to rule out ...."
D. Remarks may be added indicating possible etiology, e.g.,
   "The pattern may occur in myocardial abnormality due to
   coronary atherosclerosis, pericarditis, myxedema, etc."

ELECTROCARDIOGRAPHIC INTERPRETATION
(Variations from the following patterns can occur.)

Normal Electrocardiogram.
Intermediate position with counterclockwise rotation.

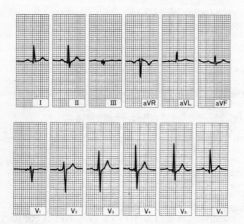

Sinus Tachycardia.
Each P wave has a normal contour and is followed by a QRS complex. Rate may vary with various stimuli.

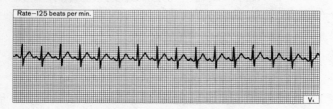

ECTOPIC ARRHYTHMIAS

Ventricular Premature Beats.
These are the result of an abnormal direction of spread of an impulse arising from an ectopic ventricular focus. A premature QRS, therefore, has a different contour than the QRS complex following the normal A-V conduction. It is abnormally broad, notched, and is followed by T waves which are opposite to the main QRS deflection. The predominant rhythm is not disturbed. R-R intervals containing premature QRS complexes are twice the length of R-R intervals which do not contain such a complex.

Lead II

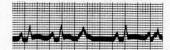

Atrial Premature Beats.

These are the result of an abnormal direction of spread of an impulse arising from an ectopic atrial focus. The distance of the ectopic focus from the sinus node determines whether the premature P wave is similar to or different from the normal P wave. The associated QRS complexes are unaltered, but the predominant rhythm is altered. If the premature beat occurs early in systole, before the ventricular conduction system has completely repolarized, the QRS following may be abnormal, resulting from an aberrant pathway.

Lead III

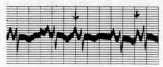

Paroxysmal Atrial Tachycardia.

Originates from an ectopic atrial focus which sends out a rapid series of regular impulses. Each P wave (which may vary from the normal) is followed by a normal QRS complex. R-R intervals are identical. Rate is unaffected by physical or functional stimuli. Rate range is usually 150 to 250 per min.

Lead I   Rate 200

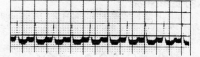

Atrial Flutter.

This rhythm is a slower variant of atrial fibrillation. The atrial rate varies from 200 to 350 per minute, but only part of the atrial impulses pass the A-V node to initiate ventricular contractions. The ratio of P waves to QRS complexes varies from 1:1 to 4:1 (usually 2:1). P waves occur at a regular rate; they are continuous, with no base line, giving a "saw-toothed" effect.

Lead II   Atrial rate   - 320

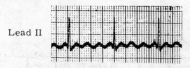

                                            Ventricular rate - 80

Atrial Fibrillation.

This is the result of an atrial rate of 350 per min. or more with irregular A-V conduction of some of the impulses

arising in the atria. No P waves are seen, but rapid, irregular, small fibrillary (f) waves may be present. QRS complexes have a normal contour but are completely irregular in
time.

Lead I 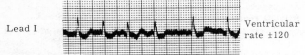 Ventricular
rate ±120

Paroxysmal Ventricular Tachycardia.

This rhythm originates from an ectopic ventricular focus
which sends out a rapid consecutive series of ventricular premature beats. It has the Ecg. appearance of similar broad
QRS complexes which appear continuous, having no intervening
isoelectric line. Atria and ventricles function independently;
thus P waves vary in location and contour and lose their normal relation to the QRS complexes. The rate is usually 150
to 200 per min. Paroxysmal ventricular tachycardia must be
differentiated from paroxysmal atrial tachycardia with intraventricular conduction defect.

Lead II 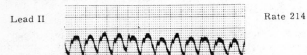 Rate 214

Ventricular Fibrillation.

Wide, continuous waves irregular in size, shape, width,
and rate. No P waves are seen, but atria can continue to beat.

Lead II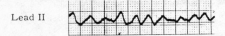

CONDUCTION ARRHYTHMIAS

Incomplete Atrioventricular Block (first degree block).

P-R interval = 0.26 sec. All P waves followed by a QRS
complex.

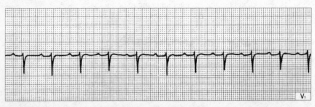

Incomplete Atrioventricular Block With Wenckebach Phenomenon.

Sinus rhythm, but all P waves are not followed by a QRS complex. P-R intervals become progressively longer because depressed A-V node becomes more refractory. When sinus impulse reaches completely refractory A-V node, P wave is not followed by a QRS complex; hence a dropped beat.

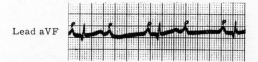

Incomplete Atrioventricular Block (2:1) (second degree block).

Sinus rhythm, but only every second P wave is followed by a QRS complex. The A-V node is completely refractory to every other atrial impulse; hence a 2:1 block with atrial rate 94, ventricular 47.

Lead aVF
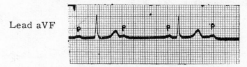

Complete Atrioventricular Block (third degree block).

P waves regular at 75/min. and completely dissociated from QRS waves, which are regular at 42/min.

Lead aVF

CORONARY INSUFFICIENCY

Coronary Insufficiency (Posterior); Consistent With Angina Pectoris.

A. Before Exercise: Low voltage QRS complexes are the only abnormality.

B. After Exercise:

1. Standard leads - Depressed $ST_{2,3}$ with diphasic $T_{2,3}$.
2. Unipolar limb leads - Depressed ST with diphasic T in aVF.

3. Unipolar precordial leads - Depressed ST with diphasic T in V₅.

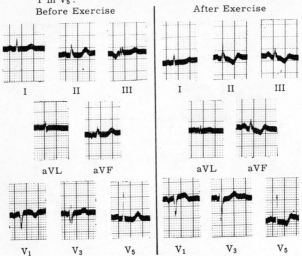

Before Exercise   After Exercise

I   II   III   I   II   III

aVL   aVF   aVL   aVF

V₁   V₃   V₅   V₁   V₃   V₅

Extensive Anterior Myocardial Infarct.
- A. Standard Leads: Notched QS_1; elevated (coved) $ST_{1,2}$ with inverted $T_{1,2}$; depressed ST_3.
- B. Unipolar Limb Leads: QS with elevated ST and inverted T in aVL.
- C. Unipolar Precordial Leads: QS with elevated ST, inverted T in V_{2-5}; notched QS, elevated ST, and inverted T in V_6.
- D. Uniformly elevated ST in precordial leads suggests ventricular aneurysms.

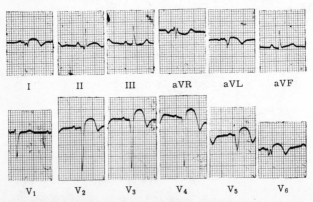

I   II   III   aVR   aVL   aVF

V₁   V₂   V₃   V₄   V₅   V₆

Posterior Myocardial Infarct.

A. Standard Leads: Depressed ST_1; $Q_{2,3}$ with elevated
   $ST_{2,3}$ and inverted $T_{2,3}$.

B. Unipolar Limb Leads: Depressed ST in aVL and Q in aVF
   with elevated ST and inverted T.

C. Unipolar Precordial Leads: Depressed ST in V_6.

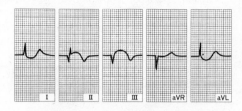

VENTRICULAR HYPERTROPHY

Left Ventricular Hypertrophy.

Axis, −30; horizontal, counterclockwise rotation.

A. Standard Leads: R_1 = 22 mm.; R_1 + S_3 = 45 mm.; depressed ST_1 with inverted T_1.

B. Unipolar Limb Leads: R in aVL = 23 mm.; depressed
   ST with inverted T in aVL; horizontal position.

C. Unipolar Precordial Leads: SV_1 + RV_5 = 51 mm.; inverted T in $V_{3,4}$; depressed ST with inverted T in $V_{5,6}$;
   counterclockwise rotation.

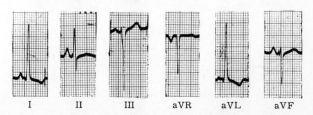

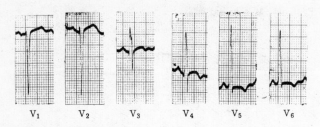

V_1 V_2 V_3 V_4 V_5 V_6

Right Ventricular Hypertrophy.
    Axis, + 150; vertical, clockwise rotation.
A. Standard Leads: Broad, deep S_1, depressed $ST_{2,3}$ and inverted $T_{2,3}$.
B. Unipolar Limb Leads: Prominent R in aVR; depressed ST with inverted T in aVF.
C. Unipolar Precordial Leads: qR complex in $V_{1,2}$; prominent R in V_1; V.A.T. = 0.05 sec. in V_1; broad and deep S in $V_{5,6}$.

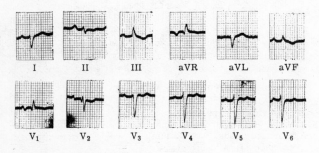

I   II   III   aVR   aVL   aVF

V_1 V_2 V_3 V_4 V_5 V_6

Acute Cor Pulmonale (Pulmonary Infarct).
A. Vertical heart.
B. Standard Leads: Prominent S_1, with inverted $T_{2,3}$.
C. Unipolar Limb Leads: Inverted T in aVF.
D. Inverted T in V_{1-4}.

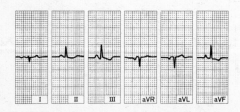

I   II   III   aVR   aVL   aVF

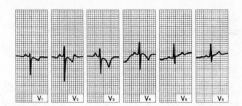

BUNDLE BRANCH BLOCK

Right Bundle Branch Block.
A. Standard Leads: QRS = 0.12; broad, deep S_1.
B. Unipolar Limb Leads: Prominent R' in aVR; depressed ST with inverted T in aVL; horizontal heart.
C. Unipolar Precordial Leads: High R' in V_1 with V.A.T. = 0.10 sec.; M-shaped QRS in V_{1-3}; inverted T in $V_{1,2}$; broad S in $V_{5,6}$.

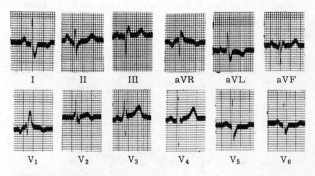

Left Bundle Branch Block.
A. Standard Leads: Monophasic QRS_1, 0.16 sec.
B. Unipolar Limb Leads: QRS in aVL resembles V_6.
C. Unipolar Precordial Leads: Elevated ST in $V_{1,3}$. M-shaped QRS in V_6 with V.A.T. = 10 sec.; inverted T in V_6.

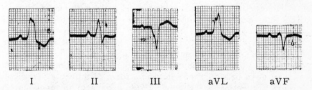

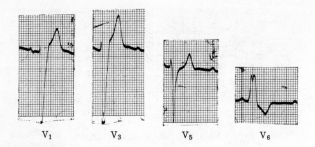

V_1 V_3 V_5 V_6

MISCELLANEOUS

Pericarditis.

A. Standard Leads: Elevation of $ST_{1,2}$ with upward convexity.

B. Unipolar Precordial Leads: Elevation of ST waves in same direction with low or inverted T's in V_{2-6}. Usually elevation of most ST segments in same direction is characteristic, may be followed by return to normal or by T-inversion in all leads involved. Inverted T waves may be permanent.

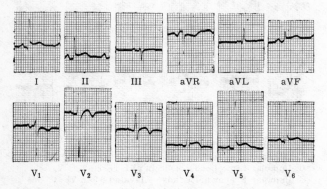

I   II   III   aVR   aVL   aVF

V_1 V_2 V_3 V_4 V_5 V_6

Digitalis Effect.

Characteristically, sagging of ST segments occurs in a direction opposite the major QRS deflection; low or inverted T waves are commonly associated. In precordial leads digitalis ST changes appear chiefly in left precordial leads. These are evidence of digitalis effect but not digitalis toxicity per se. Ventricular bigeminy usually indicates digitalis toxicity but may be seen in a normal heart as a form of multiple ventricular premature beats. Bigeminy also occurs in an inadequately digitalized, failing heart. Differentiation may be difficult.

I   II   V₅

Hyperkalemia: See p. 427.

Hypokalemia: See p. 426.

Hypocalcemia.
    Prolonged Q-T interval, due chiefly to prolongation of ST segment.

Lead II

Q-T interval = 0.48 sec.
Rate = 70

TABLE FOR DETERMINING HEART RATE*

To find heart rate, select the figure in the column L which represents the cycle length in seconds measured on the electrocardiogram. The corresponding number in column R is the rate per minute. Thus if the interval between P waves (or R waves) of two consecutive beats is 0.60, the heart rate is 100 beats per minute.

The table is accurate only if rhythm is regular. With an irregular rhythm, as in atrial fibrillation, an approximate determination of ventricular rate per minute can be made by counting the number of R waves in 15 large squares (3 seconds in length) and multiplying by 20.

L	R	L	R	L	R	L	R	L	R
0.10	600	0.38	158	0.66	91	0.94	63	1.58	38
0.11	550	0.39	155	0.67	90	0.95		1.64	37
0.12	510	0.40	150	0.68	89	0.96	62	1.68	36
0.13	470	0.41	145	0.69	87	0.97	61	1.73	35
0.14	430	0.42	142	0.70	85	0.98		1.77	34
0.15	400	0.43	138	0.71	84	0.99	60	1.82	33
0.16	375	0.44	136	0.72	83	1.00		1.86	32
0.17	350	0.45	133	0.73	82	1.01	59	1.92	31
0.18	335	0.46	129	0.74	81	1.03	58	2.00	30
0.19	315	0.47	127	0.75	80	1.05	57	2.06	29
0.20	300	0.48	125	0.76	79	1.07	56	2.15	28
0.21	284	0.49	123	0.77	78	1.09	55	2.22	27
0.22	270	0.50	120	0.78	77	1.11	54	2.30	26
0.23	260	0.51	117	0.79	76	1.13	53	2.40	25
0.24	250	0.52	115	0.80	75	1.15	52	2.50	24
0.25	240	0.53	113	0.81	74	1.17	51	2.60	23
0.26	230	0.54	111	0.82	73	1.20	50	2.70	22
0.27	222	0.55	109	0.83	72	1.23	49	2.84	21
0.28	215	0.56	107	0.84	71	1.25	48	3.00	20
0.29	206	0.57	105	0.85		1.27	47	3.15	19
0.30	200	0.58	103	0.86	70	1.29	46	3.35	18
0.31	192	0.59	101	0.87	69	1.33	45	3.50	17
0.32	186	0.60	100	0.88	68	1.36	44	3.75	16
0.33	182	0.61	98	0.89	67	1.38	43	4.00	15
0.34	177	0.62	96	0.90		1.42	42	4.30	14
0.35	173	0.63	95	0.91	66	1.45	41	4.70	13
0.36	168	0.64	93	0.92	65	1.50	40	5.10	12
0.37	164	0.65	92	0.93	64	1.55	39	5.50	11
								6.00	10

L = Heart cycle length in seconds. R = Heart rate per minute.

*Modified after Ashman and Hull: Essentials of Electrocardiography. Copyright 1937, 1941 by The Macmillan Company and used with their permission.

UPPER LIMITS OF NORMAL P-R INTERVALS*†

	Rate				
	< 70	71-90	91-110	111-130	> 130
Large adults	0.21	0.20	0.19	0.18	0.17
Small adults	0.20	0.19	0.18	0.17	0.16
Children, ages 14 to 17	0.19	0.18	0.17	0.16	0.15
Children, ages 7 to 13	0.18	0.17	0.16	0.15	0.14
Children, ages 1½ to 6	0.17	0.165	0.155	0.145	0.135
Children, ages 0 to 1½	0.16	0.15	0.145	0.135	0.125

NORMAL AND UPPER LIMITS OF NORMAL Q-T INTERVALS*‡

Cycle Length in Sec.	Heart Rate per Min.	Men and Children in Sec.	Women in Sec.	Upper Limits of Normal	
				Men and Children in Sec.	Women in Sec.
1.50	40	0.449	0.461	0.491	0.503
1.40	43	0.438	0.450	0.479	0.491
1.30	46	0.426	0.438	0.466	0.478
1.25	48	0.420	0.432	0.460	0.471
1.20	50	0.414	0.425	0.453	0.464
1.15	52	0.407	0.418	0.445	0.456
1.10	54.5	0.400	0.411	0.438	0.449
1.05	57	0.393	0.404	0.430	0.441
1.00	60	0.386	0.396	0.422	0.432
0.95	63	0.378	0.388	0.413	0.423
0.90	66.5	0.370	0.380	0.404	0.414
0.85	70.5	0.361	0.371	0.395	0.405
0.80	75	0.352	0.362	0.384	0.394
0.75	80	0.342	0.352	0.374	0.384
0.70	86	0.332	0.341	0.363	0.372
0.65	92.5	0.321	0.330	0.351	0.360
0.60	100	0.310	0.318	0.338	0.347
0.55	109	0.297	0.305	0.325	0.333
0.50	120	0.283	0.291	0.310	0.317
0.45	133	0.268	0.276	0.294	0.301
0.40	150	0.252	0.258	0.275	0.282
0.35	172	0.234	0.240	0.255	0.262

*From Ashman and Hull, ibid.
†Intervals measured in fractions of a second.
‡A nomogram for rate correction of the Q-T interval may be found on p. 96.

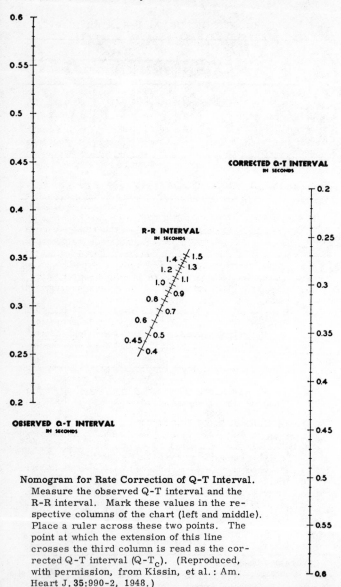

Nomogram for Rate Correction of Q-T Interval.
Measure the observed Q-T interval and the
R-R interval. Mark these values in the respective columns of the chart (left and middle).
Place a ruler across these two points. The
point at which the extension of this line
crosses the third column is read as the corrected Q-T interval (Q-T$_c$). (Reproduced,
with permission, from Kissin, et al.: Am.
Heart J. **35**:990-2, 1948.)

6...
Preparation for X-ray Examination

ROUTINE X-RAY ORDERS

Each department has its own preferences; the directions below are a general guide. Gallbladder x-rays or urography should be completed before barium studies. Barium enema should be completed before GI series if both are to be done.

Barium Enema.
1. To obtain a bowel as clear of fecal matter as possible, a clear liquid diet (no solid food) should be ordered for a 24-hour period prior to the examination. Such a diet consists of (1) water, (2) tea or coffee with or without sugar, (3) carbonated beverages such as ginger ale or Coca Cola, (4) syrup strained from canned fruits, (5) clear, fat-free chicken or beef broth, salted.
2. Less effective than the above is a light supper, consisting of toast and any of the clear liquids mentioned above, on the night before the examination.
3. Give 60 ml. (2 oz.) castor oil or 120 ml. (4 oz.) Neoloid® at 4:00 p.m. on the day before the examination. Some also prefer cleansing enemas the night before, but give no enemas on the morning of the examination.
4. To x-ray at a time specified.
5. A mild cathartic such as milk of magnesia is advisable after the examination to prevent fecal impaction.
6. Do not schedule proctoscopy or sigmoidoscopy to precede the barium enema on the same day.

Upper GI Series or Small Bowel Study.
Dangerous with colon obstruction. Valuable for diagnosis of small bowel obstruction.
1. Give no cathartic or enema on the day before.
2. Light supper, and then nothing to eat or drink and no chewing gum or cigarettes after midnight until the x-rays are completed.
3. A mild cathartic such as milk of magnesia is advisable after the examination to prevent fecal impaction.

UROGRAPHY

Intravenous Urography.
Contraindicated with iodine sensitivity. The two contrast

media most commonly used are (1) sodium diatrizoate (Hypaque®), 59.87% iodine; and (2) meglumine diatrizoate (Renografin®). No visualization should be expected with a P.S.P. kidney function test of less than 35% in two hours. (See also p. 136.)

1. Give a light supper.
2. Give 60 ml. (2 oz.) castor oil or 120 ml. (4 oz.) Neoloid® at 4:00 p.m. the day before examination.
3. Nothing by mouth after midnight until x-rays are completed.
4. Empty bladder before x-ray in a.m.
5. Some radiologists test for sensitivity by injecting 0.5 to 1 ml. of the dye I.V. and observing for reactions. If no reactions occur in ten minutes, the rest of the drug is given. There is no absolute test of sensitivity to iodides. Even if the patient does not seem to be sensitive, epinephrine, diphenhydramine, levarterenol, and sedatives should be available for I.V. use if needed.

Retrograde Urography.

Some radiologists use no special preparation for this (see p. 455).

1. Nothing by mouth after a light meal in evening.
2. Cleansing enema in the morning.
3. To cystoscopy at appointed time.

GALLBLADDER VISUALIZATION

Single Oral Method (Graham-Cole Test).

If gallbladder does not visualize, repeat the original dose on the day after the first test. The gallbladder is not likely to visualize in the presence of (1) markedly impaired liver function, (2) duct obstruction, (3) pyloric obstruction, or (4) diarrhea.

1. No enemas or cathartics before x-rays.
2. Give a fat-free supper on the evening preceding the examination.
3. At 6:00 p.m. (or 12 hours before the examination) give radiopaque medium by mouth. These agents may produce diarrhea and nonvisualization of the excreted tablets. Repeat test, giving with 4 ml. of paregoric after the tablets are taken.
4. Nothing by mouth after midnight.

Intravenous Gallbladder and Bile Duct Visualization.

This technic is usually employed in the visualization of the biliary tree after cholecystectomy. It may be used for visualization of the gallbladder if diarrhea, pyloric obstruction, or any other factor interferes with the absorption of the orally administered contrast medium. Visualization of the gallbladder or bile ducts fails in the presence of markedly impaired liver function or with obvious jaundice. The agent used is a 20% solution of sodium iodipamide (Cholografin®), containing 64.32% iodine. It is administered intravenously and the same precautions for sensitivity are observed as in kidney visualization. Serial films are taken over a prolonged period. Tomography is of great value in visualization of the bile ducts. It may cause hypotension in elderly patients. In such individuals, give medium by I.V. drip in saline over a 20-minute period.

RADIATION HAZARD

Although excessive radiation can produce genetic changes and other undesirable effects, the diagnostic value of appropriate x-rays when indicated far outweighs the relatively remote risks. If the precautions outlined below are observed at all times, it is not necessary to withhold x-ray studies or therapeutic procedures from properly selected patients.

Radiation dose depends upon kilovoltage, filters, tube distance, shielding, field coning, and duration of exposure.

Precautions.*
1. Check apparatus for optimum kilovoltage and filter.
2. Eliminate stray radiation or leakage.
3. Know the output of the machine.
4. Seek expert consultation in case of doubt.
5. Exercise special caution with children, pregnant or potentially pregnant women, and persons below age 40.
6. Avoid exposure of gonads or large areas of body.
7. Studies involving large amounts of radiation or repeated examinations should be based on good indication.
8. With fluoroscopy -
   a. Use only to study dynamics of motion, introduction of contrast media, effects of external pressure, and positioning for spot films.
   b. **Do not use** for survey or screening procedures or for reduction of fractures.
   c. Target to patient distance should be at least 18 in.
   d. Do not exceed 10 r per minute in any examination.
   e. Adapt eyes to darkness for at least ten minutes.
   f. Use protective gloves, apron, and film badge.
   g. Use smallest possible shutter opening and interval.
   h. Use 2 mm. or more of aluminum added filter.
   i. Use image amplifier whenever possible.

*A Practical Manual on Use of X-rays With Control of Radiation Hazards. Chamberlain, R.H., and Nelsen, R.J., 1959. American College of Radiology, Chicago, Illinois.

7...

Simplified Laboratory Procedures

The purpose of this chapter is to outline the simple laboratory procedures that are employed to extend and complement the physical examination of the patient. Proper evaluation of these preliminary analyses will aid in the effective choice of more complicated quantitative tests.

In ordinary office practice, about 80% of all routine laboratory analyses are within normal limits; the use of screening tests results in a saving of time and cost of laboratory examinations.

To complete the physical examination the following should be done:

A. Blood: Erythrocyte sedimentation rate, P.C.V., Hgb., WBC, differential, and serologic test for syphilis.
B. Urine: Careful urinalysis, including determination of specific gravity and pH, tests for protein and glucose, and careful examination of the urinary sediment.
C. Feces: Test for occult blood.

DRAWING BLOOD
(Venipuncture)

When the venous pressure increases as a result of constriction of veins by a tourniquet, fluid and the materials dissolved in it may leak out into the tissues from the venous end of the capillaries, resulting in a relative hemoconcentration which may interfere especially with accurate hematocrit and protein determinations; accordingly, blood should be taken immediately after applying the tourniquet.

Amount Needed.

Draw 10 ml. of blood in anticipation of doing a serologic test for syphilis and hematologic studies at the time of the patient's initial visit. Place 5 ml. in a vial containing anticoagulant for the hematologic tests and put the remaining 5 ml. into the Wassermann tube for the serologic test for syphilis. At the time the blood is drawn, place 1 drop of blood on a slide and make a smear.

Use of Anticoagulant.

Five ml. of blood provide ample material for all tests described. Double oxalate (ammonium-potassium), EDTA (ethylenediamine tetraacetic acid dipotassium salt), or heparin may be used. These are available commercially or may be made up in the office (see pp. 144-5).

HEMATOLOGY

Using the routine outlined below, one can analyze many of the physical characteristics of the blood and its components within a very short time. If abnormal features appear, accurate quantitative tests are indicated, e. g., actual blood count and icterus index. (See Chapters 9 and 10.)

Sedimentation Rate.

The Wintrobe type of graduated hematocrit tube, 100 mm. long, is recommended since it can be used for both sedimentation rate and packed cell volume determination (see below). Mixing should be complete, but care must be taken to prevent foaming. Fill the tube to the "100 mm." mark with the oxalated blood and allow to stand in a vertical position for one hour. The maximum normals are 10 mm. per hour for men and 20 mm. per hour for women. (See pp. 178-9.)

Packed Cell Volume (Hematocrit) and Leukocyte Volume.

The microhematocrit apparatus is well adapted for office use (see p. 152).

If the Wintrobe tube is to be used, after reading the sedimentation rate, centrifuge for 10 to 15 minutes at 3500 r.p.m. or until r.b.c. are completely packed. (If the centrifuge used will not reach a speed of 3500 r.p.m., it may be calibrated for packed cell volumes at lower speeds by correlating with red counts, etc.) The tube will then contain a top layer of plasma, a center layer of platelets and leukocytes, and a bottom layer of packed erythrocytes.

   A. Packed Cell Volume: This is an index of the erythrocyte count. In men, between 40 and 54 mm. is considered a normal volume of red cells; in women, between 37 and 47 mm. If the packed cell column is less than the lower limit, the patient has an anemia, and it then becomes necessary to do a complete blood count to determine the relationship between the red cell count and the hemoglobin. From a stained smear, one may judge the various changes in morphology and staining characteristics of the red cells.

   B. Leukocyte Volume: The thickness of the layer of leukocytes is an index of the white count. Roughly, 1 mm. of packed white cells corresponds to a 10,000 to 12,000 WBC. Less than 0.5 mm. of packed white cells indicates a leukopenia. The elevated counts associated with frank leukemias show up spectacularly as columns of packed leukocytes several mm. thick. From the smear one can determine the differential white cell count. Deviations from normal must be checked by more accurate methods (see p. 156).

C. Observation of the Plasma: The column of plasma provides additional diagnostic aids:

1. Jaundice (icterus index) - An increase in bilirubin concentration is readily apparent, and with a series of standard tubes it is possible to approximate the icterus index.

2. Plasma lipids - If there is an elevation of plasma lipids the plasma may have a milky appearance.

Red Cell Fragility Test.

A screening test for determining increased red cell fragility involves the use of 0.45% sodium chloride in addition to the standard equipment for counting red cells. Blood is drawn to the "0.5" mark in two red cell pipets. The first is diluted to the "101" mark with Hayem's or Gower's solution and the second pipet with 0.45% sodium chloride solution. Both pipets are shaken for two minutes and counts made from both pipets; the percentage of cells hemolyzed in the 0.45% saline solution is thus determined. Less than 30% of normal erythrocytes are hemolyzed by this technic. An abnormal increase in red cell fragility, as in congenital hemolytic icterus, will cause hemolysis of more than 70% of the cells.

Blood Coagulation. (Use specimen drawn for serologic tests.)

Blood coagulation tests are readily done in the office. The blood drawn for the serological tests and placed in a Wassermann tube should coagulate within ten to 18 minutes. Within one or two hours the clot should begin to retract, forming a firm, contracted clot from which serum will be expressed in another one or two hours. Failure of the blood to coagulate within 20 minutes may indicate hemophilia or other coagulation defects, thus indicating the need for further tests. Failure of the clot to retract indicates that either the glass tube is not absolutely clean or that thrombocytopenia exists. If the clot retracts after being freed from the walls of the tube with an applicator, failure to retract was due to improperly prepared glassware. Thrombocytopenia may be further investigated by examination of the stained blood smear for platelets and by doing a bleeding time and a tourniquet test (see pp. 159 and 160).

BLOOD CHEMISTRY

Blood Sugar in Diagnosis of Diabetes.
　　In a patient with mild diabetes, a fasting blood glucose may
be normal but postprandial blood glucose will be elevated. A
breakfast consisting of two slices of toast, about a teaspoonful
of jelly, coffee containing one or two teaspoons of sugar, and
a glass of orange or grapefruit juice will provide an amount of
glucose which will produce hyperglycemia (blood glucose over
160 or 170 mg./100 ml.) in almost any diabetic. One blood
specimen drawn 2 hours after such a meal provides a clinically useful index of glucose tolerance. A 2-hour postprandial
blood glucose level greater than 120 mg./100 ml. indicates the
possibility of diabetes mellitus. Urine should be tested for
glucose at the time the blood is drawn. (For standard urine
glucose tests, see p. 116.)

URINALYSIS

　　There is no substitute for a careful, complete urinalysis
on a suitable specimen of urine. A suitable specimen should
be acid, of a specific gravity of at least 1.010 and preferably
of 1.016 or higher. It should be examined soon after collection.

Proteinuria (Albuminuria).
　　The most convenient test for urine protein is the addition
of 3 drops of 20% sulfosalicylic acid to each ml. of urine used
in the test; the turbidity of a positive test is easily seen. If
this turbidity disappears when the urine is heated above 60°
and reappears upon cooling, the protein is of the Bence Jones
variety.
　　Labstix®, Bili-Labstix®, Albustix®, or Uristix® may be
used (see p. 113).

Glycosuria.
　　Tests for glucose should be done routinely. A convenient
screening test is available, using Galatest® powder (turns gray
to black on contact with reducing substances, e.g., glucose).
The Clinitest® method is also simple and rapid. Clinistix® and
Tes-Tape® are easy to use and specific for glucose. Labstix®
permits determination of protein, glucose, ketones, occult
blood, and pH simultaneously. (Bili-Labstix® includes bilirubin.)

Acetonuria.
　　See p. 118.

Bilirubinuria. (See p. 120.)
A. Foam Test: The presence of bile is readily and simply determined by shaking the urine; the foam produced will persist and have a distinct yellow tinge.
B. Ictotest®: See p. 120.
C. Bili-Labstix®: See p. 121.
D. Harrison Spot Test: See p. 121.

MISCELLANEOUS TESTS

Stool Examination for Occult Blood.
    In doing stool examinations, it is very simple to determine the presence of occult blood. Most physicians, if doing a complete work-up, include a rectal examination. A bit of stool that clings to the rectal glove may be tested for blood.
    A bit of stool is smeared on a clean slide free of blood. Add a few drops of glacial acetic acid, a few granules of benzidine, and mix well with the stool. The addition to this mixture of a few drops of hydrogen peroxide will produce a deep blue color if occult blood is present; traces of blue may be due to enzymes in ingested food.
    There is now available a simplified test using Hematest® tablets (see p. 280).

Bacteriology.
    Smears of exudates, sputum, etc., are easily made and examined in the office.

EQUIPMENT AND REAGENTS FOR THE OFFICE
(See also section on Solutions, Stains,
and Reagents, pp. 621-8.)

General.
Microscope
Centrifuge
Syringes - 5 and 10 ml.
Needles - 20 and 22 gauge,
    1 to 1½ inch
Wassermann tubes

Test tubes and forceps
Centrifuge tubes
Glass slides and cover slips
Pipets, serological, 1 and
    10 ml.
Bunsen burner or gas plate

Hematology.
Vials with screw tops,
    10 ml. capacity
Wintrobe hematocrit tubes
    with stand; pipets for
    filling and washing.
Anticoagulant of choice
Wright's stain

Hemacytometer with pipets
Hemoglobinometer
Saline, 0.9% and 0.45%
Hayem's or Gower's
    solutions
Hydrochloric acid, N/10
Immersion oil

Occult Blood.
Hematest® tablets. Alternatively, benzidine, glacial acetic acid, hydrogen peroxide.

Urinalysis.
20% sulfosalicylic acid (for protein determination)
Benedict's solution, Galatest® powder, Clinitest® tablets, Clinistix®, or Tes-Tape® (for glucose determination)
Sodium nitroprusside ⎫ (For acetone determination;
Glacial acetic acid ⎬ may use Acetest® tablets,
Ammonium hydroxide ⎬ Ketostix®, or Labstix® in-
pH indicator paper ⎭ stead.)
Labstix® for testing pH, protein, glucose, ketones, and occult blood simultaneously.
Bili-Labstix® for testing pH, glucose, protein, ketones, bilirubin, and blood simultaneously.

Bilirubin.
10% Ferric chloride ⎫ (Fouchet's reagent; may use
25% Trichloroacetic acid ⎬ Ictotest® tablets instead.)
10% Barium chloride

Urobilinogen and Serotonin.
Hydrochloric acid, concentrated ⎫ (Ehrlich's reagent)
Paradimethylaminobenzaldehyde ⎭

Phenylpyruvic Acid.
10% Ferric chloride ⎫ (Phenistix® may be used
HCl or acetic acid ⎬ instead.)

Bacteriology.
Gram's stain
Gram's iodine
Methylene blue
Safranine
Carbolfuchsin

Miscellaneous.
Acetone
Alcohol, ethyl or isopropyl
Nitric acid, concentrated
Applicator sticks
Distilled water

ROUTINE CAVITY PUNCTURE FLUID EXAMINATION
(Add anticoagulant to specimen.)

The outline below applies more or less equally well to all serous effusions.

Microbiologic Aspects.
   Culture all fluids. Gram's stain and acid-fast stains should be done as indicated. Special media and animal inoculation should be employed as indicated.

Cytologic Aspects. (Add anticoagulant.)
  A. Cell Counts: Do RBC and WBC in the usual way, with blood counting pipet and hemacytometer.
   1. RBC - The two most common causes of an RBC over 10,000 per cu. mm. (faintly pink-tinged fluid) are neoplasm and tuberculosis.
   2. WBC - Rarely over 500 per cu. mm. except in infections and neoplasms.
   3. Differential WBC - Centrifuge and stain smear of sediment with Wright's stain. If 80% or more of cells are small lymphocytes, tuberculosis must be ruled out. In infected nontuberculous fluids, polymorphonuclear cells predominate. Eosinophils have no known significance. Note also serosal cells, neoplastic cells, etc.
  B. Pathologic Study: Exfoliative cytologic studies are always indicated. If carcinoma is suspected, send 500 to 1000 ml. of citrated fluid to the pathology laboratory so that a "cell button" may be made of the sediment.

Physical Aspects.
  A. Note volume.
  B. Color and Transparency: Faint pink tinge in test tube suggests RBC of 10,000 per cu. mm. Pseudomonas aeruginosa imparts a greenish color. Chylous fluids have a milky white opacity. Generally, the more yellow the color, the greater the protein content. Transparency is diminished with increasing WBC or RBC.
  C. Specific Gravity: Use an ordinary hydrometer (urinometer) with the fluid cooled to a temperature of 60° F. (15.5°C.). If fluid is likely to clot, do this test first. If dilution is necessary to float the urinometer, multiply the last two figures in the specific gravity reading by the dilution to get the correct specific gravity. Such dilution makes the fluid unfit for chemical analysis or a test of clot formation.
   1. Pleural fluids have average specific gravities as follows:
     a. Cirrhotic or nephrotic - 1.015 or less.
     b. Cardiac   - 1.015 or less.
     c. Neoplastic   - 1.015 or less.

     d. Tuberculous pleurisy - 1.018 or more.
     e. Infected pleurisy   - 1.018 or more.
  2. Ascitic fluids have similar specific gravities, except that in ascitic fluid resulting from congestive heart failure specific gravity ranges from 1.014 to 1.02. In general, the specific gravity parallels the protein content of a puncture fluid specimen.
D. Odor: Fluid infected with E. coli has a fecal odor.
E. Clot Formation: In general, the higher the protein content, the more likely and more rapid the clotting.

Chemical Aspects.

A. Total Proteins: Accurate chemical determination is preferred. May be approximated from the specific gravity as follows:

$$(Sp.\ gr. - 1.007) \times 343 = Gm.\ protein\ per\ 100\ ml.$$

Therefore, a specific gravity of:
     1.010 contains 1 Gm. protein per 100 ml.
     1.015 contains 2.5 Gm. protein per 100 ml.
     1.020 contains 4.5 Gm. protein per 100 ml.
     1.025 contains 6 Gm. protein per 100 ml.

B. Globulin.
C. Test as necessary for glucose, bile, fat, etc.
D. Seromucin: Rivalta test: Place 100 ml. of water in a graduated cylinder. Add two drops of glacial acetic acid and mix. Allow one drop of the suspected fluid to fall into the column of water. If a distinct bluish-white cloud appears, the test is positive.

Differentiation of Transudates and Exudates.

Transudates are accumulations of noninflammatory fluids in the serous cavities. They are usually the result of congestive heart failure, obstruction to venous flow, or low blood protein. They have a specific gravity below 1.018, a clear or slightly cloudy, light yellow appearance, few cells, no bacteria, and less than 2.5 Gm. protein per 100 ml. (chiefly albumin). Usually, they do not clot. Chylous transudates are milky white in appearance.

Exudates are usually the result of inflammation. They have a specific gravity above 1.018. They may be clear or cloudy; serous, purulent, or hemorrhagic. They coagulate and contain over 3 Gm. % of protein (albumin, globulin, fibrinogen). They may be odorless or putrid. The cell count may vary from 500 to 40,000 per cu. mm. Polymorphonuclear leukocytes predominate in acute pyogenic infections; lymphocytes, monocytes, and eosinophils may predominate in chronic exudates. Exudates may contain seromucin, a protein found only in exudates and demonstrated by the Rivalta test.

SYNOVIAL FLUID

Using sterile technic, infiltrate skin, subcutaneous tissue, and synovial tissue with 1% procaine. Insert an 18 or 19 gauge spinal puncture needle with stilet into the joint space. Add a drop of heparin (1000 units per ml.) or a drop of 10% disodium EDTA or 2 mg. of potassium oxalate per ml. to the 1 to 2 ml. of joint fluid to be used for cytologic study. If crystals are to be examined, use 3.8% sodium citrate, one part to nine parts of synovial fluid (not suitable for chemical assay or for complement assay). Add no anticoagulant to the remaining fluid.

If the volume is small, 1 ml. is sufficient for study of appearance, cytology, type of mucin precipitate, and culture. Six to 10 ml. will be necessary if studies include clotting tendency, glucose and protein content, relative viscosity, and guinea pig inoculation.

Synovianalysis in Arthritis*

	Appearance	Viscosity	W.b.c./ cu. mm. (1) (2)	Mucin Clot (3)	Protein (avg. Gm./100 ml.)		Also Present
					Total	Glob.	
Normal	Straw-colored, clear, cloudy	High	200-600 25% neut.	Good	1.36	0.05	
Traumatic	Yellow to bloody	High	±2000† 30% neut.	Good	4.27		
Osteo-arthritis	Yellow, clear	High	±1000 20% neut.	Good	3.08	0.75	Cartilage fibrils
Rheum. fever	Yellow, slightly cloudy	Low	±10,000 50% neut.	Good	3.74	1.07	
Systemic L. E.	Straw-colored, slightly cloudy	High	±5000 10% neut.	Good			
Gout	Yellow to milky, cloudy	Low	±12,000 60% neut.	Fragile	4.18	1.54	Urate crystals
Rheum. arthritis	Yellow to greenish, cloudy	Low	±15,000 65±% neut.	Fragile	4.74	1.79	Rheumatoid factor
Tuberculous	Yellow, cloudy	Low	±25,000 50-60% neut.	Fragile	5.3	2.0	Tubercle bacilli
Septic	Grayish or bloody, turbid	Low	±80,000 90% neut.	Fragile	5.64	2.45	Bacteria

*Modified from Hollander, J.L., et al.: Synovianalysis. Bull. Rheum. Dis. 12:263-4, 1961.
†Many r.b.c.

(1) Dilute in white cell counting pipet with normal saline faintly colored with methylene blue; r.b.c.'s and w.b.c.'s are counted simultaneously in a standard hemacytometer.
(2) Thin dried smear; standard Wright's stain.
(3) To 2% acetic acid solution, add a few drops of synovial fluid; observe the clot that forms.

8...

Urinalysis and Renal Function Tests

COLLECTION AND PRESERVATION

Collection of Specimen.

A specimen voided at random will serve for ordinary qualitative tests. The urine specimen should be suitable for the type of examination to be performed. For diabetes, a 2 to 3 hour postprandial urine is desirable; for nephritis, a morning specimen will usually have a higher specific gravity which will prevent lysis of red cells, etc.

Repeated samples taken during the day are often necessary, as for proteinuria of orthostatic origin.

To collect a 24-hour urine, have patient void and discard urine at a set hour, save all urine for the next 24 hours, and then void at same hour to finish the collection.

Preservation of Specimen.

Decomposition of urine occurs especially quickly at warm temperatures. Prompt examination is to be encouraged.

Preservatives are all more or less unsatisfactory. The following are used:

A. Toluol is the best preservative of chemical constituents. Use 2 ml. toluol per 100 ml. urine.

B. Thymol: A small floating lump will preserve urine several days in a bottle. It may cause a false-positive reaction for protein.

C. Formalin: Use 1 drop per 30 ml. of urine. This amount does not affect the microscopic examination, but interferes with test for indican (Obermayer test). Formalin in too large a concentration will precipitate protein. It is a strong reducing agent and may produce reduction of copper or bismuth in tests for glucose.

D. Boric Acid: The amount of powder that can be heaped on a dime (5 grains) will delay decomposition of 120 ml. of urine. Yeasts can still grow, and uric acid crystals are precipitated.

GROSS EXAMINATION OF URINE

Color and Appearance.

Normal urine is usually pale yellow and quite clear.

A. Colorless: Dilution; diabetes mellitus or insipidus.

COMPOSITION OF NORMAL URINE

Specific Gravity in Health: 1.003-1.030

Reaction (pH) of Normal Urine: 4.6-8.0, depending on diet (avg., 6.0).

Volume: Normal range = 600-2500 ml./24 hours (avg., 1200 ml.). Night:day ratio of volume = 1:2 to 1:4, if 8:00 a.m. and 8:00 p.m. are the divisions. The night urine ordinarily does not exceed 500-700 ml., nor does it have a sp. gr. less than 1.018. (For volume in children, see p. 111.)

Titratable Acidity: Total for a 24-hour specimen ranges from 20-40 mEq. Varies with diet.

Total Solids in Grams per Liter: 30-70 Gm. (avg., 50 Gm.). Long's coefficient to estimate total solids per liter: Multiply the last 2 figures in the sp. gr. by 2.66.

Inorganic Constituents per 24 Hours:

Iron	0.06-0.1 mg.
Chlorides (as chloride)	6(4-10) Gm. (100-300 mEq.) on usual diet
Sodium	4 Gm. (170 mEq.) on usual diet
Phosphate (as phosphorus)	0.8-1.3 Gm. on usual diet
Potassium	2 Gm. (50 mEq.) on usual diet
Sulfur (total) as SO_3	2 (0.7-3.5) Gm.
Calcium	< 150 mg.
Magnesium	0.15 (0.05-0.3) Gm.
Iodine	20-450 γ
Arsenic	0.05 mg. or less
Lead	0.12 mg. maximum
Copper	0-100 μg.

Organic Constituents per 24 Hours:

		Nitrogen Equivalent
Nitrogenous, total	25-35 Gm.	10-14 Gm.
Urea ($^1/_2$ of total urine solids; varies with diet)	15-30 Gm.	7-12 Gm.
Creatinine	1.4 (1-1.8) Gm.	0.5 Gm.
Ammonia	0.7 (0.3-1) Gm.	0.4 Gm.
Uric acid	0.7 (0.5-1) Gm.	0.2 Gm.
Undetermined N (amino acid, etc.)		0.5 Gm.
Protein, as such ("albumin")	0-0.1 Gm.	
Creatine, in children	10-50 mg. (Excreted in adults with liver or muscle diseases or thyrotoxicosis.)	

Traces of Other Organic Constituents per 24 Hours:

Hippuric acid	0.6 (0.1-1) Gm.
Oxalic acid	0.02 Gm.
Indican	0.01 Gm.
Allantoin	0.03 Gm.
Purine bases	0.01 Gm.
Acetone bodies	3-15 mg.
Coproporphyrin	50-250 μg.
Phenols, total	0.1-0.3 Gm.

Glucose: 50% of people have 2-3 mg./100 ml. after a heavy meal. A patient with diabetes can lose up to 100 Gm./day.

Ascorbic Acid: Adults excrete 15-50 mg./24 hours; in scurvy, less than 15 mg./24 hours are excreted.

Amylase (diastase): 40-260 units/hour.

24-HOUR VOLUME OF URINE IN CHILDREN*

Age	Total Vol. in ml.	Sp. Gr.	Vol. in ml. / Kg. Body Wt.
2 days	130	1.004-1.005	18-40
4-5 days	70-200	1.004-1.005	56-66
6-10 days	200-300	1.003-1.004	60-95
1-2 mos.	250-420	1.004-1.007	75-110
1-2 years	500-700	1.010-1.014	45-70
3-5 years	600-1200	1.010-1.014	50-100
6-8 years	800-1300	1.010-1.019	40-80
9-12 years	1000-1500	1.010-1.020	40-65

*For volume of urine for adults, see p. 110.

B. Milky: Purulent disease of genitourinary tract; chyluria.

C. Orange: Due to santonin, cryptophanic acid; associated with urobilinogen.

D. Red: Food pigments (beets), hematuria or hemoglobinuria (see p. 134); phenolphthalein; pyramidon; sulfonal; picric acid.

E. Greenish: Jaundice (see p. 120); thymol; phenol poisoning.

F. Dirty Blue or Green: Seen when urine is putrefying; in typhus or cholera. Also due to methylene blue.

G. Dark Brown, Brown-red or Yellow: Very concentrated urine. Seen in acute febrile diseases. Also due to bile.

H. Brown-yellow or Brown-red (if Acid), or Bright Red (if Alkaline): Due to rhubarb, senna, chelidonium, cascara, Argyrol®, aloes.

I. Brown, Brown-black, or Black: Hemorrhage in urinary tract containing acid urine (acid hematin); hemoglobinuria (paroxysmal, associated with incompatible transfusion, blackwater fever); porphyria; methemoglobinuria; myoglobinuria; melanin; phenol poisoning; homogentisic acid (alkaptonuria). In porphyria, urine turns dark brown on exposure to sunlight or boiling.

Reaction (pH).

Litmus paper, nitrazine paper, or other pH indicator papers may be used. In place of indicator paper, methyl red solution may be used: Add 2 drops of 0.4% alcoholic solution of methyl red to 5 ml. urine. Red = acid; orange = neutral; yellow = alkaline.

Esch. coli infection of genitourinary tract usually produces acid urine; that due to Proteus (which splits urea to form ammonia) produces alkaline urine.

Odor.

Significant only in fresh specimen. Normally is not unpleasant; aromatic, due to volatile fatty acids. Ammoniacal odor follows bacterial action. Fruity odor of acetone appears

in ketosis. Asparagus is a source of methyl mercaptan in
urine, giving characteristic odor.

Specific Gravity.   (See p. 110.)
  A. Urinometer: Filter foam off urine. Do not let urinometer
     touch sides of container. Read graduations on stem at
     bottom of meniscus. Dilute urine, if necessary, to obtain
     enough to float urinometer, and multiply last two figures
     of specific gravity reading by the dilution factor. Do not
     use diluted urine for chemical tests.
     1. Correction factors for solutes and other solids - Spe-
        cific gravity is raised 0.001 when the following are
        added in stated amounts per 1000 ml.
        a. Urea, 3.6 Gm.   c. NaCl, 1.5 Gm.
        b. Glucose, 2.7 Gm.   d. Protein, 3.9 Gm.
     2. Correction factors for temperature - To correct for
        room temperature, add 0.001 to specific gravity for
        each 3° C. above, subtract 0.001 for each 3° C. below
        standardization temperature of urinometer.
  B. Refractometer: The content of dissolved solids is re-
     lated to the refractive index of a solution. The Goldberg
     refractometer has been calibrated to read directly the
     specific gravity of the urine. The instrument requires
     only a few drops of urine, which is a great advantage if
     the volume of urine available is less than 10-15 ml.

CHEMICAL EXAMINATIONS OF URINE

PROTEIN TESTS
(See p. 133.)

  Filter or centrifuge if urine is not clear. Protein and
bile salts cause urine to froth.

Heat and Acetic Acid Test.
  Have test tube three-fourths full of urine and boil upper
portion for two minutes. Turbidity is due to earthy phosphates or carbonates, or to protein. If turbidity fades upon
acidification of urine with 3 to 5 drops of 10% acetic acid,
turbidity is due to phosphates or carbonates, which may appear in normal urine. Faint traces of protein may be indicated only after addition of the acid. False positive tests occur with x-ray contrast media and tolbutamide metabolites.
Read as follows:

-	No cloudiness.
±	Cloudiness barely visible.
+	Definite cloudiness, but no granularity and no flocculation.
++	Granular cloudiness, but no flocculation. Seen from above, the cloud is dense but not opaque. About 0.1% protein.
+++	Dense opaque cloud, clearly flocculated. About 0.2 to 0.3% protein.
++++	Very thick precipitation, almost a solid. 0.5% or more protein.

Sulfosalicylic Acid Test.

Urine must be clear and acid. Add 3 drops of 20% sulfo-salicylic acid to 1 ml. of urine. Absence of cloudiness means absence of protein. If cloudiness persists upon boiling, it is due to protein. If the cloudiness disappears on heating but returns on cooling, it is due to Bence Jones protein. (See Bence Jones protein tests on p. 114.) Precipitate forms if urine contains tolbutamide metabolites, x-ray contrast media, or a high concentration of penicillin.

Albustix®.

Paper strips impregnated with bromphenol blue and salicylate buffer are dipped in urine. Protein produces a change in color from pale yellow to blue. If the urine is highly alkaline, a false positive test may result. Tolbutamide, radiographic contrast media, and preservatives do not react, precluding false-positive tests which often occur with sulfosalicylic acid and other reagents. The same reagents are available in tablet form (Albutest®).

Uristix®, Labstix®, Bili-Labstix®.

On the same paper strip is a small portion of Albustix® reagents for protein and other indicator papers for other determinations.

Esbach's Quantitative Protein Test.

If necessary, acidify urine. Cover bottom of an Esbach tube with pumice, fill to the "U" mark with urine, and add Esbach's (or Tsuchiya's) reagent (see pp. 623 and 627) to the "R" mark. Insert stopper and slowly invert the tube 12 times, set vertically in a cool place, and read 30 minutes later. (Without pumice, one must wait 24 hours to read tube.) The tube is marked to read in per cent or in grams of protein per liter at the top of the sediment.

Dilution of urine may be used to obtain more accurate results. If diluted urine is used, multiply the reading on the

Esbach tube by the dilution to get the correct value. Dilutions may be done as follows:

1. 1.010 to 1.014 - May dilute with equal amount of water.
2. 1.015 to 1.021 - Dilute one part of urine with two parts of water.
3. Over 1.022 - Dilute one part of urine with three parts of water.
4. If qualitative test is +++, dilute one part of urine with four parts of water.

Shevky and Stafford Quantitative Test for Protein (MacKay Modification). (See table on p. 115.)

Centrifuge urine to remove all sediment. If the heat and acetic acid test gave a ++ or less, use urine undiluted; if +++, dilute urine ten times with water; if ++++, dilute urine 20 times.

Put 4 ml. of clear centrifuged urine in special narrow-tipped tube, add 2.5 ml. of Tsuchiya's reagent (see p. 627), and mix by inversion. Let stand exactly ten minutes, then centrifuge for exactly ten minutes at 1800 r.p.m. To determine amount of protein, calculate as follows:

Protein in mg./100 ml. = Volume of ppt. × 720 × dilution.

Normal protein excretion per 12 hours is not over 100 mg.

Addis Urine Sediment Count.

See details on p. 129.

Bence Jones Protein Tests.

A. Heat and Sulfosalicylic Acid: The addition of 3 drops of 20% sulfosalicylic acid to each 1 ml. of urine will precipitate Bence Jones protein as well as albumin. After mixing the specimen containing the precipitated protein, divide the specimen equally in two similar test tubes. Place both in a water bath and heat to boiling. Remove one from the bath, cool to below 40°C., and compare the turbidity in the two tubes in good light against a dark background. Cool the hot tube and heat the previously cooled tube in the water bath, and compare again. If the cool tube shows persistently a more densely turbid floc of protein, Bence Jones protein is most likely present. If albumin is present as well, add 10% acetic acid to a fresh portion of urine until the specimen is definitely at pH 6.0 or lower and bring to a boil with frequent shaking to break up the protein floc. When the urine boils, filter while hot. The Bence Jones protein present will be in solution at boiling temperature, and thus will be present in the filtrate. Test the filtrate with sulfosalicylic acid and heat as described above.

URINE PROTEIN - PER 24 HOURS

METHOD: Put $1/10$ hour quantity of urine into a calibrated 15 ml. centrifuge tube, dilute with distilled water to 7 ml., add Tsuchiya's reagent (see p. 627) to 14 ml. Mix well by inverting three times. Centrifuge for five min. at 3500 r.p.m. Read the room temperature. The following chart shows grams of protein per 24 hours.

Grams of Protein Per 24 Hours

Ppt. Reading (ml.)	20°C.	21°C.	22°C.	23°C.	24°C.	25°C.	26°C.	27°C.	28°C.
0.05	0.52	0.55	0.57	0.60	0.63	0.66	0.69	0.72	0.75
0.10	1.0	1.1	1.1	1.2	1.3	1.3	1.4	1.4	1.5
0.15	1.6	1.6	1.7	1.8	1.8	1.9	2.1	2.2	2.3
0.20	2.1	2.2	2.3	2.4	2.5	2.6	2.8	2.9	3.0
0.25	2.6	2.7	2.8	3.0	3.1	3.3	3.4	3.6	3.7
0.30	3.1	3.3	3.4	3.6	3.8	4.0	4.2	4.4	4.6
0.35	3.7	3.8	4.0	4.2	4.4	4.6	4.8	5.0	5.3
0.40	4.2	4.4	4.6	4.8	5.0	5.3	5.5	5.8	6.0
0.45	4.7	4.9	5.2	5.4	5.7	5.9	6.2	6.5	6.8
0.50	5.2	5.5	5.7	6.0	6.3	6.6	6.9	7.2	7.5
0.55	5.7	6.0	6.3	6.6	6.9	7.2	7.6	7.9	8.3
0.60	6.3	6.6	6.9	7.2	7.5	7.9	8.2	8.6	9.0
0.65	6.8	7.1	7.4	7.8	8.1	8.5	8.9	9.4	9.8
0.70	7.3	7.8	8.0	8.4	8.8	9.2	9.6	10.1	10.5
0.75	7.8	8.2	8.6	9.0	9.4	9.9	10.3	10.8	11.3
0.80	8.4	8.8	9.2	9.6	10.0	10.5	11.0	11.5	12.0
0.85	8.9	9.3	9.7	10.2	10.7	11.2	11.7	12.2	12.8
0.90	9.4	9.8	10.3	10.8	11.3	11.8	12.4	13.0	13.6
0.95	9.9	10.4	10.9	11.4	11.9	12.5	13.0	13.7	14.3
1.00	10.4	10.9	11.4	12.0	12.5	13.1	13.7	14.4	15.1
1.10	11.5	12.1	12.6	13.2	13.8	14.5	15.2	15.9	16.6
1.20	12.5	13.1	13.7	14.4	15.0	15.8	16.5	17.3	18.1
1.30	13.6	14.2	14.9	15.6	16.3	17.1	17.8	18.7	19.6
1.40	14.6	15.3	16.0	16.8	17.6	18.4	19.3	20.1	21.1
1.50	15.7	16.4	17.2	18.0	18.8	19.7	20.6	21.6	22.6
1.60	16.7	17.5	18.3	19.2	20.1	21.0	22.0	23.0	24.1
1.70	17.7	18.6	19.5	20.4	21.6	22.3	23.4	24.5	25.6
1.80	18.8	19.7	20.6	21.6	22.6	23.6	24.7	25.9	27.1
1.90	19.8	20.8	21.7	22.8	23.8	25.0	26.1	27.3	28.6
2.00	20.9	21.9	22.9	24.0	25.1	26.3	27.5	28.8	30.1

Conversion of Centigrade to Fahrenheit Temperatures:

°C.	°F.	°C.	°F.	°C.	°F.
20	68	23	73.4	26	78.8
21	69.8	24	75.2	27	80.6
22	71.6	25	77	28	82.4

B. Toluenesulfonic Acid (Cohen and Raducha): To 2 ml. of urine in a small test tube add 1 ml. of TSA reagent; allow the reagent to flow slowly down the side of the tube. Mix. A precipitate forming within five minutes indicates presence of Bence Jones protein. A negative test excludes Bence Jones protein. Globulins will give a positive test if present at concentrations greater than 500 mg./100 ml. Rarely, the test will be positive in patients with nephrosis or acute disseminated lupus erythematosus.

TSA reagent: p-Toluenesulfonic acid   12 Gm.
Glacial acetic acid, q.s. ad 100 ml.

C. Electrophoresis: Electrophoretic examination of the urine will reveal a characteristic band in the γ or β globulin region.

Bence Jones protein is often seen in multiple myeloma and rarely in chronic leukemia, osteomalacia, osteogenic sarcoma, cancer metastases to bone, and hypertension.

GLUCOSE TESTS

Urine need not be clear but should be well mixed. In the standard copper reduction tests, protein may interfere; remove it by acidifying and filtering at boiling temperature. A high concentration of salicylates, acetanilid (present as glucuronides in urine), or urates may reduce copper to give a "false" green or even yellow color. Fructose, galactose, lactose, maltose, or a pentose may also give a false positive reduction test; in case of doubt, do fermentation tests. Homogentisic acid and uric acid will reduce copper reagent, as will other reducing agents (formaldehyde) also.

If glucose is present, test also for acetone and diacetic acid.

Qualitative Clinitest®.

This test is rapid, requires no heating, uses tablets containing sodium hydroxide and copper sulfate. Cupric ions are reduced to Cu_2O to produce the green to orange color described for Benedict's solution. Add 5 drops of urine, 10 drops of water, and one Clinitest® tablet; do not shake tube while reaction occurs, and let stand 15 seconds after reaction is completed before reading the color as in Benedict's, above.

Qualitative Galatest®.

To a small mount of the Galatest® reagent add a few drops of urine. Reducing substances react with bismuth oxychloride and sodium hydroxide to yield the gray to black color of bismuth.

Glucose Oxidase Test. (Specific for glucose.)

Clinistix® and Tes-Tape® are papers impregnated with glucose oxidase and orthotolidine. Glucose oxidase reacts with glucose to yield gluconic acid and hydrogen peroxide. Hydrogen peroxide and orthotolidine yield a blue color. Dip in urine and read color reaction. Clinistix® is a qualitative test paper, Tes-Tape® is "quantitative." Whereas other tests for glucose indicate presence of other "reducing substances" as well, the glucose oxidase test is specific for glucose. Labstix® reagent papers for protein, glucose, ketones, occult blood, and pH are attached to a small strip of plastic, permitting simultaneous analysis. (Clinistix®, Labstix®, and Bili-Labstix®, Ames Co., Elkhart, Ind.; Tes-Tape®, Eli Lilly and Co., Indianapolis, Ind.)

Benedict's Qualitative Glucose Test.

This reagent will detect 0.02% of glucose, thus being much more sensitive than Fehling's or Haines' solutions. In the reaction with reducing substances, cupric ion is reduced to Cu_2O (cuprous oxide). If only 0.1% or less of glucose is present, the precipitate may not appear until cooling.

Add 8 drops (or $1/2$ ml.) of urine to 5 ml. of Benedict's reagent (see p. 622) in a test tube. Heat to boiling and set in a bath of boiling water for 5 minutes. Read Benedict's test as follows:

Blue to cloudy green color	= Negative, 0	
Yellow-green*	= +	(Less than 0.5% glucose)
Greenish-yellow	= ++	(0.5-1% glucose)
Yellow	= +++	(1-2% glucose)
Orange to Red	= ++++	(Over 2% glucose)

*May show only after cooling.

Benedict's Quantitative Glucose Test.

Place a small quantity of powdered pumice, 10 Gm. of anhydrous sodium carbonate, and 25 ml. of quantitative Benedict's reagent (see p. 622) in a 250 ml. evaporating disk, and heat. While the mixture is boiling, add urine rapidly from a buret until the blue color begins to fade; then add urine slowly until all blue color is gone and only a gray color remains. At this point all cupric ion originally in solution is reduced. The amount of urine used contains 0.05 Gm. of glucose. To calculate Gm. of glucose/100 ml. urine, divide 5 by the number of ml. of urine used.

ACETONE TESTS
(The tests used all react also with diacetic acid.)

Ketostix®, Labstix®, Bili-Labstix®.

Paper strips are impregnated with the reagents listed below for Acetest®. The strip is dipped in the urine, and the color reaction compared with a color chart.

Acetest® Tablets.

Tablets containing sodium nitroprusside, aminoacetic acid, and disodium phosphate are available. Place 1 drop of urine on a tablet and observe in 30 seconds. A purple color indicates presence of acetone.

Legal's Test.

Place 10 ml. of urine in a test tube and add a few crystals (or 6 drops of a 20% solution) of sodium nitroprusside. Acidify with glacial acetic acid; invert tube repeatedly. Overlay carefully with strong ammonia water. Allow to stand 5 minutes. If acetone is present, a violet ring appears at the junction of the two fluids. The degree of positivity depends on the speed of the reaction.

DIACETIC ACID TEST (GERHARDT'S TEST)

This test is not very delicate, and a positive reaction indicates a significant degree of ketosis. It need not be done unless the test for acetone was positive.

Precipitate the phosphates in 5 ml. of urine with 10% ferric chloride solution, drop-by-drop; filter, and add more ferric chloride. If bordeaux red color appears, it indicates presence of 0.05% or more of diacetic acid.

Since the red color may be due to salicylates, sodium bicarbonate, etc., it is necessary to test a control: Boil 75 ml. of urine in a beaker for 15 minutes and repeat the test; if the red color persists, the reaction is due to substances other than diacetic acid, which is volatile and is removed by boiling.

Ketostix®, Labstix® or Bili-Labstix® may be used for ketones.

CALCIUM (SULKOWITCH TEST)

Either fasting or random urines may be tested. Place the patient on a neutral low-calcium diet 72 hours before test. Collect a 24-hour urine specimen. Mix equal parts of urine and Sulkowitch reagent (see p. 627), let stand 2 or 3 minutes, and read as follows:

0 = No precipitate, no urine calcium; serum calcium level 5 to 7.5 mg./100 ml. 1+ = Fine white cloud, normal urine and

blood calcium level. 2+ and 3+ = Increased urinary calcium.
4+ = Precipitate like milk, strongly suggests hypercalcemia,
as in hyperparathyroidism, overtreatment of hypoparathyroidism, overtreatment with vitamin D, lysis of bone by
metastatic neoplasm.

The progress of therapy of hypocalcemia with vitamin D
and calcium or with dihydrotachysterol may be observed by
determining calcium concentration in urine with the
Sulkowitch test.

SEROTONIN (5-HYDROXYTRYPTAMINE)

Argentaffinomas may secrete serotonin, which is metabolized to 5-hydroxyindoleacetic acid. The presence of this
compound in the urine in more than trace amounts almost invariably indicates malignant carcinoid metastatic to the liver.

Method 1.

To test for 5-hydroxyindoleacetic acid, acidify 2 ml. of
filtered urine with 2 drops of 10% HCl and extract twice with
20 to 25 ml. of ether. Evaporate pooled ether extract to dryness. Dissolve the dry residue in 1 ml. of N/10 HCl. Add 1
ml. Ehrlich's reagent (see p. 623). Boil for 2 to 3 minutes.

A distinct blue color indicates the presence of 5-hydroxy-
indoleacetic acid in abnormal amounts in the urine.

Method 2.

Run a control (known normal) urine simultaneously. Into
a test tube, pipet 0.2 ml. of urine, 0.8 ml. of water, and 0.5
ml. of 1-nitroso-2-naphthol (0.1% in 95% ethanol), and mix.
In a separate tube prepare fresh nitrous acid by adding 0.2 ml.
of 2.5% sodium nitrite to 5 ml. of 2 N sulfuric acid; let stand
10 minutes. To the first tube add 0.5 ml. of the freshly prepared nitrous acid, and mix. Add 5 ml. of ethylene dichloride
and shake. If turbid, centrifuge. Ethylene dichloride will
layer on top.

If 5-hydroxyindoleacetic acid is being excreted at a rate
in excess of 30 mg. per 24 hours, the concentration will be
sufficient to color the ethylene dichloride purple. Depth of
color is proportional to concentration. A negative result produces a colorless to yellowish upper layer.

False-positive results may be obtained if bananas have
been consumed prior to the test or if acetanilid has been ingested. False-negative results may be produced by consumption of phenothiazine derivatives.

BLOOD (NONSPECIFIC)

Peroxidase gives positive reaction, and blood is its most likely source. Other substances (e.g., pus) may also give positive reactions. For causes of hematuria see p. 134.

Guaiac Test.
In one test tube mix 2 ml. of 10% acetic acid, 5 ml. urine, and 5 ml. ether. In a second tube place 5 ml. of 95% alcohol, 2 ml. fresh hydrogen peroxide, and a pinch of powdered guaiac. Pour the guaiac solution slowly down the side of the first tube. Blood in the urine causes a blue color to appear at the zone of contact between the guaiac and the ether.

Occultest® Tablets, Hemastix®, Labstix®, Bili-Labstix®.
Blood reacts with the peroxide-orthotolidine reagent to yield a blue color. Follow directions given by the manufacturer.

Benzidine Test.
This test is extremely delicate. Saturate 2 ml. of glacial acetic acid with benzidine and pour off the clear supernatant fluid. Add 1 ml. of fresh hydrogen peroxide and 2 ml. of urine. (Note: If the blue color develops before the addition of urine, the glassware is contaminated.)

BILE PIGMENTS

In early biliary obstruction and hepatitis, bile may be demonstrable in the urine before there is any visible jaundice (see p. 208). Use fresh urine for testing.

Foam Test.
This is a rapid but not very accurate test; protein will also cause foam. Shake 5 ml. of urine in a test tube; bile produces a yellowish foam which persists.

Ictotest® Tablets.
p-Nitrobenzene diazonium p-toluene sulfonate is the active reagent. It will not yield false-positive reactions with promazine derivatives, thus avoiding confusion when screening patients for hepatotoxic reactions to these drugs. Follow directions given by the manufacturer.

Bili-Labstix®.
A dip-stick with indicators for bilirubin, protein, glucose, ketones, blood, and pH.

Harrison Test.

This is a sensitive test.   Mix 5 ml. urine and 5 ml. of a 10% barium chloride solution in a test tube.   Collect the precipitate on filter paper and spread it to dry on another filter paper.   When dry, add 1 or 2 drops of Fouchet's reagent (see p. 623) to the precipitate.   A green color appears in the presence of bilirubin.   Disregard other colors.

Barium chloride-impregnated strips of heavy filter paper may also be used.   Moisten a strip of barium chloride paper with urine and add 1 drop of Fouchet's reagent to wet area.

Iodine Ring Test.

This test is sensitive and reliable.   Layer a 10% alcoholic iodine solution on urine in a test tube.   A green ring indicates the presence of bile.

UROBILINOGEN AND UROBILIN

Urobilinogen is colorless; urobilin is its brown oxidation product.   As urine stands, urobilinogen is converted to urobilin.   Tests for urobilinogen must, therefore, be performed on freshly voided urine.   Collection in a dark bottle containing petroleum ether (sufficient to provide surface layer) and Na_2CO_3 (5 Gm. for 24-hour volume), and storage in the refrigerator will preserve urobilinogen if tests must be delayed or if total 24-hour excretion is to be measured.

Urobilistix®.

Reagent strips contain p-dimethylaminobenzaldehyde stabilized in an acid buffer as the active reagent.   Use freshly voided urine without contaminant or additive.   Dip reagent area of strip in urine.   Remove strip and tap edge of strip against urine container to remove excess urine.   Read in 60 seconds against color chart provided.   The color range provides an acceptable quantitative measure.   Porphobilinogen and p-aminosalicylic acid will react like urobilinogen.

Other Tests.

When testing for either urobilinogen or urobilin in the presence of bilirubin, precipitate the bilirubin with a few ml. of 10% $CaCl_2$ or 10% $BaCl_2$ and filter.   Precipitate can be used for Harrison test (see above); filtrate can be used for urobilinogen or urobilin tests.

Urobilinogen (Ehrlich's Test).

Genitourinary infections interfere with this test since under these circumstances nitrites are present in urine; both nitrites and bile cause an interfering green color.   Sulfonamides and procaine will produce yellowish color reactions.

Pyridium, indole, porphobilinogen, and p-aminosalicylic acid will yield a pink to red color indistinguishable from that produced by urobilinogen.

Mix 10 ml. of fresh urine cooled to room temperature and 1 ml. of Ehrlich's reagent (see p. 623) in a test tube by several inversions, and let stand 5 minutes.

A pink color is normal; cherry or darker red colors indicate abnormal amounts of urobilinogen. The test may be used as a semi-quantitative determination if the urine is diluted 1:10, 1:20, 1:30, 1:40, etc. Color reactions are normal in dilutions up to 1:20.

Urobilin (Schlesinger's Test).

To convert urobilinogen to urobilin, add a few drops of Lugol's solution. Mix 10 ml. of urine and 10 ml. saturated alcoholic solution of zinc acetate, and filter into a dry test tube.

Abnormal amounts of urobilin give the filtrate a green fluorescence which is best seen against a dark background with a light source from the side, or in sunlight against a black background. The fluorescence becomes more marked after an hour.

PORPHYRINS
(Porphobilinogen)

Perform Ehrlich's test for urobilinogen by mixing equal parts of urine and Ehrlich's reagent. Add two parts of saturated sodium acetate solution and mix. If turbid, filter. Shake with a small amount of chloroform.

Urobilinogen is soluble in chloroform; porphobilinogen is not. If after several extractions with chloroform the aqueous phase is still pink, the test is positive for porphobilinogen.

PHENYLPYRUVIC ACID

Phenylpyruvic acid is excreted in the urine in phenylpyruvic oligophrenia, in which an "error" of phenylalanine metabolism is associated with lack of skin and hair pigmentation and mental retardation.

Phenistix®.

Paper strips are impregnated with ferric ammonium sulfate, magnesium sulfate, and cyclohexylsulfamic acid. Ferric ions react with phenylketones to produce a blue-gray color. The strips are dipped in urine or pressed against a wet diaper and compared with a color chart. Thus a rough estimate of phenylketone concentration can be made in a range of 0 to 100 mg./100 ml.

Ferric Chloride Test.

To test for phenylpyruvic and related acids in the urine, add a few drops of strong HCl or acetic acid and 1 ml. of 5 to 10% ferric chloride solution to 5 ml. of urine. A deep blue-green color indicates the presence of phenylpyruvic acid. The color may fade after ten to 30 minutes.

CYSTINE

To 5 ml. of urine add 2 ml. of 5% sodium cyanide solution and allow to react for 10 minutes. Add 5 drops of 5% sodium nitroprusside solution and mix thoroughly. Cystine produces a magenta color. If no cystine is present, a pale brown or pale pink color results. The cyanide and nitroprusside solutions should be freshly prepared.

Examine urine sediment for cystine crystals.

DETERMINATION OF HEREDITARY
METABOLIC DISEASE BY URINALYSIS

Errors of Carbohydrate Metabolism.
- A. Galactosuria: Positive test for reducing substance (Benedict's, Galatest®, Clinitest®). Negative glucose oxidase test (Clinistix®, Tes-Tape®). Positive phloro-glucinol-HCl test (Tollens).
- B. Pentosuria (ʟ-Xylulose): Positive test for reducing sub-stance (Benedict's, Galatest®, Clinitest®). Negative glucose oxidase test (Clinistix®, Tes-Tape®). Positive orcinol-HCl test (Bial).
- C. Fructosuria: Positive test for reducing substance (Bene-dict's, Galatest®, Clinitest®). Negative glucose-oxidase test (Clinistix®, Tes-Tape®). Positive resorcinol-HCl test (Seliwanoff).

Errors of Amino Acid Metabolism.
- A. Cystinuria: (Cystine, ornithine, arginine, lysine.) Cystine crystals in sediment. Positive cyanide-nitroprusside test for cystine (see above).
- B. DeToni-Fanconi-Debre Syndrome: (Amino acids, glucose, phosphate.) Positive glucose oxidase test (Clinistix®, Tes-Tape®). Paper chromatography for amino acids.
- C. Wilson's Disease: (Amino acids, glucose, phosphate, uric acid.) Positive glucose oxidase test (Clinistix®, Test-Tape®). Paper chromatography for amino acids.
- D. Phenylketonuria: (Phenylpyruvic acid and other phenyl-alanine derivatives.) Positive test with Phenistix® or ferric chloride test (see p. 122).

E. Hartnup Disease: (Amino acids, indole compounds.)
   Paper chromatography.
F. Alkaptonuria: (Homogentisic acid.) Urine darkens on
   standing. Positive test for reducing substance (Benedict's, Galatest®, Clinitest®). Negative glucose oxidase
   test (Clinistix®, Tes-Tape®). Urine reduces silver on
   sensitized photographic plate.
G. Tyrosinosis: (Hydroxyphenylpyruvic acid.) Paper
   chromatography. Positive Millon test.
H. Maple Syrup Disease: (Leucine, valine, and hydroxy
   acids.) Maple syrup odor of urine. Paper chromatography.

Abnormal Porphyrin Metabolism.
A. Acute Porphyria: (Uroporphyrin I and III, coproporphyrin
   III, porphobilinogen.) Urine darkens on exposure to sunlight. Positive porphobilinogen test (see p. 122). Spectroscopic and fluorimetric identification.
B. Cutaneous Porphyria: (Uroporphyrin I and III, coproporphyrin III.) Red urine. Spectroscopic and fluorimetric
   tests.

IODIDE AND BROMIDE

To 10 ml. of urine add a few drops of fuming nitric acid
and 5 ml. of chloroform; mix gently and let stand three minutes. The chloroform settles to the bottom. Iodides produce
a pink to violet color; bromides produce a yellow color.

BARBITURATES (Modified Koppanyi Method)

Acidify 100 ml. of urine with a few drops of dilute sulfuric
acid, and then extract by shaking with 200 ml. of diethyl ether
in a separatory funnel. Allow to settle, drain water layer,
and filter the top ether layer through filter paper. Remove
the ether by evaporation at low temperature on a water bath.
If the residue is colored, dissolve it in 10 ml. of N/2 sodium
hydroxide. Acidify slightly with dilute sulfuric acid and re-
extract with ether. Evaporate the ether to dryness, and dissolve the residue in 1 ml. of dry chloroform. Transfer a few
drops to a 6 mm. test tube, add two drops of 1% anhydrous
cobalt acetate in absolute methyl alcohol, and mix. Layer on
top 5 drops of 5% isopropyl amine in absolute alcohol. A
violet interface or ring indicates the presence of barbiturates.
A trace of water prevents color development. Diphenylhydantoin (Dilantin®), glutethimide (Doriden®), and other ureides
give a positive test.
Alternates: The first ether extract may be washed with
pH 9.0 buffer to remove interfering material before proceeding

further. The acid urine may be treated with 5 Gm. of Super-Cel® to remove interfering substances. Remove the Super-Cel® by filtration before extracting with ether.

FAT

Shake equal parts of urine and ether; cloudiness due to fat disappears; decant ether onto watch glass, evaporate; fat leaves greasy deposit. Fat (but not chyle) may be seen microscopically.

MICROSCOPIC EXAMINATION OF URINE

Secure sediment by centrifuging fresh urine sample for five minutes. Draw off clear supernatant fluid, place a drop of sediment on a glass slide, and cover. Examine first with low power, then high power, and vary light intensity in order to see casts. If protein is present, look for casts, erythrocytes, leukocytes, and renal tubule epithelial cells. In cases of urinary calculi examine for red cells, leukocytes, epithelial cells, and cystine crystals. (See drawings on p. 126.)

ORGANIZED ELEMENTS
(See Addis Count, p. 129.)

Sediment from freshly voided urine should be used. The sediment may be stained with Sternheimer and Malbin stain to assist in differentiating the formed elements.

This stain is prepared, performed, and interpreted as follows:

Solution A:

Methylrosaniline chloride	3.0 Gm.
95% Ethyl alcohol	20.0 ml.
Ammonium oxalate	0.8 Gm.
Distilled water, q.s. ad	80.0 ml.

Solution B:

Safranine O	0.25 Gm.
95% Ethyl alcohol	10.0 ml.
Distilled water, q.s. ad	100.0 ml.

Mix 3 parts of solution A with 97 parts of solution B and filter. This is kept in a dropper bottle. For staining, place 1 drop of the stain in the reconstituted sediment in the centrifuge tube. Examine under a cover slip.

MICROSCOPIC EXAMINATION OF URINE SEDIMENT*

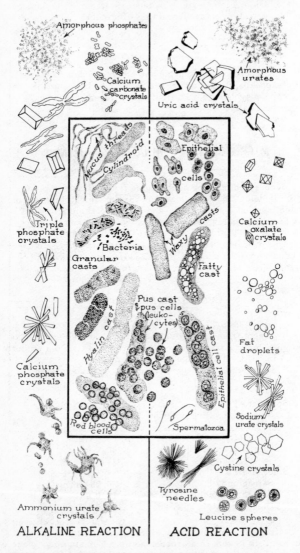

Amorphous phosphates

Calcium carbonate crystals

Amorphous urates

Uric acid crystals

Mucus threads

Cylindroid

Epithelial cells

Triple phosphate crystals

Bacteria

Granular casts

Waxy casts

Calcium oxalate crystals

Fatty cast

Pus cast pus cells (leuko- cytes)

Hyalin cast

Fat droplets

Epithelial cell cast

Calcium phosphate crystals

Sodium urate crystals

Red blood cells

Spermatozoa

Cystine crystals

Tyrosine needles

Ammonium urate crystals

Leucine spheres

ALKALINE REACTION | **ACID REACTION**

*Redrawn after Todd and Sanford. (100-200 ×.)

127

ABNORMAL URINARY SEDIMENTS

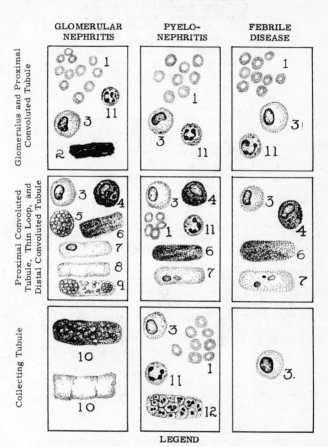

LEGEND

1. Red blood cells.
2. R.b.c. cast.
3. Tubule cell.
4. Tubule cell full of protein.
5. Tubule cell full of fat
   ("oval fat body").
6. Granular cast.
7. Hyaline cast.
8. Waxy cast.
9. Fatty cast.
10. Broad cast - granular
    or waxy.
11. White blood cell.
12. White blood cell cast.

Interpretation:
>   RBC: Unstained or slightly purple.
>   Neutrophil: Dark purple with red-purple nuclei and
>   violet granules. Some large neutrophils stain
>   light blue to colorless (glitter cells).
>   Renal tubule cells: Narrow rim of orange-purple
>   cytoplasm about dark purple nucleus.
>   Bladder epithelium: Dark blue nucleus, light blue
>   cytoplasm.
>   Squamous cells: Purple nuclei, pink cytoplasm.
>   Hyaline casts: Pink to purple.
>   Granular casts: Purple granules, pink matrix.
>   Leukocyte casts: Purple and blue cells, pink matrix.
>   Tubular epithelial casts: Small cells with purple
>   nuclei, pink matrix.
>   Waxy casts: Purple.
>   RBC casts: Unstained or light purple.

Red Cells.

These are crenated in concentrated urine and swollen in
dilute urine. If much blood is present, the plasma protein will
produce a positive protein test. Red blood cells are counted
either per high power field or by using the hemacytometer.

Leukocytes, or Pus Cells.

These shrink in a strongly acid urine, swell and clump
together in an alkaline urine. Leukocytes are counted per
high power field or by placing a small drop of urine directly
on the blood-counting chamber (see p. 148); count the cells in
the four large corner squares, and divide the sum by four and
multiply by ten to get the count per cu. mm.

Epithelial Cells.

With practice, epithelial cells from tubules, bladder, and
urethra can be distinguished. Tubule cells filled with fat can
be identified by appropriate lighting of the microscopic field
under low and high power.

Casts. (See p. 126.)

These are formed in renal tubules and are usually significant of renal disease. Several varieties can be identified
and their significance appraised by virtue of their probable
sources: Glomerular inflammation results in formation of red
cell casts high in the nephron; associated tubule inflammation
or degenerative disease may result in production of fatty casts,
waxy casts, and of the less significant hyaline and granular
casts; collecting tubules contribute broad waxy or granular
casts when urine flow through them is reduced. Leukocyte
casts signify purulent renal disease. Casts dissolve in dilute
or alkaline urine. They are seen best under reduced light.
Count casts per low power field.

Mucus Threads and Cylindroids.
Differentiate from casts.

Bacteria.
Study only in catheterized or clean specimen (see p. 289).

Parasites.
Motile forms of Trichomonas vaginalis (morphologically similar to T. hominis, p. 347) or eggs of Schistosoma haematobium (see p. 358) may be seen.

UNORGANIZED SEDIMENT

This varies with the pH of the urine. Amorphous material is of little importance. Crystals of normal urine are formed as urine cools. Crystals of abnormal urine are as follows: (See p. 126.)

1. Cystine - In some cases of calculi.
2. Leucine and tyrosine - Liver destruction.
3. Cholesterin - Excessive tissue breakdown.
4. Bilirubin and hematoidin - Of little importance.
5. Sulfonamide crystals - May be seen if patient is taking sulfonamides; hematuria may be caused by sulfonamide crystals which form in the renal tubules or excretory tract.

ADDIS URINE SEDIMENT COUNT

The Addis count is a quantitative estimate of the severity of a renal lesion, as seen in nephritis, hypertensive disease with an associated renal lesion, and collagen disease. It is not a diagnostic test.

Collection of Specimen.
A. Give a dry diet the day before the test. Nothing that will pour from a vessel should be taken (gravy, coffee, milk, tea, water, etc.). If the patient shows evidence of nitrogen retention, however, do not withhold fluids.
B. Instruct patient to void at bedtime, discard specimen, and note time on label of bottle.
C. Have him empty his bladder on arising, collect specimen in the bottle, and note time. If it is necessary to void during the night, the bottle should be used. Thus a collection of urine during a known period will be completed. Use 1 ml. of neutral formalin as a preservative. Female patients should be catheterized or should wash vulva and place cotton plug in vagina to separate labia during voiding.

Examination.

A. Determine volume of urine collected.

B. Determine specific gravity. Normally, specific gravity is over 1.027. Sediment count is not valid if specific gravity is < 1.016.

C. Determine pH (pH paper). pH must be 6.0 or less to prevent dissolution of casts and red cells.

D. Mix specimen well to disperse sediment, and place in a calibrated centrifuge tube a one-fifth hour (12 minute) aliquot. Centrifuge to pack sediment completely (1800 r.p.m. for 15 minutes; 3500 for 5 minutes).

E. Draw off supernatant carefully so as to leave 0.5 ml. in the tube. Save supernatant for protein determination. Mix the sediment in the 0.5 ml. urine and fill hemacytometer (see p. 148).

F. Count under low power all casts in six of the nine large squares. Average the counts in two or more chambers. Number counted × 100,000 = number of casts excreted in 24 hours at rate of excretion during collection of specimen. This factor is derived as follows:

$$\frac{\text{Number counted}}{0.6 \text{ cu. mm.}} \times (500 \text{ cu. mm.} \times 120) = \text{No./24 hours}$$

G. Count under high power the red cells and white cells and epithelial cells in 15 of the 25 divisions of the central sq. mm. (i.e., 240 of the smallest squares). Do not count squamous cells. Average the counts of two or more chambers. Number red cells counted x 1,000,000 = number of red cells excreted in 24 hours. Number white cells and epithelial cells counted x 1,000,000 = number of white cells and epithelial cells excreted in 24 hours. These factors are derived as follows:

$$\frac{\text{Number counted}}{0.06 \text{ cu. mm.}} \times (500 \text{ cu. mm.} \times 120) = \text{No./24 hours}$$

H. If more precise counts are desired more squares can be counted, thus reducing the multiplication factor accordingly. The upper limits of normal for 24 hours excretion by this technic are:[*]

   Casts, 100,000
   Red blood cells, 1,000,000
   White blood cells and epithelial cells, 2,000,000

I. It is advisable to place a drop of the sediment on a slide under a cover glass and to study the qualitative characteristics of the sediment in an effort to establish the type

---

[*]These normal values were established by Addis following initial publication of his method, and reflect minor changes in technic that he introduced.

of renal lesion present if possible (see p. 126). In some instances it is desirable to concentrate the sediment of the entire urine specimen into one small plug. A careful study of several preparations under cover slips may reveal the rare red blood cell cast that may help confirm the presence of glomerulitis.

Interpretation.

The Addis count is a quantitative measure that provides a means of estimating the activity and the progression or regression of a renal lesion from time to time. The diagnosis of a renal lesion requires a clinical examination and a qualitative study of the urine sediment, the types of formed elements being important in this regard (see pp. 126 and 132).

THE TWO AND THREE GLASS TESTS OF URINE FROM THE LOWER URINARY TRACT OF THE MALE

Procedure.
  A. Three Glass Test: Collect in glass containers three specimens as indicated below. Micturition should be continuous during the collection, and the separate specimens collected by changing containers at the proper intervals.
    1. "First glass" consists of the first 4 to 7 ml. of urine voided. This specimen is the urethral specimen, and contains the elements harbored in the urethra.
    2. "Second glass," the bladder specimen, contains all of the urine in the bladder with the exception of a small portion left in the bladder for the "third glass."
    3. "Third glass," the prostatic specimen, is the last voided and may contain prostatic secretions.
  B. Two Glass Test: Use two colorless beakers or drinking glasses. This test is the same as the "three glass test" with the third (prostatic) specimen omitted.

Interpretation.

The urine is examined for color, appearance, and presence of shreds or other sediment. Microscopic examination of wet smear and stained smear reveals the presence of bacteria and the possible location of infection.

RENAL FUNCTION TESTS

Tests of renal function involve study of the urine, the blood, urography, and special function tests.

Summary of Renal Physiology.

Each kidney contains about one million nephrons. Each nephron consists of a glomerulus connected to a long tubule which has three distinct divisions: the proximal convoluted

COMMON PATTERNS OF ABNORMAL URINE COMPOSITION IN DISEASE

Disease	Volume Daily	Color	Sp. Gr.	Protein†	r.b.c.†	Casts†	Microscopic (Casts and Cells and Other Findings)
Normal	600-2500	Yellow amber	1.003-1.030	0-trace (0-0.05 Gm.)	0 to occ.	0 to occ.	Hyaline casts (urine must be acid and fresh or preserved).
Diseases with high fevers	Decreased	Amber	Increased	Trace or +	0	None to few	Hyaline casts, tubule cells.
Congestive heart failure	Decreased	Amber	High; varies with renal function	1-2+	None to +	+	Hyaline and granular casts.
Eclampsia	Decreased	Amber	Increased	3-4+	None to +	3-4+	Hyaline casts.
Diabetic coma	Increased to decreased	Light	High	+	0	None to +	Hyaline casts. Glucose. Ketone bodies.
Acute glomerulo-nephritis*	Decreased	Smoky; red	Increased	2-4+	1-4+	2-4+	Blood, cellular, granular, hyaline casts. Renal tubule epith.
Degenerative phase glomerulonephritis	Normal or decreased	Light	Normal or increased	4+	1-2+	4+	Granular, waxy, hyaline fatty casts. Fatty tubule cells.
Terminal phase glomerulonephritis	Increased to decreased	Light	Low; fixed	1-2+	Trace to +	1-3+	Granular, hyaline and fatty casts. Broad casts.
Lipoid nephrosis	Decreased	Light to dark	Very high	4+	0 to trace	4+	Hyaline, granular, fatty, waxy casts. Fatty tubule cells.
Collagen disease	Normal, increased, or decreased	Light to dark	Normal or decreased	1-4+	1-4+	1-4+	Blood, cellular, granular, hyaline, waxy, fatty, broad casts. Fatty tubule cells.
Pyelonephritis	Normal or decreased	Cloudy dark	Normal or low	1-2+	None to +	None to +	Pus casts and hyaline casts. Many pus cells. Bacteria.
Benign hypertension (late)	Normal or increased	Normal or light.	Normal or low	None to +	0 to trace	None to +	Hyaline and granular casts.
Malignant hyper-tension	Normal, increased, or decreased	Light	Low; fixed	1-2+	Trace to +	1-2+	Hyaline and granular casts.

*May be anuric, or have low, fixed specific gravity. †Quantities expressed in scale of 0-4+.

tubule, the thin loop of Henle, and the distal convoluted tubule. Several nephrons connect to a collecting tubule which communicates with the renal pelvis.

The glomeruli function as ultrafilters which produce a filtrate similar in composition to plasma except that glomerular filtrate contains almost no protein. In the normal adult about 180 liters of filtrate are produced in 24 hours. Of this, the tubules reabsorb about 178 liters of water and most of the organic and inorganic solutes. Normally, some components of the filtered solutes are actively absorbed (completely or nearly so): glucose, amino acids, sodium, etc. For some solutes such as glucose, phosphate, and amino acids, the maximum reabsorptive capacity of the tubule is limited and all filtered material in excess of this limit is excreted in the urine. For example, the maximum amount of glucose which can be reabsorbed by the average normal adult kidney is 320 mg. per minute; if more is filtered, the excess is lost in the urine. Other solutes are not reabsorbed, are only passively and only partially reabsorbed, or are actively secreted by the tubule. Inulin, a carbohydrate used for renal function studies, is not at all reabsorbed by the tubule. Some urea is passively reabsorbed, but most of the filtered urea escapes reabsorption. Exogenous creatinine, H^+, K^+, phenol red (P.S.P.), Diodrast®, para-aminohippurate, and penicillin are actively secreted by the tubule cells, thus increasing excretion over the amount filtered.

Functions of the Kidney Include:

A. Elimination in solution of solid waste substances (e.g., end products of protein metabolism) and foreign substances (e.g., dyes).

B. Regulation of water balance.

C. Regulation of "acid-base" equilibrium and electrolyte excretion. This involves secretion of H^+ and production of ammonia from amino acids, principally glutamine. The H^+ and NH_4^+ produced are exchanged for Na^+ in the distal convoluted tubule, thus providing for conservation of this essential cation.

URINALYSIS IN TESTING RENAL FUNCTION

Record intake and output of fluids. The normal day output (8:00 a.m. to 8:00 p.m.) is two or three times the normal night output. This ratio is changed in renal disease, in some cases of heart failure, and in hyperaldosteronism. (See p. 110 for the usual daily urine volume.)

A fixed sp. gr. of 1.010 to 1.012 suggests renal disease.

Proteinuria.

The presence of protein in the urine indicates increased glomerular permeability and some degree of diminution of tubular reabsorption of protein. It appears in many types of renal disease. Slight proteinuria is seen in congestive heart failure, infectious diseases, after a heavy meal, and in some cases is associated with prolonged standing (orthostatic proteinuria) or with vigorous exercise.

Casts.

Casts result from precipitation of protein in the tubules. Waxy and fatty casts are suggestive of nephrosis.

Pus Cells.

These are seen in large numbers in any genitourinary infections. (Women should cleanse the vulva, spread the labia, and collect a "clean" specimen free of vaginal leukocytes.)

Hematuria.

Gross or microscopic hematuria may result from glomerulonephritis, infection, trauma (including calculi), strictures, drug poisoning, or tumors of the kidneys, bladder, or urethra.

Hemoglobinuria.

Hemoglobin is found in urine following hemolysis associated with paroxysmal nocturnal hemoglobinuria, sickle cell crises, idiosyncrasy to cold, acute severe hemolytic reaction, or transfusion reactions.

Bacteria.

Bacteria in the urine may be specific for infection, as in renal tuberculosis.

ALTERATIONS OF BLOOD COMPOSITION COMMONLY FOUND IN IMPAIRED RENAL FUNCTION

A rise in blood urea nitrogen, creatinine, and N.P.N. is seen when glomerular filtration rate is reduced or renal blood flow is greatly reduced. Phosphate and sulfate retention are common.

Low serum protein concentrations occur commonly. Edema may occur if serum albumin drops below 2.5 Gm./100 ml. or the total serum proteins below 5.5 Gm./100 ml.

Acid-base equilibrium is disturbed in nephritis. "Renal acidosis" is partly due to failure to conserve sodium during excretion of anions, e.g., chlorides, phosphates (see pp. 425 and 427).

Anemia accompanies chronic renal disease.

CONCENTRATION-DILUTION TESTS

If the patient's routine urine specimens contain no sugar or protein and have a sp. gr. of 1.025 or higher, a concentration test is unnecessary.

Principle: Urine sp. gr. is a measure of capacity of the tubules to reabsorb water from glomerular filtrate, thus concentrating the urine. A more accurate test of concentration of solute in urine is the determination of osmolality, but the apparatus required for this procedure is not generally available.

Concentration Test.

This test is unreliable in case of heart failure with edema. It is contraindicated in uremia.

A. The subject abstains from all fluid for 24 hours after the morning meal. (Do not dehydrate uremic patients who may have a large obligatory renal water loss.)

B. Collect urine specimens during the last 12 hours of the period and determine specific gravity of each.

C. Specific gravity should reach 1.025 or more. In some patients with edema, nocturnal diuresis will invalidate the test.

Dilution Test (Water Test).

This test is contraindicated in cases of cardiac or renal edema. This test may be modified for use in diagnosis of adrenal insufficiency (see p. 243).

A. Evening meal as desired. Nothing by mouth after 8:00 p.m.

B. At 8:00 a.m., empty bladder and drink 1500 ml. water within 45 minutes.

C. Void every half hour till noon (save eight specimens).

D. Sp. gr. should be 1.003 or less in at least one specimen.

E. Total quantity of voided specimens should be over 80% of intake (i.e., over 1200 ml.).

Mosenthal Modification of Concentration-dilution Tests.

A. Patient follows his usual eating and drinking habits.

B. Collect urines every two hours from 8:00 a.m. to 8:00 p.m. Collect night urine as one specimen (8:00 p.m. to 8:00 a.m.).

C. Results:

1. Sp. gr. in one specimen should exceed 1.020.
2. A difference of 0.009 or more should exist between lowest and highest sp. gr.
3. Volume of 12-hour night urine should not exceed 725 ml.

Vasopressin (Pitressin®) Concentration Test.

This test is contraindicated in pregnancy and coronary artery disease. It depends on the anti-diuretic effect of posterior pituitary extract. No preparation is needed other than abstinence from diuretics. Empty bladder. Inject subcutaneously 10 U.S.P. units of vasopressin (Pitressin®). Collect urine after 60 and 120 minutes. Highest sp. gr. should exceed 1.020.

Interpret as in concentration test above. This pituitrin test gives reliable results in presence of cardiac edema or ascites. A further application of the test is in diabetes insipidus, where urine concentration is normal after giving pituitrin but not after fluid restriction.

PHENOL RED TEST
(P.S.P., PHENOLSULPHONPHTHALEIN)

Principle: This is a measure of tubular excretion. Phenol red is removed from peritubular capillary blood by the renal tubules and excreted into the urine. Various standards of "normality" are in use.

Intravenous Method.

Be certain bladder can be completely emptied, leaving no residual urine. The bladder should not be empty at the beginning of the test because it is necessary that the patient be able to void for the 15-minute collection.

A. The patient should drink two glasses of water before and additional water during the test to ensure a urine volume sufficient to permit collection of a urine specimen at the stated time. Larger urine volumes reduce error resulting from incomplete emptying of bladder.

B. Inject 1 ml. of dye (6 mg.) I.V. Collect the total volume of urine voided at 15, 30, and 60 minutes after injection of the dye. Determine the P.S.P. content of each specimen.

C. Interpretation:

	% P.S.P. Excreted			
	15 min.	30 min.	60 min.	Total
Normal	15-27+	12-20	13-20	55-60
Renal insufficiency	< 15	< 12	< 12	< 40

Ureteral Catheterization Method (Cystoscopy).

This method can be used to study function of one kidney at a time. Have the two ureteral catheters dripping into separate test tubes containing dilute NaOH, and inject 1 ml. of P.S.P. dye I.V. Normally the dye appears within 3 minutes, as indicated by pink coloration in tubes.

Phenolsulphonphthalein (P.S.P., Phenol Red) Test for Re-
    sidual Urine.

The P.S.P. test has been modified to serve as a measure
of residual urine.

The patient empties his bladder. Exactly 1 ml. of P.S.P.,
containing 6 mg. of the dye, is given intravenously. In this
modification of the P.S.P. excretion test, the water intake is
limited to 200 ml. or less during each of the two subsequent
half-hour periods; this is necessary because the rapid filling
of the bladder in the presence of urethral obstruction may result in a loss of bladder tone and a consequent increase in
residual urine.

Collect all of the urine the patient can pass one-half hour
and one hour after injection of the dye.

Normally, the P.S.P. excretion is 50 to 60% in the first
half hour plus an additional 10 to 15% during the second half
hour.

Interpretation:

		First Spec. ($1/2$ hour)	Second Spec. (1 hour)
Normal		50%-60%	10%-15%
Residual urine	(a)	15%	25%
present	(b)	35%	25%
	(c)	25%	25%

If the initial half-hour excretion is less than, equal to, or
only slightly more than second half-hour excretion, residual
urine must be present. If the excretion curve is flat and the
morning specific gravity low, catheterization should be done
after collection of the second half-hour specimen to confirm
the presence or absence of residual urine, since under these
circumstances one cannot distinguish between severely depressed renal function and a large residual volume of urine.
If the specific gravity of the morning urine is high, renal insufficiency is unlikely and a flat excretion curve is a reliable
index of residual urine volume.

A rough estimate of residual urine volume can be calculated from the following formula:

$$\frac{Vol.^1 \; (60 - P.S.P.^1)}{P.S.P.^1} = \; ml. \; residual \; urine$$

$Vol.^1$ = Volume of first half-hour specimen.
$P.S.P.^1$ = % of P.S.P. recovered in first specimen.
60   = Expected normal P.S.P. excretion in the first
             half-hour.

(Values for the second half-hour are not used in this calculation.)

CLEARANCE TESTS

These tests are designed to measure the capacity of the kidneys to clear waste products or foreign materials (inulin, Diodrast®, etc.) from the blood into the urine. From the determination of blood concentration of the test material and the quantity eliminated in the urine, "clearance" can be calculated in terms of ml. of blood cleared per unit time.

Creatinine Clearance.

Creatinine is filtered through the glomerulus. Under ordinary circumstances the clearance of endogenous creatinine approximates the glomerular filtration rate. The clearance formula is:

$$\text{Clearance} = \frac{UV}{P}, \text{ where: }$$

U = mg. /100 ml. creatinine in urine
P = mg. /100 ml. creatinine in plasma
V = ml. of urine excreted per minute or per 24 hours.

A. Technic:
   1. Twenty-four hour endogenous creatinine clearance - The entire volume of urine excreted over a period of 24 hours is collected. A blood specimen is obtained during the forenoon of the day of the test. Creatinine concentrations are measured in urine and plasma (or serum), and the volume of urine is measured for use in the formula above.
   2. Two- to six-hour clearance periods may be employed. Fasting state is preferred for the brief clearance period. A two- to six-hour urine collection is completed and a blood specimen obtained at about the midpoint of the urine collection period. Creatinine concentrations of plasma and urine and the urine volume are determined for calculation of the clearance.
B. Interpretation: Normal values for men and women corrected to 1.73 sq. M. body surface area range from 140 to 180 L. /24 hrs. (100 to 125 ml. /min.). To correct clearance to standard 1.73 sq. M. body surface area:

$$\frac{\text{Clearance}}{\text{observed}} \times \frac{1.73 \text{ sq. M.}}{\text{estimated surface area*}} = \frac{\text{corrected}}{\text{clearance}}$$

Care in the chemical determination of creatinine is essential. False low clearance results may be observed because of noncreatinine chromogen in plasma such as occurs in some patients with cardiac disease. As a clinical test of glomerular filtration it is superior to the urea clearance.

---

*For surface area (S.A.), see nomogram, p. 634.

Urea Clearance.

Clearance has been defined as the ml. of blood completely cleared of urea per minute by the kidneys. As the blood flows through the glomeruli, the concentration of urea in the glomerular filtrate is equal to that of the blood producing the filtrate. Some urea is reabsorbed by the tubules. Thus urea clearance equals ml. of blood which contain the amount of urea removed per minute in the urine.

It has been empirically shown that with a rapid flow of urine (2 ml. or more per minute) the excretion of urea is at a maximum, hence is called "maximum clearance" (C_m). It normally ranges from 64 to 99 ml., the mean for an average adult being 75 ml. of blood cleared per minute. The formula is:

$$C_m = \frac{UV}{P}, \text{ where: } \begin{array}{l} U = \text{mg. /100 ml. urea nitrogen in urine} \\ P = \text{mg. /100 ml. urea nitrogen in plasma} \\ V = \text{ml. urine excreted per minute} \end{array}$$

If urine flow is slow (1.9 ml. or less per minute), urea excretion is disproportionately less than above. The range is 41 to 65 ml. per minute; the mean for an average adult, 54 ml. of blood per minute. This is "standard clearance" (C_s), and any value below 40 ml. is abnormal. The formula is:

$$C_s = \frac{U\sqrt{V}}{P}$$

Because the mathematical formula is not valid, standard clearance values are unreliable.

A. Technic: The patient requires no special preparation; do test in a.m., after a breakfast without coffee. Water may be consumed to insure adequate urine output. Empty bladder at 10:00 a.m. and discard urine; an indwelling catheter may be used if patient cannot empty bladder completely. Empty bladder again 60 minutes later, and label as specimen No. 1; at this time also draw 5 ml. oxalated blood. One hour later, empty bladder again and label as specimen No. 2. Determine volume and the urea nitrogen content of each specimen (U). Determine urea nitrogen content of plasma (P). Determine volume of urine secreted (V) during each of the two test hours, and choose applicable formula above. Calculate two clearances, one for each urine specimen; the results should be similar. To obtain the per cent of normal, multiply C_s by the factor 1.76; multiply C_m by 1.26.

B. Interpretation: Normal values result unless disease has destroyed over 50% of the renal parenchyma. In the presence of renal insufficiency, there is a direct relationship between the anatomical destruction of renal parenchyma and clearance test values. In normal persons, urea clearance may be affected by protein intake; C_m is increased by caffeine, small doses of epinephrine, or an ordinary meal. C_m is decreased by posterior pituitary hormone or large doses of epinephrine.

PRINCIPLES OF PRECISE TESTS OF RENAL FUNCTION

The urea clearance test is being replaced by the inulin, endogenous creatinine, and Diodrast® or PAH clearance tests, which help differentiate disease of glomeruli and tubules.

Glomerular Filtration Rate (GFR).

Inulin, a polysaccharide eliminated exclusively through the glomeruli, is neither excreted nor absorbed by the tubules. Inulin clearance, therefore, is a measure of glomerular filtration rate. Other substances may be used, the most reliable of which is sodium iothalamate, labeled with ^{131}I or ^{125}I, permitting easy assay of plasma and urine concentrations. Normal in adults is 100 to 130 ml. per minute per 1.73 sq. M. of body surface.

Renal Plasma Flow (RPF).

Para-aminohippurate, Diodrast®, and ^{131}I- or ^{125}I-labeled sodium iodohippurate at low concentration in plasma are cleared almost completely by filtration and tubular secretion as the plasma flows through the kidney. If, for example, at a plasma PAH concentration of 1 mg./100 ml., 6 mg. PAH appear in the urine per minute, 600 ml. of plasma must be passing through the kidneys per minute. The normal range is 500 to 800 ml. of plasma per minute per 1.73 sq. M. of body surface. Varying with the hematocrit, this indicates a flow through the kidneys of 1000 to 1500 ml. of whole blood per minute, or almost a third of the cardiac output at rest.

Filtration Fraction.

Ratio of volume of glomerular filtrate to the volume of plasma from which the filtrate was obtained is expressed as:

$$\frac{GFR}{RPF}$$

This ratio is called the "filtration fraction." The normal filtration fraction is $\frac{120 \text{ ml./min.}}{600 \text{ ml./min.}}$, or 0.2.

Maximal Tubular Capacity (T_m).

At high concentrations of Diodrast®, iodohippurate, or para-aminohippurate in plasma, the excretory capacity of the renal tubule is exceeded. By measuring the amount of test

material excreted under these conditions and correcting for
the amount of test material simultaneously filtered through
the glomerulus, the maximal excretory capacity of the tubule
is obtained. T_m for reabsorption of glucose, amino acids,
etc. can be determined similarly, although in this instance
the amount filtered minus the amount excreted per unit of
time equals the maximal reabsorptive capacity. (See p. 138
for values.)

RENAL FUNCTION TESTS

Determination		Normal Value
Phenolsulfonphthalein (P.S.P., Phenol red)	1 ml. I.V.	15 min. 35% (28-51) ⎫ 30 min. 17% (13-24) ⎬ 55-60% 60 min. 12% (9-17) ⎭ 120 min. 6% (3-10)
Clearance Tests: Inulin clearance Mannitol clearance Endogenous creatinine clearance	Glomerular Filtration Rate (GFR)	Corrected to 1.73 M^2 S.A. Male, 110-150 ml./min. Female, 105-132 ml./min.
Diodrast® clearance p-Aminohippurate (PAH) clearance	Renal Plasma Flow (RPF)	Male, 560-830 ml./min. Female, 490-700 ml./min.
Filtration fraction	FF equals GFR/RPF	Male, 17-21% Female, 17-23%
Urea clearance (C_u)		Standard, 40-65 ml./min. Maximal, 60-100 ml./min.
Maximal Glucose Reabsorptive capacity	Tm_G	Male, 300-450 mg./min. Female, 250-350 mg./min.
Maximal Diodrast® Excretory capacity	Tm_D	Male, 43-59 mg./min. Female, 33-51 mg./min.
Maximal PAH Excretory capacity	Tm_{PAH}	80-90 mg./min.

9...
Hematology

COLLECTION OF BLOOD SPECIMENS

Capillary Blood.

Capillary blood may be used for hemoglobin, cell counts, blood typing, bleeding or coagulation time, or for microchemical determinations. The required apparatus includes sponges and 70% alcohol, a lancet, and diluting pipets and diluting solutions. For microchemical determinations, micropipets (0.01 to 0.1 ml.) and the appropriate diluting fluids are necessary.

Choose a site on the skin which is free from circulatory abnormalities. The tip of a finger and the lobe of the ear are commonly used. In infants the big toe or heel may be used. Cleanse the skin with cotton or a sponge wet with 70% alcohol. Let the skin dry in air and make a deep puncture. Wipe away the first drop of blood, and draw blood into a pipet from the next drop as it wells from the wound. If both red and white cell counts are to be made, draw blood for the white count first since it requires a greater quantity.

Venous Blood.

Venous blood is used for blood counts, serologic tests, and various blood chemical determinations. The required apparatus includes a sterile 5-20 ml. syringe, sterile sponges, sterile needles of the required sizes (No. 23 to 19, 1 to 1 1/2 inches long are good sizes), containers for specimens, various solutions (diluting, anticoagulant, etc.), a tourniquet (blood pressure cuff or rubber tubing), and labels.

Veins of the antecubital fossa are most frequently used. Place the tourniquet firmly around the upper arm and ask the patient to close and open his fist repeatedly. While the patient does this, clean the puncture site with alcohol and let dry. Fix the skin and vein with one hand and insert the needle with a firm motion. Obtain the amount of blood needed (2.5 ml. blood provides 1 ml. serum), release the tourniquet, withdraw the needle, and give the patient a sterile sponge to press over the wound. Elevate the arm to help prevent extravasation of blood through the puncture wound while closure takes place. Remove the needle from the syringe, gently expel the blood into the prepared containers, and mix gently. The

NORMAL BLOOD ANALYSIS

Physical Properties of Blood.
  Volume: Whole blood - 65.6 ± 7.3 ml./Kg.
       (Normal = mean ± 2 σ = 51.0 - 80.2 ml./Kg.)
       Erythrocytes - 25.8 ± 2.7 ml./Kg.
       Plasma - 39.8 ± 6.1 ml./Kg.
  Sp. gr.: Whole blood = 1.055 (1.045 to 1.065).
       Serum = 1.030   Red cells = 1.080
  Viscosity (relative to water): 3.5 to 4.5.
  pH: 7.35 to 7.45.
  Total solids in whole blood: 20 (19 to 23) Gm./100 ml.
    Of these: 90% = hemoglobin.
           7% = proteins (see pp. 205 and 216).
           3% = salts and lipids.
    Total solids in serum: 6.3-8.0 Gm./100 ml.

Average Hematocrit Cell Pack. (See p. 152.)
    Men: 40-54%
    Women: 37-47%

Hemoglobin in Gm./100 ml. (General average is 14.5 Gm.)
    Men: 14-18 Gm.
    Women: 12-16 Gm.

    Total Hgb. in body: 500 to 700 Gm.
    About 0.36% of Hgb. is iron.

Normal Cell Counts.
  Red blood cells, in million per cu. mm.: (See p. 145.)
    Men: Average, 4.6-6.2
    Women: Average, 4.2-5.4
    Reticulocytes: 0.5% to 2.7% (see p. 154).
  White blood cells: 4,500 to 11,000 per cu. mm. (see p. 155).
    Myelocytes   =   0%
    Juvenile neutrophils   =   0%
    Band neutrophils   =   0-5%
    Segmented neutrophils = 40-60%
    Lymphocytes   = 20-40%
    Eosinophils   =   1-3%
    Basophils   =   0-1%
    Monocytes   =   4-8%
  Platelets, per cu. mm.: 200,000 to 400,000 (see p. 159).

Cellular Elements. (Described quantitatively, see pp. 152-5.)
  Red corpuscles: Average diameter = 7.3 μ; range, 5.5 to 8.8 μ
    Mean corpuscular volume = 87 c.μ; range, 80 to 94 c.μ
    Mean corpuscular Hgb. = 30 micromicrograms ($\gamma\gamma$);
               Range = 28 to 32 $\gamma\gamma$ (see unit p. 153).
    Mean corpuscular Hgb. concentration = 35%; range, 33 to 38%
    Color, saturation and volume indices = 0.9 to 1.1 (pp. 152-5).
  White cells: Average diameter varies from 6 to 15 μ
  Platelets: Average diameter is 2 to 4 μ

needle and syringe should be washed in tap water immediately after using; never place blood-stained needles in alcohol, since denatured blood protein will adhere firmly to the needle.

In case of difficulty in entering the cubital veins in obese persons or in children, the application of hot towels to the whole arm and hand for 20 minutes will produce vasodilatation and better filling of the veins. If veins in the cubital fossa are not available, other possibilities are the veins of the forearm or the dorsum of the hand, the femoral vein (just medial to the pulsation of femoral artery), or the jugular veins.

Hemolysis can be minimized by using perfectly clean and dry apparatus. Treat the blood gently; do not expel it through a needle.

Drawing Venous or Arterial Blood With No Exposure to Air.

For special determinations of gas content and pH of blood, the specimen must be obtained without exposure to air. Where apparatus for these determinations is available, materials and instructions will be available also.

BLOOD ANTICOAGULANTS

General Anticoagulants.
A. Salts of Ethylenediamine Tetraacetic Acid (EDTA):
These salts remove calcium from blood by chelation and thus prevent coagulation. EDTA salts preserve cellular elements better than does oxalate. EDTA is not recommended as an anticoagulant for blood to be used in chemical procedures.

Of the salts of EDTA the dry dipotassium salt is preferred for preparation of blood for sedimentation rates and packed cell volume since it is more readily soluble in blood and does not alter erythrocyte volume. It should be used in a concentration of 1 mg./ml. of blood.

Prepare a 2.5% solution of dipotassium EDTA in water. For 5 ml. of blood, place 0.2 ml. in a tube and dry at room temperature or at low heat. Add blood and mix carefully.

B. Oxalate Tubes: (For blood chemistry and hematocrit.)
1. May use 2 to 3 mg. of potassium oxalate per ml. of blood. This may cause shrinkage of cells.
2. Double oxalate for sedimentation rate and hematocrit - Potassium oxalate, 2 Gm.; ammonium oxalate, 3 Gm., water to make 100 ml. 0.2 ml. of solution is sufficient to provide anticoagulant for 5 ml. of blood. Place required amount in test tube and evaporate to dryness at room temperature or at low heat so as not to destroy the anticoagulant. Blood is added to the anticoagulant

in the tube and mixed carefully to avoid foaming. Do not use ammonium oxalate for N.P.N. or urea determinations.

C. Heparin powder or heparin solution as required.

Variations in Blood Elements According to Age

Age	Hemoglobin (in Gm. %)		Red Counts (in millions)		WBC (1000's)	Diff. Count	
	Avg.	Range	Avg.	Range	Avg.	P.M.N. (in %)	Lymph. (in %)
1st day	21	15-26	5.9	4.1-7.5	20	57	20
2nd day	20	16-24	5.7	4.0-7.3	-	55	20
6th day	18.5	13-23	5.4	3.9-6.8	13.5	50	37
2 weeks	17.5	15-20	5	4.5-5.5	12	34	55
1 month	16	13-18	4.7	4.2-5.2	11.5	34	56
2 months	12	11-14	3.9	3.4-4.4	11	33	57
3 months	11.4	10-13	4	3.5-4.5	10.5	33	57
6 months	12	11-14.5	4.5	4-5	10.5	36	55
1 year	13	11.5-15	4.6	4.1-5.1	10	39	53
2 years	13	12-15	4.7	4.2-5.2	9.5	42	49
5 years	13.5	12.5-15	4.7	4.2-5.2	8	55	36
8-12 years	14	13-15.5	5	4.5-5.4	8	60	31
12-15 years	13.4	13-15.5	5	4.3-6	8	60	40
16-60 years	Males 15-16 Females 13-15		Males = 5 Females = 4.5		8	40-60	20-50
60-70 years Over 70 yrs.	Males = 14.8 Females = 14.2 Males = 14.2 Females = 13.9				8	40-60	20-50

1. At birth, 3% of red blood cells are reticulocytes. Newborn's cells are large: M.C.V. = 110 cu. μ and mean diameter = 8 μ; normal "adult" proportions are approached at two to three months of age.

2. Variation in hemoglobin and blood count of young infants is markedly greater than after the age of one year.

3. Platelet counts are the same in infants and adults (see p. 159).

Special Anticoagulants.

A. For Uric Acid Determination: (If not done on serum.) Use 1 mg. of lithium oxalate per ml. of blood.

B. Preservative and Anticoagulant Combined: Will preserve blood six days for N.P.N., glucose, and other determinations. Use mixture of 1 mg. thymol and 10 mg. sodium fluoride (free of ammonia) per ml. of blood.

METHODS OF BLOOD EXAMINATION

Medico-legal Proof of the Presence of Blood.

The guaiac and benzidine tests (see p. 120) are reliable only when negative; Teichmann's test (hemin crystals) is reliable only when positive. The precipitin test is the only consistently reliable means of differentiating human and

animal blood; it is complicated, and is not a test specifically
for blood alone, but for any proteins of the species involved.
(See standard texts for details of technic.)

Hemoglobin Determination.

Normal values are given on p. 145.
A. Photometer Methods:
1. Cyanmethemoglobin method - Prepare a solution containing:

Sodium bicarbonate	1
Potassium cyanide	0.05
Potassium ferricyanide	0.2
Distilled water	1000

   This solution should be made fresh once a month
   and stored in a brown bottle. Pipet carefully and take
   care not to discard cyanide solutions into sinks or re-
   ceptacles containing acid (to prevent formation of hydrocyanic acid).

   When blood is diluted 1:200 in this solution, the
   hemoglobin is converted into cyanmethemoglobin. To
   4 ml. of the diluent add 20 cu. mm. of blood. Mix
   well. Read in photometer at 540 mμ (green filter).

   For this procedure a certified standard hemoglobin
   solution may be obtained from reputable laboratory
   supply firms.
2. Sheard-Sanford oxyhemoglobin method - Mix 20 ml. of
   0.1% sodium carbonate and 0.1 ml. of blood or aliquots of these (e.g., 4 ml. diluent for 20 cu. mm.
   blood); read optical density in photometer at 540 mμ
   within 30 minutes. Photometer calibration should be
   based on blood iron determination or oxygen capacity
   determination.
3. Alternative oxyhemoglobin method - In place of the
   sodium carbonate solution use distilled water; mix
   with the desired quantity of blood and add a few drops
   of ammonia water before reading in photometer.
4. Alternative oxyhemoglobin method - Oxyhemoglobin is
   unstable in water containing copper in more than trace
   quantities. It is not necessary to use copper-free
   water if the alkaline diluent is replaced by tetrasodium
   ethylenediamine tetraacetate (EDTA), which chelates
   the copper. To 4 ml. of 0.3% (0.01-M) tetrasodium
   EDTA add 20 cu. mm. blood. Mix well. Read in
   photometer at 540 mμ. There is no fading for several
   hours.
B. Sahli Method: Based on conversion of hemoglobin to acid
   hematin, which has a brown color. Fill tube with N/10
   HCl to "10" mark. Draw blood to the "20 cu. mm."
   mark in Sahli pipet, wipe tip, and expel blood into the
   Sahli tube. Rinse pipet with acid mixture, taking care to
   leave no solution in or on pipet when it is removed.

Wait 5 to 45 minutes, put tube in colorimeter, and agitate mixture, adding distilled water till a "match" is obtained with the brown glass standard. Then read level of fluid in tube. The 100% standard varies according to the technic used; it is best, therefore, to report hemoglobin in Gm./100 ml. of blood.

Red Blood Cell Counts (RBC).

A. Automated Methods; Newer Instruments: Accurate counts are readily made with new electronic instruments, some of which include diluting apparatus and computer modules. These are suited for larger laboratories.

B. Hemacytometer Method:

1. Diluting fluids - Use freshly filtered Hayem's (see p. 624) or Gower's (see p. 624) diluting fluid. (In an emergency, saline solution may be used.) Gower's solution makes r.b.c. stand out more clearly and causes less agglutination, but it stains the pipet in time.

2. Preparations for counting - Draw blood to the "0.5" mark in the red-counting pipet. Wipe tip clean and draw diluting fluid to the "101" mark. Shake three minutes, but do not "centrifuge" cells into the ends of the pipet. Expel 5 to 8 drops. Fill counting chamber by a single smooth flow of fluid under the cover glass; if the moat fills, clean the hemacytometer, shake pipet for 3 minutes, and refill the counting chamber. Allow 2 to 3 minutes for cells to settle.

3. Counting r.b.c. - Count r.b.c. in 80 of the smallest squares, and multiply the total by 10,000 to get the red cell count per cu. mm. of blood. Count those cells which touch the upper and left borders of the "R" squares (see diagram below) but not those which touch the lower and right borders. Record counts for each of the five "R" squares counted; the difference between highest and lowest counts must not exceed 20. For greater accuracy, duplicate counts should be made, using a different pipet for each count.

4. Cleaning pipets - To clean pipets, put a four- or five-hole stopper in a thistle tube, connect to suction, place pipets in stopper, and draw fluids through them in this order: water, 95% alcohol, ether, and dry in air; or water, acetone, and dry in air.

Red Corpuscles in Blood Smears.

Thin, well-stained smears are necessary for satisfactory study of red corpuscles (see p. 156). Look for maturity, size, shape, coloring, markings, and intra- or extracellular parasites. Some abnormalities are shown in the diagrams on p. 149 and discussed in the following paragraphs.

Neubauer Hemacytometer Grating

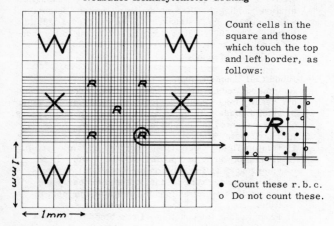

Count cells in the square and those which touch the top and left border, as follows:

● Count these r.b.c.
○ Do not count these.

The above grating consists of 9 sq. mm. and supplies a convenient scale on which to measure the size of small objects, such as parasite eggs. The chamber for blood counting is 0.1 mm. deep and is used as follows:

R = Five smaller squares, each containing 16 of the smallest squares, which measure 1/400 sq. mm. each. These 80 smallest squares are the only ones in which r.b.c. are counted, usually under high power.

W = 4 sq. mm. Count white cells here, under low power.

X = 4 sq. mm. which are used with other squares when spinal fluid cell count is made (see p. 259).

A. Anisocytosis: This is an abnormal variation in size of r.b.c. Average normal diameter is 7.3 μ, and the normal range is 5.5-8.8 μ. Microcytes are 6 μ or less in diameter, macrocytes are 9-12 μ, and megalocytes are 12-25 μ in diameter. Macrocytosis is suggestive of pernicious anemia; microcytosis is seen in iron deficiency anemia. Anisocytosis in general is seen in those anemias which are not of the aplastic type.

B. Poikilocytosis: This is unusual variation in shape of r.b.c., with many oval, club-shaped, caudate, and other non-discoid forms present. This is common in pernicious anemia and in most anemias not of the aplastic type. Judge shape only in those r.b.c. which do not touch their neighbors.

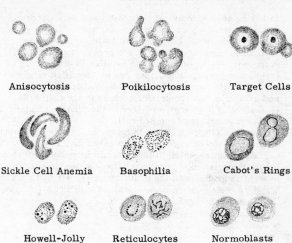

| Anisocytosis | Poikilocytosis | Target Cells |

| Sickle Cell Anemia | Basophilia | Cabot's Rings |

| Howell-Jolly Bodies | Reticulocytes (Large, basophilic) | Normoblasts |

C. Polychromatophilia: This is a bluish tinge in r.b.c. stained with Wright's stain. It is caused by an unusual affinity for basic stain which may affect only parts of corpuscles and only a few corpuscles in a smear. Normal r.b.c. are acidophilic. The blue staining is due to the youth of the cells, and is seen in many blood dyscrasias. Polychromatophilia, basophilic stippling, and increase in reticulocytes all indicate an increased number of young r.b.c. in the blood.

D. Basophilic Stippling: This is the presence in Wright-stained smears of blue granules of various sizes scattered over the pink background of the corpuscle. It occurs especially in lead poisoning, but may be found whenever polychromatophilia or an increased reticulocyte count is present. A smear may show both stippling and polychromatophilia. Stippling may occur in any severe anemia. Other names for stippling are punctate basophilia, basic degeneration, granular degeneration, and Grawitz degeneration.

E. Howell-Jolly Bodies and Cabot's Rings: These are remnants of nuclei in r.b.c. They are seen in anemias associated with splenic disease and especially after splenectomy.

F. Heinz Bodies: These consist of precipitated, denatured hemoglobin produced by the action of oxidant drugs. Heinz bodies usually occur in association with some variety of hemolytic anemia and are especially apparent following splenectomy. The bodies have been observed in thalassemia major. They are not visible in Wright's stain preparations, but, if stained with crystal violet, brilliant cresyl blue, or brilliant green, they appear as stained irregular bodies 2μ or smaller in diameter. In fresh, wet preparations, they can be identified as globular refractile bodies. They may be multiple or single and as a rule lie eccentrically, close to the cell walls. Occasionally they are found free in the plasma or may lie in evaginations of the red cell.

G. Siderocytes (Pappenheimer Bodies): In some unusual types of anemia, and often following splenectomy, erythrocytes contain granules which in turn contain iron demonstrable by the Prussian blue reaction. These granules appear as basophilic granules in the ordinary smear stained with Wright's stain. When counterstained with Prussian blue, they appear blue-green or bright blue. They range up to 2μ in diameter, and up to ten or 12 may be present in a cell.

H. Other Inclusion Bodies: Associated with the abnormal hemoglobins H and Zurich, denatured hemoglobin appears as granules when stained with brilliant cresyl blue. Hgb. H granules appear as multiple small irregular dots. The Hgb. Zurich inclusions are produced when sulfonamides induce hemolysis. The inclusions are large; they occur singly in a red cell and lie close to the cell membrane. When stained with brilliant cresyl blue the bodies appear blue; when Wright's stain is used they are polychromatophilic.

I. Spherocytosis: Spherocytes occur in some hemolytic anemias. The r.b.c. become more spherical in shape. They appear more dense, smaller in diameter, and do not form rouleaux.

J. Sickle Cells and Target Cells: Sickle cells and, in many instances, target cells are products of abnormal hemoglobin structure. Normally in the infant a typical variety of hemoglobin exists (hemoglobin F). As new erythrocytes and hemoglobin are formed, the hemoglobin structure changes to that typical of the adult (hemoglobin A, A_2). Hemoglobins may be differentiated by electrophoresis and solubility in alkali. Variants of hemoglobin have been further differentiated by identification of polypeptide chains (α, β, γ, δ) and of amino acid sequences within the polypeptide chain. When in the reduced state, one type of hemoglobin assumes a physical configuration which distorts the cell into the sickle shape; this has been labeled hemoglobin S. A large number of variants of hemoglobin have been identified, each with an abnormality of a polypeptide chain usually due to substitution of a specific amino acid. The traits producing these variants are transmitted genetically, and heterozygous and homozygous states have been demonstrated, the latter often being associated with hemolytic anemia of varying intensity. (It is interesting that Mediterranean anemia per se is characterized by target cells, but so far no abnormal hemoglobin has been found in pure thalassemia although the rate of formation of one of the polypeptide chains is impaired. The commonest variety of thalassemia major is homozygous high A_2 beta, in which the A_2/A ratio is increased and hemoglobin F is increased. In most cases of thalassemia minor, the hemoglobin is heterozygous high A_2 beta.

1. Sickle cells are abnormal forms resulting from the presence of an abnormal hemoglobin. Sickling occurs in 10% of Negroes, but only a few of these have the anemia. Methods for detection of sickling trait:

    a. Moist cover slip preparations. Cover a small drop of fresh blood on a slide with a cover-slip, seal with petrolatum or paraffin, keep at warm room temperature, and examine for sickling every 12 hours up to 72 hours. To derive percentage of circulating sickling forms, draw 4 ml. blood into a syringe containing 1 ml. of 10% formalin; examine wet preparation. Do not confuse sickling with familial ovalocytosis.

    b. Daland and Da Silva method - Acceleration of removal of oxygen from hemoglobin by use of reducing substances.

        (1) Reagents - Sodium bisulfite or ascorbic acid, 2 Gm., in 100 ml. water. (Make up fresh.)

        (2) Method - Use capillary blood, oxalated or defibrinated. Mix 2 drops of either reagent with 1 drop of blood on a glass slide. Cover, and seal cover slip with petrolatum or oil. If no sickling appears in four hours, the test is negative. Positive test: 10% or more r.b.c. show sickled form.

2. Target cells are seen in sickle cell disease, "Mediterranean" anemia, some hypochromic anemias, and liver disease. A central dot or mass of stained material in the red cell gives it the appearance of a target. "C" and "H" configurations of hemoglobin occur also. Target cells are thin cells (leptocytes) and are more resistant (less fragile) to hemolysis in hypotonic solutions. (See Fragility of Red Corpuscles, p. 155.)

K. Other Abnormal Forms: Helmet-shaped r.b.c., burr cells, and microspherocytes occur in microangiopathic hemolytic states and in the hemolytic anemias seen following insertion of heart valve prostheses. Hereditary burr cell (acanthocyte) anemia has been described.

Packed Cell Volume (P. C. V.) or Hematocrit (Hct.) Determination.

A. Technic:
1. Centrifuge whole blood (see anticoagulants, p. 144) in a hematocrit tube for 15 minutes at 3500 r. p. m. (or longer at lower speeds) until packing is complete. After centrifuging, the blood is separated into three layers: a tall bottom layer of packed r. b. c. , a narrow middle layer of w. b. c. and platelets, and a top layer of liquid plasma. The percentage of the height of the column of blood occupied by packed red cells constitutes the hematocrit. For example, if a third of the column is r. b. c. , the hematocrit is 33%.
2. Microhematocrit methods are in common use in clinical laboratories. Capillary tubes coated with anticoagulant can be filled with blood obtained by finger puncture or from a vein. One end is sealed with clay and the tube centrifuged for three minutes in a special high-speed centrifuge. By reading the packed cell height and the total height of the entire specimen, the hematocrit can be determined. Special reading devices are available.

B. Average Values: If the red cells are of normal size, RBC = 5 million and hematocrit is about 45%.
1. Men - 47% red corpuscles (range is 40 to 54%).
2. Women - 42% red corpuscles (range is 37 to 47%).

Red Blood Cell Indices.

The three traditional blood indices (volume, color, and saturation) are relative measures of the size and hemoglobin content of red cells. Corresponding absolute measures now in use are given below with hypothetical examples. Note that "Hgb." means hemoglobin. "Volume of packed r. b. c." or P. C. V. means the hematocrit. See Price-Jones curve, p. 154.

A. Mean Corpuscular Volume and Volume Index:
1. Mean Corpuscular Volume (M. C. V.) - Avg. is 87 cu. μ ; range is 80 to 94 cu. μ

Example: P. C. V. = 45%   RBC = 5, 340, 000/cu. mm.

P. C. V. in % $\times$ 10 or

$$\frac{\text{Vol. packed r. b. c. in ml./liter of blood}}{\text{Millions r. b. c./cu. mm. of blood}} = \frac{450}{5.34} = 84.2 \text{ cu. } \mu$$

2. Volume Index (V. I.) - Normal is 0. 9 to 1. 1
Example: P. C. V. = 36%   RBC = 4, 280, 000/cu. mm.

$$\begin{array}{l} \text{Observed r.b.c.} \\ \text{vol. in \% of normal} \\ \overline{\text{Observed r.b.c. in}} \\ \text{\% of normal} \end{array} = \begin{array}{l} \text{Vol. r.b.c.} \\ \text{(P.C.V.) Found} \\ \overline{\text{Normal Volume}} \\ \text{(P.C.V.)} \\ \overline{\text{RBC Found}} \\ \text{Normal RBC} \end{array} = \dfrac{\dfrac{36}{45}}{\dfrac{4.28}{5}} = 0.93$$

In determining the "index" one must assume a "normal" hematocrit and r.b.c. value. For men, the average hematocrit has been determined as about 45%; for women, it is about 40%. The average RBC for men is 5,000,000; for women, 4,500,000. The red cell volume usually varies with Hgb. content. V.I. is merely another expression of M.C.V. in terms of per cent of normal.

B. Mean Corpuscular Hemoglobin and Color Index:
1. Mean Corpuscular Hemoglobin (M.C.H.) - This is given in micromicrograms ($\gamma\gamma$) (10^{-12} Gm. or picogram). Average is 30$\gamma\gamma$; range is 28 to 32$\gamma\gamma$. Children's range is about 20 to 27$\gamma\gamma$. M.C.H. indicates the actual amount of Hgb. per red blood cell in absolute units.
Example: Hgb. = 15.6 Gm./100 ml.
RBC = 5,340,000/cu. mm.

$$\frac{\text{Gm. Hgb./liter of blood}}{\text{Millions r.b.c./cu. mm. blood}} = \frac{156}{5.34} = 29.2\gamma\gamma$$

2. Color Index (C.I.) - Normal is 0.9 to 1.1
Example: Hgb. = 9.4 Gm./100 ml.
RBC = 2,670,000/cu. mm.

$$\begin{array}{l} \text{Hgb. in \%} \\ \text{of normal} \\ \overline{\text{RBC in \%}} \\ \text{of normal} \end{array} = \begin{array}{l} \text{Gm. Hgb. found} \\ \overline{\text{Normal Hgb.}} \\ \text{RBC found} \\ \overline{\text{Normal RBC}} \end{array} = \dfrac{\dfrac{9.4}{15.6}}{\dfrac{2.67}{5}} = 1.12$$

The M.C.H. and C.I. above both serve to indicate the average amount of hemoglobin per red corpuscle. Both are higher than normal in most macrocytic anemias such as pernicious anemia, sprue, and cirrhosis of the liver; and less than normal in most secondary anemias. (See pp. 143 and 145 for normal r.b.c. values.)

C. Mean Corpuscular Hemoglobin Concentration and Saturation Index:
1. Mean Corpuscular Hemoglobin Concentration (M.C.H.C.) - This is the amount of hemoglobin in terms of per cent of the volume of a corpuscle. Average = 35%: range = 33 to 38%. Example: Hgb. 15.6 Gm./100 ml.; P.C.V. 45%.

Characteristic Red Cell Values in Three
Types of Anemia

Type of Anemia	M.C.V. (cu. μ)	M.C.H. ($\gamma\gamma$) (10^{-12} Gm.)	M.C.H.C. (Concen. %)	Cell Diameter
Normal Blood*	80-94	28-32	33-38	6.7-8.0
Macrocytic	95-160	30-52	31-38	7.5-9.6
Microcytic	72-79	22-26	31-38	6.5-8.5
Hypochromic	50-71	14-21	21-29	5.8-7.5

*Or normocytic anemia.

$$\frac{\text{Gm. Hb. /100 ml. Blood}}{\text{P.C.V.}} \times 100 = \frac{15.6}{45} \times 100 = 34.7\%$$

2. Saturation Index (S.I.) - Normal is 0.9 to 1.1.

$$\frac{\text{Color Index}}{\text{Volume Index}} = \frac{1.2}{1} = 1.2$$

Price-Jones Curve.

The Price-Jones curve shows the distribution of the sizes of red corpuscles.

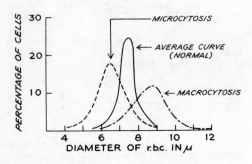

Reticulocyte Counts.

A. Regular Smear:

1. Stains - Either of the following two stains may be employed:

   a. New methylene blue N
   (Color Index No. 52030)   0.5
   Potassium oxalate   1.6
   Distilled water, q.s. ad   100

   b. Brilliant cresyl blue   1
   Isotonic saline   100

2. Technic - On a clean slide, mix well 2 drops of stain

and 2 drops of blood. Let stand in a moist chamber
for 10 minutes. (An inverted Petri dish with a moist
filter paper in the top serves the purpose.) Prepare
several thin smears from the stain-blood mixture.
Alternatively, to 0.5 to 1 ml. of stain in a small test
tube add an equal amount of blood and mix gently for
10 minutes. (If brilliant cresyl blue, 1% in saline is
used, the blood must be oxalated.) Make several thin
smears. Counterstain 2 minutes with Wright's stain,
but leave buffer on for only 1 minute. Air-dry and
count 1000 r.b.c. Reticulocytes contain a reticulum
which stains only supravitally and shows up as basophilic skeins, dots, or filaments. With a normal rate
of red cell production, 0.5 to 2.7% of circulating r.b.c.
are reticulocytes.

If oxalated blood is used, mix 5 drops of blood with
5 drops of stain in small test tube, allow to stand for
10 minutes, and make smear as above.

B. Rapid Method: Cover slide with 1% cresyl blue (in alcohol) and let dry; rub off excess stain (rub hard) with
gauze. Put small drop of blood on cover slip; invert onto
stained slide. Count while wet. Each slide will accom-
modate two cover slip preparations.

Fragility of Red Corpuscles. (See p. 102 for screening test.)
A. Method: Set up 18 clean small test tubes, each containing
1 ml. of NaCl solution, varying from 0.6% NaCl by 0.02%
steps down to 0.26% NaCl. (Prepare by mixing aliquots
of 0.6% NaCl and distilled water.) Draw 5 ml. of venous
blood (see p. 144 for method), and eject one drop through
the syringe needle into each tube. Invert each tube once
with a dry finger over the open end, and place in refrigerator for 12 to 18 hours. Record concentration of saline
at which hemolysis begins and concentration at which it is
complete (as indicated by absence of any r.b.c. at bottom
of tube). Run in parallel a control with known normal
blood to correct for variation in saline concentrations.
B. Interpretation: Normal r.b.c. will hemolyze only in NaCl
solutions of 0.44% or less, hemolysis being complete in
solutions of 0.3% NaCl; no hemolysis will occur in solutions of 0.45% to 0.6% NaCl. In hemolytic jaundice there
may be increased fragility of r.b.c. in solutions up to
0.6% NaCl with increased hemolysis in all tubes. Greater
resistance to lysis occurs with target cells or leptocytes
(thin cells).

White Cell Counts (WBC).
A. Automated Methods; Newer Instruments: Accurate counts
are readily made with new electronic instruments, some
of which include diluting apparatus and computer modules.
These are suited for larger laboratories.

B. Hemacytometer Method: (See diagram on p. 148.) Fill
   white-counting pipet with blood to the "0.5" mark, wipe
   tip clear, and fill to the "11" mark with diluting fluid
   (3% acetic acid solution; see p. 600). Shake 3 minutes,
   expel 3 to 5 drops, and fill counting chamber.

   Under low power and reduced illumination count 4 or 5
   sq. mm. of leukocytes, find the average count per sq. mm.,
   and multiply by 200 to get the leukocyte count/cu. mm. of
   blood. The greatest variation between squares should not
   exceed 12 cells. Of cells which touch borders, count only
   those on the upper and left borders (as in diagram for
   r.b.c., p. 148).

Differential White Cell Counts, Blood Smears.

A. Slide Method for Making Smear: After skin puncture, remove and discard the first drop of blood, and touch one
   end of a slide to the small newly formed drop. Place the
   end of a second slide over the drop of blood, and smear
   across the first slide as follows:

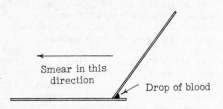

Smear in this direction

Drop of blood

1. Wash the slides thoroughly with soap and water. It is
   often necessary to clean the slides with acetone,
   detergents, etc.
2. Clean skin with 70% alcohol and dry.
3. Staining - Permit the smear to dry, and flood it with
   Wright's stain for 2 minutes. Then add 10 to 15 drops
   of distilled water or buffer of pH 6.4 and leave on for
   3 minutes while gently agitating the slide. (It may be
   necessary to alter the relative amounts of stain and
   buffer and the fixing and staining times to achieve a
   good differential stain.) Wash with water until the
   stain is removed; timing of stain varies with stain
   used. Blot dry. Examine the preparation directly
   under oil immersion, or cover first with balsam and
   cover-slip. Move the objective over the field as indicated in diagram below:

Do differential count by moving the slide
as shown at right in order to include central and peripheral areas of the smear.

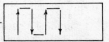

4. Restoring smears - If smears are overstained with Wright's stain, the red cells may be too red and white cells too pale and ghostlike, or stain may precipitate on smears (see also p. 628). Restore smears as follows:
   a. Flood entire slide with new Wright's stain.
   b. Allow to stand for 15 to 30 seconds.
   c. Rinse with distilled water or buffer.
   d. Allow to dry in air.

B. Coverglass Method of Making Blood Smears:
   1. Cleaning of coverslips - Immerse for two to four hours in concentrated nitric acid. Remove them to a large glass funnel set up in a sink so that tap water flows up through the funnel, agitating and rinsing coverslips for 30 minutes. Drain off water, immerse in clean 95% alcohol, and dry.
   2. Pick up a small drop of blood on the coverslip, drop another coverslip on it, and immediately separate the two slips by sliding them apart. Do not lift one coverslip from the other. Dry and stain both slips, and mount on slides with balsam or oil.

C. Examination of Blood for White Cells: (For r.b.c., see p. 147.) The term "differential count" refers to percentage distribution of types of white cells. Normal counts are given on pp. 143 and 145, and below. The usual procedure is to count 100 white cells, classifying them as polymorphonuclears (P.M.N.'s), large or small lymphocytes, mononuclears, eosinophils, basophils, and disintegrating cells. Any premature or young white cells should be noted very carefully. In case of high WBC, count 200 to 500 cells.

Schilling arranged the white cells according to age, including all leukocytes. A normal Schilling hemogram is shown below:

Total White Count	4500-11,000
Myeloblasts and promyelocytes	0%
Myelocytes	0%
Metamyelocytes	0%
Band cell neutrophils	0-5%
Neutrophils with lobulated nuclei	40-60%
Lymphocytes	20-40%
Mononuclears, eosinophils, basophils	5-10%

The neutrophils are arranged according to maturity, and a "shift to the left" means that an unusually large number of immature cells is present.

D. Peroxidase Stain for White Cells: Helps distinguish immature cells of myeloid and lymphoid series. Granules staining with peroxidase stain are found in myelocytes, metamyelocytes, neutrophils, eosinophils, and monocytes. Myeloblasts, lymphoblasts, lymphocytes, and plasma cells do not contain such granules. The granules are coarser and darker in mature neutrophils than in the more immature myeloid cells. In monocytes the granules are fine and less numerous than in the myeloid series. In infectious mononucleosis, the mononuclear cells are peroxidase-negative.

After staining by one of the methods below, count 200 leukocytes in each of the three fields, estimating the per cent of typical peroxidase-positive cells and peroxidase-negative cells. Compare with the usual differential count (see above).

1. Cover a dry blood smear with 10 drops of peroxidase stain, solution A; stain for 1.5 minutes. Add 5 drops of solution B; stain for 3 to 4 minutes. Wash well in water for 3 to 4 minutes. Counterstain with Wright's stain. (For solutions A and B, see p. 626.)
2. Goodpasture stain - See p. 624.

E. Alkaline Phosphatase Stain for White Cells: This test is useful in distinguishing chronic myelocytic leukemia from a benign myeloid reaction, particularly in the presence of leukocytosis of over 30,000. The only cells that are stained are neutrophils, both mature and metamyelocytic. Alkaline phosphatase positive granules stain brown or black. Cells are evaluated on a scale of 0 to 4+ and a score is calculated from the staining characteristics of 100 neutrophils. The method of staining and scoring and the interpretation can be obtained in Kaplow, Blood 10: 1023, 1955, and in Cartwright, Diagnostic Laboratory Hematology, 3rd Ed., Grune & Stratton, 1963, pp. 133-7.

F. Lupus Erythematosus (L. E.) Cells:

1. Draw 5 to 10 ml. of venous blood. Place in a 50 ml. flask containing 20 to 30 glass beads 3 to 5 mm. in diameter or clean metal paper clips. Swirl or shake gently for 10 to 15 minutes to defibrinate the blood.
2. Let stand 15 minutes.
3. Transfer blood and a few beads to a test tube or container and mix on a rotator or by inverting for 30 minutes.
4. Let stand at room temperature for 1 hour.
5. Centrifuge at 2000-3000 r.p.m. for 5 to 10 minutes.
6. Transfer the buffy coat to Wintrobe hematocrit tube and centrifuge again for 5 to 10 minutes.
7. Transfer the buffy coat and an equal amount of plasma to a small tube, mix well, and prepare smears. Dry rapidly and stain with Wright's stain.
8. Examine smears for clumps of platelets and neutrophilic leukocytes where the typical L. E. cell is most likely to be found (see p. 166).

BLEEDING AND BLOOD COAGULATION

Blood Platelet (Thrombocyte) Counts.
Platelets are oval or round elements, 2 to 4μ in diameter, seen in groups of two to 20 among red cells in a smear. The normal platelet count is 200,000 to 400,000 per cu. mm.

A. Rapid Method (Fonio): Puncture finger or ear lobe, wipe dry, and put drop of 14% magnesium sulfate solution over the puncture. Touch slide to finger, smear, dry, and stain with Wright's stain (see p. 628). Do r. b. c. determination simultaneously. Count platelets per 1000 r. b. c.; calculate platelet count from RBC.

B. Direct Method: Draw freshly filtered platelet solution (see p. 626) to the "0.5" mark in red cell pipet, wipe tip, then draw blood to the "0.5" mark (so that platelet solution reaches the "1.0" mark). Again wipe tip and fill pipet with platelet solution to the "101" mark. Mix and count in hemacytometer as for a red count.

C. Method of Wiener: Obtain 4 ml. of blood by venipuncture; mix well with 1 ml. of 3.8% trisodium citrate. Allow red cells to settle for 15-30 minutes but do not prolong standing lest platelets settle out. With a capillary pipet transfer some supernatant plasma containing platelets to a clean, dry tube. Mix 21 drops of clean saline with three drops of plasma, using the same capillary pipet to make sure all drops are of equal size. Shake the mixture gently and transfer to counting chamber. Allow platelets to settle and count 10 of the 4×4 (red cell counting) squares. Total counted $\times 250 \times 10 \times 10$ (or total $\times 25,000$) = platelets per cu. mm.

D. Method of Brecher and Cronkite: This technic requires phase contrast microscopy. For details see Brecher, G., and Cronkite, E. P.: J. Appl. Physiol. **3**:365, 1950; or G. E. Cartwright: Diagnostic Laboratory Hematology, 3rd Ed., pp. 80-87 (Grune and Stratton, 1963).

Bleeding Time. (Do not confuse with coagulation time.)
This test aids in diagnosis of certain bleeding diseases (see p. 160). The Ivy bleeding time is a measure of blood vessel retractability; it also varies directly with the blood prothrombin level, which in turn depends on vitamin K (see p. 422).

A. Ivy Bleeding Time: (Hemostasis bleeding time method.) Place blood pressure cuff on upper arm and inflate to 40 mm. Hg. With an alcohol sponge clean an area free of visible veins on the flexor surface of the forearm. With a sterile Bard-Parker No. 11 blade make a puncture wound 5 mm. deep and 2 mm. wide. Note time of puncture; touch wound gently with sterile filter paper to absorb blood every 30 seconds until bleeding stops. Normal is 1 to 7 minutes, but it may extend to 11 minutes in some normal subjects.

  B. Duke Bleeding Time: (Not a particularly reliable method.) Using the ear lobe, make a deep skin puncture as for a blood count. Gently remove drops of blood with filter paper. Normally the bleeding stops after 1 to 6 minutes.

Tourniquet Test. (Capillary fragility test of Hess, Rumpel-Leede sign.)

This test may demonstrate latent purpura (see p. 164). On the flexor surface of the forearm mark with ink any pink, purple, or yellow spots. Mark a circle on skin 2.5 cm. (1 inch) in diameter. Apply a blood pressure cuff and keep it inflated for 15 minutes midway between systolic and diastolic pressure. Appearance of more than ten new petechiae is a positive test which may occur with thrombopenia below approximately 70,000, nonthrombopenic purpura, and scurvy.

Coagulation Time.

Blood clotting is dependent on the interaction of several factors, as outlined on p. 162.

Blood Coagulation Tests. (See p. 164.)

Defects of the blood coagulation mechanism may be due to deficiency of essential factors or to antibodies against some component essential for coagulation.

  A. Lee and White Test Tube Method for Coagulation: Normal = 5 to 10 minutes. This method requires venous blood drawn by syringe. It is more reliable than skin puncture methods in which tissue fluids may contribute thromboplastin, which accelerates coagulation. This is the method of choice for heparinized patients.

  Technic: Place three clean, dry test tubes (13 × 100 mm. with internal diameter of 11 mm.) in a rack in a 37° C. water bath. With a clean, dry syringe and needle draw 6 ml. of venous blood, remove needle, and gently eject 2 ml. of blood into each test tube. Record time at which blood was drawn. After 5 minutes tilt the first tube to see if blood has clotted, and tilt at 1-minute intervals until the tube can be inverted without loss of blood. Agitation accelerates coagulation, so the end point is determined in tubes two and three. Now test second tube by tilting, and note the time after drawing of the blood when a firm clot is formed; check with third tube. This constitutes the clotting time. Normal values for clotting time are 9 to 15 minutes.

  B. Capillary Tube Method: Coagulation rates vary with this method, and the technic is therefore considered unreliable.

Clot Retraction Time. (Do not confuse with coagulation time.)

Normal = retraction of the clot from the walls of the tube beginning within 30 minutes, appreciable in one hour, and complete in four hours. Clot retraction is directly related to platelet count, hence is impaired in thrombocytopenia, normal in hemophilia (see p. 164).

Technic: Draw 5 ml. venous blood, transfer to test tube, and incubate at 37° C. in vertical position. Record degree of retraction after one, two, and four hours. It may be necessary to loosen the clot gently from the wall of the test tube if contraction is not apparent at the end of one hour. The degree and rate of retraction should be noted. Note also any digestion of clot or discoloration of serum.

Prothrombin Determination.

Prothrombin is an essential element in blood clotting (see p. 162) which is present in inadequate quantity in vitamin K deficiency or in various hepatic or biliary diseases. Hemorrhagic disease of newborn may be due to hypoprothrombinemia, which is prevented if expectant mothers take adequate doses of vitamin K.

Quick's Method is generally used (J. Biol. Chem. **109**:73, 1935).

A. Solutions needed for prothrombin time are as follows:
1. Sodium oxalate - Dissolve 1.34 Gm. of pure anhydrous sodium oxalate in 100 ml. of distilled water.
2. Calcium chloride - Dissolve 1.11 Gm. of pure anhydrous calcium chloride in 100 ml. distilled water.
3. Thromboplastin solution.

B. Technic:
1. Place 0.5 ml. of sodium oxalate solution in a centrifuge tube calibrated at 5 ml.
2. Draw 4.5 ml. of blood from a vein.
3. Remove needle from syringe and gently expel blood against the side of the centrifuge tube; mix and centrifuge 15 minutes at 3000 r.p.m.
4. Place plasma, thromboplastin solution, and calcium chloride solution in water bath at 98.6° F. (37° C.).
5. Add 0.1 ml. of plasma to 0.1 ml. of thromboplastin solution in a hemolysis tube. Then quickly add 0.1 ml. of calcium chloride solution and start stop-watch. (Thromboplastin and calcium chloride solutions may be mixed in equal parts and 0.2 ml. of the mixture added to the plasma in one step.)
6. Tilt tube to ascertain time of coagulation; as soon as plasma no longer flows, note time in seconds. May agitate with nichrome wire loop which will pull clot with it when it forms.

C. Interpretation: Bleeding tendency may be expected when the plasma concentration of prothrombin drops below 20%

BLOOD COAGULATION*
(Enzyme Cascade Scheme)

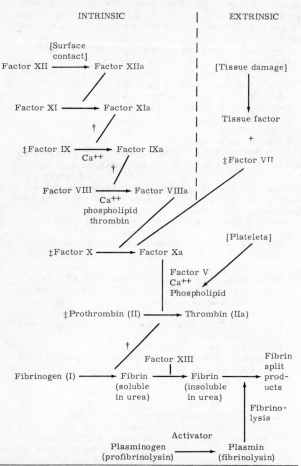

INTRINSIC   EXTRINSIC

Factor XII $\xrightarrow{\text{[Surface contact]}}$ Factor XIIa   [Tissue damage]

Factor XI $\longrightarrow$ Factor XIa   ↓

‡Factor IX $\xrightarrow{\text{Ca}^{++}}$ Factor IXa   Tissue factor

Factor VIII $\xrightarrow{\text{Ca}^{++} \text{ phospholipid thrombin}}$ Factor VIIIa   +

‡Factor VII

[Platelets]

‡Factor X $\longrightarrow$ Factor Xa

Factor V
Ca^{++}
Phospholipid

‡Prothrombin (II) $\longrightarrow$ Thrombin (IIa)

Factor XIII

Fibrinogen (I) $\longrightarrow$ Fibrin
(soluble in urea) $\longrightarrow$ Fibrin
(insoluble in urea) $\longrightarrow$ Fibrin split products

Fibrinolysis

Activator

Plasminogen (profibrinolysin) $\longrightarrow$ Plasmin (fibrinolysin)

*Nearly all the coagulation factors apparently exist as inactive
proenzymes (Roman numerals) that, when activated (Roman numerals plus **a**) serve to activate the next proenzyme in the sequence.
†Heparin acts to inhibit.
‡Plasma content decreased by coumarins.

of normal. (See also p. 164.) The curve below is an example of correlation of percentage of normal of plasma concentration and "prothrombin time." On this curve the accepted range for "successful" anticoagulant therapy with Dicumarol® or related drugs is 10 to 20% of normal. Such a standard curve must be determined for each new batch of thromboplastin.

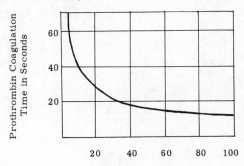

Plasma Concentration of
Prothrombin, in % of Normal

Activated Partial Thromboplastin Time.

A screening test for the integrity of thromboplastin formation employs a cephalin extract reagent (platelet factor reagent) and an activating factor (celite) to ensure a reproducible end-point. The test is sensitive to all factors except factor VII and platelets.

Normally, the clotting time of plasma using the activated platelet factor is 35 to 50 seconds. If the clotting time exceeds 50 seconds, specific tests for individual factors are indicated.

EXAMINATION OF BONE MARROW

Indications.

The aspiration and study of smears of bone marrow is often used as a diagnostic procedure in the investigation of blood dyscrasias. Although surgical removal of a biopsy specimen for section is no longer done in most cases, examination of a section of tissue may be helpful in many conditions and is necessary in the diagnosis of myelofibrosis with agnogenic myeloid metaplasia. In this condition, immature granulocytes, nucleated red cells, and giant platelets appear in the peripheral blood as a result of extramedullary hemo-

LABORATORY DIAGNOSIS OF THE MORE COMMON HEMORRHAGIC DISEASES

	Bleeding Time	Coagulation Time	Clot Retraction	Platelet Count	Prothrombin Time	Thromboplastin Generation	Capillary Fragility	Comment
Platelet Deficit								
Idiopathic thrombocytopenia (Werlhof)	↑	N	Slow, poor	↓	N		↑	Bone marrow often shows many megakaryocytes.
Secondary purpura	↑	N	Slow, poor	↓	N	Only platelets abnormal	↑	2° to marrow destruction, drug sensitivity, chronic liver disease, late renal disease, or thrombotic thrombocytopenia. Hereditary.
Coagulation Factor Deficit (Partial List)								
Hemophilia	N	↑	N	N	N	↑	N	AHF (VIII) or PTC (IX) deficiency.
Prothrombin complex deficiency	N	N or ↑	N	N	↑	N	N	Coumarin therapy; vitamin K lack; liver disease; congenital factor V, VII, X deficit.
Fibrinogen deficit	N	↑ No clot	Poor, no clot	N	N	N	N	Intravascular coagulation (consumption coagulopathy); congenital lack; severe liver disease.
Heparin therapy	N to ↑	↑	N	N	↑	↑	N	
Purpura of Sepsis or Allergy								
Septicemias; erythematous infections	N	N	N	N	N	N	N to ↑	Common in meningococcemia, subacute bacterial endocarditis, measles, etc.
Henoch-Schönlein purpura	N	N	N	N	N	N	N or ↑	Idiopathic. Drug sensitivity.
Increased Capillary Permeability; Vascular Disease								
Pseudohemophilia (Willebrand)	↑ or N	N	N	N	N or ↑	↑	N or ↑	Often hereditary; occurs in both sexes. Abnormal platelet morphology.
Thrombasthenia (Glanzmann)	N	N	Poor	N	N	N	N	
Hereditary hemorrhagic telangiectasia	N	N	N	N	N	N	N	Hereditary bleeding from trauma to telangiectases.
Senile purpura	N	N	N	N	N	N	↑ or N	Poor supporting tissue about capillaries, especially subcutaneously.
Scurvy	N	N	N	N	N	N	↑	Lack of vitamin C with decreased intercellular substance.

poietic activity. Because of myelofibrosis, failure to obtain a good specimen of marrow by aspiration is common, and biopsy is necessary for examination of the marrow.

A. Diagnostic Importance: Diseases in which diagnosis can be made with certainty only by aspiration of bone marrow:
   1. Multiple myeloma.
   2. Aleukemic leukemia.
   3. Aplastic anemia.
   4. Familial splenic anemia (Gaucher's disease).
B. Confirmatory: Diseases in which marrow studies are useful in confirmation of a diagnosis:
   1. Leukemia of all varieties.
   2. Hemolytic anemia.
   3. Pernicious anemia.
   4. "Idiopathic" thrombocytopenia and granulocytopenia.
   5. Leishmaniasis.
   6. Disseminated lupus erythematosus (L.E. cells) (see p. 166).

Procedure of Bone Marrow Aspiration.
   A. Equipment: An 18 gauge lumbar puncture or thoracentesis needle cut to one inch in length is adequate. Special needles with stylets may be purchased for bone marrow aspiration. Use dry 2 to 10 ml. syringe and dry needle.
   B. Technic of Aspiration:
      1. Sternal aspiration - Have patient supine with pillow under shoulders. Infiltrate skin with 3 ml. of 2% procaine. Enter skin at sternomanubrial junction, pointing dorsally and caudad at a 45° angle. Push and rotate needle until a slight "give" is felt and the needle is firmly held in the cancellous bone. Remove stylet, attach syringe, and aspirate 0.2 to 1 ml. If unsuccessful, replace stylet, insert needle to depth of 1.5 cm., and aspirate. "Suction pain" during strong aspiration is common. Withdraw needle and dress wound.
      2. Spinous process. Marrow may be aspirated from tip of lower thoracic or lumbar spinous process. Technic is same as for sternal aspiration.
      3. Iliac crest - This site is easily entered in children and provides the safest site for puncture because of the muscle tissue on the inner aspect. Anesthetize as above. The bone is entered 2 to 3 cm. below the crest in the midaxillary line. Less pressure is required, and there is little change in resistance as the marrow is entered. Twisting motion with gentle pressure is sufficient. It is well to begin attempts to aspirate as soon as the needle seems to be rigidly held in place, indicating that the tip is fixed in bone.

DEVELOPMENT OF LYMPHOCYTES

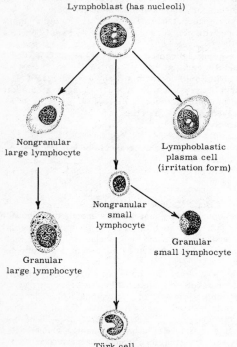

Lymphoblast (has nucleoli)

Nongranular large lymphocyte

Lymphoblastic plasma cell (irritation form)

Nongranular small lymphocyte

Granular large lymphocyte

Granular small lymphocyte

Türk cell (infections, anemia, leukemia)

"L. E." PHENOMENON
(After Berman, Axelrod, Goodman, and McClaughy.)

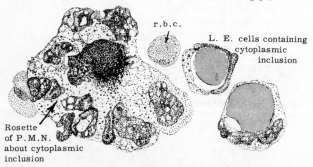

r.b.c.

L. E. cells containing cytoplasmic inclusion

Rosette of P.M.N. about cytoplasmic inclusion

DEVELOPMENT OF GRANULAR LEUKOCYTES

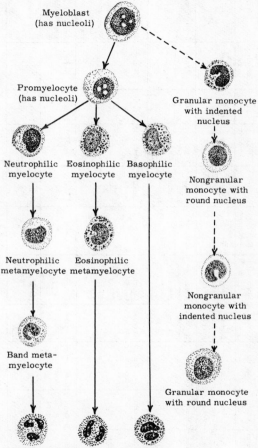

Myeloblast
(has nucleoli)

Granular monocyte
with indented
nucleus

Promyelocyte
(has nucleoli)

Neutrophilic
myelocyte

Eosinophilic
myelocyte

Basophilic
myelocyte

Nongranular
monocyte with
round nucleus

Neutrophilic
metamyelocyte

Eosinophilic
metamyelocyte

Nongranular
monocyte with
indented nucleus

Band meta-
myelocyte

Granular monocyte
with round nucleus

Neutrophilic   Eosinophilic   Basophilic
(polymorphonuclear leukocytes)

MORPHOLOGIC CHARACTERISTICS OF THE LEUKOCYTES IN BONE MARROW AND BLOOD
Modified from Wintrobe, Clinical Hematology
(Wright's Stain)

	Type of Cell	Diameter	NUCLEUS						CYTOPLASM			
			Position	Shape	Color	Chromatin	Nuclear Membrane	Nucleoli	Relative Amount	Color	Perinuclear clear zone	Granules
GRANULOCYTES	Myeloblast	10-18μ	Eccentric or central	Round or oval	Light reddish purple	Very fine mesh	Very fine	2 to 5	Scanty	Deep blue	None	None
	Progranulocyte or promyelocyte ("A" and "B")	12-18μ	Eccentric	Oval	Reddish purple	Fine, becoming gradually coarser.	Indistinct	Smaller, less distinct	Scanty to moderate	Bluish	None	5-20, coarse, blue-black.
	Myelocyte (myelocyte "C")	12-18μ	Eccentric	Oval or slightly indented	Reddish purple	Coarser but still fine compared to other cells	Indistinct	Smaller, fewer.	Moderate	Bluish to bluish-pink	None	Neutrophilic: Blue-black, fine or coarse. Eosinophilic: Red, large, coarse. Basophilic: Purplish-black, coarse, large.
	Metamyelocyte (juvenile)	10-18μ	Eccentric or central	Indented or horseshoe	Light purplish blue	Coarse	Present	Usually none	Plentiful	Pink	None	Neutrophilic, eosinophilic, basophilic.
	Polymorphonuclear neutrophil	10-15μ	Eccentric or central	2-5 or more lobules	Deep purplish blue	Rather coarse	Present	None	Plentiful	Pale pink	None	Fine pink or violet.

Group	Cell	Size	Nucleus position	Nucleus shape	Color	Chromatin	Parachromatin	Nucleoli	Cytoplasm amount	Cytoplasm color	Vacuoles	Granules
GRANULOCYTES (CONT'D.)	Polymorpho-nuclear eosinophil	10-15μ	Eccentric or central	2-3 lobes	Pale purplish blue	Coarse	Present	None	Plentiful	Bluish pink	None	Large, coarse, uniform in size, brick-red to crimson, numerous.
GRANULOCYTES (CONT'D.)	Polymorpho-nuclear basophil	10-15μ	Central	2-3 lobes	Pale purplish blue	Coarse, overlaid with granules	Present	None	Plentiful	Faint pink	None	Fewer, large, coarse, uniform, purplish-black.
LYMPHOCYTES	Lymphoblast	10-18μ	Eccentric or central	Round or oval	Light purplish red	Moderately coarse particles	Fairly dense	1-2	Scanty	Deep blue	Present	None
LYMPHOCYTES	Lymphocyte	7-18μ	Eccentric	Round or slightly indented	Deep purplish blue	Large clumps	Dense	None	Scanty or plentiful	Sky-blue, deeper blue, or pale pink	Present if cytoplasm dark	None to a few distinct, azurophilic specific granules.
MONOCYTES	Monoblast	14-18μ	Eccentric or central	Round or oval	Purplish red	Stringy, fine	Fine	1-2	Scanty to moderate	Deep blue to gray blue	None	None
MONOCYTES	Monocyte	12-20μ	Eccentric or central	Oval, round, notched, horseshoe	Pale purplish violet	Spongy	Distinct	None	Plentiful	Dirty grayish-blue	None	Numerous, fine azurophilic granules and vacuoles - like "red sand."

Cell Distribution in Bone Marrow and Peripheral Blood

Types of Cells	Marrow (%)		Peripheral Blood (%)	
	Average	Range	Average	Range
Myeloblasts	2.5	0.5-5	0	
Promyelocytes	6	1-8	0	
Neutrophil series:				
Myelocytes	15	8-20	0	
Juveniles	17.5	10-25	0	0
Bands	12.5	5-15	2	0-5
Segmented	27	15-35	50	40-60
Eosinophils	4	1-7	2	1-3
Basophils	1	0.5-1.5	0.5	0-1
Lymphocytes	13	5-20	30	20-40
Monocytes	1.5	0.5-4	5	4-8
Nucleated red cells /100 leukocytes:				
Megaloblasts	0.2	0-0.5	0	
Erythroblasts	2	0.5-4	0	
Pronormoblasts	4.5	1-8	0	
Normoblasts	15	10-20	0	

Red Blood Cells:
Morphologic Characteristics
of Normoblastic and Megaloblastic Series

Megaloblastic	Normoblastic

Promegaloblast, 19-27 μ
  Nuclei - Chromatin fine; delicate distribution; no clumping.
	Pronormoblast, 12-15 μ
	  Nucleus - Large thick strands of chromatin with clumps; nucleoli present.

Basophilic Megaloblast
  Nucleus - Fine chromatin.
	Basophilic Normoblast
	  Nucleus - Nucleoli absent; chromatin coarse.
	  Cytoplasm - Basophilic.

Polychromatic Megaloblast
  Nucleus - Chromatin still finely divided.
  Cytoplasm - Basophilic
	Polychromatic Normoblast
	  Nucleus - Smaller.
	  Cytoplasm - Pink spots or general hue.

Orthochromatic Megaloblast
  Nucleus - Chromatin has become clumped but not to extent of normal series.
	Orthochromatic Normoblast
	  Nucleus - Pyknotic
	  Cytoplasm - Acidophilic; no basophilia.
	  Diffuse Basophilia - ''Reticulocyte.''

Bone Marrow Smears.

A. Making Smears: Smears should be made immediately or after the addition of heparin, oxalate or the disodium or dipotassium salt of EDTA to the aspirated marrow. This is done as for blood (see p. 144).

B. Staining: If not stained immediately fix smear with a few drops of methyl alcohol. The dried film is placed on a level rack and covered with 8 to 10 drops of Wright's stain. After 1 minute, an equal number of drops of water of pH 7.3 to 7.5 is added, and the preparation is allowed to stand for 6 minutes. The stain is removed by gentle washing and the smear allowed to dry.

If counterstaining with Giemsa's stain is desired, pour off Wright's stain, add 20 drops of the diluted Giemsa's stain (prepared according to the directions on p. 624), and allow to stand for 15 minutes.

Bone marrow smears may be stained with Giemsa's stain for 5 to 15 minutes, according to the desires of the individual examining the smear.

Note: If the time intervals are observed and the stain has been properly filtered, precipitation of stain on the smear will not be a problem. If precipitation does occur, precipitated stain may be removed without decolorization by allowing several drops of undiluted Wright's stain to run over the surface of the smear during the washing process.

C. Counting Cells: Count 500 to 2000 leukocytes, plus the nucleated red cells seen while classifying leukocytes. Examination normally shows 10,000 to 50,000 nucleated cells per cu. mm. and a ratio of granulocytes to nucleated red cells of about 3.6:1. Note normal differential counts (see p. 170).

BLOOD TYPING
(See Transfusions, p. 431.)

International Landsteiner Types	Jansky Types	Moss Types	r.b.c. Agglutinogens	Serum Agglutinins	% of White* Americans
O	I	IV	O	ab	45
A	II	II	A	b	41
B	III	III	B	a	10
AB	IV	I	AB	o	4

*There are great racial differences in distribution.

In the table above, note that agglutinin against agglutinogen not present in the red cell is present in the plasma of each type.

Methods of Blood Typing.
The following may be used: (1) blood directly from puncture wound, (2) free r.b.c. resuspended in serum from about
a clot (about 10% r.b.c. in serum), or (3) r.b.c. suspended in
saline (about 10% r.b.c. in normal saline).
1. Mix 2 drops of r.b.c. suspension with 1 drop of potent
   typing serum as shown in diagram.

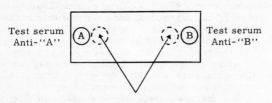

Test serum   Test serum
Anti-"A"   Anti-"B"

Patient's r.b.c. suspension

2. Rotate slide, tilt slide to mix the cells in the typing
   serum, and observe for agglutination, which should
   appear in 2 or 3 minutes if serum is potent.

In the following table, plus (+) signs indicate agglutination; minus (-) signs indicate no agglutination. It is obvious
that if a known type "A" or "B" is available, it is possible to
determine any unknown blood type. Always insist on potent
typing serum and follow manufacturer's directions. Label
tubes and slides carefully. Check every step twice. **Errors
may have fatal consequences.**

		Donor's Corpuscles Agglutinogen			
	Agglutinin	AB	A	B	O
Recipient's Serum	o	-	-	-	-
	b	+	-	+	-
	a	+	+	-	-
	ab	+	+	+	-

Transfusion reactions are usually due to destruction of
donor cells in the recipient plasma, but if a type O with high
agglutinin content in the plasma is used as a universal donor,
recipient red cells may be destroyed in type A, B, or AB
recipients.

Sub-types.

Because of the existence of sub-types, blood typing alone is not adequate to establish compatibility of two bloods. Two subgroups of A (A_1 and A_2) have been identified. Furthermore, an agglutinogen designated as H is present in almost all human erythrocytes. Anti-H sera react most strongly with group O cells and less so with A_2, A_2B, B, A_1, and A_1B, in that order. Anti-H occurs rarely in sera of A_1 and A_1B individuals.

Mixtures of known A_1, A_2, B, and O cells are available commercially. Serum can be tested against these cells to confirm the presence of specific agglutinins for more precise typing.

Direct Cross-matching.

This method eliminates most sub-type incompatibilities. To test for "warm agglutinins," do cross-matching at 98.6° F. (37° C.). Cross-matching must be done before every whole blood transfusion. As a check on selection of blood for transfusion, do typing first, then cross-match.

A. Identify and mark all containers, test tubes, and slides used. Double check each step of the procedure.

B. Preparing r. b. c. and Serum: Draw blood from recipient, allow to clot, and centrifuge. Draw off into a clean test tube the recipient's serum (RS), label the tube, and place it beside the tube containing the remaining serum and the recipient's cells (RC). Similarly obtain donor's serum (DS) and donor's cells (DC).

C. Blood from donor and recipient should be accurately typed for AB and Rh factors (see above).

D. Place four 10 × 75 mm. test tubes in a rack labeled I (RS-DC), II (DS-RC), III (RS-DC alb.) and IV (DS-RC alb.). Proceed according to the following plan:

E. Cross-Match Procedure:

1. Saline tube test (major side) (RS-DC) - Place 2 drops of the patient's serum in a test tube. Add 2 drops of 2% suspension donor cells in saline. Mix by shaking. Serofuge for 30 seconds (or centrifuge 1 to 2 minutes in bench-type centrifuge at 1000 r. p. m.). Gently resuspend cells, observing macroscopically for agglutination. Let stand at room temperature for 30 minutes. Serofuge for 30 seconds and read as before.

2. Saline tube test (minor side) (DS-RC) - Place 2 drops donor serum in a test tube. Add 2 drops of 2% suspension of patient's cells in saline. Mix by shaking. Serofuge for 30 seconds. Gently resuspend the cells, observing macroscopically for agglutination. Let stand at room temperature for 30 minutes. Serofuge for 30 seconds and read as before.

3. High protein tube converted to anti-globulin (major

side) (RS-DC alb.) - Place 2 drops of patient's serum
in a test tube. Add 1 drop of 2% suspension of donor
cells in saline. Add 3 drops of 30% bovine or human
albumin. Mix by shaking. Serofuge for 45 seconds.
Gently resuspend the cells, observing macroscopically
for agglutination. Incubate at 37° C. for 30 minutes.
Serofuge 45 seconds and read as before. Wash cells
3 times with saline, serofuging for 60 seconds (minimum) for each wash. Add 1 drop of anti-globulin
(Coombs) serum. Serofuge for 20 seconds and read
macroscopically for agglutination.

4. High protein tube converted to anti-globulin (minor
side) (DS-RC alb.) - Place 2 drops of the donor serum
in a test tube. Add 1 drop of 2% suspension of patient's
cells in saline. Add 3 drops of 30% bovine or human
albumin. Mix by shaking. Serofuge 45 seconds.
Gently resuspend the cells, observing macroscopically
for agglutination. Incubate at 37° C. for 30 minutes.
Serofuge 45 seconds and read as before. Wash cells
3 times with saline. Add 1 drop of anti-globulin serum
(Coombs). Serofuge 20 seconds and read as before.

Mixed Cell Suspensions.

Mixtures of red cells of group O containing C, D, E, c,
and e of the Rh antigens and those of the Lewis, Kidd, Duffy,
Kell, and other systems are now available commercially.
These are used according to the distributor's instructions to
detect antibodies in the recipient serum. The use of these
"check cells" is strongly recommended as part of the transfusion procedure.

Rh Factor, or Rh Agglutinogen.

Rh incompatibility was a common source of blood transfusion reactions until 1940, when the presence of the Rh agglutinogen and anti-Rh agglutinins was discovered.

Three (or four) genes, each commonly responsible for
two alternate forms and occasionally other alleles, determine
the Rh genotype. The commonly occurring factors (antigens)
have been designated as C, D, E (Fisher-Race system) or
equivalent Rh′, Rh°, Rh′′(Wiener system) and the respective
alternative forms c, d, e or hr′, hr°, hr′′. Three genes on
the determinant chromosome from each parent contribute to
the complete genotype, for example CDe/cde.

The most common antigen is D, followed by combinations
of CD and DE. The homozygous cde (Rh-negative) comprises
about 13% of the white race and is rare in Orientals and
American Indians.

An individual may produce antibody against any of the
antigenic factors not included in his genetic structure, but
such antibodies are found less frequently than anticipated,

and are not normally present. Agglutinins have been identified against Rh factors designated as D, D^U, C, c, E, e, and less common factors f, Ce, C^W, C^X, V, E^W, G, VS, C^G, and several others.

A. Formation of Anti-Rh Agglutinins:

1. In transfusions - If an Rh-negative person receives an injection of Rh-positive blood, he may produce anti-Rh agglutinins in solution in the plasma; if, within a few days or even years later, Rh-positive blood is given again, the Rh-positive erythrocytes will be agglutinated and hemolyzed, causing a transfusion reaction.

2. In pregnancy - An Rh-negative pregnant woman may be sensitized to Rh antigens by an Rh-positive fetus. If the father is Rh-positive, the fetus may be Rh-positive; if the mother happens to be Rh-negative, a few fetal Rh-positive cells may enter the maternal circulation and provoke the production of anti-Rh agglutinins (antibodies) in maternal plasma. This plasma slowly filters into the fetal circulation and destroys the Rh-positive red cells, causing erythroblastosis fetalis, with anemia and jaundice. If a pregnant or recently delivered Rh-negative woman (with anti-Rh agglutinins) is transfused with Rh-positive blood, she will have a severe transfusion reaction due to destruction of Rh-positive cells. If she is transfused with Rh-negative blood, no reaction will occur. The father's blood should not be used to transfuse either the baby or the mother.

B. Rh Typing: The technic varies with the source and characteristics of the anti-Rh serum used. Many sera are not effective if saline is used in the typing, but all human sera are suitable for typing if the cells to be typed are suspended in compatible serum. Typing should be performed for transfusion purposes by a technic such as that recorded above for typing and cross-matching. Follow instructions accompanying typing sera or consult more detailed texts for complete information.

Other Red Cell Agglutinins.

M, N, S, s, and U are closely related agglutinogens which rarely may produce isosensitization.

Certain familial agglutinogens have been discovered which will stimulate production of antibody in the recipient free of these antigens. Of these the Kell, Duffy, Lutheran, Lewis, and Kidd factors are clinically the most important. The indirect Coombs test may demonstrate the presence of antibodies to such factors in a recipient's serum. Specific antisera have been developed for identification of some of these agglutinogens in erythrocytes.

Coombs' Test (Antiglobulin Test).

When antibody to an antigen contained in an erythrocyte becomes attached to the cell, agglutination of erythrocytes may occur. Some antibodies may not produce agglutination even though the antibody globulin is attached to the erythrocytes. Certain types of antibodies, even in high concentration, may fix on blood cells and not cause agglutination in saline media; these are the blocking or incomplete antibodies.

Antibody to human globulin has been prepared in animals. When added to washed antibody-globulin—coated erythrocytes, the anti—human globulin serum will agglutinate the coated erythrocytes. In the absence of a coating of antibody globulin the erythrocytes will not be agglutinated by the anti—human globulin serum. Since the Coombs serum reacts with human globulin, it is imperative to remove all unattached plasma globulin by repeatedly washing the erythrocytes with saline.

A. Direct Antiglobulin Test: This test is carried out by mixing anti—human globulin serum with red blood cells washed in physiological saline. It is indicated for detection of antibody-coated erythrocytes in hemolytic anemia, anemia or jaundice of the newborn, and following hemolytic transfusion reactions.

  1. Procedure -

    a. Wash 0.5 ml. of blood to be tested in a 13 × 100 mm. test tube with four changes of isotonic saline.

    b. Make a 2% suspension in saline from the packed red cells.

    c. In a 10 × 75 mm. test tube place 2 drops of anti—human globulin serum. Add 1 drop of the 2% cell suspension.

    d. Incubate at 37° C. for 30 to 60 minutes.

    e. Shake tubes gently and observe for agglutination. Check with hand lens or with low-power objective of microscope.

    f. If negative, centrifuge at 1000 r.p.m. for one minute. Check for agglutination as above.

    g. Positive and negative controls should be run, using known normal cells and sensitized cells as described in the indirect test below.

  2. Interpretation - Agglutination confirms the presence of antibody on the erythrocytes.

B. Indirect Antiglobulin Test: This test is carried out by sensitizing or coating normal Group O erythrocytes or compatible erythrocytes with serum known or thought to contain blocking antibodies, and then indicating their presence with the antiglobulin serum. It is possible to demonstrate antibodies in serum using erythrocytes of known antigenic structure or to demonstrate antigenic structure of erythrocytes using antisera of known antibody content.

1. Procedure -
   a. Erythrocytes used may be -
      (1) Of known antigenic structure. (See Mixed Cell Suspensions, p. 174.)
      (2) Normal donor's cells for transfusion.
      These are prepared in a 2% suspension in saline.
   b. Incubate at 37° C. for 60 minutes equal quantities of the cell suspension and the serum to be tested (i.e., unknown serum or recipient's serum, respectively). For controls in the direct test, Rh-negative (cde) and Rh-positive (-D-) cells may be incubated with anti-D serum containing blocking antibodies. Antibody will be adsorbed onto D containing cells, but not onto Rh-negative cells.
   c. Proceed as for direct antiglobulin test, steps a through g.
2. Interpretation - Agglutination confirms the presence in the serum tested of antibody which has been absorbed onto the erythrocytes.

Medico-legal Use of Blood Groups.

A. Four Major Blood Types: These are inherited as Mendelian characteristics. Types A and B are dominant over O. All possible types of children from known parents are listed:

Parents	Children
O + O	O
O + A	O, A
O + B	O, B
A + A	O, A
A + B	O, A, B, AB

Parents	Children
B + B	O, B
O + AB	A, B
A + AB	A, B, AB
B + AB	A, B, AB
AB + AB	A, B, AB

B. M and N Agglutinogens: This sub-group of red cell agglutinogens never causes agglutinins to form in man, hence has no significance for transfusions. To get anti-M or anti-N serum, it is necessary to inject appropriate animals with human red cells of Landsteiner "O" and also of known M and N groups. It is difficult to get good anti-serum. All possible types of children from known parents are listed:

Parents	Children
M + M	M
M + N	MN
M + MN	M, MN

Parents	Children
N + N	N
N + MN	N, MN
MN + MN	M, N, MN

C. Rh Factor: See p. 174. The blood type indicates presence of genetically determined agglutinogens. Extensive tables of incidence and inheritance of the Rh factors are available.

D. Summary of Medico-legal Use: It is possible to disprove parentage by use of above three sets of blood characteristics. However, it is impossible to prove parenthood. Agglutinogens of Rh, M, N, A, or B cannot appear in blood of child unless present in one of the parents.

A parent of group M cannot have child of group N.
A parent of group N cannot have child of group M.
A parent of group O cannot have child of group AB.
A parent of group AB cannot have child of group O.

SEDIMENTATION RATE

Principle.

If blood which contains anticoagulant is permitted to stand in an upright tube, the red cells will gradually settle to the bottom. The rate at which this settling takes place is as sensitive an index of bodily reaction to injury or disease as is leukocytosis and fever. The mechanism of increased sedimentation is first a clumping of cells, after which the larger aggregates settle rapidly; such clumping is correlated with increased blood globulin and fibrinogen or a decreased blood albumin level. A normal sedimentation rate does not exclude the possibility of disease, but an increased rate is indication for further study.

Precautions Which Apply to Handling Blood by Any Method.

A. Proper anticoagulant for 5 ml. blood is 2 mg. heparin, a mixture of 4 mg. potassium oxalate and 6 mg. ammonium oxalate, or 5 mg. dipotassium EDTA (see p. 144). These do not change cell size or hematocrit.

B. Perform test within three hours after blood is drawn.

C. Maintain room temperature at 70 to 79° F. or 22 to 27° C.

Methods.

Significance of results is the same with all methods, although "normals" vary slightly with length of tube used. The rate is relatively unaffected by ordinary room temperature, bore of tube (if not less than 2 mm. in diameter), food ingestion, exercise, and patient's temperature.

The sedimentation rate is markedly increased by inclination of the tube from the vertical and also by a low hematocrit. High rates in anemia, e. g., RBC below 3.5 million, require cautious interpretation. Polycythemia decreases the sedimentation rate. Rates are the same in children and adults.

A. Wintrobe and Landsberg: Blood column is 100 mm. high. The advantage of this method is that it employs the same

tube for hematocrit and sedimentation rate. Draw 5 ml.
of blood, put in tube containing appropriate amount of
double oxalate, mix carefully (do not shake), and fill
Wintrobe tube to 10 cm. mark with a capillary pipet.
Set up vertically, and read sedimentation rate in exactly
1 hour.

B. Westergren: 1 ml. blood rises to 200 mm. To exactly
0.5 ml. of a 3.8% sodium citrate solution, add 4.5 ml.
venous blood. Invert a few times to mix. Fill a Westergren pipet exactly to the 0 mark and place vertically in a
Westergren rack. Read the upper level of red cells in
approximately 1 hour.

A modified method permits use of blood drawn into
EDTA anticoagulant (see p. 144). Dilute 2 ml. of EDTA
treated blood with either 0.2 ml. saline or 0.2 ml. 3.8%
sodium titrate. Mix well. Fill Westergren tube as above.
Normals: Under age 50 - Males, 15 mm./hour;
females, 20 mm./hour.
Over age 50 - Males, 20 mm./hour;
females, 30 mm./hour.

C. Sources of Error: Improper anticoagulant; tube not vertical; dirty tube; bubbles caused by too vigorous mixing.

Interpretation of Sedimentation Rates.

The value of sedimentation rates is that they indicate possible presence of organic disease, as in persons suspected of
having only psychogenic disease, or to follow the course of
disease.

A. Rapid: Usually found in - (1) Any extensive inflammation,
cell destruction, or toxemia. In acute infections, increased rate may lag behind rise in fever and leukocytosis; in recovery, sedimentation rate may return to normal rapidly. (2) Pregnancy, after the second month.
(3) Puerperium, 40 to 120 mm./45 minutes (Westergren)
for five to eight days; back to normal after two months.
(4) In tuberculosis (especially miliary) and (5) active rheumatic fever, sedimentation rate is used to follow the
course of the disease. (6) Acute myocardial infarction
(rapid increase). (7) Active rheumatoid arthritis (not
much elevated in osteoarthritis). (8) Nephrosis (low
blood albumin, anemia). (9) All types of shock. (10) Active syphilis (moderate acceleration). (11) Postoperative
states (variable periods). (12) Any active infectious disease, acute or chronic. (13) Salpingitis, appendicitis
(often normal), due to absorption of purulent or necrotic
material. (14) Infected, necrotic, or malignant tumors.
(15) Liver disease (depends on blood proteins; see above).
(16) Menstruation (slight acceleration).

B. Slow: Usually found in - (1) Newborn infant. (2) Polycythemia. (3) Congestive heart failure. (4) Allergic conditions. (5) Sickle cell anemia.

10...

Chemical Analysis of Blood and Urine

CHEMICAL CONSTITUENTS
OF BLOOD AND BODY FLUIDS

Interpretation of Laboratory Tests.

Normal values are those that fall within two standard deviations from the mean of the population. This normal range encompasses 95% of the population. Many factors may affect values and influence the normal range; by the same token, various factors may produce values that are normal under the prevailing conditions but outside the 95% limits determined under other circumstances. These factors include age, race, sex, environment, and diurnal and other cyclic variations.

Normal values vary with the method employed, the laboratory, and conditions of collection and preservation of specimens. With increasing awareness of the proper application of laboratory control of performance and of method, variations in normal values occur less frequently. The normal values established by individual laboratories should be clearly expressed to ensure proper interpretation by the physician.

Interpretation of laboratory results must always be related to the condition of the patient. A low value may be the result of deficit or of dilution of the substance measured, e. g., low serum sodium. Deviation from normal may be associated with a specific disease or with some drug consumed by the subject - e. g., gout and treatment with chlorothiazides or with antineoplastic agents are associated with elevated serum uric acid concentrations. (See accompanying tables.)

Values may be influenced by the method of collection of the specimen. Inaccurate collection of a 24-hour urine specimen, variations in concentration of the randomly collected urine specimen, hemolysis in a blood sample, addition of an inappropriate anticoagulant to a blood sample, and contaminated glassware or other apparatus are examples of causes of erroneous results.

Note: Whenever an unusual or abnormal result is obtained, all possible sources of error must be considered before responding with therapy based on the laboratory report. Laboratory medicine is a specialty, and experts in the field should be consulted whenever results are unusual or in doubt.

180

Albumin, Serum. See Protein, serum.

Aldolase, Serum. Normal (Bruns): 3-8 units/ml. Males, < 33 units; females, < 19 units (Warburg and Christian).

A. Precautions: Serum should be separated promptly. If there is to be any delay in the determination, the serum should be frozen.

B. Physiologic Basis: Aldolase, also known as zymohexase, splits fructose-1,6-diphosphate to yield dihydroxyacetone phosphate and glyceraldehyde-3-phosphate. Because it is present in higher concentration in tissue cells than in serum, destruction of tissue results in elevation of serum concentration.

C. Interpretation: Elevated levels in serum occur in myocardial infarction, muscular dystrophies, hemolytic anemia, metastatic prostatic carcinoma, leukemia, acute pancreatitis, and acute hepatitis. In obstructive jaundice or cirrhosis of the liver, serum aldolase is normal or only slightly elevated.

Ammonia, Blood. Normal (Conway): 40-70 μg./100 ml. whole blood.

A. Precautions: Do not use anticoagulants containing ammonia. Suitable anticoagulants include potassium oxalate, EDTA, and heparin that is ammonia-free. The determination should be done immediately after drawing blood. If the blood is kept in an ice-water bath it may be held for up to 1 hour.

B. Physiologic Basis: Ammonia present in the blood is derived from two principal sources: (1) In the large intestine, putrefactive action of bacteria on nitrogenous materials releases significant quantities of ammonia. (2) In the process of protein metabolism, ammonia is liberated. Ammonia entering the portal vein or the systemic circulation is rapidly converted to urea in the liver. Liver insufficiency may result in an increase in blood ammonia concentration, especially if protein consumption is high or if there is bleeding into the bowel.

C. Interpretation: Blood ammonia is elevated in hepatic insufficiency or with liver by-pass in the form of a portacaval shunt, particularly if protein intake is high or if there is bleeding into the bowel.

D. Drug Effects on Laboratory Results: Elevated by methicillin, ammonia cycle resins, chlorthalidone, spironolactone. Decreased by monoamine oxidase inhibitors, oral antimicrobial agents.

Amylase, Serum. Normal: 80-180 Somogyi units/100 ml. serum. (One unit equals amount of enzyme which will produce 1 mg. of reducing sugar from starch at pH 7.2.)

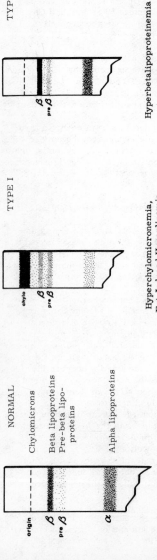

NORMAL

Chylomicrons

Beta lipoproteins

Pre-beta lipo-
proteins

Alpha lipoproteins

**Lipoprotein Groups (Paper Electrophor-
esis).** (Slightly modified and reproduced, with permission, from Diagnosis News 2 (5), May 1969. Based on
material from Levy, R.I., and
Frederickson, D.S.: Diagnosis and
management of hyperlipoproteinemia.
Am J Cardiol 22:576-83, 1968.)

TYPE I

**Hyperchylomicronemia,
Fat-Induced Hyperlipemia**

Triglycerides much higher than choles-
terol.
Plasma creamy.
Usually familial and manifest in child-
hood.
Lipemia retinalis, eruptive xanthomas,
hepatosplenomegaly, abdominal pain.
Fat tolerance markedly abnormal
(chylomicrons on any fat intake).
Postheparin lipolytic activity low.
Glucose tolerance normal.

TYPE II

Hyperbetalipoproteinemia

Cholesterol higher than triglycerides.
Plasma clear.
If familial, manifest in childhood.
Xanthomatosis: tendon, tuberous, xan-
thelasma, arcus.
Accelerated atheromatosis.
Glucose tolerance usually normal.
Carbohydrate inducibility normal.
Postheparin lipolytic activity normal.
Fat tolerance normal.

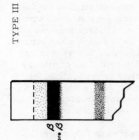

TYPE III	TYPE IV	TYPE V

"Broad Beta Disease"

Cholesterol and triglycerides equally elevated.

Plasma clear, cloudy, or milky.

Usually familial and manifest in adulthood.

Xanthomatosis: planar, "tubero-eruptive," tendon, arcus.

Accelerated atheromatosis.

Glucose tolerance often abnormal.

Carbohydrate inducibility abnormal.

Postheparin lipolytic activity normal.

Fat tolerance slightly abnormal.

Endogenous Hyperlipemia

Triglycerides higher than cholesterol.

Plasma clear, cloudy, or milky.

Often familial, usually manifest in adulthood.

Occasionally eruptive xanthomas and hepatosplenomegaly.

Atherosclerosis frequently associated.

Glucose tolerance usually abnormal.

Carbohydrate inducibility usually abnormal.

Uric acid often abnormal.

Postheparin lipolytic activity normal.

Fat tolerance usually normal.

Mixed Hyperlipemia

Triglycerides much higher than cholesterol.

Plasma creamy.

When familial, usually manifest in adulthood.

Abdominal pain, lipemia retinalis, eruptive xanthomas, hepatosplenomegaly.

Glucose tolerance often abnormal.

Carbohydrate inducibility usually abnormal.

Postheparin lipolytic activity low or normal.

Fat tolerance abnormal.

A. Precautions: If storage for more than 1 hour is necessary, blood or serum must be refrigerated.
B. Physiologic Basis: Normally, small amounts of amylase (diastase) originating in the pancreas and salivary glands are present in the blood. Inflammatory disease of these glands or obstruction of their ducts results in regurgitation of large amounts of enzyme into the blood.
C. Interpretation:
  1. Elevated in acute pancreatitis, obstruction of pancreatic ducts (carcinoma, stone, stricture, duct sphincter spasm after morphine), mumps, occasionally in the presence of renal insufficiency, occasionally in diabetic acidosis, and occasionally with inflammation of the pancreas from a perforating peptic ulcer.
  2. Decreased in hepatitis, acute and chronic; pancreatic insufficiency, and occasionally in toxemia of pregnancy.
D. Drug Effects on Laboratory Results: Elevated by morphine, codeine, meperidine, methacholine, pancreozymin, sodium diatrizoate, cyproheptadine, perhaps by pentazocine, thiazide diuretics. Pancreatitis may be induced by indomethacin, furosemide, chlorthalidone, ethacrynic acid, corticosteroids, histamine, salicylates, and tetracyclines. Decreased by barbiturate poisoning.

Amylase, Urine. Normal: Varies with method. 40-250 Somogyi units/hour.
A. Precautions: If the determination is delayed more than 1 hour after collecting the specimen, urine must be refrigerated.
B. Physiologic Basis: See Amylase, Serum. If renal function is adequate, amylase is rapidly excreted in the urine. A timed urine specimen (i.e., 2, 6, or 24 hours) should be collected and the rate of excretion determined.
C. Interpretation: Elevation of the concentration of amylase in the urine occurs in the same situations in which serum amylase concentration is elevated. Urinary amylase concentration remains elevated for up to 7 days after serum amylase levels have returned to normal following an attack of pancreatitis. Thus the determination of urinary amylase may be useful if the patient is seen late in the course of an attack of pancreatitis. An elevated serum amylase with normal or low urine amylase excretory rate may be seen in the presence of renal insufficiency.

Bicarbonate, Serum or Plasma (measured as CO_2 content). Normal: 24-28 mEq./L. or 55-65 Vol.%.
A. Precautions: Plasma or serum is preferably drawn under oil and handled anaerobically.
B. Physiologic Basis: Bicarbonate–carbonic acid buffer is

one of the most important buffer systems in maintaining
normal pH of body fluids. Bicarbonate and pH determinations on plasma serve as a basis for assessing "acid-
base balance."
C. Interpretation:
1. Elevated in -
   a. Metabolic alkalosis (arterial blood pH increased)
      due to ingestion of large quantities of sodium bi-
      carbonate, protracted vomiting of acid gastric
      juice, accompanying potassium deficit.
   b. Respiratory acidosis (arterial blood pH decreased)
      due to pulmonary emphysema or hypoventilation due
      to oversedation, narcotics, or inadequate artificial
      respiration.
2. Decreased in -
   a. Metabolic acidosis (arterial blood pH decreased)
      due to diabetic ketosis, starvation, persistent diar-
      rhea, renal insufficiency, ingestion of excess acidi-
      fying salts, or salicylate intoxication.
   b. Respiratory alkalosis (arterial blood pH increased)
      due to hyperventilation.

Bilirubin, Serum. Normal: Direct (glucuronide), 0.1-0.4
mg./100 ml. Indirect (unconjugated), 0.2-0.7 mg./100
ml.
A. Precautions: The fasting state is preferred to avoid
turbidity of serum. For optimal stability of stored serum, samples should be frozen and stored in the dark.
B. Physiologic Basis: Destruction of hemoglobin yields
bilirubin, which is conjugated in the liver to the diglucu-
ronide and excreted in the bile. Bilirubin accumulates
in the plasma when liver insufficiency exists, biliary
obstruction is present, or the rate of hemolysis increases. Rarely, abnormalities of enzyme systems involved in bilirubin metabolism in the liver (e.g., absence
of glucuronyl transferase) result in abnormal bilirubin
concentrations.
C. Interpretation:
1. Direct and indirect forms of serum bilirubin are elevated in acute or chronic hepatitis, biliary tract obstruction (cholangiolar, hepatic, or common ducts),
   toxic reactions to many drugs, chemicals, and toxins,
   and Dubin-Johnson and Rotor's syndromes.
2. Indirect serum bilirubin is elevated in hemolytic diseases or reactions and absence or deficiency of glucuronyl transferase, as in Gilbert's disease and
   Crigler-Najjar syndrome.
D. Drug Effects on Laboratory Results: Elevated by acetaminophen, chlordiazepoxide, novobiocin, acetohexamide. Many drugs produce impairment of liver function.

Calcium, Serum. Normal: 9-10.6 mg./100 ml. or 4.5-5.3
mEq./L. (Ionized 4.2-5.2 mg./100 ml. or 2.1-2.6
mEq./L.)

A. Precautions: Glassware must be free of calcium. The
patient should be fasting. Serum should be promptly
separated from the clot.

B. Physiologic Basis: Endocrine, renal, gastrointestinal,
and nutritional factors normally provide for precise regulation of calcium concentration in plasma and other body
fluids. Since some calcium is bound to plasma protein,
especially albumin, determination of the plasma albumin
concentration is necessary before the clinical significance
of abnormal serum calcium levels can be interpreted
accurately.

C. Interpretation:
1. Elevated in hyperparathyroidism, secretion of para-
thyroid-like hormone by malignant tumors, vitamin D
excess, milk-alkali syndrome, osteolytic disease such
as multiple myeloma, invasion of bone by metastatic
cancer; Paget's disease of bone, Boeck's sarcoid, and
immobilization.
2. Decreased in hypoparathyroidism, vitamin D deficiency
(rickets, osteomalacia), renal insufficiency, hypoproteinemia, malabsorption syndrome (sprue, ileitis,
celiac disease, pancreatic insufficiency), and severe
pancreatitis with pancreatic necrosis.

Calcium, Urine. Daily Excretion: Ordinarily there is a
moderate continuous urinary calcium excretion of
50-150 mg./24 hours, depending upon the intake.

A. Procedure: The patient should remain upon a diet free of
milk or cheese for 3 days prior to testing; for quantitative
testing a neutral ash diet containing about 150 mg. calcium per day is given for 3 days. Quantitative calcium
excretion studies may be made on a carefully timed 24-
hour urine specimen. The screening procedure with the
Sulkowitch reagent is simple and useful.

B. Interpretation: On the quantitative diet a normal person
secretes 125± 50 mg. of calcium per 24 hours. Normally,
a slight (1+) cloud reaction (Sulkowitch) occurs if milk
and cheese are not present in the diet. In hyperparathyroidism, the urinary calcium excretion usually exceeds
200 mg./24 hours. Urinary calcium excretion is elevated
in almost all situations in which serum calcium is high.

Carbon Dioxide Combining Power, Serum or Plasma.
Normal: 24-29 mEq./L. or 55-75 Vol. %.
Plasma or serum CO_2 combining power is elevated or decreased in the same clinical circumstances as plasma or serum bicarbonate. Anaerobic handling of the specimen is not

necessary. The method is the same as for bicarbonate determination except that the serum or plasma is exposed to an "alveolar" air concentration of CO_2 (i. e., 40-50 mm. Hg partial pressure or 5-6% CO_2) prior to the determination.

See Bicarbonate, above, for interpretation.

Ceruloplasmin and Copper, Serum. Normal: Ceruloplasmin, 23-50 mg./100 ml.; copper, 70-150 μg./100 ml.

A. Precautions: None.

B. Physiologic Basis: About 5% of serum copper is loosely bound to albumin and 95% to ceruloplasmin, an oxidase enzyme that is an alpha$_2$ globulin with a blue color. In Wilson's disease, serum copper and ceruloplasmin are low and urinary levels of copper are high.

C. Interpretation:

1. Elevated in pregnancy, hyperthyroidism, infection, aplastic anemia, acute leukemia, and cirrhosis of the liver.

2. Decreased in Wilson's disease and accompanied by increased urinary excretion of copper.

Chloride, Serum or Plasma. Normal: 96-106 mEq./L. or 340-375 mg./100 ml.

A. Precautions: Determination on whole blood yields lower results than those obtained using serum or plasma as the specimen. Always use serum or plasma.

B. Physiologic Basis: Chloride is the principal inorganic anion of the extracellular fluid. It is important in maintenance of acid-base balance even though it exerts no buffer action. When chloride as HCl or NH_4Cl is lost, alkalosis follows; when chloride is retained or ingested, acidosis follows. Chloride (with sodium) plays an important role in control of osmolarity of body fluids.

C. Interpretation:

1. Elevated in renal insufficiency (when Cl intake exceeds excretion), nephrosis (occasionally), renal tubular acidosis, ureterosigmoid anastomosis (reabsorption from urine in gut), dehydration (water deficit), and overtreatment with saline solution.

2. Decreased in gastrointestinal disease with loss of gastric and intestinal fluids (vomiting of acid gastric juice, diarrhea, gastrointestinal suction), renal insufficiency (with salt deprivation), overtreatment with diuretics, chronic respiratory acidosis (emphysema), diabetic acidosis, excessive sweating, adrenal insufficiency (NaCl loss), hyperadrenocorticism (chronic K^+ loss), and metabolic alkalosis ($NaHCO_3$ ingestion; K^+ deficit).

Chloride, Urine.

Urine chloride content varies with dietary intake, acid-base balance, endocrine "balance," body stores of other

electrolytes, and water balance. Relationships and responses
are so variable and complex that there is little clinical value
in urine chloride determinations other than in balance studies.

Cholesterol, Plasma or Serum. Normal: 150-280 mg./100
ml.
A. Precautions: The fasting state is preferred.
B. Physiologic Basis: Cholesterol concentrations are determined by metabolic functions which are influenced by
heredity, nutrition, endocrine function, and integrity of
vital organs such as the liver and kidney. Cholesterol
metabolism is intimately associated with lipid metabolism.
C. Interpretation:
1. Elevated in familial hypercholesterolemia (xanthomatosis), hypothyroidism, poorly controlled diabetes
mellitus, nephrotic syndrome, chronic hepatitis, biliary cirrhosis, obstructive jaundice, hypoproteinemia
(idiopathic, with nephrosis or chronic hepatitis), and
lipemia (idiopathic, familial).
2. Decreased in acute hepatitis and Gaucher's disease,
occasionally in hyperthyroidism, acute infections,
anemia, malnutrition.
D. Drug Effects on Laboratory Results: Elevated by bromides, anabolic agents, trimethadione, oral contraceptives. Decreased by cholestyramine resin, haloperidol,
nicotinic acid, salicylates, thyroid hormone, estrogens,
clofibrate, chlorpropamide, phenformin, kanamycin,
neomycin, phenyramidol.

Cholesterol Esters, Plasma or Serum. Normal: 65-75% of
total serum or plasma cholesterol.
A. Precautions: None.
B. Physiologic Basis: Cholesterol is esterified in the intestinal mucosa and in the liver. Cholesterol exists in
plasma or serum as the free form (25-33% of total) and
as the ester (67-75% of total). In the presence of acute
hepatic insufficiency (as in acute hepatitis), the concentration of esters is reduced.
C. Interpretation:
1. Elevated along with cholesterol in absence of hyperbilirubinemia (see Cholesterol, above). The ratio of
ester/total cholesterol under these circumstances is
normal. With hyperbilirubinemia, absolute values
may be elevated, but not in the same proportion as
total cholesterol, so that the ester/total cholesterol
ratio is less than 65%.
2. Decreased in acute hepatitis. Cholesterol esters may
be decreased also in chronic hepatitis and chronic
biliary obstruction; in these situations the decrease in
cholesterol ester exceeds the decrease in total choles-

terol, which results in an ester/total cholesterol ratio of less than 65%.

Creatine Phosphokinase (CPK). Normal: Up to 36 I.U.; varies with method.

A. Precautions: The enzyme is unstable, and the red cell content inhibits enzyme activity. Serum must be removed from the clot promptly. If assay cannot be done soon after drawing blood, serum must be frozen.

B. Physiologic Basis: CPK splits creatine phosphate in the presence of ADP to yield creatine + ATP. Skeletal and heart muscle and brain are rich in the enzyme.

C. Interpretation: Normal values vary with the method.
  1. Elevated in the presence of muscle damage such as with myocardial infarction, trauma to muscle, muscular dystrophies, polymyositis, and severe muscular exertion. Following myocardial infarction, serum CPK concentration increases rapidly (within 3-5 hours), and remains elevated for a shorter time after the episode (2 or 3 days) than does GOT or LDH.
  2. Not elevated in pulmonary infarction parenchymal liver disease.

Creatine, Urine (24 Hours). Normal: See table below.

Urine Creatine and Creatinine, Normal Values (24 Hours)

	Creatine	Creatinine
Newborn	4.5 mg./Kg.	10 mg./Kg.
1-7 months	8.1 mg./Kg.	12.8 mg./Kg.
2-3 years	7.9 mg./Kg.	12.1 mg./Kg.
4-4$\frac{1}{2}$ years	4.5 mg./Kg.	14.6 mg./Kg.
9-9$\frac{1}{2}$ years	2.5 mg./Kg.	18.1 mg./Kg.
11-14 years	2.7 mg./Kg.	20.1 mg./Kg.
Adult male	0-50 mg.	25 mg./Kg.
Adult female	0-100 mg.	21 mg./Kg.

A. Precautions: Collection of the 24-hour specimen must be accurate. The specimen may be refrigerated or preserved with 10 ml. of toluene or 10 ml. of 5% thymol in chloroform.

B. Physiologic Basis: Creatine is an important constituent of muscle, brain, and blood; in the form of creatine phosphate it serves as a source of high-energy phosphate. Normally, small amounts of creatine are excreted in the urine, but in states of elevated catabolism and in the presence of muscular dystrophies, the rate of excretion is increased.

C. Interpretation:
   1. Elevated in muscular dystrophies such as progressive muscular dystrophy, myotonia atrophica, and myasthenia gravis; muscle wasting, as in acute poliomyelitis, amyotrophic lateral sclerosis, and myositis manifested by muscle wasting; starvation and cachectic states, hyperthyroidism, and febrile diseases.
   2. Decreased in hypothyroidism, amyotonia congenita, and renal insufficiency.

Creatinine, Plasma or Serum. Normal: 0.7-1.5 mg./100 ml.
   A. Precautions: Other materials than creatinine may react to give falsely high results.
   B. Physiologic Basis: Creatinine, which is derived from creatine, is excreted by filtration through the glomeruli of the kidney. Endogenous creatinine is apparently not excreted by renal tubules. Retention of creatinine is thus an index of glomerular insufficiency. Creatinine clearance closely approximates the inulin clearance and is an acceptable measure of filtration rate.
   C. Interpretation: Creatinine is elevated in acute or chronic renal insufficiency, urinary tract obstruction, and impairment of renal function induced by some drugs. Values of less than 0.8 mg./100 ml. are of no known significance.
   D. Drug Effects on Laboratory Results: Elevated by ascorbic acid, barbiturates, sulfobromophthalein, methyldopa, and phenolsulfonphthalein, all of which interfere with the determination of the alkaline picrate method (Jaffe reaction).

Creatinine, Urine. See table on p. 189 for normal values.

Enzymes, Serum. See specific enzyme.

Globulin, Serum. See Proteins below.

Glucose, Whole Blood, Plasma, Serum. Normal: Fasting blood glucose (Folin), 80-120 mg./100 ml. Fasting blood glucose (true), 60-100 mg./100 ml. Plasma and serum levels are slightly higher than those of whole blood, i.e., true glucose, 70-110 mg./100 ml.
   A. Precautions: If determination is delayed beyond 1 hour, sodium fluoride, about 3 mg./ml. blood, should be added to the specimen. The filtrates may be refrigerated for up to 24 hours. Errors in interpretation may occur if the patient has eaten sugar or received glucose solution parenterally just prior to the collection of what is thought to be a "fasting" specimen. Whole blood, plasma, or serum may be used.

B. Physiologic Basis: The glucose concentration in extracellular fluid is normally closely regulated, with the result that a source of energy is available to tissues and no
glucose is excreted in the urine. Hyperglycemia and
hypoglycemia are nonspecific signs of abnormal glucose
metabolism.

C. Interpretation:
1. Elevated in diabetes mellitus, hyperthyroidism, adrenocortical hyperactivity (cortical excess), hyper-
pituitarism, and hepatic disease (occasionally).
2. Decreased in hyperinsulinism, adrenal insufficiency,
hypopituitarism, hepatic insufficiency (occasionally),
functional hypoglycemia, and by hypoglycemic agents.

D. Drug Effects on Laboratory Results: Elevated by corticosteroids, chlorthalidone, thiazide diuretics, furosemide,
ethacrynic acid, triamterene, indomethacin, oral contraceptives (estrogen-progestin combinations), isoniazid,
nicotinic acid (large doses), phenothiazines, and paraldehyde. Decreased by acetaminophen, phenacetin, cyproheptadine, pargyline, and propranolol.

**Iodine, Protein-bound (PBI), Butanol Extractable (BEI), Or-
ganic; Serum.** Normal: PBI, 4-8 μg./100 ml.; BEI,
3-6.5 μg./100 ml. (See Thyroid tests, p. 226.) Thyroxine (T_4), 2.9-6.4 μg./100 ml.

A. Precautions: Avoid iodine contamination of glassware and
the use of iodine on the skin prior to venipuncture. The
patient need not be fasting.

B. Physiologic Basis: Thyroid hormone is normally the only
organic iodine compound present in blood in significant
concentration. The protein-bound iodine is, therefore, a
measure of circulating thyroxine.

C. Interpretation:
1. Elevated in hyperthyroidism, thyroiditis (during active
stage), and pregnancy. Factitiously high levels may
result from (1) administration of large doses of thyroid
hormone (desiccated thyroid, thyroxine), (2) ingestion
of inorganic and organic iodides, and (3) administration of organic iodides used in x-ray diagnostic tests
(cholecystograms, urograms, myelograms, bronchograms, uterosalpingograms). These diagnostic compounds may produce elevated iodine levels for 1 year
or more.
2. Decreased in hypothyroidism, after use of mercurial
diuretics (effect is only of few days' duration), during
administration of reserpine, or during administration
of triiodothyronine (which suppresses thyroxine production by the thyroid gland).

D. Drug Effects on Laboratory Results: Elevated by sulfobromophthalein, oral contraceptives (estrogen-progestin

combinations), estrogens, pyrazinamide, chlormadinone, and Metrecal®. Decreased by salicylates, anabolic steroids, progestogens, bishydroxycoumarin, diphenylhydantoin, para-aminobenzoic acid, tolbutamide, tolazamide, and thiocyanate.

Iron, Serum. Normal: 50-175 µg./100 ml.
  A. Precautions: Syringes and needles must be iron-free. Hemolysis of blood must be avoided. The serum must be free of hemoglobin.
  B. Physiologic Basis: Iron concentration in the plasma is determined by several factors, including absorption from the intestine, storage in intestine, liver, spleen, and marrow, breakdown or loss of hemoglobin, and synthesis of new hemoglobin.
  C. Interpretation:
    1. Elevated in hemochromatosis, hemosiderosis (multiple transfusions, excess iron administration), hemolytic disease, pernicious anemia, hypoplastic anemias, often in viral hepatitis. Spuriously elevated if patient has received parenteral iron during the 2-3 months prior to determination.
    2. Decreased in iron deficiency with infections, nephrosis, and chronic renal insufficiency, and during periods of active hematopoiesis.

Iron-binding Capacity, Serum. Normal: Total, 300-360 µg./100 ml. Unsaturated, 150-300 µg./100 ml.
  A. Precautions: None.
  B. Physiologic Basis: Iron is transported as a complex of the metal binding globulin transferrin or siderophilin. Normally this transport protein carries an amount of iron which represents about 30-40% of its capacity to combine with iron. Thus the "unsaturated" iron binding capacity is normally 60-70% of the total capacity.
  C. Interpretation of Unsaturated Iron Binding Capacity:
    1. Elevated in the presence of low serum iron or iron deficiency anemia, acute or chronic blood loss, pregnancy, and acute hepatitis.
    2. Decreased in the presence of high serum iron, hemochromatosis, hemosiderosis, hemolytic disease, pernicious anemia, acute and chronic infections, cirrhosis of the liver, uremia, and malignancy.

Lactic Dehydrogenase, Serum, Serous Fluids, Spinal Fluid, Urine. Normal: Serum, 200-450 units/ml. (Wroblewski-LaDue), 80-120 units/ml. (Wocher); serous fluids, lower than serum; spinal fluid, 15-75 units/ml. (Wroblewski-LaDue); urine, up to 8300 units/24 hours (Wroblewski-LaDue).

A. Precautions: Any degree of hemolysis must be avoided because the concentration of LDH within red blood cells is 100 times that in normal serum. Heparin and oxalate may inhibit enzyme activity.

B. Physiologic Basis: LDH catalyzes the interconversion of lactate and pyruvate in the presence of NADH or $NADH_2$. It is distributed generally in body cells and fluids.

C. Interpretation: Elevated in all conditions accompanied by tissue necrosis, particularly those involving acute injury of the heart, red cells, kidney, skeletal muscle, liver, lung, and skin. Marked elevations accompany hemolytic anemias, and the anemias of vitamin B_{12} and folate deficiency, and polycythemia rubra vera. The course of rise in concentration over 3-4 days followed by a slow decline during the following 5-7 days may be helpful in confirming the presence of a myocardial infarction; however, pulmonary infarction, neoplastic disease, and megaloblastic anemia must be excluded. Although elevated during the acute phase of infectious hepatitis, enzyme activity is seldom increased in chronic liver disease.

Lactic Dehydrogenase Isoenzymes. Normal serum levels are as follows:

	Percent of Total (and Range)
Isoenzyme 1	28 (15-30)
2	36 (22-50)
3	23 (15-30)
4	6 (0-15)
5	6 (0-15)

A. Precautions: As for LDH (see above).

B. Physiologic Basis: LDH consists of five separable proteins, each made of tetramers of two types or sub-units, H and M. The five isoenzymes can be distinguished by kinetics, electrophoresis, chromatography, and immunologic characteristics. By electrophoretic separation, the mobility of the isoenzymes corresponds to serum proteins α_1, α_2, β, γ_1, and γ_2. These are usually numbered 1 (fastest moving), 2, 3, 4, and 5 (slowest moving). Isoenzyme 1 is present in high concentrations in heart muscle (tetramer H H H H) and in erythrocytes and kidney cortex. Isoenzyme 5 is present in high concentrations in skeletal muscle (tetramer M M M M) and liver.

C. Interpretation: In myocardial infarction, the α isoenzymes are elevated - particularly LDH 1 - to yield a ratio of LDH 1:2 of > 1.0. Similar α isoenzyme elevations occur in renal cortex infarction and with hemolytic anemias.

LDH 5 and 4 are relatively increased in the presence
of acute hepatitis, acute muscle injury, dermatomyositis,
and muscular dystrophies.
D. Drug Effects on Laboratory Results: Decreased by clofibrate.

Lipase, Serum. Normal: 0.2-1.5 units.
A. Precautions: None. The specimen may be refrigerated
up to 24 hours prior to the determination.
B. Physiologic Basis: A low concentration of fat splitting
enzyme is present in circulating blood. In the presence
of pancreatitis, pancreatic lipase is released into the
circulation in higher concentrations, which persist, as a
rule, for a longer period than does the elevated concentration of amylase.
C. Interpretation: Serum lipase is elevated in acute or ex-
acerbated pancreatitis and in obstruction of pancreatic
ducts by stone or neoplasm.

Magnesium, Serum. Normal: 1.5-2.5 mEq./L.
A. Precautions: None.
B. Physiologic Basis: Magnesium is primarily an intracellular electrolyte. In extracellular fluid it affects
neuromuscular irritability and response. Magnesium
deficit may exist with little or no change in extracellular
fluid concentrations. Low magnesium levels in plasma
have been associated with tetany, weakness, disorientation, and somnolence.
C. Interpretation:
1. Elevated in renal insufficiency and in overtreatment
with magnesium salts intravenously or intramuscularly.
2. Decreased in chronic diarrhea, acute loss of enteric
fluids, starvation, chronic alcoholism, chronic hepatitis, and hepatic insufficiency.

Nonprotein Nitrogen (NPN), Blood, Plasma, or Serum.
Normal: 15-35 mg./100 ml.
A. Precautions: See Urea, below.
B. Physiologic Basis and Interpretation: See Urea, below,
and Creatinine, above.

Phosphatase, Acid, Serum. Normal: Bodansky units, 0.5-2;
King-Armstrong, 1-5; Gutman, 0.5-2; Shinowara,
0-1.1; Bessey-Lowry, 0.1-0.63.
A. Precautions: Avoid hemolysis of the specimen, which
releases erythrocyte phosphatase to give factitiously high
results. Serum may be refrigerated 24-48 hours prior
to determination.
B. Physiologic Basis: Phosphatase active at pH 4.9 is pres-

ent in high concentrations in the prostate gland and in erythrocytes. In the presence of carcinoma of the prostate which has gone beyond the capsule of the gland or has metastasized, serum acid phosphatase concentration is increased.

C. Interpretation: Increased in carcinoma of the prostate, metastatic or invasive beyond the capsule of the gland, and occasionally in acute myelocytic leukemia.

Phosphatase, Alkaline, Serum. Normal in adults: Bodansky, 2-5 units; King-Armstrong, 5-13; Gutman, 3-10; Shinowara, 2.2-8.6; Bessey-Lowry, 0.8-2.3. Normal in children: Bodansky, 5-14; King-Armstrong, 15-30; Bessey-Lowry, 2.8-6.7.

A. Precautions: Serum may be kept in refrigerator 24-48 hours, but values may increase slightly (10%). The specimen will deteriorate if not refrigerated. Do not use fluoride or oxalate.

B. Physiologic Basis: Alkaline phosphatase is present in high concentrations in growing bone and in bile. Concentration in circulating blood reflects phosphatase activity in bone growth and repair. If hepatic excretory ducts become occluded, phosphatase concentration in the blood increases.

C. Interpretation:
   1. Elevated in -
      a. Children (normal growth of bone).
      b. Osteoblastic bone disease - Hyperparathyroidism, rickets and osteomalacia, neoplastic bone disease (osteosarcoma, metastatic neoplasms), ossification as in myositis ossificans, Paget's disease (osteitis deformans), and Boeck's sarcoid.
      c. Hepatic duct or cholangiolar obstruction due to stone, stricture, or neoplasm.
      d. Hepatic disease resulting from drugs such as chlorpromazine, methyltestosterone.
   2. Decreased in hypothyroidism and in growth retardation in children.

D. Drug Effects on Laboratory Results: Elevated by acetohexamide, tolazamide, tolbutamide, chlorpropamide, allopurinol, sulfobromophthalein, carbamazepine, cephaloridine, furosemide, methyldopa, phenothiazine, and oral contraceptives (estrogen-progestin combinations).

Phosphorus, Inorganic, Serum. Normal: Children, 4-7 mg./100 ml. Adults, 3-4.5 mg./100 ml. or 0.9-1.5 mM./L.

A. Precautions: Glassware cleaned with phosphate cleaners must be thoroughly rinsed. The fasting state is neces-

sary to avoid postprandial depression of phosphate associated with glucose transport and metabolism.

B. Physiologic Basis: The concentration of inorganic phosphate in circulating plasma is influenced by parathyroid
gland function, intestinal absorption, renal function, bone
metabolism, and nutrition.

C. Interpretation:

1. Increased in renal insufficiency, hypoparathyroidism,
and hypervitaminosis D.

2. Decreased in hyperparathyroidism, hypovitaminosis D
(rickets, osteomalacia), malabsorption syndrome
(steatorrhea), some forms of renal tubular insufficiency, postprandial state, and after insulin.

Potassium, Serum or Plasma. Normal: 3.5-5 mEq./L.;
14-20 mg./100 ml.

A. Precautions: Avoid hemolysis, which releases erythrocyte potassium. Serum must be separated promptly from
the clot or plasma from the red cell mass to prevent diffusion of potassium out of erythrocytes.

B. Physiologic Basis: Potassium concentration in plasma
determines the state of neuromuscular and muscular
irritability. Elevated or decreased concentrations of
potassium impair the capability of muscle to contract.

C. Interpretation:

1. Increased in renal insufficiency (especially in the
presence of increased rate of protein or tissue breakdown); adrenal insufficiency; and too rapid administration of potassium salts, especially intravenously and
with spironolactone (Aldactone®) administration.

2. Decreased in -

a. Inadequate intake (starvation).

b. Inadequate absorption or unusual enteric losses -
Vomiting, diarrhea, or malabsorption syndrome.

c. Unusual renal loss - Secondary to hyperadrenocorticism (especially hyperaldosteronism) and to
adrenocorticosteroid therapy, metabolic alkalosis,
use of diuretics such as chlorothiazide and its derivatives and the mercurials, and renal tubular
defects such as the De Toni-Fanconi syndrome and
renal tubular acidosis.

d. Abnormal redistribution between extracellular and
intracellular fluids - Familial periodic paralysis,
testosterone administration.

D. Drug Effects on Laboratory Results: Elevated by triamterene, phenformin. Decreased by degraded tetracycline, phenothiazines, and sodium polystyrenesulfonate
resin.

Proteins, Serum or Plasma (Includes Fibrinogen). Normal:
See Interpretation, below.

A. Precautions: Serum or plasma must be free of hemolysis.
Since fibrinogen is removed in the process of coagulation
of the blood, fibrinogen determinations cannot be done on
serum.

B. Physiologic Basis: Concentration of protein determines
colloidal osmotic pressure of plasma. The concentration
of protein in plasma is influenced by the nutritional state,
hepatic function, renal function, occurrence of disease
such as multiple myeloma, and metabolic errors. Variations in the several fractions of plasma proteins may
signify the presence of specific disease.

C. Interpretation:

1. Total protein, serum - Normal: 6-8 Gm./100 ml.
See Albumin and Globulin fractions, below.

2. Albumin, serum or plasma - Normal: 3.5-5.5 Gm./
100 ml.

a. Elevated in dehydration, shock, hemoconcentration,
administration of large quantities of concentrated
albumin "solution" intravenously.

b. Decreased in malnutrition, malabsorption syndrome,
acute or chronic glomerulonephritis, nephrosis,
acute or chronic hepatic insufficiency, neoplastic
diseases, and leukemia.

3. Globulin, serum or plasma - Normal: 1.5-3 Gm./100
ml.

a. Elevated in hepatic disease, infectious hepatitis,
cirrhosis of the liver, biliary cirrhosis, and hemo-
chromatosis; disseminated lupus erythematosus;
acute or chronic infectious diseases, particularly
lymphopathia venereum, typhus fever, leishmaniasis, schistosomiasis, and malaria; multiple myeloma; and Boeck's sarcoid.

b. Decreased in malnutrition, congenital agammaglobulinemia, acquired hypogammaglobulinemia,
and lymphatic leukemia.

4. Fibrinogen, plasma - Normal: 0.2-0.6 Gm./100 ml.

a. Elevated in glomerulonephritis, nephrosis (occasionally), and infectious diseases.

b. Decreased in accidents of pregnancy (placental
ablation, amniotic fluid embolism, violent labor),
acute and chronic hepatic insufficiency, and congenital fibrinogenopenia, and occasionally with
prostatic carcinoma.

Protein Fractions as Determined by Electrophoresis

	Percentage of Total Protein
Albumin	52-68
α_1 globulin	2.4-4.4
α_2 globulin	6.1-10.1
β globulin	8.5-14.5
γ globulin	10-21

Some Constituents of Globulins

Globulin	Representative Constituents
α_1	Thyroxine binding globulin
	Transcortin
	Glycoprotein
	Lipoprotein
α_2	Haptoglobin
	Glycoprotein
	Macroglobulin
β	Transferrin
	Lipoprotein
	Glycoprotein
γ	γG
	γM
	γA

Sodium, Serum or Plasma. Normal: 136-145 mEq./L.
  A. Precautions: Glassware must be completely clean.
  B. Physiologic Basis: Sodium constitutes 140 of the 155 mEq. of cation in plasma. With its associated anions it provides the bulk of osmotically active solute in the plasma, thus affecting the distribution of body water significantly. A shift of sodium into cells or a loss of sodium from the body results in a decrease of extracellular fluid volume with consequent effect on circulation, renal function, and nervous system function.
  C. Interpretation:
    1. Increased in dehydration (water deficit), CNS trauma or disease, and hyperadrenocorticism due to hyperaldosteronism or to corticosterone or corticosteroid excess.
    2. Decreased in adrenal insufficiency; renal insufficiency, especially with inadequate sodium intake; renal tubular acidosis; as a physiologic response to trauma or burns (sodium shift into cells); unusual losses via the gastrointestinal tract, as in acute or chronic diarrhea, in-

testinal obstruction or fistula, and in unusual sweating with inadequate sodium replacement. In some patients with edema associated with cardiac or renal disease, serum sodium concentration is low even though total body sodium content is greater than normal; water retention and abnormal distribution of sodium between intracellular and extracellular fluid contribute to this paradoxical situation. Hyperglycemia occasionally results in shift of intracellular water to the extracellular space, producing a dilutional hyponatremia.

Transaminase Enzyme Tests, Serum or Serous Fluid. Normal: Glutamic oxaloacetic transaminase (SGOT), 5-40 units. Glutamic pyruvic transaminase (SGPT), 5-35 units.

A. Precautions: None.

B. Physiologic Basis: Glutamic oxaloacetic transaminase, glutamic pyruvic transaminase, and lactic dehydrogenase are all intracellular enzymes involved in amino acid or carbohydrate metabolism. The enzymes are present in high concentrations in muscle, liver, and brain. Elevations of concentrations of these enzymes in the blood indicate necrosis or disease, especially of these tissues.

C. Interpretation: Elevated in myocardial infarction; acute infections or toxic hepatitis; cirrhosis of the liver; liver neoplasm, metastatic or primary; and in transudates associated with neoplastic involvement of serous cavities. SGOT is elevated in muscular dystrophy, dermatomyositis, and paroxysmal myoglobinuria.

D. Drug Effects on Laboratory Results: Elevated by a host of drugs, including anabolic steroids, androgens, clofibrate, erythromycin (especially estolate) and other antibiotics, isoniazid, methotrexate, methyldopa, phenothiazines, oral contraceptives, salicylates, acetaminophen, phenacetin, indomethacin, acetohexamide, allopurinol, bishydroxycoumarin, carbamazepine, chlordiazepoxide, desimipramine, codeine, morphine, meperidine, tolazamide, propranolol, and guanethidine.

Urea and Urea Nitrogen, Blood, Plasma, or Serum. Normal: BUN, 8-20 mg./100 ml.

A. Precautions: **Do not use** ammonium oxalate or "double oxalate" as anticoagulant, for the ammonia will be measured as urea (see Method). Do not use too much oxalate, for it will impair urease activity.

B. Physiologic Basis: Urea, an end-product of protein metabolism, is excreted by the kidney. In the glomerular filtrate the urea concentration is the same as in the plasma. Tubular reabsorption of urea varies inversely with rate of urine flow. Thus urea is a less useful measure of

glomerular filtration than is creatinine, which is not reabsorbed. BUN varies directly with protein intake and
inversely with the rate of excretion of urea.
C. Interpretation:
   1. Elevated in -
      a. Renal insufficiency - Nephritis, acute and chronic;
         acute renal failure (tubular necrosis), urinary tract
         obstruction.
      b. Increased nitrogen metabolism associated with
         diminished renal blood flow or impaired renal func-
         tion - Dehydration from any cause, gastrointestinal
         bleeding (combination of increased protein absorp-
         tion from digestion of blood, plus decreased renal
         blood flow).
      c. Decreased renal blood flow - Shock, adrenal in-
         sufficiency, occasionally congestive heart failure.
   2. Decreased in hepatic failure, nephrosis not compli-
      cated by renal insufficiency, and cachexia.
D. Drug Effects on Laboratory Results: Elevated by many
   antibiotics that impair renal function, guanethidine,
   methyldopa, indomethacin, isoniazid, propranolol, and
   potent diuretics (decreased blood volume and renal blood
   flow).

Uric Acid, Serum or Plasma. Normal: 3-7.5 mg./100 ml.
A. Precautions: If plasma is used, lithium oxalate should be
   used as the anticoagulant; potassium oxalate may interfere with the determination.
B. Physiologic Basis: Uric acid, an end-product of nucleo-
   protein metabolism, is excreted by the kidney. Gout, a
   genetically transmitted metabolic error, is characterized
   by an increased plasma or serum uric acid concentration,
   an increase in total body uric acid, and deposition of uric
   acid in tissues. An increase in uric acid concentration
   in plasma and serum may accompany increased nucleo-
   protein catabolism (blood dyscrasias, therapy with anti-
   leukemic drugs), thiazide diuretics, or decreased renal
   excretion.
C. Interpretation:
   1. Elevated in gout, toxemia of pregnancy (eclampsia),
      leukemia, polycythemia, therapy with antileukemic
      agents, and renal insufficiency.
   2. Decreased in acute hepatitis (occasionally), treatment
      with allopurinol, probenecid.
D. Drug Effects on Laboratory Results: Elevated by thiazide
   diuretics, ethacrynic acid, spironolactone, furosemide,
   ascorbic acid, and triamterene. Decreased by salicylates
   (small doses), methyldopa, clofibrate, phenylbutazone,
   cinchophen, sulfinpyrazone, and phenothiazines.

BLOOD CHEMISTRY

Preparation of Protein-free Blood Filtrate.

Measure carefully one volume of blood from a pipet and add to this eight volumes of N/12 sulfuric acid. Wait until the mixture becomes dark and then add one volume of 10% sodium tungstate solution.

Filter repeatedly until the filtrate is crystal clear. This filtrate may be used for any determination not involving protein of the blood.

Note that the dilution is 1:10.

Macromethod for Blood Sugar.

A. Reagents:
1. Alkaline copper tartrate solution (see p. 622).
2. Molybdate phosphate solution (see p. 625).
3. Standard sugar solution - Stock solution of 1% glucose in saturated benzoic acid solution will keep indefinitely.
   a. Standard containing 10 mg. glucose/100 ml.: Pipet 1 ml. stock solution into 100 ml. saturated benzoic acid solution. Each 2 ml. of this standard contains 0.2 mg. glucose.
   b. Standard containing 20 mg. glucose/100 ml.: Pipet 2 ml. of stock solution into 100 ml. of saturated benzoic acid solution.

B. Procedure: Place 2 ml. of the prepared blood filtrate in a Folin-Wu blood sugar tube; in two other tubes add 2 ml. of each of the above standards. Add to each tube 2 ml. of the alkaline copper tartrate and boil in a water bath for six minutes. Cool in water bath; when cool, add 2 ml. of the molybdate-acid solution. Dilute to 25 ml. mark and read in colorimeter with standard that most nearly matches the color or read in photometer at 420 mμ.

C. Calculation: Set known standard at 20.
1. Using standard with 0.2 mg. glucose/2 ml.

$$\frac{20}{\text{Unknown reading}} \times 100 = \text{mg. glucose/100 ml. whole blood.}$$

2. Using standard with 0.4 mg. glucose/2 ml.

$$\frac{20}{\text{Unknown reading}} \times 200 = \text{mg. glucose/100 ml. whole blood.}$$

Folin Micromethod for Blood Glucose.

A. Reagents: (See Appendix.)
1. Sulfuric acid-sulfate solution.
2. Potassium ferricyanide solution.
3. Sulfate-tungstate solution.
4. Cyanide-carbonate solution.
5. Ghatti-gum iron solution.

6. Standard glucose solution - Add 980 mg. of glucose to 300 ml. water. Dissolve 1 Gm. benzoic acid in 400 ml. distilled water. If heat is necessary, allow to cool, mix, and dilute to 1 liter.

B. Procedure: To 4 ml. of sulfate-tungstate reagent add 0.1 ml. of blood collected from the finger or ear. Clean the pipet well by drawing the reagent up into it and blowing it out several times. Add 1 ml. of the acid-sulfate reagent, mix well, and centrifuge for three minutes.

Transfer 2 ml. of the clear supernatant fluid and 2 ml. of water to a 25 ml. tube. Set up another tube containing 4 ml. of the standard. To each add 1 ml. of the ferri-cyanide solution and then add 1 ml. of the cyanide-carbonate solution.

Heat both tubes in a boiling water bath for eight minutes and add 5 ml. of ghatti-gum solution after cooling. Dilute to 25 ml. and compare in the colorimeter or read in photometer at 520 mμ.

C. Calculation: Set standard at 20 mm.

$$\frac{20}{\text{Unknown reading}} \times 100 \text{ mg.} = \text{glucose}/100 \text{ ml. whole blood}$$

Blood Glucose and Acetone, Rapid Method.*

A. Reagents:
1. Trichloroacetic acid, 20% in water.
2. Sodium (or potassium) hydroxide, 20% in water.
3. Ammonium hydroxide, concentrated.
4. Sodium nitroprusside, 20% in water.
5. Standard glucose solutions. Dilute one part of the 1% stock solution of glucose described previously (p. 201) with nine parts of distilled water to make a standard which, when employed in the test, will be equivalent to 200 mg./100 ml. Other dilutions can be made accordingly.

B. Procedure:
1. To 4 ml. of 20% trichloroacetic acid add 4 ml. of blood (may be oxalated) or plasma. Shake or mix thoroughly in a corked tube. Centrifuge for a few minutes or filter.
2. For blood sugar - To 1.5 ml. of 20% sodium hydroxide add 3 ml. of clear supernatant solution or filtrate from Step 1. Add glass bead and heat to boiling for about one minute or heat in boiling water bath for five minutes. Read color by daylight or white light.
   a. Colorless to tinge of yellow = Hypoglycemia
   b. Pale or lemon yellow   = Normal range

*Jager, I.: J. Lab. & Clin. Med. **42**:474 (1953).

    c. Deep yellow   = Hyperglycemia
    d. Orange   = Severe hyperglycemia

    For standard solutions, add 2 drops of 20% tri-
chloroacetic acid to 3 ml. of standard; add 1.5 ml. of
20% sodium hydroxide and heat as for blood.

3. For blood acetone - To 1.5 ml. or remainder of filtrate or supernatant fluid add 2 drops of 20% sodium
nitroprusside. Carefully overlay ammonium hydroxide solution. A purple ring indicates acetone, as
in the test for acetone in urine. The depth of color of
the ring gives a rough indication of acetone concentration.

4. Alternative test - Make serial dilutions of serum or
plasma as follows: straight plasma, 1:1, 1:2, 1:4,
1:8, 1:16. Place 1-2 drops of each well-mixed dilution on a separate Acetest® tablet. Acetone concentration can be expressed as the highest yielding a
distinct purple color.

Blood Glucose Screening Test.

    Dextrostix® provides a rapid screening test that is simple
and reliable between blood glucose levels of 40 and 250 mg./
100 ml. Cellulose reagent strips impregnated with glucose
oxidase and a chromogen indicator system are coated with a
semipermeable membrane. Capillary or venous blood is applied to the strip, allowed to permeate the strip for one minute, and washed off completely. The blue color developed is
compared with a chart provided with the strips. See package
enclosure for detailed instructions.

TABLES OF NORMAL VALUES

The normal values listed are those in which there is agreement as determined by accurate and accepted technics. (Modified after Castleman, B., and McNeely, B.U.: New England J. Med. **276**:167, 1967.)
For each ml. of serum needed, draw 2.5 ml. of blood.

BLOOD, MISCELLANEOUS VALUES

Determination	Normal Value
Hematocrit Studies	
Packed cell volume	Men: 47% (40-54) Women: 42% (37-47)
Mean corpuscular volume	82-92 cubic micra (c. μ)
Mean corpuscular hemoglobin	28-32 micromicrograms ($\mu\mu$g.)
Mean corpuscular hemoglobin concentration	32-37%
Diameter of red cells	7.3 micra (avg.)
Bleeding Time	
Ivy	1-7 minutes
Coagulation Time	
Lee-White	6-18 minutes
Clot Retraction	Begins in 1-3 hours
Activated Partial Thromboplastin Time (Activated PTT)	35-50 seconds
Fragility of Red Cells	Begins 0.45-0.38% NaCl
	Complete 0.36-0.30% NaCl
Sedimentation Rate	
Westergren	Less than 20 mm./hour
Wintrobe	0-10 mm./hour

BLOOD, PLASMA, OR SERUM: CHEMICAL CONSTITUENTS
(Values vary with procedures used.)

Determination	Material Analyzed	Amount* Req./ Fasting State	Normal Value
Acetone bodies	Plasma	2 ml.	0.3-2 mg./100 ml.
Aldolase	Serum	4 ml.	3-8 units/ml. (Bruns). Male < 33; female < 19 units (Warburg and Christian).
Aldosterone†	Plasma		0.003-0.01 μg./100 ml.
Amino acid N	Plasma	2 ml. fasting	3.0-5.5 mg./100 ml.
Ammonia‡	Blood	2 ml.	40-70 μg./100 ml.
Amylase	Serum	2 ml.	80-180 Somogyi units/100 ml.
Base, total serum	Serum	2 ml.	145-160 mEq./L.
Bilirubin	Serum	2 ml.	Direct, 0.1-0.4 mg./100 ml. Indirect, 0.2-0.7 mg./100 ml.
Calcium	Serum	2 ml. fasting	9.0-10.6 mg./100 ml. 4.5-5.3 mEq./L. (varies with protein concentration)
CO_2: Content Combining power	Serum or plasma	1 ml.	24-29 mEq./L. 55-65 Vol.% 55-75 Vol.%
Carotenoids	Serum	2 ml. fasting	50-300 μg./100 ml.
Ceruloplasmin	Serum	2 ml.	23-50 mg./100 ml.
Chloride	Serum	1 ml.	96-106 mEq./L. 340-375 mg./100 ml. (as chloride)
Cholesterol	Serum	1 ml.	150-280 mg./100 ml.
Cholesterol esters	Serum	1 ml.	50-65% of total cholesterol
Copper	Serum	5 ml.	70-150 μg./100 ml.
Cortisol†	Plasma		5-18 μg./100 ml.

*Minimum amount required for any procedure.
†Consult laboratory concerning amount required and special instructions.
‡Do not use anticoagulant containing ammonium oxalate.
§Separate serum immediately and freeze.

Determination	Material Analyzed	Amount* Req./ Fasting State	Normal Value
Creatine phospho-kinase (CPK)§	Serum	3 ml.	0-36 IU
Creatinine	Blood or serum	1 ml.	0.7-1.5 mg./100 ml.
Epinephrine†	Plasma		0.1 µg./L.
Norepinephrine†	Plasma		0.5 µg./L.
Fatty acids, total	Serum		9-15 mM./L.
Fibrinogen	Plasma	2 ml.	0.2-0.4 Gm./100 ml.
Glucose (Folin)	Blood	0.1-1 ml. fast.	80-120 mg./100 ml. (fasting)
Glucose (true)	Blood	0.1-1 ml. fast.	60-100 mg./100 ml.
Glucose (true)	Serum or plasma	0.1-1 ml. fast.	70-110 mg./100 ml.
Glucose tolerance	Blood		(See p. 226.)
Haptoglobin	Serum	1 ml.	40-70 mg. Hgb. binding capacity/100 ml.
Iodine, BEI	Serum	10 ml.	3-6.5 µg./100 ml.
Iodine, PBI (thy-roid hormone)	Serum	5 ml.	4-8 µg./100 ml.
Iodine, thyroxine	Serum	5 ml.	2.9-6.4 µg./100 ml.
Iron	Serum	5 ml.	65-175 µg./100 ml.
Iron binding capac-ity, total	Serum	5 ml.	250-410 µg./100 ml.
Lactic acid†	Blood (in iodoacetate)		0.44-1.8 mM./L. 4-16 mg./100 ml.
Lactic dehydro-genase	Serum	1 ml.	215-450 units/ml. (Wroblew-ski-LaDue) (<240 IU/L.)
Leucine amino-peptidase	Serum	2 ml.	50-200 units/ml.
Lipase	Serum	2 ml.	0.2-1.5 units (ml.of N/10 NaOH)
Lipids, total	Serum		500-600 mg./100 ml.
Magnesium	Serum	2 ml.	1.5-2.5 mEq./L.; 1.8-3.0 mg./100 ml.
Nonprotein nitrogen‡	Serum or whole blood	1 ml.	15-35 mg./100 ml.
Osmolality	Serum	5 ml.	285-295 mOsm./Kg. water
Oxygen: Capacity	Blood	5 ml.	16-24 Vol.% (varies with Hgb. concentration).
Arterial content	Blood	5 ml.	15-23 Vol.% (varies with Hgb. concentration).
Arterial pO₂†	Blood	5 ml.	75-100 mm. Hg (sea level)
Arterial % sat.			94-100% of capacity
pCO₂†	Art. blood	5 ml.	35-45 mm. Hg
pH (reaction)†	Art. blood	2 ml.	7.35-7.45
Phenylalanine	Serum	1 ml.	0-2 mg./100 ml.
Phosphatase, acid	Serum	2 ml.	

Normal values (units): 1-5 (King-Armstrong), 0.5-2 (Bodansky), 0.5-2 (Gutman), 0-1.1 (Shinowara); 0.1-0.63 (Bessey-Lowry).

Phosphatase, alk.	Serum	2 ml.	

Normal values (units): Adults: 5-13 (King-Armstrong), 2-4.5 (Bodansky), 3-10 (Gutman), 2.2-8.6 (Shinowara); 0.8-2.3 (Bessey-Lowry); Children: 15-30 (King-Armstrong), 5-14 (Bodansky), 2.8-6.7 (Bessey-Lowry).

Phosphorus, inorganic	Serum	1 ml. fasting	3-4.5 mg./100 ml. (children, 4-7 mg.) 0.9-1.5 mM./L.
Phospholipid	Serum	2 ml.	145-200 mg./100 ml.
Potassium	Serum	1 ml.	3.5-5.0 mEq./L. 14-20 mg./100 ml.

*Minimum amount required for any procedure.
†Consult laboratory concerning amount required and special instructions.
‡Do not use anticoagulant containing ammonium oxalate.
§Separate serum immediately and freeze.

Determination	Material Analyzed	Amount*Req. Fasting State	Normal Value
Protein: Total	Serum	1 ml.	6-8 Gm./100 ml.
Albumin	Serum	1 ml.	3.5-5.5 Gm./100 ml.
Globulin	Serum		1.5-3 Gm./100 ml.
Fibrinogen	Plasma	1 ml.	0.2-0.6 Gm./100 ml.
Separation by electrophoresis:			
Albumin			52-68% (3.2-5.5 Gm.)
Globulin α_1			2.4-4.4% (0.2-0.4 Gm.)
α_2			6.1-10.1% (0.5-0.9 Gm.)
β			8.5-14.5% (0.6-1.1 Gm.)
γ			18.7-21.0% (0.7-1.7 Gm.)
Prothrombin clotting time	Plasma	2 ml.	By control.
Pyruvic acid†	Blood (in iodoacetate)		0.07-0.22 mM./L. 0.6-2.0 mg./100 ml.
Serotonin†	Blood		0.05-0.20 µg./ml.
Sodium	Serum	1 ml.	136-145 mEq./L. 310-335 mg./100 ml. (as Na)
Sulfate	Plasma or serum	2 ml.	0.5-1.5 mEq./L.
Transaminase (SGOT, SGPT)	Serum	1 ml.	10-40 units/ml.
Triglycerides	Serum	1 ml.	< 165 mg./100 ml.(5.4 mEq./L.)
Triiodothyronine (T_3) uptake†	Serum	3 ml.	10-14.6%
Urea nitrogens	Serum or whole blood	1 ml.	8-20 mg./100 ml.
Uric acid	Serum	1 ml.	3-7 mg./100 ml.
Specific gravity	Blood	0.1 ml.	1.056 (varies with Hgb. and protein concentration).
	Serum	0.1 ml.	1.0254-1.0288 (varies with protein concentration).
Blood volume (Evans Blue dye method)			Adults, 2990-6980 ml. Women, 46.3-85.5 ml./Kg. Men, 66.2-97.7 ml./Kg.

*Minimum amount required for any procedure.
†Consult laboratory concerning amount required and special instructions.

MISCELLANEOUS VALUES

Determination	Material Analyzed	Normal Value
Urobilinogen Fecal	Feces	40-280 mg./24 hours.
Urine	Urine	0.4 mg./24 hours.
ᴅ-Xylose absorption	Urine 5 hr. sample	5-8 Gm./5 hr. after ingestion 25 Gm. ᴅ-xylose
Congo Red	Serum	More than 60% retention in serum after 1 hour.
Insulin tolerance	Blood	Glucose level decreases to half of fasting level in 20-30 min.; returns to fasting level in 90-120 min.
Tolbutamide response	Blood	See p. 239. Endocrine function.
Fecal fat	Feces	Less than 30% of dry weight.

URINE VALUES

Determination	Normal Values

Addis test	Maximum in 24 hours:
	   Red cells: 1,000,000
	   White and epithelial: 2,000,000
	   Casts: 100,000
	   Protein: 30 mg.

Amylase	40-260 units/hour
Calcium	< 150 mg./24 hours
Copper	0-100 μg./24 hours
Creatine	< 100 mg./24 hours (see p. 189)
Creatinine	15-25 mg./Kg./24 hours
Lead	< 120 μg./24 hours

Porphyrins
  Coproporphyrin
  Uroporphyrin
	
	0-160 μg./24 hours
	0-26 μg./24 hours

Titratable acidity	20-40 mEq./24 hours
Uric acid	250-750 mg./24 hours
Urobilinogen	0-4 mg./24 hours

Hormone Excretion	Values per 24 Hours
Follicle stimulating hormone (FSH)	Before puberty: < 5 mouse uterine units (m.u.u.) Adult to menopause: 5 to 50 m.u.u. Postmenopausal and castration: up to 150 m.u.u. Adult male: up to 50 m.u.u.
Aldosterone	2-26 μg. Varies with Na and K intake.
11-17 Hydroxysteroid	Varies with method used. Men: 4-12 mg.; women: 4-8 mg.

17-Ketosteroid	Varies with method used.
	  Under 8 years: 0-2 mg.
	  Adolescent: 2-20 mg.
	  Men: 10-20 mg.
	  Women: 5-15 mg.

Catecholamine
  Epinephrine
  Norepinephrine
  Vanilmandelic acid (VMA)
	
	< 10 μg.
	< 100 μg.
	To 9 mg.

Estrogens (total)	Men: 4-25 μg.; women: 4-60 μg.

VITAMINS: SERUM VALUES

Vitamin A	Serum	15-60 μg./100 ml. 50-200 I.U./100 ml.
Thiamine	Serum	0.07-0.88 μg./100 ml.
Riboflavin	Serum	13-85 μg./100 ml.
Nicotinic acid	Serum	10-30 μg./100 ml.
B$_{12}$	Serum	100-900 $\mu\mu$g./ml.
Folic acid	Serum	5-24 μg./ml.
Ascorbic acid	Plasma	0.4-1.5 mg./100 ml.
	W.b.c.	25-40 mg./100 ml.

11...

Liver Function Tests

The varied functions of the liver, its functional reserve, and its tremendous capacity for regeneration render evaluation of "liver function" exceedingly difficult. It is also true that many of the "tests of liver function" are in a sense artificial since they employ agents with which the liver does not normally deal. Some signs of altered liver function assume significance only when interpreted in the light of adequate history and physical examination, for the same abnormal results of chemical and physiological tests may be obtained in other than hepatic disease (e.g., elevated globulin values and associated zinc turbidity values in infectious disease; elevated alkaline phosphatase in certain diseases of bone).

Liver function tests are most often employed to determine:

1. Presence of liver disease.
2. Type of liver disease.
3. Extent and progression of liver disease.

For the reasons mentioned above, the first two purposes of liver function testing are inadequately fulfilled. Carefully performed, however, the tests employed will indicate progression of disease or recovery.

Many tests that might be of value are too expensive or difficult to be readily available. In this discussion only those which can be performed in the average well-equipped laboratory and clinic will be considered.

TESTS OF EXCRETION BY THE LIVER

BILE PIGMENT

Serum bilirubin concentration depends on the rate of removal of bilirubin formed from destruction of hemoglobin. Increased bilirubin concentrations in the blood may result from (1) increased destruction of hemoglobin (hemolysis), or (2) decreased excretion or retention, due to either cellular or excretory duct disease of the liver.

Types of Bilirubin.

In the plasma, bilirubin is present as "indirect" reacting bilirubin, which is not water soluble; and "direct" reacting esterified bilirubin (bilirubin-glucuronide), which is water soluble. In the Van den Bergh reaction, the water-soluble ester reacts readily with diazo reagent ("direct reaction"): the addition of alcohol renders the unesterified bilirubin soluble so that diazotization may occur ("indirect reaction").

Bilirubinuria.

When bilirubin-glucuronide ("direct"-reacting) concentration in blood plasma exceeds 0.2 to 0.4 mg./100 ml., it will appear in the urine. Finding bilirubin in the urine is a valuable bit of evidence indicating hyperbilirubinemia due to hepatic cellular or duct disease; the urine tests may be positive before clinical levels of jaundice are reached.

URINE UROBILINOGEN

Urobilinogen is normally formed from bilirubin by bacterial action in the bowel. Normally, all urobilinogen absorbed from the gut is excreted by the liver, only up to 4 mg. appearing in the urine in 24 hours.

Urine Urobilinogen Increased (>4 mg./24 hours).

A. Impaired liver function or partial duct obstruction.
B. "Overloading" of the liver as a result of increased urobilinogen production following hemolytic disease.

Urine Urobilinogen Absent.

If biliary duct obstruction is complete, no bilirubin enters the gut, no urobilinogen is formed, and none is found in the urine or feces.

With these facts in mind, a study of the illustrations on pp. 210 and 211 reveals most of the causes of variation in urinary urobilinogen excretion.

FECAL UROBILINOGEN

If the hepato-biliary system is functioning normally, fecal urobilinogen varies directly with rate of r.b.c. hemolysis.

Fecal Urobilinogen Increased.

Occurs when blood destruction is increased and when biliary obstruction is relieved.

In the case of hemolysis, the daily excretion is related to the existing total body hemoglobin mass. If there is a reduced total body hemoglobin mass, accelerated rates of

BILIRUBIN-UROBILINOGEN CYCLE
(Solid Arrows = Bilirubin-Glucuronide.
Dotted Arrows = Urobilinogen)

NORMAL

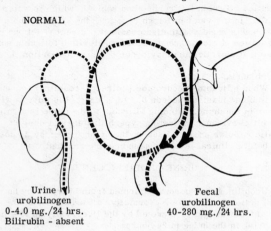

Urine
urobilinogen
0-4.0 mg./24 hrs.
Bilirubin - absent

Fecal
urobilinogen
40-280 mg./24 hrs.

HEMOLYTIC JAUNDICE
Bilirubin formation increased

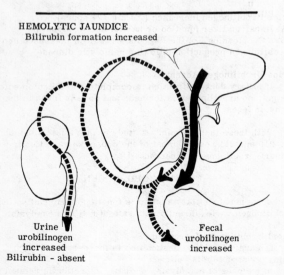

Urine
urobilinogen
increased
Bilirubin - absent

Fecal
urobilinogen
increased

BILIRUBIN-UROBILINOGEN CYCLE
(Solid Arrows = Bilirubin-Glucuronide.
Dotted Arrows = Urobilinogen)

HEPATITIS

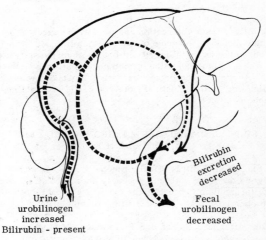

Urine
urobilinogen
increased
Bilirubin - present

Bilirubin
excretion
decreased

Fecal
urobilinogen
decreased

OBSTRUCTION

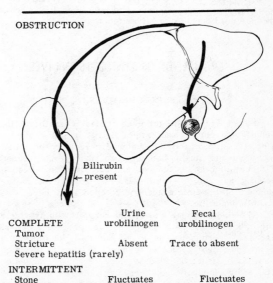

Bilirubin
← present

	Urine urobilinogen	Fecal urobilinogen
COMPLETE		
Tumor		
Stricture	Absent	Trace to absent
Severe hepatitis (rarely)		
INTERMITTENT		
Stone	Fluctuates	Fluctuates

hemolysis may only yield an amount of urobilinogen that would be within normal limits for an individual with normal hemo-globin mass.

Fecal Urobilinogen Absent.

Occurs with exclusion of bilirubin from the gut in com-plete biliary tract obstruction and in extreme cases of hepato-cellular disease. Absence of urobilinogen in feces is im-portant in indicating biliary tract obstruction; persistent ab-sence is a strong indication of malignant obstructive disease. Decreased fecal urobilinogen excretion may occur when anti-biotics which alter intestinal flora are used (tetracyclines, streptomycin, etc.).

SULFOBROMOPHTHALEIN (BROMSULPHALEIN®)
(B.S.P.) EXCRETION

Excretion of intravenously injected B.S.P. is almost en-tirely via the liver. This is probably the most satisfactory artificial medium for testing the excretory capacity of the liver when jaundice is absent. In the opinion of many, the most satisfactory test is that which measures retention 45 minutes after injection of B.S.P. in a dose of 5 mg./Kg. body weight. Minor elevation of retention may result from anemia, heart failure, thyrotoxicosis, and infectious diseases which produce mild reduction of liver function.

EVALUATION OF SYNTHESIS IN LIVER

SERUM PROTEINS

Because serum albumin and at least a small fraction of globulin are synthesized in the liver, serum proteins are affected both quantitatively and qualitatively in liver disease. In any disease causing hepatocellular damage the concentration of serum albumin decreases. In many liver diseases, serum globulin may rise to such levels as to maintain normal or in-creased total protein concentration even when there is severe albumin depletion.

The changing levels of serum albumin thus provide valu-able indices of severity, progress, and prognosis in hepatic disease. Decreased albumin and elevated globulin levels in serum indicate hepatocellular origin of jaundice or liver dis-ease. In obstructive jaundice, serum protein changes occur late, after secondary hepatocellular damage has occurred. Cholangitis and biliary cirrhosis, however, result in liver damage which may not be accompanied by protein alteration. Furthermore, serum protein changes may return to normal before convalescence from hepatitis is complete, and serum protein changes occur also in other than hepatic diseases. Interpretation of the significance of serum protein measurements thus requires care and judgment.

Special tests of serum protein alterations are as follows:
1. Total protein determination plus electrophoresis.
2. Cephalin-cholesterol flocculation.
3. Thymol turbidity.
4. Zinc turbidity.

Since tests 2, 3, and 4 are dependent upon globulin increase and, perhaps, upon alteration of albumin-globulin relationships, they provide a simple means of detecting changes in serum protein content. Because serum proteins are altered in many diseases, these tests are not specific for liver disease. They are of value, however, in differentiating cellular from obstructive hepatic disease, and, employed with appropriate reservations, they are of assistance in following the progress of hepatic disease. Persistent elevation of thymol or zinc turbidity may indicate persistently active hepatocellular disease; confirmation should be sought from other tests as indicated in the table on p. 216.

PROTHROMBIN CONCENTRATION

Prothrombin deficiency may occur as a result of (1) inadequate absorption of fat-soluble vitamin K because of absence of bile from the intestinal tract, or (2) inability of a damaged liver to convert vitamin K to prothrombin. A normal prothrombin concentration does not rule out abnormal liver function.

Low Prothrombin in the Presence of Jaundice.

When a low prothrombin level is found in a jaundiced patient, give 2 to 4 mg. vitamin K, I.V. or I.M., and measure prothrombin concentration 24 hours later.
A. A return of prothrombin concentration to approximately 85 to 100% of normal indicates that the capacity of liver cells to synthesize prothrombin is good.
B. A poor response indicates hepatocellular disease, either primary or following prolonged obstructive disease.

Low Prothrombin in the Absence of Jaundice.

In the absence of jaundice, a low prothrombin level usually indicates serious liver damage, and a failure of response to large doses of water-soluble vitamin K given parenterally (60 to 70 mg.) confirms the presence of severe liver damage. This is true also if jaundice is present.

CHOLESTEROL AND CHOLESTEROL ESTERS

Decrease of Both Substances.

With disease or damage of liver parenchyma, serum cholesterol and cholesterol esters may diminish. If cholesterol ester concentration is extremely low, parenchymal damage is usually extensive and the prognosis is poor. Persistently low cholesterol ester concentration or ester/total ratio indicates continuing hepatocellular damage; a rise in cholesterol ester often heralds improvement.

Increase of Total But Decrease of Esters.

With biliary obstruction, total cholesterol may rise but the cholesterol ester concentration is usually unaffected.

DETOXIFICATION

The liver removes noxious materials or renders them harmless by conjugation of toxic substances with amino acids, glucuronate and inorganic radicals (such as sulfate), by oxidation or reduction, and by excretion, etc.

Hippuric Acid Test. (Infrequently performed.)

This is a convenient function test which depends upon the conjugation of sodium benzoate with glycine to yield hippuric acid, which is excreted in the urine. Because of the irregularity of absorption of sodium benzoate when given orally, it is better to employ the intravenous route of administration. After injection of 1.77 Gm. of sodium benzoate intravenously, at least 0.7 Gm. hippuric acid will be excreted in the urine within 1 hour if liver and kidney function are normal. Acceptance of low values is permissible only if impaired renal function is not responsible for retention of hippuric acid.

EVALUATION OF ENZYME ACTIVITY

SERUM ALKALINE PHOSPHATASE

The concentration of this enzyme often increases in the plasma of an icteric patient. It is normally present in the liver and excreted in the bile, so that elevation of serum alkaline phosphatase may be a manifestation of retention; at least this is a convenient explanation for the observation that serum alkaline phosphatase concentration increases in obstructive jaundice. In acute and chronic hepatocellular disease, serum alkaline phosphatase is increased, but not to the degree characteristic of obstructive jaundice. In hemolytic disease, normal levels are the rule. In occasional cases of metastatic carcinoma of the liver, serum alkaline phosphatase may increase in the absence of jaundice. It is well to remember that phosphatase measurements may be normal early in the obstructive disease and with relief of obstruction. Such diseases as Paget's disease of bone, hyperparathyroidism, and rickets, which are associated with high serum alkaline phosphatase concentration, must be ruled out.

SERUM TRANSAMINASE

Liver and muscle are rich in enzymes of the Krebs cycle. Among such enzymes are a group involved in the transfer of NH_2 groups from amino acids to keto acids, thus providing for metabolism of amino acids. Destruction of muscle or of liver cells releases the enzymes, with resultant increase in concentration in the plasma. In obstructive jaundice and particularly in acute hepatitis, the levels of glutamic-oxaloacetic transaminase and of glutamic-pyruvic transaminase rise to very high levels (300 to 1500 units; normal is 5 to 40 units), as does the lactic dehydrogenase concentration also (normal, 200-450 units). Chronic hepatitis may produce moderate elevations of serum transaminase. Liver cell destruction incident to neoplastic disease metastatic to the liver will produce moderate elevation of transaminase concentration in the serum.

In many cases there seems to be a correlation between the differences in the degree of elevation of SGOT and SGPT and the cause of jaundice. Elevation of SGPT is greater than elevation of SGOT in extrahepatic obstruction, acute hepatitis, and toxic hepatitis; the reverse is true in cirrhosis of the liver, intrahepatic neoplasm, and hemolytic jaundice.

Other enzymes present in the liver are under investigation and may prove useful and reliable in the future. Among these are leucine aminopeptidase (obstructive jaundice, hepatic metastases), 5'-nucleotidase (obstructive jaundice), and isocitrate dehydrogenase (acute hepatitis).

SELECTION OF LIVER FUNCTION TESTS

Individual liver function tests are limited in significance and often are not specific for liver disease. These tests supplement the thorough examination of the patient. By employing a battery of tests, choice of which differs in the jaundiced and nonjaundiced patient, differential diagnosis may be facilitated. Serial repetition of a group of tests may be the only means of determining prognosis.

Some of the tests offer criteria for cure. Selection and interpretation must be based on the principles and limitations of the tests and must be correlated with clinical findings.

LIVER FUNCTION TESTS

LIVER FUNCTION	TESTS USED		NORMAL VALUES	USUAL RESPONSES TO TESTS	
				Hepatocellular Disease	Obstructive Disease
Excretion	Serum bilirubin	Direct	0.1-0.4 mg./100 ml.	Elevated	Elevated
Bile pigment		Indirect	0.2-0.7 mg./100 ml.	Elevated	Elevated
	Bilirubin, urinary		Absent	Present	Present
	Urobilinogen Urinary		0-4/24 hr.	Increased	Absent or variable
	Fecal		40-280 mg./24 hr.	Decreased	Absent or variable
Bromsulphalein®	B.S.P. (5 mg./Kg.)		0-5% retention after 45 minutes.	Retained	Rarely retained in non-jaundiced patients after relief of obstruction.
Synthesis	Serum protein	Albumin	4.5-5.5 Gm./100 ml.	Decreased	Normal or decreased
Protein		Globulin	1.5-3.0 Gm./100 ml.	Increased	Normal or decreased
	Cephalin flocculation (S)		0-1+ in 48 hrs.	Positive	Negative
	Thymol turbidity (S)		0-5 units	Increased	Normal
	Zinc turbidity (S)		0-12 units	Increased	Normal
Prothrombin from Vit. K	Prothrombin response		(See p. 211)	Poor	Rapid and complete
Cholesterol-cholesterol ester	Serum levels		150-240 mg./100 ml.	Slightly decreased	Greatly increased
			60% of total cholesterol	Greatly decreased	Slightly increased
Detoxification	Hippuric acid synthesis		Over 0.7 Gm. hippuric acid excreted in urine in 1 hr. after 1.77 Gm. sodium benzoate I.V.	Decreased	Normal
Miscellaneous	Serum alkaline phosphatase		2-4.5 Bodansky U. 5-13 King-Armstrong U.	Normal to slight increase	Increased
	Serum transaminase SGOT, SGPT		5-40 units	Increased	Normal or slightly increased

Suggested Liver Function Tests.

A. Jaundice Absent: Urine bilirubin, urine urobilinogen,
   serum bilirubin, Bromsulphalein® excretion, transami-
   nases, cephalin-cholesterol flocculation, thymol turbidity,
   zinc turbidity.

B. Jaundice Present: As above (but omitting B.S.P.), plus
   alkaline phosphatase, prothrombin response, serum proteins.

C. Possible Metastatic Cancer: Alkaline phosphatase, trans-
   aminases, bilirubin. If alkaline phosphatase and transam-
   inases are elevated in the presence of normal bilirubin
   and normal or slightly increased BSP retention, one
   should suspect metastatic cancer in the liver.

12...
Endocrine Function and Tests

Hormones are biologic substances which influence the biochemical reactions that occur in all bodily functions.

Disturbances in secretion of hormones are most frequently clinically apparent in the history and physical examination. Particular attention should be given to such items as changes in body weight, rate of growth, age at onset of puberty and menstruation; regularity, length, and amount of the menstrual flow; history of polyuria or polydipsia, libido, development of primary and secondary sex characteristics, quality of the hair and nails, condition and pigmentation of the skin, blood pressure, and body build and fat distribution. In addition to the routine hemogram and urinalysis, features of the history and physical examination provide indications for special laboratory and x-ray investigations. Surgical procedures, such as biopsy of bone or culdoscopy, may be required to obtain diagnostic data. The laboratory testing of endocrine function and the measurement of specific hormones establish the definitive diagnosis.

A great many specific tests of endocrine function are available to the clinician. The most useful and important of these have been outlined below, arranged in most cases in relationship to the gland whose performance they measure.

ANTERIOR PITUITARY

The anterior pituitary elaborates the following: (1) follicle-stimulating hormone (FSH), (2) interstitial cell–stimulating hormone (luteinizing hormone, LH, ICSH), (3) corticotropin (adrenocorticotropic hormone, ACTH), (4) thyroid-stimulating hormone (TSH), (5) prolactin (luteotropic hormone, LTH), (6) growth hormone (GH), and (7) melanocyte-stimulating hormone (MSH).

These hormones are large protein molecules, either glycoproteins (TSH, FSH, ICSH) or simple proteins (GH, LTH, ACTH, MSH).

The regulation of hormones elaborated by the endocrine glands is both complex and varied. The tropic hormones of the anterior pituitary are regulated by CNS factors (hypothalamic releasing hormones) as well as by the products of their specific target organs. A delicate balance is thus provided, as well as a mechanism for response to changes in environment. Antidiuretic hormone (ADH) is regulated by osmotic pressure and volume. Parathormone is controlled by calcium and phosphorus concentrations; norepinephrine and epinephrine by direct neural stimuli; and insulin secretion by blood glucose concentrations. MSH secretion is inhibited by glucocorticoids and causes skin pigmentation when cortisol is absent.

Clinical tropic hormone deficiencies may be single or multiple, caused by pressure (chromophobe tumors, craniopharyngioma) or intrinsic disorder (hemorrhage, infarction, functional hypopituitarism). If single, deficiency is most often of gonadotropins and leads to failure of development or involution of the sexual organs. Less often, TSH or ACTH are diminished. Tropic hormone excess is most often associated with pituitary tumors.

GROWTH HORMONE (GH)

Actions.

GH stimulates growth of all nonendocrine tissue in the body and may affect secretion of adrenal medulla and pancreas. Normal plasma levels are less than 3 mμg./ml. (females higher than males), and after insulin hypoglycemia rises to approximately 25 mμg./ml. It increases nonesterified fatty acids. Also, in diabetic and acromegalic patients it is diabetogenic. Only monkey and human GH produce nitrogen retention in man. GH may stimulate the growth of malignant craniopharyngioma.

Clinical Disorders.
  A. Deficiency: Dwarfism.
  B. Excess: Gigantism (prepuberal); acromegaly (post-puberal).

Methods of Evaluation.
Make studies of visual fields and growth records; x-ray of sella turcica and of hands for bone age and tufting of phalanges, as well as of spine for overgrowth of vertebrae and spur formation; BMR, serum phosphorus, glucose tolerance, insulin tolerance (**caution**). In acromegaly, plasma levels are greater than 10 mμg./ml. and do not suppress after glucose loads. In GH deficiency, low levels fail to increase after a hypoglycemic challenge.

CORTICOTROPIN (ACTH)

Actions.
Corticotropin stimulates production of all adrenocortical hormones (transient stimulatory effect on aldosterone) and causes hyperplasia of the adrenal cortex. In the adrenal it promotes increased protein synthesis, accelerates glycolysis, and increases steroidogenesis. Extra-adrenal actions include mobilization of nonesterified fatty acids from fat depots.

Clinical Disorders.
A. Deficiency: Pituitary adrenal insufficiency.
B. Excess: Cushing's disease. (Corticotropin-like substances elaborated by malignant tissue, particularly in the lung, pancreas, or prostate, may also lead to Cushing's disease.)

Methods of Evaluation.
Make x-ray of sella turcica; study basal excretion of 17-hydroxysteroids; assess diurnal patterns; study plasma cortisol levels. (See also Cushing's syndrome, p. 245.) Corticotropin lack is indicated by (1) failure of adrenocortical function; (2) low 24-hour urinary excretion of 17-ketosteroids and 17-hydroxycorticoids, which increase stepwise in response to daily corticotropin administration; or (3) a failure of hydroxycorticoid excretion to increase following administration of metyrapone, which blocks the production of cortisol and results in increase of corticotropin production by the intact hypophysis (see p. 247); (4) normal or slightly reduced aldosterone excretion; (5) normal plasma ACTH levels are barely detectable − less than 0.5 mU./100 ml. plasma.

THYROID-STIMULATING HORMONE (TSH)

Actions.
TSH stimulates thyroid hormone production and accelerates its proteolytic release from thyroglobulin. It causes thyroid hyperplasia.

Clinical Disorders.
A. Deficiency: Pituitary myxedema, hypothyroidism.
B. Excess: May cause hyperthyroidism and hyperplasia in thyrotoxicosis; may intensify existing diabetic state. A separate exophthalmogenic factor may arise in the pituitary.

Methods of Evaluation.
Deficiency is suggested by increase in parameters of thyroid function after TSH is given. See p. 227 for tests of hyperthyroidism and hypothyroidism.

GONADOTROPINS: FOLLICLE-STIMULATING HORMONE (FSH) AND LUTEINIZING HORMONE (LH)

Actions.

FSH stimulates growth of ovarian follicle in women and spermatogenesis in men. In women, LH is responsible - after the initial action of FSH - for estrogen secretion, follicle maturation, ovulation, and corpus luteum formation. In men, LH stimulates Leydig cells and production of androgens and estrogens in the testis. Plasma levels of LH show a mid-cycle surge at ovulation for several days. Levels during the luteal phase are somewhat lower than during the follicular phase of menstrual cycle.

Clinical Disorders.
  A. Deficiency: Hypogonadism, infertility.
  B. Excess: Precocious puberty, functional uterine bleeding, persistent corpora lutea or corpus luteum cysts.

Methods of Evaluation.

Methods include study of urinary excretion of gonado-tropins in 24 hours; radioimmunoassay of LH and FSH in plasma; clinical estimation of gonadal function in male or female; clinical improvement and increase in urinary 17-keto-steroid, testosterone, and estrogen excretion following in-jection of chorionic gonadotropin indicate pituitary gonado-tropin deficiency.

Pituitary gonadotropins are usually the first tropic hor-mones to be lost when the pituitary is affected by starvation, pressure, or loss of blood supply. The determination of these hormones and their fractionation (FSH excretion high in menopausal women, LH extremely high in young men) permit estimation of anterior pituitary function. The action of pla-cental chorionic gonadotropic hormone resembles that of LH.

The patient should not receive androgen, estrogen, corti-cotropin (ACTH), or corticosteroid therapy for one month prior to collection of specimen.

The procedure is as follows: Urine is collected over a 24-hour period and the determination performed as soon as possible. If there is to be a delay, the urine should be kept under refrigeration; a chemical preservative is not usually added.

Very little gonadotropin is excreted until puberty, when it increases rapidly. The normal range for men and women between puberty and the climacteric is 5 to 50 mouse uterine units (0 to 25 rat units) per 24 hours. In women, relative peaks in gonadotropin excretion occur at ages 14 to 16 and 50 to 60. Postmenopausal women may excrete up to 800 mouse uterine units per 24 hours (five times more than men and 20 times more than normally menstruating women). Excretion levels vary greatly at all ages.

Maximum gonadotropin excretion in menstruating patients occurs about two weeks before the next expected period.

Subnormal gonadotropin excretion occurs with diminution of hypothalamic or pituitary function. Excessive quantities of estrogen inhibit FSH production, and increased excretion of gonadotropins occurs with gonadal failure in men or women. The test thus helps in differentiating primary gonadal failure from that secondary to pituitary failure. Small amounts of FSH (2.5 to 3 mouse uterine units per 12 hours) are excreted in anorexia nervosa; none is excreted in panhypopituitarism. High levels of FSH are usually found in gonadal dysgenesis and in Klinefelter's syndrome.

Prolactin (LTH).

Prolactin stimulates the production of progesterone and may maintain the corpus luteum of pregnancy. It increases mammary growth and causes lactation in the steroid-prepared breast.

POSTERIOR PITUITARY

The posterior pituitary elaborates (1) antidiuretic hormone (ADH, vasopressin), with pressor and antidiuretic action, only the latter of which is of importance in man; and (2) oxytocic hormone, which may play a role in parturition.

Elaboration of ADH is initiated by increase in the extracellular fluid osmotic pressure; by direct nervous system stimulation of the hypothalamus; and, to a minor degree, by extracellular fluid volume. It may be formed by neurosecretory cells in the supraoptic or paraventricular nuclei of the hypothalamus, and travel along axons to the posterior lobe where it is stored. Lesions at any of these sites interfere with ADH release to the body.

Actions.

ADH increases renal tubular reabsorption of water (antidiuretic action), and raises blood pressure by constricting arteries and capillaries (vasopressor effect). Oxytocic hormone stimulates smooth muscle of the intestine, the uterus, and other organs (oxytocic effect).

Clinical Disorders.

A. Deficiency of ADH: ADH deficiency produces diabetes insipidus if the anterior pituitary is still functioning.
B. Excess ADH; Syndrome of Inappropriate ADH Secretion: Findings consist of hyponatremia, normal BUN, urinary sodium loss, competent circulatory system, and in-

creased urinary osmolality. These findings are similar to the observations made after exogenous administration of ADH to man. This syndrome is seen most frequently in pulmonary neoplasms but is reported in CNS disorders, tuberculous meningitis, head trauma, pneumonia, intrathoracic tumors, myxedema, and acute intermittent porphyria. Neoplastic tissue in some cases has been shown to possess ADH activity.

Methods of Evaluation.

Study for intracranial lesion (lumbar puncture, skull film, electroencephalogram), serologic test for syphilis, chest x-ray (metastases), bone marrow studies (multiple myeloma, eosinophilic granuloma). However, 45% are classified as idiopathic. Differentiate diabetes insipidus from psychogenic diuresis by hypertonic saline test; from chronic nephritis or ADH-resistant diabetes insipidus (10 to 15% of cases) by administration of vasopressin (Pitressin®). The simple measurement of a urine volume of more than 5 L./day is strong presumptive evidence of deficiency.

A. Water Restriction: While this is quite simple, careful supervision is necessary so that losses of 3 to 5% of body weight are avoided. Be extremely careful in children. Volume and concentration (specific gravity or mOsm./Kg.) are determined at each voiding. Urine flow should reach less than 0.5 ml./minute and urine concentration should be greater than 800 mOsm./Kg. (sp. gr. 1.020).

B. Hypertonic Saline Test (Carter-Robbins Test, Hickey-Hare Test): This test is used to differentiate psychogenic polydipsia from diabetes insipidus. Caution is required, since dehydration may cause vasomotor collapse in patients with diabetes insipidus. Administration of hypertonic saline solution may be hazardous in cardiac or renal disease.

Antidiuretic therapy is stopped until urine output reaches its original level. The patient may be cautiously dehydrated for eight to 12 hours, or this step may be omitted. Just before the test, the patient drinks 20 ml. of water per Kg. body weight in 1 hour. Urine is collected at 15-minute intervals.

When the urine flow exceeds 5 ml. per minute, 2.5% saline solution is given I.V. at a rate of 0.25 ml. per Kg. body weight per minute for 45 minutes.

In normal subjects and in psychogenic polydipsia, a marked reduction in urinary flow will occur during the saline infusion or during the two 15-minute periods immediately following it.

In 85 to 95% of patients with true diabetes insipidus, the urine flow does not decrease with the saline infusion, but administration of 0.1 unit of vasopressin (Pitressin®)

will inhibit diuresis in the absence of renal disease.

C. Response to Vasopressin (Pitressin®): This test also differentiates diabetes insipidus from chronic nephritis and pitressin-resistant polyuria due to other causes, e.g., potassium depletion, hypercalcemia. Be sure vasopressin is thoroughly mixed in the vial.

Urine volume and specific gravity and symptoms of polyuria and polydipsia are observed before and after repeated subcutaneous injections of 0.2 ml. (4 units) vasopressin every three or four hours day and night for 24 hours or before and after one-hour infusion of aqueous vasopressin (5 milliunits per minute).

Patients with chronic nephritis or vasopressin-resistant diabetes insipidus experience no relief of symptoms during test period. In diabetes insipidus or psychogenic polydipsia, symptoms may improve, urine volume may decrease, urine specific gravity may increase to 1.015 or more, and urine osmolality may rise above serum osmolality.

D. Nicotine Stimulation: Numerous untoward reactions (nausea, vomiting, perspiration) limit the usefulness of this test. 0.5 to 1 mg. of nicotine base to non-smokers and doses as high as 3 mg. to habitual smokers are given I.V. to patients undergoing water diuresis. The normal response to intravenous nicotine is secretion of vasopressin, 80% reduction in urine flow, and rise in osmolality. Responsiveness to nicotine but not to hypertonic stimulus suggests that osmoreceptor centers are functionally separate from vasopressin sensory centers.

THYROID

The thyroid elaborates thyroxine and 3,5,3-triiodothyronine $(T_3)(3-7:1)$ which circulate; and thyroglobulin in colloid. Thyroxine and triiodothyronine (T_3) are iodine-containing amino acids. Thyroglobulin is a protein with a molecular weight of 675,000.

About one-third of the iodine absorbed from the intestine into the plasma is trapped by the thyroid gland (a process blocked by thiocyanate, perchlorate, and iodine itself). The amino acid tyrosine is iodinated to monoiodo- and diiodotyrosine (blocked by the antithyroid goitrogens, propylthiouracil and methimazole). Molecules of this compound couple to form triiodothyronine (T_3) and thyroxine (T_4), which are stored in the thyroglobulin molecule until they are released to the circulation by proteolysis (accelerated by TSH or cold environment and decreased by iodine). A specific plasma protein system binds T_4 and, to a lesser extent, T_3. T_4 is also bound to thyroxine-binding prealbumin and albumin. The residual binding capacity is decreased in thyrotoxicosis and nephrosis and increased by myxedema, normal pregnancy, estrogen administration, or iodide or propylthiouracil therapy of thyrotoxicosis. Free thyroxine is present in serum at a mean concentration of 2.76 mμg./100 ml. T_3 is more potent than T_4 and has more rapid onset and cessation of action. Iodine may be released to the circulation from mono- and di-iodotyrosine and reused in hormone synthesis.

Antibodies to thyroglobulin (and possibly to thyroid follicular epithelium also) have been demonstrated in the sera of patients with Hashimoto's thyroiditis, in about 80% of patients with primary myxedema, and in about 60% of patients with thyrotoxicosis. Experimentally these antibodies may result in direct cytotoxicity to thyroid tissue. Various types of cretinism may be traced to abnormalities in virtually any step of the pathway from iodine uptake to release of active hormone. The thyroid hormones inactivate TSH and inhibit its production by the anterior pituitary, possibly through neurohypophysial action; conversely, a decreased level of circulating thyroid hormone increases TSH production.

A long-acting thyroid stimulator (LATS), a 7S gamma globulin, has been identified that is not thyrotropin; the pituitary is not directly involved in its production. LATS may be an integral component in the pathogenesis of hyperthyroidism. A role in the production of ophthalmopathy and pretibial myxedema is also suggested for LATS.

Actions.

Thyroid hormones affect the rate of metabolism, growth, development, and differentiation. The thyroxine effect appears in 7 to 12 hours after administration, is greater at 4 to 8 days, and disappears in 4 to 8 weeks. The T_3 effect appears in 4 to 8 hours and lasts for 3 days. Careful adjustment of dosage may reduce hypercholesterolemia without increasing total body metabolism. There is no evidence that this reduction is a specific effect of a separate chemical analog.

Clinical Disorders.

In infants and children, deficiency of hormone (often due to defects in hormone synthesis) may cause cretinism or juvenile myxedema, with failure of growth and development and mental retardation. In adults, hypothyroidism manifested by cold intolerance, decreased sweating, weight gain, constipation, skin and hair changes, amenorrhea or menorrhagia, and slow tendon reflexes is not unusual.

Excess thyroid hormone causes thyrotoxicosis, with clinical evidence of autonomic nervous system overactivity and hypermetabolism. Exophthalmos, myopathy, and skin lesions may or may not be present.

Methods of Evaluation.

Inquire as to intake of goitrogens (rutabaga, turnips, kale, cabbage, cobalt) or iodine, physical examination, BMR, protein-bound iodine or butanol-extractable iodine determination, free thyroxine, radioactive iodine uptake by thyroid, excretion in urine, or incorporation in protein-bound iodine; erythrocyte uptake of ^{131}I-ʟ-triiodothyronine (T_3 uptake), blood cholesterol (especially when determined before and after trial of therapy with thyroid), electrocardiogram, response to TSH and to thyroxine suppression, exophthalmometer readings, chest films, bone age films, and barium swallow and thyroid scintigram to show substernal thyroid.

It is now possible to assess defects in the formative stages of thyroid hormone and to detect antibodies to thyroid components. Each test of thyroid function must be correlated with the clinical findings.

Comparison of the Various Thyroid Tests.

Properly performed, the BMR is useful in the diagnosis of both hypothyroid and hyperthyroid states; it is relatively free from drug-induced interference, and is particularly valuable in following the course of the patient under treatment.

Borderline hypothyroidism is best detected by the following tests: free thyroxine, protein-bound iodine (PBI) or butanol-extractable iodine (BEI), T_3 red blood cell uptake, blood cholesterol, and occasionally by therapeutic trial of desiccated thyroid or, for prompter results, T_3. In children a fall in blood cholesterol after thyroid administration is a valuable index of hypothyroidism. An elevated blood cholesterol is seldom associated with pituitary myxedema.

In hyperthyroid states, the free thyroxine, the PBI, and the thyroid uptake of ^{131}I 6 hours or less after oral or I. V. administration are most valuable. They assess diffuse thyroid hyperfunction more accurately than toxic nodules.

Thyroid function is best assayed by the use of several of the tests listed above. If inorganic iodine has been taken (e.g., Lugol's solution, kelp), the BEI or the free thyroxine test should be used since nonhormonal iodine is usually insoluble in butanol. The serum PBI may be decreased to the hypothyroid range by the administration of T_3. Cobalt or other antithyroid drugs, thyroid, exogenous iodine, and phenylbutazone may depress radioiodine uptake. Radioiodine excretion in 24 hours is valid only if renal function is good. Scintigraphic studies are useful to show the size, shape, and location and the relative functional activity of different parts of the thyroid gland, information most useful where malignancy is suspected. In subacute thyroiditis, the PBI, sedimentation rate, thyroglobulin-reacting antibodies, and white blood count are often elevated. After iodine or thyroid administration, PBI may be high and iodine uptake low.

A. Free Thyroxine: This measurement is the closest approximation of the level of thyroxine affecting the cell. It is not affected by pregnancy or other factors modifying thyroid-binding globulin.
   1. Procedure - Performed on serum.
   2. Interpretation - The normal mean value is 2.76 mμg./ 100 ml. The hyperthyroid mean value is 13.08 mμg./ 100 ml. (four times the normal) and the hypothyroid mean value is 0.38 mμg./100 ml. (one-seventh of the normal). The mean value in pregnancy is 2.35 mμg./ 100 ml.

B. Other Tests to Determine Concentration of Hormone in Blood:
   1. T_4-iodine - T_4 is separated from iodinated materials by column or thin layer chromatography. The iodine content of the separated T_4 is measured.
   2. T_4 by binding displacement - This method is not dependent on iodine measurement. Extracted hormone is added to a solution of labeled T_4, serum protein, and buffer.
      The displacement of labeled T_4 is compared to a standard curve obtained by adding known increments of T_4 to the binding mixture. Iodinated materials have little influence in this technic.

C. Protein-Bound Iodine (PBI); Butanol-Extractable Iodine (BEI): Butanol-extractable iodine (BEI) should be determined if the total blood iodine (normally 5 to 15 μg./100 ml.) is elevated. Iodine contamination of syringes, skin, test tubes, etc. used in the test must be rigorously avoided. X-ray contact media, thyroid, thyroxine, oral contraceptives, stilbestrol, and some phenothiazines increase PBI; T_3, testosterone, methyltestosterone, norethandrolone (Nilevar®), methandrostenolone (Dianabol®), diphenylhydantoin (Dilantin®), mercurial diuretics, and large doses of chlorpromazine reduce PBI.
   1. Procedure - The skin is sterilized without the use of iodine, and 10 ml. of whole blood are withdrawn into iodine-free glassware.
   2. Interpretation - Some variation exists in different laboratories. Average range of normals is 5 to 8 μg. of PBI and 4 to 7 μg. of BEI per 100 ml. of serum. Elevated PBI levels may occur in patients with acute thyroiditis, in the presence of pregnancy, following ingestion of iodides or thyroid (effect lasts 2 to 4 weeks), or in those who have had pyelograms, cholecystograms, and particularly bronchograms and myelograms (effect lasts 1 to 5 years, invalidates BEI). High PBI levels in acute thyroiditis often fall to less than normal in the postacute and chronic phases of the disease.
      In almost all patients with thyrotoxicosis, the levels of PBI are elevated; in about 80% of patients

with myxedema, the PBI levels are reduced; in mild hypothyroidism, levels often fall within the lower limits of normal (4-6 μg./100 ml.) and complementary tests, such as the T_3 uptake, should be used.

D. Radioactive Iodine (^{131}I) Uptake: The rate of uptake of a tracer dose of ^{131}I is particularly valuable (as in the PBI) in the diagnosis of hyperthyroidism. The excretion of radioactive iodine in the urine is elevated in hypothyroidism and reduced in hyperthyroidism, although considerable day-to-day variation in intake may occur.

A scintigram may be plotted using a scintillation counter, and is recorded on paper by a scanning device positioned over the neck. Most thyroid carcinomas do not accept radioiodine, and this condition is found four times as frequently in nonfunctioning or multiple nodules.

Prior administration of antithyroid drugs, thyroid, or iodine-containing medications will invalidate radioiodine studies for two to four weeks, and organic iodine x-ray contrast media reduce uptakes for a much longer time. Pregnant women should not be given radioiodine; lactating women should not receive more than 5 μc.

1. Procedure - A tracer dose of 50 to 100 μc of ^{131}I (with the use of a scintillation detector, 1 to 10 μc) may be administered orally or I.V. After ten minutes, one hour, six hours, or 24 hours, radioactivity may be measured over the thyroid or in the urine and expressed as a percentage of the dose given.

2. Interpretation - Diffuse toxic goiters usually take up more radioiodine than do toxic nodular goiters or thyroid remnants with recurrent activity following surgery or radioiodine. Hyperthyroid patients often show less than normal suppression of ^{131}I uptake following the administration of triiodothyronine (T_3), 75 μg. daily for one week. When this test is performed following antithyroid drug therapy, a patient whose uptake suppression is less than 65% often relapses.

Radioiodine uptake studies are most useful in detection of hyperthyroidism. The uptake may be high in iodine-deficient goiter, but since the iodine remains unbound it is rapidly discharged following the administration of potassium thiocyanate.

	^{131}I Uptake					^{131}I Excretion in urine in 24 hours
	Oral			I.V.		
	One hour	Six hours	24 hours	One hour	24 hours	
Normal	9-19%	7-25%	10-50%	up to 11%	10-40%	40-70%
Hyperthyroidism	>20%	>25%	> 50%	>11%	> 40%	5-40%
Hypothyroidism	< 9%	< 7%	<10-15%	< 5%	<10-15%	70-90%

E. Erythrocyte Uptake of ^{131}I-L-Triiodothyronine (T_3 Red Cell Uptake) (Resin Uptake Test):

1. Procedure - This test requires no administration of radioactive material. Three ml. of freshly drawn whole blood are used, or a patient's serum may be sent by mail to the laboratory where fresh red cells or a resin of a standard type are added. The sample is then mixed with tracer amounts of ^{131}I-T_3, incubated and shaken, and measured for radioactivity in a well-type scintillation counter. The red cells are then separated and washed with saline, and the radioactivity of the red cell mass is determined and corrected for the hematocrit. The test indicates the saturation of thyroid-binding globulin. Greater saturation of this carrier protein in hyperthyroidism permits ^{131}I-T_3 to enter the red cells more readily; conversely, the relative unsaturation which occurs in hypothyroidism could allow less ^{131}I-T_3 to enter the red cells. Current technics using resin T_3 uptake have different values. Check with the reporting laboratory.

2. Interpretation - Normal uptake ranges from 11 to 17% in females and 11 to 19% in males. Results are not invalidated by the ingestion of kelp or iodine medication, but opinion is divided concerning the effect of prior x-ray contrast media. The test demonstrates hyperthyroidism more reliably than deficiency and is particularly useful in pregnancy, where the BMR, PBI, and radioiodine uptake levels are high but (in the absence of hyperthyroidism) the T_3 red cell uptake is low. Estrogen administration also reduces uptake levels. The uptake rises in nephrosis, liver failure, carcinomatosis, pulmonary insufficiency, tachycardias, and after the administration of anticoagulants.

F. Basal Metabolic Rate (BMR): The BMR is a determination of the amount of oxygen consumed by a patient in the basal state within a given interval. It is difficult to perform accurately because many patients are unable to remain at a basal level while breathing in a closed system.

1. Procedure - The patient should eat nothing after the evening meal and ideally should remain at rest in the morning until the test is completed. A sedative may be administered at bedtime the night before the test if the patient is otherwise unable to sleep. If it is necessary for the patient to travel on the morning of the test, he should be allowed to rest in a relatively dark, quiet room for at least 30 minutes before the test.

Oxygen consumption is measured for two six-minute periods with the patient awake and completely at rest. In nervous patients, the somnolent metabolic rate (SMR, 8 to 13% lower than the BMR) may be determined following the administration of pentobarbital sodium, I.V.

The graph with the least slope is usually the most accurate, and an adequate base line should be apparent. Repeated determinations are more reliable than a single observation.

2. Interpretation - The normal BMR is usually determined from tables, according to age, sex, and surface area. In men it is about 40 Cal. and in women about 35 Cal./sq.M./hour. The BMR is given in percent of this normal, and the normal variation is ± 15%. Minimal metabolic activity is reached during sleep and averages 90% of the waking BMR. Maximal metabolism occurs during exercise, when it may be increased 600 to 800% above the BMR. The BMR increases approximately 7% for each Fahrenheit degree of fever.

Extrathyroidal factors which increase the BMR include failure to achieve basal rate, food or drug ingestion, leakage of oxygen from the apparatus or through a perforated eardrum, patient activity, congestive heart failure, pregnancy, obstructions of the tracheobronchial tree, and infections; excess of metabolizing cells, as in leukemia or polycythemia; and such endocrine diseases as acromegaly, pheochromocytoma, and diabetes insipidus.

Extrathyroidal factors which decrease the BMR include use of exhausted soda lime, beginning the test with underexpansion of the chest, malnutrition, Addison's disease, nephrosis, postinfectious asthenia, and shock.

G. TSH Stimulation Test: Thyrotropin stimulates the thyroid gland inactivated by thyroid or by the lack of endogenous TSH (in pituitary myxedema). The degree of response may be demonstrated by the usual thyroid function tests. Hypersensitivity to proteins is a contraindication, but the test may be performed while the patient is taking thyroid.

1. Procedure - After determination of BMR and particularly PBI and radioactive iodine uptake, give pituitary thyroid-stimulating hormone (TSH), 10 U.S.P. units I.M. After 24 hours the tests done previously are repeated.

2. Interpretation - Normal response is a two-fold increase in the radioactive iodine uptake. Primary hypothyroidism shows little or no response. Long-standing pituitary insufficiency may require three to seven days of TSH stimulation.

H. Antithyroglobulin Antibody Titer: High titers are found in chronic (Hashimoto's) thyroiditis and in some cases of myxedema. The test may be useful in establishing the etiology of the hypothyroid state.

THYROCALCITONIN
(Calcitonin)

Thyrocalcitonin is a 32 amino acid peptide produced in the parafollicular cells of the thyroid (ultimobranchial body embryologically). The main effect in man is to inhibit bone resorption; it lowers serum calcium and phosphorus. Hypocalcemia decreases thyrocalcitonin secretion; hypercalcemia increases thyrocalcitonin secretion. A syndrome of thyrocalcitonin excess - medullary carcinoma of the thyroid - is recognized in man. Little effect on calcium homeostasis is observed.

PARATHYROID

Parathyroid hormone has been isolated as a pure and single protein with a molecular weight of approximately 8500. Its production by the gland varies inversely with the plasma level of ionized calcium, which is ordinarily maintained within normal limits.

Actions.

Parathyroid hormone acts by controlling metabolic reactions which (1) increase calcium and phosphorus reabsorption from bones; (2) increase calcium reabsorption and phosphate excretion in the renal tubule; (3) increase absorption of calcium from the gastrointestinal tract; and (4) decrease calcium secretion in the lactating breast. Secondary hyperparathyroidism may follow renal insufficiency.

Clinical Disorders.
  A. Deficiency: Tetany (acute deficiency); hypoparathyroidism (chronic deficiency), often with epileptiform seizures.
  B. Excess: Hyperparathyroidism with symptoms of hypercalcemia, renal calculi, bone reabsorption, sometimes peptic ulcer, hypertension, pancreatitis.

Methods of Evaluation.

X-ray of the bones of the hands, teeth, and skull, I.V. pyelogram, serum calcium (repeated, as often inaccurate in unspecialized laboratories), serum phosphorus, urine calcium, serum alkaline phosphatase, bone biopsy. Calcium and phosphorous tolerance, reabsorption, and excretion tests (see below). Ellsworth-Howard test (see p. 234). Test response of elevated calcium level to cortisone administration. Reduced blood magnesium levels (1.5-1.8 mg./100 ml.) are frequent in hypoparathyroidism. Serum protein should be de-

DISEASES OF CALCIUM AND PHOSPHORUS METABOLISM
(Compiled From Albright)

(L = low. N = normal. H = high. VH = very high.)

Cause	Disease Entity	Serum			Urine on Low-Ca Diet	
		Ca	P	Alk. P'tase	Ca	P
Vitamin D deficit and deficient calcium absorption	Rickets (child)	L to N	L	H to VH	L	L
	Osteomalacia (adult) (often accompanies steatorrhea)	L to N	L	H	L	L
Vitamin D excess	"Hypercalcemia with metastatic calcification"	H	L to H	N	H	H
Parathormone excess	Hyperparathyroidism; osteitis fibrosa (generalized) if Ca and P intake is low	H*	L†	H to VH (but normal if no bone dis.)	H	H
Parathormone deficiency	Hypoparathyroidism	L	H	N	L	L
Associated with renal disease: Glomerular disease	Renal "rickets" is secondary to hyperparathyroidism	L	H‡	N or H	L	L
Tubular disorders	Osteomalacia;					
	1. Fanconi syn.	L to N	L	N to H	H	H
	2. Renal tubular acidosis	L to N	L	N to H	H	N to H
Endocrine disease other than parathyroid	Osteoporosis:					
	1. Postmenopausal	N	N	N	N to H	N
	2. Thyrotoxicosis	N to H	N	N	N	N
	3. Cushing's disease	N	N	N	N to H	N
	4. Acromegaly	N	N§	N	N to H	N
	5. Addison's disease	N to H	N	N	-	-
Miscellaneous (not all involve calcium and phosphorus except as disease of bone)	Osteoporosis of:					
	1. Disuse with age	N	N	N	N to H	N to H
	2. Immobilization	N to H	N	N	H	H
	Paget's disease	N	N to H	H to VH	N to H	H
	Polyostotic fibrous dysplasia	N	N	N to H	N	N
	Metastatic neoplasm	N to H	N	N** to H	N to H	H
	Multiple myeloma	N to H	N to H	N	N to H	N to H
	Boeck's sarcoid	N to (?)H	N	N to H	H	N
	Hypercalcemia and excess alkali intake (Burnett's syndrome)	H	N to H	N	N	N

*90% (>11 mg./100 ml.)

†90% (<3 mg./100 ml.)

‡Serum P high in renal disease due to retention by kidneys.

§May be high.   **Phosphatase is high if bone is being formed.

termined, as one-half of serum calcium is protein-bound.
(See chart, p. 232.) Specific tests are noted below.

A. Serum Calcium: Hyperparathyroidism is suggested by
   the repeated finding of serum calcium levels above 11 mg./
   100 ml. Hypercalcemia also occurs in multiple myeloma,
   sarcoidosis, the milk-alkali syndrome, vitamin D intoxication, acute osteoporosis, Addison's disease, after
   electroshock therapy, in the presence of metastatic malignant disease with or without bone involvement, and in
   thyrotoxicosis.

   On a neutral ash diet containing about 100 mg. of
   calcium per day, the normal person excretes 125 ±
   50 mg. of calcium per 24 hours. If milk or cheese is
   not present in the diet the urine normally forms a slight
   cloud when Sulkowitch reagent is added (see p. 118). In
   hyperparathyroidism, which may be intermittent, hypercalcemia is usually associated with a daily urinary excretion greater than 200 mg. Hypercalcemia due to this
   cause is usually unaffected by corticoids (hydrocortisone,
   100 mg. per day, or prednisone, 20 mg. per day, for one
   week), which decrease hypercalcemia in sarcoidosis,
   infantile hypercalcemia, metastatic malignancy, the
   usual case of vitamin D intoxication, and miliary tuberculosis. Bone biopsy and tracer studies are just now
   emerging as diagnostic tools.

B. Tubular Reabsorption of Phosphate (TRP) (Gordan): This
   test may indicate hyperparathyroidism in patients with
   good renal function and a daily phosphate intake of 800
   mg. or more. False positives may occur with uremia
   and in some cases of renal tubular disease, sarcoidosis,
   and osteomalacia.

   1. Procedure - A constant diet containing moderate
      amounts of calcium and phosphate is given for three
      days. Fasting blood is drawn in the morning when a
      timed four-hour urine specimen is collected.

      Urine phosphate (UP) and creatinine (UC) (in mg.
      excreted/min.) and serum phosphate (SP) and creati-
      nine (SC) (in mg./100 ml.) are determined. Formula:

      $$\text{TRP (in \%)} = 100 \left\{ 1 - \frac{\text{UP} \times \text{SC}}{\text{UC} \times \text{SP}} \right\}$$

   2. Interpretation - TRP is above 78% on a normal diet,
      higher on a low-phosphate diet (430 mg. per day for
      3 days). In hyperparathyroidism, the TRP is 74% or
      less after a normal diet, 85% or less on a low-phos-
      phate diet.

C. Deprivation of Phosphate: A low-phosphate diet (e.g.,
   2000 Calories, 430 mg. phosphate, 700 mg. calcium)
   for three to six days may produce pathologically lowered

blood phosphate levels and definitely elevated calcium levels in hyperparathyroidism but not in normal persons. Such a diet appears to be diagnostically useful in patients with borderline chemical values.

D. Phosphate Clearance:
1. Procedure - The patient eats an otherwise unrestricted 800 mg. phosphate per day diet, a 12-hour urine collection is made, and the serum phosphorus is assayed midway through the collection. Simultaneous blood urea nitrogen or nonprotein nitrogen determinations are performed.
2. Interpretation - Phosphate clearance is normally 6 to 17 ml. per minute, higher in hyperparathyroidism despite severe renal dysfunction. In hypoparathyroidism, phosphate clearance is below 6 ml. per minute even though hypocalcemia has been corrected.

E. Calcium Tolerance Test:
1. Procedure - On a constant diet, three consecutive 24-hour urines are collected and measured for phosphate. On the second day, a four-hour infusion of 1 L. of normal saline solution containing calcium gluconate-glucoheptonate (in a quantity sufficient to provide 15 mg. of calcium/Kg. ideal body weight) is given.
2. Interpretation - A normal response consists of a marked reduction of urinary phosphate on the day of calcium infusion and a rebound increase on the third day. In hyperparathyroidism, minor alterations in urinary phosphate excretion are observed.

F. Ellsworth-Howard Test: This test distinguishes hypoparathyroidism from pseudohypoparathyroidism, in which the level of parathyroid hormone is adequate but the renal tubules are unresponsive. Anaphylactoid reactions to parathyroid extract may occur. Be sure the extract used is phosphuretic in humans and renal function is adequate.
1. Procedure - The fasting patient is given 2 ml. (200 units) of parathyroid extract I. V. The urinary phosphorus content is determined hourly for three hours prior to and for three to five hours following the injection.
2. Interpretation - Following the injection of parathyroid extract in normals, there is a five-fold to six-fold increase in urine phosphorus excretion. In hypoparathyroidism, following the injection of parathyroid extract, there is a ten-fold or greater increase in urine phosphorus excretion; with pseudohypoparathyroidism, there is at most a two-fold increase.

G. Serum Parathyroid Hormone: Radioimmunoassay methods have been developed but will not be readily available for some time.

PANCREAS (ISLET CELLS)

Glucagon (hyperglycemic-glycogenolytic factor, HGF), a polypeptide from the alpha cells, accelerates gluconeogenesis and causes hyperglycemia, glycosuria, ketonuria, and increased nitrogen excretion in the normal and diabetic human.

Insulin, elaborated by the beta cells in islet tissue, is a zinc- and sulfur-containing protein with a molecular weight calculated under specific conditions to be 5734. It is almost entirely utilized by the body; only a trace is excreted in the urine. Increased plasma levels of insulin can now be detected by several experimental methods, and insulinase and an insulinase inhibitor have been found in the liver. Insulin appears to be present in plasma in both an unbound and a bound state. Factors inhibitory to insulin have been found in the serum of patients with diabetic ketosis and insulin resistance.

Actions.

Insulin production is decreased by low blood glucose levels and increased by hyperglycemia. Insulin acts in part by facilitating the transport of hexoses and amino acids across the cell membranes. This results in a lowered blood glucose, an increase in the peripheral utilization of glucose, the suppression of hepatic glucose production from glycogen, and a transient decrease in serum inorganic phosphate and potassium.

Clinical Disorders.
A. Deficiency: Diabetes mellitus.
B. Excess: Hypoglycemia.

Methods of Evaluation of Hyperglycemia.

Physical examination; blood glucose, acetone, and carbon dioxide; urine glucose, acetone, and ketone bodies; and glucose tolerance test (see below).

Many factors influence carbohydrate metabolism: intestinal absorption of glucose, hepatic glycogen metabolism, skeletal muscle mass, insulin and its antagonists and the enzymes which destroy it, glucagon and thyroid, anterior pituitary hormone, and adrenal hormones.

A. Glucose Tolerance Test: Serial blood glucose determinations after glucose loading may be indicated when the diagnosis of diabetes mellitus cannot be made on the fasting blood glucose level alone, when hyperadrenocorticism or acromegaly is suspected, in the study of abnormalities of liver function or gastrointestinal absorption, and in the study of hypoglycemia. Such tests are unreliable in the presence of severe infection, following a period of fasting in which the patient receives less than 50 Gm. of carbohydrate daily, or following the injection of insulin.

Tolerance tests are unnecessary in the presence of fasting hyperglycemia or severe established diabetes mellitus. If the blood glucose value is within the normal fasting range two hours after a meal which contains 50 to 100 Gm. of carbohydrate, diabetes mellitus may be excluded without further testing. True blood glucose levels between 100-120 mg./100 ml. are suggestive of diabetes mellitus and should prompt a glucose tolerance test.

1. Procedure - On the morning of the test the patient fasts and receives no insulin.
    a. Oral glucose tolerance test - A fasting blood glucose sample is drawn; the patient urinates and takes by mouth 500 ml. of a cooled solution containing 100 Gm. of glucose. Blood and urine glucose determinations are performed at 30, 60, 90, 120, and 180 minutes. In persons with hypoglycemia, determinations may be made hourly to the seventh hour.
    b. Intravenous glucose tolerance test - This procedure avoids the uncertainties of glucose absorption from the intestine. The patient receives an intravenous infusion of 0.5 Gm. of glucose per Kg. body weight as a 20% glucose solution over a 30-minute period, and blood and urine specimens are collected at 30, 60, 90, 120, and 180 minutes.
2. Interpretation -
    a. Oral test - The test is considered normal if the fasting blood glucose is less than 100 mg./100 ml., the peak value is less than 160 mg./100 ml., and the two-hour value is less than 120 mg./100 ml.
    b. Intravenous test - Normally the initial blood glucose is not elevated, and the blood glucose level does not exceed 250 mg./100 ml. upon completion of the infusion, falls below the initial level at two hours, and returns to the preinjection level between the third and fourth hours.
B. Insulin Tolerance Test: This test is now used primarily to determine insulin resistance in patients with suspected hyperadrenocorticism or acromegaly. In states such as anterior pituitary or adrenocortical insufficiency, where an increased insulin responsiveness is expected, caution is imperative. The dose should be reduced to at least one-third.
1. Procedure - After preparation as for the glucose tolerance test, a fasting blood glucose specimen is drawn, 0.1 unit crystalline zinc insulin per Kg. of ideal body weight is injected I.V., and further blood samples are obtained at 20, 30, 45, 60, 90, and 120 minutes.

ABNORMAL GLUCOSE METABOLISM IN THE
LIVER DURING UNCONTROLLED DIABETES*

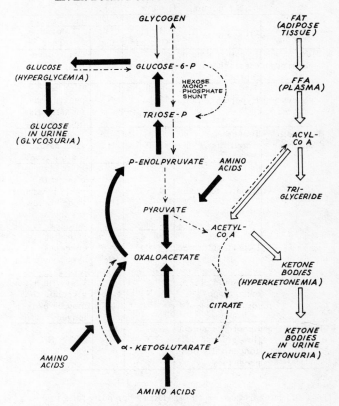

Activity of Pathway

⟹ Greater than normal   -----→ Probably below normal

→ Normal   ·-·-·→ Markedly impaired

⟹ Increased gluconeogenesis

URINE AND BLOOD CHANGES IN DISEASES OF CARBOHYDRATE METABOLISM

N = normal. L = low. H = high.

Cause	Disease Entity	Urine Glucose	Blood Glucose	
			Fasting	Tolerance Test
Slow absorption	Hypothyroidism, steatorrhea (sprue)	N	N	Oral curve flat; I.V. curve N.
Rapid absorption	Hyperthyroidism	N to H postprandially	N	High, early peak; occasionally diabetic curve.
Metabolic disorder	Diabetes mellitus	H	N to H	Peak high with slow return to fasting level
	Hepatic disease	N to H	L to H	Peak high, often with rapid return to and below fasting in 3 to 4 hours.
	Hyperinsulinism	N	L to N	N or flat curve at hypoglycemic levels
	Addison's disease, hypopituitarism	N	L to N	Flat with hypoglycemia that may be prolonged.
Renal disease	Renal glycosuria (low glucose T_m), congenitally or in pregnancy.	H	N	N

2. Interpretation - Blood glucose normally falls to 50% of the fasting level in 10 to 30 minutes and returns to normal levels in 90 to 120 minutes. A greater or more prolonged fall indicates abnormal insulin sensitivity; a lesser response suggests insulin resistance.

C. Other Tests for Hyperglycemia:

1. Sodium tolbutamide test - The normal person given 1 Gm. of sodium tolbutamide (Orinase®) I.V. in 10 ml. of distilled water or saline over a period of two minutes shows a precipitous fall in blood glucose to an average of 55% of the pretest level at 40 minutes and a rapid return to the fasting level at 2 hours. By contrast, the blood glucose of the diabetic falls slowly

for 2 hours (average level, 90% of pretest level at 40
minutes). This test demonstrates the rise in insulin
activity after tolbutamide administration. It is relatively unaffected by age, obesity, liver disease, steroid treatment, or thyrotoxicosis. A progressive loss
of tolbutamide sensitivity develops during pregnancy.

2. Corticoid glucose tolerance test - The standard glucose tolerance test reveals gross impairment of carbohydrate tolerance in established diabetes. The
early diabetic state is suggested if the tolerance curve
becomes diabetic when the test is repeated after oral
administration of cortisone acetate, 50 mg. (or prednisone, 10 mg.), 8 hours and again 2 hours before re-
testing.

3. Glycosuria - See p. 116 for testing urine for glucose.

Methods of Evaluation of Hyperinsulinism.

Hypoglycemia is most often due to excess insulin dosage,
but it may also result from a number of other organic or
functional causes roughly divisible into (1) those which occur
only in the postabsorptive or fasting state; and (2) the reactive hypoglycemias, which follow carbohydrate ingestion
and subsequent rise in blood glucose with excessive insulin
release.

A. I.V. Tolbutamide Test: One Gm. of sodium tolbutamide
is given I.V. to subjects in the fasting state. Patients
with insulinomas have a greater maximal drop in blood
glucose levels and a more prolonged phase of hypoglycemia than do normal subjects. Caution is imperative.

B. Fasting Tests: Organic hypoglycemia is suggested by a
fall in blood glucose below 50 mg./100 ml. after a provocative fast of 5 to 72 hours climaxed by vigorous exercise.

C. Glucagon Test: Normal persons given 1 mg. of glucagon
I.M. 6 to 8 hours after eating show a blood glucose rise
of 50 to 100 mg./100 ml. with a peak at 45 minutes and a
return to normal by 2 hours. In the presence of organic
hypoglycemia due to hyperinsulinism, the blood glucose
rises more rapidly to a peak at 30 minutes, and falls to
or below the fasting level in 90 minutes and to markedly
hypoglycemic levels (caution) in 2 hours.

D. Insulin Concentration: Plasma insulin levels can now be
measured with radioimmunoassay technics that are more
reliable than bioassay methods. By immunoassay, the
insulin concentration in peripheral venous plasma of fasting normal humans is 0-70 μU./ml.

DIFFERENTIAL DIAGNOSIS OF HYPOGLYCEMIC STATES*

Condition	Fasting Blood Sugar	5-Hour Glucose Tolerance Test	3-Hour Intravenous Tolbutamide Tolerance Test	Leucine Tolerance Test	48 to 72-Hour Fast With Exercise	Glucagon Tolerance Test	Epinephrine Tolerance Test
Islet cell tumor	Normal or low	Normal or diabetic	Sustained hypoglycemia	Normal or sustained hypoglycemia	Hypoglycemia	Normal	Normal
Extrapancreatic tumors	Normal or low	Normal or diabetic	Normal	Normal	Hypoglycemia	Normal	Normal
Liver disease	Normal or low	Diabetic	Normal or diabetic	Normal	Hypoglycemia	Abnormal	Abnormal
Malnutrition	Low	Diabetic	Normal or diabetic	Normal	Hypoglycemia	Abnormal	Abnormal
Hypopituitarism and hypo-adrenalism	Normal or low	Normal	May have excessive drop in first hour but returns toward normal by 2-3 hours	Normal	Normal or hypoglycemia	Normal	Normal
Reactive (functional) hypoglycemia	Normal	Normal or low at 2 hours with hypoglycemia between 1.5 and 4 hours	Normal (may show early marked drop)	Normal	Normal	Normal	Normal
Early diabetes mellitus	Normal	Diabetic during first 2 hours with hypoglycemia between third and fifth hour	Diabetic	Normal	Normal	Normal	Normal
In Children: Prematurity	Low	Diabetic	Diabetic	Normal	Hypoglycemia	Abnormal	Abnormal
Leucine sensitivity	Normal or low	Normal	Normal	Significant hypoglycemia	Normal blood sugar	Normal	Normal
Glycogen storage disease	Low	Diabetic	Diabetic	Normal	Hypoglycemia	Abnormal	Abnormal

*Modified after B. R. Boshell (Mod. Treat. 3:337, 1966) and reproduced, with permission, from Current Diagnosis and Treatment, 1970. Brainerd, Krupp, Chatton, and Margen, Eds. Lange, 1970.

Tests for Acetone.

Ketone bodies are not normally present in blood or urine. In diabetic acidosis, however, ketonuria is usually readily demonstrated by the purple color which forms with a nitro-prusside tablet (Acetest®) or powder. Elevated blood levels of ketone bodies develop later in acidosis, and may be estimated by adding a drop of serum or plasma to the nitro-prusside tablet or powder. If a deep purple color appears promptly, a drop of serum is mixed with a drop of water, and this 1:1 dilution is retested; if a color again appears, 1:4 and 1:8 dilutions are tested to obtain a quantitative result, which is helpful in guiding treatment and estimating prognosis.

ADRENAL CORTEX

The adrenal cortex produces four major groups of hormones: (1) glucocorticoids (cortisol, cortisone), (2) androgens (androstenedione, dehydroepiandrosterone), (3) mineralocorticoids (aldosterone, deoxycorticosterone, corticosterone), and (4) estrogens and progesterone.

The steroid production by the adrenal cortex is controlled by a number of factors originating in the hypothalamic-pituitary system. ACTH is the major tropic substance of this system. Aldosterone is under minimal control of ACTH, and its secretion is mainly influenced by volume receptors, angiotensin II, and potassium concentration. The plasma concentration of cortisol, in turn, regulates ACTH secretion. This "feed-back" mechanism does not seem operative for aldosterone secretion.

Transcortin, a globulin, avidly binds cortisol and corticosterone, and is the main carrier protein at normal concentrations. Estrogens increase transcortin levels. Steroids bound to transcortin are inactive, but are in equilibrium with free unbound steroids.

Actions.

The mineralocorticoids increase reabsorption of sodium and chloride, increase excretion of potassium, and allow an exchange of intracellular potassium with extracellular sodium. Aldosterone is most effective in this regard. The glucocorticoids affect protein, carbohydrate, and fat metabolism, raising blood glucose, increasing gluconeogenesis and protein catabolism (with resulting osteoporosis), metabolizing hepatic fat depots, decreasing tubular reabsorption of urates, increasing uropepsin secretion, and lysing eosinophils and lymphocytes.

Clinical Disorders of Adrenal Steroids.
  A. Deficiency:
    1. Acute - Addisonian crisis; Waterhouse-Friderichsen syndrome.
    2. Chronic - Addison's disease.
  B. Excess:
    1. Principal glucocorticoids - Cushing's syndrome.
    2. Principal androgen excess - Adrenogenital syndrome in females, macrogenitosomia in males.
    3. Aldosterone excess - Primary hyperaldosteronism.

Methods of Evaluation of Glucocorticoids and Androgens.
    Evaluation of adrenocortical function may depend upon the following: (1) Physical examination, noting particularly pigmentation of skin and mucous membranes, pubic and axillary hair growth, blood pressure, and the presence of edema; (2) determination of serum sodium, potassium, chloride, CO_2, urea, and protein; (3) x-ray studies of the bones for osteoporosis and of the adrenal region, with or without retroperitoneal pneumography and tomography; (4) determination of blood and urine levels of 17-ketosteroids, 17-hydroxycorticoids, aldosterone, and specific excretory products such as androsterone and etiocholanolone, pregnanetriol, and pregnenetriolone; (5) specific function tests such as the water-loading test and the response of hormone excretion levels to stimulation by exogenous ACTH, inhibition of ACTH production by corticoids, or inhibition of 11-oxygenation by metyrapone; and (6) in the absence of interfering factors the number of circulating eosinophils, normally between 100 and 300/cu.mm., varies inversely with adrenocortical activity.
  A. Urinary 17-Hydroxycorticoids, 17-Ketosteroid Excretion, Ketogenic Steroids, or Free Cortisol: The basal 24-hour urine excretion of 17-hydroxycorticoids is the most frequently used test in assessing adrenocortical activity. Paraldehyde, quinine, colchicine, iodides, sulfamerazine, and chlorpromazine interfere with the Porter-Silber steroid determination by the Norymberski method. 17-Hydroxycorticoids are metabolites of cortisol and cortisone. Urinary 17-ketosteroids are metabolites of (1) adrenocortical steroids such as cortisol, (2) adrenal androgens, and (3) gonadal androgens.
    The test therefore reflects the activity of the adrenal cortex and the gonads in the male and the adrenal cortex in the female. There is diurnal variation in excretion of 17-hydroxycorticoids and 17-ketosteroids of adrenal origin. False increase in levels may be due to nonspecific chromogens. The contribution of testosterone metabolites to the ketosteroids in the urine is minimal.
    17-Ketosteroid levels determined by the Zimmerman reaction are greatly reduced by probenecid (Benemid®)

and meprobamate administration. These drugs should
be withdrawn for several days before urine collections.

The patient should not be receiving androgens or
cortisol when specimens are collected. Testosterone
propionate is excreted in the urine and is measured as
17-ketosteroids; methyltestosterone does not appear in
the urine.

1. Procedure - A 24-hour urine specimen is collected in
   a jug containing 5 ml. of 2% thymol in glacial acetic
   acid.
2. Interpretation - High levels of excretion of both 17-
   hydroxycorticoids, 17-ketosteroids, ketogenic steroids, and urinary free cortisol are found in adrenocortical carcinoma and adrenocortical hyperplasia,
   and of 17-ketosteroids and pregnanetriol in the adrenogenital syndrome. Low levels of excretion are found
   in hypopituitarism, Addison's disease, myxedema,
   and occasionally in anorexia nervosa. (See table on
   p. 246.)

B. Plasma Cortisol: Unconjugated cortisol (free and protein
   bound) concentrations vary diurnally. At 8 a.m., the
   average concentration in plasma is 12 μg./100 ml. (range,
   5-18 μg./100 ml.). Diurnal variation is striking. In normal humans observing customary day-night activity, the
   highest levels occur at about 8 a.m. and the lowest levels
   shortly after midnight.

C. Tests for Adrenocortical Insufficiency:
   1. Water excretion test (Soffer) -
      a. Procedure - The patient fasts overnight. In the
         morning he empties his bladder, and drinks 1500
         ml. of water (about 20 ml. per Kg. body weight)
         over a period of 15 to 45 minutes. A five-hour
         urine specimen collected from the beginning of the
         test is measured. During the five-hour period the
         patient reclines or sits except while voiding. The
         test may be repeated two hours after the oral ad-
         ministration of 50 mg. of cortisone.
      b. Interpretation - Normal individuals excrete 1200
         ml. or more of urine over the five-hour collection
         period. Patients with Addison's disease may ex-
         crete less than 800 ml. of urine. False-positive
         results may occur if the rate of absorption of water
         from the gastrointestinal tract or its elimination by
         the kidneys is decreased, e.g., in patients with
         nephritis, cirrhosis, celiac disease, or cardiac
         failure.
            Patients with adrenal insufficiency (primary, or
         secondary to hypopituitarism) show substantial in-
         crease in diuresis when retested following cortisone.

2. Corticotropin (ACTH) response test (Thorn test) - If responsive adrenocortical tissue is present, the administration of potent corticotropin results in an increased secretion of adrenocortical steroids, increase in plasma cortisol, producing eosinopenia and increased urinary excretion of 17-ketosteroids and 17-hydroxycorticoids. If ACTH has been absent because of pituitary insufficiency, its daily administration leads to a stepwise increase in adrenocortical response over a period of 2 to 3 days.

Adrenal response to corticotropin is retarded in myxedema as well as in hypopituitarism. Allergic eosinophilia may mask a fall in eosinophils. The patient should be free of the effects of large doses of androgens, cortisone, and corticotropin before urinary steroids are measured.

a. Procedure -
   (1) The 4-hour corticotropin test may be used for screening. The eosinophil count or plasma cortisol is measured before 25 U.S.P. units of corticotropin are administered in a 4-hour infusion. Four hours later, another eosinophil count is done or plasma control measured.
   (2) Eight-hour intravenous corticotropin test - 25 U.S.P. units of corticotropin in 500 ml. of normal saline are administered I.V. as a continuous 8-hour infusion. An eosinophil count or plasma cortisol level is determined at the beginning and at the end of the 8-hour period. Twenty-four-hour urine collections are made on a control day prior to the test and on the day of corticotropin administration. Urinary excretion levels of 17-ketosteroids, 17-hydroxycorticoids, ketogenic steroids, or urinary free cortisol on each specimen are compared with the control value.
   (3) As an alternative to the intravenous test, 40-80 U.S.P. units of corticotropin gel (repository corticotropin injection) or corticotropin zinc may be given I.M. twice daily over the testing period. Corticotropin gel should not be used in suspected adrenal insufficiency.
   (4) The patient with Addison's disease may be protected from an untoward reaction to ACTH by the administration of 0.1 to 0.25 mg. of fludrocortisone; urinary steroid levels are not appreciably altered.
   (5) A synthetic ACTH preparation (24 amino acid) has made possible a rapid intramuscular test. 0.25 mg. I.M. will more than double normal plasma cortisol in less than 1 hour.

b. Interpretation - The four-hour corticotropin screening test normally decreases circulating eosinophils
by more than half. In tests (2) or (3) above, normal subjects respond with an 80 to 100% fall in
eosinophil levels, a two-fold to five-fold increase
in 17-hydroxycorticoids, and a two-fold increase
in 17-ketosteroid excretion levels (see chart on
p. 246). Plasma cortisol increases by three or
four times.

When Cushing's syndrome is present due to
adrenocortical hyperplasia, 17-hydroxycorticoid
excretion levels may reach 75 to 100 mg. per 24
hours. The response is usually absent in the presence of the usually more autonomous adrenal carcinoma. ACTH stimulation of patients with the
adrenogenital syndrome produces an excessive response in 17-ketosteroid levels, not noted in cases
of "idiopathic hirsutism."

In Addison's disease, the four-hour corticotropin
test elicits a fall of less than 50% in circulating
eosinophils. In the eight-hour intravenous corticotropin test and the corticotropin gelatin solution
alternate, the addisonian patient shows little or no
change in circulating eosinophils, urinary or plasma hormone levels.

Patients with hypopituitarism and ACTH insufficiency show varying responses depending upon
the degree of adrenocortical involution. Repetition
of the test on three to five consecutive days shows
a gradual rise in 17-ketosteroid and 17-hydroxy-
corticoid output and an increasing eosinopenia.
Plasma cortisol usually shows an increase of three
to four times in four hours.

All tests other than the intravenous administration of corticotropin are subject to occasional false-
negative responses due to extravascular inactivation
of corticotropin.

D. Adrenocortical Inhibition Tests:
1. Tests with dexamethasone - Tests to determine the
suppressibility of ACTH by glucocorticoids may be
carried out using dexamethasone. Dexamethasone has
relatively little effect on sodium or potassium balance
and does not interfere with steroid determinations.
a. Procedure - Twenty-four-hour urine specimens
are collected for analysis on three successive days.
After the first specimen is obtained, 0.5 mg. dexamethasone is given every six hours by mouth for
two days. Excretion level is measured on each
24-hour urine specimen.

In normal individuals the repeated administration of the 0.5 mg. dose reduces by 50% the basal ex-

AVERAGE DAILY URINARY EXCRETION OF 17-KETOSTEROIDS AND 17-HYDROXYCORTICOSTEROIDS BEFORE AND AFTER STANDARD ACTH STIMULATION*

	Total 17-Ketosteroids (mg./24 hrs.)	After ACTH	17-Hydroxy-corticosteroids (mg./24 hrs.)	After ACTH
Normal children up to 8th year	Gradual increase from 0 to 2.5	2×	In proportion to body weight	3×
Boys and girls, 8-18 years	Increase to adult levels at age 16	2×		3×
Normal men†	8-25 / 5-20	2×	9 ± 4‡	3-5×
Normal women§	5-15 / 4-10	2×	7 ± 3‡	3-5×
Eunuchs	7-17			
Testicular tumors	N to very high			
Adrenal adenoma	L to N (wide fluctuation)	No constant change	10-30 (wide fluctuation)	>50 / 4-7×
Adrenocortical carcinoma	N to very high	No response	>30-80	No response
Adrenocortical hyperplasia	N to high	>30	>20-100	>50 / 3-5×
Addison's disease	Men, 1-10 / Women, 0-5	No significant rise	Lower than normal	No significant rise
Panhypopituitarism	0.5-5	Little rise	Lower than normal	Slow progressive rise
Gout	Often 50% below normal	2×	Normal	3-5×

*25 U. S. P. units of ACTH in 500 to 1000 ml. of saline or 5% dextrose in water are infused intravenously over exactly 8 hours. There is a constant spontaneous diurnal variation in urine output of these steroids, minimal at midnight.

†In normal men a gradual fall in 17-ketosteroids occurs from 30 years on.

‡Levels vary with methods used.

§In women an abrupt fall occurs at 30 years of age which continues until the age of 50 or 60. Concurrent elevation of estrogen output may occur.

cretion level of 17-hydroxycorticoids per 24 hours by the end of the second day. If suppression of excretion is not obtained, the test is repeated with a dose of 2 mg. every 6 hours for 2 days.

b. Interpretation - The increased steroid excretion which occurs in patients with adrenocortical hyperplasia is usually suppressed only by the larger (2 mg.) doses, whereas the steroid excretion of patients with autonomous adrenocortical neoplasms may not be suppressed even with higher doses.

2. Rapid dexamethasone test - One mg. of dexamethasone at midnight will reduce normal plasma levels to less than 5 μg./100 ml. by 8:00 a.m. This will effectively rule out adrenal overactivity.

3. Tests with metyrapone (Metopirone®) - Inhibition of 11-beta-hydroxylase by metyrapone results in reduced blood levels of cortisol and loss of cortisol inhibition of ACTH. The ability of the pituitary to respond to this stimulus by release of ACTH may be measured by noting the increment in 17-ketosteroids, 17-hydroxycorticoids, or the metabolite of 11-deoxycortisol (compound S), produced by the adrenal and excreted in the urine. Compound S is formed by the adrenal cortex after inhibition of cortisol (hydrocortisone) formation. The rise in urinary 17-hydroxycorticoids is a result of increased amounts of this metabolite.

a. Procedure -

(1) I.V. - Metyrapone, 30 mg./Kg. body weight in 1 L. of normal saline, is given I.V. for 4 hours, starting between 8:00 and 10:00 a.m. The same procedure is followed on another day, except that 25 U.S.P. units of ACTH are added to the metyrapone infusion to compare the functional capacity of maximally stimulated adrenals with the response evoked by the endogenous ACTH released after administration of metyrapone alone.

(2) Oral - A basal 24-hour urine 17-hydroxycorticoid measurement is obtained. 0.75 Gm. of metyrapone are given every 4 hours for 6 doses. A second 24-hour urine for 17-hydroxycorticoid levels is obtained the day **following** the drug administration.

b. Interpretation - Normal subjects may double their basal 24-hour 17-hydroxycorticoid excretion after metyrapone, and ACTH adds nothing to this response. Hypopituitary patients show no increase in excretion with metyrapone, but their response to exogenous ACTH is adequate. Addisonian patients

respond to neither stimulus. Intravenous metyrapone causes a vigorous response in patients with
adrenal hyperplasia, but adrenal tumors fail to
respond. Chlorpromazine blocks metyrapone responses.

Clinical Disorders of Mineralocorticoids.

A. Primary Hyperaldosteronism: Primary hyperaldosteronism is usually due to adrenocortical adenoma. The
principal manifestations of excess aldosterone secretion
are hypertension and hypokalemia. Urinary aldosterone
levels are high and plasma renin activity is reduced or
absent. (These laboratory determinations are not every-
where available.)

The most effective screening technic to determine
whether hypertension is due to hyperaldosteronism or
not is the serum potassium measurement. The disease
must be suspected if more than 50 mEq. of potassium
are excreted in 24 hours and the serum potassium level
is below 3 mEq. per liter. The patient should be on a
high salt intake (2 Gm. of salt with each meal for 4 days
before electrolyte measurements and electrocardiography are done). The Ecg. changes are those of prolonged
hypertension and hypokalemia.

The patient with hyperaldosteronism frequently com-
plains of severe headache. Potassium depletion causes
weakness, paresthesias, flaccid paralysis, polyuria,
and nocturia. Transient correction of hypokalemia by
administration of spironolactone (Aldactone®), 400 mg.
daily in divided doses for 3 days, is presumptive evidence of primary hyperaldosteronism. A diabetic glucose tolerance curve is present in about half of cases.

Isosthenuria which does not respond to vasopressin is
also due to potassium depletion.

Sodium retention causes hypernatremia and dilutional
anemia due to increased plasma volume (low hematocrit).
Autonomic dysfunction is manifested by a postural fall
in blood pressure without changes in the pulse rate.

Desoxycorticosterone acetate (DOCA®), 20 mg. I.M.
daily in divided doses for 3 days, causes no change in
aldosterone production if an aldosterone-producing tumor
is present.

B. Secondary Hyperaldosteronism: Excessive secretion of
aldosterone is seen in edematous states such as cirrhosis with ascites, nephrosis, congestive heart failure,
and toxemia of pregnancy; in nonedematous states such
as malignant hypertension; in unilateral renal arterial
narrowing; and after diuretic therapy. Useful differential
diagnostic aids are: (1) low serum sodium concentrations,

(2) blood volume, usually reduced in hypertensive patients, and (3) normal or elevated plasma renin activity.

ADRENAL MEDULLA

The adrenal medullary hormones are catecholamines: (1) epinephrine and (2) norepinephrine (arterenol), probably the parent compound from which epinephrine is formed by addition of a methyl group.

Preganglionic sympathetic nerve fibers from the intermediolateral cell column release acetylcholine at adrenal medullary cells to stimulate hormone production. Norepinephrine is released at all postganglionic sympathetic nerve endings.

Actions.

Epinephrine is sympathomimetic, increases cardiac output and rate, systolic blood pressure, blood glucose, hepatic glycogenolysis, basal metabolic rate, and sweating, and causes mydriasis and skin-vessel constriction. By contrast, norepinephrine causes bradycardia, peripheral vasoconstriction, and rise in diastolic blood pressure, and has much less prominent metabolic effects.

Clinical Disorders.
  A. Deficiency: Hypotension. Idiopathic spontaneous hypoglycemia (failure of epinephrine response to hypoglycemia).
  B. Excess: Paroxysmal or persistent hypertension, headaches, sweating, tachycardia, elevated BMR and blood glucose.

Methods of Evaluation.
Chemical assay of epinephrine or norepinephrine in blood or urine; provocative and blocking tests for pheochromocytoma, glucose tolerance test, BMR, x-rays of suprarenal area.

Adrenal medullary hyperactivity, as in pheochromocytoma, produces symptoms and signs, including hypertension, through the release of large amounts of epinephrine and norepinephrine into the blood stream. The most satisfactory single diagnostic procedure is the discovery of plasma levels in excess of 0.5 μg. per liter of norepinephrine. Jaundice, azotemia, and tetracycline administration also cause high levels.

When pheochromocytoma is suspected and hypertension is intermittent, or the basal blood pressure is less than 170/110, a provocative test with histamine (see p. 250) may cause a characteristic rise in the blood pressure and in the urine and plasma catecholamines. Higher levels of basal blood pressure are best investigated by the phentolamine test.

The levels of urinary catecholamines and their metabolites (such as vanillylmandelic acid [VMA], normetanephrine, and metanephrine) are greatly increased (10 to 100 times) in the presence of pheochromocytoma. The usual 24-hour excretion of epinephrine is up to 50 μg.; of the metabolite, VMA, 2.5 μg./mg. of creatinine and less than 1.3 mg./24 hours for 1 ml. metanephrine. The ingestion of caffeine, salicylates, or bananas will invalidate the VMA measurement. Tetracyclines, vasopressors, and methyldopa can influence catechol determination. Monoamine oxidase inhibitors may cause a rise in metanephrine and a low VMA. The pressor amine output at rest is about half that during normal daily activity. If the urine contains increased amounts of epinephrine (40% of cases), the tumor is almost always in one of the adrenal areas or the organ of Zuckerkandl. If urine contains increased amounts of norepinephrine (60% of cases), the tumor may still be expected to be in or near one of the adrenal areas in two-thirds of cases, and in the remaining one-third all possible sites must be considered.

In both provocative and blocking tests, control blood pressure must be taken and the pressure must restabilize after venipuncture before the drug is given. Hypotensive drugs, e. g., rauwolfia, chlorothiazide, or sedatives will confuse the results if given within 24 hours before testing. No diagnosis of pheochromocytoma should be based on these tests alone.

A. Histamine Provocative Test: **Caution:** Histamine may cause a severe blood pressure rise in hypertensive patients, and phentolamine should be available as an antidote.

   1. Procedure - A cold pressor test is first performed by placing the patient's forearm in a water-ice bath for one minute after basal blood pressure readings have been obtained, and then recording postimmersion blood pressure readings at 30-second intervals for three minutes or until the basal state is again achieved. At this time, 0.01 to 0.05 mg. of histamine phosphate in 0.5 ml. of isotonic saline is injected rapidly I.V. and the blood pressure readings are again followed to a basal level at 30-second intervals.

   2. Interpretation - Normal subjects experience flushing, headache, and slight blood pressure fall. An elevation in blood pressure significantly greater than the cold pressor response within two minutes of the injection, or an increase in the basal levels of plasma catecholamines following histamine stimulation, may indicate pheochromocytoma.

B. Phentolamine Blocking Test: This test is used for the
diagnosis of pheochromocytoma in the hypertensive phase.
Barbiturates interfere with the test.

1. Procedure - When the resting patient has achieved a
basal blood pressure level, 5 mg. of phentolamine
(Regitine®) are given rapidly I.V. and the blood pressure is determined at 30-second intervals. Maximum
effect appears in 2 minutes and lasts 3 to 4 minutes.
If a pheochromocytoma is strongly suspected, a dose
of 1 mg. should be administered to avoid profound
and prolonged hypotension.

2. Interpretation - In normal individuals, phentolamine
causes a slight transient fall in blood pressure. In
the presence of pheochromocytoma with hypertension,
a fall in systolic blood pressure of more than 35 mm.
Hg, and a fall in diastolic blood pressure of more than
25 mm. Hg appearing in 2 minutes and lasting for at
least $2^{1/2}$ minutes is characteristic.

OVARIES (FOLLICLE)

The ovarian follicles elaborate (1) estradiol, which is
interconvertible in the body with estrone, and (2) estriol,
formed from estradiol or estrone, which is present in largest
amounts during pregnancy.

Estradiol is secreted in FSH-prepared ovarian follicle
under stimulation by LH. It is excreted in urine in the conjugated form with glucuronic acid after inactivation in liver.

Actions.

Estrogens stimulate endometrial growth and proliferation
in the follicular phase of menstruation, cornify vaginal epithelium, control development of secondary sex characteristics;
act on anterior pituitary to suppress FSH; counteract effects
of androgens, stimulate the teat and duct system of the breast,
close epiphyses and check advance of postmenopausal osteoporosis, retain water and sodium, stimulate growth of the
uterus in pregnancy, and sensitize the uterus to the oxytocic
action of posterior pituitary hormone.

Clinical Disorders.

A. Deficiency: Before puberty - eunuchoidism; after puberty - weight gain, hot flashes, nervousness, menopause,
atrophy of sex organs, and osteoporosis.

B. Excess: In women, endometrial hyperplasia. In men,
estrogen administration or failure of liver to inactivate
endogenous estrogens may lead to gynecomastia and deficient spermatogenesis. Prolonged excess in men may
stimulate carcinoma of the breast.

Methods of Evaluation.

Physican examination, vaginal smear, endometrial biopsy, x-rays of bones for osteoporosis or bone age, urinary estrogen and gonadotropin, response of patient to "medical D and C" (menstrual flow in response to progesterone administration proves estrogen presence).

The presence of estrogen may be detected clinically through study of the cornification of the vaginal cells, biopsy of a proliferating endometrium, or the production of bleeding after the parenteral administration of 10 mg. of progesterone for 5 days or a single injection of 250 mg. of hydroxyprogesterone caproate (Delalutin®) (which requires the prior action of estrogen on the endometrium). Reliable routine methods have been developed for measuring estradiol, estrone, and estriol in urine.

Urine levels of follicle-stimulating hormone and the response of manifestations of hypogonadism to the administration of chorionic gonadotropins have the same significance in women as in men. The absence of urinary FSH may indicate pituitary failure, whereas an excess may represent ovarian failure.

OVARIES (CORPUS LUTEUM)

Ovarian corpus luteum elaborates progesterone. Corpus luteum is formed by stimulation of FSH and LH; progesterone is formed and corpus luteum maintained into pregnancy if necessary through stimulation by LH and LTH. Progesterone is excreted as pregnanediol conjugated with glucuronic acid.

Actions.

Progesterone furthers proliferation of estrogen-prepared endometrium and induces secretion in luteal phase of menstruation, develops and maintains placenta in pregnancy, stimulates the lobule and alveolar systems in breasts, suppresses the motility of the uterus and decreases its sensitivity to oxytocin, suppresses FSH production, lessens stimulation of LH and LTH production, and promotes estrogen excretion and conversion to estriol.

Clinical Disorders.
  A. Deficiency: Some abortions during first trimester of pregnancy. In nonpregnant women, menorrhagia.
  B. Excess: Acne, pseudopregnancy.

Methods of Evaluation.

The presence of progesterone may be demonstrated by the discovery of a proliferative endometrium on biopsy or by the 0.2 to 0.6° F. elevation in the basal body temperature, at the onset of ovulation, which is known to be due to progesterone. Urinary pregnanediol and plasma progesterone are effective measurements of progesterone production.

PREGNANCY TESTS

Most pregnancy tests depend upon the production of chorionic gonadotropin by the developing trophoblastoderm, a process which may occur by the twelfth day following nidation. Pregnancy may also be tentatively diagnosed by the persistence of the elevated luteal temperature phase in the basal temperature chart kept by the patient; or by the failure of three intramuscular injections of 1:2000 neostigmine methylsulfate at daily intervals to induce menstrual flow.

Excretion of unusually large amounts of gonadotropin occurs in the presence of hydatidiform mole and chorionepithelioma in the female and of embryonal carcinoma of the testis in the male.

SEROLOGIC TESTS

Hemagglutination Inhibition Test (Pregnosticon®).
This test utilizes (1) red blood cells sensitized to HCG (human chorionic gonadotropin), (2) urine, and (3) anti-HCG serum. When antibodies are bound on "coated" red cells, hemagglutination results. The addition of urine from a pregnant woman blocks the reaction between antibody and red cells. Clumping indicates pregnancy; no clumping means no pregnancy.

Agglutination Inhibition Test (Gravindex®).
This test utilizes (1) anti-HCG serum, (2) urine, and (3) HCG antigen (latex particles). Interpretation is as above. The HCG-latex particles replace the sensitized red cells.

MALE GONADS (TESTES)

From Leydig cells, the testis elaborates testosterone and its metabolic forms, androsterone and dehydroepiandrosterone (also from adrenal cortex). Luteinizing hormone from the pituitary stimulates the formation of testosterone, which is inactivated and conjugated in the liver and excreted as glucuronide. Testosterone production rates in men are 2-8 mg. per day; in women, 0.5 to 2.5 mg. per day.

Actions.
Testosterone in small doses supports spermatogenesis; in larger doses, suppresses it. It maintains sex organs and controls development of male sex characteristics, inhibits pituitary LH, promotes long-bone growth without closure of epiphyses, and has many anabolic effects (e. g., retention of sodium, chloride, water, decrease in gluconeogenesis).

Clinical Disorders.
  A. Deficiency: Before puberty, eunuchoidism or crypt-orchism. After puberty, asthenia, loss of beard and potency, atrophy of sex organs, hot flashes, nervousness, depression, and osteoporosis. Partial deficiency syndromes may occur (e. g., Klinefelter, Del Castillo).
  B. Excess: Masculinization as with adrenocortical tumors, Leydig cell tumors, testicular teratomas and seminomas. Administered excess may depress spermatogenesis which "rebounds" to supra-normal level after withdrawal.

Methods of Evaluation.
  A. Physical examination, noting pubic and temporal hair, prostate, and testes; the study of male hypogonadism or sperm deficiencies involves testicular biopsy, examination of the semen and spermatozoa count (see p. 255), and such urinary hormone determinations as indicate androgen production (17-ketosteroid excretion) or inhibition or lack of the pituitary gonadotropins (FSH determination). The absence of hyaluronidase from semen may indicate an obstructive lesion of the ducts leading from the testes, where the enzyme is produced. Urinary testosterone and plasma testosterone measurements are available. Plasma testosterone cells in adult men are between 0.4 and 1 μg./100 ml. In castrates, the concentration is 0.015 μg./100 ml.; in women, 0.050 μg./100 ml.; in children, 0.015 μg./100 ml.
  B. Gonadotropin Stimulation Test: Hypogonadism originating in the testis is accompanied by high excretory levels of follicle-stimulating hormone, whereas FSH excretion is low when the defect is in the pituitary. Evidences of hypogonadism will disappear and 17-ketosteroid excretion will rise in a patient with hypopituitarism when gonadotropins are administered. This treatment is ineffective when the defect originates in the gonad.
    The patient should not be receiving endocrine therapy at the time of testing.
    Chorionic gonadotropin is given I. M. in a daily dose of 2000 I. U. for 3 weeks. The patient is watched for

abatement of evidences of hypogonadism: in men, sperm count, testicular biopsy, 17-ketosteroids, testosterone, secondary sex characteristics; in women, vaginal smear for estrogenic effect, secondary sex characteristics.

Disappearance of the evidences of hypogonadism indicates hypogonadism secondary to pituitary failure.

. . .

CHROMOSOMAL SEX DETERMINATION

Tissues may be stained to show the presence of a chromatin mass adhering to the inner surface of the cell nuclear membrane. The presence of a typical chromatin mass is interpreted to indicate the presence of the female XX sex chromosomal pattern. Smears obtained by vigorous scraping of the buccal mucosa yield cells suitable for such studies. The chromatin-positive pattern characterizes 30 to 50% of the epithelial nuclei of normal females (referred to as chromatin-positives) and up to 4% of the nuclei of normal males (chromatin-negatives). Most patients with gonadal dysgenesis (Turner's syndrome) are chromatin-negative, but persons with true Klinefelter's syndrome are chromatin-positive. Patients with pseudohermaphroditism have a chromosomal sex corresponding to their gonadal sex. It is not yet possible to equate chromosomal sex with genetic sex.

. . .

SEMINAL FLUID

Examination of seminal fluid is an integral part of the evaluation of infertility.

Collection.
The ejaculate should be obtained after at least 4 days of abstinence from intercourse. It is best produced by masturbation in the physician's office. This ensures that the entire specimen is collected in a clean, dry glass or plastic container. Condoms must not be used since sperm are quickly killed on contact with them. The specimen must be examined within 2 hours after collection. If collected outside the office by masturbation or coitus interruptus, the container should be protected from extremes of temperature during delivery to the laboratory.

Observations.

The ejaculate should be observed for time required for liquefaction following ejaculation, viscosity, volume, and the number, motility, and morphology of sperm.

Motility.

Place a small drop of well mixed seminal fluid on a warm (37° C.) slide. Cover with a clean cover slip ringed with petrolatum. With the high dry objective, focus through the depth of the fluid and count 200 spermatozoa, noting the number of nonmotile and the number of motile (showing progressive movement) sperm. In some laboratories, the observations are repeated every 2 to 3 hours to evaluate the viability of sperm. The initial index of motility is of most value.

Sperm Count. (Do in duplicate.)

Draw seminal fluid to 0.5 mark in WBC pipet. Dilute to 11 mark with the following solution:

> Sodium bicarbonate, 5 Gm.
> Distilled water, 100 ml.
> To the solution add formalin (neutral), 1 ml.

Mix well and fill the hemocytometer chamber. Allow 2 minutes for sperm to settle in the chamber. Count spermatozoa in four large squares and multiply the result by 50,000 to obtain the number of sperm per ml.

Morphology.

Smears are made like thin blood smears. Two staining methods are suitable:

> (1) Usual Papanicolaou stain as for exfoliative cytology. Prepare smear and fix immediately in 95% ethanol or 50% ethanol-ether before the smears dry. Stain in routine manner.
>
> (2) Meyer's hematoxylin stain. Make a thin smear and dry in air. Flood the slide with 10% formalin for 1 minute. Wash. Stain with Meyer's hematoxylin for 2 minutes. Wash with water. Dry in air.

Examine 200 or more sperm with oil immersion objective and record numbers of normal and abnormal forms. Note presence of white, red, and epithelial cells.

Normal Values.

> 1. Average volume is 4 ml. (3 to 7 ml.).
> 2. Liquefaction should be complete within 30 minutes after ejaculation.
> 3. Normal sperm count is 60 to 200 million/ml.
> 4. 75% of sperm should show normal motility and morphology.

13...

Cerebrospinal Fluid Examination

Collection of Specimens.
Spinal fluid may be obtained by lumbar, cisternal, or ventricular puncture as described below. Normal values for C.S.F. are given on p. 258.

LUMBAR PUNCTURE

See p. 603.

CISTERNAL PUNCTURE

Cisternal puncture is an essentially dangerous procedure (because of proximity of needle to medulla) which should be undertaken only by an experienced physician and only if absolutely necessary.

Indications.
For comparison of pressure rise upon jugular compression (block) or to obtain C.S.F. when lumbar puncture is not feasible. It is rarely indicated.

Interpretation.
Observe resting pressure and rise upon jugular compression to rule out spinal fluid block.

VENTRICULAR PUNCTURE

Because of the risk of damage to brain tissue or hemorrhage, this is a dangerous procedure which should be undertaken only when urgently indicated and with great care in infants when puncture by other routes is impractical. It is performed for investigation of hydrocephalus and intracranial lesions.

Interpretation of Abnormalities.
Greatly elevated protein values suggest chronic inflammation (e.g., toxoplasmosis). After withdrawal of fluid, air can be introduced to give contrast in x-ray pictures.

Lumbar Puncture, Normal:

Pressure

Reclining -	Newborn	30-80 mm. of water.
	Children	50-100 mm. of water.
	Adults	70-200 (Avg. = 125.)
Sitting -	For all ages	Normal if fluid rises to level of foramen magnum. (Avg. adult: 350-400 mm. of water.)

Volume of cerebrospinal fluid in adults:

Total	120-140 ml.
Lateral ventricles	10-15 ml. each.
Rest of ventricular system	5 ml.
Cranial subarachnoid spaces	25 ml.
Spinal arachnoid spaces	75 ml.
Appearance	Clear and colorless
Specific gravity	1.003-1.008
Cells per cu. mm.: Adults	0-5 mononuclears
Infants	0-20 mononuclears
Total protein	20-45 mg./100 ml.
Electrophoresis: Albumin	55-69%
α_1 globulin	3-8%
α_2 globulin	4-9%
β globulin	10-18%
γ globulin	7-16%
Glucose (varies with blood glucose)	50-85 mg./100 ml.
Chlorides, as sodium chloride	700-750 mg./100 ml. (120-130 mEq./L.)
Colloidal gold (gold sol)	0000110000
Urea nitrogen	5-20 mg./100 ml.
Creatinine	0.4-2.2 mg./100 ml.
Non-protein nitrogen	12-30 mg./100 ml.
Uric acid (below blood level)	0.3-1.5 mg./100 ml.
Amino acids	30% of blood
Calcium	4-7 mg./100 ml. (2-3 mEq./L.)
Carbon dioxide	40-60 vol./100 ml. (25 mEq./L.)
Lactic acid	8-27 mg./100 ml.
Magnesium	3.0-3.5 mg./100 ml.
Potassium	12-15 mg./100 ml. (3-4 mEq./L.)
Phosphate, total	1.2-2.0 mg./100 ml.
Sodium	325 mg./100 ml. (140 mEq./L.)
Cholesterol	0.06-0.22 mg./100 ml.

Cisternal Puncture (Other values are as above).

Total Proteins	10-25 mg./100 ml.

Ventricular Puncture (Other values are as above).

Total Proteins	5-15 mg./100 ml.

COMBINED PUNCTURE

Indications.
To determine the location of a spinal block which interferes with the flow of cerebrospinal fluid.

Interpretation of Abnormalities.
If fluid is obtained from the upper but not the lower
puncture site, an obstruction may lie between the two levels.
This may be outlined by the introduction of radiopaque material
for x-ray examination. The material can be partially removed through the lower needle.

EXAMINATION OF SPINAL FLUID
(For Normal Values, see p. 258.)

Always obtain three or four specimens of 2 to 4 ml. each
in sterile tubes. (See table, p. 262.)

Gross.
A. Color: Normal C.S.F. is clear and colorless. Xanthochromic fluid means either old hemorrhage or very high
protein content. Red or pink fluid indicates recent
hemorrhage.
B. Opacity: Cloudy fluid suggests high cell count (infection).
C. Pellicle: Pellicle on top of fluid left standing for one to
three hours suggests tuberculous meningitis.

Cell Counts.
A. Diluting the Fluid:
1. Draw Unna's polychrome methylene blue to the "1"
mark in a r.b.c. counting pipet and fill pipet to "101"
mark with spinal fluid. This colors white cells blue
and red cells yellow.
2. Turbid fluid - When many white cells are present (e.g.,
turbid or purulent fluid), better counts are obtained
with a w.b.c. pipet and w.b.c. counting fluid. (See p.
155.)
3. Bloody fluid - When significant numbers of red cells
are present in the fluid, the possibility of traumatic
bleeding must be considered. Fresh r.b.c. are intact
and their margin is smooth. Older cells have crenated
appearance.
B. Count: Count nine large squares in the counting chamber
(see p. 148) for both red and white cells: The total multi-
plied by 1.1 gives the number of cells per cubic milli-
meter.

Differential Count.

Usually made on sediment from centrifuged specimen, treated like blood smear and stained with Wright's stain.

Globulin Tests.

These are of no value if spinal fluid is bloody.

A. Pandy: Place 1 to 2 ml. of a saturated solution of phenol in a small test tube and add 1 drop of spinal fluid. Some authors recommend the use of 5 or 10% phenol solution. Cloudiness against a black background indicates increased amounts of globulin. Report as 0, +, ++, +++, or ++++.

B. Ross-Jones (Nonne-Apelt Reaction, Phase 1): Carefully layer 0.5 ml. of clear spinal fluid over 1 ml. of a saturated solution of ammonium sulfate. A thin white ring appearing at the juncture of the liquids, which disappears on mixing, indicates a 1+ reaction. Heavy cloudiness persisting after mixing is a 4+ reaction.

Total Proteins. (Quantitative method of Dennis and Ayer.)

Place 1.2 ml. of clear spinal fluid, 0.8 ml. of distilled water, and 2 ml. of 5% sulfosalicylic acid in a small test tube and mix by inversion. Allow to stand for five minutes, then read in colorimeter against a known standard protein suspension. Make known suspension by mixing 2 ml. of a standard protein solution with 2 ml. of 5% sulfosalicylic acid. If the unknown is too heavy with protein, dilute and compare. Consider dilution factor in the calculation.

$$\frac{mm. \ Standard}{mm. \ Unknown} \times 50 = mg. \ of \ protein/100 \ ml. \ of \ fluid.$$

Electrophoresis shows predominantly albumin in normal CSF.

Glucose Test.

The concentration of glucose in the spinal fluid is markedly influenced by the concentration of glucose in the blood. Therefore, the measurement of C.S.F. glucose should always be accompanied by measurement of blood glucose.

A rapid, semi-quantitative test for C.S.F. glucose may be performed as follows:

To 2 ml. of fresh spinal fluid add 1 drop of 10% formaldehyde and keep in refrigerator. Place 1 ml. of Benedict's solution in each of five small test tubes (75 × 12 mm.) and add spinal fluid in amounts given in chart below. Boil for five minutes, read and determine the mg./100 ml. glucose; reduction in tube five only means 10 to 20 mg./100 ml., etc.

Tube No.	ml. C.S.F.	Reductions					
1	0.05	+	0	0	0	0	0
2	0.10	+	+	0	0	0	0
3	0.15	+	+	+	0	0	0
4	0.20	+	+	+	+	0	0
5	0.25	+	+	+	+	+	0
mg./100 ml. glucose		50	40-50	30-40	20-30	10-20	0-10

Chlorides.

The usual normal concentration of chlorides in the spinal fluid is 700 to 750 mg./100 ml. (120-130 mEq./L.). The concentration of C.S.F. chlorides in various disease states generally reflects the concentration of blood chlorides. Thus a person with serious hypochloremia (e.g., in advanced tuberculous meningitis) would show also low chlorides in the spinal fluid. However, no diagnostic value can be ascribed to spinal fluid chloride concentration.

Bacteriologic Examination.

Smears and cultures for bacteria should be made of all fluids when indicated.

A. Smears: Make smears directly if fluid is very turbid, otherwise from sediment of centrifuged C.S.F. All smears should be stained with Gram's stain. If no characteristic bacteria are found, acid-fast bacilli should be looked for with Kinyoun or Ziehl-Neelsen stain. If a pellicle forms on fluid after standing, it should be smeared on slide and stained for acid-fast bacilli. (See p. 292.) An India ink preparation is required for Cryptococcus.

B. Cultures: Cloudy fluid should be streaked on chocolate agar, Sabouraud's agar, and blood agar plates and inoculated into blood broth and thioglycollate medium. All media are incubated at 37° C., some in candle jars (for 10% CO_2 atmosphere). Sediment of centrifuged fluid should be cultured on special media for tubercle bacilli and fungi and inoculated into guinea pigs. (See p. 292.) Mice should be inoculated intraperitoneally if coccidioidomycosis is suspected.

C. Special Presumptive Tests for Tuberculous Meningitis: Levinson test, tryptophan test, etc., are of little value.

D. Virus Isolation: In some forms of aseptic meningitis (e.g., when caused by herpes simplex, mumps, ECHO, or Coxsackie) viruses can be isolated from the C.S.F. by inoculation of tissue cultures and animals. In arthropod-borne encephalitis (e.g., caused by St. Louis or Western equine viruses) this is not practical; diagnosis depends upon the rise in specific antibody titer.

THE CEREBROSPINAL FLUID IN DIFFERENTIAL DIAGNOSIS

Disease	Initial Pressure	Appearance	Cells per cu. mm.	Protein mg./100 ml.	Glucose mg./100 ml.	Colloidal Gold	Remarks
Normal lumbar puncture	70-200 mm. H$_2$O	Clear, color-less, no clot	0-5 lymphs	20-45	50-85	0000110000	In fasting afebrile individuals.
Acute purulent meningitis (bacterial)	Increased	Opalescent to purulent clot	500-20,000, mostly polys	50-1,000+	0-45	Variable	Organisms in sediment or clot, culture positive.
Tuberculous meningitis	Increased	Opalescent fi-brin web, pell.	10-500, mostly lymphs	45-500+	0-45	Variable	Sugar and chloride values falling progressively.
Syphilitic meningitis, early, acute	Increased	Clear to tur-bid; occasional clot	25-2,000, mostly lymphs	45-400+	15-75	1st zone or midzone curve	Often positive serologic test in C.S.F. and blood.
Late C.N.S. syphilis	Usually normal	Normal	Normal or increased	Normal or increased	Normal	Depending on activity	Often positive serologic test in C.S.F.
Aseptic meningeal reaction (brain or extradural abscess, thrombosis, etc.)	Usually normal	Clear or tur-bid; often xanthochromic	Increased	Normal or increased	Normal	Variable	Culture of C.S.F. nega-tive. Similar reactions occur with use of intra-thecal drugs.
Poliomyelitis, acute	Usually normal	Usually clear and colorless	Increased	Increased	45-100	Normal or midzone	
Viral encephalitis (arthropod-borne)	Normal or increased	Normal	0-100, mostly lymphs	Normal or increased	45-100	Variable	Proved by serological tests.
Viral meningo-encephalitis*	Normal or increased	Normal	0-2,000+, mostly lymphs	Normal or increased	Normal	Variable	Proved by virus isolation and serological tests.
Postinfectious encephalitis	Usually increased	Normal	Slightly increased	Normal or increased	Increased	Variable	
Traumatic ("bloody") tap	Normal	Bloody	Many r.b.c. (fresh)	Increased	Normal	Normal	Most blood in first tube. Least blood in last tube.
Cerebral hemorrhage, ventricular, subarachnoid	Slightly increased	Bloody, super-natant yellow	Many r.b.c. (crenated or fresh)	Increased	Variable	Normal	Blood present in all specimens equally.
Toxoplasmosis, congenital	Increased	Xanthochromic	50-500, mostly monos.	Increased up to 2000	Variable		Toxoplasma in stained smear.

*"Aseptic meningitis" caused by mumps, herpes simplex, lymphocytic choriomeningitis, Coxsackie, ECHO, and other viruses.

Condition	Pressure	Cells	Appearance	Total protein	Colloidal gold	Sugar	Serology	Remarks
Subdural hematoma	Usually increased	Usually increased	Clear or yellow	Normal	Normal or increased	Variable	Normal	If papilledema present, lumbar puncture contraindicated.
Brain tumor	Usually increased	Usually increased	Clear, occasionally xanthochromic	Normal or increased	Usually increased	Normal or increased	Variable	Little fluid obtained.
Spinal cord tumor (subarachnoid block)	Normal or low	Normal or increased	Often xanthochromic	Normal or increased	Usually increased	Normal or increased	Variable	
Multiple sclerosis	Low	Normal or increased	Normal	Normal or increased	Normal	Normal	Normal	50% of cases have normal C.S.F. 1st or midzone.
Uremia	Usually increased	Usually increased	Normal	Normal or increased	Usually increased	Variable	Variable	C.S.F. N.P.N. is high.
Diabetic coma	Low	Increased	Normal	Normal or increased	Increased	Normal	Normal	May have spasticity, weakness, convulsions.
Alcoholism	Occasionally increased	Normal or increased	Normal	Normal or increased	Normal	Normal	Normal or increased	

TYPICAL CURVES OF LANGE'S COLLOIDAL GOLD TEST (Gold Sol)

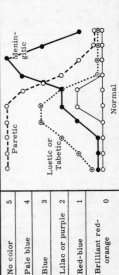

Colors in Test Tubes		Dilutions of spinal fluid with 0.4% NaCl (10 tubes)
No color	5	
Pale blue	4	
Blue	3	
Lilac or purple	2	
Red-blue	1	
Brilliant red-orange	0	

Curves: Meningitic — Paretic — Luetic or Tabetic — Normal

"GRADES" OF SYPHILITIC SPINAL FLUID (Stokes)

	Grade I	Grade II	Grade III
Serology	- -	±	++
Number of white cells/mm.	5-25	25-100	7-100+
Protein increase	+	++	+++
Colloidal gold curve	0000000000	0023454310	5555554310

Note: Grade III fluid denotes marked activity and is definite indication for intensive therapy.

After adequate penicillin therapy, the cells tend to disappear first; the colloidal gold curve and the serology may remain abnormal for long periods.

15...

Sputum Examination

Study sputum for specific diagnosis of diseases of respiratory tract suggested by symptoms or signs.

Collection of Specimen.
Insist that patient bring up sputum from "deep down" by coughing. Saliva is of no value. Collect in sterile dish or cup. Examination to be significant has to be prompt. In addition, collect 24-hour sputum in paraffined paper container to judge amount and physical characteristics. If bronchoscopy is done, specimens of secretions and bronchial washings are desirable. Always obtain specimen before starting chemotherapy; reexamine at intervals. Transtracheal aspiration may reflect lung flora better than sputum.

Examinations.
A. Gross Appearance: Amount per 24 hours, color, odor, layering, consistency, etc. Look for:
   1. Bronchial casts in late pneumonia or chronic bronchitis.
   2. Dittrich plugs in chronic bronchitis, bronchiectasis, bronchial asthma.
   3. "Lung stones" may be found in chronic tuberculosis.
B. Microscopic Examination: Select flecks of mucus, pus, cheesy material. Examine wet preparation and stained smear (see p. 266). The presence of more than a few squamous epithelial cells suggests heavy admixture of saliva and nasopharyngeal mucus. Such specimens do not reflect processes in the bronchi or lungs.
   1. Unstained - Look for fungi, parasites, Curschmann's spirals and Charcot-Leyden crystals (spirals and crystals both found in bronchial asthma), clumps of pus cells, red cells, fat globules, "sulfur granules," elastic fibers (indicate lung destruction).
   2. Stained - Gram's for predominating bacteria, Kinyoun or Ziehl-Neelsen for acid-fast bacilli, Wright's for eosinophils in bronchial asthma, etc.
C. Bacteriologic Examination:
   1. Routine culture on blood agar plates. Streak two plates in series to assure well-isolated colonies.

2. If mycotic disease is suspected, culture on anaerobic blood agar plates, Sabouraud's agar. If sulfur granules (Actinomyces) are found, wash in saline and inoculate into thioglycollate medium.

3. Culture for tubercle bacilli; concentrate (see p. 292).

4. Special cultures for Mycoplasma - Specimens are inoculated into special PPLO broth or special agar, each supplemented with 30% human ascitic fluid or serum. Incubation at 37°C. continues for 2-7 days, and subculture onto solid media is then necessary. Minute colonies, largely buried in the agar, may be detected with a hand lens. For transfer and microscopic examination, blocks of agar are cut from the plate. Special staining methods (Dienes) or immuno-fluorescence can be applied to such agar blocks.

5. Animal inoculation - Inoculate sputum into guinea pigs for tuberculosis (see p. 292); into mice for pneumococci, Coccidioides, some viruses; into eggs and tissue cultures for viruses.

6. In children, throat swabs should be cultured because sputum often cannot be obtained. Throat swabs may reflect lung flora. If a tracheal tube is in place, aspirated material should be cultured.

7. Patients under treatment with antibiotics often have large numbers of yeasts in their sputum. This usually has no etiologic significance.

D. Cytologic Study for Neoplastic Cells: (See also Chapter 23.) From a fresh sputum specimen, tissue fragments or blood-tinged material are selected and smeared over five slides with the aid of another glass slide so as to form thin and uniform films. The wet films are immersed in a mixture of equal parts of 95% alcohol and ether for 30 minutes.

From ether-alcohol mixture, slides are transferred to 95% alcohol for one minute and subsequently handled as ordinary tissue sections and stained with hematoxylin-eosin.

Scan slides under low power for tumor fragments or groups of neoplastic cells, then study individual cells under the high-dry objective for hyperchromatism, loss of polarity of cell, marked variation of size and shape of cell and nucleus, relatively large or multiple nuclei, distinct nucleoli, etc.

E. Agents Isolated From Sputum by Special Methods (see C4 above): The agent of psittacosis and the viruses of influenza, mumps, poliomyelitis, measles, and herpes simplex; adenoviruses; respiratory syncytial, parainfluenza, Coxsackie, ECHO, and other may be found. Send fresh sputum or nasopharyngeal washings promptly to virus laboratory, preferably in a sterile glass vial packed in dry ice.

MICROSCOPIC FINDINGS IN SPUTUM

Pigmented alveolar
epithelium

Alveolar epithe-
lium with fatty
degeneration

Alveolar epithe-
lium with
myelin granules

Pus cells

Red blood
corpuscles

Elastic
fibers

Fibrinous cast
of small bronchus

Curschmann's
spirals

Giant multinucleated macro-
phage with numerous
ingested particles

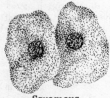
Squamous
epithelial cells

Squamous metaplasia of bronchial
epithelium with degenerative changes

Bronchial epithe-
lial cells

Squamous
carcinoma

Squamous
carcinoma epithe-
lial pearl

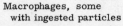
Adenocarcinoma.
Cells with secretory vacuoles.
Macrophages, some
with ingested particles

Carcinoma
mitoses

15...

Examination of Secretions of the Gastrointestinal Tract

CONSTITUENTS OF NORMAL SALIVA

Amount of secretion in 24 hours - 1000 to 1500 ml.
pH - 6.3 to 6.85 (5.75 to 7.05 if collected without loss of CO_2).
    pH in mouth is usually 7.5 to 8.0.
Sp. gr. - 1.002 to 1.008.
Total solids - 0.5 Gm./100 ml.
Sodium - 17.4 (8.7-24) mEq./L.
Potassium - 14.1 (13-16) mEq./L.

NORMAL GASTRIC CONSTITUENTS IN ADULTS

Constituents	Normal Residuum	Appetite Juice*
Water (%)	99.02	99.45
Total solids (%)	0.98	0.55
Organic solids (mucin, ferments, etc.) (%)	0.53	0.41
Inorganic solids (%)	0.45	0.14
Specific gravity	1.006-1.009	1.007
pH	0.9-1.5	0.9-1.5
Total acidity: In C.U.† or mEq./L.	10-50	20-100
Free HCl: In C.U.† or mEq./L.	0-30	25-50
Chlorides (as Cl), as Gm./100 ml.	0.5-0.6	
Total nitrogen (avg. = 66 mg./100 ml.)	51.75	
Non-protein nitrogen ⎫	20-30	
Urea nitrogen ⎬ in mg./100 ml.	1.3-4	
Total sulfur ⎪	7	
Total phosphorus ⎪	5	5
Amino acid N ⎪	3-9	3-9
Ammonia N ⎭	2-3	2-3

Digestive Factors.
    Intrinsic factor of Castle (anti-pernicious anemia factor), pepsin and hydrochloric acid (for protein digestion), rennin (curdles milk), gastric lipase (weak lipolytic ferment).

*In cephalic phase of gastric secretion; that which occurs as a result of seeing, smelling, or tasting food.
†Clinical units or degrees (see p. 270).

NORMAL GASTRIC CONSTITUENTS IN
INFANTS AND CHILDREN

At birth the stomach secretes small amounts of pepsin, rennin, and free acid. About 4% of apparently normal children have achlorhydria, and this percentage gradually increases with age (after the age of 60, 30% have achlorhydria). During the first year the volume of residuum is 2 to 5 ml., pH = 2.6 to 3.0. There is a steady increase in volume and acidity until the age of 15 to 20 years when adult levels are reached.

Maximum Response to Histamine Varies With Age as Follows:

	1 mo.	6 mos.	1 yr.	2 yrs.	5 yrs.	10 yrs.	15 yrs.
Free Acid*	0-20	0-59	12-80	15-95	20-90	53-113	49-115
Total Acid*	15-40	5-71	25-105	26-106	38-102	61-145	61-128

*Clinical units or degrees or mEq./L.

ABNORMAL GASTRIC CONSTITUENTS

These may include the following:
1. Blood. This is the most important abnormal finding.
2. Food remnants many hours after eating. (See emptying time, p. 272.)
3. Large amounts of mucus or bile.
4. Sarcinae, pyogenic organisms, Boas-Oppler bacillus, yeast cells.
5. Tissue fragments, large amounts of epithelium.
6. Parasites and ova.
7. Organic acids, e.g., lactic acid, seen in absence of HCl.
8. Tubercle bacilli, in pulmonary tuberculosis. (See method, p. 292.)

ROUTINE GASTRIC JUICE EXAMINATION

Gross Examination.
A. Amount: Normal fasting stomach content is 50 to 100 ml.
B. Color: Normal is opalescent, colorless.
   1. Blood is red or the color of coffee grounds if acid hematin is formed.
   2. Fresh bile is yellow; old bile is green.
   3. In stasis, food colors may remain.

GASTRIC CONTENTS IN DISEASE

	Gastritis (Acute or Chronic)	Duodenal Ulcer	Gastric Ulcer	Gastric Carcinoma*
Mucus (+ if increased)	+++	Negligible	Negligible	++
Yeasts and Sarcinae (+ if present)	+	Absent		++
Lactic acid	+	Absent	Absent	++
Blood (+ if present)	Sometimes	Usually absent	++	+++
Total acidity	Low, 10°†	High, 50°† and up	Varies	Low
Free acidity	Low or absent	High, 30°† and up	Normal or low	Often absent
Rate of gastric evacuation	Varies	Early: fast Late: slow	Varies	Slow

*Some of the findings due to associated achlorhydria.
†The sign (°) refers here to clinical units or mEq./L.

C. Odor: Normal is sour or slightly rancid. May be fecal in intestinal obstruction, ammoniacal in uremia.
D. Character: Note thickness of three layers on standing: Mucus on top, opalescent fluid next, and "bread-like" residue on bottom.
E. Reaction: Test with litmus and nitrazine papers (p. 111).
F. Rate of Secretion:
   1. Mean values for basal rate of secretion of acid - Age 20-29, 2.5 mEq./hour; age 50-59, 2 mEq./hour; over age 60, 1.5 mEq./hour.
   2. Mean values for 12-hour nocturnal secretion in normal individual: Volume, 580 ml.; free acid, 29 mEq./L. or 16.85 mEq./12 hours.

Chemical Examination.
A. Blood: May be due to trauma of passing a tube. Do Hematest®, guaiac, or benzidine tests (see p. 120).
B. Qualitative Test for Free HCl (Töpfer's test): To 5 drops of gastric juice in evaporating dish add 1 to 2 drops of 0.5% alcoholic solution of dimethyl-amino-azobenzene (Töpfer's reagent). Cherry-red color occurs with HCl.
C. Titration for Acid:
   1. Transfer 5 ml. of gastric juice to an evaporating dish, add 20 ml. H_2O. Add 3 drops of Töpfer's reagent (see above) and 3 drops of phenolphthalein, and titrate with N/10 NaOH until the last trace of red color disappears. This is the amount of NaOH necessary to neutralize the free HCl; this value times 20 equals the clinical units

of free HCl. Now continue titrating until red color of
phenolphthalein appears. The total number of ml. of
NaOH used (in both titrations) times 20 equals the
clinical units of total acidity.

2. Units of measurement -
   a. Clinical units are defined as the number of ml. of
      N/10 NaOH required to neutralize 100 ml. of
      gastric contents. This unit is also called a degree
      [using the degree sign (°)]. Each C. U. or degree
      is equal to 0.00365 Gm. of HCl or 1 mM. or mEq.
      acid per liter.
   b. Milliequivalents of H^+ per liter equals number of
      ml. of N/10 NaOH required to neutralize acid in
      100 ml. of gastric content (or ml. of 1-N NaOH
      required to neutralize acid in 1 liter of gastric con-
      tent). One mEq./L. = 1 clinical unit.
   c. The normality (HCl) of gastric juice is calculated
      by dividing C. U. or milliequivalents by 1000.
   d. In the fasting state, gastric contents ordinarily
      contain 0.15 to 0.25% HCl. For gastric juice the
      maximum concentration of HCl is about 0.58%,
      which corresponds to an HCl normality of about
      0.160, or 160 mEq. of HCl/L. It is interesting
      that in the blood the concentration of total base is
      also in the range of 160 mEq./L.
   e. The pH of gastric contents bears no constant
      relationship to any other measuring unit of acidity.
      The free (rather than total) acid primarily deter-
      mines the pH, which usually varies in fasting con-
      tents from 2.0 to 1.0, and this pH range corre-
      sponds to an HCl normality of about 0.05 to 0.10.
      If the normality drops to 0.01 or so, the pH may be
      about 3.0, and it takes very little food or other
      diluent to bring the pH to 7.0.

D. Lactic Acid (Kelling's Test): Usually seen only in achlorhydria. Add 2 drops of 10% ferric chloride to one test
   tube-full of water, mix, and divide into two test tubes.
   Add one ml. of gastric juice to one tube and compare.
   Lactic acid gives canary yellow color. Much lactic acid
   (over 0.1%) suggests gastric carcinoma.

E. Pepsin: Mix 10 ml. gastric juice with 10 ml. N/10 HCl.
   Divide in three tubes. Boil one for negative control; add
   pepsin to one as positive control. Place one Mett tube
   in each and incubate overnight.

Microscopic Examination.

Place one drop of sediment on slide, and cover. Look
for undigested food particles, blood, mucus, bacteria, tissue
fragments, parasites, sarcinae, yeasts. Oppler-Boas bacilli
are large nonmotile rods which stain brown with Gram's stain
and form lactic acid; they occur in stasis in absence of HCl.

Exfoliative cytologic preparations of fresh gastric washings should be employed in the search for gastric neoplasms.

GASTRIC TEST MEALS

Technics.

Give nothing by mouth after supper; test in morning. (For technic of intubation, see p. 273.)

A. Diagnex Blue® Test: (Gastric intubation is not required for this test.) Azure A carbacrylic resin dissociates in the presence of acid to yield free azure A, which is then excreted in the urine. In the absence of free acid in the stomach, no azure A will be released and none will appear in the urine.

The test meal consists of caffeine with sodium benzoate to stimulate gastric secretion and azure A resin granules as the indicator substance. Urine is analyzed for azure A by a simple colorimetric procedure. Follow the directions supplied by the manufacturer.

B. Histamine Test Meal (to determine achlorhydria): Do not give histamine to patients with history of allergy, asthma, etc. With tube in place, aspirate for ten minutes to empty stomach. Give histamine, 0.3 to 0.5 mg. subcut. (or may use 0.1 mg./10 Kg. body weight), or Histalog®, 50 mg. I. M., and continue to collect samples. Divide samples into 10- or 15-minute specimens; total time of collection may vary from 30 to 60 minutes. Normal response (mEq./ hour): mean, 11.8; upper limit of normal, 18.7.

C. Augmented Histamine Test (Kay) Modified to Employ Betazole (Histalog®): With tube in place, collect basal secretion continuously for 1 hour (four 15-minute periods). Give betazole (Histalog®), 1.5 mg./Kg. body weight I. M. (Some patients may complain of faintness, headache, or flushing; pallor or flushing may be observed.) Collect gastric juice continuously for 60 to 90 minutes, collecting each 15-minute specimen separately. The largest volume secreted in any half hour after the betazole is measured and the free and total acidity are then determined. Secretion is expressed in mEq./hour. (Normal volume is 150-250 ml./hour.) Normal secretion is 0.1-42.1 mEq. (mean 17.1) in men and 0.3-28.2 mEq. (mean 9.4) in women. Secretion less than 11 mEq./hour in men or 5 mEq./ hour in women practically excludes the possibility of duodenal ulcer.

D. Alcohol Test Meal, Fractional Analysis: Insert Levin or Rehfuss tube, withdraw all residuum, and inject 200 ml. of 5% alcohol (or 100 ml. of 7% alcohol). Leave tube in place and withdraw 10 ml. of specimens every 15 minutes for two hours. Determine free and total acidity.

Interpretation of Tests of Gastric Function.

A. Acidity: If the fasting specimen contains free acid as determined by development of a red color upon addition of Töpfer's reagent, there is little information that can be gained by continuing with "test meals." Absence of free acid must be proved by application of test meals.

   1. Anacidity and achylia gastrica are found in pernicious anemia, gastric mucosa atrophy, riboflavin deficiency, in virtually all cases of carcinoma of the stomach, and in about 3% of normal adults (this increases to 30% of normal people over the age of 60).

   2. Hypersecretion and hyperchlorhydria occur commonly in duodenal ulcer and are characteristic of the Zollinger-Ellison syndrome (multiple endocrine adenomas) associated with pancreatic islet cell tumors which secrete gastrin. In the Zollinger-Ellison syndrome the ratio of basal to maximal acid output (BAO/MAO) is greater than 60% (normal, 10-20%).

B. Emptying Time: Normal = three to six hours. Gastric retention is indicated by presence of food for longer than six hours after eating, by large residuum, and by yeasts and other organisms. An obstructing lesion of pylorus is the common cause.

Special Gastric Examinations.

A. Insulin (Hypoglycemia) Test of Gastric Secretion: Normally hypoglycemia produces a "cephalic" stimulus which, via the vagus, initiates gastric secretion. Production of hypoglycemia has been used to test completeness of section of vagus fibers after vagotomy.

   1. Method - Pass stomach tube. Take fasting specimen of blood for glucose determination and fasting specimen of gastric juice for free acid titer. Give 15 units of regular insulin I.V. Take blood for glucose determination every 30 minutes for two hours; take 15-minute samples of gastric juice for titration.

   2. Interpretation - If hypoglycemia is produced (Folin blood glucose 50 mg./100 ml. or less; "true" blood glucose 40 mg./100 ml. or less), a rise in gastric juice secretion volume and acidity indicates intact vagal fibers; failure to obtain such a response suggests but does not prove complete vagus section. It is necessary to have proof of positive response prior to vagus section.

B. Cytologic Method for Diagnosis of Gastric Carcinoma: A fasting sample of gastric juice is aspirated, centrifuged immediately, and processed according to the method of Papanicolaou or modifications thereof (see p. 393).

C. Tubercle Bacilli: Gastric washings. (See p. 292.)

GASTROINTESTINAL TUBES AND THEIR USE

Indications for Intubation.
  A. To obtain gastric juice for analysis.
  B. Tube-feeding.
  C. Duodenal drainage. Instill magnesium sulfate into duodenum.
  D. Preoperative decompression in gastrointestinal obstruction; this may make surgery unnecessary (see pp. 445 and 447).
  E. Postoperative decompression in case of vomiting and distention (see pp. 445 and 452).
  F. Removal of ingested poisons (see p. 458).

Contraindications to Intubation.
  Avoid retching in cases of aneurysm, heart failure, hypertension, or marked arteriosclerosis. Use tube with care in case of gastric ulcer. Do not use after corrosive poisons have been swallowed.

Types of Tubes. (May be rubber or newer plastic variety.)
  A. Ewald tube is a large oral tube, size 30 F. or larger, used in emptying stomach of particulate matter, as after Ewald or motor meals. Used in tube-feeding patients.
  B. Rehfuss tube is a small oral tube with a heavy perforated metal "olive" at its tip. Olive helps patient swallow tube, falls into dependent part of stomach. Used for obtaining gastric juice or emptying stomach.
  C. Levin tube is the most generally used stomach tube. It is a round-tipped nasal catheter, size 14 or 16 F., with four openings in its terminal three inches (8 cm.). It is used for obtaining gastric juice, gastric decompression, or duodenal drainage.
  D. Wangensteen tube is a Levin-type tube impregnated with lead in its terminal end to help in entering duodenum, for intestinal decompression. Has nine openings in terminal ten inches.
  E. Miller-Abbott tube is a tube, size 16 F., with two lumens which is used for decompression in small bowel obstruction. A small channel serves to inflate a balloon in the tip of the tube after it has passed into the midportion of the duodenum. The larger channel is proximal to the balloon and serves for aspiration. Modifications of this tube exist.

Technic of Intubation.
  The average distance from teeth through cardia is 18 inches (46 cm.); from cardia through pylorus is 11 inches (28 cm.). Nasal route is two inches (5 cm.) farther than oral route.

Cover patient with waterproof apron and give him an emesis basin to hold. Reassure the patient; explain that retching may be controlled by active panting. Marked pharyngeal spasm can be overcome by local anesthesia. Use water for lubricant. If patient begins to cough, withdraw the tube; it is probably in trachea.

A. Oral tubes made of rubber are kept in icewater until inserted. Plastic tubes should not be chilled because they become rigid if cold. Push tube into pharynx, tell the patient to swallow, and simultaneously push in three to four inches (7 to 10 cm.) of tube. Introduce a total of 20 inches (50 cm.) from teeth, and aspirate to make sure tip is in stomach. In case of difficulty, have patient swallow water and push tube in while swallowing. Patient may swallow Rehfuss tube without help; when it is withdrawn, pharyngospasm may hold the "olive"; if so, have patient swallow icewater while doctor pulls firmly on tube. The Ewald tube is forced down by doctor; tell patient to swallow; push tube in firmly as larynx descends.

B. Nasal tubes are easier to introduce. Keep tube in water at room temperature. Push tube into nostril along base of nose (aim toward occiput, not up) until it is felt to bend into pharynx; tell the patient to swallow, and simultaneously push in six or seven inches (15 to 18 cm.) of tube. Introduce a total of 22 inches (56 cm.), then aspirate. Tube may coil up in pharynx and cause gagging.

DUODENAL DRAINAGE
(See p. 447 for decompression.)

Indications.
A. For diagnosis of liver or biliary tract disease. Drainage may be done periodically to help diagnose exacerbations of chronic infections early so that they can be controlled.
B. For other diagnostic purposes relating to parasites, pancreatic enzymes, etc.
C. For therapeutic drainage in cholangitis or biliary obstruction.

Technic for Diagnostic Drainage.
A. Give nothing by mouth after midnight.
B. In the morning, insert a weighted tube (Rehfuss, Levin; see p. 273) to a length of 20 inches (50 cm.). Withdraw gastric specimen.
C. With patient erect or lying on his right side before the fluoroscope, feed and massage tube into middle third of the duodenum. Now aspirate duodenal contents for five to 30 minutes and label "A"; this evacuation specimen is of little value for bile study.

D. Slowly inject 50 ml. of warm 33% magnesium sulfate
solution through the tube to relax sphincter of Oddi.
Clamp tube for five minutes, then drain for 30 minutes
and label "B." Gallbladder bile is first dark, then
lighter. If no "B" bile is obtained, inject another 50 ml.
of magnesium sulfate. If still unsuccessful, inject 30
ml. of olive oil.

E. During the final period of 30 minutes, try to collect
yellow hepatic bile. Label it "C."

Examination for Diagnosis.
A. Note density, color, flocculi in all three specimens.
Test for bile, blood, reaction, ferments as desired.

B. Microscopy: This is important in detecting early cholelithiasis (gall sand). Note pus cells, bacteria, cellular
elements, crystals.

C. Giardia or other parasites may be present.

D. Culture for bacteria, especially typhoid bacilli.

Interpretation.
A. Absence of dark "B" bile indicates loss of gallbladder
function. No bile may appear in common duct obstruction.

B. In cholelithiasis, many cholesterol and calcium bilirubin
crystals appear in "B" and "C" bile. The cholesterol
crystals may be perfect or atypical, or may be mixed
with cellular detritus. The calcium bilirubinate comes
as yellow or reddish particles the size of a pinhead.

C. In biliary tract inflammation there is much yellow cellular and bacterial material in "B" and "C" bile.

D. Blood may be grossly visible in advanced carcinoma.

COMPOSITION OF PANCREATIC JUICE

Obtain specimen by duodenal drainage (see p. 274); it is
mixed with bile. The flow of pancreatic juice is stimulated by
an injection of secretin. Secretin is a hormone normally produced by upper intestinal mucosa in response to the presence
of acid. The flow of pancreatic juice begins five minutes after
a meal, is at its height in two to three hours, lasts six to
eight hours in all.

Gross and Chemical Characteristics of Pancreatic Juice.
A. Volume per 24 hours = 500 to 800 ml.

B. Specific Gravity = 1.007.

C. Total Solids = 1.5 to 2.5 Gm./100 ml.

D. Alkalinity: pH = 7.0 to 8.2; 10 ml. of pancreatic juice =
10 to 13 ml. of N/10 NaOH and is more effective than bile
or succus entericus in neutralizing acid gastric juice.

E. Bicarbonate = 70 to 100 mEq./L.

F. Sodium = 100 to 150 mEq./L.

G. Potassium = 2 to 8 mEq./L.

H. Chloride = 50 to 95 mEq./L.

Digestive Enzymes (Ferments).

Are all produced by the same type of pancreatic cell. They are more powerful than the corresponding enzymes produced by other organs. In pancreatic injury or duct obstruction the serum concentration of diastase and lipase increases; urinary diastase is increased. These facts are used in diagnosis.

A. Trypsin is pancreatic protease. There are 100 to 200 units per liter. It is much more active than pepsin.

B. Diastase is pancreatic amylase, or amylopsin. It is not present in the newborn. Concentration: 1000 to 2000 units per liter.

Test for diastase in duodenal specimen: Add 2 ml. of a 1 to 10 dilution to 2 ml. of a 1% starch solution; incubate at 37° C. for 30 minutes. Add one drop of Gram's iodine solution; if any blue color remains, it indicates defective diastase secretion.

C. Steapsin or lipase. Concentration: 30,000 to 60,000 units per liter.

D. Maltase breaks down maltose.

E. Rennin curdles milk.

F. Two peptidases, amino- and carboxy-poly-peptidases.

Fibrocystic Disease: Sweat Test.

Abnormally high concentrations of sodium and chloride appear in sweat obtained from patients with fibrocystic disease. Sweat may be collected on electrolyte-free gauze pads or by iontophoresis. (Check with laboratory for details of technic.)

	Normal (mEq./L.)	Fibrocystic Disease (mEq./L.)
Chloride	4-60	60-160
Sodium	10-90	80-190

There may be some overlap between "high normal" and "low normal" levels. The test should be repeated if any doubt exists.

COMPOSITION OF BILE

Gross and Chemical Characteristics of Bile.

A. Volume per 24 Hours: 700 to 1000 ml.

B. Specific Gravity: Hepatic duct, 1.010; gallbladder, 1.026 to 1.032.

C. Total Solids:

	Hepatic Duct (Gm./100 ml.)	Gallbladder (Gm./100 ml.)
Bile salts	1.8	8.7
Fatty acids and lipids	0.24	1.8
Cholesterol	0.16	0.87

D. pH: Hepatic duct, 7.5 (6.2-8.5); gallbladder, 6.0 (5.6-8.0).

E. Sodium: 134 to 156 mEq./L.

F. Potassium: 3.9 to 6.3 mEq./L.

G. Chloride: 83 to 110 mEq./L.

H. Bicarbonate: 38 mEq./L.

FECES EXAMINATION

The specimen should be obtained without the use of oils or enemas, and should be free of barium. It should be examined as soon as possible, preferably while still warm. Saline cathartics are sometimes indicated in making examinations for typhoid carriers and amebiasis.

Marking Stool for Timed Collection.

This is easily done by feeding a capsule containing 0.2 Gm. powdered charcoal to mark the beginning of the collection, followed by another capsule at a definite interval to mark the end of the collection. Capsules containing 0.3 Gm. of carmine are also used. Total gastrointestinal passage time is normally one to three days (may be four days).

Gross Examination.

A. Amount: The average daily output of moist feces by adults is 80 to 170 Gm. (average, 100 Gm.). In rare cases a high-vegetable diet may produce up to 350 Gm. of daily fecal output, representing 75 Gm. of solids. In starvation, 7 to 8 Gm. of sticky green-black feces are excreted per day. Solids constitute only 25% of fecal matter:
   1. Food residues.
   2. Remains of intestinal and digestive secretions.
   3. Bacteria. These constitute one-third the weight of dried feces.
   4. Various cellular elements.

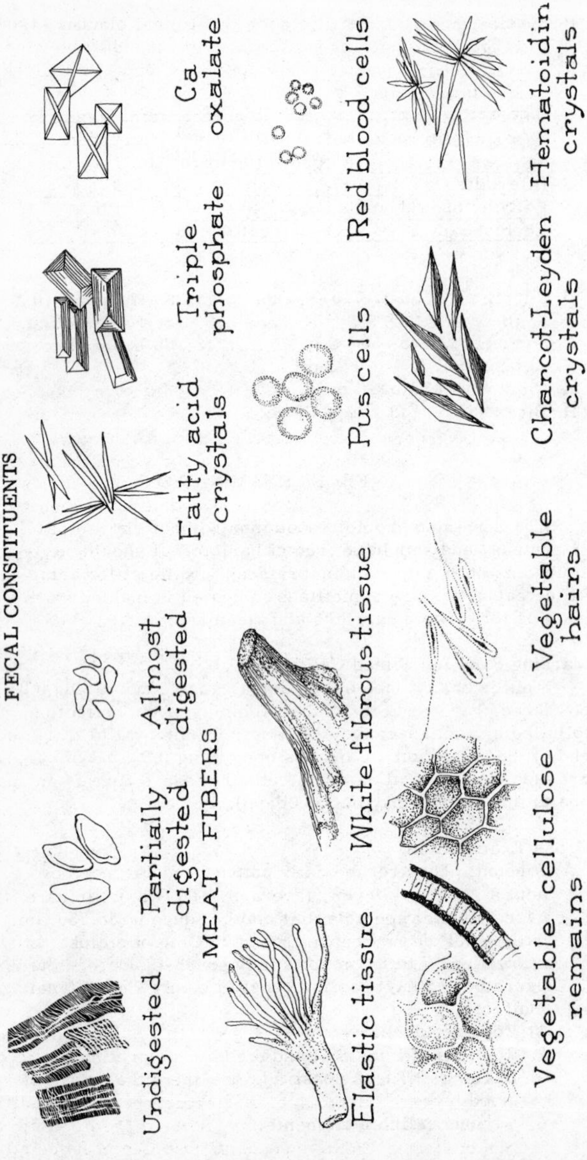

FECAL CONSTITUENTS

MEAT FIBERS

Undigested — Partially digested — Almost digested

Elastic tissue — White fibrous tissue

Vegetable cellulose remains — Vegetable hairs

Ca oxalate — Triple phosphate — Fatty acid crystals — Red blood cells — Pus cells — Charcot-Leyden crystals — Hematoidin crystals

5. Substances excreted into the intestines. Mucus is normally present in small amounts, but may be very plentiful in dysentery, etc. Mucous shreds may look like tapeworms.

B. Color: The diet is the most important determining factor. The usual brown color is due to urobilin and stercobilin, two pigments derived from bilirubin.
1. Brown - Average well-balanced diet.
2. Light brown - Milk diet.
3. Brownish-black - High-meat diet.
4. Yellow - Rhubarb, santonin, senna, fats.
5. Green - Calomel, spinach, unchanged biliverdin.
6. Black - Bismuth or iron salts, or blood.
7. Grayish-white (clay-colored) - Biliary obstruction.
8. Red - Bleeding in colon or rectum; undigested beets or tomatoes.

C. Odor: Normal odor of feces is not highly disagreeable and is due to indole and skatole. It is made more unpleasant by methane, hydrogen sulfide, and methyl mercaptan. Meat diets produce a most marked odor, milk and vegetable diets produce almost none (e.g., stools of infants). A very foul odor indicates alkaline reaction; highly acid feces smell sour or rancid.

D. Reaction: The pH of feces does not vary widely, ranging from 7.0 to 7.5. However, a heavy intake of lactose may produce an acid reaction.

E. Consistency: Normal feces are soft but formed. The longer the total gastrointestinal passage time, the firmer the feces usually are. Children tend to have softer stools.

F. Parasites: Examine grossly and microscopically (see pp. 336-41).

G. Effect of Oral Antibiotics: Treatment with oral antibiotics for more than a few days will frequently produce marked changes in the character of feces. The stools may become bulky, contain more undigested material, often have a greenish-gray color, and are frequently odorless. There may be a marked increase in mucus. Diarrhea with watery stools may occur.

Chemical Examination.

A satisfactory fecal emulsion is made by dipping a small round wooden applicator stick into several portions of the fecal specimen and mixing adherent feces in a test tube containing 2 to 5 ml. water.

A. Blood: Blood in the stool is of great importance in diagnosis; it may be the only sign of ulcerative, neoplastic or inflammatory disease of the gastrointestinal tract. It requires 100 ml. or more of blood from the upper gastrointestinal tract to produce a tarry stool. Chemical detection of less than this depends on reaction of heme pigments with benzidine, guaiac, or orthotolidin.

Benzidine and guaiac tests may give color reactions with inorganic iron, bismuth, and enzymes from w.b.c.'s or undigested food.

1. Hematest® tablets are reliable and simple to use. Hemoglobin reacts with a peroxide-orthotolidin reagent to yield a blue color. False-positive reactions are rare. Follow manufacturer's instructions.

2. Gum guaiac (not a screening test) - On a piece of clean filter paper (not paper towels) or a clean blood-free slide, smear a small amount of feces. Add 2 drops glacial acetic acid and mix. Add 2 drops fresh, saturated solution of gum guaiac in 95% alcohol and 2 drops H_2O_2 (3%). Blue color is positive reaction; green color that fades is negative. Avoid contamination of reagents or filter paper with blood.

3. Benzidine test - Emulsify about 1 ml. of stool in 10 ml. H_2O containing 5 drops glacial acetic acid. Centrifuge slowly for one minute to separate large stool particles. To 1 ml. benzidine solution (see p. 622) in a clean Hgb.-free test tube, add 0.5 ml. of the acid extract of stool and 0.5 ml. fresh 0.6% H_2O_2 solution (in that order). Let stand at least five minutes for development of color (green, blue, then purple). Intensity of color parallels concentration of Hgb. Read at 15 minutes to allow for development of maximum color.

B. Hydrobilirubin (Urobilin): With mortar and pestle mix a few grams of fresh feces with an equal quantity of 10% mercuric chloride solution. Let stand six to 24 hours. Urobilin gives a deep red color; bile gives a green color.

C. Urobilinogen: Quantitative fecal and urine urobilinogen determinations are sufficiently difficult so that they should be performed in a clinical or hospital laboratory. (Ref.: Watson, C. J., and Hawkinson, V., Am. J. Clin. Path. **17**:108, 1947; Watson, C. J., et al., Am. J. Clin. Path. **14**:605, 1944.)

Microscopic Examination.

A. Cells: Usually a suspension of feces is placed on a slide covered with a cover glass, and examined promptly under high power.

1. Epithelial cells indicate increased gastrointestinal irritation.

2. Red cells are not seen normally.

3. Leukocytes, especially P.M.N.'s, are best seen if 1 drop of 10% acetic acid is added to 1 drop of fecal emulsion on a slide. A small number of leukocytes is normal. Large numbers are seen in gastrointestinal inflammations. Macrophages and leukocytes may be seen in chronic cases of amebic dysentery with second-

ary bacterial invasion. Eosinophils are numerous in amebiasis, especially during the acute phase, and in "intestinal allergy."

B. Crystals (use low power):

1. Calcium oxalate crystals, fatty acid crystals, and triple phosphate (ammonium-magnesium-phosphate) crystals are common and not significant.

2. Hematoidin crystals are yellow needles occurring in groups or sheaves after intestinal hemorrhage.

3. Charcot-Leyden needles are seen occasionally in parasitic infections, especially amebiasis.

C. Undigested Food (use low power):

1. Vegetable matter - Vegetable cells in various stages of decomposition are seen. Vegetable hairs look much like Strongyloides larvae.

2. Animal matter - Muscle fibers may be recognized by their striations. Elastic fibers do not swell when 10% acetic acid is added, as does connective tissue.

3. Undigested starch turns blue upon addition of 1 drop of Lugol's solution.

4. Fat - Neutral fat globules can be stained with Sudan III or IV. The dye is prepared as a saturated solution in 70% alcohol. To a 1 or 2 mm. pellet of feces on a glass slide, add 2 or 3 drops of alcoholic solution of Sudan III or IV. Mix well with an applicator stick. Add 1 drop of 0.9% saline solution, cover with a cover slip, and examine under the microscope. Record as 0 to ++++, as follows: (Normal = 0 to ++)

	Droplets of Fat Under Entire Cover Slip
0 to +	0-2
+	3-5
++ to +++	Intermediate amounts
++++	Half of visible material

D. Parasites: See pp. 336-41.

Pathogenic Agents Which May Be Revealed by Feces Examination.

A. Direct Smear Examination:

1. Ascaris
2. Amebas
3. Balantidium
4. Clonorchis
5. Diphyllobothrium
6. Enterobius
7. Fasciola
8. Fasciolopsis
9. Hookworm
10. Hymenolepis
11. Giardia
12. Paragonimus
13. Schistosoma
14. Strongyloides
15. Taenia
16. Trichuris

B. Anal Smear Examination (Scotch Tape and Slide or Paraffined Swab): Enterobius.

C. Culture Technics:
   1. Shigellae   4. Amebas
   2. Cholera vibrios   5. Dientamoeba
   3. Salmonellae
D. Virus Isolation in Tissue Culture and by Animal Inoculation:
   1. Aseptic meningitis (Coxsackie) viruses
   2. Enteroviruses (including poliomyelitis virus)
   3. ECHO virus
   4. Adenoviruses
   5. Infectious hepatitis virus

16...
Microbiologic Examination

BACTERIOLOGIC SPECIMENS

Principles of Collection and Handling.
 A. Avoid contaminating yourself, materials, and surrounding areas. Treat all specimens as potential sources of infection, and collect them in closed sterile containers.
 B. Collect specimens from areas where suspected organisms are most likely to be found (e.g., spreading edge of lesion; see chart, p. 284) and at a time when their growth is probable (e.g., blood culture when fever is rising or at peak).
 C. Collect scanty material on two sterile cotton swabs. Use one for culture. From the other prepare smears by rotating swab lightly over slide.
 D. Collect specimens prior to use of antiseptics or antibiotics when possible. Sulfonamides administered systemically can be antagonized in the specimen by using culture media containing 5 mg. para-aminobenzoic acid per 100 ml. The action of penicillin is blocked in the specimen if culture media contain penicillinase. Thioglycollate medium neutralizes antibiotics to some extent.
 E. Label all specimens clearly and completely.
 F. Send to laboratory promptly after collection.

Routine Procedure When No Specific Technic is Indicated.
 A. Routine Smear: Prepare smears and stain by Gram's method. Smear pus like blood film. Centrifuge fluids aseptically and smear and culture sediment. Grind solids and tissues in mortar aseptically with sterile sand. Suspend ground material in broth; smear and culture.
 B. Routine Culture: Culture all specimens on blood agar and in thioglycollate medium. Technic: Plate one loopful of broth, or touch swab to one corner of plate and streak from that corner with sterile wire loop. Place one drop of specimen, or twirl swab, into thioglycollate broth. Apply specialized culture methods as indicated in addition to routine culture.

Special Technics May Be Indicated as Follows:
 A. Hanging drop of liquid cultures or suspensions of bacteria for motility.

BACTERIOLOGIC DIAGNOSIS OF SPECIFIC MICROORGANISMS FROM CLINICAL INFECTIONS*

Organism	Principal Sources of Clinical Specimens	Preferred Culture Media	Special Conditions and Additional Tests Usually Required
Staphylococcus	Pus or exudate from site of infection; blood stream, spinal fluid, urine.	Blood agar plates; trypticase-soy broth; brain broth (3 weeks).	Aerobic or micro-aerophilic. Presence of hemolysis; coagulase reaction; mannitol fermentation.
Streptococcus	Sputum, blood stream, spinal fluid, exudates, pus.	Blood agar plates; trypticase-soy broth; blood broth.	Aerobic or micro-aerophilic. Type of hemolysis; growth in 6.5% NaCl broth - enterococci. Immunofluorescence.
Pneumococcus			Hemolysis - alpha type; solubility in bile; typing with specific serum.
Gonococcus	Exudates from genitalia, eye, joints.	"Chocolate" agar plates incubated in 10% CO_2 (candle jar).	Intracellular diplococci on smear. Oxidase test.
Meningococcus	Blood stream, spinal fluid, nasopharynx, skin petechiae.		Intracellular diplococci on smear. Oxidase test; maltose fermented.
Corynebacterium diphtheriae	Nasopharynx, wounds, eye.	Löffler's slants; potassium tellurite medium; blood agar plates.	Typical morphology on smear. Virulence test; Schick skin test.
Clostridium	Wounds, exudates, pus, blood stream.	Blood agar plates; thioglycollate medium; chopped meat broth.	Strictly anaerobic. Type of hemolysis; milk coagulation; morphology.
Mycobacterium tuberculosis	Sputum, exudates, pus, spinal fluid, urine.	Petragnani's, Loewenstein's, or Dubos's media (2-4 weeks).	Guinea pig inoculation. Acid-fast stain; concentration.
Actinomyces	Sputum, exudates, pus.	Thioglycollate medium; blood agar plates.	Sulfur granules in specimen. Aerobic and anaerobic culture.
Escherichia coli- Enterobacter- Klebsiella group	Urine, blood stream, spinal fluid, exudates, pus, sputum.	Blood agar plates, MacConkey's or eosin-methylene blue (EMB) agar. Blood broth.	Lactose fermented (paracolon bacilli ferment lactose slowly).

Organism	Specimen	Culture media	Identification
Mycoplasma pneumoniae	Sputum, throat.	Special Mycoplasma agar and broth.	Special stains of impression smears.
Salmonella	Feces, blood stream, urine, exudates.	MacConkey's or EMB agar plates; SS agar plates; tetrathionate broth; triple sugar iron agar.	Identified by slide agglutination with specific serum; patient's serum for agglutination test - H and O agglutination.
Shigella	Feces		Identified by slide agglutination with specific serum.
Proteus–Pseudomonas group	Urine, exudates, blood stream, spinal fluid.	Blood agar plates; nutrient agar plates. EMB agar.	Characteristic pigment, odor, "swarming"; lactose not fermented.
Pasteurella	Blood stream, sputum, exudates, pus.	Blood agar plates; cystine agar.	Patient's serum for agglutination test.
Brucella	Blood stream, exudates.	Trypticase-soy agar and broth, incubated in 10% CO_2 (candle jar).	Patient's serum for agglutination or precipitin tests.
Hemophilus species	Spinal fluid, blood stream, sputum, exudates.	"Chocolate" agar plates; blood agar plates in 10% CO_2.	Typing with specific serum. Precipitin test in spinal fluid.
Bacteroides	Exudates, blood stream.	Chopped meat broth; thioglycollate medium; blood agar plates.	Strictly anaerobic. Typical morphology.
Treponema pallidum	Primary or secondary syphilitic lesion.	None	Fluorescence microscopy; serologic tests (STS, TPI, FTA-ABS).
Leptospira	Blood stream, urine.	Serum broth.	Dark-field microscopy.
Borrelia recurrentis	Blood stream.	Blood broth.	Stained blood film; serologic tests.
Yeasts and fungi	Skin, nails; exudates, pus; sputum, blood.	Blood agar plates; Sabouraud's medium.	Serologic tests on patient's serum.

*Reproduced, with permission, from Jawetz, Melnick, and Adelberg: Review of Medical Microbiology, 9th Ed. Lange, 1970.

B. Dark-field Microscopy: Objects in focus appear brightly illuminated on dark background. This is the best method for spirochetes and some fungi. Special equipment needed is a dark-field condenser instead of an ordinary condenser, "funnel stop" in the oil immersion objectives, and a strong, concentrated source of parallel light. Place immersion oil between condenser and slide and between cover slip and objective. Examine fresh material (e.g., syphilitic lesion exudate) without stain, or dried material on glass slide stained with fluorescent antibody.

C. Immunofluorescence: Microorganisms in a smear may be identified by specific antiserum labeled with fluorescein, examined by fluorescence microscopy in ultraviolet light.

D. Anaerobic Cultures: Culturing bacteria in the absence of oxygen is achieved by (1) displacing air with nitrogen or hydrogen or (2) adding reducing substances (e.g., thioglycollate medium).

Some organisms (e.g., neisseriae, brucellae) prefer an atmosphere of 10% CO_2 in air. This is easily obtained by burning a candle in a closed jar. The candle goes out when CO_2 concentration reaches 10%.

E. Blood Agar Media for Hemolysis: "Beta" hemolysis means complete dissolution of red blood cells; it results in clearing of a previously turbid blood agar plate or blood broth. "Alpha" hemolysis means partial alteration of pigment of red blood cells, resulting in a green zone around colonies. To establish type of hemolysis it is often necessary to make blood agar pour plates in addition to surface culture. Add blood and culture suspension to melted agar cooled to 45° C. (113° F.) and pour into Petri dishes in 15-ml. amounts.

F. Oxidase Test for Neisseriae: Oxidase, an enzyme produced by neisseriae (and some other bacteria), can be detected by dyes. Drop 1% aqueous dimethyl-paraphenylene-diamine hydrochloride on suspected colonies on chocolate or blood agar. Neisseria colonies will turn pink, maroon, and finally black. This test is used routinely to detect colonies of gonococci.

G. Coagulase Test for Pathogenic Staphylococci: Production of coagulase by staphylococci indicates pathogenicity; add a loopful of suspected colony from blood plate to 0.5 ml. of citrated rabbit plasma diluted 1:5 with physiological saline. Place tube in water bath at 37° C. (98.6° F.) and examine at 30-minute intervals for signs of clotting. If a clot forms within two hours, the organism is coagulase positive. Most such pathogenic staphylococci are also hemolytic, reduce tellurite (jet black colonies on tellurite agar), and ferment mannitol.

Specific Culture and Smear Methods.

A. Blood Culture and Smears:

1. Blood culture technic - Use great care with sterile equipment and materials. Apply tourniquet. Prepare skin area in antecubital fossa with weak (2%) tincture of iodine. Remove iodine with 70% alcohol. Withdraw 12 ml. of blood. Add 2 ml. of blood to sterile tube with citrate, mixing well, and add remainder of blood to flask containing 50 to 100 ml. blood culture media. This will support growth of aerobic and anaerobic organisms. Take citrated blood to laboratory. Pour two infusion agar plates with 1 ml. blood in each, incubating one aerobically, the other anaerobically. Keep all cultures at 37° C. (98.6° F.), and examine every other day for three weeks by making stained smears and subcultures.

2. Special blood culture methods for the following -

   a. Brucella - Inoculate 10 ml. of the patient's blood into 50 ml. of tryptose phosphate broth, and incubate at 37° C. in an atmosphere of 10% CO_2. Subculture every three to four days onto slants of liver infusion agar which are kept sealed at 37° C. for three weeks.

   b. Pasteurella tularensis - Inoculate blood onto glucose-cystine blood agar slants and incubate for six to ten days.

3. Usefulness of blood cultures and smears - Cultures are essential for the proper diagnosis and treatment of bacteremias and septicemias. Blood cultures should be taken in all cases of fever of unknown origin. Draw blood during chill, while fever rises, or during height of fever. Blood smears are most useful in parasitic diseases (see p. 344) and spirochetal infections.

   a. Positive blood cultures are commonly found in infections (chiefly early in the disease) with these organisms: Aerobacter, Bacteroides, Brucella, Klebsiella, coliform bacteria, Pseudomonas, Proteus, meningococcus, pneumococcus, salmonellae, staphylococci, streptococci, Pasteurella, etc. Culture media should contain substances to neutralize sulfonamides (PABA) or antibiotics (e.g., penicillinase) which the patient may be receiving. Whenever possible, blood culture should be obtained **before** instituting therapy (see above).

   b. Positive blood smears are found often in the following diseases: Leptospirosis (Weil's disease), relapsing fever, filariasis, kala-azar, malaria, trichinosis, and trypanosomiasis.

   c. Positive results from inoculation of blood into experimental animals or tissue cultures often appear early in the following diseases: Leptospirosis, rat-

bite fever, relapsing fever, rickettsial diseases
(see p. 307), some viral diseases (e.g., poliomyelitis).

d. Quantitative blood culture - Estimation of number of
organisms present per ml. of blood is important
when qualitative culture is positive. For technic
see p. 287.

B. Eye Cultures: Collect material from conjunctiva with
small cotton swabs or curet, avoiding contact with margins
of lids. Corneal specimens must be obtained by curet.
Take swab or specimen in broth tube to laboratory.
Plate on blood agar aerobically and in 10% CO_2 (candle
jar). Make a smear of conjunctival secretions and stain
with Giemsa's stain.

C. Ear and Mastoid Cultures: Collect material on cotton
swab and remove solid material from external canal for
fungus study. Smear and culture. It may be possible to
aspirate material through the drum.

D. Nasopharyngeal Cultures: (Avoid external nares, "nose"
culture.) Introduce sterile glass or plastic tube into nostril as deeply as is comfortably possible. Pass sterile
cotton swab on wire through tube. Rotate in nasopharynx
and withdraw. Place into broth. Plate on blood agar and
chocolate agar aerobically and in candle jar (meningococci).

E. Throat Culture: Pass two sterile cotton swabs over each
tonsillar area and over posterior pharyngeal walls.
Make smears and culture on blood agar. Stain smear
with Löffler's alkaline methylene blue for tentative diagnosis of diphtheria. If suggestive diphtheria-like organisms are seen, culture also on Löffler's serum slants
and tellurite blood agar plates. Stain another smear with
gentian violet (one minute) for Vincent's organisms (pale
spirochetes and dark, cigar-shaped fusiform bacilli).
Culture for Mycoplasma (see p. 265).

F. Sputum Cultures: See p. 264.

G. Spinal Fluid: Always collect three specimens in sterile
tubes and send to laboratory promptly (cell count, chemistry, serology, and bacteriology). If fluid is cloudy,
make direct smear and stain with Gram's stain. Incubate
C.S.F. at 37° C. overnight if prompt culture is not feasible. Many organisms will grow in C.S.F. If fluid is
fairly clear, centrifuge ten minutes, smear sediment,
and culture on blood agar, in thioglycollate medium, and
on chocolate agar in 10% CO_2 (candle jar). For examination for tubercle bacilli, fungi, and viruses, see p. 261.

H. Wounds and Ulcers: Collect material on cotton swab.
Make smears, always culture both aerobically (blood
agar) and anaerobically (thioglycollate).

I. Surgical Biopsies: Divide in half. Place one piece in
formalin for pathological sections, the other half in ster-

ile saline and take to laboratory. Grind up with sterile
sand in mortar, suspend in broth, and culture aerobically
and anaerobically, always including thioglycollate. Inject part of suspension subcutaneously into guinea pigs
(for tubercle bacilli).

J. Stool Cultures: Obtain stool specimen from defecation,
rectal or anal swab. Suspend small amount in broth and
streak a blood agar plate and a differential medium for
non-lactose fermenting bacteria (e.g., SS agar, desoxy-
cholate agar, eosin-methylene blue agar, or bismuth
sulfite agar). If typhoid is suspected, first enrich for 18
hours in selenite F medium, then streak. Colorless colonies on differential media are non-lactose fermenters.
(See pp. 290 and 291.)

K. Gastrointestinal Cultures: Stomach washings for tubercle
bacilli (see p. 292), bile drainage, and surgical specimens are treated like stool specimens.

L. Urine Culture: From males satisfactory specimens can
usually be obtained by cleansing the meatus with mercury
bichloride solution (1:1000) and collecting the midportion
of urine in a sterile container. From females satisfactory midstream specimens can often be obtained after
cleansing the vulva and spreading the labia. Catheterization may be necessary. Specimens from each ureter can
be obtained by the urologist. All urine specimens must
be delivered to the laboratory promptly and examined
within one hour (or refrigerated). Make a Gram stain of
urine or of centrifuged sediment. When bacteria are
readily seen microscopically their number exceeds 10,000
per ml. of urine. Many bacteria multiply rapidly in urine.

Culture of urine must be quantitative because the urine
of normal persons may contain up to about 1000 bacteria
per ml. from urethral flora or unavoidable contamination
during collection. Spread 0.1 ml. urine on a blood agar
plate (or incorporate into a pour plate). Similarly inoculate urine diluted 1:100 and 1:10,000. In addition, inoculate a loopful of urine into thioglycollate medium and onto
a blood agar plate for direct disk sensitivity tests. Incubate all media at 37°C. overnight. Count colonies and
estimate the number of bacteria per ml. of urine.

Finding more than 100,000 colonies per ml. of one
type of organism in fresh, properly collected urine always
indicates active infection. Finding less than 1000 colonies
per ml. - often of several kinds - suggests that the organisms come from normal flora. Intermediate counts (e.g.,
between 5000 and 50,000 per ml.) do not permit definitive
interpretation from a single specimen and should be repeated with a fresh specimen. Such counts, if obtained repeatedly, may indicate persistent, chronic, or suppressed
infection. If present in a single specimen only, they suggest contamination.

[Cont'd. on p. 293.]

SOME IMPORTANT GRAM-NEGATIVE INTESTINAL BACILLI

Organism	Fermentation Reactions							Triple Sugar Iron Agar or Kligler's Iron Agar		
	Motility	Glucose	Lactose	Sucrose	Salicin	Mannitol	Xylose	H₂S Prod.	Slant	Butt
E. coli	+	AG	AG	±	±	AG	AG	-	A	AG
A. aerogenes	±	AG	AG	AG	AG	AG	AG	-	A	AG
Paracolon bacteria	±	AG	d±	-	±	AG	AG	±	±A	AG
K. pneumoniae	-	AG	±	±	±	±	±	-	±	AG
S. typhosa	+	A	-	-	-	A	±	+	-	A
S. paratyphi (A)	+	AG	-	-	-	AG	±	-	-	AG
S. paratyphi (B) (schottmülleri)	+	AG	-	-	-	AG	AG	+	-	AG
S. typhimurium	+	AG	-	-	-	AG	±	+	-	AG
S. choleraesuis	+	AG	-	-	-	AG	AG	+	-	AG
S. enteritidis	+	AG	-	-	-	AG	AG	+	-	AG
Sh. dysenteriae	-	A	-	-	-	-	-	-	-	A
Sh. flexneri	-	A	-	±	-	A	-	-	-	A
Sh. sonnei	-	A	dA	dA	-	A	-	-	-	A
P. vulgaris	+	AG	-	AG	AG	-	±	+	-	AG
Ps. aeruginosa	+	A	-	±	-	-	-	-	-	±A
Alcaligenes faecalis	+	-	-	-	-	-	-	-	Alk	Alk

(±) Variable. (A) Acid (yellow). (AG) Acid and gas. (+) Positive. (-) Negative. (d) Delayed. (Alk) Alkaline.

DAY-BY-DAY PROCEDURES FOR BACTERIOLOGIC EXAMINATION OF STOOLS

First Day	Streak stool suspension on EMB or MacConkey's and SS agar or desoxycholate-citrate agar. Inoculate into selenite F broth or tetrathionate broth.					
Second Day	Pick clear, colorless colonies to lactose broth and to Kligler's iron agar (KIA) or triple sugar iron agar (TSI). Streak on SS agar; transfer later to lactose broth and KIA and urea medium.					
Third Day	Examine lactose broth for motility of organisms, continue incubation for two weeks. Note reaction on KIA or TSI and separate into one of the following groups:					
	I A/AG H_2S - (or +) E. coli A. aerogenes	II -/- H_2S - A. faecalis Ps. aeruginosa (some strains)	III -/AG H_2S + S. schottmülleri S. enteritidis S. typhimurium Proteus } Some Paracolon } strains	IV -/AG H_2S - S. paratyphi Paracolon Shigella newcastle	V -/A H_2S + S. typhosa Paracolon	VI -/A H_2S - Sh. dysenteriae Sh. paradysenteriae Sh. sonnei, dispar, alkalescens Ps. aeruginosa } Some Proteus } strains
	Legend: Slant/Butt: A = acid (yellow) AG = acid and gas H_2S + = present (black) H_2S - = absent (not black)					

Motility: In lactose broth young coliforms (I, II) and salmonellae (II, IV, V) are usually motile, shigellae (VI) usually nonmotile.

Sugar Reactions: Inoculate sugar tubes (sucrose, mannitol, xylose); reactions shown on p. 290. If these sugars are fermented - but lactose only very slowly (two weeks' observation) - the organism may be a paracolon bacillus.

Smell: Pseudomonas cultures smell sweetish; proteus cultures have distinctly ammoniacal odors.

Agglutination Tests: Grow the organism in a pure culture and make a heavy suspension in saline. Place drops (1 drop = 0.05 ml.) of sera to be tested on the ruled area of a glass slide. Using a sterile loop, mix each drop with a loopful of 1:3 salmonella grouping serum (A, to E and VI), shigella grouping serum, or E. coli diagnostic serum; rock the slide for 1 minute and observe agglutination against proper control.

METHODS OF EXAMINATION FOR TUBERCLE BACILLI

Whenever possible every specimen should be examined by:

1. Direct smear of caseous or purulent fragment;
   stain with acid-fast method (see p. 620).
2. Smear from concentrated material.
3. Culture from concentrated material on special egg-
   glycerin or Dubos medium with penicillin.
4. Guinea pig inoculation.

Specimen	Microscopic			Culture	Guinea Pig
	Direct	Concentrated			
Sputum	+	Clorox®-NaOH concentrate		NaOH-alum concentrate	NaOH-alum concentrate
Urine	-	Centrifuged sediment		Centrifuged sediment	Centrifuged sediment
Pus	+	Clorox®-NaOH concentrate		NaOH-alum concentrate	NaOH-alum concentrate
Spinal fluid	Pellicle	Centrifuged sediment		Centrifuged sediment and pellicle or NaOH-alum concentrate	Centrifuged sediment and pellicle or NaOH-alum concentrate
Pleural, pericardial, ascitic, or joint fluid	Centrifuged sediment	NaOH-alum concentrate		NaOH-alum concentrate	NaOH-alum concentrate
Gastric washing	-	NaOH-alum concentrate		3-day pool NaOH-alum concentrate	3-day pool NaOH-alum concentrate

Concentration Technics:

1. Clorox®-NaOH - For smears only. To 10 ml. sputum add 10 ml. concentrating solution (1 part 50% chlorine bleaching agent, e.g., Clorox®, plus 1 part 8% NaOH). Mix well, add 2 ml. benzene, petroleum ether, or high-test gasoline, shake for ten min., and centrifuge at high speed. Tubercle bacilli will be found at interface between two layers. Scoop up with loop passed through gasoline and smear on new clean slide.

2. NaOH-alum - Mix equal parts of specimen and concentrating solution (4% sodium hydroxide with 0.2% potassium alum and bromocresol purple indicator). Shake vigorously and place in incubator for 30 to 60 minutes. Neutralize with 25% hydrochloric acid (drop-by-drop) until indicator shows neutral pH. Centrifuge for 10 minutes, decant supernatant, and use sediment.

If cultures are negative in the presence of signs of urinary tract infection, consider tuberculosis or ureteral obstruction. Ureteral specimens are normally sterile (have no normal flora); any bacteria found in them must be considered significant.

M. Vaginal and Cervical Cultures: Collect specimen on a sterile swab through a speculum. Place swab in broth tube and take to laboratory immediately. Also make direct wet preparation (for trichomonas) and smear (for gonococci). Culture on blood agar and chocolate agar in 10% CO_2. Smears for cytologic examination are prepared and treated as for sputum (see p. 264). For Mycoplasma (PPLO), inoculate special media and observe by special methods (see p. 265).

N. Urethral and Prostatic Material: Collect pus or expressed secretions on swab. Smear and culture as in M, above. For Mycoplasma (PPLO), see p. 265.

O. Transudates and Exudates: Centrifuge material at high speed for ten minutes. Culture sediment on blood agar and in thioglycollate broth. Make gram-stained smear, and send "button" to pathology laboratory for sections.

P. Skin, Hair, and Nails: Collect in sterile Petri dish or, if suppurative, on a sterile cotton swab. Inoculate blood agar and Sabouraud's agar. Make smear and examine with Gram's stain. For fungi, immerse specimen in 10 to 20% KOH under cover glass and study microscopically.

Q. Autopsy Material: Secure sterile heart blood by needle or sterile capillary pipet. Specimens are secured from organs by first searing the surface with small soldering iron, then puncturing through seared area with pipet. From exposed surfaces, take swab. Culture all material on aerobic and anaerobic blood agar plates and in broth and thioglycollate medium. Terminal dissemination of intestinal organisms throughout the tissues frequently occurs; these organisms may overgrow important pathogens in liquid culture.

R. Antibiotic Sensitivity Tests: See p. 537.

WATER STANDARDS AND EXAMINATION

Requirements for Drinking Water.
A. Solids: Total solids should not exceed 1000 parts per million (p. p. m.).
   1. Clay or silt - Below 500 p. p. m. (30 gr. per gallon).
   2. Fluorides - Below 0. 9 p. p. m. The fluoride concentration is directly related to the temperature of the area.
   3. Lead - 0. 05 p. p. m. or less.
   4. Copper - 1 p. p. m. or less.
   5. Zinc - 5 p. p. m. or less.
   6. Iron (total) - 0. 3 p. p. m. or less.

7. Sulfates - 250 p. p. m. or less, as $SO_4^=$.
8. Chlorides - 250 p. p. m. or less, as chloride ion.
9. Specific limits are also set for various chemical pollutants, including alkyl benzene sulfonate (detergents), cyanide, chloroform extractables, barium, cadmium, carbon, nitrate, and silver.

B. Hardness: The hardness of water is due to calcium and magnesium carbonates. (Sulfates and chlorides are also present.)
  1. Soft water contains 50 p. p. m. or less of these.
  2. Very hard water contains over 150 p. p. m. of these.
  3. Great Lakes water contains about 100 p. p. m. of these.

C. Bacteria: Organism count should not exceed 100 per ml. following 24 hours incubation on ordinary agar plates at 37° C. (98. 6° F.). E. coli should not be present. Five samples of 10 ml. each are examined. To use chlorine as disinfectant, need 0. 2 to 0. 5 p. p. m.

D. Oxygen: 4 to 10 p. p. m. of oxygen should be present. Fish will die if oxygen concentration is below 4 p. p. m.

E. Radioactivity: ^{226}Ra, 3 micromicrocuries per liter; ^{90}Sr, 10 micromicrocuries per liter; total gross beta activity, 1000 micromicrocuries per liter.

Water-borne Diseases.

Diseases may also be carried from the water source to the host by means of flies, excreta, shellfish, ice, etc.

A. Diseases Commonly Borne by Water: Ascariasis, cercarial dermatitis (schistosomes), cholera, diarrheas (bacterial and viral), bacterial dysentery (shigellae), amebic dysentery (Entamoeba histolytica), filariasis (Dracunculus medinensis, guinea worm), infectious hepatitis (viral), paratyphoid and enteric fevers, schistosomiasis, typhoid fever (salmonellae), Weil's disease (leptospira), fluorine poisoning (mottled teeth), lead poisoning, melioidosis(?).

B. Diseases Only Rarely Borne by Water: Hookworm disease, oxyuriasis, poliomyelitis, trichuriasis, tularemia.

Bacteriologic Examination of Water.

Fitness for human use is judged by two standards:

A. The total number of bacteria (cultured in a standard fashion) should not exceed 100 per ml.

B. Coliform bacteria (E. coli, A. aerogenes, etc.) should be absent altogether or present only occasionally in small numbers. This guards against pollution with excreta.

Steps in the Examination of Water.

The examination is carried out by Public Health Laboratories according to methods presented in detail in Standard Methods of Water Analysis, American Public Health Association. In brief, the following steps are included:

A. Collection of Water Sample: Representative samples of

water are repeatedly collected from the source in sterile
bottles of not less than 50 ml. capacity, and examined in
the laboratory without delay. The samples may have to
be packed in ice for shipment.

B. Total Bacterial Count: The total number of bacteria per
ml. of water is estimated by quantitative culture on agar
plates.

C. Tests for Coliform Bacteria: Coliform bacteria suggestive of fecal contamination are detected by their ability
to ferment lactose with the production of gas (presumptive test) and subsequent cultural identification of these
organisms by bacteriologic methods (confirmed test).

MILK STANDARDS AND EXAMINATION

Examination of Milk for Quality.

A. Standards of Quality and Purity:
1. Total solids should not exceed 12.5%.
2. Non-fat solids should be at least 8.5%.
3. Butter fat should be at least 3.5%. (The ratio of fats
to total solids may be used to detect skimming or
watering.)
4. Antibiotic test to check for presence of antibiotics.
5. Mastitis test to check for intensity of mastitic infection.
6. Pesticide residual test to check for pesticide residue.

B. Pasteurization: Pasteurization is heat treatment of milk
designed to kill pathogenic agents but not all bacteria.
Remember that "pasteurization does not make bad milk
good, but makes good milk safe." For safety, all milk
should be pasteurized, particularly to guard against
brucellosis, perhaps Q fever, etc. Two methods of
pasteurization are available: (1) Short-time, high-
temperature method (most common): 161° F. for 15
seconds; (2) vat method: 145° F. for 30 minutes.

Test of pasteurization: The phosphatase test is a useful indicator of adequate pasteurization. Normally, unheated milk always contains phosphatase, an enzyme
capable of liberating phenol from phosphoric-phenyl
esters. When milk is heated at 145° F. for 30 minutes,
most of the enzyme is destroyed.

The test measures colorimetrically the phosphatase
activity of milk samples. If activity is in excess of a
standard amount, pasteurization has been inadequate.

Milk-borne Diseases (Raw Milk).

A. Bacterial: Dysenteries (shigellae), typhoid and paratyphoid fevers (salmonellae), summer diarrhea (proteus
and coliform bacteria), streptococcal infections, undulant
fever (brucellosis), tuberculosis (bovine), diphtheria.

B. Viral and Rickettsial: Foot and mouth disease, poliomyelitis (rare), hepatitis, Q fever.
C. Intoxications: Milk sickness, etc.

Bacteriologic Examination of Milk.

Both the total number and the kind of bacteria are determined. The total number of bacteria per ml. of milk is
a measure of the effectiveness of the sanitary precautions
observed in obtaining and handling the milk. The methods
followed generally are those detailed in Standard Methods for
the Examination of Dairy Products, American Public Health
Association.

A. Total Bacterial Count: This may be estimated in one of
three ways -
1. Direct microscopic count of a stained smear prepared
from milk in a standard fashion.
2. Standard plate count by culturing dilutions of milk on
agar plates and counting the colonies that develop.
3. Reduction tests based on the ability of bacteria present
in large numbers to decolorize rapidly a standard
amount of dye (e.g., methylene blue) added to the
milk. The speed of decolorization is roughly proportional to the number of bacteria present.
B. The Type of Organisms Present: These are identified by
the usual bacteriologic methods.
1. Coliform organisms are detected by their fermentation
of lactose with formation of acid and gas, and cultural
characteristics.
2. Streptococci are detected by their hemolysis on blood
agar plates. Some α-hemolytic streptococci, however,
are found in most milk samples (S. lactis).
3. Salmonella organisms must be isolated by enriching
the milk in tetrathionate broth, then streaking on
selective media.
4. Brucella organisms are difficult to culture from milk.
Therefore the sediment from centrifuged milk specimens is inoculated subcutaneously into guinea pigs.
Brucella can be demonstrated three to five weeks
later in the animal's organs.
   Brucellosis in infected animals can more readily
be established by finding agglutinating antibodies in
their sera or milk, or by a positive skin test.
5. Tubercle bacilli are difficult to demonstrate in milk.
Tuberculin testing of cows is a better index of animal
infection. If desired, sediment from centrifuged milk
is mixed with cream and injected subcutaneously into
guinea pigs. The guinea pigs may be tuberculin-
tested three to four weeks later, and autopsied eight
weeks after inoculation. Tubercle bacilli can be
demonstrated in the lymph nodes and other organs of
infected guinea pigs.

17...

Serologic Diagnostic Methods

Basis for Serologic Reactions.

When certain substances are introduced into the animal body the tissues respond with the formation of special gamma globulins. These gamma globulins are called "antibodies" and are capable of combining in a specific manner with the substances called "antigens" that evoked their formation. Complete antigens are large molecules, usually proteins. Smaller units (haptens) may combine with proteins to form complete antigens.

The major classes of antibodies and their characteristics are listed in the following table:

Classification of Immunoglobulins (Ig) (WHO)

	Former Designation	Sed. Const.	Mol. Wt.	Cross Placenta	Elicit PCA†	% CHO	Average Conc. in Serum mg./100 ml.	Examples
IgG	γG 7Sγ	7S	140,000	Yes	Yes	2%	1200	Rh blocking antibody, bacterial agglutinating antibodies, antitoxin.
IgA	γA γ1A β_{2}A	7S-13S	60,000-600,000	No	No	10%	300	Antibodies in secretions
IgM	γM γ1M β_{2}M 19Sγ	19S‡	900,000	No	No	12%	150	Human anti-A iso-antibody. Early antibody to many antigens.
IgD	γD	7S	150,000	No	No	?	3	?
IgE	γE	8S	200,000	No	No	10%	< 0.1	Skin-sensitizing antibody in ragweed allergy

†Passive cutaneous anaphylaxis.
‡IgM macroglobulins can be broken into 7S units by treatment with reagents that break S–S bonds (e. g., mercaptoethanol).

Antigen-antibody reactions are highly specific. An antibody will react only with the species of antigen which evoked its formation. This can be illustrated as the combination of a given chemical configuration with its complementary image:

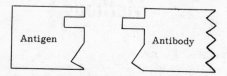

Serologic and immunologic methods utilize the specificity of antigen-antibody reactions for the diagnosis of disease. In particular, diseases due to infectious agents are characterized by the development of specific antibodies against the responsible microorganism. The presence of a specific antibody in the serum thus suggests past or present infection of the person with the microorganism. Detection in the test tube of specific antibodies is, therefore, a valuable tool in the diagnosis of diseases suspected to be of infectious origin, particularly if the etiologic agent cannot be recovered.

While antigen-antibody reactions are specific, cross reactions will occur in serologic procedures and immunologic tests between antigens possessing closely related chemical groups and antibodies. Knowledge of this possibility will avoid confusion.

Time for Taking Specimens.

For most conclusive results, always obtain one specimen of blood serum as early as possible in the disease, another about ten days later, and a third about four weeks after onset of the illness.

Manner of Drawing Blood.

For proper performance of all serologic tests the blood serum must be obtained properly. Venous blood is drawn with aseptic precautions (see p. 142) and permitted to clot in a sterile test tube. The clot is separated from the test tube wall and left at refrigerator temperature overnight to permit clot retraction. The tube is then centrifuged and the clear serum, free from hemolysis, is transferred by sterile pipet into another tightly stoppered, sterile tube. The serum should be kept cold and brought to the laboratory as quickly as possible.

Interpretation of Results.

If antibodies are present in the same concentration (titer) in all three specimens obtained as described on p. 292, they were almost certainly acquired in the past and have nothing to

do with the present illness. If, on the other hand, their concentration (titer) rises very markedly in the course of the illness (i. e., from the first to the third specimens), they help to
establish the definite diagnosis. The initial antibody response
is predominantly IgM; later, IgG.

TYPES OF ANTIGEN-ANTIBODY REACTIONS

Toxin-antitoxin Neutralization.

Certain bacteria, e. g., Corynebacterium diphtheriae or
Clostridium botulinum, produce soluble toxins. Antibodies to
these toxins, i. e., antitoxins, are able to neutralize them
when mixed in proper proportions. This reaction takes place
in the absence of complement (see p. 311). This principle is
useful in the typing of botulinus toxin and in the virulence test
for diphtheria bacilli.

Agglutination Tests.

Certain organisms evoke the production of antibodies in
patients and these antibodies can agglutinate the causative
organisms in vitro.
 A. Indications:
  1. Identification of isolated bacteria by slide or tube test
     (see p. 291) by mixing with known sera.
  2. Measurement of antibody concentration in patient's
     serum by mixing serum dilutions with diagnostic anti-
     gens, especially the following:
     a. Salmonella species (typhoid, paratyphoid fevers,
        etc.).
     b. Brucella (undulant fever).
     c. Proteus OX19, OX2, OXK (rickettsial diseases;
        see p. 307).
     d. Pasteurella pestis (plague).
     e. Pasteurella tularensis (tularemia).
     f. Leptospira species (leptospirosis).
  3. Other diseases - In primary atypical pneumonia caused
     by the Eaton agent (Mycoplasma pneumoniae), cold
     agglutinin tests are frequently positive (see p. 304);
     a nonspecific agglutination reaction with streptococcus
     MG is also occasionally positive. Sera from patients
     with rheumatoid arthritis often agglutinate sensitized
     sheep cells (see p. 305).
 B. Technic of Agglutination Tests:
  1. Tube method - Make serial twofold dilutions of serum
     with saline in the following manner. Place 0.5 ml.
     saline in each of a series of small test tubes. Add
     0.5 ml. serum to first tube, mix well by drawing up
     and expelling repeatedly from pipet, and transfer 0.5
     ml. to second tube. Proceed similarly until last tube

of the row is reached, then discard 0.5 ml. To each
tube add 0.5 ml. of a bacterial suspension standardized for density. Shake the rack of tubes, then incubate overnight at 37°C. (98.6°F.) or 50°C. (122°F.).

A positive reaction (++++) consists in complete
clumping of the bacteria with complete clearing of the
supernatant fluid. A negative reaction (-) consists of
uniform turbidity in the suspension without clumped
sediment.

2. Slide agglutinations are often useful for rapid identification of bacteria. A suspension of unknown organisms from a fresh culture is mixed with a drop of
specific antiserum on a glass slide. On another area
of the same slide the organisms are mixed with a drop
of saline. After standing or gentle rotation of the slide
for a few minutes, the slide is observed grossly and
under the microscope. A positive result is indicated
by rapid clumping of bacteria and loss of motility in
the serum drop but not in the saline drop (high dry
objective, subdued light) (see p. 291).

A similar rapid slide agglutination test may be performed with commercial salmonella or brucella antigens for the identification of antibodies in unknown sera.

C. Interpretation of Agglutination Tests for Infection With
Salmonellae (Typhoid, Paratyphoid), Coliform Organisms, Etc.:

1. "O" and "H" antigens and antibodies - Many motile
bacteria have two principal antigenic components:

a. The somatic "O" antigen (= Ohne Hauch) is obtained when thick suspensions of bacteria are treated
with an equal quantity of absolute alcohol with
vigorous stirring and shaking. Incubate the mixture
for 12 to 24 hours at 37°C. (98.6°F.), then shake
well. Add a quantity of saline equal to the amount
of alcohol added, to reduce alcohol concentration
to 33%, and store in refrigerator. Adequate "O"
antigens are obtained from E. coli by heating the
culture for one hour in boiling water bath.

b. The flagellar "H" antigen (= Hauch) is prepared by
growing the bacteria on agar in Blake bottles and
washing the growth off with saline containing 0.5%
formalin. Shake well, and store in the refrigerator.

In "H" antigens the formalin treatment preserves
the flagellar structures on the surface while in "O"
antigens the treatment removes them. A third
group of somatic "K" antigens are thermolabile,
and occur as envelopes surrounding the cell body.
They may interfere with "O" agglutination and must
sometimes (e.g., in E. coli serotypes) be destroyed
by heating before the "O" antigen can be determined.

One important "K" antigen is the Vi antigen of virulent typhoid bacilli.

2. Factors in interpretation - For the diagnosis of infection by serologic tests the following are important:

a. The best proof of active disease (e.g., typhoid) other than identification of the organism is the finding of a rising agglutination titer when serum is secured from the patient at intervals during the second and third weeks of the illness.

b. Significant agglutination titers may persist in the blood for years after clinical or subclinical infection or after vaccination. The finding of a single positive agglutination test therefore does not prove the existence of active disease.

c. There are some cross-reactions between various enteric organisms encountered in agglutination tests. The organism agglutinated by the patient's serum in the highest dilution is ordinarily considered the most significant.

d. The following antigenic patterns are often encountered in salmonella infections:

	Titers observed with antigens		
	"O"	"H"	"Vi"
2nd and 3rd weeks of active typhoid fever	1:80 and rising	< 1:40	Low
Vaccination in the past	< 1:40	1:80 or more, not rising	Low
Carrier state	< 1:40	< 1:40	1:40 or more

Similar "receptor analysis" can occasionally be carried out in other infections caused by gram-negative bacteria.

Precipitin Tests.

Antibodies against soluble antigens ("precipitins") are often demonstrable by their formation of a visible precipitate as the result of antigen-antibody reaction. As the precipitate is often soluble in excess of either antibody or antigen, the two have to be mixed in accurate proportions. Precipitin tests are used clinically for the diagnosis of syphilis (see p. 306), for the grouping of β-hemolytic streptococci, for the serologic identification of proteins (e.g., identification of blood stains), and in some other bacterial, parasitic, and mycotic infections.

Opsonocytophagic Tests.

Antibodies which enhance the ability of leukocytes to ingest bacteria are called "opsonins." They can be demonstrated by mixing patient's fresh citrated blood with a suspension of bacteria and comparing the degree of phagocytosis with that of controls. Such tests are occasionally employed in brucellosis but are of doubtful significance for diagnosis.

Bacteriolysin Test.

Antibodies can occasionally be demonstrated by their ability to dissolve bacteria. While the antigen-antibody reactions described above take place in the absence of complement, the latter is an essential component in this and the following reactions. Complement is a substance present in most fresh mammalian sera and destroyed by heating at 56° C. (138° F.) for 30 minutes. This procedure is called "inactivation" of a serum. In most tests complement is used in the form of pooled guinea pig serum of established satisfactory potency (fresh or reconstituted from the dehydrated state).

In a test for bacteriolysis, suspensions of the organism are mixed with serum which is being tested for antibodies. Complement is added and the mixture incubated at 37° C. (98.6° F.) for one hour, or (in the case of cholera) injected intraperitoneally into guinea pigs. Control mixtures containing normal serum are included in the test. At the end of the incubation period the organisms in contact with specific antibodies will have dissolved, while those mixed with normal serum should be unchanged. The test is used mainly in cholera and leptospirosis (as agglutination-lysis).

Fluorescent Antibody Technics.

A new serologic technic is based on the conjugation of antibody molecules with fluorescent dyes (e.g., fluorescein, rhodamine). Such "labeled" antibody may be used to locate antigen microscopically because of the high specificity of the antigen-antibody bond. By ultraviolet light microscopy, fluorescent-labeled antibody can rapidly identify specific microorganisms in smears from cultures, pus, tissue, or exudates, and can establish the localization of antigens in tissue section. This technic is used for bacteriologic and virologic diagnosis and for the study of "hypersensitivity" diseases.

This technic can also be used for indirect staining:

antigen + its antibody A + anti-A-antibody-fluorescent
(e.g., + (e.g., antivirus + (e.g., antihuman globulin
virus)   human antibody)   from rabbit)

Such indirect technics permit the localization of some antigens or antibodies which cannot otherwise be established with present methods. Reagents are now available commercially.

Complement Fixation Tests.

The reaction consists of two parts:
A. Part I - Mechanism of Reaction: Specific antibody com-

bines with ("fixes") complement only in the presence of corresponding specific antigen:

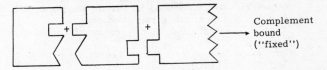

Specific Antigen + Antibody + Complement

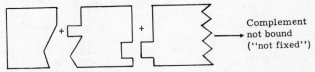

Non-specific Antigen + Antibody + Complement

B. Part 2 - Test for Presence of Free (Not Bound) Complement: "Hemolytic system" is added to above mixture of antigen + antibody + complement. "Hemolytic system" consists of sheep cells + anti-sheep cell hemolysin (i.e., serum from rabbits repeatedly injected with sheep cells). If free complement is present, it will combine with and hemolyze the sheep cells (i.e., if the original antigen did not fit the antibody, the two did not combine, hence no complement was bound).

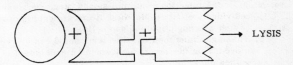

Sheep cells + Hemolysin + Complement

This complement fixation test is negative. Hemolysis is present.

If free complement is not present (because it was all bound by original antigen-antibody combination), the sheep cells will remain intact:

Sheep cells + Hemolysin

This complement fixation test is positive. No hemolysis.

Between parts 1 and 2, the antigen-antibody-complement mixture is incubated for varying periods at 37° C. (98.6° F.) or kept at refrigerator temperature for "fixation" of complement prior to addition of the indicator "hemolytic" system.

C. Complement fixation tests are used commonly in the diagnosis of the following diseases:
   1. Viral diseases (see p. 308).
   2. Rickettsial diseases (see p. 307).
   3. Fungous diseases (especially coccidioidomycosis, histoplasmosis, blastomycosis).
   4. Complement-fixing anti-nuclear antibody is found in certain "hypersensitivity" diseases.
   5. Complement-fixation tests are occasionally employed in the diagnosis of brucellosis, parasitic diseases (cysticercosis, trichinosis, echinococcosis), gonorrheal arthritis, and syphilis (see p. 306).

Sheep Cell Agglutination Test for Infectious Mononucleosis (Paul-Bunnell Test, "Heterophil Agglutination Test").

This is a nonspecific reaction based on the finding that persons with infectious mononucleosis develop a high titer of sheep cell agglutinating antibodies.

A. Technic: See Davidsohn, J. A. M. A. 108:289, 1937.
B. Problems of Interpretation:
   1. Normal persons may have agglutination titers up to 1:112.
   2. After the injection of animal serum (e.g., antitoxin), individuals often develop high titers of agglutinins (which will agglutinate sheep cells).
   3. The agglutinins mentioned under 1 and 2 can be removed from the serum by absorption with boiled guinea pig kidney.
   4. The agglutinins developing in mononucleosis are not absorbed with boiled guinea pig kidney but are absorbed by washed and boiled beef red cells.

Cold Agglutination Test.

In some cases of "primary atypical pneumonia" (PAP) substances appear in the serum which are capable of agglutinating human group O red cells in the cold, but not at room temperature or at 37° C. (98.6° F.). The test is performed by making serial twofold dilutions of the patient's serum in saline and adding an equal amount of a 1% suspension of washed human group O red cells. The mixtures are shaken well and left in the refrigerator overnight. A positive result is indicated by finding clumped cells immediately on removing the tubes from the refrigerator which do not remain clumped after the tubes have been at room temperature for three to four hours. Control tubes with normal serum and with saline-red cell mixtures are included.

The degree of positivity of this test depends on the etiology and to some extent the severity of the illness. PAP caused by adenoviruses is never associated with a positive cold agglutination test. PAP due to the Eaton agent (Mycoplasma pneumoniae) gives cold agglutination tests in proportion to the severity of the illness. Early treatment of such cases with tetracycline drugs interferes with the development of a positive test. Results of the test correlate fairly well with specific serologic tests for Mycoplasma infection.

Antistreptolysin Titer.

Persons infected with β-hemolytic streptococci often develop antibodies against the hemolysin O produced by the streptococcus. This antibody can be tested for by its ability to inhibit hemolysis of red cells by a standardized streptococcus hemolysin. The test should be carried out only in a laboratory having considerable experience and standardized reagents at its disposal. A reliable technic is indicated by Rantz, L. A., et al., Am. J. Med. **5**:3, 1948.

Finding persistently high antistreptolysin titers (in excess of 125 units) suggests recurrent or persistent infection with hemolytic streptococci and reaction to such infection, e.g., in rheumatic fever. **Note:** Adequate penicillin therapy of hemolytic streptococcus infections often interferes with the development of antistreptolysin in high titer.

Serologic Tests for Rheumatoid Arthritis.

Most patients with active rheumatoid arthritis possess an unusual serum protein which is capable of reacting with gamma globulin. This 19S globulin ("rheumatoid factor") can be demonstrated by several serologic tests. Most of these tests consist of the agglutination of particles (latex, bentonite, tannic acid-treated red blood cells, etc.) coated with human 7S gamma globulin, by diluted serum from rheumatoid patients. The interaction of rheumatoid factor (19S) and 7S gamma globulin can also be demonstrated as a precipitin reaction and may represent an antigen-antibody reaction.

Virus Neutralization Tests.

In many viral infections it is not practical to attempt to isolate the etiologic agent. The diagnosis usually rests on the demonstration that antibodies capable of neutralizing the infectious agent appeared in the course of the illness. It is essential, therefore, to obtain at least two and preferably three specimens of the patient's serum during the illness: the first as early as possible after onset of the illness; the second ten to 14 days later; and the third about four weeks after onset of the illness.

The sera must be obtained in an aseptic manner (see p. 142) and must be kept refrigerated. The laboratory test consists of mixing suitable proportions of serum with infectious material, inoculating it into susceptible laboratory animals, fertile eggs, or tissue cultures, and observing the presence or absence of protection from viral effects.

The viral diseases in which neutralization tests are commonly available are indicated in the table on p. 308.

Virus Hemagglutination-Inhibition Test.

A number of viruses (e.g., influenza, Newcastle, mumps, encephalitides) agglutinate erythrocytes, and this reaction may be specifically inhibited by antiserum. This reaction forms the basis of a number of diagnostic tests for viral infections.

To standardized amounts of virus, serial dilutions of the serum under test are added (after heating the serum for 30 minutes at 56° C.), and the mixture is shaken well. An equal amount of 0.5% suspension of human, chicken, or other erythrocytes is added and the mixture incubated at room temperature for 45 to 60 minutes. Care must be taken not to disturb the test tubes or racks. The tubes are then read for agglutination of the red blood cells. The titer of a given serum is defined as the highest dilution of serum which effects complete inhibition of red cell agglutination.

SEROLOGIC TESTS FOR SYPHILIS

Commonly Used Serologic Tests for Syphilis (S.T.S.).

The tests below are accepted in the 1955 Manual of the Public Health Service, U.S. Department of Health, Education, and Welfare (Serologic Tests for Syphilis, Public Health Service Publ. No. 411, U.S. Government Printing Office, Washington 1955). Others are occasionally used. Adherence to the published standard method is essential in obtaining reliable results.

If more than one test is desired it is customary to perform one complement-fixation and one flocculation test. The greater the agreement between different tests and the results of different laboratories, the more confidence may be placed in reports of these serologic findings. The different technics estimate the presence of reagin, not of specific antibody directed against T. pallidum.

A. Complement Fixation Test: Kolmer-Wasserman.
B. Flocculation Tests: Hinton, Kahn, Kline, Mazzini, APHA Reference Test.
C. VDRL (Venereal Disease Research Laboratory).

See the above manual for the standard technic of these tests.

[Cont'd. on p. 310.]

RICKETTSIAL DISEASES OF IMPORTANCE

Group	Disease	Etiologic Agent	Rash	Occurrence	Vector	Weil-Felix OX19	OX2	OXK
Typhus	Epidemic typhus	R. prowazeki	Central	World-wide	Lice	++++	+	0
	Murine typhus	R. mooseri	Short duration	World-wide	Rat flea	++++	+	0
	Brill's disease*	R. prowazeki	Central	East Coast U.S.	None	++++	+	0
Spotted Fevers	Rocky Mountain spotted fever	R. rickettsi	Peripheral	North and South America	Ticks	+++	++	0
	Mediterranean (boutonneuse) fever	R. conori	Primary and palms and soles	Mediterranean	Dog ticks	++++	++	0
	South African tick fever	R. rickettsi	Primary lesion	South Africa	Ticks	+++	+++	++
	Other spotted fevers	Various	Various	Australia, India, Russia	Ticks	+++	++	Occ.
Rickettsialpox		R. akari	Primary lesion, central rash	New York, Boston	Mites	0	0	0
Scrub typhus Tsutsugamushi fever		R. orientalis	Primary lesion, central rash	Japan, Burma, Malaya, New Guinea	Mites	0	0	+++
Q fever		Coxiella burneti	None	World-wide	(Air-borne)	0	0	0

Diagnosis Based On:

1. Exposure to known vectors in endemic areas.
2. Clinical appearance.
3. Isolation of rickettsiae (infrequently done; see p. 309).
4. Results of Weil-Felix test on early and later serum specimens; rise in titer is diagnostic.
5. Results of complement fixation tests with acute and convalescent sera; rise in titer is diagnostic.
6. Response to chemotherapy is often suggestive.

Therapy: Chloramphenicol (Chloromycetin®) or the tetracyclines are the drugs of choice.

*Brill's disease is a recrudescence of an old typhus infection.

LABORATORY METHODS FOR THE DIAGNOSIS OF DISEASES DUE TO SOME VIRUSES AND RELATED AGENTS

Disease	Etiologic Agent	Specimen Submitted for Examination	Test	Remarks
Adenovirus infection (respiratory, eye), pharyngoconjunctival fever	Adenoviruses.	Throat swabs, conjunctival scrapings, blood, etc.	Virus isolation, C-F, virus neutralization.	Tissue culture.
Croup (infantile)	Parainfluenza, respiratory syncytial viruses.	Throat swab; blood serum, acute and convalescent.	Virus isolation, hemagglutination-inhibition.	Tissue culture. Different viruses in different years.
Dengue	Dengue virus.	Blood serum, acute and convalescent.*	Virus neutralization.	Not often available.
Encephalitis (Japanese B, St. Louis, western and eastern equine, Venezuelan)	Specific viruses.	Blood serum, acute and convalescent.* Brain (autopsy).	Virus neutralization, complement fixation. Virus isolation.	Only rise in titer diagnostic.
Gingivostomatitis, herpes labialis, cold sores, encephalitis, genital herpes	Herpes simplex virus.	Vesicle fluid, saliva, spinal fluid,† Blood serum, acute and convalescent.*	Virus isolation. Virus neutralization, complement fixation.	In eggs, mice, rabbits, tissue culture. Only rise in titer significant. Most adults have antibodies.
Herpangina, pleurodynia, aseptic meningitis	Coxsackie A and B.	Throat washings, stools.† Spinal fluid.† Blood serum, acute and convalescent.*	Virus isolation, neutralization, C-F.	Many different virus types. Tissue culture. Suckling mice.
Inclusion conjunctivitis	Trachoma-like agent.	Epithelial scrapings of conjunctiva of lower lid.	Stained smear, egg inoculation.	Elementary bodies seen. Occurs especially in newborn.
Infectious mononucleosis	Unidentified.	Blood for white blood cell count. Blood serum, acute and convalescent.*	WBC and differential, Paul-Bunnel test.	Atypical lymphocytes. Rising heterophil agglutination titer.
Influenza	Influenza viruses A, B, C (several subtypes).	Throat washings.† Blood serum, acute and convalescent.*	Virus isolation, hemagglutination-inhibition, C-F.	In eggs, mice, or tissue culture. Only greater than four-fold increase in titer diagnostic.
Keratoconjunctivitis, epidemic	Adenovirus, type 8.	Swabs or scrapings from conjunctiva. Blood serum, acute and convalescent.*	Virus isolation, virus neutralization.	Tissue culture.
Lymphocytic choriomeningitis	LCM virus.	Blood serum, acute and convalescent.*	Virus neutralization.	Only rise in titer diagnostic.
Lymphogranuloma venereum	LGV agent.	Pus or tissue biopsy.† Blood serum, acute and convalescent.*	Skin test (Frei), agent isolation.	Elementary bodies. In eggs and mice.

Disease	Agent	Specimens	Tests	Remarks
Mumps	Mumps virus.	Saliva, spinal fluid.† Blood serum, acute and convalescent.*	Virus isolation, hemagglutination-inhibition, C-F.	In eggs. Only rise in titer significant.
Meningitis, aseptic (viral)	Coxsackie, ECHO, polio, H. simplex, mumps, LCM, etc.	Spinal fluid, blood serum, acute and convalescent.*	Virus isolation, neutralization, C-F.	Tissue culture, eggs, suckling mice.
Poliomyelitis	Poliomyelitis virus.	Feces, nasopharyngeal washings.† Blood serum.*	Virus isolation, C-F, neutralization.	In monkeys, tissue culture.
Primary atypical pneumonia (PAP) ("viral pneumonia")	Mycoplasma, adenoviruses, others.	Throat swabs, sputum. Blood serum, acute and convalescent.*	Cold hemagglutinins, virus isolation, C-F, virus neutralization.	Cold agglutination negative in adenovirus infection. Tissue culture.
Psittacosis	Psittacosis agent.	Sputum, blood.† Blood serum, acute and convalescent.*	Agent isolation, complement fixation.	In mice and eggs. Cross-reactions occur (LGV).
Rabies	Rabies virus.	Brain tissue (autopsy).	Smears for Negri bodies, fluorescent antibody test. Virus isolation.	Virus demonstration in animal and human brain. In mice.
Rickettsial diseases (see p. 307)	Various rickettsiae.	Whole blood. Blood serum, acute and convalescent.*	Rickettsia isolation, complement fixation, Weil-Felix test.	In guinea pigs. Only rise in titer significant. For results see chart on p. 307.
Toxoplasmosis	Toxoplasma (a protozoon).	Spinal, ventricular fluid, lymph node. Blood serum, acute and convalescent.*	Toxoplasma isolation, neutralization test, complement fixation.	In mice. Often not available. Special dye test.
Trachoma	Trachoma agent.	Epithelial scrapings from conjunctiva of upper tarsus.	Stained smear. Agent isolation.	Elementary bodies seen. In fertile eggs.
Variola (smallpox)	Variola virus.	Scrapings from base of fresh lesion. Vesicle fluid. Dried crusts from lesions.	Stained smear, virus isolation, complement fixation.	Special fixation and stain. In eggs and rabbit cornea. Crusts serve as antigen.
Yellow fever	Yellow fever virus.	Blood serum† from first week. Blood serum, acute and convalescent.* Liver tissue (autopsy).	Virus isolation, virus neutralization, histologic diagnosis.	In mice or monkeys. Only rising titer diagnostic. Midzonal necrosis and "Councilman" bodies.

*Collect sterile blood as early as possible in disease and again two and four weeks after onset of illness. Let blood clot, send sterile serum to laboratory, keep refrigerated, label adequately.

†Collect materials as early as possible in disease, ship to laboratory frozen, without thawing. Maintain aseptic precautions, label adequately.

Antigens for S. T. S.

The causative agent of syphilis, T. pallidum, has not yet been grown in vitro. Thus antigens prepared from virulent T. pallidum are not available. Experimentally, antigens from the Reiter strain of treponemes appear to have significant specificity in complement-fixation tests. They are used with increasing frequency.

It has been found empirically that sera from syphilitic individuals will flocculate or fix complement in the presence of alcoholic extracts of beef heart muscle to which cholesterol and lecithin have been added. Such standardized extracts (cardiolipin-lecithin antigens) are employed in most S. T. S. used for the assay of reagin. Living treponemes from animal lesions are employed in the TPI (see p. 311).

Fluids to Be Tested by S. T. S.

A. Patient's Serum: Draw 5 to 10 ml. of sterile venous blood and permit to clot in dry sterile test tube. Blood samples should not be taken during high fever or soon after anesthesia or alcohol intoxication, for these and other conditions (see below) tend to give false-positive reactions.

Centrifuge the clotted blood and remove the cell-free serum. Store in refrigerator until test can be performed. Just prior to test the serum is inactivated at 56° C. (133° F.) for 30 minutes to destroy complement.

B. Spinal Fluid: Collect 3 ml. spinal fluid in sterile test tube, free from blood cells (see p. 606).

Interpretation of Results of S. T. S.

A. In untreated adults the S. T. S. will become positive in 60 to 80% of cases in the primary stage (four to eight weeks after exposure), whether primary lesions are present or not. If manifest secondary lesions develop, the blood test will be positive in 90 to 100% of the cases and the spinal fluid in 30 to 70%. In late (tertiary) syphilis, the blood is positive - if visceral lesions are developing - in 60 to 80% of cases. If there are no visceral lesions but C. N.S. involvement, the spinal fluid is a better guide. Note, however, that in tabes dorsalis, both blood and C.S.F. may be negative in the presence of progressive symptoms and signs. In general paresis both blood and C.S.F. are almost always positive.

B. In the newborn, and in infants up to ten weeks, the blood test may reflect the mother's reaction and does not necessarily indicate infection of the infant. It is important, therefore, to follow titers of infants born of mothers with positive serology but without evidence of activity of the disease (e.g., adequately treated).

C. Antisyphilitic therapy usually results in gradual reversion of positive serologic tests to negativity. This, however,

may take many months. A positive blood test in an adequately treated individual is therefore no justification for
extending or repeating therapy unless there is evidence of
activity of the disease or rise in complement fixation
titer. Antisyphilitic therapy, particularly with penicillin,
administered to dark-field–positive, seronegative individuals often interferes with the development of a positive
S. T. S.

D. Anticomplementary Specimens: Occasionally blood samples are encountered which fix complement in the absence
of beef heart antigen. Such specimens cannot satisfactorily be examined by the complement fixation test. This
occurs particularly in hemolysed or contaminated specimens. Such samples can be submitted to precipitation or
flocculation tests. "Anticomplementary" means neither
positive nor negative result.

E. Biologic false-positive serologic reactions for syphilis
occur in 0.01 to 0.1% of all positive tests. Commonly
they are weakly positive (except in yaws, pinta, and
bejel, where they are the same as in syphilis).

Such biologic false-positive reactions may occur in
yaws, pinta (mal del pinto), bejel (all closely related
spirochetal infections), 50 to 100% of cases; leprosy, 40
to 70% of cases; infectious mononucleosis, 10 to 50% of
cases; malaria, 10 to 40% of cases; rat-bite fever and
relapsing fever, 20 to 50% of cases; all protozoan and
viral infectious diseases, occasionally; all diseases
associated with abnormally high globulin levels; all immunization and vaccination procedures; any fever of long
duration; all "collagen diseases."

Unless supported by clinical findings, never accept the
result of a single serologic test for syphilis as proving the
diagnosis. Always request at least two examinations. Consider conditions commonly responsible for biologic false-
positive reactions.

Quantitative S. T. S.

Any serologic test for syphilis may be carried out with
dilutions of serum, and the highest dilution giving a ++++ reaction may be reported. This permits evaluation of trends in
serologic response (result of therapy, indication of relapse,
follow-up of infants).

Number of units = serum dilution giving ++++ reaction
× 4.

Treponema Pallidum Immobilization Test (TPI).

Serum from individuals with syphilis contains an antibody
which results in the rapid immobilization of actively motile
T. pallidum. This test has the greatest diagnostic specificity
because it measures a true antibody against the etiologic

organism of syphilis rather than the development of reagin against a lipid extract of mammalian tissue which shows only accidental relationship to the presence of syphilis. Therefore, TPI can conclusively differentiate between biologic false-positive tests and true syphilitic positives. The test is not easy to perform and is available only in a few central laboratories. The FTA-ABS test (below) is preferable.

Fluorescent Antibody Tests for Syphilis.

An indirect fluorescent antibody test employing killed, virulent T. pallidum as antigen and patient's serum absorbed with sonicated Reiter spirochetes as antibody (FTA-ABS) is as specific and as sensitive as the TPI test.

Another immunofluorescence test is being used for the identification of T. pallidum in early syphilitic lesions. Exudate is dried on slides, then stained with fluorescein-labeled anti-syphilis serum and examined with ultraviolet light in the dark field. T. pallidum fluoresces brightly.

C-REACTIVE PROTEIN*

C-reactive protein (CRP) is a substance in the serum of certain patients which reacts with the somatic C polysaccharide of pneumococci. It can be detected by a precipitin reaction with pneumococcus polysaccharide, but is more commonly measured by precipitation with specific antiserum prepared in rabbits.

CRP is a β-globulin, perhaps bound to serum lipid. It is not found in the serum of normal individuals, but appears within 14 to 26 hours following inflammation or tissue injury. It is consistently found in the serum of patients with bacterial infections, active rheumatic fever, acute myocardial infarction, and widespread malignant disease. It is also commonly present in rheumatoid arthritis, virus infections, and active tuberculosis, but only rarely in chronic leukemia, multiple myeloma, and limited primary neoplasm.

The laboratory determination for CRP thus forms a nonspecific test for the presence of inflammation, tissue injury, or necrosis.

---

*For details see Roantree, R. J., and Rantz, L. A.: Arch. Int. Med. **96**:674, 1955.

18...

Medical Parasitology

Donald Heyneman, PhD*

Parasitology in its broadest sense is concerned with organisms, animal or plant, living on or in other organisms that serve as their hosts. From the biologic point of view, parasitism is a category of association of living beings in which one partner (the parasite) maintains itself at the expense of the energy of the other (the host). Bacteria (including rickettsiae and spirochetes), fungi, and viruses are parasites in this sense, but medical parasitology is usually restricted to the animal parasites, chiefly protozoa and helminths, that produce a state of disease in man. Microbial human parasites are included, for convenience, in the field of microbiology, with the specialized subbranches of virology, rickettsiology, bacteriology, etc. Another major category, medical entomology, includes noxious and venomous arthropods and those that serve as vectors or as intermediate hosts. Medical entomology is a commonly accepted misnomer that includes ticks, mites, and spiders as well as insects of medical importance. Arthropod intermediate hosts are named but not considered in detail in this chapter.†

Parasitism as a way of life is an integral part of nature, one that represents a biologic complex whose physiologic and ecologic adaptations are just beginning to be unraveled. With increased understanding of this phenomenon should come a far better notion of human medical parasitology, including the relatively small numbers of parasites it is concerned with, and the still smaller number of diseases they produce.

Pathogenicity - the ability to produce disease - is not the same as infection. Although the difference is often disregarded, infection (the presence of internal parasites) without resulting disease is a common and perhaps a more natural condition than is infection with disease. Disease often occurs, especially when the host-parasite relationship is in imbalance

*Research Parasitologist, G.W. Hooper Foundation, and Professor of Parasitology, Department of International Health, University of California Medical Center, San Francisco, California.

†For a discussion of venomous arthropods, see Chapter 34, Arachnids & Insects, in: Dreisbach: Handbook of Poisoning, 6th Ed. Lange, 1969.

(as may occur in an evolutionarily recent or maladapted host-parasite association, or where the host is weakened, mal-nourished, immunologically deficient, under stress, or suf-fering from another disease). However, disease does not **necessarily** follow infection. Asymptomatic cases are, in fact, generally far more common. The medical view neces-sarily focuses on the host-parasite imbalance manifested by disease, but this view must also encompass parasitism in its wider state in order to evaluate the many cases of parasitism where treatment may not be required. It is also important to recognize the abundance and wide distribution of human para-sites, especially in the tropics. In Africa and many parts of Asia, parasitism is essentially a normal condition, with near-ly every child and most adults harboring one or more species.

Importance of Morphologic Identification.

Recognition and differentiation of the animal parasites of man, often involving separation of pathogenic from very sim-ilar nonpathogenic forms, demands precise knowledge of their morphology. Except in a comparatively few instances, the diagnostic cultural, biochemical, and serologic procedures of the bacteriologist are not available to the parasitologist. As the diagnosis of a parasitic infection rests upon demonstration of the parasite - and this demonstration depends upon mor-phologic recognition - it is essential that those responsible for handling clinical specimens be well trained microscopists. Proficiency in this phase of laboratory work is gained by ex-tensive practical experience with properly collected and processed clinical specimens. The diagnosis and differentia-tion of protozoan diseases, whether intestinal or systemic, often present unusual difficulties. Differentiation of intesti-nal amebas demands particular care, especially in light in-fections. The medical technologist must not only recognize the various species of smaller nonpathogenic amebas but must also distinguish the nonpathogenic small race (Entamoeba hartmanni) from the larger form (E. histolytica) that is re-sponsible for pathogenic amebiasis.

Cultivation Technics.

The use of cultivation procedures as a means of diagnosis in parasitology is limited. Effective methods are available for detection of some of the intestinal amebas and flagellates (Entamoeba histolytica, Dientamoeba fragilis, Trichomonas hominis, etc.) and blood and tissue flagellates (Leishmania donovani, Trypanosoma cruzi, etc.), and for their mainte-nance in the laboratory.

Serologic Technics.

Serologic tests may be of practical value in distinguishing past from recent or current infection, often useful in public health surveys. Specific tests provide corroborative diagnoses. The complement fixation test for amebiasis; the complement fixation, agglutination, and precipitin tests for leishmaniasis; and the complement fixation test for Trypanosoma cruzi infections have been of diagnostic value. The dye test for toxoplasmosis is widely used, though a more critical one is still being sought. Serologic as well as intradermal tests are particularly useful in diagnosis of those helminth infections, such as trichinosis, larva migrans, echinococcosis, and schistosomiasis, in which it is difficult and sometimes impossible to demonstrate the causative organism.

Histopathologic Technics.

Certain parasites produce characteristic tissue changes that make possible a histopathologic diagnosis. For example, biopsy of the rectum, the urinary bladder, or the liver is often the only reliable method of diagnosis in schistosomiasis. Muscle biopsy is indicated for trichinosis, and spleen or sternal puncture is often necessary for a positive diagnosis of kala azar.

Epidemiology.

The solution of problems associated with the epidemiology, prevention, and control of parasitic diseases of man requires a knowledge of the geographic distribution, life histories, and habits not only of parasites but of their vectors and hosts as well. The elimination of parasitic infections from a community thus depends upon the combined efforts of laboratory worker, field investigator, and clinician - often with the assistance of the social worker, agricultural engineer, sanitarian, and nutritionist.

•   •   •

On the following pages information pertinent to the more important parasites of man is presented, as well as a consideration of the diseases produced by them and a description of the laboratory methods and procedures employed for their detection in clinical specimens. For more extensive information on this subject the following references should be consulted:

1. Audy, J. R., Dunn, F. L., and Goldsmith, R. S., Infectious Diseases: Protozoal, Ch. 24, pp. 719-31, in: Current Diagnosis and Treatment, 1970. Brainerd, H., Krupp, M. A., Chatton, M. J., and Margen, S., Eds. Lange, 1970.
2. Belding, D. L., Textbook of Parasitology, 3rd Ed. Appleton-Century-Crofts, 1965.
3. Brown, H. W., Basic Clinical Parasitology, 3rd Ed. Appleton-Century-Crofts, 1969.

4. Burrows, R. B. , Microscopic Diagnosis of the Parasites of Man. Yale Univ. Press, 1965.

5. Chandler, A. C. , and Read, C. P. , Introduction to Parasitology, 10th Ed. Wiley, 1961.

6. Cheng, T. C. , The Biology of Animal Parasites. Saunders, 1964.

7. Dunn, F. L. , Audy, J. R. , and Goldsmith, R. S. , Infectious Diseases: Metazoal, Ch. 25, pp. 732-51, in: Current Diagnosis and Treatment, 1970. Brainerd, H. , Krupp, M. A. , Chatton, M. J. , and Margen, S. , Eds. Lange, 1970.

8. Faust, E. C. , Beaver, P. B. , and Jung, R. C. , Animal Agents and Vectors of Human Disease, 3rd Ed. Lea and Febiger, 1968.

9. Faust, E. C. , and Russell, P. F. , Craig and Faust's Clinical Parasitology, 7th Ed. Lea and Febiger, 1964.

10. Hunter, G. W. , Frye, W. W. , and Swartzwelder, J. C. , A Manual of Tropical Medicine, 4th Ed. Saunders, 1966.

11. Jawetz, E. , Melnick, J. L. , and Adelberg, E. A. , Review of Medical Microbiology, 9th Ed. Lange, 1970.

12. Jeffrey, H. C. , and Leach, R. M. , Atlas of Medical Helminthology and Protozoology. Livingstone, 1966.

13. Maegraith, B. , Exotic Diseases in Practice. Heinemann, 1965.

14. Maegraith, B. G. , Kershaw, W. E. , and Dagnall, D. , Techniques in Tropical Pathology. Oliver and Boyd, 1961.

15. Manson-Bahr, P. H. , Manson's Tropical Diseases, 16th Ed. Williams and Wilkins, 1966.

16. Markell, E. K. , and Voge, M. , Medical Parasitology, 2nd Ed. Saunders, 1965.

17. Spencer, F. M. , and Monroe, L. S. , The Color Atlas of Intestinal Parasites. Thomas, 1961.

THE LIFE CYCLE OF THE MALARIAL PARASITE

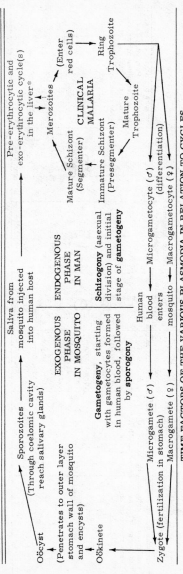

TIME FACTORS OF THE VARIOUS PLASMODIA IN RELATION TO CYCLES

Species	Length of Sexual Cycle (in mosquito at 77° F.)†	Incubation (Prepatent) Period (in man)	Length of Asexual Cycle (in hours)
P. vivax (vivax malaria)	9 days	11 - 13 days	48 hours
P. malariae (malariae malaria)	15 - 21 days	15 - 16 days	72 hours
P. falciparum (falciparum malaria)	10 days	9 - 10 days	24 - 48 hours
P. ovale (ovale malaria)	15 days	14 - 15 days	48 hours

*P. falciparum apparently does not reinfect liver cells, hence is a self-limiting infection, although it is usually more severe than the other malarias. Typical relapses occur in the other malarias, either by continuous multiplication in liver cells or by periodic reinvasion of the blood stream. Possible reinfection of liver tissue by blood stream merozoites is shown by the dotted arrow.

†Period varies depending upon temperature.

OUTSTANDING DIFFERENTIAL CHARACTERISTICS OF THE PLASMODIA

Species	Parasitized Erythrocyte	Parasite	Erythrocytes Showing Typical Forms			Invasive Characteristics*
Plasmodium vivax (vivax malaria).† Preva- lent in temperate zones. Commonest type.	Cell enlarged, often pale; Schüff- ner's dots in all forms but rings. Multiple infec- tions fairly com- mon.	All forms in peripheral blood. Ame- boid tropho- zoite large, irregular in shape, scat- tered brown pigment gran- ules. Mero- zoites 12-24 (average 16).	Ring Trophozoite / Red Cell / Parasite	Mature Ameboid Trophozoite	Segmenter / Merozoites	Tendency to attack retic- ulocytes, not mature erythro- cytes. Parasitemia usually 8,000 to 50,000/cu.mm. of blood (average: 20,000).
Plasmodium malariae (malariae malaria).† Comparatively rare. Temperate zone and subtropics.	Cell normal in size and color; stippling absent. Multiple infections rare.	All forms in peripheral blood. Cyto- plasm com- pact, usually rounded, though band forms com- mon. Pig- ment appears early; dark, coarse. Merozoites 6-13 (aver- age 8); rosette.	Ring Trophozoite	Band Form / Mature Trophozoite	Segmenter / Pigment	Attacks primarily older ery- throcytes. Parasitemias lower than other malarias, up to 20,000/cu.mm. of blood (average: 6,000).

			Ring Trophozoite	Macrogametocyte	Microgametocyte	
Plasmodium falciparum (falciparum malaria),† Predominant throughout tropical regions, particularly Africa. Chloroquine-resistant forms in Southeast Asia, South America, possibly Africa.	Cell normal in size and color. A few large red dots (Maurer's clefts) sometimes seen. Schüffner's dots absent. Multiple infections very common.	Only rings and gametocytes in peripheral blood. Merozoites small, 8-32 (average: 24).			Red Cell Ghost	Invades erythrocyte regardless of age, often in multiple form. Parasitemias may exceed 500,000/cu.mm., 10-40% of red cells. Infected red cells agglutinate, forming thrombi and emboli, blocking capillary walls, with resulting obstruction and ischemia as primary cause of pathology.
Plasmodium ovale (ovale malaria),† Rare; chiefly in Africa, though with sporadic worldwide distribution.	Parasitized cells enlarged, often fringed, oval or irregular in shape. Schüffner's dots abundant, found in ring stages. Multiple infections common.	All forms in peripheral blood. Similar to vivax but slightly smaller. Merozoites in rosette or cluster, 4-16 (average: 8).	Young (signet-ring) trophozoite showing early appearance of Schüffner's dots	Early segmenter developing in fimbriated erythrocyte	Mature schizont with 8 merozoites	Similar to vivax. Infects up to 30,000 cells per cu. mm. (average: 9,000).

*The invasive characteristics of the different plasmodia parallel the variations in severity of the disease. Parasitemia and severity of reaction are strongly affected by state of immunity or previous exposure and by level of nutrition.

†Clinical names (benign tertian for vivax, malignant tertian or estivoautumnal for falciparum, quartan for malariae) are now replaced by names of causative agents.

INTESTINAL PROTOZOA OF MAN

Infections world-wide; incidence depends on sanitation level. Entamoeba histolytica present in 3-30% of population; serious disease more characteristic of tropical than temperate areas, but usually much less common than asymptomatic infection. Incidence of Giardia lamblia varies with age; most common in children, rare in adults in most studies. Balantidium coli is comparatively rare; possibly transmitted from infected swine, though most hog infections are B. suis, not infective to man. Only these three commonly accepted pathogenic forms included below. Pathogenicity of other species is rare or questionable.

Parasite	Enters Man	Infective Form	Life Cycle in Man	Exit	Reservoir Host
Entamoeba histolytica	Mouth by contamination	Cyst	Becomes trophozoite in intestine. May invade mucosa and/or other organs of body, chiefly liver.	Cysts and/or trophozoites in feces (latter not infective).	Man.*
Giardia lamblia			Duodenum and bile passages.		Man.
Balantidium coli			May invade mucosa of large intestine.		Man, pig, monkey.

Nonpathogenic protozoa are commonly found in the feces of man. Microscopists must learn to distinguish them from the recognized pathogenic forms. The commoner organisms: Amebas - Entamoeba hartmanni, E. coli, Endolimax nana, Dientamoeba fragilis, Iodamoeba bütschlii (rarer); Flagellates - Chilomastix mesnili, Trichomonas hominis. Their main importance is that they are a sign of environmental pollution with fresh feces and may elicit unnecessary treatment or inaccurate diagnosis.

Trichomonas vaginalis, known only in the trophozoite stage, inhabits the human vagina and urethra of male and female. Produces vaginitis with severe itching and mucopurulent discharge in small proportion of cases. T. vaginalis is world-wide in distribution, occurring in 10-40% of women examined. It is mainly transferred by coitus but may also be transferred by treatment of the female, however, should always include treatment of her sexual partner. A flagellate identical with T. vaginalis found in the vagina of monkeys.

*Experimentally in monkey, pig, rat, dog, cat, but these hosts are not natural reservoirs.

INTESTINAL PROTOZOAN DISEASES OF MAN

Disease and Etiology	Possible Clinical Features	Laboratory Diagnosis
Amebiasis E. histolytica	Flask-shaped ulcers formed in mucosa of large bowel which appear as pinpoint dots on surface, with little inflammation but extensive undermining below surface. Localized in cecum and whole large bowel, especially on flexures and sigmoid colon. There is no eosinophilia in uncomplicated protozoan infections. **Blood:** Leukocytosis, anemia. **Symptoms:** Dysentery, bloody diarrhea, sometimes followed by constipation; abdominal pain and discomfort, gas distention; appetite disturbance, weight loss, headache, nervous manifestations, localized tenderness. **Complications:** Liver abscess (single or multiple) with liver enlargement and congestion. Pain, swelling, leukocytosis, anemia, fever. Lung abscess primary or, more commonly, secondary to liver abscess. Peritonitis (bacterial) with usual manifestations. Ulcerations and abscesses of other organs or tissues, manifestations depending upon site infected. (Incubation Period: acute, 8-10 days; chronic, 2 months-years.)	Examine feces by smear, concentration, culture. Abscess and ulcer material (as for feces).
Giardiasis G. lamblia	Duodenitis, perhaps choledochitis. Mucosal inflammation, possible mechanical and toxic interference with absorption of vitamin A and fats, resulting in diarrhea and steatorrhea.	Examine feces by smear, concentration.
Balantidiasis Bal. coli	Limited to large intestine where parasites localize, with pathology and symptoms that may resemble amebic dysentery. Most cases asymptomatic with high natural resistance; acute or chronic disease rare. The latter may produce extensive ulceration.	Examine feces by smear, concentration, culture.

Prevention: Proper disposal of human feces, with particular attention to the preschool child. Family and neighborhood hygiene is most important.

Toxoplasma gondii is a crescent-shaped protozoon found intracellularly in tissues and free in body fluids which causes toxoplasmosis. Method of transmission to adults is unknown. The fetus in utero is infected across the placenta. May be symptomatic or latent. Acute prenatal form involves all the viscera and is usually quickly fatal. Subacute or chronic prenatal toxoplasmosis shows predominantly C. N. S. manifestations and eye signs. Postnatal infection may be a rare, fulminating, erythematous, typhus-like infection; a lymphatic form resembling infectious mononucleosis; a chronic form with chorioretinitis, encephalitis, or synovial and osteoarticular involvement. Generally, however, infection in man is mild or asymptomatic. Infection is world-wide and extremely common (13-59% by intracutaneous test): disease is rare. Diagnostic laboratory methods: Isolation of the organism from C. S. F. or autopsy material. The complement fixation test and the Sabin-Feldman dye test are the most commonly employed serologic procedures, but useful direct agglutination and indirect hemagglutination tests are currently under development. C. S. F. protein in subacute and chronic forms is high, usually over 500 mg./100 ml.

BLOOD FLAGELLATES OF MAN

Incidence depends upon prevalence of vertebrate reservoirs and insect hosts, and varies with human habitation, habits, and agricultural practices.

Parasite and Distribution	Fly Host	Enters Man	Life Cycle in Man	Exit	Cycle in Fly	Reservoir Host*
Leishmania donovani. Asia, Africa, tropical South America, Middle East, Mediterranean basin.	Phlebotomus† (sandfly)	Plug of leptomonads injected with bite of fly.	Become leishmania (L-D bodies) in cells of reticuloendothelial system.			Man, dog, various wild dogs, foxes or jackals, wild rodents.
Leishmania tropica. Asia, South and Central America, Middle East, Europe.	Phlebotomus† (sandfly)		Become leishmania (L-D bodies) in endothelial cells of skin.	Sucked into fly with blood of host.	Become leptomonads in the intestine of the fly.	Man, various wild rodents, possibly dog.
Leishmania brasiliensis. Central and South America.	Phlebotomus† (sandfly)		Become leishmania in endothelial cells of skin and (secondary) mucous membranes of nasopharynx.			Man, various wild rodents, possibly dog.
Trypanosoma gambiense. Central and West Africa.	Glossina palpalis, others (tsetse fly)	Fly bites; metacyclic trypanosome injected with saliva.	Trypanosome in lymph and blood; later in spinal fluid.		Become crithidial and then metacyclic trypanosomes in the intestine and salivary glands of fly.	Man, domestic animals.
Trypanosoma rhodesiense. Central and East Africa.	Glossina morsitans, others (tsetse fly)					Man, wild game animals.
Trypanosoma cruzi. Central and South America.	Panstrongylus megistus (kissing bug) and other reduviid bugs	Metacyclic trypanosome in feces scratched into skin or rubbed into mucous membrane of eye.	Becomes leishmania in tissue cells (particularly cardiac muscle) and trypanosome in blood stream.	Sucked into bug with blood of host.	Become crithidial and then metacyclic trypanosomes in the hind intestine of bug.	Man, dog, cat, fox, armadillo, opossum (Didelphis), rodents.

*Varies in each area, e.g., in India and Africa, the dog apparently is not involved in L. donovani transmission whereas it is the principal reservoir in China and the Mediterranean. In many areas, reservoir hosts and vectors are still unknown.
†Various species involved, depending upon locality; vector usually specific for each region. Some vectors incriminated epidemiologically but not yet proved experimentally; others still unknown.

BLOOD FLAGELLATE DISEASES OF MAN

Disease & Etiology	Clinical Features	Laboratory Diagnosis
Kala azar (visceral leishmaniasis) L. donovani	Chronic febrile disease, causing hyperplasia and then blockage of cells of the reticuloendothelial system, particularly spleen and liver. Irregular fever (may spike twice a day) with chills, sweating, diarrhea, edema, cachexia, leukopenia, anemia. Splenomegaly and leukopenia characteristic. (Incubation Period: 2-9 months.) Untreated cases usually end fatally; with proper treatment, fatality is under 5%.	Blood: Thick and thin smears,* culture in N.N.N. or Tobie's diphasic blood agar. CF test diagnostic; nonspecific tests such as Napier & Chopra serum tests for screening; skin test for past infection. Nasal scrapings, lymph node biopsy, sternal marrow and splenic or hepatic aspirate: Stained smears, culture, inoculation of hamsters.
Oriental sore (cutaneous leishmaniasis) L. tropica	Endothelial cells and lymphoid tissue of skin parasitized. Itching red papule → scaling → crusted ulcer → enlargement of ulcer → healing. May be multiple. [Incubation Period: Several days to months, depending on strain, (1) dry (urban), relatively benign, slowly-ulcerating form; or (2) moist (rural), acute, rapidly-ulcerating zoonotic form.]	Ulcer curettings (from margin, not center, of ulcer): Stained smears, culture.
American leishmaniasis (espundia, uta, forest yaws; mucocutaneous leishmaniasis) L. brasiliensis	Initial lesions similar to oriental sore, but this enlarges, producing a weeping "saucer" ulceration. Destructive and deforming secondary lesions occur at mucocutaneous junctions particularly of the nasopharynx. Produces fever, pain, malaise, and anemia. (Incubation Period: Indeterminate.) Initial lesion appears in a few days, complications in a few months to many years. Nutrition probably very important in severity. Several distinct diseases grouped here.	Ulcer curettings (from margin, not center, of ulcer): Stained smears, culture.
Sleeping sickness West African - T. gambiense; East African - T. rhodesiense	Local lesion at fly bite followed by fever, adenitis, rash, transitory edemas. May fulminate (T. rhodesiense) or go on to meningoencephalitis and meningomyelitis, with mental and physical wasting leading to coma and death (T. gambiense). (Incubation Period: T. gambiense, 1-3 weeks, T. rhodesiense, 1-2 weeks.)	Blood: Thick and thin smears, concentration, culture. Spinal fluid: Sediment smears. Lymph node fluid: Smears, culture.
Chagas' disease T. cruzi	Acute, usually in children: Febrile illness with generalized adenopathy lasting a few months; placental infection may be common. Chronic: Cardiac involvement, particularly of right ventricle, consisting of degeneration of the cardiac muscle. Patient seldom lives beyond 50 yrs. Megacolon may be a sequel. Anemia of children in hyperendemic areas probably due to other factors than blood sucking by insect vector. Romaña's sign (palpebral edema) most probably an allergy to insect bite. (Incubation Period: 1-2 weeks.)	Blood: Thick and thin smears only in initial phases. Culture. Xenodiagnosis: See p. 343. Complement fixation most reliable serologic test.

*Direct blood film stains seldom positive except in heavy infections; buffy coat smear or culture better. Spleen impression smear from autopsy material or inoculation of hamster causing fatal infection is a better indicator.

COMMON INTESTINAL ROUNDWORMS OF MAN - PATHOLOGY

Disease and Etiology	Clinical Features	Laboratory Diagnosis
Enterobiasis, pinworm infection Enterobius vermicularis	Symptomless to perianal itching and irritation. Vaginal itch when female worms leave anus and enter genital passage. Nervousness, insomnia in persistent or heavy infections, especially from biting fingernails after scratching infected rectal area.	Cellulose (Scotch) tape swab (see p. 342).
Trichuriasis Trichuris trichiura	Depend on worm load. Symptomless to chronic debilitating diarrhea and anemia with damage to physical and mental development. Lower right quadrant pain is a common complaint. Chronic diarrhea, bloody stools, and tenesmus in heavier infections. Weight loss, wasting, rectal prolapse in massive trichuriasis - especially in children. Worms visible attached to mucosa under sigmoidoscopy in heavy infections, mucosa hyperemic, friable, edematous. Stools are mucoid and sticky with streaks of blood, numerous Charcot-Leyden crystals, eosinophils, and Trichuris eggs.	Feces: Direct smear, concentration (see pp. 337 and 339).
Ascariasis Ascaris lumbricoides	**Larvae** (migratory phase): Rarely pneumonitis with cough, hemoptysis, hemorrhages, lung consolidation, focal eosinophilic inflammation.* Eosinophilia (usually under 30%) during larval migration, falls rapidly afterwards.\ **Adults** (intestinal phase): Symptomless to serious intestinal mechanical complications (pancreatitis, appendicitis, diverticulitis), especially after disturbance of worms causing obstruction or perforation; metabolic complications (malabsorption, nutritive drain). Nausea, vomiting, aggravation of malnutrition.	Feces: Direct smear, concentration (see pp. 337 and 339).

*Inflammatory and eosinophilic reactions (without hemorrhage) particularly intense and rapid in previously exposed (sensitized) individuals.

| Hookworm infection
Necator
americanus,
Ancylostoma
duodenale | **Larvae** (migratory phase): Intense skin invasion may produce "ground itch," pruritic vesicular lesions followed by lung reactions (less intense than in ascariasis): cough, tracheal irritation, eosinophilia. Nausea, vomiting, dyspnea may result from larvae of Ancylostoma ("Wakana disease" in Japan).
Adults (intestinal phase): Hypochromic microcytic anemia is the chief clinical feature, varies with intensity and duration of infection, iron intake, nutritive state, age and condition of patient. Hypoproteinemia, edema, trophic skin disorders, reduction growth and mental development may follow. Allergic urticaria, diarrhea, abdominal pain in heavy infections. Intestinal malfunction through malabsorption and possible metabolic disturbance probably of considerable importance, particularly in children and undernourished populations. | Feces: Direct standardized smear to count eggs or examine after concentration (see pp. 337 and 339), cultivation of feces on filter paper strips in test tubes (Harada-Mori technic, see p. 345). |
| Strongyloidiasis
Strongyloides
stercoralis | **Larvae:** Invasion of skin may cause "ground itch," similar to hookworm. Malaise and cough, pulmonary infiltration may occur; high eosinophilia with larvae in focal lesions in colon, abdominal lymph nodes, liver, lungs following autoreinfection.
Adults: Alternate diarrhea and constipation; inflammation of intestinal mucosa; may be hemorrhage and microulceration with watery, mucoid diarrhea, colicky abdominal pain, tenderness, flatulence. Heavier infections produce atrophy of mucosa, ulcerous enteritis, edema, and fibrosis of intestinal wall. Extreme cases (usually after autoreinfection) with rapid deterioration, asthenia, anorexia, and death or chronic invalidism. Intestinal malfunction with impaired protein digestion and fat absorption may produce a condition similar to sprue. | Feces: Larvae (not eggs) in direct smear, concentration. Cultivation of feces on filter paper strips in test tubes (Harada-Mori technic, see p. 345). |

Prevention: Hookworm, Ascaris, Strongyloides - Prevent soil and vegetable pollution by proper disposal of feces. Raise nutritional level, particularly iron intake with hookworm, to prevent geophagia. Control human and other infection reservoirs.

Enterobius - Personal cleanliness, prevent dispersion of eggs, clean surroundings, mass treatment of family.

EXTRAINTESTINAL ROUNDWORM INFECTIONS OF MAN - LARVAL WORM PATHOLOGY

Disease and Etiology	Clinical Features	Laboratory Diagnosis
Trichinosis Trichinella spiralis	**Adults** (intestinal phase): Irritate and inflame the intestinal mucosa, with nausea, vomiting, diarrhea, and pain. **Larval migration and penetration** (1-6 weeks after infection): Muscular rheumatic pains, edema of the eyes, face, and hands. Irregular, persistent sweating and fever; difficulty with breathing, swallowing, and speech; rash and high eosinophilia (50-90%). **Larval encystment** (muscle phase) (after 6 weeks): Cachexia, toxic edema, skin eruptions, anemia, dehydration, and gradual subsidence of muscular pains. Fatalities usually occur 4-6 weeks after ingestion of heavily infected pork by nonimmune individual. Usually a home-butchered hog implicated.	Biopsy material: Examination by compression tissue between glass slides or by digestion (see p. 343). Intradermal test (see p. 342), rapid flocculation, complement fixation, precipitin tests.
Cutaneous larva migrans, creeping eruption. Ancylostoma braziliense and other nonhuman hookworms, species of animal Strongyloides, Gnathostoma spinigerum,* and possibly other nematodes.	Intracutaneous, violently itching, serpiginous tunnels, which are caused by wandering of hookworm larvae unable to complete normal penetration, migration, and development. Worms move about in the area of initial penetration, producing irregular papulovesicular lesions. Dry crust may form with local eosinophilia and cellular infiltration. This condition usually is transitory but larvae may also penetrate to deeper tissues, produce pulmonary infiltration and be recovered in sputum. The larvae may last several weeks to months, moving at intermittent periods of 1-3 cm. per day.	Clinical signs sufficient - no worms identified to date except in experimental animals.

*Normally a stomach worm of cats and other fish-eating mammals. Human infection by ingestion of uncooked fish, frogs, snakes or birds (in turn infected via a copepod, Cyclops), releasing larva that wanders in subcutaneous tunnels or deeper tissues. May produce cutaneous nodules or abscesses; rarely may cause ocular involvement.

Visceral larva migrans. Toxocara canis, T. cati and Toxascaris leonina (dog and cat ascarids); also Ancylostoma caninum, A. braziliense, Capillaria hepatica, possibly Ascaris lumbricoides var. suum and filariae of the genus Dirofilaria, other animal nematodes.	Chiefly in children ages 1-4, often benign, asymptomatic; later there may develop 20-90% eosinophilia and hepatomegaly. Fever, cough, joint and muscle pains, anorexia, weight loss, nervousness, abdominal pain, pneumonitis, splenomegaly all reported. Symptoms vary with number and location of larvae and patient's allergic response. Chief result of wandering of larvae is indication of a series of focal eosinophilic inflammations succeeded by granulomatous reactions. Endophthalmitis reported in young adolescents who apparently harbored larvae in their tissues from childhood.	Heavy infections show larvae and eosinophilic granulomatous lesions in liver biopsy. Chiefly a clinical diagnosis (persistent hypereosinophilia, hepatomegaly, hyperglobulinemia and frequent pneumonitis); hemagglutination technic useful for confirmation.
Eosinophilic meningoencephalitis Angiostrongylus cantonensis	Mild to intractable headache with 25% eosinophilia in CSF, low-grade fever, stiffness in neck and back, local hyperesthesias or paresthesias, facial paralysis. Caused by ingestion of larvae of rat lungworm from uncooked land snails and slugs or paratenic hosts. Reported in Taiwan, Thailand, Vietnam, Hawaii, Tahiti, New Caledonia, and other South Pacific islands.	Worms rarely observed in brain at autopsy or in CSF; pleocytosis with eosinophilia is the chief diagnostic sign.

Prevention: Trichinella - Sufficient cooking of pork (U.S. Government does not inspect for Trichinella). Hookworm and ascarids of dogs and cats - Avoid contamination in play areas, sand boxes; avoid undue contact, licking, etc., by family pets. Prevent pica by small children.
Angiostrongylus - Proper cooking of molluscs (possibility of infection from shrimp or crab juices in salad or direct infection by larvae on raw vegetables or lettuce).
Note: All except Trichinella (itself a zoonosis) are normally animal parasites in which only the larval worms are found in man as a result of chance exposure, often from family pets. The pathology observed is caused by the ill-adapted and fruitless wandering of these larvae and the host's reaction to them, resulting in worm entrapment and destruction with accompanying allergic responses or mechanical damage. The majority of moderate or even high infections normal to man elicit no noticeable response and remain undiscovered (e.g., high rate of trichinosis found in postmortem examinations).

COMMON INTESTINAL ROUNDWORMS OF MAN - LIFE CYCLES

Parasite & Distribution	Man Ingests	After Liberation in Duodenum	Adult Behavior	Propagation	Reservoir Host
Enterobius vermicularis. Cosmopolitan, urban.	Egg (infective in 4 hours)	Larvae become adult in ileum or lower bowel.	Female lives for 12 days to 2 months, and then moves into perianal region, lays eggs, and dies. Male minute.	Eggs on perianal skin, fingernails, clothing, dust; rarely in feces.	Man only host
Trichuris trichiura*	Egg (infective in 3-6 weeks)	Larvae mature in mucosa of cecum or sigmoid of colon. No blood migration.	Worms probably live several years, attached to mucosa by anterior end; pathogenic in heavy infection.	Eggs in feces, ingested as contaminants on food, soil, or fingers.	Man only known host
Ascaris lumbricoides*	Egg (infective in 2-3 weeks)	Larvae enter blood stream; to right heart; break out into alveoli of lungs; carried up trachea to esophagus; swallowed, enter intestine.	Ascaris: Live free in small intestine about 1 year. Necator lives 10-15 years, A. duodenale 4-5 years, attached to mucosa small intestine. Strongyloides: Parthenogenetic female parasitic, embedded in mucosa chiefly in jejunum. Infection often long-lived via autoreinfection; difficult to cure.	Eggs in feces, develop in soil, adhesive, ingested as contaminant.	Man only host. Pig ascaris does not infect man.
Necator americanus, *† Ancylostoma duodenale*†	Filariform larvae penetrate skin			Hookworm larvae enter skin; Ancylostoma often via ingestion. †	Man only host
Strongyloides stercoralis*‡				Eggs hatch in mucosa, larvae passed in feces. ‡	Man, dog; differentiation not certain.
Trichinella spiralis	Larvae encysted in raw pork	Worms mature in mucosa, larvae enter blood stream encyst in striated muscles.	Adults die after producing about 1500 larvae in 3 weeks.	Hogs eat uncooked garbage or infected rats. Infection via pork.	Hog, rat, flesh-eating mammals.

*Cosmopolitan, mainly tropical and subtropical areas with poor sanitation and favorable soil and moisture conditions. Ancylostoma, tolerant of low temperatures, with more northern, temperate distribution; Necator, chiefly tropical. Ascaris probably commonest helminth of man; Trichuris commonest in wet tropics.

†Hookworm soil cycle: Eggs hatch in soil ⟶ 2 stages rhabditiform larvae ⟶ infective filariform larvae ⟶ enters through skin or buccal mucosa via water.

‡Biphasic cycle of Strongyloides:

Parasitic cycle: Direct - No intervening reproduction in soil
Indirect - One or more freeliving generations

Freeliving reproductive cycle in soil

TISSUE ROUNDWORMS OF MAN - CHIEFLY FILARIAE, LIFE CYCLES

Parasite & Distribution	Intermediate Host	Mode of Human Infection	Site of Worm Maturation	Larvae Found In	Exit	Larval Development In	Reservoir Host
Wuchereria bancrofti Brugia malayi Tropics and subtropics	Culex, Aedes, Anopheles, Mansonia, and other mosquitoes	Filariform larvae actively leave mosquito at time of biting, usually enter skin via puncture	In lymph vessels and nodes	Bloodstream (nocturnal periodicity*; certain strains subperiodic or nonperiodic).	Microfilariae taken up by insect when biting	Thoracic muscles; larvae migrate to proboscis (8-15 days)	For subperiodic form B. malayi only; cats, dogs, monkeys (in Malaya)
Loa loa Tropical Africa	Chrysops (deer or mangrove flies)	Probably same	In subcutaneous tissues	Bloodstream (diurnal periodicity)	Same	Abdomen; larvae migrate to proboscis	Primates?
Onchocerca volvulus Tropical Africa, Venezuela, and mountainous portions of Central America	Simulium (buffalo gnat)	Probably same	Same. Host reaction produces nodule around cluster of adults	Subcutaneous tissues; eye (no periodicity)	Same	Thoracic muscles, larvae do not concentrate in proboscis	Man
Dracunculus medinensis Africa, India, Far and Middle East, Indonesia	Cyclops (water flea)	Infected Cyclops accidentally ingested in water	Digested out of Cyclops, worm migrates into tissues, female to skin	Adult female in skin causes host to form blister near head of worm. Blister then filled with larvae, bursts when skin immersed in water, discharging larvae. New blister later forms as female moves to new site.	Cyclops feeds on larva, which penetrates gut, develops in hemocoel (18-21 days)	Man

*Periodicity of microfilarial appearance in peripheral blood. May be nocturnal, with almost all microfilariae in circulating blood from 10 p.m. until 4 a.m., after which microfilariae confined to pulmonary capillaries. Other strains or species show a modified nocturnal pattern (subperiodic) or a daytime appearance in peripheral blood (diurnal periodicity), usually correlated with biting habits of vector.

TISSUE ROUNDWORMS OF MAN - CHIEFLY FILARIAE, PATHOLOGY

Disease & Etiology	Clinical Features	Laboratory Diagnosis
Bancroft's filariasis W. bancrofti Malayan filariasis B. malayi	Filariae in afferent lymphatics or lymph nodes (of lower extremities, male genitalia, vulva, mammary gland) may cause inflammation followed by intensely fibrotic reaction involving whole area in a mass of scar tissue. Pain, fever, chills, toxemia, eosinophilia. Chronic stage (after disappearance of microfilariae) varies from microscopic lesion to lymph varicosity to marked elephantiasis. High eosinophilia and superficial lymphadenopathy in Malayan filariasis. Pathology probably a general and focal sensitization response.	Blood: Thick and thin smears, concentration (see p. 344). Intradermal test gives useful group filaria reaction; indirect hemagglutination, fluorescent antibody tests under development.
Loiasis Loa loa	Fugitive swelling ("Calabar swelling") in skin due to local edema and skin reaction against migrating adult worm. The latter commonly moves across surface of eyeball or under skin at bridge of nose (best times for removal with local anesthesia). Eosinophilia with occasional proteinuria produced.	
Onchocerciasis O. volvulus	Small cutaneous fibrous skin nodules with filariae entwined in center. Microfilariae in nodule, neighboring tissues, or in normal skin far from nodules, rarely in blood. Skin reactions particularly common in Africa: reduction of elastic fibers, depigmentation, progressive thickening, pruritus, papulovesicular lesions or hyperkeratotic patches with microfilariae in scrapings. Eosinophilia and transient urticaria during incubation. Ocular involvement leading to blindness a common result of prolonged infection. Conjunctiva and vitreous humor with numerous microfilariae. Pathology due to mechanical action toxins, hypersensitive response of patient; ocular symptoms after 7-9 years.	Microfilariae in nodule aspirate or skin snip: repeated skin snips may be required: scapular region area of choice. Cutaneous manifestations, eosinophilia, ocular lesions, pruritus may follow diethylcarbamazine (Hetrazan®) therapy.
Dracontiasis D. medinensis	Asymptomatic until reddish papular lesion appears, usually on legs. Lesion forms blister bearing head of female worm and numerous larvae. Blister bursts when immersed in water, releasing larvae. Urticaria, pruritus, allergic symptoms, eosinophilia. Accidental rupture of worm may produce intense inflammatory reaction with secondary infection.	Local lesion, with head of worm and larvae in blister. X-ray reveals calcified worm; reflected light shows worm under skin. Intradermal test.

Prevention: Protection against insect bites or ingestion of Cyclops in water. Insect control and water filtration with mass treatment in endemic areas.

Note: "Eosinophilic lung" describes a host allergic response to migration of microfilariae that are trapped in lungs, producing an allergic, asthma-like response. Probably caused by human filariae or closely related species, as completion of worm development and microfilariae production required. Diagnosed by: Clinical signs, eosinophilia (3000 or more absolute count, usually over 35%), high hemagglutination or complement fixation titer that drops following diethylcarbamazine (Hetrazan®) therapy, elevated sedimentation rate, mottled lung lesions visible under x-ray.

TAPEWORM DISEASES OF MAN

Disease & Etiology	Clinical Features	Laboratory Diagnosis
Hymenolepiasis Hymenolepis nana	Symptomless to systemic toxemia, depending on worm load. Eosinophilia, nervous manifestations, with or without diarrhea, and pain. Heavy worm load, probably following autoreinfection, may produce convulsions, insomnia, dizziness.	Feces: Direct smear or concentration to show eggs.
Taeniasis saginata Taenia saginata	Abdominal and hunger pains, chronic indigestion, weight loss, persistent diarrhea or alternating with constipation; nervous manifestations. Eosinophilia.	Feces: Not reliable. Recovery of gravid segments which actively crawl from anus; can be found in underwear or bed linen. Segments or eggs may be rare in feces.
Taeniasis solium Taenia solium	**Intestinal:** Same as T. saginata. **Cysticercosis:** Symptoms may vary with number of larvae and site in tissues. Foreign body response with inflammation followed by fibrosis and necrosis of parasite, later calcification. Shows affinity for C.N.S., symptoms resemble brain tumor, epilepsy, and other disorders. Chief site: Subcutaneous tissues, eye, brain.	Feces: Recovery of gravid segments. Recovery of larva by biopsy from infected tissue. Detection of calcified larvae by x-ray.
Hydatid disease Echinococcus granulosus, E. multilocularis	E. granulosus produces unilocular cysts, 80-90% in liver and lungs. The host becomes sensitized following escape of fluid through fissures. Pressure symptoms. Anaphylactic shock may occur upon rupture. Cachexia results from secondary metastases. Pulmonary or cerebral emboli may occur. Manifestations resemble cholelithiasis, or renal, hepatic, or intestinal colic, sometimes of long standing. E. multilocularis produces uncontrolled, untreatable metastases in liver with final destruction of most of the parenchyma.	Cyst contents in urine. Sputum: Direct smear. Serology: Complement fixation, flocculation, precipitin, hemagglutination, intradermal tests. X-rays for pulmonary cysts or calcified cysts elsewhere. Clinical history and picture of great value.
Diphyllobothriasis (fish tapeworm disease) Diphyllobothrium latum	Symptomless to marked systemic toxemia. Pain, weight loss, diarrhea, eosinophilia. Severe macrocytic anemia, similar to pernicious anemia, found in a small number of cases (70% from Finland), where there is a tendency for this type of anemia). Worm competes for vitamin B$_{12}$ with host.	Feces: Direct smear or concentration to show eggs.

Prevention: Hymenolepis nana, proper disposal of feces; avoidance of accidental ingestion of grain beetles and moths (or larvae); control of rodents. Taenia saginata and Taenia solium, cook beef and pork well; hydatid disease (very difficult), do not pet dogs in endemic areas, protect food from flies. Diphyllobothrium latum, cook fish well.

TAPEWORMS OF MAN

Diphyllobothrium latum, 80-100% in highly endemic areas; Taenia saginata, commonest of the large tapeworms; Hymenolepis nana, probably most common in man. Echinococcus granulosus, 3-16% in some endemic areas; Taenia solium, where pork is eaten raw (rare in U.S.).

Parasite & Distribution	Cycle in Intermediate Host			Cycle in Definitive Host		Summary of Hosts
	Infection	Route	Fate	Maturation of Worm	Exit	
Taenia saginata (beef tapeworm) World-wide	Ingestion of egg (cattle)	Egg hatches in intestine; **oncosphere** released, penetrates intestine, enters	Encysts in muscles or organs, forms a **cysticercus** larva (bladderworm) in cattle called Cysticercus bovis.	Man ingests cysticercus in raw beef; scolex attaches to duodenum, becomes adult in 6-12 months.	Gravid segments per anus	**Definitive:** Man **Intermediate:** Cattle, buffalo, giraffes, llamas, goats.
Taenia solium (pork tapeworm) World-wide	Ingestion of egg (hogs, man); auto-reinfection (man)†	bloodstream of vertebrate.	Similar to T. saginata, cysticercus larva (in hogs) called C. cellulosae.	As for T. saginata, but infection source is under-cooked pork.		**Definitive:** Man **Intermediate:** Hogs, man (autoreinfection†)
Echinococcus granulosus (hydatid worm). Sheep-raising countries	Ingestion of egg (sheep, accidental ingestion in man)		Forms **hydatid cyst** with thousands of infective scoleces in fluid, although cysts may also be sterile. Chiefly in liver, also in lungs, rarely in brain.	Sheep dogs ingest hydatid "sand" (infective scoleces) from hydatid cyst in sheep carcass. Worms attach to canine intestinal wall; become adult.	Eggs in feces	**Definitive:** Dogs, all canids; rarely cats **Intermediate:** Sheep, hogs, cattle, man‡

			Cysticercoid		Eggs in feces	Man; rats and mice; gerbil in Africa (chiefly a rodent infection, found primarily in mice; also commonest tapeworm of man, possibly distinctive strain in man).
Hymenolepis nana (dwarf tapeworm) World-wide	Ingestion of egg by man or rodent (direct cycle) or by various insects (indirect cycle)	Egg hatches in intestine; oncosphere released. In man, it invades villus; in insect, it penetrates gut and enters hemocoel.	Cysticercoid larva, containing scolex of future adult worm, formed either in villus of human host or hemocoel of insect.	In man, larva leaves villus, attaches to small intestine, becomes adult. If infected insect ingested, cysticercoid digested out, hatches, attaches, grows to adult in 10-12 days.* Cysticercoid derived either from insect or direct egg-to-cysticercoid cycle in man can produce infection.	Eggs in feces	Man; rats and mice; gerbil in Africa (chiefly a rodent infection, found primarily in mice; also commonest tapeworm of man, possibly distinctive strain in man).
Diphyllobothrium latum (fish or broad tapeworm). Northern Europe, Great Lakes, Chile, Argentina, Orient	Water flea ingests swimming embryo (coracidium) hatched from egg in water.	Hooked embryo penetrates gut wall, develops into procercoid larva in hemocoel.	Freshwater fish eats water flea: larva digested out in intestine, penetrates to muscles or various organs, becomes 3rd stage larva (plerocercoid or sparganum).	Man ingests fish with sparganum; larva liberated in intestine, attaches to intestinal wall, becomes adult.	Eggs in feces into water	Definitive: Fish-eating mammals Intermediate: Water fleas (Diaptomus), then various freshwater fish§

*Following ingesting of infected beetle with cysticercoids, internal reinfection (autoreinfection) is possible. When initial human infection is from an egg infection, immunity is rapidly and strongly induced against succeeding generations of H. nana. No such immunity results from initial cysticercoid infection via beetle, therefore an autoreinfection generation can develop, after which host is usually immune.

†Eggs from adult worms may hatch if flushed into duodenum by reverse peristalsis. Oncosphere then can penetrate intestine, pass via bloodstream to all tissues and organs where cysticerci form. More commonly, this condition follows accidental ingestion of eggs from infected human feces.

‡Man is a "dead-end" intermediate host only. Man cannot serve as the final host for development of adult E. granulosus.

§Larvae often are passed through successive predaceous fish; they are digested free, penetrate intestine, and reestablish themselves in organs or muscles of each in turn. Pike and similar game fish often are cause of infection in man.

FLUKES OF MAN

Parasite & Distribution	Definitive Host — Enters Man	Definitive Host — Habitat	Intermediate Host Cycle Outside Man — Exit	Intermediate Host Cycle Outside Man	Reservoir Hosts
Schistosoma haematobium; Mediterranean basin, Africa. Egypt is classical focus	Cercaria penetrates skin	Vesical and pelvic venous plexuses draining urinary bladder.	Terminal-spined large egg in urine or feces	Egg hatches to release swimming miracidium in water. Invades appropriate snail. (Clonorchis egg ingested by snail.) → In snail tissues each miracidium becomes a sporocyst, which forms a number of embryos (sporocysts or rediae, depending on species) which in turn produce many cercariae.	Man, monkeys
Schistosoma mansoni; Africa, Brazil, Venezuela, Puerto Rico, Dutch Guiana, West Indies, Antilles		Branches of inferior mesenteric veins draining rectum and sigmoid.	Lateral-spined large egg in feces		Man, baboon, monkeys, opossums, wild rats in Brazil, Africa
Schistosoma japonicum; Japan, East Asia, Philippine Islands		Same as for **S. mansoni**, but occurs chiefly in superior mesenteric veins draining small intestine.	Round, small-spined egg in feces*		Man, horses, hogs, sheep, goats, cows, dogs, cats, water-buffalo, rodents
Fasciolopsis buski; East and South Asia	Ingested metacercaria on water plants or other vegetation	Small intestine attached to intestinal wall.		Cercariae swarm from snail → Encyst on water plants (**Fasciola** and **Fasciolopsis**),	Man, pigs
Fasciola hepatica; World-wide, sheep and cattle-raising countries		Major bile ducts after migrating from intestine through peritoneal cavity, liver capsule, and parenchyma.			Sheep, cattle, other herbivores. Man accidental host
Clonorchis sinensis†; South Asia; immigrants in America	Ingested metacercaria in raw fish	Bile ducts migrating from intestine through ampulla of Vater.	Egg in bile to feces	or invade fish (**Clonorchis**), or crayfish, or crab (**Paragonimus**),	Man, dogs, cats, fish-eating mammals
Paragonimus westermani; Asia, North and Central Africa, America (P. kellicotti)	Ingested metacercaria in crayfish, crab	Encysted in lungs, pleural and peritoneal cavities, liver, migrating from intestine through peritoneal cavity.	Egg in sputum or feces	or directly penetrate human skin (**Schistosoma**).	Man, wildcats, foxes, wolves, dogs, rats, pigs, weasels

*Spine may be hidden in some views or be too small to be seen.

†Other locally common and medically significant fish-borne flukes found in man: Heterophyes heterophyes (Egypt, Turkey, Orient), Metagonimus yokogawai (Orient - common), Opisthorchis felineus (common in Eastern Europe and Siberia; rare in Central or Western Europe), O. viverrini (very common in Thailand, Laos).

FLUKE DISEASES OF MAN

Disease & Etiology	Clinical Features	Laboratory Diagnosis
Schistosomiasis Bilharziasis Schistosoma haematobium Schistosoma mansoni Schistosoma japonicum	**Initial:** Skin penetration by cercariae produces itching, erythema, petechiae, usually a hypersensitization following repeated exposures. Eosinophilia in latter case, with fever. **Maturation of worms:** Fever, liver tenderness and enlargement, edema, diarrhea; eosinophilia variable. **Adult worms:** Systemic and histologic changes due mainly to reaction against eggs acting as foreign bodies. Symptoms vary with duration, frequency, and severity of exposure and degree of host reaction, itself related to age, nutrition, and concurrent infections. Generally with bowel and vesical disturbances, lasting for months to years. **Chronic disturbances:** Portal hypertension with resulting esophageal varices or intestinal fibrosis. Fibrosis, thickening, calcification in bladder wall (S. haematobium), thickening of small intestine (S. japonicum), prolapse of rectum (S. mansoni), loss of gut motility, local tissue and organ dysfunction.	**Urine:** Direct smear for eggs, sedimentation and hatching of miracidia in diluted urine for S. haematobium, preferably in last portion of fluid passed. **Feces:** Direct smear, concentration for S. mansoni or japonicum eggs. Rectal biopsy and sigmoidoscopy (S. mansoni, S. japonicum); intravenous pyelography and cystoscopy (S. haematobium). **Blood:** Precipitin (circumoval or CHR) test (see p. 343).
Fasciolopsiasis Fasciolopsis buski	Localized inflammation of jejunum or duodenum, followed often by ulceration at sites of worm attachment. Diarrhea with foul-smelling stools; abdominal pain. In severe infections fibrosis, ascites, anorexia, nausea, vomiting, toxemia, prostration.	**Feces:** Direct smear, sedimentation (see pp. 338, 340).
Fascioliasis Fasciola hepatica	Worm migrations cause tissue necrosis and fibrosis. Bile duct damage resembles that for Clonorchis. Picture like any biliary derangement (gallbladder, choledochus involvement). Eosinophilia. Infection runs a chronic course of many years.	**Feces:** Direct smear, sedimentation (see pp. 338, 340). Duodenal drainage; complement fixation, skin tests.
Clonorchiasis Clonorchis sinensis	Similar hepatic involvement. Large numbers of parasites cause diarrhea, jaundice, cachexia, eosinophilia. Proliferation and desquamation of biliary epithelium, dilatation, and thickening of the wall occur. Severe symptoms of liver dysfunction, recurring jaundice with hepatomegaly may follow. Long-continued chronic course common.	Direct smear, sedimentation (see pp. 338, 340); eggs in biliary drainage.
Paragonimiasis Paragonimus westermani	**Lung:** Parasites are embedded, usually in pairs, in subpleural cysts (eggs act as foreign bodies) with inflammation, eosinophilia, and fibrous capsule formation. Chronic cough with fever, brown sputum, hemoptysis, severe chest pain, bronchial pneumonia or pleural fluid common. May enter any organ and produce local symptoms, e.g., abdominal pain, diarrhea, C.N.S. involvement. Similar lesions in other tissues.	**Sputum:** Direct smear. **Feces:** Direct smear, sedimentation (see pp. 338, 340); complement fixation, etc.

Prevention: Schistosomes: Eradicate snails, stay away from all freshwater bodies. Liver flukes: Eat only well-washed and cooked vegetables; avoid raw salads of wild plants growing in flooded regions (fascioliasis, fasciolopsiasis); eat only well-cooked or fried fish (clonorchiasis). Paragonimus: Do not eat or handle raw freshwater crab or crayfish meat.

LABORATORY EXAMINATION FOR PARASITES

FECES
(See also p. 277.)

Specimen Collection.

Collect specimen in a clean, dry container and examine as soon as possible. Characteristic movement of Entamoeba histolytica trophozoites are only seen in a direct smear examined while the specimen is still warm. Specimens following administration of oil, bismuth, or barium are unsatisfactory. Repeated examinations are advisable; at least three to six should be examined preferably on consecutive days since the time of appearance of parasites in the feces is variable. If mucus or blood streaks are present, these must be examined since trophozoites or cysts of intestinal protozoa may be distributed irregularly throughout the specimen. Fluidity, stickiness, form, and odor are important factors to consider in diagnosis.

Preservation and Shipment of Specimens to Be Examined for Trophic and Encysted Protozoa.

A. PVA (Polyvinyl Alcohol) Method of Brooke and Goldman: Excellent for ameba, especially if permanent slides are required. For collection of field specimens and for mass surveys, the MIF method (see p. 337) is recommended.

1. Reagent - Modified Schaudinn's solution is prepared by mixing 5 ml. of glacial acetic acid, 1.5 ml. glycerol, and 93.5 ml. Schaudinn's solution (two parts saturated aqueous mercuric chloride and one part 95% ethyl alcohol).

    Heat the above solution to 75° C.; while stirring, slowly add 5 Gm. polyvinyl alcohol (PVA) powder (Dupont's Elvanol®, Grades 71-24 or 71-30). This final solution should be clear and free of lumps after cooling. It is used at room temperature, and lasts for several months.

2. Preparation of specimens -
    a. One specimen should be sent without above fixative to be used for detection of protozoan cysts and helminthic ova. This specimen can be used for temporary or permanent smears or for concentration procedures (see p. 339).
    b. Second specimen is prepared by thoroughly mixing with three or more parts of fixative in a small vial. To prepare slides a small amount of this fecal mixture (recent or months old) is spread thinly over about one-third of the slide. After drying for three or more hours at 37° C. or overnight at room

temperature, the smear is stained by the iron hematoxylin method (see p. 340). This procedure is particularly suitable for the preservation and staining of the trophic forms of intestinal protozoa. To obtain satisfactory stained fecal smears containing cystic stages the excess clear PVA solution is decanted from the vial and a small amount of the remaining fixed fecal material is placed on a piece of facial tissue or toilet paper. The excess PVA solution is allowed to absorb for five to ten minutes, leaving a moist fecal residue. Gently scrape up a small amount of the residue with the sharp edge of a broken applicator stick and smear with gentle brushing strokes on a slide. Drop smear immediately into 70% alcohol to which iodine has been added to produce a port wine color, and stain by the iron hematoxylin method (see p. 340). To insure satisfactory preparations of both cystic and trophic forms, the preparation of both types of smears is recommended.

B. MIF (Merthiolate-Iodine-Formalin) Method of Sapero and Lawless: This is becoming the standard method for mass surveys, collection of bulk material, or parasitologic field studies. Fecal specimens are fixed and stained immediately, and can be examined at any time within several months of collection. This method is particularly good for protozoa.

1. Reagents - MIF stock solution is made from 250 ml. distilled water, 200 ml. tincture of merthiolate (No. 99, Lilly 1:1000), 25 ml. formaldehyde, U. S. P. , 5 ml. glycerol. Store in brown bottle. Lugol's solution (5% iodine in 10% potassium iodide in distilled water), not over one week old, forms the second solution.

2. Preparation of specimens - For each specimen to be collected, have ready 2.35 ml. MIF stock solution in a Kahn test tube with cork stopper and 0.15 ml. Lugol's solution in a second Kahn tube with a rubber stopper. Combine the two solutions just before adding the fecal specimen. Break up about 0.25 Gm. feces into the combined solution, mix thoroughly, and stopper well. (May be examined immediately on a slide, 1 drop fecal preparation and 1 drop distilled water; or stored in a well stoppered tube, where the stain will be retained for several months.)

Standardized Direct Fecal Smear Examination.

Follow directions given by Beaver strictly (J. Parasitol. , **35**:125-135, 1949; **36**:451-456, 1950). Place a glass slide over a calibrated photometer (a Weston Master is just as good) and set the reading at 20 f. c. Add a drop of saline and with the tip of an applicator comminute feces progressively until the needle moves down to the preset reading. A preparation of 2 mg. (^{1}/500 ml.) is preferable. Cover with a coverglass and examine all the microscopic fields, counting the various eggs and looking for cysts and trophozoites of protozoa. A drop of iodine solution (Lugol's, Craig's, or D'Antoni's) will help differentiate nuclear detail of amebae. This method permits quantitation of worm loads as well as examination for all signs of parasites (e.g., 500 × egg count for ^{1}/500 ml. preparation).*

Where standardized smear or precise comparative readings are not required, two smears can be made on a single slide, one mixed with 1 drop of physiologic saline, the second in 1 drop of iodine solution. The former is for living material, the latter for helminth eggs and nuclear detail in protozoan cysts. This is still the most simple and widespread diagnostic procedure followed. It permits rapid examination of the unaltered specimen, including protozoan trophozoites, exudative cells, Charcot-Leyden crystals, and other diagnostically helpful objects.

Negative-Stain Direct Fecal Smear Examination.

Prepare normal fecal smear in saline to which 1-2 drops of 1% isotonic eosin are added. Background material and **dead** parasites turn uniformly pink. Stain will not penetrate living trophozoites, causing them to stand out markedly as clear, translucent organisms against a pink background. A rapid and useful procedure.

Isotonic eosin, 1%, and brilliant cresyl blue, 0.2%, makes a good vital stain, causing living material to appear as shiny pale blue-green objects on the pink background.

Kato Cellophane Thick Smear Technic (Kato and Miura, 1954).

This procedure permits rapid examination of a large number of samples (up to 70 per hour) for eggs of the common helminths. It is not suitable for protozoa or minute helminth eggs (Clonorchis, Heterophyes) or for highly fibrous or gaseous samples. Its speed and economy have enabled Japanese public health workers to make as many as 20,000,000 fecal examinations in a year.

  A. Materials:
    1. Wettable cellophane of medium thickness (40 to 50 micra), cut in strips 22 × 30 mm.
    2. Glycerine–malachite green solution: 100 ml. pure glycerine, 100 ml. water, 1 ml. 3% aqueous malachite green.

---

*The most widely used quantitative procedure for fecal egg counts is still the 0.1 N sodium hydroxide dilution method using calibrated flasks (Stoll, 1923; Stoll and Hausheer, 1926), which was developed for hookworm egg counts. Cf. WHO Technical Report 255, Annex 2, 21-6, 1963.

The cellophane strips should be soaked in the glyc-
erine mixture for at least 24 hours before use.
B. Procedure:
1. Place 50 to 60 mg. feces (4-mm. cube) on a clean slide.
2. Cover with a glycerine-soaked cellophane strip, press
   to spread feces in an even layer (a No. 5 rubber stopper is satisfactory). Feces need not be spread to all
   areas of cellophane; a circumference equal to the
   width of the strip is sufficient.
3. Allow to stand at room temperature for one hour (or
   20 to 30 minutes at 40° C. in a dry incubator). This
   dries and clears the specimen. (Do not overdry, as gas
   bubbles will form and air cells will surround the eggs.)
4. Examine entire film under low magnification (50 ×
   magnification can be used by experienced microscopists).

Rapid low-power scanning of a relatively large sample
obviates the need for concentration procedures for most infections (except as noted above).

Concentration.
Parasites are often so few in number that they cannot be
detected without employing a concentration procedure.
A. Formalin-Ether Sedimentation Technic (Ritchie): Best
   for trematode eggs; though excellent for all parasites,
   including protozoan cysts.
1. Emulsify portion of stool (a mass 2 to 3 cm. in diameter) in 30 to 50 ml. saline. (For specimens that have
   previously been preserved in formalin, start with 2,
   below. Tap water may be used instead of saline in
   this case if desired.)
2. Strain about 10 ml. of the emulsion through two layers
   of wet gauze into a 15 ml. centrifuge tube with a conical tip. The remainder of the emulsion may be used
   for other concentration technics, direct smears, or
   for preservation.
3. Centrifuge at moderate speed (1000 r.p.m.) for a few
   minutes and then decant supernatant.
4. Resuspend sediment in fresh saline, centrifuge, decant as before. Repeat as necessary, if supernatant
   is particularly cloudy.
5. Add 10 ml. of 10% formalin to the sediment, mix
   thoroughly, and allow to stand for ten minutes or
   longer.
6. Add 3 ml. of ether, stopper the tube, and shake vigorously for 15 to 20 seconds.
7. Centrifuge immediately at 2000 r.p.m. for about two
   minutes. Four layers should result: (1) at the bottom, a small amount of sediment containing most of
   the parasites and eggs; (2) a layer of formalin; (3) a

fluffy plug of fecal debris on top of the formalin; and
(4) at the top, a layer of ether.

8. Free the plug of debris from the sides of tube by ring-
ing with an applicator stick, and decant the top three
layers.

9. Mix the remaining sediment with the small amount of
fluid that drains back from the sides of the tube and
prepare iodine or unstained mounts in the usual manner for microscopic examination.

B. Zinc Sulfate Centrifugal Flotation Technic (Faust,
D'Antoni, and Sawitz): Most efficient method for protozoan cysts, for Hymenolepis nana, and for nematode eggs.
Not suitable for operculated eggs (trematodes other than
schistosomes and Diphyllobothrium latum).

1. Emulsify 1 ml. of feces in 10 ml. of tap water.

2. Filter through two layers of gauze.

3. Centrifuge mixture for one minute at 2600 r. p. m. and
pour off supernatant fluid.

4. Add fresh water, mix well, and centrifuge again. Repeat this process three or four times.

5. For the final emulsification, substitute 33% zinc sulfate solution (sp. gr. 1.180) for the tap water.

6. Centrifuge the suspension for one minute at top speed.

7. Eggs and cysts rise to surface (trophozoites destroyed).

8. Disturbing the supernatant as little as possible, transfer several loopsful of the surface film to a glass
slide. Add a drop of iodine, mix, cover with coverglass, and examine microscopically.

Heidenhain's Iron Hematoxylin Staining Method For Intestinal Protozoa.

There are numerous modifications of the iron-hematoxylin
stain, any one of which will give good results if properly
handled. The process of decolorization is the most vital step.
This can be mastered only by experience.

A. Staining Solutions:

1. Schaudinn's fixative - Two parts saturated mercuric
chloride in water, one part 95% ethyl alcohol. Before
using add 5 ml. glacial acetic acid to 100 ml. of the
stock solution.

2. Hematoxylin stain (stock solution) - Dissolve 10 Gm.
hematoxylin powder in 100 ml. absolute ethyl alcohol.
Let stand several weeks to ripen before use. For use,
5 ml. of the ripened hematoxylin is added to 95 ml.
distilled water.

3. Mordant - Dissolve 5 Gm. ferric ammonium sulfate in
100 ml. distilled water and filter.

B. Procedure:

1. Make thin fecal smear on glass slide with toothpick or
applicator.

2. Before drying occurs, immerse slide in Schaudinn's fluid which has been heated to 45° C. Fix for five to 15 minutes at this temperature or for 30 minutes at room temperature.
3. Staining in Coplin jars -

70% iodine alcohol	5 minutes
70% alcohol	2 minutes
50% alcohol	2 minutes
Tap water	2 minutes
Distilled water	Rinse
5% aqueous alum (mordant)	60 minutes at 50° C.
Distilled water (2 changes)	Rinse
0.5% hematoxylin	60 minutes at 50° C.
Differentiate in 1% aqueous iron alum (a critical step)	Usually 3-5 minutes
Tap water (running)	15 to 20 minutes
50% alcohol	2 minutes
70% alcohol	2 minutes
95% alcohol	2 minutes
Isopropyl alcohol	2 changes of 2 minutes
Carbol xylol	5 minutes
Xylol (2 changes)	5 minutes

Mount in xylol-balsam, xylol-Damar or Permount® with a coverglass of No. 1 thickness.

Cultivation of Intestinal Protozoa.

Numerous types of special media have been developed for the cultivation of the intestinal amebas and flagellates as well as for the ciliate Balantidium coli. Among these are Boeck-Drbohlav's Locke-egg-serum medium, Nelson's egg yolk-alcoholic extract medium, and Balamuth's egg yolk infusion-liver extract medium. Consult standard texts for details of preparation.

URINE

Collect urine in clean, dry container, avoiding fecal contamination. Study centrifuged sediment. Trophozoites of Trichomonas vaginalis, unhatched eggs of Schistosoma haematobium, and intact scoleces or hooklets of Echinococcus granulosus may appear in the urine. Viable S. haematobium eggs will hatch only after dilution of urine.

SPUTUM

Examine for parasites as a direct smear under a cover glass. If the sputum is thick, bloody, or pus-laden, mix with equal volume 1 to 2% sodium hydroxide; stir, let settle, and study sediment. Larvae of Strongyloides stercoralis, scoleces of Echinococcus granulosus, eggs of Paragonimus westermani, or migrating nematode larvae may be present in the sputum. Charcot-Leyden crystals and eosinophils can also be observed in wet mounts or after wet fixation and staining.

Gastric washings for night-swallowed sputum will often yield Paragonimus eggs or migrating nematode larvae better than will sputum or feces (owing to less detritus).

Duodenal aspirates are useful for nematode eggs and are particularly helpful for eggs of Clonorchis and other bile-dwelling parasites.

SPINAL FLUID

Examine centrifugate directly under the microscope. Make smears, stain with Giemsa's stain, and examine. Culture some of the sediment, as for blood. Inoculate guinea pigs or mice if necessary. Eosinophilia may indicate eosinophilic meningoencephalitis (see p. 327).

VAGINAL SECRETIONS

Wet preparation may be examined directly for Trichomonas vaginalis. Cultures can be made by experienced technicians.

GRAHAM CELLULOSE TAPE TECHNIC FOR DIAGNOSIS OF ENTEROBIASIS

With the help of a tongue depressor, press the adhesive side of a small strip or loop of cellulose tape (e.g., Scotch Tape®) over the anal and perianal surfaces, preferably at night. Then place tape with adhesive side down in a drop of toluene on a microscopic slide. Examine for eggs or worms which have adhered to the tape.

IMMUNOLOGIC TESTS
(See p. 367.)

Intradermal tests for Schistosoma, Trichinella spiralis (Bachmann test), and Echinococcus granulosus (Casoni test) are very sensitive and sufficiently specific. Antigen for Schistosoma is made from extracts of adult worms or cercariae; for Trichinella, from larvae digested from muscles of laboratory-infected rats. Hydatid antigen consists of fluid obtained from hydatid cysts found in man, sheep, cattle, or hogs.

The complement fixation, circumoval, and CHR (Cercarien-Hüllen-Reaktion) tests are very sensitive and sufficiently specific in the diagnosis and follow-up of schistosomiasis. Normal living eggs or cercariae of the species under suspicion are incubated overnight in blood serum from the patient. A peculiar precipitate will form around them. The circumoval test is species-specific and becomes negative several months after successful therapy. A recently developed hemagglutination test (Kagan, 1955) uses sheep red cells sensitized with tannic acid and coated with schistosome antigen, which are agglutinated by serum agglutinins. Intradermal tests with saline extracts of cercariae or adult schistosomes are helpful only in screening cases since they are group-specific but not species-specific.

Although reliable complement fixation, precipitin, agglutination-hemagglutination, and fluorescent antibody tests have been developed for the diagnosis of a number of the parasitic infections of man, they have had only limited application as yet, although improvement and increased practical use is anticipated. Improved antigen purification and preparation methods and standardization of procedures, often with the help of central diagnostic laboratories, such as the USPHS National Communicable Disease Center in Atlanta, Georgia, will make possible world-wide diagnostic and epidemiologic surveys employing these newly developed and improved tools. Tests employing small filter paper squares with a drop of test blood or serum serologically studied in a central diagnostic laboratory are particularly suitable for field surveys.

MUSCLE BIOPSY FOR TRICHINELLA SPIRALIS

Small pieces of deltoid, biceps, or gastrocnemius muscle are removed from the vicinity of their tendinous attachment under local anesthesia. (1) Examine small pieces of muscle compressed between two glass slides microscopically for encysting or encysted larvae. (2) Digest muscle in artificial gastric juice (pepsin and hydrochloric acid) and examine sediment for motile larvae.

XENODIAGNOSIS

Laboratory-bred triatomid bugs (obtainable from Gorgas Memorial Laboratory, Panama City, Panama, and various other laboratories working on Trypanosoma cruzi) are fed on patients suspected of having Chagas' disease. Two weeks later, they are examined for the presence of the parasite in their intestinal contents. Suitable only for the early stages of disease when parasites are blood-borne.

BLOOD

Combined Thin and Thick Films.

A. Making Films: Cleanse finger, ear lobe, heel, or toe (of children) thoroughly with acetone and allow to dry. Prick skin deeply to cause a few drops of blood to flow freely. On one end of a meticulously clean slide free of fingerprints or oil film make a thin smear as for a blood count. For the preparation of the thick film deposit a large drop of blood at the other end of the slide and spread it out evenly with the corner of another slide to a diameter of about 20 mm. The film should not be too thick since it may crack and peel when dry. Dry slide in a flat position so that distribution of blood will be even. Protect from dust and insects; avoid excessive heat. Allow to dry in air for at least eight to 12 hours or for two hours in incubator at 37° C. Keep free from dust or contamination with excreta of flies or roaches. Stain as soon as practicable, as freshly stained material gives distinctly superior results.

B. Staining Films: Fix thin-filmed end of slide in methyl alcohol for two to three minutes. **The thick film must not be fixed.** Immerse slide for 30 minutes in a mixture of one drop of concentrated Giemsa's stain to each ml. of phosphate-buffered distilled water (pH 7.2). Wash off with buffered water and air dry. Examine with oil-immersion objective. (For further details, see references.) Hematoxylin stain is preferred for microfilariae since nuclear detail and sheaths (if present) stain more distinctly.

Concentration of Microfilariae.

Hemolyze 10 ml. or more of citrated blood with 50 ml. of a 2% solution of saponin in physiologic saline. Centrifuge in conical centrifuge tubes and examine the sediment. Chylous urine and scrotal aspirates should always be centrifuged to attempt recovery of microfilariae.

Serum Tests for Leishmania donovani.

The Napier aldehyde test and the Chopra antimony test are based on an increase in the euglobulin fraction of the blood serum. Sometimes, but not always, they aid in diagnosis. Complement fixation, precipitin, agglutination, and intradermal tests also are specific and useful for special purposes. (See references for further details.)

Cultures for Blood Flagellates.
  A. Leishmania donovani: Culture centrifuged cells from
     citrated blood, bone marrow, liver, lymph nodes, or
     spleen pulp aspirates in N. N. N. (Novy, MacNeal,
     Nicolle) medium or Tobie's diphasic blood agar medium
     at 20° to 24° C. for one to four weeks.
  B. Leishmania tropica and L. brasiliensis: Culture scrap-
     ings or aspirated material from border of lesions as for
     L. donovani. (Not found in blood.)
  C. Trypanosoma gambiense and T. rhodesiense: Culture
     centrifuged **citrated** blood, lymph node aspiration fluid,
     or spinal fluid in special media developed for these
     organisms.
  D. Trypanosoma cruzi: Culture blood as for Leishmania
     donovani.

Culture for Nematode Larvae in Feces (Harada-Mori Culture).
     This technic is superior to the old charcoal cultures for
isolation, identification, and quantitation of larval nematodes
in the stool. It consists of a filter paper strip with a thick
fecal layer placed on the middle portion, inserted in a test
tube with water high enough to wet the paper but not wash off
the feces. Infective larvae migrate to the bottom of the tube
and can be removed easily for study or spotted with a low-
power lens for survey work. (Details can be found in WHO
Technical Report 255:27-30, 1963.)

PROTOZOA IN FECES (× 1200)

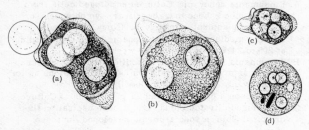

Entamoeba histolytica. (a, b) Trophozoite or vegetative form with ingested red cells; (c) small race or E. hartmanni with food vacuoles (not red cells); (d) cyst with 4 nuclei and chromatoidal bodies (large race).

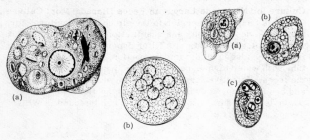

Entamoeba coli. (a) Trophozoite with vacuoles and inclusions; (b) cyst with 8 nuclei showing eccentric nucleoli.

Endolimax nana. (a) Trophozoite; (b) precystic form; (c) tetranucleate cyst.

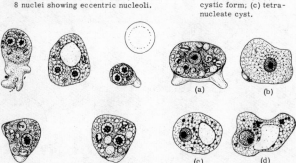

Dientamoeba fragilis. Trophozoites. (No cysts are found.) Mononuclear form (lower left) occasionally found.

Iodamoeba bütschlii. (a) Trophozoite; (b) precystic form; (c, d) cysts showing dense glycogen vacuole (unstained) and varied form.

[Simple double circles represent the size of red cells.]

Drawings on pp. 346-358 by P.H. Vercammen-Grandjean, D.Sc.

PROTOZOA IN FECES (× 1200)

Trichomonas hominis. (a) Normal and (b) rounded trophozoites (latter frequently seen in smear preparations).

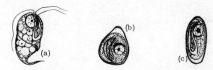

Chilomastix mesnili. (a) Trophozoite; (b, c) cysts.

Enteromonas hominis. (a, b) Trophozoites; (c) dividing trophozoite; (d, e) cysts.

Retortamonas intestinalis. (a, b) Trophozoites; (c) cyst.

The intestinal flagellates shown above (but not Giardia, below) are rare and apparently harmless; they are probably present only when personal or community hygiene is poor.

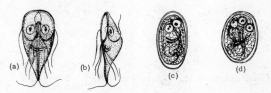

Giardia lamblia. (a) Face and (b) profile of vegetative forms; (c, d) binucleate and tetranucleate cysts.

[Simple double circles represent the size of red cells.]

PROTOZOA IN FECES

(a)   (b)   (c)

Isospora hominis. (a) Unsegmented oocyst; (b) seg-
mented into 2 sporoblasts, develop after passage
in feces; (c) degenerate oocyst. (× 1200)

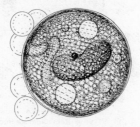

Balantidium coli. Cyst. (× 1000)

PROTOZOA IN GENITAL TRACT (× 1200)

  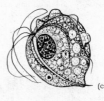

(a)   (b)   (c)

Trichomonas vaginalis. (a, c) Normal trophozoites; (b) round form
after division (often distorted in stained preparations). (No
cysts are found.)

[Simple double circles represent the size of red cells.]

PROTOZOA IN BLOOD AND TISSUES

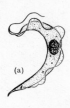 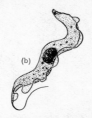 

Trypanosoma gambiense (or T. rhodesiense, indistinguishable in practice).
(a, b) Blood forms; (c) crithidial form (intermediate type; kinetoplast not
yet anterior to nucleus), found only in tsetse fly, Glossina spp. (× 1200)

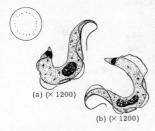 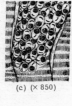

Trypanosoma cruzi. (a, b) Trypanosome blood forms; (c) leishmaniae in heart
muscle; (d, e) crithidial forms found in intermediate host, a triatomid bug,
and in culture.

Leishmania donovani. (a) Large re-
ticuloendothelial cell of spleen with
Leishman-Donovan bodies; (b) flagellate forms, leptomonads, found only
in sandfly gut or culture. (× 1000)

Toxoplasma gondii. (a) In large
mononuclear cells; (b) free in
tissue fluids (**not in blood**).
(× 1000)

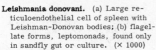

[Simple double circles represent the size of red cells.]

PROTOZOA IN BLOOD (× 850)

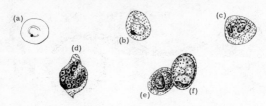

Plasmodium vivax. (a) Young signet ring trophozoite; (b) ameboid trophozoite showing Schüffner's dots in enlarged red cell; (c) mature trophozoite;
(d) mature schizont; (e) microgametocyte; (f) macrogametocyte with compact peripheral nucleus.

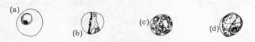

Plasmodium malariae. (a) Developing ring form of trophozoite; (b) band
form of trophozoite (note absence of granules); (c) mature schizont in
"rosette" with 8 merozoites; (d) mature microgametocyte.

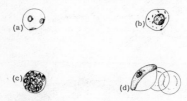

Plasmodium falciparum. (a) Ring stage (multiple infection, including a
surface or accolé form); (b) mature trophozoite showing clumped pigment
in cytoplasm and Maurer's dots in erythrocyte; (c) mature schizont; (d)
mature macrogametocyte. Only rings and gametocytes are usually found
in peripheral blood.

Plasmodium ovale. (a) Young signet ring trophozoite showing early development of Schüffner's dots; (b) ameboid trophozoite developing in fimbriated
erythrocyte; (c) mature schizont showing 8 merozoites.

[Simple double circles represent the size of red cells.]

MICROFILARIAE IN BLOOD OR SKIN (× 300)

SHEATHED FORMS

Wuchereria bancrofti. Nocturnal or subperiodic, in blood, lymph, or hydrocele fluid. 225-300 × 8-10 μ. Tail free of nuclei, body curves sinuous.

Brugia malayi. Nocturnal or subperiodic, in blood, lymph, or lymphocele fluid. 160-250 × 5-6 μ. Two nuclei in tip of tail, body curves kinked.

Loa loa. Diurnal periodicity, in blood. 250-300 × 6-9 μ. Nuclei to tip of tail.

NONSHEATHED FORMS

Mansonella ozzardi. Nonperiodic, in blood. 170-240 × 4-5 μ.

Onchocerca volvulus. Nonperiodic, in skin and connective tissue lymphatics (rare in blood). 300-350 × 5-9 μ.

Dipetalonema streptocerca. Nonperiodic, in blood or skin. 180 × 2-3μ.

Dipetalonema perstans. Nonperiodic, in blood. 200 × 4 μ.

[Simple double circles represent the size of red cells.]

TREMATODES (ADULT FLUKES)

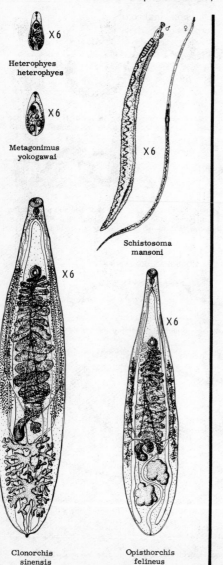

Heterophyes
heterophyes
X6

Metagonimus
yokogawai
X6

Schistosoma
mansoni
X6

Clonorchis
sinensis
X6

Opisthorchis
felineus
X6

Paragonimus
westermani
X0.6

Fasciola
hepatica
X0.6

Fasciolopsis
buski
X0.6

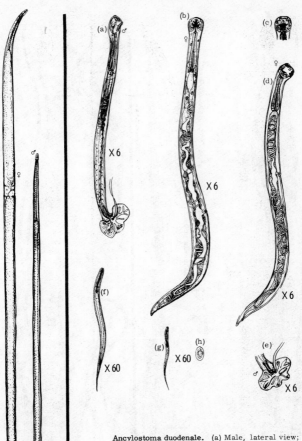

Ancylostoma duodenale. (a) Male, lateral view; tail in ventral view to show copulatory bursa; (b) female, anterior in dorsal view and posterior in lateral view.
Necator americanus. (c) Head, dorsal view; (d) female, lateral view; (e) male, ventral view of tail to show copulatory bursa.
Both A. duodenale and N. americanus. (f) Filariform or infective larva; (g) rhabditiform larva; (h) ovum.

Ascaris lumbricoides

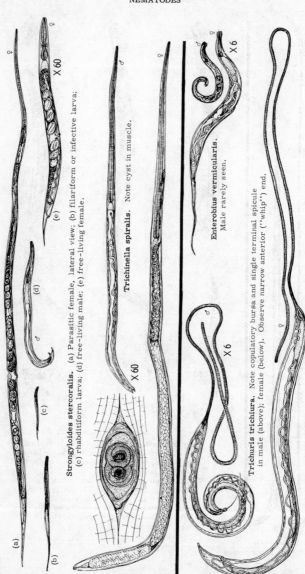

Strongyloides stercoralis. (a) Parasitic female, lateral view; (b) filariform or infective larva; (c) rhabditiform larva; (d) free-living male; (e) free-living female.

Trichinella spiralis. Note cyst in muscle.

Enterobius vermicularis. Male rarely seen.

Trichuris trichiura. Note copulatory bursa and single terminal spicule in male (above); female (below). Observe narrow anterior ("whip") end.

CESTODES (TAPEWORMS)

(See ova on p. 358.)

Hymenolepis nana. Rostellar hooks present (see p. 354). Normal worm size: 1-7.5 cm. (0.5-3 inches).

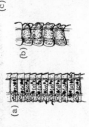

Hymenolepis diminuta. (a) Mature proglottids; (b) gravid proglottids; (c) unarmed scolex and beginning of strobila. Normal worm size: 30-90 cm. (1-3 feet).

X2

Taenia saginata and T. solium. (a) Gravid proglottid of T. saginata with many more uterine ramifications than in T. solium (see [e] at right); (b) T. saginata, unarmed scolex and beginning of strobila; (c) armed scolex of T. solium with beginning of strobila; (d) mature proglottid of T. saginata or T. solium; (e) gravid proglottid of T. solium. Normal worm size: T. saginata, 4-6 meters (15-20 feet); T. solium, 1.5-3 meters (6-10 feet).

Diphyllobothrium latum. (a) Cross-section through scolex; (b) scolex and neck; (c) mature proglottid; (d) gravid proglottid. Normal worm size: 3-9 meters (10-30 feet).

CESTODES

Diphyllobothrium latum. (a) Scolex; (b) same, cross-section.

Taenia saginata and T. solium. (a) Scolex of T. saginata; (b) scolex of T. solium, showing armed rostellum; (c) same, end view.

Hymenolepis diminuta. Scolex and neck, showing unarmed rostellum.

Hymenolepis nana. (a) Scolex with hooked rostellum retracted; (b) same with rostellum everted.

Echinococcus granulosus. (a) Adult scolex; (b) end view of adult scolex rostellum, showing arrangement of 2 hook rows; (c) hooks; (d) larval scolex from hydatid fluid, invaginated; (e) same, evaginated; (f) entire adult worm; normal size, 2-8 mm. (1/8-3/8 inches).

357

OVA OF TREMATODES (× 300)

Schistosoma haematobium. Terminally spined embryonated ovum (containing miracidium).

Schistosoma mansoni. Laterally spined embryonated ovum (containing miracidium).

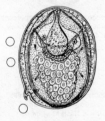

Paragonimus westermani. Unembryonated operculated ovum.

Schistosoma japonicum. Embryonated ovum with small lateral spine, often not visible.

Clonorchis sinensis. Small operculated and embryonated ovum.

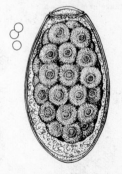

Heterophyes heterophyes or Metagonimus yokogawai

Fasciola hepatica or Fasciolopsis buski. Unembryonated operculated ovum.

[Simple circles represent the size of red cells.]

358

OVA OF NEMATODES (× 300)

**Ancylostoma duodenale or
Necator americanus.** Note
shape, thin shell, 4-8 cell
stage.

Ascaris lumbricoides. (a) Fertilized unembryonated ovum; (b) unfertilized
ovum; (c) fertilized decorticated ovum.

Trichuris trichiura

Strongyloides stercoralis. (a) Embryonated
ovum (rarely seen); (b) rhabditiform larva
usually seen in feces.

Trichostrongylus orientalis.
Unembryonated ovum.
(Rare in man.)

Enterobius vermicularis.
Embryonated ovum.
Note flattening on one
side, thin shell.

OVA OF CESTODES (× 300)

Taenia saginata, T. solium, or Echinococcus granulosus. (Eggs essentially
identical.) Observe 6-hooked hexacanth larva or oncosphere.

Diphyllobothrium latum.
Unembryonated,
operculated ovum.

Hymenolepis diminuta.
Note size; colored
yellow from bile
stain.

Hymenolepis nana. Note
polar filaments, shape
of egg. Color usually
clear, not bile-stained.

[Simple circles represent the size of red cells.]

19...

Medical Mycology

For purposes of convenience, fungous infections are divided into superficial and deep mycoses. The superficial fungous infections of skin, hair, and nails are often chronic and resistant to treatment but rarely affect the general health of the patient. The deep mycoses produce systemic involvement and are often fatal.

SUPERFICIAL MYCOSES
(Dermatomycoses)

The fungi involved in "ringworm" and "athlete's foot" are collectively called dermatophytes. They belong to the genera Microsporum, Trichophyton, Epidermophyton, and others (see p. 360). Laboratory identification is made by direct microscopic examination or by culture on Sabouraud's medium and blood agar at 37°C. for several days and at 22° C. for two to three weeks. In collecting specimens, first cleanse the surface with 70% alcohol, then scrape or cut off a superficial slice of epidermis or remove hairs with forceps. Place the specimen in a drop of 10 to 20% potassium hydroxide solution and apply a cover glass. Examine after 30 minutes for mycelia and spores (see p. 365).

Treatment is by removal of infected hairs; by applying topical antifungal agents, e.g., undecylenates; or by giving griseofulvin, 250 mg. (or 10 mg./lb.) orally one to four times daily, especially in T. rubrum infection.

DEEP MYCOSES

Actinomycosis.
  A. Etiologic Organisms:
    1. Anaerobic Actinomyces israelii (bovis) occurs in gums and tonsils of healthy individuals. It apparently spreads and becomes pathogenic when tissues are devitalized from other causes (trauma, infection). It often responds to chemotherapy.
    2. Aerobic Nocardia asteroides and other species occur in world-wide distribution in soil. They are often resistant to chemotherapy.
  B. Clinical Features: About 90% are of anaerobic type. Indurated lesions with multiple sinuses draining pus in characteristic locations should suggest actinomycosis.

Common Superficial Mycoses

Organism	Disease	Remarks
Microsporum canis	Tinea capitis	In dogs, cats, and children.
Microsporum audouini	Tinea capitis	Treatment-resistant, in children.
Microsporum gypseum	Tinea capitis and cruris, kerion	On body or scalp.
Malassezia furfur	Tinea versicolor	On trunk, neck, arms.
Trichophyton schoenleini	Favus	Yellow scutula on scalp, loss of hair.
Trichophyton mentagrophytes (gypseum)	Kerion, tinea barbae, inter-digital lesions, tinea cruris	Ringworm of hairy areas, "athlete's foot" of interdigital folds, soles, etc.
Trichophyton rubrum and other species		
Epidermophyton floccosum		

With few exceptions, all the organisms named above could be found in a given lesion of dermatomycosis. Identification of the organism is made by morphologic and cultural criteria in special cases only. Ordinarily, demonstration of a dermatophyte is sufficient.

Initial or predominant lesions may be cervicofacial, pulmonary, or abdominal.
C. Diagnosis:
  1. Demonstration of "sulfur granules" in pus, sputum, or biopsy specimen. Fish out granules and wash in saline. Granules consist of a central mass of mycelium and peripheral clubs; they are hard and can be crushed under a cover glass. With Gram's stain the central mass stains purple blue and the clubs stain red (same in histologic secretions; see p. 365).
  2. Actinomyces israelii can be cultured anaerobically in veal infusion broth or thioglycollate medium. Nocardia will grow on blood agar plates. Animal inoculation is unsatisfactory.
D. Differential Diagnosis: The clinical picture of actinomycosis is occasionally simulated by rat-bite fever (Streptobacillus moniliformis), Bacteroides infections, erysipeloid (Erysipelothrix infections), and staphylococcal actinophytosis (botryomycosis).

Blastomycosis.
A. Etiologic Organism: Blastomyces dermatitidis. Its

natural habitat is uncertain but it probably occurs in soil. The disease is found particularly in the Mississippi Valley and the southeastern United States.

B. Clinical Features: Blastomycosis is more frequent in males than in females. It often begins in the lungs, suggesting inhalation as route of infection.

    1. Cutaneous form - Often self-limited, with good prognosis. Local, indurated, granulomatous lesion, draining pus.

    2. Systemic form - Widespread, progressive granulomata with poor prognosis.

C. Diagnosis:

    1. Demonstration of budding yeast forms 8-20 microns in diameter, with double-contoured cells, in wet preparations from pus, sputum, or biopsy material (see p. 365).

    2. Culture of organism on Sabouraud's medium and identification by mycologist.

    3. Positive skin test with yeast-phase antigen is often present. (With histoplasmin and coccidioidin, reactions are negative.)

    4. Complement-fixing antibodies may be found in serum of progressive cases.

Coccidioidomycosis.

A. Etiologic Organism: Coccidioides immitis. In endemic areas (arid Southwest of United States, especially San Joaquin Valley of California, West Texas, Arizona) the organism is found in soil and dust. Airborne infection during hot, dusty months occurs even on casual exposure (e.g., traveling through endemic region). Occurrence in Italy and South America is questionable.

B. Clinical Features:

    1. Primary infection ("valley fever") - Mild respiratory influenza-like illness, often followed by erythema nodosum and pleurisy. Occasionally, thin-walled pulmonary cavities appear. The great majority of cases recover with complete healing. A few (principally in dark-skinned races) progress to granulomatous stage.

    2. Progressive granulomatous stage - Systemic involvement, with widespread lesions, closely resembling tuberculosis. Mortality is greater than 50%.

C. Diagnosis:

    1. Identification of characteristic "spherules," with double-contoured walls and filled with endospores, in sputum or other discharges examined directly under microscope (see p. 365). Endospores are not highly infectious.

    2. Culture of discharge on Sabouraud's medium gives fluffy white growth. (Caution: Highly infectious arthrospores are present.)

3. Inoculate sputum or pus intraperitoneally into mice.
4. Coccidioidin skin test - 1:100 dilution of standard
   material gives positive reaction within two to three
   weeks after exposure and primary infection. Lower
   dilutions give more cross-reactions with other fungous
   diseases.
5. Precipitin test - Precipitating antibodies usually
   appear in the course of primary infection and tend to
   disappear again with healing.
6. Complement-fixing antibodies are often of very low
   titer in primary infection. They tend to increase in
   titer in progressive disease, and imply an unfavorable
   prognosis.

Histoplasmosis.

A. Etiologic Organism: Histoplasma capsulatum. Infection
   is probably airborne in many parts of the world, particularly in the central United States. The fungus grows
   abundantly in bird feces (chicken houses) and bat guano
   (caves) and produces massive infection with severe clinical disease upon exposure in such places. In endemic
   areas a small inoculum from dust gives widespread subclinical childhood infection.
B. Clinical Features:
   1. Primary infection is probably respiratory and often
      asymptomatic, particularly in children in endemic
      areas. Pulmonary calcifications seen in tuberculin-
      negative adults who have positive histoplasmin skin
      tests have been assumed to be manifestations of healed
      pulmonary histoplasmosis.
   2. Granulomatous pulmonary lesions with widespread
      systemic dissemination occur in progressive, usually
      fatal cases.
C. Diagnosis:
   1. Identification of small oval intracellular forms in
      smears of blood, bone marrow, lymph nodes, or
      biopsy specimens.
   2. On blood agar at 37° C., colonies are yeast-like,
      smooth, and white. On Sabouraud's agar at 20° C.,
      white, cottony colonies develop with large (8-20
      microns), thick-walled, spherical spores with finger-
      like projections, the typical tuberculate chlamydo-
      spores (see p. 365).
   3. Histoplasmin skin test - Positive reaction is evidence
      of past infection. Some cross-reactions occur.
   4. Complement fixation tests positive within four weeks.

Cryptococcosis (Torulosis).

A. Etiologic Organism: Cryptococcus neoformans (Torula),
   world-wide in distribution, found in soil. Grows abundantly in bird feces (e.g., pigeon roosts).

B. Clinical Features: Infection usually occurs by inhalation of dust. Initial lesions are usually in the lung or skin, commonly self limited, and are rarely diagnosed. Clinical disease is most commonly a chronic meningitis.

C. Diagnosis:
1. Wet preparations from skin, sputum, or centrifuged spinal fluid show round yeast cells with thick mucoid capsules, occasional budding (see p. 365). Use India ink preparation.
2. On Sabouraud's agar cryptococci grow in large, moist, shiny colonies. Smears from such colonies show typical yeast cells. Urea is hydrolyzed.
3. Cryptococcus grows in mice injected intraperitoneally or intracerebrally with spinal fluid or culture.

Candidiasis (Moniliasis).

A. Etiologic Organism: Candida albicans (Monilia), present on normal mucous membranes in mouth, vagina, and intestine. Systemic moniliasis occurs rarely.

B. Clinical Features: Monilial infection usually is associated with other debilitating conditions or lowering of normal resistance. Oral moniliasis (thrush) occurs in infants. Dermatitis of skin of hands may occur after maceration in water. Monilial vulvovaginitis is seen particularly in diabetic and pregnant women. Monilial bronchitis, pneumonitis, meningitis, and endocarditis occur rarely. Dissemination may be favored by treatment with antibiotics, particularly the tetracyclines.

C. Diagnosis:
1. Identification of budding yeast and hyphal forms in fresh wet preparations.
2. Culture on Sabouraud's medium yields yeast colonies.

Mucormycosis.

A. Etiologic Organism: Rhizopus oryzae, rarely cultured but seen in histologic preparations in thrombosed blood vessels and adjoining tissue as nonseptate hyphae with surrounding neutrophilic and giant cell response.

B. Clinical Features: Symptoms referable to the nervous system; respiratory, gastrointestinal, or urinary tract; skin, or eye. Usually superimposed on another debilitating disease, e.g., diabetes mellitus. Removal of local lesion (e.g., kidney) occasionally results in cure.

C. Diagnosis: Usually only in histologic sections.

Sporotrichosis.

A. Etiologic Organism: Sporotrichum schenkii is primarily a saprophyte of plants; it is world-wide in distribution. Contact infection occasionally occurs in animals and man.

B. Clinical Features: Local and systemic forms have been observed (usually lymphatic type). Prognosis is good.

C. Diagnosis: In smears and sections of tissue the organism is occasionally seen as a small, cigar-shaped, gram-positive body inside monocytes and giant cells. Cultures on Sabouraud's agar show leathery colonies with clusters of pyriform conidia (see p. 365).

Maduromycosis (Madura Foot).

A. Etiologic Organisms: Nocardia sp., Monosporium apiospermum, other filamentous fungi. The disease occurs particularly in the tropics, and is associated with local trauma on feet and legs.

B. Clinical Features: A chronic, indurated swelling with multiple sinuses draining serosanguinous or "oily" fluid containing colored granules. Lower extremities are mainly involved.

C. Diagnosis: Based on clinical appearance and finding of typical granules; microscopy and culture.

Chromoblastomycosis.

A. Etiologic Organisms: Hormodendrum, Phialophora organisms occur world-wide in nature. Most human cases occur after trauma to the skin of the legs.

B. Clinical Features: Localized tumors, progressing slowly.

C. Diagnosis: Small brown septate bodies found in pus or sections; culture.

Rhinosporidiosis.

A. Etiologic Organism: Rhinosporidium seeberi is endemic in India and Ceylon and occurs sporadically in the United States and other parts of the world. Infection is usually contracted while swimming in stagnant water.

B. Clinical Features: Sessile or pedunculated friable polyps on mucous membranes of nose, eyes, larynx, and external genitalia in children and young adults.

C. Diagnosis: Oval or round spores 7 to 9 micra wide in smears; spore-filled sporangia in sections.

Treatment of Deep Mycoses.

Actinomycosis often responds to sulfonamides, penicillin, or tetracyclines, alone or in combination; aerobic nocardia may respond to sulfonamides, but often resists treatment. **Blastomycosis** often responds to hydroxystilbamidine, 100 to 200 mg. I.V. daily; or amphotericin B, 50 to 100 mg. daily I.V. **Cryptococcus meningitis** may respond to amphotericin B, 50 to 100 mg. I.V. daily and 1 mg. intrathecally every other day. **Coccidioidomycosis (disseminated)** may be benefited by amphotericin B, 50 to 100 mg. I.V. daily. In coccidioidal meningitis, give also amphotericin B, 0.5 to 1 mg. intrathecally every other day. **Candidiasis** is treated with gentian violet, sodium propionate, parahydroxybenzoic acid, or nystatin applied topically.

Chemotherapy has been suggested for other deep mycoses, but its usefulness has yet to be evaluated.

COMMON MYCOTIC ORGANISMS

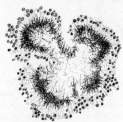

Actinomyces bovis
sulfur granule
0.2-2 mm.

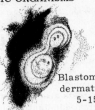

Blastomyces
dermatitidis
5-15 μ

Unruptured
spherule

Ruptured
spherule

Coccidioides immitis
Spherules with endospores in pus
15-75 μ

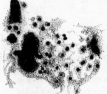

Histoplasma
capsulatum in
mononuclear cell
2-5 μ

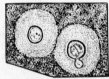

Cryptococcus
neoformans
5-12 μ

Microsporum
audouini
10-15 × 40-120 μ

Microsporum
gypseum
8-10 × 30-50 μ

Sporotrichum schenkii
Clusters of pyriform conidia
20-60 μ

Histoplasma capsulatum
Tuberculate Spores in
Culture at 20° C. 8-20 μ

20...

Skin Tests

Skin tests are diagnostic procedures performed by the intradermal administration of diagnostic materials or their application to the surface of the skin. In order to be useful, skin tests have to be properly performed, accurately read, and correctly interpreted.

TECHNIC OF SKIN TESTS

Instruments and materials must be sterile. The skin must be carefully cleaned, but irritation is to be avoided. Gentle sponging with 70% alcohol usually is sufficient. Most skin tests are performed on the flexor surface of the forearm, but other skin areas are equally satisfactory.

Intracutaneous Injection.

A short bevel, fine gauge (No. 26 or 27) needle is introduced below the upper layers of the epithelium but not into the subcutis. A properly placed needle permits the injection of 0.1 ml. of fluid, raising a round bleb. This is the most reliable technic, and is used commonly for tuberculin and histoplasmin tests, coccidioidin test in adults, and many others.

Transcutaneous Administration.

The skin is cleaned and dried. With a lance or needle, short scratches are made in the epidermis, not deeply enough to draw blood. The scratches should be one-eighth inch long and about two inches apart on the flexor aspect of the forearm. One drop of the allergen test fluid is applied to each scratch and left undisturbed for ten minutes. Used commonly in testing for pollen or food allergens.

Patch Tests.

These depend on the ability of the test substance to diffuse into the skin. The test substance is adsorbed onto a small patch of gauze which is affixed to the skin with adhesive tape, allowing the patch to remain in contact with the skin for 24 hours. Sterile, unimpregnated gauze must surround the patch and separate it from the area where the adhesive tape touches

the skin (to distinguish reactions to the patch from reactions
to adhesive). Used sometimes for tuberculin test in children,
but less reliable than intradermal test.

IMMUNOLOGIC BASIS FOR SKIN TESTS

Most skin test reactions may be placed in one of the
following three groups:

Toxin-antitoxin Neutralization.
The action of toxin or antitoxin is responsible for the observed reaction. In the Schick and Dick tests, toxin is injected into the skin. Unless neutralized by circulating antitoxin, the toxin provokes erythema and induration within 12 to
72 hours. A positive reaction thus indicates the absence of
adequate antitoxin levels. In the Schultz-Charlton reaction,
antitoxin is injected into an area of suspected scarlet fever
rash. If blanching occurs, the erythrogenic toxin has been
neutralized by specific antitoxin. This identifies the rash and
confirms the diagnosis.
Toxin-antitoxin neutralization tests do not involve hypersensitivity reactions.

Anaphylactic Type of Hypersensitivity (Immediate Reactions).
This type of reaction is characterized by the following
features:
A. The reaction is "immediate." Erythema and wheal formation appear within five to 20 minutes and disappear
   within one hour after injection or application of the
   allergen.
B. The reaction is associated with specific circulating antibodies and can be passive transferred by means of
   serum. (See Prausnitz-Küstner reaction, p. 371.)
C. The reaction is mainly a vascular one, without much cellular infiltration and induration.
D. Examples of "immediate reactions" of this type are
   allergy to pollen and horse serum sensitivity.

Tuberculin Type of Hypersensitivity (Delayed Reactions).
This type of reaction is characterized by the following
features:
A. The reaction is "delayed." Erythema and induration
   appear in 24 to 48 hours and may last for several days.
B. The reaction is not intimately associated with circulating
   antibodies and cannot be transferred passively by means
   of serum. Passive transfer is possible by means of leukocytes or leukocyte extracts from a sensitive individual.
C. The reaction is largely infiltrative and inflammatory, with
   little acute change in vascular permeability (which is
   paramount in the anaphylactic type).

D. Examples of "delayed reactions" are tuberculin, coccidioidin, histoplasmin, and Frei tests.

DESCRIPTION OF SOME COMMON SKIN TESTS

Toxin-antitoxin Neutralization Tests.
A. Schick Test: For determining susceptibility to diphtheria.
  1. Material - Diluted diphtheria toxin containing 1/50 M. L. D. (minimal lethal dose for a guinea pig) in 0.1 ml. is available commercially.
  2. Technic - After cleansing the skin of the forearm, 0.1 ml. is injected intradermally. A positive test consists of an area of erythema 1 to 2 cm. in diameter reaching its maximum intensity about the fourth day. Pigmentation of the area may persist for weeks.
  3. Interpretation - A positive test means that the individual does not have sufficient circulating antitoxin to neutralize the injected toxin and therefore that he is susceptible to diphtheria. The converse is true for the negative reactor.
      Present-day purified toxins rarely give false-positive reactions attributable to sensitivity. Moreover, reactions due to sensitivity tend to fade much more quickly than a positive Schick test. If it is desired to include a check on possible sensitivity, 0.1 ml. of heated (and therefore inactivated) toxin is injected into the other arm. If this control site develops the same reactions as the site injected with active toxin, sensitivity is present to the injected protein.
  4. Test for toxoid sensitivity - Before immunization of adults the Moloney test for sensitivity to toxoid should be performed. This is usually done by injecting 0.1 ml. of diphtheria toxoid diluted 1:20 instead of the heated toxin control. A positive test indicates sensitivity to the toxoid, and immunization has to start with exceedingly small doses.
B. Dick Test: For the determination of susceptibility to the erythrogenic toxin of hemolytic streptococci. It consists of observing the reaction to intradermally injected erythrogenic streptococcus toxin. The development of erythema indicates a positive test. A negative Dick test merely indicates probable immunity to the erythrogenic toxin but not to streptococcic infection. A Dick-negative person is unlikely to develop scarlet fever but is as likely as a Dick-positive person to develop other streptococcic diseases or sequelae. Therefore, the test is of little importance and is rarely done.
C. Schultz-Charlton Reaction: For the diagnosis of scarlet fever rash. The rest consists of the injection of anti-

toxin to streptococcic erythrogenic toxin (or scarlet
fever convalescent serum) into an area of rash. Blanching in 12 hours suggests specific neutralization and confirms the diagnosis of scarlet fever. This test is of
little importance and is rarely done.

Immediate Reaction Type of Skin Tests.

A. Test for Sensitivity to Horse Serum: Before injecting
   horse serum (e.g., tetanus or diphtheria antitoxin) into
   any patient, ascertain possible sensitivity to horse serum.
   Similar precautions and tests apply to certain drugs,
   especially penicillin. Inquire about previous injections
   of serum or reactions to drugs, history of allergy, hay
   fever, etc., and perform sensitivity test as follows:
   1. Technic - Always have a vial of 1:1000 epinephrine and
      a small syringe and needle ready when doing any test
      for serum sensitivity or administering serum. Of the
      two tests, the skin test is more reliable. If no evi-
      dence of hypersensitivity is obtained by the tests,
      serum is administered undiluted by the route indicated.
      a. Skin test - Cleanse skin, then inject intradermally
         0.1 ml. of horse serum diluted 1:10 with saline.
         Appearance of wheal 1 to 3 cm. in diameter within
         15 minutes suggests sensitivity to horse serum.
      b. Conjunctival test - Examine conjunctivas for
         presence of inflammation. Instill one drop of horse
         serum diluted 1:10 into one conjunctival sac, one
         drop of saline into the other as control. The con-
         trol conjunctiva should appear normal after three
         to five minutes. In persons hypersensitive to horse
         serum the test conjunctiva will show reddening,
         itching, and lacrimation within 15 to 30 minutes.
   2. Unfavorable reactions following serum administration -
      a. Immediate anaphylaxis - Exceedingly rare if skin
         tests are negative. Consists of asthma, nausea,
         vascular collapse, and shock within five to 60 min-
         utes after serum administration. Give 1 ml. of
         1:1000 epinephrine subcut. at first sign of reaction,
         and other supportive measures. Unless patient re-
         sponds promptly, give hydrocortisone, 100 mg. I.V.
      b. Febrile reaction - Occurs even when skin test was
         negative. Chills, fever, nausea within one to six
         hours after serum was administered I.V. Use
         supportive measures, no epinephrine.
      c. Serum sickness - Occurs often, even when skin test
         was negative. Fever, pruritus, edema, urticaria,
         lymphadenopathy, arthralgia, occasionally arthritis
         with effusion, develop usually seven to 11 days after
         serum injection. Rarely, an accelerated reaction
         of the same type develops one to six days after
         injection of serum or drug (e.g., penicillin).

      d. Treatment - Epinephrine is helpful. Corticotropin
        (ACTH) or corticosteroids tend to suppress the
        symptoms of hypersensitivity reactions.
  3. If the skin test is positive -
      a. Obtain antiserum from another animal species
        (e.g., rabbit or goat) and repeat skin test with it.
        Avoid implicated drug.
      b. Desensitize patient to horse serum.
  4. Desensitization is carried out as follows: Inject
     gradually-increasing doses of horse serum diluted
     1:10. Begin with 0.1 ml., then 0.2 ml. and 0.5 ml.
     subcut. at 30-minute intervals. If no significant re-
     action is observed, give 0.1 ml. undiluted horse
     serum subcut. followed by 0.2 ml. and 0.5 ml. at 30-
     minute intervals. If a given dose is followed by a
     slight reaction, give the same or a smaller dose after
     30 to 60 minutes together with 1 ml. of 1:1000 epi-
     nephrine. Increase doses steadily until 2 or 3 ml. can
     be given without reaction. Repeat every 30 to 60 min-
     utes until the full dose of serum has been given. Sim-
     ilar desensitization is possible with drugs, e.g.,
     streptomycin.
  5. Treatment of severe reactions - After a severe re-
     action it is unwise to continue serum administration
     and desensitization. If severe reaction should occur
     during desensitization, treat with:
      a. Epinephrine, 1:1000, 1 ml., subcut. or I.V.
      b. Atropine sulfate, 0.5 mg. subcut.
      c. Antihistaminic drugs, e.g., diphenhydramine
        (Benadryl®), I.V.
      d. Artificial respiration and oxygen if necessary; ex-
        ternal warmth.
      e. Hydrocortisone, 50 to 100 mg. I.V.
B. Direct Skin Tests for Allergens: (Respiratory, contact,
  drug, or food.)
  1. Technic - In allergic work-up the patient is ordinarily
     tested by either the scratch or the intradermal
     method for sensitivity to a variety of allergens. Test
     substances are available commercially or may be
     specially prepared. The usual positive response con-
     sists of a wheal and erythema appearing five to 30 min-
     utes after contact with the allergen.
  2. Interpretation - In interpreting such reactions the
     following must be kept in mind:
      a. A negative skin test does not rule out systemic
        sensitivity.
      b. A positive skin test does not necessarily mean that
        allergic symptoms are related to the particular
        allergen.
      c. Individuals may at times give positive reactions to
        many test substances, at other times to none.

C. Prausnitz-Küstner Reaction: A method used to demonstrate presence of a substance by passive transfer of serum. Used in dermatology and investigation of allergy.
1. Technic - Obtain serum from the patient and inject 0.2 to 0.3 ml. intradermally into a normal person. Twelve to 18 hours later inject the suspected antigen into the area thus prepared with the serum and into another comparable skin area, as control.
2. Interpretation - A positive reaction (erythema, wheal) at the test (but not the control) site indicates successful transfer of specific antibodies and, by inference, demonstrates that the patient possesses anaphylactic hypersensitivity to the allergen.
D. Penicillin Hypersensitivity: Use skin test of penicilloyl-polylysine, native penicillin, or its degradation products.
E. Foshay's Test: Rarely used in tularemia and brucellosis for the detection of circulating specific antigen. Immediate positive reaction to intradermal injection of specific antiserum is considered useful in diagnosis.
F. Extracts of parasitic worms (e.g., trichinella) may give immediate and delayed reactions (see below).

Delayed Reaction Type of Skin Tests.
A. Tuberculin Test (Mantoux test, Pirquet reaction): An individual who has been infected with the tubercle bacillus gives a skin reaction of the delayed type when tuberculoprotein is administered. In addition to the local skin reaction, focal and general reactions may occur in very hypersensitive individuals, e.g., persons with erythema nodosum or phlyctenular conjunctivitis. In such persons, therefore, only very minute quantities of test substances must be injected.
1. Test materials -
a. Old tuberculin (O.T.), a concentrated filtrate of broth in which tubercle bacilli have been grown.
b. Purified protein derivative (P.P.D.), obtained by chemical fractionation of O.T. Both O.T. and P.P.D. are available commercially, standardized in terms of biologic reactivity as tuberculin units (T.U.). Equivalent values are given below.

Approximate Tuberculin Equivalents

Tuberculin Units (T.U.)	"Strength"	P.P.D. (mg./dose)	O.T. Dilution
1	1st	0.00002	1:10,000
5	Intermediate	0.0001	1:2000
250	2nd	0.005	1:100

2. Technic - The initial test dose most commonly is 5 T.U., but this should be reduced to 1 T.U. if the in-

dividual is expected to be hypersensitive. Higher doses are injected when lower doses have given negative results. 0.1 ml. of suitable strength test material is injected into the cleansed skin of the forearm. Readings are taken 48 and 72 hours later.

3. Reading and interpretation - The tuberculin test is considered positive if induration of 10 mm. diameter or more follows injection of 5 T.U. Erythema has no specific meaning. In very strongly positive reactions there may be central necrosis. A positive tuberculin test indicates only that the individual has been infected with tubercle bacilli in the past; it does not indicate present, active disease, resistance, or immunity. The test is most helpful if there is evidence of recent "conversion," i.e., change from tuberculin-negative to tuberculin-positive in a few months. This clearly indicates recent infection and requires study to rule out active disease.

Tuberculin tests may be falsely negative during illnesses which induce "anergy," e.g., miliary tuberculosis, measles and other exanthemata, Boeck's sarcoid, and Hodgkin's disease or in persons receiving corticotropin (ACTH) or corticosteroids.

B. Candida: Skin test material used to test for reactivity to a universal antigen or the presence of anergy.

C. Ducrey Test: (Ito-Reenstierna test, chancroid skin test, dmelcos test; for the diagnosis of chancroid.) Ducrey vaccine (a suspension of Hemophilus ducreyi) is injected intradermally. A positive reaction (erythema and induration) in one to three days denotes past infection with H. ducreyi; hypersensitivity may persist for years.

D. Brucellergen Test: (For the diagnosis of brucellosis.) Intradermal injection of a suspension of brucella organisms may give positive results in 12 to 48 hours. However, the test is not reliable, and agglutination or precipitin reactions are usually preferred if the organism cannot be isolated from the patient.

E. Tularemia Skin Test: Essentially similar to brucellergen test. Not reliable; little used.

F. Frei Test: (For the diagnosis of lymphogranuloma venereum.) The antigen consists of a suspension prepared from infected chick embryos and is injected intradermally. A control injection with uninfected chick embryo material must be included in the test. A positive reaction consists of induration and erythema five to 20 mm. in diameter in 48 hours. Reading of the control injection must be negative. A positive reaction is suggestive of past infection with one of the agents of the lymphogranuloma-psittacosis group.

G. Skin tests for mumps and herpes simplex are available, denoting past infection with these viruses. The reaction (after intracutaneous injection of virus material) is often faint and fleeting. It may reach its maximum erythema and edema in one to 48 hours.

H. Echinococcus Skin Test: (Casoni reaction; for the diagnosis of hydatid disease.) Antigen (hydatid fluid) obtained from human or animal sources gives immediate or delayed reactions after intradermal injection.

I. Trichinella Skin Test: (For the diagnosis of trichinosis.) Commercial antigens are of doubtful value because they are too insensitive. An acid-soluble protein fraction of trichina larvae gives good specificity of delayed reaction.

J. Coccidioidin Test: (For diagnosis of past infection with Coccidioides immitis.) This test is essentially similar to the tuberculin test. The fungus is grown in synthetic medium for long periods and the broth is filtered and concentrated. Usual test strength is 1:100, giving a positive reaction with induration and erythema in 24 to 48 hours. Hypersensitivity is commonly acquired as a result of subclinical infection following transient and minimal exposure to infectious arthrospores. Hypersensitivity persists for life. The test is occasionally negative in disseminated coccidioidomycosis. Cross-reactions with other fungous infections are noted with lower dilutions of coccidioidin.

K. Histoplasmin Test: (For the diagnosis of past infection with Histoplasma capsulatum.) Histoplasmin is prepared similarly to tuberculin and coccidioidin. Usual test strength is 1:100. Positive test indicates past infection. Cross-reactions with other fungous infections are apparently rather high.

L. Blastomycin Test: (For the diagnosis of past infection with Blastomyces.) Test material is a suspension of yeast phase blastomycetes. Test, interpretation, and reading are similar to those of the coccidioidin test.

M. Nickerson-Kveim Test: (For the diagnosis of Boeck's sarcoid.) An extract of sarcoid tissue (especially lymph node or spleen) injected into the skin of a person with Boeck's sarcoid results in a small papule which persists for months. Excision of this papule after four to eight weeks discloses a microscopic pattern resembling other sarcoid lesions. The basis of the reaction is not known and the test is not quite reliable.

N. Toxoplasma Skin Test: Injection of test material prepared from a suspension of killed organisms gives a delayed reaction in some persons with positive serologic tests, no reaction in others. The test is unreliable for diagnosis and is used mainly for epidemiology.

O. Nonbacterial Regional Lymphadenitis ("Cat Scratch Fever") Test: Pus from active cases is diluted 1:5, heated at 60° C. for ten hours, and stored at 4° C. Intradermal injection of 0.1 ml. gives a delayed reaction in persons with this disorder, no reaction in others.

21...

Epidemiology

PRECAUTIONS IN HANDLING INFECTIOUS DISEASES

General Precautions.
  A. Patient: If possible, isolate patient in a private room
     with running water. The patient must have his individual
     thermometer, water bottle, and other utensils. Supply
     him with paper handkerchiefs, paper sputum cup, and
     paper bags as discard containers. Instruct patient on
     safe behavior.
  B. Attendants: Doctors and nurses must wear masks and
     gowns when working with or examining a patient. The
     gown is considered contaminated on the outside and must
     be folded inside out when taken off. Hands must be
     washed thoroughly with soap and water after every con-
     tact with patient or his immediate surroundings.
  C. Miscellaneous: All dishes, glasses, and other utensils
     used by the patient must be disinfected after use, prefer-
     ably by boiling for 15 to 20 minutes. Discarded con-
     tainers, sputum cups, etc. must be wrapped and auto-
     claved or incinerated.

Enteric Infections.
     In enteric infections, in addition to the above precautions,
the urine, feces, and bath water of the patient are considered
contaminated. Prior to discarding these excreta they must be
treated with strong disinfectant (e. g., Lysol®). Laundry must
be collected with care and autoclaved or boiled before being
washed.

Respiratory Infections.
     In highly infectious respiratory disease (e. g., "open"
pulmonary tuberculosis), the patient must be maintained in
strict isolation in a private room. Patient, doctors, nurses,
and attendants must wear masks. The patient must be taught
to cover his mouth and nose when coughing or sneezing.
Special attention must be paid to collection and disposal of
discharges from respiratory tract. Tuberculin-negative individuals must be tested at regular intervals to determine conversion to positive tuberculin reaction permitting follow-up.

DELOUSING MEASURES

Ten per cent DDT in talcum is very effective in all forms of pediculosis. Treatment must be repeated two or three times at intervals of one week. All infested clothing must be steamed or autoclaved. The body and head must be washed thoroughly two or three days after DDT application.

MISCELLANEOUS

Diseases of Animals Transmissible to Man.

Anthrax
Arbor virus infection (encephalitis, hemorrhagic fevers, yellow fever, etc.)
Brucellosis
Erysipeloid
Filariasis
Glanders
Leptospirosis
Pasteurella multocida infection
Plague
Psittacosis (ornithosis)
Rabies
Rat-bite fever
Relapsing fever
Rickettsioses
Salmonellosis
Schistosomiasis
Tuberculosis
Tularemia
Trypanosomiasis

Some Causes of Persistent Fever of Unknown Origin (FUO).*

If the usual diagnostic procedures (including thorough bacteriologic and serologic studies) fail to reveal the diagnosis, consider early biopsy or exploratory laparotomy.

A. Infections (Bacterial, Fungal, Parasitic; Rarely Viral): Consider especially tuberculosis, liver and biliary tract disease, bacterial endocarditis, abdominal abscess, and urinary tract disease.

B. Neoplasms: Consider especially those involving the kidneys, lungs, thyroid, liver, pancreas; lymphomas, leukemias, and myeloma.

C. Hypersensitivity Diseases: Visceral angiitis, disseminated lupus erythematosus, periarteritis nodosa, scleroderma, dermatomyositis, rheumatic fever, and drug fever.

D. "Periodic Fever": Determine etiocholanolone levels.

E. Neurogenic or Endocrine Disorders: Consider lesions of brain stem and thalamus; encephalitis, hyperthyroidism.

F. Factitious Fever: Malingering.

G. Miscellaneous: Consider sarcoidosis, thrombophlebitis, infarctions, poisons, drugs.

---

*R.G. Petersdorf and P. Beeson, Medicine **40**:1, 1961.

EPIDEMIOLOGIC FEATURES OF SOME INFECTIOUS DISEASES

Disease	Etiologic Agent	Transmission	Incubation Period	Isolation	Immunity From Disease	Artificial Immunization	Control
Actinomycosis	Actinomyces israelii (anaerobe), Nocardia asteroides (aerobe).	Usually endogenous (tonsils, crypts, teeth).	?	None	?	None	?
Adenovirus infection (respiratory, eye)	Adenoviruses (more than 30 types)	Droplets, contact.	2-10 days	None	Yes	Vaccine (killed); oral vaccine (living) not acceptable at present.	Immunization in military: oral vaccine (living).
Ancylostomiasis (hookworm disease)	Hookworms: A. duodenale, Necator americanus.	Contaminated soil; skin contact.	2-10 weeks	None	No	None	Sanitary disposal of feces. Wearing of shoes.
Anthrax (many names)	Bacillus anthracis	Contact, inhalation, ingestion of contaminated animal tissue.	1-4 days	Of lesions	Partial	For animals only	Proper sterilization of infected tissues, hides, bristles, wool, etc.
Ascariasis	Round worm: Ascaris lumbricoides	Feces to mouth.	2 mos.	None	No	None	Sanitary disposal of feces. Hygiene.
Blastomycosis	Blastomyces dermatitidis (fungus)	Inhalation of dust from soil.	?	None	?	None	?
Brucellosis (undulant fever)	Brucella abortus, suis, melitensis.	Contact with infected animals. Ingestion of milk, etc.	6-60 days or longer	None	?	For animals only (living vaccine)	Eradication of disease in animals. Pasteurization of milk.
Carrion's disease (Verruga-Oroya fever)	Bartonella bacilliformis	Sandfly.	21 days	None	?	None	Vector control
Chancroid (soft chancre)	Hemophilus ducreyi	Sexual contact.	1-10 days	Modified	No	None	Prevention of exposure
Chickenpox (varicella)	Virus (identical with herpes zoster)	Respiratory droplets. Occasionally crusts from lesions.	2-3 weeks	10 days after exposure until 1 week after vesicles appear	Yes	Hyperimmune globulin (human)	Isolation
Cholera	Vibrio cholerae	Feces, vomitus, contaminated water & food; flies.	Few hrs. to 5 d.	Absolute	?	Vaccine (killed)	Sanitation, hygiene, vaccination.

Disease	Etiologic agent	Source and mode of transmission	Incubation period	Isolation/quarantine	Immunity	Immunization	Control measures
Choriomeningitis, lymphocytic	Virus	Contact with mice	8-14 days	None	Yes	None	Eradication of mice
Coccidioidomycosis	Coccidioides immitis	Inhalation of fungus spores (dust)	7-21 days	None	Partial	None	Dust control in endemic areas
Common cold	Many viruses	Person-to-person contact (droplets)	1-4 days	Short	?	Specific vaccines available against RS virus, myco-plasma, etc.	Experimental vaccines against several viruses
Dengue	Virus	Bite of Aedes aegypti mosquito	3-15 days	Screens until afebrile	Partial	None	Mosquito abatement
Diarrhea of newborn	Viruses: ECHO and others. Bact.: E.coli serotypes, others.	Respiratory droplets. Fecal contamination.	2-21 days	Absolute	?	None	Isolation, sterile technic in nursery.
Diphtheria	Corynebacterium diphtheriae	Respiratory droplets from cases and carriers	2-5 days	Strict until repeated cultures are negative	Yes	Active: toxoid Passive: antitoxin	Active immunization of population
Dysentery, amebic	Entamoeba histolytica	Feces of infected man; water, food, flies.	Days to months	None (enteric precautions)	No	None	Carrier control, food sanitation, water.
Dysentery, bacillary	Shigella species	Feces of infected man; water, food, flies, etc.	1-7 days	Strict until cultures are negative	No	None (chemo-prophylaxis with antimicrobials)	Breaking transmission chain; chemotherapy.
Encephalitis, arthropod-borne viral	Viruses (St. Louis, equine, Japanese B, West Nile, etc.)	Bite of infected mosquitoes and other arthropods	4-21 days	Screens until afebrile	Yes	Formolized virus suspensions in some instances	Control of specific vectors
Favus	Trichophyton schoenleini	Hair, skin, toilet articles.	?	Modified (skull cap)	No	None	Hygiene; chemo-therapy?
Filariasis	Wuchereria species (see p. 329)	Bite of infected arthropods	1 month to years	Impractical	No	None	Control of vectors; treatment of patients
Food infection	Salmonellae, occasionally streptococci.	Meat, eggs, rodents.	6-48 hours	Exclude from food handling	No	None	Food sanitation
Food intoxication	Staphylococcal enterotoxin	Ingestion of bakery or dairy products, meats.	2-8 hours	None	No	None	Food sanitation
	Botulinus toxin	Ingestion of poorly processed canned food	12-48 hours	None	Fatal disease	Antitoxin (type-specific) for early treatment	Proper canning methods

[Cont'd.]

EPIDEMIOLOGIC FEATURES OF SOME INFECTIOUS DISEASES (Cont'd.)

Disease	Etiologic Agent	Transmission	Incubation Period	Isolation	Immunity from Disease	Artificial Immunization	Control
Gas gangrene	Various clostridia (spore-forming anaerobes)	Contamination of wounds with soil, manure, etc.	8-24 hours	None	No	Antitoxin of doubtful value	Prompt and thorough debridement of wounds. Penicillin?
Glanders	Malleomyces mallei	Secretions, skin, feces of infected horses.	1-5 days	Absolute	Yes	None	Destruction of infected horses
Gonorrhea	Neisseria gonorrhoeae	Contact of mucous membrane with infective pus.	1-8 days	Modified	No	None (chemoprophylaxis effective)	Sex hygiene; treatment of cases.
Granuloma inguinale	Donovania granulomatis	Venereal contact with active lesions.	Days to months	Modified	No	None	Sex hygiene
Hepatitis, infectious	Virus	Contact? Water? Shellfish. Fecal contamination.	15-35 days	Modified	Yes	Gamma globulin after exposure	Sanitation, food hygiene.
Hepatitis, serum (homologous)	Virus	Blood, plasma, blood products, syringes, needles, instruments.	2-4 mo. or longer	None	Probable	Gamma globulin in older patients	Thorough sterilization; careful selection of blood donors.
Herpes simplex	Virus	Droplets, saliva.	?	None	?	None	Hygiene in children
Impetigo contagiosa	Staphylococci and streptococci	Contact with lesions.	1-5 days	Modified	? No	None	Hygiene, chemotherapy
Inclusion conjunctivitis	Chlamydia	Mother's cervix to infant's eyes; venereal disease.	7-12 days	Modified	?	None	Sex hygiene. Antimicrobial therapy.
Infectious mononucleosis	? Virus	Respiratory contact? Saliva?	7-14 days	None	? Yes	None	?
Influenza	Type A, B, C viruses, many subtypes.	Respiratory contact.	1-4 days	During acute illness	Short-lived and type-specific	Possible with formolized virus. Resistance partial and short-lived.	?
Keratoconjunctivitis, epidemic	Virus (adenovirus type 8)	Contact with infected eye, hands, physicians' instruments, solutions.	7-10 days	Modified	Probable	Experimental vaccine (killed)	Hygiene. Physician's technic.
Leishmaniasis	Leishmania donovani, etc.	Contact, bite of insects (e.g., sandfly).	Weeks to 6 mo.	Modified	?	None	Control of insects; hygiene.

Leprosy	Mycobacterium leprae	? Personal contact	Years	Modified if treated	?	None	Treatment of active cases
Lymphogranuloma venereum	Chlamydia	Venereal contact	1-6 weeks	Modified	?	None	Sex hygiene; treatment of active cases.
Malaria	Plasmodium vivax, malariae, falciparum.	Bite of infective female Anopheles mosquito	Variable	Modified (screens)	?	None	Mosquito control, treatment of cases
Measles (rubeola)	Virus	Respiratory contact, droplets.	10-15 days	From 7 days after exposure to 5 days after rash starts	Yes	Live virus vaccine given with gamma globulin	Universal vaccination of all children 12 months or older
Meningitis, aseptic	Coxsackie, ECHO, polio, herpes viruses, etc.	Fecal and respiratory contact	Variable	Modified	Specific	Against some viruses	?
Meningitis, meningococcic	Neisseria meningitidis	Respiratory contact, droplets.	2-10 days	Strict	?	None (sulfonamide prophylaxis no longer effective)	Avoidance of overcrowding. Penicillin treatment.
Mumps (epidemic parotitis)	Virus	Respiratory contact, droplets.	7-26 (us. 18-21) d.	Modified	Yes	Live vaccine	Isolation, vaccination.
Ophthalmia neonatorum	Neisseria gonorrhoeae	Contact with infected mucous membrane	1-3 days	Strict	No	None (prophylaxis effective)	Instillation of penicillin ointment or 1% AgNO$_3$ into eyes of newborn
Pappataci fever (sandfly fever)	Virus	Bite of infected Phlebotomus (sandfly)	2-6 days	Screening	Yes	None	Control of insects
Paratyphoid fevers	Salmonella species, especially S. paratyphi, S. schottmilleri, S. enteritidis.	Water, food, flies, excreta of infected man.	1-14 days	Strict	Yes	Vaccine of doubtful value	Sanitation; chemotherapy.
Pertussis (whooping cough)	Hemophilus pertussis	Respiratory contact, droplets.	2-21 (us. 5-10) d.	Modified	Yes	Phase I vaccine (killed)	Immunization in early life
Pharyngoconjunctival fever	Adenoviruses (see above)	Respiratory contact, swimming.	3-8 days	Modified	Yes	Type specific	Immunization not acceptable at present
Plague	Pasteurella pestis	Infected rodents, fleas; discharge from lesions; sputum.	2-10 days	Strict	Yes	Formolized or live avirulent vaccine	Rodent and flea control; chemoprophylaxis with sulfonamides.

[Cont'd.]

EPIDEMIOLOGIC FEATURES OF SOME INFECTIOUS DISEASES (Cont'd.)

Disease	Etiologic Agent	Transmission	Incuba-tion Period	Isolation	Immunity From Disease	Artificial Immunization	Control
Pneumonia: Bacterial	Pneumococcus, Staph., Strep., Hemophilus sp., Klebsiella.	Respiratory contact, droplets.	1-7 days	"Aseptic medical technic".	Partial type-specific	Experimental only	Avoidance of crowding, exposure, alcohol, malnutrition, cross-infection.
Nonbacterial	Viruses, rickettsiae, foMyco. pneumoniae.	Contact, droplets, fomites, animals.	2-30 days	Modified	? Yes	Against some specific agents	Differs with etiology.
Poliomyelitis	Virus types I, II, III.	Respiratory secretions and feces of infected persons.	7-21 days	Until end of febrile period	Type-specific	Vaccines, live attenuated virus.	Active immunization, boosters.
Psittacosis (ornithosis)	Chlamydia	Excreta of infected birds; rarely sputum of man.	6-15 days	Strict	Yes	Experimental only	Treatment of infected birds. Limit bird-man contact.
Q fever (see Rickettsial diseases, p. 307).							
Rabies (hydrophobia)	Virus	Saliva of infected animals, bite.	10 days to 6 months	Modified	Yes (but high fatality)	After bite, hyper-immune serum and duck embryo vaccine (killed). Animal vaccination with live vaccines.	Control of stray dogs and cats; animal vaccination. Impound and observe all animals that have bitten humans.
Rat-bite fever	Spirillum minus, Streptobacillus.	Bite of infected rodents.	3-30 days	None	?	None	Control of rodents.
Relapsing fever	Borrelia recurrentis, B. duttoni.	Bite of ticks, lice, infected arthropod feces; infected rodents.	3-12 days	Modified	Yes	None	Delousing, tick repellents.
Ringworm	Microsporum, Trichophyton, and other fungi.	Lesions of infected man and animals, clothing, etc.	?	Modified	No	None	Hygiene, especially in children; sterilization of barbers' tools.
Rocky Mountain spotted fever (see Rickettsial diseases, p. 307).							

Rubella (German measles)	Virus	Droplets, respiratory discharges.	14-21 days	Exclude from school 10 days after exposure	Yes	Live vaccine	Exposure of girls before child-bearing age. Live vaccine.
Sandfly fever (see Pappataci fever, p. 379).							
Scabies	Sarcoptes scabiei	Contact with infected man, clothing, bedding, etc.	? 48 hours	Modified	No	None	Hygiene. Treatment of infested persons.
Scarlet fever (see Streptococcal infections, below).							
Schistosomiasis (see p. 335).							
Septic sore throat (see Streptococcal infections, below).							
Smallpox (variola)	Virus	Respiratory droplets or contact with lesions.	7-16 (usually 12) days	Absolute until all scabs are off	Yes	Smallpox vaccine; read reaction at 3 and 9 days. Refrigerate vaccine.	Repeated vaccination; strict case isolation, quarantine. Early treatment of close contacts with methisazone (Marboran®).
Streptococcal infections (erysipelas, sepsis, sore throat, scarlet fever, etc.)	Group A β-hemolytic streptococci; occasionally anaerobic streptococci.	Droplets inhaled from carriers or cases; ingestion of contaminated food; entrance of streptococci into wounds, vagina, etc.	1-5 days	While clinically ill, respiratory precautions.	Partial, type-specific.	Not accepted	Avoidance of crowding, restriction of carriers, chemoprophylaxis (sulfonamides, penicillin).
Syphilis	Treponema pallidum	Contact with infectious lesion, transfusions; transplacental.	1-6 (us. 3) weeks	Modified	?	Chemoprophylaxis after exposure	Sex hygiene. Treatment of infectious cases.
Tetanus (lockjaw)	Clostridium tetani	Contamination of wounds with dirt containing spores.	4-21 days or longer	None	Highly fatal	Active: toxoid Passive: antitoxin (human)	Active and passive immunization. Debridement of wounds.
Trachoma	Chlamydia	Contact with infectious discharges of eyes and nose; fomites.	?	Modified	?	Experimental vaccines	Hygiene; treatment of infectious cases with tetracycline or sulfonamide.
Trichinosis	Trichinella spiralis	Ingestion of insufficiently cooked infected meat.	6-7 days	None	?	None	Adequate cooking or freezing, storage.

[Cont'd.]

EPIDEMIOLOGIC FEATURES OF SOME INFECTIOUS DISEASES (Cont'd.)

Disease	Etiologic Agent	Transmission	Incubation Period	Isolation	Immunity From Disease	Artificial Immunization	Control
Tuberculosis	Mycobacterium tuberculosis	Discharges from lesions of infected man. Infected cow's milk.	Variable	Strict in "open" cases	?	BCG (live vaccine) in selected cases only	Case-finding, segregation, treatment; "test and slaughter" program in cattle.
Tularemia	Pasteurella tularensis (Francisella)	Contact with infected animals (rabbits, etc.), ticks, deer fly. Laboratory contact.	1-10 days	Yes	Yes	Only experimental	Avoidance of contact with vectors and animal hosts.
Typhoid fever	Salmonella typhi	Water, food contaminated with excreta of infected man.	3-38 (usually 10-14) days	Strict until 2 successive negative stool cultures	Yes	Typhoid vaccine	Sanitation, immunization.
Typhus fever (see Rickettsial diseases, p. 307).							
Vaccinia (cowpox)	Virus	Contact with fresh lesion (especially if skin disorder, eczema present).	3-4 days	Modified	Yes	Smallpox vaccine. Methisazone	Avoidance of vaccinating in presence of skin disease.
Varicella (see Chickenpox, p. 376).							
Variola (see Smallpox, p. 381).							
Vincent's angina (trench mouth)	Anaerobic spirochetes and fusiform bacteria	Not contagious except for underlying disease, e.g., herpes simplex stomatitis.	?	None	No	None	Mouth hygiene, chemotherapy.
Weil's disease (leptospirosis)	Leptospira icterohaemorrhagiae, L. canicola, etc.	Ingestion of food and water contaminated with rat or dog urine.	4-19 days	None	Yes	None	Sanitation
Yaws (frambesia)	Treponema pertenue	Contact with infectious lesions, fomites, flies.	1-3 mos. or more	Modified	?	None	Prevention of contact; insect control; penicillin
Yellow fever	Virus	Bite of infected mosquitoes (Aedes, Haemagogus, etc.).	3-6 days	Modified (screening)	Yes	Living avirulent virus vaccine (strain 17 D)	Immunization, mosquito control.

22...

Biologic Products for Prophylaxis and Therapy

Active Immunity.

Some biologic products used for prophylaxis exert their effect through the stimulation of active immunity. This is manifested in part by the production of antibodies in the injected individual. Such relative active immunity commonly lasts for years, and can be restimulated by recall ("booster") injections. The production of active immunity is the method of choice, whenever possible, in the long-term prevention of infectious disease. Active immunization has to be carried out **before** the individual is exposed to the infectious disease.

Passive Immunity.

Other biologic products are used **after** the individual has been exposed to the infectious disease, or even after onset of symptoms of the disease. These products exert their effect through the mechanism of passive immunity: Antibodies preformed in an animal or man (see p. 391) are administered to the individual exposed to or suffering from the disease. The antibodies thus introduced will give a measure of protection for some days or weeks; in the ill patient the antibodies (particularly antitoxins) will neutralize the toxins formed by the invading microorganisms and thus give the host time to produce his own antibodies. **Passive immunity is always short-lived.**

BIOLOGIC PRODUCTS USED FOR THE PRODUCTION OF ACTIVE IMMUNITY

Improvements and changes are frequently made in biologicals dispensed by the large drug manufacturers. Dosage schedules likewise frequently change. Follow the manufacturer's instructions which accompany the biologic product used.

Toxins.

Certain bacteria (e. g., diphtheria and tetanus bacilli) produce potent poisons called exotoxins. These thermolabile antigenic substances are excreted into culture media and can be readily obtained by filtering the organisms out. Toxins were previously used in immunization procedures in neutral mixtures with antitoxins. Toxin-antitoxin mixtures are unstable and have been almost abandoned in favor of toxoids as immunizing agents.

Toxoids (Anatoxins).

Toxoids are obtained from toxins by treatment with formalin or heat. Toxoids are just as antigenic as toxins, capable of stimulating antitoxin production, but they have lost their poisonous property. Consequently they are useful immunizing agents, particularly against diphtheria and tetanus. Staphylococcus toxoid is occasionally used in recurrent staphylococcal infections.

A. Preparations: Toxoid may be dispensed as:
1. Plain fluid toxoid, i. e., fluid formol-toxoid.
2. Alum-precipitated toxoid, in which the toxoid has been precipitated from the original solution with potassium and aluminum sulfate and then resuspended in saline.
3. Absorbed toxoid, in which the toxoid molecules have been adsorbed onto aluminum hydroxide or other similar colloids for slower absorption from the tissues.

B. Administration: Plain fluid toxoid is administered I. M. in three doses at intervals of two to four weeks. Alum-precipitated or aluminum hydroxide—adsorbed toxoid is given in three doses one month apart. In all cases a booster dose should be given one year after the original immunization. Tetanus and diphtheria toxoids are often administered together to children (in addition to or combined with pertussis vaccine). Adequate antibody levels can ordinarily be expected about one month after completion of the course of immunization. (See p. 388 for initial immunization schedule of children.)

C. Test for Hypersensitivity: Whereas adsorbed or precipitated toxoids are well tolerated by children, adults often have marked reactions to them. Therefore, fluid toxoids are preferred in adults. Their administration should be preceded by a skin test (see Moloney test, p. 368) with toxoid to rule out hypersensitivity, which would make administration of full doses hazardous. This is particularly important with diphtheria toxoid.

Bacterial Vaccines (Bacterins).

These consist of heavy suspensions of killed or nonvirulent live bacteria which are injected I. M., subcut., or intracutaneously. They are intended to confer partial resistance to the natural disease, but never give complete immunity.

A. Anthrax: Live attenuated bacterial or spore suspensions, used in animals only; moderately effective.

B. Brucella: Several types of live attenuated bacteria, e. g., strain 19, for animals only; moderately effective.

C. Cholera: Suspension of killed cholera vibrios; not very effective. Give 0.5 to 1 ml. subcut. two to three times at ten-day intervals; subsequently, give 1 ml. once every six months when exposed to cholera. Marked local and systemic toxic reactions are common.

D. Dysentery, Bacillary: Suspension of several types of killed dysentery bacilli; of questionable value.

E. Pertussis (Whooping Cough): Suspension of killed Phase I H. pertussis in saline, adsorbed onto aluminum hydroxide, or precipitated with alum; effectively prevents or modifies pertussis. Pertussis vaccine may be mixed with diphtheria or tetanus toxoid and inactivated poliomyelitis vaccine for initial immunization of children (see schedule, p. 388).

F. Plague: Suspension of killed virulent or live avirulent plague bacilli used to give partial protection to persons exposed in endemic areas; live avirulent vaccine is probably more effective. Dosage and schedule depend on preparation.

G. Tuberculosis: Suspension of live, avirulent bacteria, strain BCG, indicated only for tuberculin-negative individuals heavily exposed to infectious cases of tuberculosis (e.g., family contacts, medical personnel). BCG (bacille Calmette-Guérin) results in some degree of resistance to progressive tuberculosis.

H. Typhoid Vaccine: Suspension of killed typhoid (Salmonella typhosa) organisms; moderately effective. For adults, give two doses of 0.5 to 1 ml. each subcut. four to six weeks apart. Recall ("booster") injection of 0.1 ml. intracutaneously should be given once a year or 0.5 ml. subcut. every three years. It is doubtful that paratyphoid A (S. paratyphi) or paratyphoid B (S. schott-mülleri) vaccines are effective. They produce marked vaccine reactions.

Viral and Rickettsial Vaccines.

These consist of concentrated suspensions of inactivated virulent or live avirulent particles, or of antigens derived from them. Many are prepared in embryoned eggs and should not be administered to persons of known hypersensitivity to eggs. For dosage schedules and routes of administration, follow manufacturer's directions.

A. Adenovirus: Cell culture–grown, inactivated vaccine (types 3, 4, 7) for military recruits temporarily unavailable. Live vaccine for oral use, experimental, effective.

B. Encephalomyelitis, Equine (Eastern or Western Type): Formalin-killed virus, for immunization of laboratory personnel and animals; not very effective.

C. Influenza: Formalin-killed virus strains representing types A and B and prevalent subtypes; moderately effective if the antigens of the infecting strain are represented in the vaccine. Vaccinate every year in high-risk patients.

D. Japanese B Encephalitis: Killed virus, similar to encephalomyelitis vaccine.

E. Measles: Live virus vaccine given together with small amount of gamma globulin (very effective). Inactive vaccine undesirable.

F. Mumps: Attenuated, egg-cell-grown live virus vaccine; highly effective.

G. Poliomyelitis: Formalin-killed (occasionally also ultraviolet irradiated) viruses of three types available. Moderately effective in preventing paralysis. Live virus vaccine, taken orally, very effective.

H. Q Fever: Killed rickettsiae and soluble antigens for immunization of heavily exposed persons and laboratory personnel; moderately effective.

I. Rabies: Killed virus (grown in embryonated duck eggs) injected into persons bitten by animals suspected of rabies, in addition to rabies antiserum (see p. 392); efficacy uncertain. Live avirulent egg-adapted virus (Flury strain) for immunization of animals; effective. Cell culture–grown live virus (experimental).

   Note: Injections of killed vaccine prepared from animal nerve tissue may lead to demyelinating encephalitis.

J. Rocky Mountain Spotted Fever: Killed rickettsiae and soluble antigens prepared in chick embryo yolk sac, used for the protection of persons exposed to the bites of ticks which carry the disease; moderately effective.

K. Rubella (German Measles): Cell culture–grown, live vaccine; effective. Produces arthritis in 40% of adults.

L. Smallpox: Active vaccinia virus in the form of glycerolated calf lymph. The virus loses viability if exposed to elevated temperatures and so must be kept refrigerated until used. A more stable dried vaccine is still experimental. The vaccine can be administered by multiple pressure or abrasion methods. The skin is cleansed with ether or alcohol and permitted to dry before vaccine fluid is applied. A properly performed vaccination with a good "take" results in effective immunity to smallpox; lasts one to three years.

   Reaction to vaccination in susceptible individual goes through regular stages as follows:

   1. "Primary take" - Papule (two to four days), vesicle (four to eight days), pustule (nine to 13 days), scab (13 to 18 days), scar.

   2. Accelerated reaction - In previously vaccinated persons (partially immune), an "accelerated reaction" takes place, with all stages of the reaction occurring

within less than ten days. The "immediate reaction" (24 to 48 hours) is limited to a papule, but without vesiculation. It may be elicited by inactive vaccine and should NOT be accepted as proof of immunity.

If there is no evidence of a "take" with vesicle formation (primary or accelerated reaction), the individual must be revaccinated with potent vaccine, applied with vigor.

Contraindication to smallpox vaccination: widespread eczema or other exudative skin lesions, because of danger of developing generalized vaccinia.

Methisazone (Marboran®) may be used in exposed persons to prevent smallpox.

M. Typhus, Epidemic: Killed rickettsiae and soluble antigens prepared from yolk sacs of infected chick embryos; very effective.

N. Typhus, Scrub: Similar to Rocky Mountain spotted fever vaccine; not very effective.

O. Yellow Fever: Live avirulent virus (strain 17D) distributed in dehydrated form and reconstituted before subcutaneous administration; very effective.

ACTIVE IMMUNIZATION AGAINST INFECTIOUS DISEASES

Biologic products used for active immunization are frequently modified. The schedule of administration, dose, and recommended method of choice vary with the product and change often. Always consult the manufacturer's package insert and follow its recommendations.

RECOMMENDED IMMUNIZATION OF ADULTS FOR TRAVEL

Every adult, whether traveling or not, must be immunized with tetanus toxoid. Purified toxoid "for adult use" must be used to avoid reactions. Every adult should also have primary vaccination for poliomyelitis (oral live trivalent vaccine), for diphtheria (use purified toxoid "for adult use"), and for smallpox. Every traveler must fulfill the immunization requirements of the health authorities of different countries. These are listed in "Immunization Information for International Travel" (U.S. Public Health Service, Division of Foreign Quarantine, 7915 Eastern Ave., Silver Spring, Maryland 20910.)

Immunization suggestions for travel in different parts of the world are listed on pp. 389-90.

RECOMMENDED SCHEDULE FOR ACTIVE
IMMUNIZATION OF CHILDREN

Age	Product Administered	Test Recommended
2-3 mos.	DPT(1), oral poliovaccine(2) trivalent, or type 1	
3-4 mos.	DPT, oral poliovaccine trivalent, or type 3	
4-5 mos.	DPT, oral poliovaccine trivalent, or type 2	
10-11 mos.		Tuberculin test
12 mos.	Measles vaccine(3)	
15-19 mos.	DPT, oral poliovaccine trivalent, smallpox vaccine(4)	Read primary take of smallpox in 1 week
2 yrs.	Mumps vaccine(5)	Tuberculin test(6)
3-4 yrs.	DPT, rubella vaccine(7)	Tuberculin test
6 yrs.	TD(8), smallpox vaccine, oral poliovaccine trivalent	Tuberculin test
8-10 yrs.		Tuberculin test
12-14 yrs.	TD, smallpox vaccine	Tuberculin test

(1) DPT: Toxoids of diphtheria and tetanus, alum-precipitated or aluminum hydroxide–adsorbed, combined with pertussis bacterial antigen. Suitable for young children. Three doses of 0.5 ml. injected I. M. at intervals of four to eight weeks. Fourth injection of 0.5 ml. I. M. given about one year later.

(2) Oral live poliomyelitis virus vaccine: Either trivalent (types 1, 2, and 3 combined) or single type. Trivalent given at six to eight week intervals three times, then booster one year later. Monovalent type 1, then type 3, then type 2 given at six-week intervals, then booster of trivalent vaccine one year later. Inactive (Salk type) trivalent vaccine available but not recommended.

(3) Live measles virus vaccine, 0.5 ml. injected I. M. With attenuated (Edmonston) strain, human gamma globulin, 0.01 ml./lb. injected into opposite arm at the same time, to lessen reaction to vaccine. This is not advised with "further attenuated" (Schwarz) strain. Inactive measles vaccine should not be used.

(4) Live smallpox vaccine (vaccinia virus), usually supplied as calf lymph, must be used fresh, before expiration date, and must be stored at low temperature. Administered by multiple pressure technic. Site must be inspected at seven days for evidence of "primary take" or at three to four days for evidence of "accelerated reaction." Some vesicles must be found to indicate immunizing proliferation of virus. Papule without vesication not acceptable as evidence of "take." Do not vaccinate in presence of eczema in child, or sibling, or when there is known immunologic deficiency.

Tetanus.

Booster injection of 0.5 ml. tetanus toxoid, for adult use, every five to seven years, assuming completion of primary immunization. (All countries.)

Smallpox.

Revaccination with live smallpox vaccine (vaccinia virus) by multiple pressure method every three years. W. H. O. certificate requires registration of batch number of vaccine. The physician should ascertain a "take" by observing vesicle formation after administration of either liquid or freeze-dried effective vaccine. (All countries.)

Typhoid.

Suspension of killed Salmonella typhi. For primary immunization, inject 0.5 ml. subcut. twice at an interval of four to six weeks (0.25 ml. for children under 10 years). For booster, inject 0.5 ml. subcut. (or 0.1 ml. intradermally) every three years. (All countries.) Paratyphoid vaccines are not recommended and probably ineffective at present.

Yellow Fever.

Live, attenuated yellow fever virus, 0.5 ml. subcut. W. H. O. certificate requires registration of batch number of vaccine. Vaccination available in U. S. A. only at approved centers. Vaccination must be repeated at intervals of 10 years or less. (Africa, South America.)

Cholera.

Suspension of killed vibrios, including prevalent antigenic types. Two injections of 0.5 ml. and 1 ml. are given I. M. four to six weeks apart. This must be followed by 0.5 ml. booster injections every six months during possible exposure. Protection depends largely on booster doses. W. H. O. cer-

---

(5) **Live mumps virus vaccine** (attenuated), 0.5 ml. I. M.

(6) **The frequency** with which tuberculin tests are administered depends on the risk of exposure and the prevalence of tuberculosis in the population group.

(7) **Rubella live virus vaccine** (attenuated) can be given between age one and puberty, but preferably prior to entry into kindergarten. The entire contents of a single-dose vaccine vial, reconstituted from the lyophilized state, are injected subcutaneously. The vaccine must **not** be given to women who are pregnant or are likely to become pregnant within three months of vaccination. Adult women must also be warned that there is a 40% likelihood of developing arthralgia and arthritis (presumably self-limited) within four weeks of vaccination.

(8) **Tetanus toxoid and diphtheria toxoid,** purified, suitable for adults.

tificate is valid for six months only. (Middle Eastern countries, Asia, occasionally others.)

Plague.

Suspension of killed plague bacilli given I. M. , two injections of 0.5 ml. each, four to six weeks apart, and a third injection six months later. (Middle Eastern countries, Asia, occasionally South America and others.)

Typhus.

Suspension of inactivated typhus rickettsiae given I. M. , two injections of 0.5 ml. each, four to six weeks apart. Booster doses of 0.5 ml. every six months may be necessary. (Southeastern Europe, Africa, Asia.)

Hepatitis.

No active immunization available. Temporary passive immunity may be induced by I. M. injection of human gamma globulin, 0.01 ml./lb. every two to three months.

BIOLOGIC PRODUCTS USED FOR THE PRODUCTION OF PASSIVE IMMUNITY

All these products are sera from humans or animals convalescent from or artificially immunized against a specific toxin or infectious agent. Many of them are concentrated and purified. **Always perform test for hypersensitivity before administering an animal serum.** If the person gives evidence of hypersensitivity by skin test (see p. 366), test with a preparation derived from a different animal or attempt desensitization by the procedure described on p. 370.

Antitoxins.

(Serum from horse, sheep, rabbit, or goat, specifically immunized.) These substances specifically neutralize bacterial and other toxins. The following are employed:
  A. Botulism Antitoxin: Prepared against the toxin of
     Clostridium botulinum, types A and B. Administer
     10, 000 units of the divalent antitoxin I. V. every three to
     four hours when botulism is suspected. Effective only
     before full-blown neurologic symptoms appear.
  B. Diphtheria Antitoxin: A concentrated globulin fraction
     from pooled serum of animals immunized against the
     toxin of Corynebacterium diphtheriae; effective if administered prior to organic damage by the toxin. When the
     presumptive clinical diagnosis of diphtheria is made,
     antitoxin must be administered immediately without waiting for laboratory confirmation. Depending on the severity of the case, inject 10,000 to 200,000 units I. V. or I. M.

C. Gas Gangrene Antitoxin: Trivalent material containing antitoxin against Clostridium welchii, Cl. septicum, and Cl. oedematiens. Inject 10,000 to 50,000 units I.M. or I.V. into a patient who has sustained a wound possibly contaminated with spores of gas gangrene organisms. The efficacy of gas gangrene antitoxin is very doubtful.

D. Tetanus Antitoxin: A concentrated globulin fraction obtained from the serum of horses or cattle immunized against the toxin of Clostridium tetani. For prophylaxis for a deep and possibly contaminated wound, inject 1500 to 6000 units I.M. An individual previously immunized with toxoid should instead (or in addition) receive a booster injection of tetanus toxoid. Active immunization with toxoid should follow tetanus antitoxin in all wounded persons. Hyperimmune human gamma globulin is much preferable to horse globulin for prevention or treatment of tetanus (see p. 392).

Antivenins.

Commercial antivenins are available against the venoms of poisonous snakes (rattlesnakes, vipers, and cobras), spiders, and scorpions. (Follow manufacturer's instructions.)

Antisera.

These substances contain high concentrations of specific antibodies against bacteria or viruses. They tend to limit dissemination of the infectious agent and to prevent its establishment and multiplication in tissues. They usually have no effect against toxins and other microbial products. In general, antibacterial sera have very low therapeutic effectiveness. Such previously used sera as pneumococcus (type specific), meningococcus, and scarlet fever antisera have been virtually abandoned. Antiviral sera have their greatest effectiveness if administered early in the incubation period of the disease but are of little or no benefit after the onset of specific symptoms.

A. Human Gamma Globulin: (See review by Gitlin, Gross, and Janeway in New England J.Med. 260:21, 72, 121, and 170, 1959.) Immune Serum Globulin, U.S.P., is a commercial preparation of gamma globulin derived from large pools of human plasma by low-temperature ethanol fractionation. The preparation contains about 165 mg. of gamma globulin per ml. of solution, representing a 25-fold concentration of antibody-containing globulins of plasma, glycine as stabilizer, and merthiolate as preservative. Such concentrated gamma globulin is injected I.M. or subcut., NEVER I.V. It is employed clinically in the following conditions:

1. Agammaglobulinemia with recurrent bacterial infections - Inject 0.3 to 0.45 ml. of solution per lb. body weight (150 mg. gamma globulin/Kg.) once each month,

but twice initially. Antimicrobial drugs must also be used to control active infections.

2. Measles - To **prevent** clinical disease in nonimmune persons (and interfere with development of active immunity), give 0.1 ml. of solution per lb. during the first six days after exposure. To **attenuate** the disease (and permit development of active immunity), give 0.02 ml. of solution per lb. during the first six days after exposure, or 0.04 ml. of solution between the sixth and eighth to tenth days after exposure. Gamma globulin has no effect after the rash has appeared. Complete prevention is indicated in very young or debilitated unvaccinated children. Gamma globulin is also administered with live measles vaccine to reduce reactions.

3. German measles - Susceptible women during the first four months of pregnancy may receive 0.1 ml. of solution per lb. body weight promptly after exposure.

4. Infectious hepatitis - 0.01 to 0.02 ml. of solution per lb. once or twice during the incubation period may prevent or modify the disease.

5. Serum hepatitis - 0.06 ml. per lb. after multiple transfusions given to adults over 40 years of age to avoid serious disease.

B. Hyperimmune Gamma Globulin: (Obtained from hyperimmunized man or animals. See review by Kabat, E. A., in New England J. Med. **269**:247, 1963.)

1. Tetanus - Hyperimmune human gamma globulin eliminates problems of hypersensitivity, is retained longer, and is more effective than horse antitoxin for prophylaxis or treatment. After injury in nonimmunized persons, 250 to 500 units of human hyperimmune tetanus globulin yield serum levels of 0.03 to 0.06 unit of antitoxin per ml. for several weeks.

2. Vaccinia - Hyperimmune human gamma globulin, 0.6 to 1 ml./Kg., can be given for complications of smallpox vaccination.

3. Pertussis - Hyperimmune gamma globulin, 2.5 ml., injected into infants promptly after exposure, may be effective in preventing the disease. Doubtful value.

4. Rabies - Hyperimmune concentrated horse serum is used in conjunction with vaccine for prevention of rabies following animal bites. Follow W. H. O. recommendations. Hyperimmune human globulin is experimental.

5. Rubella, varicella, or mumps may be aborted by early use of gamma globulin possessing high antibody titer.

6. Bacterial infections - Gamma globulin injected in doses of 10 ml. every two to five days in combination with antibiotics has been claimed effective in controlling chronic infections caused by staphylococci, Pseudomonas and Proteus organisms, and other bacteria. The evidence is inconclusive.

23...

Pathologic Examination

EXFOLIATIVE CYTOLOGIC STUDY; PAPANICOLAOU SMEAR

Examination for characteristic neoplastic cells in the exfoliated cells from the secretions, exudates, transudates, or scrapings of various internal organs and tissues may permit a diagnosis of early malignancy which cannot be established by other technics. Exfoliative cytology has been so valuable in the detection of early cancer of the uterine body and uterine cervix that it is usually performed as a routine part of the annual examination of all adult women.

Exfoliated cells may also be obtained from the oral mucosa, trachea and bronchi, stomach, rectum and colon, urinary tract, serous sac fluids, cyst fluids, synovial fluids, C.S.F., glandular excretions, and exudates. Methods for obtaining, collecting, and preserving such materials may vary slightly according to the pathologist's preference. Staining and interpretation of the smears should be done only by properly trained and experienced pathologists or cytologists.

Vaginal Aspiration and Cervical Scrapings.*

A. Vaginal Smears: Material from the vagina can be obtained by aspiration or with a cotton swab, spatula, or cut tongue depressor as shown on p. 394.

B. Cervical Scrapings: After vaginal fluid is obtained, a vaginal speculum (moistened in warm water) is inserted and the cervix is visualized. No lubricant should be used. With use of a cotton swab, spatula, or cut tongue depressor, the second specimen is taken from the region of the squamocolumnar junction. Since most cancers of the cervix develop in this area, over 90% of them will be detected by these scrapings. (Specimens should always be taken from any area of the cervix which is clinically abnormal.)

---

*The combined smear technic shown and described on pp. 394-96 is that recommended by the Cytopathology Laboratory, Johns Hopkins University School of Medicine. Modified, redrawn, and reproduced, with permission, from John K. Frost and Betty Jane McClellan, Clinical Cytopathology Techniques for Specimen Preparation, 2nd Ed., 1962.

Materials Needed:
One cervical spatula, cut
 tongue depressor, or cotton swab.
Two glass slides (one end frost-
 ed). Identify by writing the
 patient's name on the frost-
 ed end with a lead pencil.
One speculum (without lubricant).
One bottle of fixative (97% ethyl
 alcohol) for dip-in, spray-on,
 or drop-on fixative.

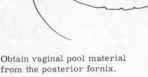

A

B

Obtain vaginal pool material
from the posterior fornix.

Place adequate drop 1
inch from end of slide,
smear (see E, p. 396),
fix, and dry.

General Rules in Obtaining Specimens.
 (1) The fixative should be open and ready for use.
     Cells dry rapidly once they are smeared, so the
     cells must be fixed immediately after the smear
     has been made.
 (2) Talcum powder or starch should be wiped from the
     gloved finger before the smear is made so that it
     will not obscure the cells.
 (3) Cotton swabs, if used, must not be contaminated by
     epithelium from the manufacturer's, examiner's, or
     patient's skin. They should be prepared just before use
     by picking up a small amount of nonabsorbent cotton with

[Cont'd. on next page.]

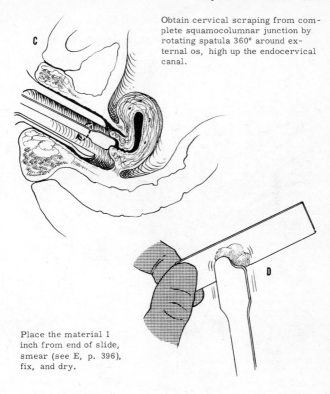

Obtain cervical scraping from complete squamocolumnar junction by rotating spatula 360° around external os, high up the endocervical canal.

Place the material 1 inch from end of slide, smear (see E, p. 396), fix, and dry.

the tip of an applicator stick and rolling against the coat sleeve or clean towel.

(4) The speculum must be introduced with no lubricant. If necessary, normal saline or vaginal fluid may be used to moisten the speculum and assist introduction.

(5) Bleeding and douching within the previous 24 hours are not contraindications to specimen collection. Specimens should be obtained when the first opportunity arises. These conditions do yield a higher percentage of unsatisfactory specimens, however, and the patient should be advised that it may be necessary to repeat the study in order to ward off anxiety if repeat study should become necessary.

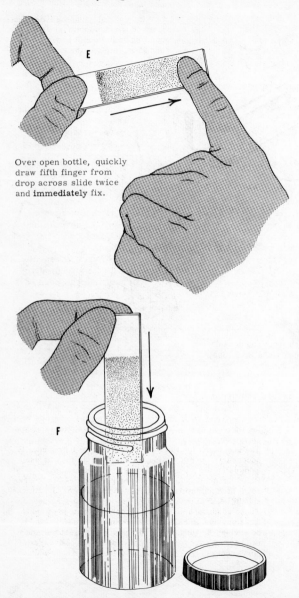

Over open bottle, quickly
draw fifth finger from
drop across slide twice
and **immediately** fix.

Although vaginal smears detect only 50% of cervical cancers, they are more apt to show malignant cells from the endometrium, fallopian tubes, ovaries, and peritoneum. In addition, they may reveal Trichomonas or Candida infections and can be used for hormonal evaluation.

Mailing the Specimens.
Various spray-on, dip-in, and drop-on fixatives are now available for rapid fixing and drying of smears. Each slide should be labeled. After drying, the slides should be placed in a mailing container for slides, so that contamination and breakage are avoided. A history form should be submitted for each case.

Laboratory Reports.
The cytologic report from the pathology laboratory usually describes the cell specimens as (1) normal, repeat in one year; (2) abnormal, repeat immediately or in not more than three months; or (3) positive, take biopsy. Commonly included in the report are the degree of inflammation, the presence of pathogens, and hormonal evaluation.

Follow-up of abnormal and positive smears is essential.
Note: In no case, including that of the positive smear, is treatment justified until definitive diagnosis has been established through biopsy studies.

BACTERIOLOGIC EXAMINATION OF AUTOPSY MATERIAL

Culture blood and organs when bacterial etiology is to be proved. Consult bacteriology laboratory regarding directions for collecting and transporting specimens.

To Secure Cultures.
Sterilize surface of organ with red-hot spatula until dry. Cultures are obtained with sterile glass pipet or syringe and 18 to 20 gage, three-inch needle by aspiration through seared area of atrium or ventricle. For solid viscera, break surface in seared dry area with sterile sharp instrument and plunge cotton swab into the substance of the organ. Place swab in tube containing a small amount of sterile broth. For leptomeninges, the swab should be directed through seared area of meninges into an adjacent unheated area.

Smears.
Smears may yield valuable information. Prepare and stain in the usual manner.

AVERAGE WEIGHTS OF ORGANS (in grams)

| ORGAN | CHILDREN | | | | ADULTS | | |
	Newborn	1 Year	6 Years	12 Years	Average Men	Average Women	Range
Brain and meninges	335-380	910-925	1200-1250	1250-1400	1375	1260	1100-1600
Spinal cord (minus dura)	3-5	- - -	- - -	23	28	28	27-30
Hypophysis (pituitary)	- - -	- - -	- - -	0.56	0.68	0.59*	0.3-0.77
Epiphysis (pineal body)	- - -	- - -	- - -	- - -	0.1565	0.1575	0.15-0.20
Thyroid	1.6-3	3	8.5	12-20	30	34	11-60
Thymus (decr. after 15 yrs.)	9-14	17-25	20-26	20-38	14	14	5-25
Parathyroids: Upper pair	- - -	- - -	- - -	- - -	0.028	0.028	
Lower pair	- - -	- - -	- - -	- - -	0.038	0.038	
Heart (greatest at 50)	17-24	37-44	90-94	124-160	300	250	240-360
Lung: Right	21-32	64-75	121-145	200-250	550	400	350-570
Left	18-35	57-75	112-145	190-250	450	350	325-480
Liver	78-150	280-300	450-640	900-960	1600	1500	1200-1800
Stomach	7.5	30	- - -	70	135	135	120-180
Spleen	7.2-11	20-26	52-60	88-93	165	150	80-300
Pancreas	2.6-3	- - -	- - -	70	90	85	60-120
Appendix							1-14
Kidney (each) (Left is larger)	11.5-14	35	55-70	80-95	160	140	120-180
Adrenal (each) larger	3-4	1-2	3.3	3.5-5	6	6	4-10
Prostate (incr. with age)	- - -	- - -	1.8	- - -	20		15-40
Testis and epididymis (each)	0.4	- - -	- - -	- - -	20		15-30
Ovary (each)	0.2-0.5	- - -	- - -	2.5		5	2-8
Uterus: Virgin	- - -	- - -	- - -	- - -		40	30-50
Multiparous	- - -	- - -	- - -	- - -		100	60-120

*In pregnancy, up to 1.

TOXICOLOGIC EXAMINATION

When the identity of the poison is unknown, the specimens listed below should be obtained. Each specimen should be placed in a separate clean container. Label clearly, seal with sealing wax, and lock in refrigerator or take sealed and labeled specimens to the toxicologist personally. Get a signed receipt for the specimens; it may be necessary to appear as a witness if legal procedure follows (see also p. 458).

If liquid preservative is required because of inability to deliver specimen to a toxicologist at once or due to lack of refrigeration, use 100 ml. of 95% Ethyl Alcohol, U.S.P., per 100 Gm. of specimen. Formalin interferes with toxicologic examination.

A. Body Fluids for Examination: (From living patient or postmortem.)
   1. Blood - 50 to 500 ml. or Gm. (may be clotted).
   2. Cerebrospinal fluid - 10 to 100 ml.
   3. Urine - All available.
   4. Vomitus or stomach contents - All available.
   5. Intestinal contents - All available.
B. Body Tissues: Brain, 500 Gm. Liver, 500 Gm. One kidney. One lung. Hair, 10 Gm. Nail clippings, 10 Gm. Muscle, 200 Gm. Bone, 200 Gm.

AVERAGE MEASUREMENTS OF CARDIOVASCULAR STRUCTURES

Heart: Organ as a whole	$13 \times 9 \times 6.5$ cm.
Thickness of atria	1-2 mm.
Thickness of left ventricle	7-15 mm.
Thickness of right ventricle	2-5 mm.
Circumference of mitral valve	7.5-11 cm. (2 fingers)
Circumference of aortic valve	7.5-8 cm.
Circumference of pulmonic valve	8.5 cm. to 9 cm.
Circumference of tricuspid valve	10-13 cm. (3 fingers)
Pulmonary artery circumference	Above heart - 8 cm.
Aorta:	
Circumference above heart	7.4 cm.
Circumference of descending thoracic aorta	4.5-6 cm.
Circumference of abdominal aorta	3.5-6 cm.

CAPACITY OF HOLLOW ORGANS IN ADULTS (in ml.)

Anterior male urethra, 7-10
Colon, about 4000
Esophagus, 100
Gallbladder, 30-50 (avg., 35)
Heart, 120-180

Pericardial cavity, 10-30
Renal pelvis, 7-10
Stomach, 1000 (newborn, 30)
Urinary bladder, 250-500
   (up to 3000 in retention)

24...

Radioisotopes

DEFINITIONS

Isotopes.—Atoms of an element having the same atomic number (number of protons in the nucleus characteristic of the element) but different mass numbers (number of protons plus neutrons, thus different atomic weights). Isotopes may or may not be radioactive. Chemical behavior is characteristic for the element. Isotopes are designated by atomic weight as a superscript before the chemical symbol, e.g., ^{24}Na; ^{131}I; ^{32}P.

Radioactivity.—The phenomenon of emitting radiation during spontaneous atomic nuclear disintegration, e.g., α, β, γ radiation. Atoms of a particular radioactive isotope emit a characteristic radiation at a rate which is always the same fraction of the number of atoms present.

Nuclear Disintegration.—A spontaneous change in which a nucleus emits a particle (α or β particle, neutron, with or without a γ ray), leaving a nucleus with a different atomic number (i.e., a different element). The nuclei of any particular radioisotope always disintegrate in the same manner.

Decay Constant.—A time-rate of disintegration, specific for each isotope.

Half-life.—The time required for disintegration of half the nuclei originally present.

TYPES AND SOURCES OF RADIATION

Alpha Particle.—The nucleus of a helium atom, comprising two protons and two neutrons.

Beta Particle.—An electron (either negatively or positively charged) originating from a nuclear disintegration.

Gamma Ray.—An electromagnetic wave which may be emitted upon nuclear disintegration. Alpha and/or beta particles may be emitted simultaneously.

EQUIPMENT AND METHODS USED FOR MEASURE-
MENT OR DETECTION OF RADIATION

Electroscope. —Radiation passing through an electroscope will ionize gas or air within it, causing leaves of the charged instrument to drop.

Ionization Chamber. —An instrument for measuring radiation quantity as a function of primary and secondary ionization produced by the radiation. One type, the electroscope, is usually used to measure large amounts of radiation. Gas-filled detectors may be used for this purpose or, as in the Geiger-Müller tube, may be used as a counter.

Scintillation Detector. —A device for measuring the light energy (by means of a photomultiplier tube) produced in certain crystals or liquids by radiation. To complete the radiation counter, the number of pulses generated by the detector must be counted by a scaler which registers or totals the pulses, or by a count rate meter which registers the rate at which the pulses occur.

Autoradiograph. —A photographic film which has been exposed to a source of radiation in such a way as to indicate the disposition of the radioactive material in the source.

Monitoring Devices. —These include film badges, pocket ionization chambers, or any radiation detector used for protective purposes to detect exposure to radiation.

UNITS OF RADIOACTIVITY

Curie (c). —The principal unit of radioactivity which results from 3.70×10^{10} nuclear disintegrations per second.

Millicurie (mc). —One-thousandth (0.001) of a curie.

Microcurie (μc). —One millionth (10^{-6}) of a curie.

Nanocurie (nano-c). —One billionth (10^{-9}) of a curie.

UNITS OF DOSAGE

Rad. —Unit of dosage. It corresponds to absorption of 100 ergs per gram of any absorber.

Roentgen (r). —A unit of radiation dose from x-rays or gamma rays. It corresponds to absorption of 83 ergs, or 5.26×10^7 million electron volts (mev) per gram of dry air.

CLINICALLY USEFUL RADIOISOTOPES

Atomic No.	Wt.	Stable Element	Useful Radioisotope	Half-life	Type of Radiation	Clinical Uses — Diagnostic	Clinical Uses — Therapeutic
33	75	Arsenic	^{74}As	17.5 days	beta + beta - gamma	Positron emitter used to localize brain tumors.	None
35	80	Bromine	^{82}Br	35.7 hours	beta - gamma	Chloride distribution in body water.	None
20	40	Calcium	^{47}Ca	5.3 days	beta - gamma	Localization of bone tumors. Calcium metabolism.	None
6	12	Carbon	^{14}C	5730 years	beta -	Metabolism of organic compounds.	None
24	52	Chromium	^{51}Cr	26.5 days	gamma	Red cell and blood volume determination. Red cell tag for red cell survival and spleen scan. Cardiac output. Tagged serum albumin to detect enteric protein loss.	None
27	59	Cobalt	^{57}Co	270 days	gamma	Vitamin B_{12} tagged with ^{57}Co, ^{58}Co, or ^{60}Co in diagnosis of pernicious anemia and malabsorption syndromes.	^{60}Co is used as a source for external, interstitial, and intracavitary irradiation.
			^{58}Co	72 days	beta - gamma		
			^{60}Co	5.3 years	beta - gamma		
29	63 65	Copper	^{64}Cu	12.9 hours	beta - gamma	Copper metabolism (Wilson's disease)	None
9	18	Fluorine	^{18}F	112 minutes	beta +	Bone scan	None
79	197	Gold	^{198}Au	2.7 days	beta - gamma	Space occupying lesions of liver.	Colloidal suspension for malignant disease of pleura and peritoneum. Gold seeds for interstitial or intracavitary therapy.
1	1	Hydrogen	^{3}H	12.3 years	beta -	Metabolism of organic compounds. Total body water determination.	None
26	56	Iron	^{59}Fe	45 days	beta - gamma	Hemoglobin metabolism. Red cell survival and volume determination. Iron absorption and metabolism. Determine iron binding.	None

				Half-life	Radiation	Uses	Therapeutic/Other
49	115	Indium	^{113m}In	1.7 hours	gamma	Lung and liver scan.	None
53	127	Iodine	^{125}I	56–60 days	gamma	Thyroid activity and scanning. Serum thyroxine (or triiodothyronine) binding capacity. Blood volume determination with RISA (radioiodinated serum albumin) or PVP. Determination of cardiac output with RISA. Determination of left-to-right cardiac shunt with methyl and ethyl iodide. Liver function evaluation, detection of space occupying lesion of liver with rose bengal or iodipamide. Renal function evaluation with ^{131}I labeled contrast media. Absorption and excretion studies with labeled fat, RISA, or PVP. Lung scanning with aggregated RISA. Placental localization.	^{131}I in hyperthyroidism. Ablation of thyroid gland. Carcinoma of thyroid, primary or metastatic, which takes up iodine. Labeled iodized oil (Lipiodol®) or iodinated poppyseed oil (Ethiodol®) to treat regional lymph nodes involved by cancer.
			^{131}I	8.1 days	beta – gamma		
			^{128}I	25 minutes	beta – gamma	Short-lived isotopes may be useful for repeated studies.	None
			^{132}I	2.33 hours	beta – gamma		
			^{133}I	21 hours	beta – gamma		
36	84	Krypton	^{85}Kr	10.3 years	beta – gamma	Cerebral blood flow. Detection of cardiac right-to-left or left-to-right shunts.	None
12	24	Magnesium	^{28}Mg	23 hours	beta – gamma	Magnesium metabolism. Body magnesium determination.	None
80	198	Mercury	^{197}Hg	2.7 days	gamma	Tumor and space occupying lesion of brain and kidney. Kidney function. Spleen scan after treating red cells with ^{203}Hg labeled 1-bromo-mercuri-2-hydroxypropane.	None
			^{203}Hg	47.9 days	beta – gamma		
42	96	Molybdenum	^{99}Mo	66 hours	beta – gamma	Liver scan.	None

CLINICALLY USEFUL RADIOISOTOPES (Cont'd.)

Atomic No.	Atomic Wt.	Stable Element	Useful Radioisotope	Half-life	Type of Radiation	Clinical Uses — Diagnostic	Clinical Uses — Therapeutic
15	31	Phosphorus	^{32}P	14.3 days	beta −	Tumor localization. Tissue metabolism. Thyroid scanning for cancer. Avascular bone necrosis. Red cell, white cell, and platelet survival after tagging with ^{32}P-diisopropyl-fluorophosphate.	Blood dyscrasias, including polycythemia vera, chronic leukemia. Rarely in lymphosarcoma, acute leukemia, mycosis fungoides, multiple myeloma. Intracavitary instillation of colloidal suspension in malignant disease of peritoneum and pleura, and of bladder. External application in skin cancers.
19	39	Potassium	^{42}K	12.4 hours	beta − gamma	Localization of brain and breast tumors. Potassium metabolism.	None
88	226	Radium	^{223}Ra	11.2 days	alpha gamma	None	Tumor irradiation.
			^{224}Ra	3.64 days	alpha gamma		
			^{226}Ra	1620 years	alpha gamma		
			^{228}Ra	6.7 years	beta −		
86	222	Radon	^{219}Rn	3.92 seconds	alpha gamma	None	Seeds (capsules of gas) implanted into accessible tumors.
			^{220}Rn	54.5 seconds	gamma		
			^{222}Rn	3.8 days	gamma		
37	85	Rubidium	^{86}Rb	19.5 days	beta − gamma	Substitute for K in determination of body K.	None
34	79	Selenium	^{75}Se	120 days	gamma	Detection of pancreatic tumors and parathyroid tumors with ^{75}selenomethionine.	None

No.	Mass	Element	Isotope	Half-life	Radiation	Diagnostic uses	Therapeutic uses
11	23	Sodium	^{22}Na	2.6 years	beta-gamma	Circulation time. Sodium body space. Radiocardiography, Placental localization. Skin graft timing.	Intracavitary radiation in urinary bladder carcinoma.
			^{24}Na	15 hours	beta-gamma		
38	88	Strontium	^{85m}Sr	65 days	gamma	Bone metabolism. Localization of osseous metastases.	None
			^{87}Sr	2.8 hours	gamma	Bone scan.	
			^{90}Sr	19.9 years	beta-	None	Applicator used mostly in ophthalmology.
16	32	Sulfur	^{35}S	87 days	beta-	Extracellular space volume. Sulfur metabolism.	None
43	99	Technetium	^{99m}Tc	6 hours	gamma	Brain scan with ^{99m}Tc pertechnetate. Scan lung, liver, spleen, placenta with ^{99m}Tc-albumin.	None
39	89	Yttrium	^{90}Y	64.6 hours	beta-	None	Incorporated into ceramic microspheres to embolize nutrient arteries to tumors of lung, prostate, bone, liver.
54	131	Xenon	^{133}Xe	5.27 days	beta-gamma	Cerebral blood flow. Detection of cardiac left-to-right shunt.	None

25...

Diets

Vitamin Requirements.
See Chapter 26.

Mineral Requirements.
A. Calcium: 1.2 to 1.4 Gm. for children and adolescents; 1 Gm. for adults; 1.5 to 2 Gm. for pregnant and lactating women.
B. Iron: 15 mg. for children and menstruating women; 1 mg. for healthy adults.
C. Copper: 1 to 2 mg.
D. Iodine: 0.12 to 0.30 mg.
E. Sodium: 2 to 5 Gm.
F. Phosphorus: 1 to 1.5 Gm. (2.5 to 3 Gm. during pregnancy).
G. Potassium: 1 to 4 Gm.

Fluid Requirements.
See Chapter 27.

TYPES OF DIETS

General Information for the Dietitian.
1. Type of diet.
2. Nature of illness.
3. Patient's appetite.
4. Total daily grams of protein, carbohydrate, and fat.
5. Size and frequency of feedings.
6. Fluid intake desired.
7. Patient's environmental and economic status.

Acid Ash Diet. (Produces excess of acid ash.)

Meat broth	Bread, cereal	Sugar, honey, jelly
Meat, fish, chicken	Crackers	Peanuts, walnuts
Cheese, eggs	Puddings (not fruit)	Corn, asparagus
Rice, pastes	Tea, coffee, cream	Prunes, plums
Pastry, cookies	Butter or substitute	Cranberries

Use only one of the following at any one meal: Fruit, fruit pies, vegetable, or milk.

Avoid:

Dried lima beans
Spinach, beet tops,
chard
Dried apricots, figs

Molasses
Olives
Carrots
Raisins

Alkaline Ash Diet. (Produces excess of alkaline ash.)

Cream vegetable soups
Any fruit (except plums,
prunes, and cran-
berries)
Ice cream, sherbets
Pudding, jello
Milk, fruit juice (except
prune juice)

Tea, coffee
Jelly, jam, honey
Sugar, syrup
Butter or substitute
Shortening, oil
Salad dressing
Any vegetable (except
corn or asparagus)

Use only one of the following at any one meal: Meat, fish,
eggs, corn, asparagus, bread, cereals, crackers, pastry,
rice, pastes.

Avoid (Except as Permitted Above):

Cheese
Meat

Fish
Chicken

Peanuts
Walnuts

Bland Diet.

Normal diet free of tough particles, coarse fibers,
strongly flavored foods, spices and condiments.

Meat broth
Puréed vegetable
soup
Ground beef, lamb,
roasted or broiled
Milk, cheese

Rice, pastes
Fine grain
cereals
Vegetables and
fruits, cooked
and puréed

Plain desserts
Weak tea
Coffee substitutes
Sugar, jelly, jam
Butter or substitute

Avoid:

Whole grain cereals
Aromatic vegetables
(cabbage, onions, etc.)
Tomatoes
Celery
Cucumbers

Dried peas or
beans
Citrus fruits
Pineapple
Plums
Figs, raisins

Fried, greasy foods
Spices and condi-
ments
Pickles
Berries
Nuts

Diabetic Diet.

Calculation of diabetic diets has been greatly simplified
by the advent of the standard American Diabetic Association
exchange diets.

A. Steps in Formulation of a Diabetic Diet:
1. Estimate optimum weight (correct obesity or malnutrition).
2. Estimate basal caloric requirement.

    3. Estimate additional caloric requirement for activity.
    4. Select the diabetic exchange diet corresponding to total estimated caloric need.
    5. Instruct patient in use of the seven simple food exchange lists.

B. Estimate Optimal Body Weight:
    1. See weight chart on p. 633.
    2. Based on height and body frame.

C. Estimate Basal Caloric Requirement: **Definition:** Calories required by a fasting patient resting in bed; ten calories per pound; or total optimal body weight (lb.) × 10.

D. Estimate Additional Caloric Requirement for Activity:
    1. Sedentary worker - Add 50% above basal requirements.
    2. Manual laborer - Add 80-100% above basal requirements.
    3. Bed restriction - Add 30% above basal requirements.

E. Select the Diabetic Association exchange diet corresponding to the estimated caloric need. There are eight choices. Note that each diet has calories distributed approximately as follows: Carbohydrate, 40% of total estimated calories; protein, 20% of total estimated calories; fat, 40% of total estimated calories.

F. Diabetic Association Exchange Diets Available:

	Calories	Carbohydrate	Protein	Fat
1.	1000	90 Gm.	60 Gm.	45 Gm.
2.	1200	125 Gm.	60 Gm.	50 Gm.
3.	1500	150 Gm.	70 Gm.	70 Gm.
4.	1800	180 Gm.	80 Gm.	80 Gm.
5.	2000	210 Gm.	90 Gm.	90 Gm.
6.	2200	250 Gm.	90 Gm.	90 Gm.
7.	2500	250 Gm.	100 Gm.	120 Gm.
8.	3000	300 Gm.	130 Gm.	140 Gm.

    Each of the above diets is modeled around seven basic food groups. Each group is listed in a separate table. Each food in a list, in the amount specified, is approximately equal in composition to any other food in the same list and may be exchanged with others. This permits simplicity of understanding, explanation, and use.

    The seven lists of food exchanges include:

List 1: Vegetables, insignificant carbohydrates
List 2: Vegetables, 7 Gm. carbohydrate per portion
List 3: Fruits
List 4: Breadstuffs
List 5: Meat or protein
List 6: Fat
List 7: Milk

The lists are identical for each of the diets. Increase
or decrease in calories is accomplished by the number of
exchanges allowed.

Example

Male (actual weight 135 lb.)
Height: 5 feet 7 inches
Frame: Medium
Occupation: Salesman

Estimated optimal weight:
   145 lb. (see table on p. 633)
Estimated basal caloric need:
   145 × 10 = 1450 Calories
Estimated additional calories for activity:
   +60% = 870 Calories   1450 Calories
               870 Calories
Total estimated caloric need: 2320 Calories
Diet prescribed: 2200 Calorie A.D.A. Exchange Diet

Elimination Diets.
  These diets consist of foods which seldom cause allergy.
Foods which are prone to produce allergic reactions are eliminated (e. g., wheat, milk, egg, fish, nuts, spices, the cabbage group of vegetables, oranges, apples, bananas, berries,
tea, coffee, honey). Elimination of these allergens in various
combinations leaves a list of available foods difficult to prepare from the standpoint of basic food requirements and palat-
ability without the aid of special recipes. These are beyond
the scope of this book. (See A. Rowe: Elimination Diets and
the Patient's Allergies, 2nd Ed. Lea & Febiger, 1944.)

High-Protein, High-Carbohydrate, Low-Fat Diet.
  Fortify the low-fat diet (p. 410) with foods high in protein
and CHO but low in fat content. Large amounts of lean meat
or fish, eggs, skimmed milk or buttermilk, cottage cheese,
cereals, breads, fruit juices, sugar, jelly, and rock candy
should be used. These may be supplemented with protein
hydrolysates and concentrated CHO preparations.

Low-Calorie Diets. (Reducing diets.)
 A. Eat only the amount and type of foods listed. Candy or
   sweet or alcoholic beverages are not allowed.
 B. One serving of fruit or vegetable = one-half cup. Interchange as indicated (see p. 414).
 C. One 10% vegetable = one 10% fruit = two 5% vegetables or
   fruits = one-half 20% vegetable or fruit (see fruit and
   vegetable list on p. 414).
 D. No fried foods or gravy.

800 Calories (Daily Intake)

Clear broth
4 × 4 × 1/2 inch serving lean
  meat, fish, or poultry
Small serving lean meat, fish,
  poultry, or 1/2 cup cottage
  cheese
2 glasses skimmed milk or
  buttermilk
5% vegetable - 5 servings

10% vegetable - 1 serving
10% fruit or juice - 1 serving
5% fruit or juice - 3 servings
1 egg, not fried
1/2 slice bread
Coffee or tea, no sugar or
  cream
1 tsp. butter or substitute

1200 Calories (Daily Intake)

Clear broth
4 × 4 × 1/2 serving lean meat,
  fish, poultry, or 2 eggs, or
  1/2 cup cottage cheese
Small serving lean meat, fish,
  poultry, or 1 egg, or 1 oz.
  cheddar cheese
2 glasses skimmed milk or
  buttermilk
5% vegetable - 3 servings

10% vegetable - 2 servings
20% vegetable - 1 serving
10% fruit or juice - 3 servings
15% fruit or juice - 1 serving
1 egg, not fried
1 slice bread
Coffee or tea, no sugar or
  cream
1 tsp. butter or substitute

Low-Fat, Nongasforming Diet.

Cook without fat. The objective is to provide 45 Gm. of
fat per day. Highly seasoned foods are avoided.
  A. Soups: Clear broth, soups made with skimmed milk,
     vegetable soup.
  B. Meats and Meat Substitutes: Lean beef, lamb, veal, dark
     meat of fowl, white meat of chicken, turkey without skin,
     white fish, shellfish, liver, cottage cheese (dry, edam),
     eggs (one daily).
  C. Starches: Bread (white, whole wheat, rye), cereals, rice,
     potatoes, pastes.
  D. Vegetables: All except those listed below.
  E. Fruits and Fruit Juices: All except those listed below.
  F. Desserts: Angel food cake, fruit whips with egg white,
     gelatin, Jello®, Junket® or plain pudding with skimmed
     milk, sherbet, water ices, jam, jelly, honey.

Avoid:

Rich, greasy soups
Pork, ham, bacon
Gravy
Cabbage
Cauliflower
Brussels sprouts

Pickles
Peppers
Dried peas and
  beans
Biscuits, muffins
Waffles, pancakes

Gumdrops, jelly beans
Coconuts
Whole milk, cream
Eggnogs, milk shakes
Ice cream, chocolate
Oils, mayonnaise

Broccoli	Raw apples	Potato chips, corn
Onions	Avocados, melons	chips
Turnips	Spices, condiments	Snack crackers
Olives	Rich pastry, cookies	Nuts, peanut butter
Radishes	Marshmallows	Fried foods

Low Saturated Fat Diet. (Polyunsaturated fats increased.)

This diet is similar to the low-fat diet (above) except that the additional foods listed below are allowed. Detailed diets plus recipes are available from local heart associations and from the American Heart Association, 44 East 23rd St., New York City.

Low-fat cottage cheese
Eggs, up to 3 per week (egg whites ad lib.)
Gumdrops, jelly beans, marshmallows
Spices
Fats: Oils - cottonseed (Wesson®), corn (Mazola®), saf-
flower, soy bean, walnuts. Margarines - Award®,
Mazola®, Emdee®. Avocados and olives (sparingly).
(Use 5-6 Tbsp. vegetable oil or substitute each day.)

Low-Purine Diet.

Avoid: More than one serving weekly of meat, poultry, or fish. The following are to be completely avoided:

Meat soup, broth	Anchovies
Liver, kidney, brains	Sardines
Sweetbreads	Herring
Liverwurst, other sausage	Meat extracts, gravies
Meat sauces	Lima or fried beans
Whole grain cereals	Lentils
or bread	Radishes, celery
Asparagus, cauliflower	Onions
Spinach, eggplant	Alcohol, tea, coffee
Watercress	Spices, condiments
Mushrooms	Mincemeat
Peas	Highly seasoned foods

Low-Residue Diet.

Give meat finely ground or roasted or as tender chops or steak, vegetables and fruits (except those listed below). These should be cooked and puréed.

Avoid:

Whole grain cereals	Onions	Coconut
Coarse dark bread	Garlic	Seed fruits
Cabbage	Leeks	Raisins
Cauliflower	Turnips	Milk
Brussels sprouts	Radishes	Jams
Broccoli	Cucumbers	Nuts

Meulengracht Diet.

  7:30 a.m.: Tea, white bread, butter.

10:00 a.m.: Oatmeal and milk, white bread, butter.

  1:00 p.m.: Meat or fish balls; meat, vegetable or fish gratin; broiled chops; tamales, omelet, mashed potatoes, vegetable purées, soups, puddings, white bread, butter, tea.

  3:00 p.m.: Cocoa.

  6:00 p.m.: Sliced tender meats, cheese, white bread, butter, tea.

Patient may eat as much as he wishes.

Salt-Restricting Diets.

The average American diet contains 6 to 15 Gm. salt per day. The low-salt, salt-free, low-sodium, Karell, and rice diets are salt-restricting diets. Salt substitutes containing no sodium may be used for flavoring.

A. Low-salt Diet: The average diet with no salt at the table. Contains 4 to 6 Gm. salt per day.

B. Salt-free Diet: The average diet with no salt used in preparing food or at the table. Contains 2 to 4 Gm. salt per day.

C. Low-sodium Diet: Contains 350 mg. sodium (Na) in the entire diet. Prepared without salt, baking powder, or baking soda.

    2 servings ($4 \times 4 \times 1/2$ inch) of beef, lamb, veal, chicken, salmon, halibut, turkey, duck, rabbit; 1 egg daily.

    No more than 6 slices of salt-free, unleavened bread.

    No more than 2 servings ($3/4$ cup) cooked cereals, puffed rice or wheat, rice, or pastes.

    3 to 4 servings ($1/2$ cup) of fresh or frozen (NOT CANNED) vegetables.

    3 to 4 servings ($1/2$ cup) of fresh, canned, or frozen fruits.

    Unsalted butter, vegetable oils, shortenings, mayonnaise.

    Fruit juices, tea, coffee, salt-free dried milk (Lonalac®).

    Sweets, puddings made with dried milk, tapioca, cornstarch and flavorings. Pie made with vegetable shortening, flour and water, and fruit filling (see above). Unsalted nuts or popcorn, plain gelatin.

    Flavorings: Cocoa, chocolate, maple, peppermint, lemon, orange, and vanilla. Spices: Cinnamon, allspice, nutmeg, paprika, ginger, pepper, dried mustard, thyme, rosemary, parsley, bay leaves, sesame seeds, caraway seeds, mace, sage, vinegar.

Avoid:

All food or medicinal preparations which contain added
SODIUM as salt, baking powder or soda, sodium benzoate, etc.

Canned or dehydrated soups, bouillon cubes.

Canned, seasoned, smoked, or dried meats or fish,
sweetbreads, cheese of any kind.

Baked products, cereals, or flours employing baking
powder or soda (bread, muffins, crackers, pastries,
waffles, pancakes, etc.).

Canned vegetable or fruit juices, sauerkraut, dandelion
greens, celery, kale, beet greens, spinach, chard,
frozen peas, or lima beans.

Liquid milk or milk products. No "ready to use" preparations such as pudding mixes, pie fillings or crust,
prepared gelatine desserts, commercial syrups, molasses or candy, seasoning or condiments containing
salt.

D. Karell Diet: 800 ml. of milk daily given in quantities of
200 ml. at desired intervals. No other food or fluid.
Contains approximately 500 mg. of sodium.

E. Rice Diet: 300 Gm. of rice, 20 Gm. of protein (no animal
protein), 5 Gm. of fat, 150 mg. of sodium, carbohydrates
as fruits or fruit juices to make 2000 Calories, vitamins,
and 1000 ml. of water daily.

Rice - Brown, white, wild, or puffed; boiled or steamed. Give 1 1/2 cups 3 times daily.

Sugar - Granulated, brown, or powdered. Pure sugar candy.

Fruit juices - Five 8-oz. glasses per day. Fresh fruit preferred. Canned fruit if nothing but sugar has been added.

Fruit - Any fresh fruit; canned or dried fruit if nothing but sugar has been added.

Avoid:

Salt - in preparing or eating.

Fats - in preparing food.

Limit fluids to 1000 ml. fruit juice daily. No water.

Avocados, nuts, or dates.

Baking powder.

Any medication containing sodium.

Tomato or other vegetable juices.

Sippy Diets.

Buffering, non-irritating foods given on STRICT
SCHEDULE.

Stage   I - 3 oz. (90 ml.) equal parts milk and cream
every hour from 7:00 a.m. to 7:00 p.m.
Night feedings if necessary.

Stage II - Stage I plus addition of fine-grain cereals, cooked eggs, toast, butter, mashed potatoes. Give these foods as one additional serving the first day, two the second day, etc., and as desired by the fourth day. Orange and fruit juices may be taken as desired if distaste for milk occurs.

Stage III - Three meals daily with 6 oz. (120 ml.) milk and cream mixture at 10:00 a.m., 2:00 p.m., and 8:00 p.m.; add to Stage II puréed vegetables, cottage cheese, rice, pastes, plain puddings, gelatin desserts. Alkalies are given on alternate hours between meals and formula. AVOID meats, fish, poultry, cheese (other than cottage cheese), raw vegetables, fried foods, spices and condiments, meat soups, tea, or coffee.

Stage IV - Stage III plus three or four servings weekly of boiled or broiled beef, lamb, chicken, or fish.

CARBOHYDRATE COMPOSITION OF FRUITS AND VEGETABLES

Five Per Cent.

Artichokes	Chard	Rhubarb
Asparagus	Cucumbers	Sauerkraut
Bamboo shoots	Eggplant	Spinach
Beet greens	Endive	Strawberries
Broccoli	Green peppers	String beans
Brussels	Lemons	Summer
sprouts	Lettuce	squash
Cabbage	Okra	Tomatoes
Cantaloupe	Peaches*	Watercress
Cauliflower	Radishes	Watermelon
Celery	Romaine	Zucchini
	lettuce	

Ten Per Cent.

Applesauce (no	Celery root	Oranges
sugar)	Cherries*	Peaches
Apricots*	Cranberries	Pears*
Beets	Gooseberries	Pineapples*
Blackberries	Grapefruit	Pumpkins
Canned peas	Honeydew melon	Rutabagas
Carrots	Leeks	Tangerines
Casaba melon	Onions	Winter squash

*Water-packed.

Fifteen Per Cent.

Apples	Currants	Pears
Apricots	Figs*	Pineapples
Blueberries	Grapes	Plums
Cherries	Loganberries	Raspberries

Twenty Per Cent.

Bananas	Green beans	Parsnips
Corn	Guavas	Pomegranates
Figs	Kumquats	White
Fresh green peas	Mangoes	potatoes

*Water-packed.

26...

Vitamins*

The body requires calories, proteins, vitamins, minerals, and perhaps fat. Deficiency disease may occur if intake or absorption of any of these is decreased or if losses or requirements are increased. Early signs of vitamin deficiency are often nonspecific and are easily overlooked. Manifest deficiency follows inadequate diet (alcoholism, obesity, therapeutic, poverty, or habitual); decreased absorption (anorexia, vomiting, diarrhea, intestinal disease); or increased need (infection, pregnancy, growth, thyrotoxicosis). Vitamin deficiencies are usually multiple, particularly of the fat-soluble or B complex groups.

The water-soluble vitamins (vitamin C, vitamin B complex) are diffusible; except in the case of vitamin B_{12} in pernicious anemia, deficiencies rarely result from impaired passage across the intestinal wall. Storage in the body is slight, and deficient diet is followed by signs of deprivation in about four months. Because these vitamins are readily excreted in the urine, toxic accumulations in the body are rare.

The fat-soluble vitamins (vitamins A, D, E, and K) are absorbed with lipids so that absorption difficulties may be expected with steatorrhea or biliary obstruction. The body has great storage capacity for these vitamins; except in the case of vitamin K, signs of deprivation do not appear until after more than a year of deficient intake. Toxic levels in the body may accumulate, as the fat-soluble vitamins are not appreciably excreted in the urine.

Both water-soluble and fat-soluble vitamins may be synthesized by intestinal flora.

The best and only certain source of all the vitamins is a well-balanced diet. Crude sources of vitamins such as brewer's yeast or wheat germ may provide unknown factors absent in purified or synthetic vitamins. Therapeutically, vitamins are most often given in five to ten times the daily maintenance allowance. Water-soluble vitamins should be given in divided doses to prevent excessive urinary waste.

Canning and cooking procedures may cause vitamins to be destroyed or lost, particularly when cooking water is discarded. When a restricted diet is unavoidable, a daily supplement of purified vitamins is useful.

---

*Therapeutic doses of vitamins are given on pp. 521-2.

WATER-SOLUBLE VITAMINS

Vitamin C.
   A. Sources: Citrus fruits, tomatoes, leafy green vegetables,
      Irish potatoes. Copper utensils, heating, air contact,
      and alkalinity all reduce vitamin C content of foods.
      Vitamin C may have to be added to infants' formulas; it
      is present in breast milk.
   B. Manifestations of Deficiency:
      1. Symptoms and signs -
         a. Early - Impaired wound healing and impaired resis-
            tance to infection and other stress.
         b. Late - Scurvy, bone changes, fragile capillaries
            with multiple hemorrhages.
      2. Laboratory findings -
         a. The ascorbic acid level in plasma, the white cells,
            and platelets may be determined chemically. Levels
            are low in deficiency states and in some normal in-
            dividuals.
         b. Test for deficiency - The administration of 15 mg.
            of ascorbic acid I.M. per Kg. of body weight, with
            determination of plasma ascorbic acid levels at two,
            three, four, and five hours, produces a maximum
            rise in level of less than 0.4 mg. per 100 ml. in
            deficiency states.

Vitamin B$_1$ (Thiamine).
   A. Sources: Whole-grain cereals (wheat, rice, barley),
      green vegetables, liver, lean meat (especially organ
      meats), and peanuts. The vitamin is produced synthet-
      ically; no natural tissue is a rich source. One Gm. of
      Dried Yeast Tablets, U.S.P., contains not less than
      0.2 mg.
   B. Manifestations of Deficiency:
      1. Symptoms and signs -
         a. Early - Multiple vague complaints suggesting neu-
            rasthenia. Anorexia and paresthesias also occur.
         b. Late - Loss of appetite; polyneuritis, particularly
            of legs; Wernicke's syndrome; beriberi heart (pal-
            pitation, tachycardia, high-output failure, edema);
            electrocardiographic changes (flat T wave and pro-
            longed Q-T interval); constipation, and growth
            failure. Need for thiamine is increased with high-
            carbohydrate intake or increase in metabolism.
      2. Laboratory findings - Blood thiamine levels do not de-
         pendably indicate deficiency. Thiamine deficiency is
         characterized in the laboratory by elevated blood
         pyruvic acid levels (above 1.2 mg./100 ml.), lowered
         blood lactic acid/pyruvic acid ratios after glucose is

given; and elevated urinary excretion of pyruvic acid.
Measurement of cardiac size and determination of
venous pressure and circulation time are useful.

Basal blood pyruvic acid concentrations above 1.2
mg./100 ml. may indicate impaired pyruvic acid
metabolism in the absence of the vitamin. Measurement of cardiac size, venous pressure, and circulation time help to characterize beriberi heart.

C. Toxic Effects of Excess: Thiamine overdosage may produce toxicity through formation of excessive amounts of
acetylcholine; epinephrine is an effective antidote.

Vitamin B₂ (Riboflavin).

A. Sources: Milk, liver, lean meat, and leafy green vegetables, and Dried Yeast Tablets, U.S.P., 1 Gm. (containing 0.04 mg. of riboflavin).

B. Manifestations of Deficiency:
  1. Symptoms and signs - Cheilosis, vascular keratitis,
     glossitis (magenta tongue), and seborrhea (symptoms
     may develop slowly after deprivation, indicating pos-
     sible storage form of vitamin in body); poor growth,
     lack of vigor, malaise, weakness, weight loss, scrotal
     dermatitis, photophobia.
  2. Laboratory findings - Serum riboflavin levels below
     3 mcg./100 ml. and reduced urinary levels in 24-hour
     specimens or following load tests occur with deficiency.

Nicotinic Acid (PP Factor).

A. Sources: Dried Yeast Tablets, U.S.P., 1 Gm. (containing 0.25 mg. of nicotinic acid), whole-grain cereals,
lean beef and pork, and peanuts.

B. Manifestations of Deficiency:
  1. Symptoms and signs -
     a. Early - Reduction of cellular respiration produces
        multiple vague complaints, lassitude, indigestion,
        and nervous instability. Isoniazid therapy may
        aggravate the deficiency.
     b. Late - Pellagra with dermatitis, diarrhea, demen-
        tia, glossitis, stomatitis. Death may occur.
  2. Laboratory findings - The niacin metabolite, N^1-methyl-
     nicotinamide, may be made fluorescent and hence
     measured. Urinary excretion of this material is de-
     creased in mild and severe nicotinic acid deficiency,
     but there is great overlap of values between deficient
     patients and those showing no evidence of deficiency.
     The anemia of pellagra may vary from microcytic to
     macrocytic.

C. Toxic Effects of Excess: After I.V. administration, fall
of blood pressure may be severe; anaphylactic reactions
occur rarely.

Vitamin B₆ (Pyridoxine).

A. Sources: As for other members of vitamin B complex.
The average adult requirement is approximately 1.5 to 2
mg./day.

B. Manifestations of Deficiency:

1. Symptoms and signs - Convulsive seizures (infants),
seborrheic dermatitis, cheilitis, keratitis, weight
loss, anorexia, drowsiness, weakness, severe neur-
opathy. Pyridoxine is essential for normal neuronal
function and may have a role in production of arteriosclerosis and prevention of dental caries. Deficiency
may develop during treatment of tuberculosis with
isoniazid. Deficiency also increases urinary oxalate
excretion, which has been implicated in the formation
of renal calculi.

2. Laboratory findings - Elevation of blood urea is prolonged beyond 12 hours after a test dose of DL-alanine,
and xanthurenic acid excretion is increased after tryptophan is given. Pyridoxine returns xanthurenic acid
excretion to normal.

Folic Acid (Pteroylglutamic Acid).

A. Sources: As for other vitamins of the B complex. The
average diet contains 0.15 mg. of total folic acid activity;
0.05 mg. of crystalline folic acid daily prevents depletion
of serum folic acid.

B. Manifestations of Deficiency:

1. Symptoms and signs - Folic acid coenzymes catalyze
the synthesis of purines and thymine, the methylated
pyrimidine of DNA (desoxyribonucleic acid). In deficiency states, it is thought that the characteristic
leukopenia, macrocytic anemia, and megaloblastic
marrow result when insufficient RNA (ribonucleic
acid) is converted to permit the doubling of DNA necessary for chromosome production and consequent
cell division. Diarrhea, gingivitis, and failure to
grow may appear. Deficiency develops slowly and is
difficult to produce because intestinal microorganisms
synthesize the vitamin. Excessive use of folic acid
antagonists, as in the treatment of leukemias and
lymphomas, may cause a syndrome not unlike that
occurring after massive irradiation, characterized by
leukopenia, bloody diarrhea, depression, coma, and
death.

2. Laboratory findings - Excretion of less than 1.5 mg.
of folic acid after an oral dose of 5 mg. indicates
severe tissue depletion or malabsorption. Comparison of excretion rates after oral and parenteral doses
may demonstrate malabsorption. Marked increase in
urine levels of the abnormal metabolite formimino-

glutamic acid (FIGLU) after ingestion of 20 Gm. of histidine is a sensitive indicator of folic acid deficiency.

Vitamin B_{12} (Cyanocobalamin).

A. Sources: Cyanocobalamin is present in a large variety of foods, particularly liver.

B. Manifestations of Deficiency:

1. Symptoms and signs - Deficiency of this vitamin is manifested by pernicious anemia with typical macrocytic cells in blood and gastrointestinal epithelium, gastric achylia, glossitis, changes in the nervous system, and megaloblastic hyperplasia of the bone marrow. Like folic acid (above), vitamin B_{12} is involved in DNA and RNA activity.

2. Laboratory findings - Normally, after an oral dose of 0.5 mcg. of vitamin B_{12}-labeled Co^{58} or Co^{60}, less than 50% is excreted in the stools, more than 6% in the urine. If a urine specimen is lost, a false-positive test may result. Microbiologic assays of serum vitamin B_{12} levels normally average 0.02 mcg./100 ml.

FAT-SOLUBLE VITAMINS

Vitamin A.

A. Sources: Fish liver oil, leafy green and yellow vegetables, whole milk, butter, cheese, eggs, and human milk.

B. Manifestations of Deficiency:

1. Symptoms and signs -
   a. Early - Dryness of the skin, night blindness, photophobia, follicular keratosis (in adults).
   b. Late - Xerophthalmia, atrophy and keratinization of skin, keratomalacia. All mucous membranes may be involved.

2. Laboratory findings - Plasma vitamin levels may be measured by colorimetric or spectrophotometric means, but may not parallel the nutritional state as well as the level of serum carotene, where concentrations less than 80 I.U./ml. (50 mcg./100 ml.) are presumptive of low dietary intake or impaired absorption.

C. Toxic Effects of Excess: Ingestion of more than 50,000 units of vitamin A daily over a six-month period may cause a syndrome characterized by subcutaneous swelling, hyperostoses, anorexia, pruritus, scaly lips, bleeding fissures at the corners of the mouth, excoriated skin, sparse and coarse hair, hepatomegaly and splenomegaly, leukopenia, anemia, increased serum lipids, and a bleeding tendency, probably due to hypoprothrombinemia. Such persons may have plasma vitamin A levels from 400 to 2000 units/100 ml. The symptoms and signs and the bone lesions disappear over two or three months after withdrawal of the vitamin.

Vitamin D₂ (calciferol, from irradiation of ergosterol), and
   Vitamin D₃ (from irradiation of 7-dehydrocholesterol).

A. Sources: Fish liver oil, egg yolk, salmon, herring, tuna, sardines, and pig and beef liver. Natural foodstuffs are often limited in content. Vitamin D₃ is formed in the skin as the result of exposure of 7-dehydrocholesterol to ultraviolet light.

B. Manifestations of Deficiency:
   1. Symptoms and signs - Rickets in children (low serum phosphorus, elevated serum alkaline phosphatase), delayed bone growth, defective tooth structure, tetany in infants (low serum calcium), osteomalacia in adults.
   2. Laboratory findings - X-rays of bones are characteristic in infantile rickets, suggestive in adult osteomalacia. In both conditions, serum calcium and phosphorus levels are normal or reduced, serum alkaline phosphatase levels elevated (usual diagnostic titer is 20 to 40 units/100 ml.).

C. Toxic Effects of Excess: Individual variations, exposure to ultraviolet light, and calcium intake affect tolerance to large doses of vitamin D. Continued daily doses of 1800 to 150,000 U.S.P. units may mobilize calcium from bone and cause metastatic calcification in soft tissues. The early symptoms of intoxication (those of hypercalcemia) include anorexia, nausea, headache, polyuria, and diarrhea; in children, pallor and lassitude. Later, weakness, fatigue, renal damage with azotemia, metastatic calcification, and depression appear. Hypochromic normocytic anemia may occur in adults. Serum and urine calcium should be determined frequently when large doses of vitamin D must be given; an increase in serum calcium to above 11 mg./100 ml. is justification for discontinuing vitamin D therapy.

Vitamin E.

It is not yet possible to assign a specific physiologic function to vitamin E, but it apparently is an anti-oxidant. It is possible, by altering the fat and protein content and other components of a vitamin E—deficient diet, to induce a wide variety of signs and symptoms in experimental animals. Many observations in experimental animals cannot be repeated in man.

There is no evidence that vitamin E is required in the diet of normal persons. It is estimated that the daily adult requirement varies between 10 and 30 mg./day. Creatinuria

and pentosuria, associated with a difficulty of fat absorption,
may be relieved by vitamin E, but there is no other evidence
of significant pharmacodynamic action or therapeutic application.

Vitamin E is abundantly available in an ordinary diet.
Rich sources are lettuce, wheat-germ oil, alfalfa, molasses,
peas, and whole rice.

Vitamin E is apparently essential, and may be of benefit
in patients with malabsorption, in those whose diets are low
in fats, and in some infants with macrocytic or hemolytic
anemias.

Vitamin K.

A. Sources: Soybeans, hog liver fat, cabbage, alfalfa, egg
   yolk, and spinach. Deficiency rarely results from lack
   in diet if intestinal synthesis is not impaired.

B. Manifestations of Deficiency: Hypoprothrombinemia and
   hemorrhage in the form of epistaxis, spontaneous bleeding
   into the skin, bowel, or bladder, or excessive bleeding at
   the site of local trauma. . Hypoprothrombinemia may be
   due to overdosage of bishydroxycoumarin or secondary to
   the administration of large doses or prolonged use of
   salicylates, sulfonamides, and barbiturates. The newborn infant has low plasma levels of several coagulating
   factors in the prothrombin complex. Small doses of
   vitamin K administered to newborn infants may be of
   some value in decreasing neonatal hemorrhage. It is
   especially indicated for infants with greater susceptibility to neonatal hemorrhage (prematurity, anoxia). The
   value of vitamin K has yet to be clearly established.

C. Toxic Effects of Excess: With the possible exceptions
   noted above, the routine administration of vitamin K to
   newborn infants has been discontinued, as hemolytic anemia, hyperbilirubinemia, jaundice, hepatomegaly, and
   death may follow large doses.

27...

Fluid and Electrolyte Balance

Millequivalents in Acid-Base Chemistry.

To convert mg. /100 ml. to mEq. /L. :

$$\text{mEq. /L.} = \frac{\text{mg. /100 ml.} \times 10 \times \text{valence}}{\text{atomic wt.}}$$

For CO_2, $\text{mEq. /L.} = \dfrac{\text{Vol. \% } \times 10}{22.2}$

	Valence	Atomic Wt.
Cations (Base +)		
Sodium	1	23
Potassium	1	39
Calcium	2	40
Magnesium	2	24
Anions (Acid $^-$)		
CO_2 ($HCO_3{}^-$)	1	(22.2 liters/mol)
Chloride	1	35.5
Phosphorus*	Varies with pH At pH 7.4 =1.8	31
Protein	mEq. /L. =	(Gm. /100 ml. × 2.43)

Electrolytes of Plasma and Interstitial Fluid. †

Normal concentrations of electrolytes in plasma and interstitial fluid are listed in the following table:

Cations (Base +)	mEq. /L.	Anions (Acid $^-$)	mEq. /L.
Sodium	142	Bicarbonate	28
Potassium	5	Chloride	103
Calcium	5	Organic Acids	6
Magnesium	3	Phosphate	1
Total	155	Sulfate	1
		Protein	16
		Total	155

*Phosphorus, if reported in this fashion, is better reported as millimols/L. $\left[\text{mM./L.} = \dfrac{\text{mg. /100 ml.} \times 10}{31} \right]$

†Interstitial fluid contains almost no protein.

ACIDOSIS AND ALKALOSIS

Alteration of pH of Extracellular Fluid by Change of Bicarbonate Buffer $\frac{[H^+][HCO_3^-]}{[B^+][HCO_3^-]}$; Causes, Signs and Symptoms

Physiological State	Change in Numerator $[H^+][HCO_3^-]$	Change in Denominator $[B^+][HCO_3^-]$	Causes	Signs and Symptoms
Respiratory acidosis High pCO2 pH < 7.4	Increases due to pulmonary retention of CO_2.	Lags behind change in numerator, but increases to compensate and restore normal ratio and pH.	Retention of H_2CO_3 as result of increased alveolar CO_2 tension. 1. Impaired airway - Asthma, bronchiolitis. 2. Impaired diffusion - Emphysema, pulmonary fibrosis, pulmonary edema. 3. Impaired respiratory muscles - Poliomyelitis. 4. Respiratory center depression - Morphine.	Alteration of respiration according to cause. Dyspnea common. Cyanosis often present.
Metabolic acidosis Low serum HCO_3^- pH < 7.4	Lags behind denominator as lung blows off CO_2 to compensate and restore normal ratio and pH.	Decreases as result of displacement by other anions or loss of $NaHCO_3$.	A. Loss of Base: 1. Lower GI tract loss, as in fistulae and diarrhea. 2. Renal loss of base. B. Decrease of $B \cdot HCO_3$ due to increase of other anions: 1. Increase of organic acids, as in diabetes, starvation, renal failure, and dehydration. 2. Acid salt ingestion - NH_4Cl; $CaCl_2$.	Respiratory rate and depth increased. Dehydration evident. Coma.
Respiratory alkalosis Low pCO2 pH > 7.4	Decreases due to hyperventilation.	Lags behind numerator but decreases to compensate and restore ratio and pH.	Reduced alveolar CO_2 tension: Hyperventilation, as occasionally in encephalitis, improper use of respirator. Commonest cause is functional hyperventilation.	"Overbreathing" (deep, rapid respiration), tetany, convulsions.
Metabolic alkalosis High serum HCO_3^- pH > 7.4	Lags behind denominator as respiration changes to retain CO_2 and restore ratio and pH.	Increases as result of loss of Cl^- or ingestion of HCO_3^-.	A. Loss of HCl in gastric juice. B. Ingestion of alkali: $NaHCO_3$, $CaCO_3$. C. Secondary to potassium deficit. D. Hyperadrenocorticism (especially aldosteronism) with potassium deficit.	Respiratory rate and depth decreased. Tetany; convulsions. Often asymptomatic.

Electrolytes of Intracellular Fluid.

Cations	mEq./L.	Anions	mEq./L.
Potassium	140	Bicarbonate	10
Magnesium	45	Organic acid phosphate	100
Sodium (variable)	10	Sulfate	20
Total	195	Protein	65
		Total	195

Volume and Electrolyte Content of Gastrointestinal Secretions and Sweat
(Modified from Lockwood and Randall, Bull. N.Y. Acad. Med. **25**:228, 1949.)

	Avg. 24-hr. Vol. in ml.	Electrolytes in mEq./L.			
		Na$^+$	K$^+$	Cl$^-$	HCO$_3^-$
Extracellular fluid		145	3	111	28
Gastric juice					
Containing acid	2500	10-110	1-32	8-155	0
Achlorhydria		8-120	1-30	100	20
Bile	500	130-160	2-12	90-120	38
Pancreatic juice	700	110-150	2-8	50-95	70-110
Small bowel suction	100-6000	80-150	2-8	40-135	30
Ileostomy					
Recent	100-4000	100-150	5-30	90-140	30
Adapted	100- 500	50	3	20	15-30
Cecostomy	100-3000	50	8	40	15
Feces (formed)	100	<10	<10	<15	<15
Sweat	500-10,000	0-100	0-5	0-100	0

Acid-Base Balance.

Minor alterations of ion concentration occur in interstitial fluid in response to physical laws governing the production of an ultrafiltrate of plasma (Gibbs-Donnan effect).

The pH of extracellular fluid depends on the buffer systems of the "weak acids" present. Of lesser importance are the buffer systems of phosphate and protein. The principal buffer system is that of $\dfrac{(H^+)\ (HCO_3^-)}{(B^+)\ (HCO_3^-)}$

When these substances are present in a ratio of 1:20 $\left[\text{normally,}\ \dfrac{(H^+)\ (HCO_3^-)}{(B^+)\ (HCO_3^-)} = \dfrac{1.35\ \text{mEq./L.}}{27\quad \text{mEq./L.}} \right]$, pH will be maintained at about 7.4. A change in ratio due to an increase of the numerator (carbonic acid portion) or a decrease of the denominator (base portion) produces acidosis, with decrease in pH. A decrease of the numerator (carbonic acid portion) or an increase of the denominator (base portion) produces alkalosis, with increase in pH.

POTASSIUM DEFICIT AND HYPOKALEMIA

Causes.
   A. Poor Intake: Starvation or upper gastrointestinal tract obstruction.
   B. Poor Absorption: Steatorrhea, short bowel syndrome, regional enteritis.
   C. Loss: (1) Gastrointestinal due to emesis, fistulae, diarrhea, suction. (2) Renal due to congenital tubular defect, renal failure, diabetic acidosis (diuresis), alkalosis. Continuous renal excretion even in face of lack of intake or absorption. Effects of diuretics. (3) Cutaneous due to burns or freezing with loss of interstitial fluid.
   D. Endocrine: Adrenocortical hormone excess, testosterone, insulin, glucose.
   E. Idiopathic: (Intracellular storage.) Familial periodic paralysis.

Clinical Manifestations.
   A. Symptoms and Signs: Weakness of muscles, including those of respiration; ineffectual respiratory effort with "fish mouth" breathing; intestinal ileus.
   B. Ecg. as Serum K$^+$ Decreases: Decreased amplitude and broadening of T wave, prominent U wave, sagging S-T segments. A-V block (see below). Changes in serial records and response to administration of potassium are confirmatory.

Correlation of the Serum Potassium Concentration and the Electrocardiogram
(Provided there is no parallel change in Na and Ca)

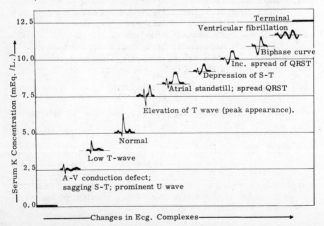

POTASSIUM "EXCESS" AND HYPERKALEMIA

Causes.
   Retention due to:
   A. Failure of the Kidney to Excrete Potassium: Anuria, severe oliguria, severe dehydration.
   B. Overdosage with potassium salts, especially via parenteral route when given too rapidly.

Clinical Manifestations.
   A. Symptoms and Signs: Muscle weakness and paralysis; paresthesias; abdominal distention; diarrhea.
   B. Ecg. as Serum K^+ Rises: Peaked T waves of increased amplitude; atrial arrest; spreading QRS; biphasic QRS-T; ventricular fibrillation. (See diagram on p. 426.)

MAINTENANCE OF FLUID BALANCE

The human organism requires replacement of continuous insensible losses of water through the lungs and skin and the water used for excretion of waste by the kidney. If water and electrolyte losses in the human being are not replaced, dehydration with serious consequences follows within a few days.

Average Daily Requirement of Water and Electrolyte (Assuming Normal Food Consumption)*

	Infant (2-10 Kg.)	Child (10-40 Kg.)	Adolescent or Adult (60 Kg.)
Basal Cal. /Kg.	55-60	60-35	30
Water loss (ml.)			
Urine	200-500	500-800	800-1200
Feces	25-40	40-100	100
Insensible	75-300 (1.3 ml. /Kg. /hr.)	340-600	600-1000 (0.5 ml. /Kg. /hr.)
Total	300-840	840-1500	1500-2300
Water allowance (ml.)			
Total	330-1000	1000-1800	1800-2500
ml. /Kg.	100-165	45-100	30-45
Salt requirement (mEq./Kg./24 hrs.)			
Sodium	1.5	20-50	50-75
Potassium	1.5	20-25	25-50

*Modified after Butler and Talbot, New Eng. J. Med. **231**:585, 1944.

CORRECTION OF ABNORMAL PHYSIOLOGIC STATES

Each patient presents an individual problem. Only general instructions can be given for replacement and maintenance therapy. Many formulas are in common use for determining the amounts of water, sodium, etc., to be administered, but there are so many exceptions to these formulas that they are often of little value. The patient's clinical condition, weight, urine volume and specific gravity, hematocrit, and serum sodium, potassium, chloride, carbon dioxide, urea, and protein provide signposts of therapy.

Condition	Symptoms and Signs	Treatment (see table, p. 430)
Shock	Low BP; pulse rapid; cold, clammy skin. Oliguria, high sp. gr.	Blood, plasma, or substitute in sufficient quantity (see p. 431).
Water deficit	Great thirst; urine scanty with high sp. gr., often high Na^+ concentration. High serum Na^+ and urea.	Water made isotonic with 5-6% glucose. Later, as water loss is replenished, give electrolyte solutions as required.
Salt deficit	No thirst; BP low, orthostatic fainting; cramps; nausea and vomiting. Urine scanty, low in Na^+ and Cl^- (except in Addison's disease).	Physiologic salt solution if deficit is mild. Concentrated (2-3%) salt solution if deficit is severe. Later, as salt deficit is repaired, add dextrose in water, etc.
Metabolic acidosis	Dehydration; rapid, deep respiration; coma; ketonuria; low serum CO_2.	Saline or Hartmann's solution, 40-80 ml./Kg. $M/6$ sodium lactate in smaller quantities determined by degree of acidosis. Dextrose in water to make up water deficit. Darrow's solution (KNL) if severe K^+ depletion exists.
Metabolic alkalosis	Dehydration; slow, shallow resp.; tetany; low urine volume; high serum CO_2; K^+ deficit common.	Physiologic salt solution. Dextrose in water. Solutions containing potassium but NOT bicarbonate or lactate.
Anuria or severe oliguria (acute renal insufficiency)	Uremia, hyperkalemia.	Limit fluid to maintenance only. Diet restriction to permit severe limitation of fluid and protein intake. Cautious electrolyte replacement.

Variations in Requirements of Water and Electrolytes.

Allowances in the chart on p. 427 must be altered for:

A. Dehydration: Salt and water are both depleted. Give 40 to 80 ml./Kg. of salt-containing solution.

B. Sweating: Insensible loss may be more than doubled.

C. Increased Metabolic Rate and Fever: Insensible loss may be more than doubled, obligatory urine volume increased.

D. Renal Inadequacy:

    1. Increased fluid loss - If polyuria and low specific gravity of urine result, intake must be increased to cover obligatory loss.

    2. Fluid retention - If oliguria results, allowance must be diminished accordingly.

E. Unusual Losses From Gastrointestinal Tract or Burns: Replace water, electrolyte, plasma, blood as indicated.

Parenteral Maintenance of Normal Requirements.

A. Ordinarily, maintenance can be achieved in the average adult suffering no unusual losses (A-E, above) by giving:

    1. Isotonic sodium chloride solution (0.9%), 500 ml.

    2. Dextrose, 5 or 10% in water, 2000 to 2500 ml.

B. Requirements for Prolonged Parenteral Therapy: If parenteral maintenance must be continued longer than 3 to 5 days, potassium losses should be replaced. Potassium solutions should be administered SLOWLY (25 mEq. of K^+ or 2 Gm. KCl in 2 to 3 hours) in order to avoid raising plasma concentration over 6 to 7 mEq./L. Because of the danger of producing high plasma (extracellular fluid) potassium concentrations, potassium solutions should NEVER be administered unless renal function is good. (See hyperkalemia, p. 427.)

Equivalent Values of Salts Used for Therapy

Salt	Gm.	mEq. of Cation per Amount Stated
I.V. or oral		
NaCl	9	155
NaCl	5.8	100
NaCl	1	17
$NaHCO_3$	8.4	100
Na lactate	11.2	100
KCl	1.8	25
K acetate	2.5	25
$\begin{cases} K_2HPO_4 \\ KH_2PO_4 \end{cases}$	1.84 0.4	25
$CaCl_2$	0.5	10
Ca gluconate	2	10
$MgCl_2$	0.5	10
Oral		
K citrate	3	25
K tartrate	5	27

COMPOSITION OF SOLUTIONS FOR PARENTERAL INFUSION*

	Ionic Concentration in mEq./L.							
	Na⁺	K⁺	Ca⁺⁺	Mg⁺⁺	NH₄⁺	Cl⁻	HCO₃⁻ Equiv.	PO₄≡
Isotonic saline (0.9%)	155					155		
Ringer's solution	147	4	6			157		
Ringer's lactate (Hartmann's)	130	4	4			111	27	
M/6 sodium lactate	167						167	
Darrow's solution (KNL)	121	35				103	53	
Potassium chloride, 0.2%, in 5% dextrose		27				27		
Polysal®	140	10	5	3		103	55	
"Modified duodenal solution" with invert sugar	80	36	4.6	2.8		63	60	
"Gastric solution" with invert sugar	63	18			70	151		
Ammonium chloride, 0.9%					170	170		
Examples of "Maintenance Solutions":								
Levulose or dextrose with electrolyte #48	25	20		3		22	23	3
Levulose or dextrose with electrolyte #75	40	35				40	20	15
Levulose and dextrose with electrolyte (Butler's II)	57	25		6		50	25	13
Dextrose in 0.2% saline	34					34		
Dextrose in 0.33% saline	51					51		
Dextrose in 0.45% saline	77					77		

AMPULS (Note Directions with ampul.) CONTENTS PER AMPUL

Potassium phosphate†, 20 ml.		40						40
Potassium chloride†, 20 ml.		40				40		
KMC†		25	10	10		45		
Calcium gluconate, 10%, 10 ml.			4.5				4.5	
Sodium bicarbonate§, 7.5%, 50 ml.	45						45	
Sodium lactate§, molar, 40 ml.	40						40	

*Many other types of solutions are commercially available and may be used.

†Dilute to 1 L.

§Dilute as indicated by manufacturer.

TRANSFUSIONS

Choice of Material for Transfusion.
A. Shock Due to Hemorrhage or Decreased Blood Volume: Whole blood - fresh, stored, or preserved.
B. Shock Resulting From Trauma, Burns or Infection: Plasma - liquid, frozen, or dried; plasma substitutes.
C. Chronic Anemia: Whole blood or resuspended red blood cells.
D. Leukopenia and Thrombocytopenia: Large amounts of fresh whole blood. Leukocyte or thrombocyte concentrates.
E. Prothrombin Factor "Deficiency" Not Corrected by Vitamin K: **Fresh** whole blood.
F. Hemophilia: Factor VIII (AHF) cryoprecipitate or other concentrate. Factor IX complex concentrate. Whole blood or plasma administered within six hours of collection.

Average Volume of Transfusions

Age	Whole Blood (ml.)	Plasma (ml.)
Newborn	25-50	25-75
1 yr.	100	75-150
3 yrs.	200-300	200-300
10 yrs.	200-400	200-300
Adult	400-600	250-300

PRODUCTS USED FOR TRANSFUSION

Whole Blood.
Certain precautions are necessary in checking donor and blood for transfusion. No donor should be used who has a hemoglobin under 12 Gm. or who has a history of syphilis, malaria, infectious hepatitis, chronic allergic disease, or drug sensitivity. The donor's serologic test for syphilis should be negative. Do Rh typing on both donor and patient (see p. 174). Cross-match blood (see p. 173).

Blood for transfusion is drawn into A.C.D. (acid-citrate-dextrose) anticoagulant, which markedly prolongs viability of erythrocytes (see p. 621).

The blood must be stored at 39 to 50° F. (4 to 10° C.). Properly stored blood may be used for transfusion until 21 days after withdrawal from the donor. Blood should not be used if over 21 days "old."

Salts of ethylenediamine tetraacetic acid and heparin are now used as anticoagulants in some blood banks.

Plasma.
A. Liquid Plasma: Should contain 5% dextrose to prevent precipitation of fibrin at room temperature. The pro-

thrombin titer diminishes rapidly after 72 hours. Liquid
plasma may be kept at room temperature for 3 years.
Recent evidence indicates that hepatitis virus is attenuated or destroyed in plasma that has remained at room
temperature or a little above for 6 months.

B. Frozen Plasma: Plasma frozen within 72 hours after
blood is drawn may be stored indefinitely at -4° F.
(-20° C.). Reliquefy at 98.6° F. (37° C.) in a water bath
and use promptly. Frozen plasma retains its full content
of labile constituents (prothrombin, complement, antibodies). Hepatitis virus is also preserved; frozen plasma should therefore not be used unless no other substitute for blood is available.

C. Dried Plasma: Plasma dried after freezing within 72
hours after blood is drawn is stable at room temperature
for five years if kept in an airtight container. Reliquefy
with 0.1% solution of citric acid and administer within one
hour. Dried plasma retains its full content of labile constituents. Hepatitis virus is preserved also.

Red Blood Cell Suspensions.

These are of value in supplying red cells with a limited
amount of fluid. Aspirate plasma from the settled red cells
(preferably packed by centrifuging) and replace with 100 ml.
of 5% dextrose in saline. Water will hemolyze the cells.
Both cells and diluent must be cold when mixed.

Serum Albumin.

Serum albumin is prepared as a 25% solution with a low
salt content (less than M/10 concentration); its viscosity is
approximately that of whole blood. One hundred ml., containing 25 Gm. of albumin, has the osmotic equivalent of 500
ml. of plasma. It is stable at room temperature and can be
added to crystalloid solutions. In shock, 100 to 200 ml. (containing 25 to 50 Gm.) is recommended; if dehydration is also
present, additional fluids must be given. It is free of
hepatitis virus.

Other Blood and Plasma Substitutes.

A number of "plasma expanders" are available. These
have high molecular weight and desirable viscosity. One advantage is the absence of hepatitis virus. Dextran, the most
commonly employed, is a water-soluble biosynthetic polysaccharide available as a 6 to 12% solution in isotonic saline.
For shock give 500 to 1000 ml. at a rate of 20 to 40 ml./minute
to maintain systolic blood pressure at 85 to 90 mm. Hg. Use
for an emergency period only while blood and plasma are being prepared. Newer low molecular weight dextran preparations appear to be suitable and less likely to produce anaphylactoid reactions.

28...

Oxygen, Carbon Dioxide, and Helium Therapy

OXYGEN

Principles of Oxygen Therapy.
Oxygen inhalation is used for the treatment of hypoxia (oxygen want). Effectiveness depends upon the cause and correction of the hypoxia.
  A. Hypoxic Hypoxia: Oxygen is most effective with hypoxia due to inadequate oxygenation of normal lung, or inadequate oxygenation due to pulmonary disease. Mechanisms preventing oxygen from reaching or traversing the alveoli must be corrected.
  B. Anemic Hypoxia: Oxygen is only fairly effective when diminished hemoglobin or hemoglobin chemically bound to a toxic substance limits the amount of oxygen which the blood can transport. Treatment must be aimed primarily at transfusion or release of hemoglobin from toxic substances.
  C. Stagnant Hypoxia: Oxygen is only fairly effective when slowing of the circulation results in inadequate blood oxygen transport. Shock, hypovolemia, or congestive heart failure must be corrected.
  D. Histotoxic Hypoxia: Oxygen is not very effective following cellular poisoning with inadequate tissue oxygenation. Cyanide or excessive doses of anesthetics or barbiturates may be the offenders.

Methods of Administration.
Optimal concentrations of oxygen (in per cent) at a given rate of flow (in L./min.) must be determined for each patient. **Ultimately, the objective is effective oxygenation of arterial blood. If there is doubt, determine O_2 saturation or pa_{O_2} (partial pressure of oxygen in arterial blood).**
  A. Tent: Used to administer oxygen concentrations which will not exceed 40 to 60% at a flow rate of 10 L./min. Temperature and humidity may be varied by a rheostat which determines the rate of oxygen-air circulation through the tent system. Flood the tent with oxygen at the rate of 15 L./min. for 30 minutes; then reduce the flow to 10 L./min. Repeat each time the tent is opened. The efficiency of the apparatus is directly proportional to the care taken in tucking in the edges and opening the tent.

B. Catheter: Use a 12 or 14 F. urethral catheter, or a
plastic tube of similar bore. The terminal inch should be
perforated with four to six small holes. The catheter
should be fastened with adhesive tape over the nose and
forehead and attached via a metal or glass cannula to a
length of tubing leading to the outlet of a humidifying
bottle. The inlet leads to the oxygen tank. Bubbling the
oxygen through three inches of water is adequate as a
humidifying measure.

1. Nasopharyngeal placement - After lubricating well with
   lubricating jelly, slip the catheter along the floor of the
   nose until it just reaches the back of the pharynx; withdraw one inch. This position allows concentrations of
   35 to 40% oxygen in the inspired air at a flow rate of
   6 to 8 L. /min. The same result may be achieved by
   use of a metal "Y" tube whose tips fit comfortably
   just inside both nostrils. The stem of the tube should
   be attached to a flexible metal forehead plate which
   can be fastened with adhesive or a headband. The
   catheter is more reliable.

2. Oropharyngeal placement - Slip the catheter into the
   oral pharynx via the nose until the patient begins to
   swallow; withdraw slightly. The tip should be just behind the uvula. In this position concentrations of oxygen in the inspired air vary from 45 to 70% at a flow
   rate of 6 to 8 L. /min.

C. Masks: These produce concentrations of oxygen approach-
ing 100%. Precautions: Remove masks every two hours,
dry, and powder. If used with pure oxygen for over 48
hours, check repeatedly for evidence of pulmonary edema
as a manifestation of oxygen poisoning.

1. B. L. B. (Boothby-Lovelace-Bulbulian) mask - A nasal
   or oronasal mask whose oxygen inlet opens into a two-
   way chamber; gas flows into the mask on inspiration
   and is expired into the bag on exhalation. If the oxygen
   flow is less than 6 L. /min., dangerous accumulation
   of carbon dioxide may occur. Sponge rubber disks on
   each side of the mask neck act as inspiratory and expiratory valves. Room air enters these valves when
   the bag collapses on inspiration. Eighty to 100% oxygen may be administered at a flow rate of 8 to 12 L.
   per minute. The oxygen concentration is proportional
   to the flow rate. The amount of room air varies also
   with the rate and depth of inspiration.

2. Meter mask, O. E. M. (Oxygen Equipment Manufacturers) type - A nasal or oronasal mask. A flutter valve
   between the mask and bag allows entry of oxygen into
   the mask and prevents passage of exhaled carbon dioxide into the bag. A safety valve allows ingress of room
   air if the oxygen flow is inadequate. A meter attached

to the tank reducing valve is interposed between the tank and mask; it has a series of graduated orifices through which room air is sucked in amounts proportionate to the diameter of the hole. The concentration of oxygen leaving the meter is printed on the regulating disk. Forty to 100% oxygen may be administered; 100% oxygen requires a flow rate of 10 to 15 L./min.

3. Positive pressure attachment for meter mask - A disk containing orifices of progressively smaller sizes is attached over the expiratory valve. The largest allows normal expiration. The others produce gradually increasing resistance to exhalation and hence increased positive pressure as their diameter diminishes. Pressure may be accurately adjusted from 1 to 4 cm. of water. In a variation of this type mask, a plug replaces the expiratory valve and a tube through the plug is led to a graduated glass tube inserted perpendicularly in a one quart glass bottle partially filled with water; pressure may be varied from 1 to 7 cm. of water.

4. Intermittent positive pressure breathing (I.P.P.B.) - The most effective apparatus for positive pressure breathing. Oxygen or compressed air is provided at pre-set pressures up to 25 cm. of water on inspiration only. It must be remembered that the volume of air provided at the alveolar level is the primary consideration. Apparatus containing both volume and pressure controls are therefore desirable. Nebulized water or medication can be simultaneously delivered. The slightest inspiratory effort triggers a valve so sensitive that a demand of −1 mm. of water can start a rapid inspiratory flow. Oxygen or air so administered reaches otherwise ill-ventilated areas of the lung, especially if used with nebulized bronchodilators. When the desired pressure is reached, the valve shuts off further flow until the next inspiratory cycle. Manual resuscitation is possible in apneic patients. The Bennett and the Bird respirators are two of the most efficient of the pressure breathing devices now available. **They require training in use and maintenance.** The Emerson has a motor driven air compressor which may be substituted for oxygen. Many small portable units utilizing the same principle are available for emergency resuscitation.

FIRE REGULATIONS FOR USE OF OXYGEN: NO SMOKING, LIVE FLAMES, or CAUTERY in room with tent or near catheter or patient with a mask.

USE NO OIL ON ANY OXYGEN REGULATOR OR OTHER EQUIPMENT.

CARBON DIOXIDE

Carbon dioxide stimulates the respiratory center and is useful in the prevention of postoperative atelectasis.

Methods of Administration.
Five per cent carbon dioxide with 95% oxygen is administered through a mask. One per cent carbon dioxide produces a detectable increase in ventilation; 9% produces a maximal increase in ventilation but results in narcotic effects. Concentrations of 5% or more may cause disorientation, apprehension, dyspnea, or headache. **Caution:** Carbon dioxide should **not** be used as a respiratory stimulant when hypoventilation and resulting hypercapnia are present.

HELIUM

Helium is an inert, nontoxic gas which can replace nitrogen in inhaled air. Helium (80%) with oxygen (20%) is efficacious in the treatment of respiratory obstruction because its low density enables an increased flow through the restricted airway. It is one of the important therapeutic procedures in the treatment of status asthmaticus. Oxygen concentration can be raised according to the needs of the patient. Flow meters calibrated for oxygen read one-third below actual flow when this mixture is used.

AEROSOL THERAPY

Purpose.
Bronchodilatation, antibiotic therapy, or wetting action.

Equipment.
A. Nebulizer: Glass apparatus to disperse solution into particles fine enough to reach minute pulmonary radicles.
B. Pressure Source: Hand bulb, oxygen tank with or without intermittent positive pressure valve, or motor driven air compressor.

Methods of Administration.
A. Nebulizer With Hand Bulb (Vaponephrine®, Vapojet®, or De Vilbiss No. 40 type): The lips are loosely closed over the mouthpiece. The bulb is compressed with inspiration. Five natural breaths are followed by one maximal inhalation which is held for three seconds. Wait one minute and repeat the cycle one or more times as necessary.
B. Oxygen Tank:
1. Ideal aerosol therapy is achieved by an intermittent positive pressure unit with attached nebulizer using

oxygen or compressed air as a power source (see p. 435).

2. The nebulizer may be attached to an oxygen tank or air compressor by a length of pressure tubing. A "Y" glass tube is inserted between the tank and nebulizer, one limb of the Y opening to the outside. Oxygen flow is regulated at 6 L. per minute. The mouth piece is placed loosely between the lips. The open limb of the Y is closed off as the patient inhales maximally and holds his breath for three seconds. The Y tube is released with exhalation.

C. Air Compressor: A motor driven air compressor can replace the oxygen tank as a power source.

D. Nebulizer With Mask: The oxygen tank or air compressor may be attached to a nebulizer incorporated into a plastic mask which is fitted with an expiratory valve. Thus a continuous flow of oxygen or air laden with the aerosol is breathed.

E. Extremely effective aerosol therapy can be achieved with the intermittent positive-pressure apparatus (see p. 427).

Drugs Employed.

A. Bronchodilators: Use 5 drops **plus** 15 drops of water.
   1. Epinephrine, 1:100 solution.
   2. Isoproterenol (Isuprel®), 1:100 or 1:200 solution.
   3. Racemic epinephrine (Vaponefrin®), 1:80 solution.

B. Antibiotics: (Precede with bronchodilator and follow with saline aerosol as well as oral rinse with water.) (Now rarely used.)
   1. Crystalline penicillin G - 50,000 to 100,000 units in 1-2 ml. of water per treatment.
   2. Streptomycin - 0.25 to 0.5 Gm. in 1-2 ml. of water.
   3. Oxytetracycline (Terramycin®) aerosol - 50 to 100 mg. in 1 to 2 ml. of water.

C. Wetting Agents:
   1. Ethyl alcohol, 50%, in oxygen humidifying bottle in place of water for treatment of acute pulmonary edema.
   2. Superinone (Alevaire®), 1 to 5 ml., may be used with the bronchodilators and antibiotics mentioned above. It may be used in a 1:1 dilution in the oxygen humidifying bottle for its mucolytic action. This drug may be very irritating.

29...

Surgery

PREOPERATIVE CARE

Examination.

A. Complete history should be taken and a thorough physical examination performed before every major surgical procedure. All significant complaints and physical findings should be evaluated by proper consultation or appropriate procedures. Question the patient about sensitivity to morphine and specific antibiotics, reactions to previous operations (e. g., bleeding tendency, poor wound healing, keloid formation, thrombophlebitis, and transfusion reactions), and chronic constipation and use of laxatives. Discuss the patient's fears (pain, death, anesthesia) with him.

B. Complete blood count and urinalysis.

C. Blood N. P. N., sodium, potassium, chloride, carbon dioxide, organ function tests, and indicated films.

D. If indicated, do bleeding and clotting times, sedimentation rate, hematocrit, and platelet count.

E. Blood typing (including Rh factor) in all major surgical procedures, and in others as indicated.

F. Material for culture and pathologic specimens should be sent to the laboratory accompanied by an informative clinical summary.

G. Patients over 50 years of age should have an Ecg. and two-hour postprandial blood glucose for baseline and screening; status of pulmonary function should be considered, especially for evidence of bronchospasm.

H. Obtain signed permit for operation from the patient or his legal guardian.

Preparation of Uncomplicated Cases.

A. Enema: Unless contraindicated, a tap water or soapsuds enema should be given on the evening before the operation in order to prevent postoperative bowel discomfort.

B. Evening Sedation: Give hypnotic dose of a sedative to allay apprehension and insure a good night of sleep.

C. Intake: Give nothing by mouth after midnight.

D. Local Preparation: On the ward, shave the surgical site and wash with soap and water. In the operating room, wash the area well for five minutes with a detergent solution or soap and water, then apply an antiseptic agent (e. g., quaternary ammonium chloride).

E. Pre-anesthetic Medication: (See p. 487.) The following combinations are usually given subcut. :

1. Meperidine hydrochloride (Demerol®), 100 mg. ($1\frac{1}{2}$ gr.), **or** morphine sulfate, 10 to 15 mg. ($\frac{1}{6}$ to $\frac{1}{4}$ gr.), with -
2. Atropine sulfate, 0.4 mg. ($\frac{1}{150}$ gr.), **or** scopolamine hydrobromide, 0.4 to 0.6 mg. ($\frac{1}{150}$ to $\frac{1}{100}$ gr.). (Give no atropine to patients with glaucoma.)
   These drugs are given one to one and one-half hours before the anesthetic together with sodium pentobarbital, 0.1 Gm. ($1\frac{1}{2}$ gr.). Elderly patients with marked hypothyroidism or diffuse chronic hepatitis do not tolerate morphine well. (For children's dosages, see p. 487.)

F. Have the patient empty his bladder before going to the operating room. If pelvic surgery is to be performed, use an indwelling catheter. If a stomach tube will be needed, it should be passed before surgery. Consideration should be given to the discomfort it may cause.

Preparation of Patients With Complications.

A. Shock: (See p. 12 for newer concepts of shock.)
   1. Types of shock in surgical patients -
      a. Hypovolemic (inadequate circulating intravascular volume).
         (1) Hemorrhage.
         (2) Trauma - Loss of blood or plasma, electrolyte fluid shifts.
         (3) Burns - Loss of plasma and electrolytes, trauma, infection.
         (4) Dehydration - Loss of fluids and electrolytes.
      b. Infection (vasoconstriction, venous pooling, diminished venous return, diminished cardiac output [especially in "gram-negative" or endotoxin shock]).
      c. Vascular obstruction (pulmonary or peripheral emboli).
      d. Anesthesia (spinal anesthesia with excess vasodilatation, or excess myocardial depression with diminished cardiac output which may occur with halothane [Fluothane®]).
   2. Objectives of management - Monitoring by clinical observation and supplemental technics is essential. All must be begun quickly and almost simultaneously.
      a. Restore adequate circulating blood volume.
      b. Support respiratory and cardiac function.
      c. Control infection.
      d. Improve function of peripheral circulation.
      e. Correct initiating causes.
      f. Provide symptomatic relief.
   3. Monitoring the course of the patient in shock -
      a. Clinical observation of blood pressure, pallor or cyanosis, pulse and respiratory rate, mental acuity, mottling of skin, cold perspiration, venous collapse, fluid intake and urinary output, and temperature.

    b. Central venous pressure should be used as a guide to the rate and volume of fluid administration. Constant judicious medical observation is necessary to ensure best results. A plastic catheter is placed in the superior vena cava or right atrium via the basilic or external jugular vein. By means of a four-way stopcock the catheter is connected to (a) a source of fluid and (b) a simple vertical manometer graduated in cm. of water. The zero point of the manometer must be at the level of the right atrium (see pp. 442 and 443).

      Note: Central venous pressure is not a measure of blood volume but an indication of the ability of the heart to accept and expel the blood brought to it. The trend of the central venous pressure is more important than any single reading. If the level rises to 12 cm. of water, reduce fluid input to a minimum and consider digitalization.

    c. Cardioscope - Continuous observation of rate and rhythm.

    d. Blood pressure - Frequent cuff determinations. Continuous recording of mean brachial artery pressure is very effective. If the brachial artery outflow is led through a densitometer, repeated and accurate determinations of the cardiac output can be made by dye dilution technics.

      85 mm. Hg should be regarded as the critical systolic level in the administration of fluids, vasopressors, or vasodilators as clinically indicated.

    e. Respiratory rate, rhythm, and volume as well as the labor involved in breathing and evidence of airway obstruction should be continuously observed.

    f. Urinary output measured by an indwelling catheter. Aim at a minimum flow of no less than 50 ml./hour.

    g. Equipment for rapid, repeated, and accurate determination of serum electrolytes, pH, pO_2, and pCO_2 should be available as well as a physician experienced in their interpretation.

    h. Blood volume studies done serially are invaluable as a guide to volume replacement.

    i. Hematocrit, hemoglobin, and pulse rate are not dependable guides for volume replacement.

    j. Immediately and repeatedly chart all significant clinical and laboratory data in an intelligible graphic form.

4. Therapeutic measures - Begin treatment promptly.

    a. Control initiating factors such as hemorrhage, and immobilize fractures.

    b. Keep patient supine, free of pain, and reassured. Normal room temperature is optimal.

c. Restore adequate circulating blood volume (75 ml./
   Kg. body weight). Start fluid replacement at once.
   With hemorrhage, whole blood is imperative; but
   plasma, serum albumin, human plasma fractions
   (Plasmanate®), plasma expanders (low molecular
   weight dextran [dextran 40; Rheomacrodex®]),
   Ringer's injection, 0.9% saline solution, and 5%
   dextrose solution (in approximately that order) are
   also temporarily effective.

   Intelligent use of central venous pressure, frequently determined, is an invaluable guide for rate
   and volume of fluid given (see para. b, above).

   (1) Whole blood - Obtain blood sample for C. B. C.,
       hematocrit, grouping, and cross-matching before
       starting the initial infusion. If whole blood has
       been lost, use properly grouped and cross-
       matched blood for replacement, if possible. In
       severe shock, 500-1000 ml./hour or more may
       be required. Carefully monitor central venous
       pressure every five to ten minutes. Continue
       transfusions until systolic pressure is 85 mm.
       Hg, central venous pressure reaches 12 cm. of
       water, hemoglobin is 12 Gm./100 ml., and cir-
       culating blood volume reaches 75 ml./Kg. body
       weight. Elderly individuals or patients with left
       ventricular disease may begin to develop pul-
       monary edema at a central venous pressure of
       12 cm. of water and may require slowing of rate
       of flow plus rapid parenteral digitalization (see
       p. 498). Group O (universal donor) blood may be
       used without cross-matching if necessary to save
       life.

   (2) Plasma, serum albumin, or Plasmanate® - Plas-
       ma and its products can be stored for emergency
       use. They are specifically indicated when plasma
       loss has led to hemoconcentration, as in burns or
       peritonitis. Pooled plasma may transmit homol-
       ogous serum hepatitis. Normal Human Serum
       Albumin, U.S.P., or sodium-poor serum albu-
       min contains 25 Gm. albumin per 100 ml. and is
       equivalent in osmotic pressure to 500 ml. of
       plasma; it is very expensive. Plasmanate® is
       a solution of albumin, alpha-globulin, and beta-
       globulin; its osmotic activity is equal to that of
       plasma. Plasmanate® and serum albumin will
       not transmit homologous serum hepatitis.

   (3) Plasma expanders - These agents are solutions
       of large inert organic molecules of low molecular
       weight. They are slowly lost from the vascular
       compartment and thus serve to increase plasma

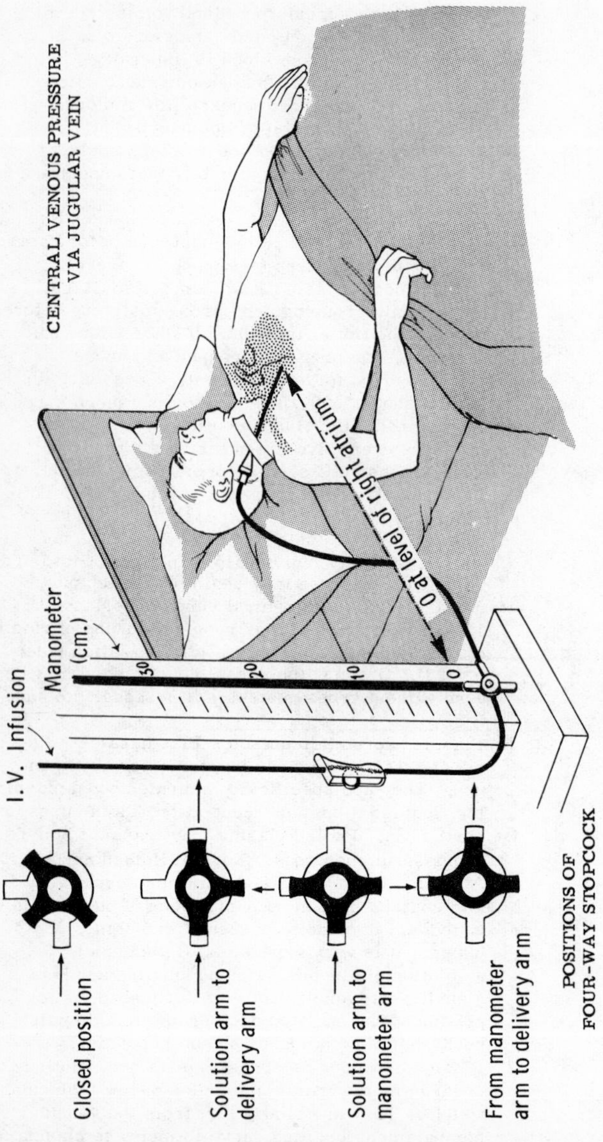

CENTRAL VENOUS PRESSURE
VIA JUGULAR VEIN

0 at level of right atrium

I. V. Infusion

Manometer
(cm.)

Closed position

Solution arm to
delivery arm

Solution arm to
manometer arm

From manometer
arm to delivery arm

POSITIONS OF
FOUR-WAY STOPCOCK

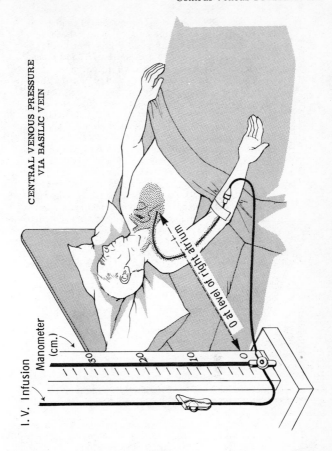

CENTRAL VENOUS PRESSURE
VIA BASILIC VEIN

I.V. Infusion

Manometer
(cm.)

0 at level of right atrium

volume. The only one recommended is dextran, preferably of low molecular weight. (Dextran 40 [Rheomacrodex®] has a molecular weight of approximately 40,000.) Administer 500 to 1000 ml. I.V. at a rate of 20 to 40 ml./minute. Use cautiously in patients with cardiac or renal insufficiency to avoid pulmonary edema. Anaphylactoid reactions have been reported. Dextran may interfere with tests for blood grouping and cross-matching. These should be done prior to administration of dextran.

(4) Saline, glucose, Ringer's injection - These fluids will expand blood volume for about one hour until blood or plasma can be obtained.

d. Blood pressure control - This may be achieved by administration of fluids, judicious use of vasoconstrictor and perhaps vasodilator drugs, and corticosteroids in pharmacologic doses to enhance vasodilatation.

If the systolic blood pressure spontaneously remains above 85 mm. Hg, do not use vasopressor drugs. If it drops below this point, consider their use, aiming at 85 mm. Hg as the optimal peak level. The most commonly used vasoconstrictors now available for this purpose are metaraminol (Aramine®), levarterenol bitartrate (Levophed®), and mephentermine (Wyamine®).

Vasodilator drugs which dilate peripheral arterioles, improving flow rate and resulting in diminution of visceral venous pooling, increase in venous return, and cardiac output appear to produce favorable effects. Further investigation is warranted. The agents being evaluated for this purpose include phenoxybenzamine (Dibenzyline®) and phentolamine (Regitine®).

Isoproterenol (Isuprel®) is being used to improve cardiac output because of its inotropic effect (increased force of myocardial contraction). Its ultimate role appears promising.

Hydrocortisone is being used in doses of 100 mg. every four hours for its vasodilator effect (especially in endotoxin shock) together with antibiotic therapy. Used in this manner, gradual diminution of the dose is not necessary.

e. Ensure adequate ventilation with a plastic airway. Mechanical intermittent positive pressure with humidified oxygen should be used to provide proper oxygenation and to alleviate any excessive labor in breathing if warranted (see p. 435). Aspirate excessive secretions; a tracheostomy with a cuffed

tracheal tube may be necessary to adequately clear
the airway and provide effective use of intermittent
positive pressure.

   f. Treat infection with appropriate antibiotics and
drainage of accumulations of purulent material.

   g. Surgical relief of acute major embolic obstruction
if indicated.

B. Liver Disease: In all forms of surgery, if there is diffuse liver disease, give a high-carbohydrate, high-
protein, low-fat diet. Protein should supply 20% of the
caloric intake. Such patients are often dangerously sensitive to morphine. They are less sensitive to codeine.
Check plasma proteins and prothrombin concentration.
If the latter is low, give vitamin K and repeat the test.

C. Anemia: Give iron or blood transfusion if indicated.

D. Diabetes: Must be controlled before and after surgery.

E. Dehydration and Acidosis: See p. 428.

Preparations for Special Procedures.

A. Gastric Surgery: In the presence of pyloric obstruction
the stomach must be allowed to regain its muscle tonus
by the use of decompression. This may take several days.
A Levin tube is inserted through the nose as shown on p.
447. To lavage the stomach, allow patient to drink 2 L.
of water with continuous suction. The type and amount of
fluid intake and amount of gastric fluid lost must be recorded accurately in order to judge replacement therapy.
A nasogastric tube may be very distressing to the patient.

B. Intestinal Obstruction: The treatment of choice is intestinal intubation and suction with the Miller-Abbott or the
Harris tube. The Miller-Abbott tube is a 10 to 12 foot
tube with a double lumen and an inflatable balloon on the
tip. The tube is passed through the nose into the stomach.
With the patient on his right side, the tube is pushed into
the stomach one to two inches at a time at short intervals
with the object of passing it through the pylorus. Fluoroscopic aid is frequently necessary. After the tube passes
the pylorus the empty balloon may be inflated with air or
filled with 3 ml. of elemental mercury. The latter
assists the peristaltic action of the intestine in carrying
the tube through the intestinal canal. Suction is applied
at the proximal end of the tube; careful measurement of
fluid lost is necessary to judge replacement therapy (see
p. 425).

C. Colon Surgery: Give neomycin, 1 Gm., and tetracycline,
0.5 Gm., by mouth at 8:00 a.m., 12:00 noon, 4:00 p.m.,
8:00 p.m., and 12:00 midnight on the day before surgery
and at 4:00 a.m. on the day of surgery. If neomycin is
unavailable, give succinylsulfathiazole or phthalylsulfathiazole, 5 Gm. 4 times daily for 5-7 days. Preliminary

ESTIMATION OF BODY SURFACE AREA IN BURNS

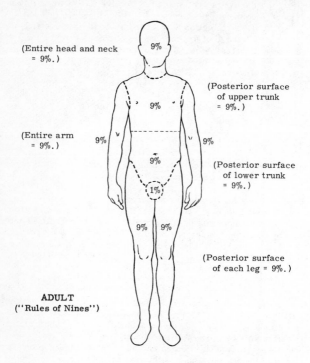

(Entire head and neck = 9%.)

(Posterior surface of upper trunk = 9%.)

(Entire arm = 9%.)

(Posterior surface of lower trunk = 9%.)

(Posterior surface of each leg = 9%.)

ADULT
("Rules of Nines")

Variations from Adult Distribution in Infants and Children (in %)*

	New-born	1 yr.	5 yrs.	10 yrs.	
Head	19	17	13	11	
Both thighs	11	13	16	17	
Both lower legs	10	10	11	12	
Neck	2				
Anterior trunk	13				
Posterior trunk	13				
Both upper arms	8				These % remain
Both lower arms	6				constant at all
Both hands	5				ages.
Both buttocks	5				
Both feet	7				
Genitals	1				
	100				

*After Berkow.

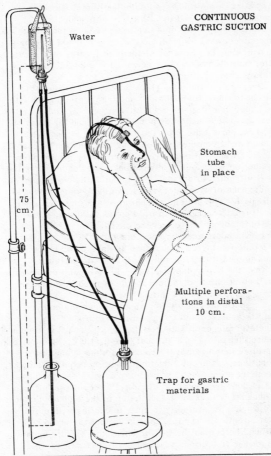

**CONTINUOUS
GASTRIC SUCTION**

Water

Stomach
tube
in place

75
cm.

Multiple perfora-
tions in distal
10 cm.

Trap for gastric
materials

Pass the nasogastric tube through the nose into the
stomach and test its location by aspirating with a large syringe.
If the stomach is empty, have the patient drink some water.
Secure the tube to the forehead, connect the second tube from
the trap to the long glass tube in the rubber stopper of the
water reservoir, and place the free rubber tubing from the
water reservoir in the empty bottle. Invert the reservoir and
hang it on the stand.

purgation, a minimum residue diet, and preoperative
enemas are required in both types of preparation.

D. Rectal Surgery: Enemas are often used on the evening before surgery. Low-residue diet may be used (see p. 411).

E. Thyrotoxicosis: Several methods of treatment are available, but the most widely accepted is subtotal thyroidectomy after adequate preparation.

Preparation includes (1) A thiouracil to return the
patient to the euthyroid state and then iodine to involute
the hyperplastic gland prior to surgery; (2) a high caloric
diet (up to 6000 Calories per 24 hours; and (3) sedation
and rest during the hyperthyroid state.

The most commonly used drug combination is propylthiouracil and iodine. Propylthiouracil stops hormone
production, and four to eight weeks are required for the
BMR to return to normal. Because of the occasional
occurrence of agranulocytosis, a weekly blood count is
indicated. The patient must immediately report fever,
sore throat, or rash. In mild cases, 100 mg. t.i.d.
orally is adequate. In severe cases, 100 to 200 mg.
every six hours may be necessary.

Iodine is started about 10 to 20 days prior to surgery
when the BMR is +10% or the PBI $<$ 8 mcg./100 ml. It
shrinks the hyperplastic gland. Lugol's solution or saturated solution of potassium iodide is used in a dose of
5 to 10 drops daily. Continue for a week after surgery.

The patient is ready for surgery when the euthyroid
state is achieved and the gland is firm.

F. Prostatic Surgery: Check B.U.N., N.P.N., or serum
creatinine. Do a P.S.P. test (see p. 136). Every effort
must be made to improve impaired kidney function pre-
operatively. Chronic urinary retention requires slow
decompression (possibly over a period of several days);
this is done by means of an indwelling catheter. It may
be necessary to place the catheter in the bladder through
a suprapubic cystotomy wound. In dealing with urinary
tract infection it is most important that the urine be
cultured before antibiotics or chemotherapeutic agents
are given. Infections will recur if obstruction is not
eliminated.

POSTOPERATIVE CARE

Parenteral Fluids and Replacement Therapy.

The following schedule may be used to meet basal requirements and to replace abnormal fluid and electrolyte loss.
It applies only to patients with normal kidney function who cannot tolerate oral feedings.

Replacement of Measured Gastrointestinal Fluid Losses

Fluid Source	Replacement*
Stomach (containing HCl)	(1) $^2/_3$ of volume lost as 0.9% saline. (2) $^1/_3$ of volume lost as glucose in water. (3) 2 mEq. (0.16 Gm.) of potassium*/100 ml.
Stomach (free of HCl)	(1) All as 0.9% saline. (2) Add 2 mEq. (0.16 Gm.) potassium*/100 ml.
Small bowel or biliary tree	(1) All as Ringer's lactate. (2) Add potassium* to make 50-75 mEq. (4-6 Gm.) per day total.

Pancreatic fistula	(1) Feed back by stomach tube the juice collected, or
	(2) Give intravenously:
	   (a) $^2/_3$ of volume as M/6 sodium lactate.
	   (b) $^1/_3$ of volume as 0.9% saline.
	   (c) Add 2 mEq. (0.16 Gm.) potassium*/ 100 ml.

*Potassium given as potassium chloride.

A. Approximate Daily Basal Requirements:
   1. 500 ml. of normal saline I V. (none in the first 24 hours postoperatively).
   2. 2500 ml. of 5 to 10% glucose in water I.V.
   3. 25 mEq. (2 Gm.) of potassium chloride per liter of fluid given slowly if parenteral therapy is continued longer than three to five days.
   4. 50 to 100 Gm. of amino acids if parenteral therapy is continued over one week.
   5. In case of gastrointestinal fluid loss by intubation or vomiting, the fluids listed in the table above must be added to the basal daily requirements.
B. Careful charting of losses is mandatory. Laboratory analysis of electrolyte content of fluids lost is most desirable. Where the facilities for electrolyte measurement are not available, replacements can be approximated fairly well if volumes and sources of fluids lost are known (see also pp. 423-30).
C. Daily weights are extremely important as a guide to fluid retention.

Early Ambulation.
    Early ambulation following major surgical procedures has helped to prevent many of the complications and much of the discomfort formerly experienced by the postoperative surgical patient. Early ambulation shortens the convalescence. The patient is spared the use of the bedpan and is less likely to suffer with nausea, vomiting, and gas pains. The incidence of postoperative pneumonia, atelectasis, and pulmonary emboli appears to be reduced. Incisional hernias have not been more frequent.

The patient sits up on the day of the operation and takes a few deep breaths. He is assisted to the bathroom on the next day and then gradually increases his activity, leaving the hospital earlier than was previously permitted. Diet depends on the nature of the procedure and the patient's desires.

Care of Bed Patients.

These require observation for minor as well as severe complications; they are to be treated as indicated.

A. Position in Bed: This varies with the type of surgery. The supine position with or without a small pillow is the position of choice immediately after surgery, especially major abdominal procedures. The patient should be rolled first to one side and then the other for 15 to 20 minutes every hour. This procedure is aimed at prevention of atelectases.

B. Watch for Shock and Hemorrhage: Check the surgical dressing, BP, pulse, and respiration every 15 to 30 minutes for two to five hours. Watch for sudden onset of pallor, cold sweat, tachycardia, drop in BP, thirst, and apprehension as possible evidences of hidden hemorrhage. Drop in hemoglobin may lag far behind hemorrhage.

C. Parenteral Fluids: Blood and plasma are rarely given immediately after surgery unless blood loss has been severe. Most surgeons replace blood loss during the operative procedure and do not permit the patient to return to his bed until shock has been controlled (see pp. 428 and 439).

D. Pain: Severe pain is combated by the use of narcotics. Give meperidine hydrochloride (Demerol®), 100 mg. (1 1/2 gr.); morphine sulfate, 8 to 10 mg. (1/8 to 1/6 gr.); or dihydromorphinone hydrochloride (Dilaudid®), 2 to 4 mg. (1/30 to 1/15 gr.) every three to four hours as necessary.

E. Fluids and Foods by Mouth: After nausea disappears, a clear liquid diet is offered. Avoid fruit juices and milk. When peristalsis has returned, a soft diet can be given, and finally a general diet. Following gastrointestinal tract surgery, at least five to seven days should elapse before a general diet is offered.

F. Restlessness and Discomfort: If possible, use sedatives in full hypnotic doses rather than narcotics for these conditions. Patients past middle age may develop hallucinations from barbiturates and should be carefully watched (see p. 486).

G. Urination: All major surgical procedures are attended by temporary suppression of urinary output; patients usually excrete only about 500 ml. of urine during the first 24 hours after surgery no matter how much parenteral fluid is given. Saline should not be given during the first 24 hours postoperatively unless necessary to replace known losses of sodium, as in renal, adrenal, or gastrointestinal disease. After 24 hours, the urinary output should be around 1000 ml. daily. Check intake and output on patients who have undergone any major surgical procedure. If patient does not void in eight to 12 hours (some wait as long as 24 hours) or is uncomfortable, use one of the measures outlined on p. 452. If the bladder can be percussed above the symphysis pubis, it is full.

H. Bowels: Because of inactivity, the patient may become constipated. If necessary, give mineral oil, or milk of magnesia and mineral oil, 30 to 60 ml. (1 to 2 oz.), every evening, or morning and evening. It is probably wiser to try a saline enema before even such a mild cathartic as milk of magnesia is used. Fecal impactions are often relieved by a warm 200 ml. oil retention enema (mineral or vegetable oil). This should be retained for four hours, expelled, and followed with a saline or soap-suds enema.

Minor Complications of Surgery.

A. Nausea and Vomiting: Prochlorperazine (Compazine®) and diphenhydramine hydrochloride (Benadryl®) may be effective in the control of nausea and vomiting. The former may be given orally in doses of 5 to 10 mg. ($1/12$-$1/6$ gr.) every four to six hours, or deep I.M. in doses of 10 mg. ($1/6$ gr.) every six hours; rare instances of hepatitis have been reported. The latter may be given orally or I.M. in doses of 50 mg. ($3/4$ gr.) every four hours; it may have a marked sedative effect.

1. Nausea - This commonly accompanies inhalation anesthesia. If transient, it requires no treatment. If it persists, insert a stomach tube and draw off any fluid or gas present (see p. 447). This may relieve the nausea at once.

2. Vomiting - Aspirate the stomach contents and then remove the tube. Remember that narcotics may cause both nausea and vomiting. If this is suspected, watch the patient for more than the usual amount of retching and for itching about the nose. If the vomiting persists, insert a stomach tube and tape in place (see p. 447). Use continuous suction and keep the stomach decompressed. Following a period of this, apply the suction intermittently, giving fluids in the meantime to see if they can be retained. Good fluids to use are warm tea or carbonated beverages; or ask the patient what he desires to drink. When fluids are retained, discontinue the suction. While continuous suction is being used, make an accurate record of intake and output and replace all fluids lost. Maintain a satisfactory urine output. Observe for metabolic alkalosis (see p. 424).

B. Distention and Gas Pains:
1. Gastric distention - Aspirate the stomach and start continuous suction with a nasogastric tube (see p. 447). Give supportive I. V. fluids.
2. Intestinal distention - First insert a rectal tube in an attempt to remove the gas. If this is not effective and suture lines in the intestines are healed, give a warm tap water enema. More stimulating enemas may be necessary. Avoid the use of gas-forming foods such as milk and fruit juices.

   Since most postoperative distention is due to an adynamic ileus, continuous suction with a nasogastric tube is an effective measure. Breathing 100% oxygen by mask will sometimes give striking relief.

C. Acute Urinary Retention (see p. 450): This is a frequent problem because patients are not accustomed to urinating in the recumbent position. Sphincter spasm is also a factor. Unless contraindicated, the measures below may be of help if the patient has not voided for eight to 12 hours or has the urge to void but cannot. A patient should not be permitted to go more than 24 hours without voiding postoperatively.
1. Hot applications to the perineum. Have women sit on bedpan; have men stand next to the bed.
2. Give warm water enema or more stimulating enema.
3. Catheterize only as a last resort. Use a small catheter (12 to 16 F.) and sterile precautions. Women may be catheterized every eight hours without great risk of incurring cystitis. Men should not be catheterized so often unless prostatism exists, in which case an indwelling catheter should be introduced. An indwelling catheter should also be used if the patient will need repeated catheterizations. Indwelling catheters should be of the Foley type, which has a small inflatable bulb at its tip for instillation of air or water. The bulb rests against the bladder neck and prevents the catheter from coming out.

D. Hiccup: Try simple methods first such as breathholding, firm traction on the tongue, or splinting the diaphragm by spreading the lower end of the rib cage. Medical measures include sedatives (rectally), local or general anesthesia, antispasmodics (atropine sulfate, 0.3 to 0.6 mg. subcut.), amyl nitrite inhalations, CO_2 inhalations by rebreathing in a paper bag or 5 to 10% CO_2 by face mask for three to five minutes, and tranquilizers, e.g., chlorpromazine or promazine. In severe and intractable hiccup which is considered to be a threat to life, phrenic block or crush may be necessary, but this is rarely required.

Major Complications of Surgery.
A. Shock: See p. 439.

B. Hemorrhage: See p. 10.

C. Pulmonary Embolism: Approximately 90% of postoperative pulmonary emboli originate from thrombi developing
in deep leg veins. Only 0.2% of these emboli are fatal.
Pelvic surgery may also be followed by pelvic vein thrombosis and embolism. Early ambulation is believed by
some to reduce the incidence of venous thrombosis in the
legs. Pulmonary emboli may precede clinical evidence of
phlebothrombosis or thrombophlebitis. Phlebothrombosis
is characterized by pain, tenderness along the course of
the deep veins of the calves, swelling, cyanosis, and a
positive Homans' sign. Thrombophlebitis is characterized by pain, swelling, fever; red and tender, cordlike
thrombosed veins; and leukocytosis. At times it may be
difficult to differentiate between the two. Medical treatment of venous thrombosis of the legs is considered the
treatment of choice if the surgical procedure does not
contraindicate it (potential danger of bleeding from a
fresh wound). Unusual care must be taken.

1. Medical management - Wrap feet and legs snugly up to
the knees. Remove and rewrap the bandages every
eight hours. Elevate the feet. Do not put pillows
under the knees. Employ anticoagulant therapy to prevent propagation of thrombi. Hourly exercise of the
legs and thighs is important.

2. Emergency treatment of pulmonary embolism should
be started at once. Give papaverine hydrochloride
60 mg. (1 gr.) immediately, I. V., and repeat every
four hours, I. M. If dyspnea or cyanosis is present,
give oxygen. Give narcotics for pain.

3. Surgical treatment - Bilateral femoral vein ligation
following pulmonary embolism from thrombosed leg
veins has been proved ineffective. However, if the
source is in the legs and there are repeated pulmonary
emboli in spite of optimum medical management, ligation should be done. If this procedure is ineffective,
inferior vena cava ligation should be considered.

D. Atelectasis: Prevention is the best treatment. The
patient should lie flat in bed unless the type of surgical
procedure warrants otherwise. Change position hourly.
Deep breathing, coughing, I. P. P. B., and balloon blowing
are valuable preventive aids.

If atelectasis does occur, make the patient attempt to
dislodge the mucous plug by coughing; splint his chest
with the hands during the procedure to diminish pain at
the site of abdominal surgery. If these measures fail, a
catheter should be inserted into the trachea and aspiration
attempted. Part of the value of this procedure is the
violent coughing which it induces.

E. Adynamic Ileus: See Distention and Gas Pains, p. 452.

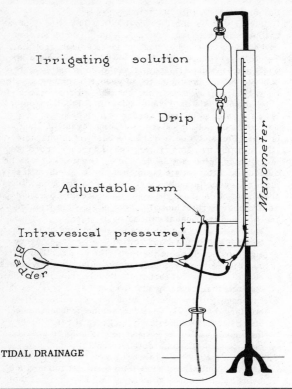

Irrigating   solution

Drip

Manometer

Adjustable arm

Intravesical pressure

Bladder

TIDAL DRAINAGE

Tidal drainage is used to maintain normal bladder tone, to develop reflex emptying of the bladder, and to reduce urinary infection in bladder paralysis due to spinal cord lesions. It operates "automatically" and intermittently, utilizing the principle of the siphon.
1. Mildly antiseptic irrigating solution drips into the system, filling the bladder through an indwelling catheter.
2. As the bladder distends, fluid begins to rise in the manometer and siphon tubing until the height of the siphon is reached.
3. Siphoning action then empties the bladder.
4. When the intravesical pressure falls below the pressure height of the siphon, drainage stops and the cycle begins again.

To determine the height for setting the adjustable arm, raise the siphon tubing, fill the bladder with 300 to 400 ml. of fluid, and then gradually lower the siphon. When the siphon begins operating fasten the adjustable arm. As the bladder tone improves, gradually raise the arm setting so that the same amount of fluid will always cause the siphon to operate. The time of discontinuing the tidal drainage must be determined clinically.

UROLOGIC ORDERS

Orders for I.V. Pyelography.
See p. 97.

Orders for Cystoscopy (Including Retrograde Pyelogram).
Cystoscopes are usually 21 to 24 F. Children's size is
16 F. Resectoscopes are 16, 22, 24, and 27 F.
A. Precystoscopic: Give a soapsuds enema on the night before and also in morning. Have the patient eat a light
breakfast. Give three to five glasses of fluids during the
hour before cystoscopy (water, milk, coffee, etc.). If
general anesthetic or thiopental (Pentothal®) is used, give
atropine sulfate one hour before and omit fluids.
B. Postcystoscopic: Force fluids. Give an opium and belladonna suppository, 15 or 30 mg. ($^{1}/4$ or $^{1}/2$ gr.) for pain
if necessary. Morphine sulfate, 10 mg. ($^{1}/6$ gr.) or
aspirin compound tablets may also be used. For dysuria,
give hot packs to bladder and perineum, hot sitz baths,
or 60 ml. warm glycerin by rectum.

General Care of Urologic Patients.
A. Record fluid intake and output. Keep daily intake over
3000 ml.
B. Catheterization requires sterile technic. Clean genitalia
well with soap and water, but not alcohol. Use a flexible
16 or 18 F. catheter. Instill 20 ml. of 10% mild silver
proteinate before removing catheter.
C. If there has been urinary retention, decompress gradually with indwelling catheter (Foley in men, mushroom
in women).
D. Indwelling catheters require constant care. Irrigate
daily or oftener with sterile boric acid solution or with
1:10,000 potassium permanganate. The tube connecting
the catheter should have a lumen 1 cm. in diameter
throughout; never let the tube dip into the fluid in the
bottle. Sterilize tubing daily. Pin the bed sheet around
the tubing to hold it in place.

BLAKEMORE-SENGSTAKEN TUBE
(For Arresting Hemorrhage From Esophageal Varices)

Technic of Introducing Tube.
A. Attach the tubing of a blood pressure manometer to a "Y"
glass tube. Connect one limb of the "Y" to the esophageal
balloon, the other to a blood pressure bulb.
B. Passing Tube: Lubricate the tube with jelly and pass it
through the nares into the stomach to the "50 cm."
mark. Facilitate swallowing with sips of water.

C. Securing Tube in Esophagus:
1. Inflate stomach balloon with 200 ml. air by means of a syringe, and then clamp this tube.
2. Withdraw the Blakemore-Sengstaken tube until resistance is felt.
3. Inflate the esophageal balloon to a pressure of 25 mm. Hg (about 40 to 60 ml. of air). If 150 to 200 ml. of air are required to achieve a pressure of 25 mm., deflate balloons and readjust position. Esophageal contractions and respiratory and cardiac impulses may intermittently raise pressure to 70 mm. Hg, but minimal pressure of 25 mm. should be maintained. Clamp tube of esophageal balloon. Check pressure frequently to detect leakage.

Maintenance of Tube.
Irrigate stomach with 50 ml. warm saline and then aspirate all contents. Connect stomach tube to constant suction for 24 hours. Irrigate tube hourly. If there is no evidence of bleeding after 48 hours, deflate the balloons in situ for 24 hours. If no further bleeding occurs, remove gently. Observe carefully for further bleeding.

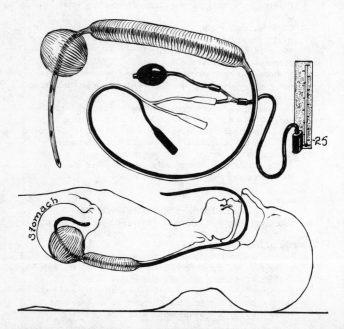

STAGES AND PLANES OF ANESTHESIA

The 4 small black rectangles represent zones, as follows:

1. Conjunctival column - Disappearance and reappearance of lid reflex.
2. Pharyngeal column - Appearance of swallowing (upper border of plane i) and of vomiting (lower border of Stage II).
3. Laryngeal column - Disappearance of carinal reflex.

The large plus and minus signs refer to the presence or absence of the indicated reflex.

Respiration Column.

Thoracic and abdominal inspiration is shown moving away from the mid-line; expiration, toward the mid-line. Regularity, rate, and depth are shown for each stage and plane, in comparison with the normal.

[Modified and reproduced, with permission, from Goodman and Gilman, The Pharmacological Basis of Therapeutics, 2nd Ed., Macmillan, 1955, as modified from Guedel, Inhalation Anesthesia, Macmillan, 1951.]

STAGES OF ANESTHESIA	RESPIRATION (Thoracic / Abdominal)	PUPIL SIZE (No Medication / Morphine 15 mg / Morphine 15 mg and Atropine 0.4 mg / Morphine 15 mg)	EYE-BALL ACTIVITY	Corneal	Conjunctival	Pharyngeal	Laryngeal	Cutaneous	Peritoneal	SOMATIC MUSCLES
I ANALGESIA	(waveform)	(pupils)	VOLUNTARY	+	+	+	+	+	+	NORMAL TONE
II DELIRIUM	(waveform)	(pupils)	+++ +++ +++	+	+	+	+	+	+	UNINHIBITED ACTIVITY
III SURGICAL — PLANE i	(waveform)	(pupils)	FIXED	+ −	−	+	+ +	+ −	+	RELAXATION • SLIGHT
III SURGICAL — PLANE ii	(waveform)	(pupils)	FIXED	+ −	−	−	−	−	+ −	• MODERATE
III SURGICAL — PLANE iii	(waveform)	(pupils)	FIXED	−	−	−	−	−	−	• MARKED
III SURGICAL — PLANE iv	(waveform)	(pupils)	FIXED	−	−	−	−	−	−	• MARKED
IV MEDULLARY PARALYSIS	(waveform)	(pupils)		−	−	−	−	−	−	• EXTREME

30...

Poisons and Toxins

PRINCIPLES OF TREATMENT OF ACUTE POISONING

The physician must be able to give instructions for emergency therapeutic measures before he sees the patient. Once he sees the patient, makes the diagnosis, and arranges for the preservation of the poison or of gastric contents, urine, and blood (for toxicologic analysis), the following general procedures should be carried out: (1) Removal of the poison from the skin, eyes, respiratory tract, or gastrointestinal tract. (The latter is accomplished by emesis, lavage, and catharsis; and by neutralization and precipitation.) (2) Detoxification of poison by specific antidotes after absorption across mucous membranes. (3) Symptomatic therapy with physiologic antidotes.

Removal of Poisons. (Immediate measures.)
  A. Skin Contamination: Flood continuously with water while removing contaminated clothes. Use no chemical antidotes.
  B. Eye Contamination: Same as skin. Wash for five minutes (acid) or 20 minutes (alkali) while holding lids apart. If sterile fluorescein shows erosion, wash for another five minutes.
  C. Inhalation of Toxic Gases: Remove patient from contaminated environment. Establish an effective airway. Give oxygen by pressure mask. Use hand or mechanical ventilator for respiratory arrest.
  D. Ingested Poisons:
    1. Dilution, adsorption, and delay of gastric emptying (if patient is conscious) - Give two glasses of water or fruit juice to dilute the poison; two glasses of milk, flour in water, or beaten eggs to dilute and delay emptying; and one glass of water with two heaping teaspoons of activated charcoal as adsorbent.
    2. Emesis - If the patient is conscious, inducing vomiting is the best means of removing poison from the body. Do not induce vomiting if acids, alkalies, kerosene, or convulsants have been ingested. Any of the following may be used:
      a. Syrup of ipecac, 20 ml. Emesis occurs in 15 to 60 minutes.

    b. Apomorphine, 0.03 mg./lb. I.M. Emesis occurs
       rapidly. If depression follows, give levallorphan
       (Lorfan®), 0.01 mg./lb. I.M.

    c. Finger in throat (especially after the above).

    d. Table salt, powdered mustard, or strong soapsuds
       in a glass of water.

3. Gastric lavage - Lavage is the treatment of choice if
   less than two hours have elapsed since exposure. Do
   not perform lavage more than 30 minutes after alkalies,
   acids, or kerosene have been ingested. Avoid a large
   tube. Use a small, flexible, well lubricated Levin
   tube passed very cautiously. If the patient is unconscious, the lavage tube should preferably be passed
   through a cuffed endotracheal tube to avoid pulmonary
   aspiration. Save clean specimens of gastric aspirate
   before adding activated charcoal. Place in a clean
   bottle, seal, and refrigerate. Obtain a written receipt
   for the specimen from the coroner's representative.
   Aspirate all materials used for lavage.

    Gastric lavage fluids -

   a. Warm tap water.

   b. 1% salt water.

   c. Activated charcoal - Mix 4 to 5 tsp. in a glass of
      water, stir to a soupy consistency, and give orally.
      Trade names include Nuchar C®, Darco G60®, and
      Norit A®.

4. Catharsis - Give cathartics after emesis or gastric
   lavage to clear poisons from the gastrointestinal tract.
   Do not give cathartics after ingested acids or alkalies.
   Do not give irritant cathartics (aloes, cascara). Following emesis or lavage, give 30 Gm. (1 oz.) of sodium sulfate dissolved in one glass of water. In phenol
   poisoning, give 30 to 60 ml. (1 to 2 oz.) of castor oil.

Detoxification After Absorption.

    There are only a few specific antidotes.

A. Dimercaprol (BAL): Mercury and arsenic poisoning.

B. Nitrites and Thiosulfate: Cyanide poisoning.

C. Calcium: Oxalic acid poisoning.

D. Calcium Disodium Edathamil (EDTA, Versenate®): Lead
   poisoning.

E. Methylene Blue: Nitrite poisoning (e.g., coronary vasodilators).

F. Ethyl Alcohol (50%): Methyl alcohol poisoning.

G. Oxygen (100%): Carbon monoxide poisoning.

H. Nalorphine (Nalline®) or Levallorphan (Lorfan®): Morphine
   and derivatives.

I. Snake Venom Antiserum: Snake bite.

J. Atropine: Mushroom poisoning.

K. Dialysis: Where indicated.

Toxic Symptoms and Disorders Requiring Treatment.
Treat symptoms of target organs.

LEGAL ASPECTS OF POISONINGS

The physician should save specimens of the poison itself. He should also save washings in clean containers for toxicologic examination when indicated. In forensic cases, these specimens may be sealed with sealing wax and placed in a locked refrigerator. In such instances, deliver the specimens to the toxicologist personally and get a signed receipt for the specimen. If refrigeration is lacking, preserve the specimen with equal quantities of 95% alcohol; do not use formalin, as this interferes with toxicologic examination.

TREATMENT OF SPECIFIC POISONINGS

ACIDS, CORROSIVE

Symptoms include severe pain in the throat and upper gastrointestinal tract, marked thirst, bloody vomitus, and difficulty in swallowing, breathing, and speaking. There is discoloration and destruction of affected skin and mucous membranes, collapse, and shock.

Treatment.
  A. Ingested:
    1. Dilute immediately by giving large quantities of milk or water to drink; give beaten eggs (at least 12) as a demulcent.
    2. Gastric lavage should be performed within 30 minutes only. (Perforation may occur if passage of a tube is attempted.) Pass a Levin tube very gently and lavage with 2 to 4 qt. of warm tap water. Do not give chemical antidotes.
    3. Relieve pain and treat shock.
  B. Skin Contact: Flood with water for 15 minutes. Use no chemical antidotes; the heat of the reaction may cause additional injury. Relieve pain and treat shock.
  C. Eye Contact: Flood with sterile water for 5 minutes, holding the eyelids open. Relieve pain.

ALCOHOL, ETHYL

The principal manifestation of ethyl alcohol poisoning is C.N.S. depression and mucous membrane irritation, with nausea and vomiting.

Erroneous diagnosis may be made because of ingestion of barbiturates or paraldehyde, head injury, schizophrenia, insulin hypoglycemia, and coma of unknown cause.

The term acute alcoholism is frequently used erroneously to denote the acute alcoholic withdrawal syndrome that occurs in chronic alcoholics who have been deprived of alcohol. It usually begins six to 24 hours after withdrawal, progressing from tremor with mild hallucinosis and "rum fits" to frank delirium tremens with complete disorientation, paranoid agitation, hallucinations, seizures, fever, and tachycardia. The blood alcohol level is usually zero or very low.

Treatment of Acute Alcoholic Intoxication.

1. Emergency measures - Remove unabsorbed alcohol by gastric lavage with tap water. Instill 4 Gm. (60 gr.) of sodium bicarbonate.
2. General measures - (Similar to those for barbiturate poisoning.)
   a. Maintain airway.
   b. Keep patient warm.
   c. Give strong coffee orally or rectally, or give caffeine with sodium benzoate, 0.5 Gm. I.M., no more frequently than once every three or four hours for three or four doses.
   d. If the patient is comatose, treat as for barbiturate poisoning (see p. 466).
   e. With nausea, vomiting, and intractable retching, prochlorperazine (Compazine®), 10 mg., may be administered slowly, deeply I.M. It may be repeated in four to six hours, or the oral route may then be used in doses of 10-15 mg. every four to six hours.
   f. In acute alcoholic excitation, use either phenothiazine tranquilizer, I.M., every two to six hours (see p. 485); or paraldehyde orally, rectally, or I.M. (see p. 486).

ALCOHOL, METHYL

Methyl alcohol is a mucous membrane irritant and C.N.S. depressant which has an affinity for the optic nerve. Its end-products produce a metabolic acidosis. The minimum lethal dose is 30 to 60 ml. (1 to 2 oz.). Symptoms include headache, abdominal pain, dyspnea, nausea, vomiting, and blindness. Examination reveals flush or cyanosis, excitement or depression, delirium, coma, and convulsions.

Treatment.

Rid the stomach of alcohol and combat metabolic acidosis.
1. Lavage well with 1 to 2% sodium bicarbonate solution.

2. Keep patient in a dark room; check carbon dioxide combining power.
3. Intravenous fluids to combat metabolic acidosis.
4. Sodium bicarbonate, 5-15 Gm. orally every two to three hours.
5. Give ethyl alcohol, 100 proof (50%), 3-20 ml. orally every two to four hours for three to four days, to block the metabolism of methyl alcohol until it is excreted.

ALKALIES

The strong alkalies are common ingredients of household cleaning compounds and may be detected by their "soapy" texture. They exert a local effect on mucous membranes and may produce shock. Symptoms include burning pain in the upper gastrointestinal tract, nausea, vomiting, and difficulty in swallowing and breathing. Examination reveals destruction and edema of the affected skin and mucous membranes, bloody vomitus and stools, dyspnea, and shock.

Treatment.
  A. Ingested:
   1. Dilute immediately with 2 qt. water or milk.
   2. Allow vomiting.
   3. Follow with 1 pt. (500 ml.) of dilute vinegar (one part vinegar to six parts water) or fruit juice.
   4. Gastric lavage should be performed within the first hour only. (Perforation may occur if passage of a tube is attempted after one hour.) Gently pass a Levin tube and lavage with 2 to 4 qt. water or dilute vinegar, using 200 ml. (one glass) portions and removing as much as possible of the liquid each time.
   5. Relieve pain and treat shock.
  B. Skin Contact: Wash with running water until the skin no longer feels soapy. Relieve pain and treat shock.
  C. Eye Contact: Wash with sterile water continuously for 20 minutes, holding the lids open. Relieve pain.

AMITRIPTYLINE, IMIPRAMINE, AND RELATED DRUGS

Amitriptyline (Elavil®), imipramine (Tofranil®), desipramine (Norpramin®, Pertofrane®), protriptyline (Vivactil®), and nortriptyline (Aventyl®) are related drugs used as antidepressants.

Deaths have occurred following doses of imipramine exceeding 1.5 Gm. in adults and as little as 70 mg./Kg. in an infant. On the other hand, adults have survived doses exceeding 5 Gm.

These compounds block parasympathetic responses, and their effects are potentiated by amine oxidase inhibitors.

Overdoses of these agents cause coma, clonic movements or convulsions, fall of blood pressure, respiratory depression, mydriasis, and disturbances of cardiac rhythm and conduction. These cardiac disturbances can include sinus tachycardia, cardiac ischemia, and various degrees of atrioventricular or intraventricular block. Ventricular fibrillation immediately precedes death.

Treatment.
  A. Emergency Measures:
   1. Remove ingested drug by gastric lavage, emesis, and catharsis.
   2. If respiration is depressed, give artificial respiration (see p. 8).
   3. Maintain blood pressure by giving fluid (see p. 444). Avoid vasoconstrictor agents.
   4. Control convulsions by barbiturates (see p. 486). Succinylcholine is also useful.
   5. Control sinus tachycardia by the administration of pyridostigmine, 15 mg. orally every ten minutes, until a response is obtained; then repeat as necessary. Control conduction abnormalities by the intravenous infusion of 1/6 M sodium lactate with continuous ECG monitoring.
  B. General Measures: Both osmotic diuresis and dialysis have been used to remove overdoses. Treat cardiac arrest.

AMPHETAMINE, METHAMPHETAMINE, DEXTROAMPHETAMINE

These are sympathomimetic drugs usually used for their C.N.S. stimulating effect. Acute poisoning produces marked sympathomimetic and stimulant effects.

The symptoms include sinus tachycardia or life-threatening arrhythmia, convulsions, spasms, dilated pupils, gasping respirations, violent psychosis, respiratory failure, and shock. Death may result from cardiopulmonary arrest.

Treatment.
   1. Restrain.
   2. Give chlorpromazine (Thorazine®), 75-100 mg. I.M., or sodium phenobarbital, 0.12 Gm. I.V. (or both).
   3. If possible, remove ingested drug by emesis or gastric lavage followed by catharsis.
   4. Administer fluids for prevention or treatment of shock. Do not use vasopressors.

ANTICOAGULANTS

Bishydroxycoumarin, ethyl biscoumacetate, phenindione, and warfarin are used medically to inhibit the clotting mechanism. Abnormal bleeding occurs only after prolonged administration. The M. L. D. of bishydroxycoumarin and warfarin is 0.1 Gm.; of phenindione, 0.2 Gm.; of ethyl biscoumacetate, 0.6 Gm.

The principal manifestation of poisoning with the anticoagulants is bleeding: hemoptysis, hematuria, bloody stools, hemorrhages into organs, widespread bruising, and bleeding into joint spaces. Phenindione may also cause jaundice, hepatomegaly, skin rash, and agranulocytosis.

Treatment.
  A. Emergency Measures: Discontinue the drug at the first sign of bleeding. If ingestion of more than ten times a daily therapeutic dose is discovered within two hours, remove by gastric lavage and catharsis.
  B. General Measures: Give menadiol sodium diphosphate, 75 mg. I. M. one to three times daily. For more rapid effect, give 10 to 50 mg. of phytonadione (Mephyton®) I. V. as the diluted emulsion. Give transfusions of fresh blood or plasma if hemorrhage is severe. Absolute bed rest must be maintained to prevent further hemorrhages.

ANTIHISTAMINES

Antihistamines are used for the treatment of allergies, colds, insomnia, anxiety, dizziness, and motion sickness. Therapeutic doses cause a high incidence of untoward effects, including drowsiness, dryness of the mouth, headache, blurred vision, tinnitus, skin rash, nervousness, tachycardia, nausea, constipation, and urinary retention. Toxic doses may have either a depressant effect, with drowsiness, disorientation, ataxia, hallucinations, stupor, and coma; or an excitant effect, with agitation, fever, nystagmus, tachycardia, tremors, hyperreflexia, and convulsions. Agranulocytosis and aplastic anemia have been reported in certain cases of chronic antihistamine poisoning.

Treatment.
  A. Acute Poisoning:
    1. Emergency measures - Delay absorption by giving tap water, milk, or activated charcoal, and then remove by gastric lavage or emesis with tap water and follow with catharsis.
       If coma and respiratory depression are present, use resuscitative measures. **Caution:** Do not use

stimulants.   Maintain normal BP by giving levarterenol (Levophed®), 4 to 16 ml. of 0.2% solution per
liter of normal saline by slow I. V. drip.
   Control convulsions by cautious ether administration or with I. V. barbiturates.
2. Treat agranulocytosis.
B. Chronic Poisoning: Discontinue drug at onset of symptoms.

ARSENIC

Arsenic is found in pesticides and industrial chemicals.
Symptoms of poisoning usually appear within one hour after
ingestion but may be delayed as long as 12 hours. They include abdominal pain, difficulty in swallowing, persistent
vomiting, diarrhea, urinary suppression, and skeletal muscle
cramps. Severe thirst and shock may follow.

Treatment.
1. Induce vomiting with the finger, or give 1 tbsp. table
   salt or 1 tsp. powdered mustard in water Stat. Follow
   with 500 ml. (1 pt.) of milk.
2. Gastric lavage with 2 to 4 qt. of warm tap water, 200
   ml. (one glass) at a time.
3. Relieve pain and treat shock.
4. Treat diarrhea.
5. Dimercaprol injection (BAL) - Use 10% solution in oil
   (100 mg. per ml.). The side effects are usually over
   in 30 minutes. They include nausea, vomiting, headache, generalized aches, and burning sensations
   around the head and face. Side effects may be reduced
   if ephedrine, 25 mg. ($3/8$ gr.), or diphenhydramine
   (Benadryl®), 50 mg. ($3/4$ gr.) is given orally 30 minutes
   before dimercaprol.
   a. Severe poisoning - Give I. M. , 3 mg. /Kg. for each
      injection (1. 8 ml. /60 Kg.):
         First and second days - One injection every four
            hours day and night.
         Third day - One injection every six hours for
            four doses.
         Fourth and subsequent days - One injection twice
            daily for ten days or until recovery is complete.
   b. Mild poisoning - 2. 5 mg. /Kg. for each injection
      (1. 5 ml. /60 Kg.):
         First and second days - One injection every four
            hours for four doses.
         Third day - One injection twice daily.
         Fourth and subsequent days - One injection once
            or twice daily or until recovery is complete.

BARBITURATES

The barbiturates are C.N.S. depressants. The clinical manifestations of barbiturate poisoning may be mild or severe, depending upon the type, dose, and time of ingestion. The M. L. D. is 1-2 Gm. (15-30 gr.).

Mild symptoms of barbiturate poisoning include drowsiness, slow or slurred speech, and mental confusion which, together, may be mistaken for alcoholic intoxication. These may be followed by sleep progressing to stupor, rapid and deep breathing, florid facies, fever, dehydration, and, occasionally, serum filled skin blebs. From this point on, coma and areflexia may appear, and eventually shock and respiratory failure.

An accurate blood level four to six hours after ingestion is valuable for prognosis and as an indication of how intensive treatment should be. A 24-hour urine drug content determination is an excellent guide to the volume of fluids which may contribute to urinary excretion of the drug, especially if the urine is alkalinized. Unfortunately, these tests are difficult and not readily available.

Treatment.

Remove the poison; combat anoxia; prevent or treat shock; maintain fluid balance; prevent pulmonary complications; and administer stimulants as indicated. The critical factor in the management of barbiturate poisoning is constant medical and nursing attendance to maintain physiologic responses until the danger of respiratory failure and shock has passed. Although this may occur at any time in the first one to four days following ingestion of a large dose, it is most likely to occur during the state of profound coma, when reflexes are absent and the patient does not respond to noxious stimuli.

A. Conscious Patient:
1. Induce vomiting with finger, or 1 tbsp. of salt or 1 tsp. of powdered mustard in water.
2. Gastric lavage with 2 to 4 qt. of warm tap water, preferably containing 1 heaping tbsp. of activated charcoal per 200 ml. (one glass) of water (if less than two hours have elapsed since time of ingestion).
3. Instill sodium or magnesium sulfate, 30 Gm. (1 oz.), in 200 ml. (one glass) of water at end of lavage.
4. Give black coffee sweetened to taste.
B. Unconscious Patient: Do not induce vomiting.
1. Gastric lavage as in conscious patient. If less than two hours have elapsed since ingestion, pass Levin tube gently to avoid stimulating vomiting with possible aspiration.
2. Saline cathartic as in conscious patient.
3. Provide an unobstructed airway. Pull the tongue

forward, insert an oropharyngeal airway, and aspirate mucus. Tracheostomy may be necessary if coma is prolonged and mucus cannot be sucked out. I.P.P.B. may be advisable if respiration becomes shallow or cyanosis appears (see p. 435).

4. Start nasopharyngeal oxygen by catheter (see p. 434).

5. Protect the eyes with petrolatum gauze pads.

6. Check and record the following **every hour:** Rate and quality of the pulse, blood pressure, reaction of the pupils, rate and depth of respiration, temperature and color of skin (cyanosis), reflexes (corneal, pupillary, tendon), and response to painful stimuli (pinching or pinprick).

7. Parenteral fluids - If heart failure is absent and renal function is adequate, give 1 L. of 0.45% sodium chloride and 1-2 L. of 5% dextrose I.V. daily to maintain a urine output of 1-1.5 L./day. Venous pooling with relative hypovolemia may occur, resulting in shock. Monitor with central venous pressure (see pp. 13, 440).

8. Alkalinize the urine to increase excretion of the drug.

9. In the event of shock, use a vasopressor such as levarterenol (Levophed®) or metaraminol (Aramine®) (see pp. 494 and 580). Adequate fluid therapy is important.

10. Procaine penicillin G, 300,000 units twice daily I.M., as prophylaxis against pneumonia.

11. Insert indwelling catheter; watch for bladder distention.

12. In intercostal muscle or diaphragmatic paralysis (rare), a total body respirator may be lifesaving.

13. Hemodialysis is proving increasingly effective in elimination of barbiturates. It should be used when serum barbiturate levels are high.

14. C.N.S. stimulants (see p. 492) - The use of the analeptic drugs in barbiturate, belladonna, and bromide poisoning is the subject of some controversy. At present it seems clear that supportive care as outlined above is the most essential aspect of therapy. Analeptic drugs such as pentylenetetrazol (Metrazol®), picrotoxin, caffeine, bemegride (Megimide®), ethamivan (Emivan®), and amphetamine have been used; but, in the presence of severe respiratory depression, these drugs are not likely to be effective. They do not shorten the duration of depression but only stimulate the medullary centers for short periods of time. It is probable that the initial stimulation will be followed by greater depression. Complications of stimulant therapy are cardiac failure, cardiac arrhythmias, hyperthermia, and kidney damage with anuria.

BELLADONNA (Atropine, Scopolamine, etc.)

The belladonna alkaloids are parasympathetic depressants with variable C.N.S. effects. Symptoms include dryness of mouth, thirst, difficulty in swallowing, and blurring of vision. The physical signs include dilated pupils, flushed skin, tachycardia, fever, delirium, delusions, paralysis, and stupor. A rash may appear over the face, neck and upper trunk.

Treatment.

Remove the poison by lavage and catharsis and counteract excitement.

1. Stimulate vomiting with the finger, or with 1 tbsp. table salt or 1 tsp. powdered mustard in 200 ml. (one glass) of water.
2. Gastric lavage with 2 to 4 qt. of water, preferably containing 4 heaping tbsp. of activated charcoal per quart.
3. Follow lavage with sodium or magnesium sulfate, 30 Gm., in 200 ml. (one glass) of water.
4. Short-acting barbiturates such as secobarbital (Seconal®), 0.1 Gm. (1 1/2 gr.), by mouth if patient is excitable.
5. Maintain clear airway and treat respiratory complications as in barbiturate poisoning.
6. Alcohol sponge baths to control high temperatures.

BROMIDES

Bromide poisoning may be acute or chronic and results from ingestion of excessive amounts. The action is that of C.N.S. depressant. Acute poisoning is rare. Symptoms include anorexia, constipation, drowsiness, apathy, and hallucinations. Physical examination reveals dermatitis, conjunctivitis, foul breath, furred tongue, sordes, unequal and irregular pupils, ataxia, abnormal reflexes (often bizarre), toxic psychosis, delirium, and coma. With preparations containing acetanilid, cyanosis may be marked.

Treatment.

Remove poison by lavage and catharsis, give C.N.S. stimulants (see p. 492), and replace bromide ion with chloride ion.

1. Remove all sources of bromide.
2. In acute poisoning, lavage copiously with tap water to remove unabsorbed bromides, and later to remove those secreted across the mucous membrane into the stomach. Follow with sodium or magnesium sulfate, 30 Gm. (1 oz.), in 200 ml. (one glass) water.
3. Give sodium chloride (in addition to regular dietary intake) as follows: (1) 1000 ml. saline twice daily I.V.,

or (2) 1 to 2 Gm. as salt tablets every four hours orally.
4. Force fluids to 4 qt. daily.
5. Mercurial diuretics (see p. 503), 2 ml. I.M. every two to three days for four or five doses, will aid in elimination of bromides.

CARBON MONOXIDE

Carbon monoxide is responsible for many deaths and near deaths resulting from inhalation of automobile exhaust or from the use of unvented gas- or coal-burning heaters. It is also used for suicidal purposes. It combines with hemoglobin to form a relatively stable compound (carboxyhemoglobin) which secondarily causes tissue anoxia. Manifestations are headache, faintness, giddiness, tinnitus, vomiting, cherry-red mucous membranes, blotchy red skin, vertigo, "inebriation," loss of memory, fainting, collapse, paralysis, and unconsciousness. The patient's blood is also bright red and will remain so when boiled or shaken with one to two volumes of sodium hydroxide. Normal blood becomes black or brown-black under such circumstances.

Treatment.
1. Remove from toxic atmosphere and keep warm. Open windows. Loosen clothing and maintain absolute rest.
2. Give inhalation of 100% oxygen by mask for one hour and/or artificial respiration.
3. Give 50 ml. 50% sucrose solution I.V. for cerebral edema, if necessary.
4. Caffeine and sodium benzoate, 0.5 Gm. I.M. as a C.N.S. stimulant.

CARBON TETRACHLORIDE

Carbon tetrachloride is used as a solvent and cleansing agent and is very common in industry and in the home. It is a local irritant and a protoplasmic poison which may severely damage the heart, liver, and kidneys. It enters the body by ingestion or inhalation. It is especially damaging in association with ingestion of alcohol. Symptoms include headache, hiccup, nausea, vomiting, diarrhea, abdominal pain, drowsiness, visual disturbances, neuritis, and intoxication. The early signs are jaundice, tender liver, oliguria, and uremia; nephrosis and cirrhosis may occur later.

Treatment.
Remove the poison by lavage and catharsis; treat cardiac, hepatic, and renal complications symptomatically.

1. Remove from exposure; keep recumbent and warm.
2. Lavage copiously with tap water and give sodium or magnesium sulfate, 30 Gm., in 200 ml. (one glass) water at once.
3. Give inhalations of 100% oxygen by mask for one hour and/or artificial respiration, if respirations are depressed.
4. Treat as a toxic hepatitis.
5. Avoid alcoholic beverages.

CYANIDES: HYDROCYANIC ACID
(Prussic Acid, Rat Poison, Cyanogas®, Cyanogen)

Hydrocyanic acid and the cyanides cause death by inactivation of the respiratory enzyme, preventing utilization of oxygen by the tissues. The clinical combination of cyanosis, asphyxia, and the odor of bitter almonds on the breath is diagnostic. Respiration is first stimulated and eventually depressed. A marked drop in blood pressure may occur.

Treatment.
Act quickly. Use nitrites to form methemoglobin, which combines with cyanide to form nontoxic cyanmethemoglobin. Then give thiosulfates to convert to thiocyanate the cyanide released by dissociation of cyanmethoglobin.

1. Place in open air in recumbent position. Remove contaminated clothing; give artificial respiration.
2. If ingested, stick finger down throat immediately. Do not wait until lavage tube has arrived; death may occur within a few minutes.
3. Amyl nitrite inhalations for 15 to 30 seconds every two minutes.
4. Give the following at once and repeat if symptoms recur:
   a. Sodium nitrite, 3%, 10 to 15 ml., or 1%, 50 ml., I.V., taking two to four minutes to give injections, and -
   b. Sodium thiosulfate, 25%, 50 ml. I.V.
5. Combat shock.
6. Give 100% oxygen by forced ventilation.

DIGITALIS

The principal manifestations of poisoning with digitalis, digitoxin, and related drugs are vomiting and irregular pulse. Other signs include anorexia, nausea, diarrhea, yellow or white vision, delirium, slow pulse, fall of BP, and ventricular fibrillation. The Ecg. may show lengthened P-R interval, heart block, ventricular extrasystoles, ventricular tachycardia, and a depressed ST segment.

The M. L. D. of digitalis is 3 Gm. (45 gr.); of digitoxin, 3 mg. ($^1/_{20}$ gr.).

Treatment.

A. Emergency Measures: Delay absorption by giving tap water, milk, or activated charcoal and then remove by gastric lavage or emesis followed by catharsis. Do not give epinephrine or other stimulants, which may induce ventricular fibrillation.

B. General Measures: Give potassium chloride, 2 Gm. dissolved in water, every hour orally; or 0.3% in 5% dextrose slowly I. V. until the Ecg. shows improvement. If kidney function is impaired, serum potassium must be determined before potassium chloride is given. Propranolol (Inderal®) appears effective in digitalis-induced arrhythmias (see p. 500).

FLUORIDES SOLUBLE IN WATER
(Insect Powders)

Symptoms include vomiting, diarrhea, salivation; shallow, rapid, and difficult respiration; convulsive seizures; small, rapid pulse; coma, and cyanosis. Interference with calcium metabolism causes severe damage to the vital centers and may result in death due to respiratory failure. The sweat may contain sufficient fluoride to cause a burning sensation on the skin of anyone touching the patient.

Treatment.

Remove the poison by lavage with a precipitating agent; give supportive treatment.

1. Lavage with lime water; 1% calcium chloride, calcium lactate, or calcium gluconate; or large quantities of milk to form insoluble calcium fluoride.
2. Give I. V. calcium gluconate, 10%, 10 to 20 ml.; or calcium chloride, 5%, 10 to 20 ml.
3. Sodium or magnesium sulfate, 30 Gm., in 200 ml. (one glass) water.
4. Give white of eggs beaten in milk as demulcent.
5. Treat shock (see p. 439) and give supportive measures.

GASOLINE AND RELATED COMPOUNDS
(Kerosene, Petroleum Ether, Paint Thinner, Benzine)

Gasoline poisoning may result from inhalation or ingestion. More severe symptoms result from inhalation because the C. N. S. is more quickly reached by this route. Acute

manifestations are vomiting, pulmonary edema, bronchial
pneumonia, vertigo, muscular incoordination, weak and irregular pulse, twitchings, and convulsions. Chronic poisoning also causes headache, drowsiness, dim vision, cold and
numb hands, weakness, loss of memory, loss of weight,
tachycardia, mental dullness or confusion, sores in mouth,
dermatoses, and anemia. The M. L. D. is 10 to 30 ml.

Treatment.
Remove the patient to fresh air, and lavage with salad oil
or large amounts of warm saline (or both), taking extreme
care to prevent aspiration. Give sodium sulfate, 30 Gm.
(1 oz.) in 200 ml. of water, and follow with liquid petrolatum,
120 ml. Observe the patient closely for three to four days for
symptoms of respiratory involvement.

IODINE TINCTURE

Symptoms include oral or abdominal pain and vomiting
and diarrhea, which may be bloody. The mucous membranes
are stained brown and are edematous. Shock and dehydration
may appear as well as asphyxiation or edema of the glottis.
Convulsions may occur. Uremia may occur as a result of
kidney damage.

Treatment.
Remove the poison by lavage with inactivating agents and
treat symptoms; give supportive treatment.
1. Lavage with 1% sodium thiosulfate, or thin flour or
   starch paste (1 heaping tbsp. per pt.).
2. Sodium or magnesium sulfate, 30 Gm. in 200 ml. (one
   glass) water.
3. Give whites of eggs beaten in milk, salad oil, or
   cream, as demulcents.
4. Symptomatic measures as indicated.
5. Anticonvulsant drugs if indicated (see p. 488).

LEAD

Lead poisoning may occur by ingestion or by inhalation of
lead fumes or lead dust. Lead has a local astringent and generalized toxic effect. Poisoning is manifested by metallic
taste, dry throat, thirst, abdominal colic, vomiting, diarrhea,
constipation, headache, leg cramps, black stools, oliguria,
stupor, convulsions, palsies, and coma. Chronic lead poisoning may produce peripheral neuritis and blood changes. Lead
may be deposited in bone.

Treatment. [Do not use dimercaprol (BAL).]

Remove the poison by lavage with a precipitating agent and by catharsis; give EDTA to form a soluble un-ionizable lead complex that is excreted in the urine.

A. Acute Poisoning:
1. Lavage with dilute magnesium or sodium sulfate solution to precipitate lead sulfate if ingested.
2. Give sodium or magnesium sulfate, 30 Gm. in 200 ml. (one glass) water.
3. Calcium disodium edetate (EDTA, Versenate®) - This agent forms a soluble unionizable lead complex that is excreted in the urine. It has been used successfully in the treatment of lead poisoning. Give continuously I. V. (2% solution) or intermittently I. M. (20% solution containing 0.5% procaine) in a total dose range of 10 to 50 mg. per Kg. per 24 hours for a course of five to seven days. The drug is nephrotoxic and should not exceed a dose of 5 Gm. per 24 hours. EDTA may be given orally, 1 Gm. four times daily.
4. Hemodialysis is effective.

B. Chronic Poisoning:
1. Remove permanently from exposure.
2. Courses of EDTA may be employed, especially when hematologic complications have occurred, e.g., basophilic stippling, reticulosis, and anemia.

MERCURY

Mercury poisoning occurs by ingestion or inhalation. Mercury is a general protoplasmic poison. Poisoning is manifested by metallic taste, salivation, thirst, burning of the throat, discoloration and edema of oral tissues, abdominal pain, vomiting, bloody diarrhea, and shock. Oliguria or anuria (as a manifestation of renal tubular necrosis) may occur.

Treatment.

Remove poison by lavage and catharsis, and inactivate by use of dimercaprol (BAL).
1. Give whites of eggs beaten with milk or water as demulcent.
2. Lavage copiously with water, preferably containing 4 heaping tbsp. activated charcoal per quart.
3. Sodium or magnesium sulfate, 30 Gm. in 200 ml. (one glass) of water.
4. Dimercaprol (BAL) - Begin injections at once as for arsenic poisoning (see p. 465).
5. Give 1000 ml. of physiologic saline at once. Maintain good hydration. Chart fluid intake and output as well as weight and urinary findings daily.

6. Supportive measures. Be prepared to treat acute renal insufficiency if necessary.
7. Hemodialysis is a very effective means of eliminating this metal.

MORPHINE, OPIUM, HEROIN, AND DERIVATIVES

Morphine acts primarily on the C.N.S., causing depression and narcosis. Manifestations of poisoning include headache, nausea, excitement, depression, pinpoint pupils, slow respiration, rapid and feeble pulse, shock, and coma.

Treatment.

Combat C.N.S. and respiratory depression.
1. **For nonaddicts**, give nalorphine (Nalline®), 5 to 10 mg. I.V.; may repeat twice at 15-minute intervals.
2. **For addicts**, give nalorphine (Nalline®), 2 mg. subcut.; may repeat twice at 15-minute intervals.
3. If swallowed, also employ gastric lavage with potassium permanganate, 1:2000 (1 Gm. in 2 qt. of water). Use plain water if potassium permanganate is not available. Repeat. Morphine is excreted into stomach. Other measures mentioned above should also be employed.
4. Instill sodium sulfate, 30 Gm. in 200 ml. (one glass) water at end of lavage.
5. Insert airway if respirations are markedly depressed.
6. Artificial respiration manually or with mechanical resuscitator.
7. 100% oxygen if cyanosis is present, preferably with positive pressure.
8. Treat shock (see p. 439).

MUSHROOM POISONING

Amanita muscaria produces parasympathetic stimulation by muscarine; occasionally an atropine-like alkaloid produces convulsions. Symptoms begin one to two hours after ingestion and include salivation, slow pulse, miosis, abdominal cramps, diarrhea, nausea and vomiting, confusion, excitement, shock, and coma. The prognosis is good. Atropine is specific.

Amanita phalloides, A. brunnescens, and A. verna produce similar effects six to 15 hours after ingestion due to widespread cell damage, especially in the liver, kidney, brain and heart. Symptoms are characterized by abdominal pain, nausea, vomiting, bloody diarrhea, and dehydration; in one to three days, jaundice, anemia, heart failure, anuria, shock, and coma usually follow. The prognosis is poor. There is no specific antidote.

Treatment.

A. Poisoning Due to Amanita muscaria:
1. Atropine sulfate, 2 mg. ($1/30$ gr.) subcut. immediately and repeat every 30 minutes as necessary to control vagal symptoms. **Caution:** Amanita muscaria may have an atropine-like effect. Observe the patient carefully, and discontinue the antidote if signs of atropinization appear (see p. 468).
2. Stimulate emesis.
3. Lavage copiously with 2 to 4 qt. of tap water.
4. Sodium or magnesium sulfate, 30 Gm. in 200 ml. (one glass) of water.
5. Relieve pain; give barbiturates for excitement.
6. Force fluids orally, and parenterally if necessary.
7. Bismuth subcarbonate, 1 Gm., every two hours for diarrhea.
8. High saline enemas.

B. Poisoning Due to A. phalloides Type Toxin: As above except that atropine is of no help; lavage, emesis, and catharsis must be repeated at least three times the first day; glucose and blood must be given as indicated; and anuria, heart failure, and shock must be treated.

OXALIC ACID

Oxalic acid, a component of bleaching powder, is a powerful local irritant which precipitates ionized calcium. Poisoning is manifested by burning in the mouth and throat, violent abdominal pain, bloody vomitus, dyspnea, tremors, oliguria, hypocalcemic convulsions, and shock.

Treatment.

Precipitate with calcium salts by mouth, and give calcium salts parenterally to inactivate absorbed drug.
1. Give calcium lactate or any other calcium salt, 30 Gm. in 200 ml. (one glass) of water; one glass of lime water; or large amounts of milk to precipitate insoluble calcium oxalate.
2. Lavage with 2 to 4 qt. of tap water and remove excess.
3. Whites of eggs beaten in milk, as demulcent.
4. Calcium gluconate or lactate, 10%, 10 ml. I.V.; and calcium salts, 1 to 2 Gm. orally four times a day.
5. Symptomatic measures as indicated.

PHENOLS AND DERIVATIVES
(Carbolic Acid, Lysol®, Cresols, Stock Dips, Creosote)

These substances are local corrosives and also have systemic effects on nervous and circulatory systems. Poisoning is manifested by a burning sensation in the upper gastrointestinal tract, thirst, nausea, vomiting, erosion of mucous membranes, dark vomitus, oliguria, shock, and respiratory failure.

Treatment.

Remove the agent by lavage and catharsis, and give supportive treatment.

1. Delay absorption by giving tap water, milk, or universal antidote and then remove by repeated gastric lavage with tap water, or emesis.
2. Follow lavage or emesis with 60 ml. castor oil or olive oil, followed by sodium or magnesium sulfate, 30 Gm. in 200 ml. (one glass) of water.
3. **Do not** use alcohol or mineral oil for lavage.
4. Symptomatic measures as indicated.
5. External burns - Wash with rubbing alcohol and then soap and water.

PHENOTHIAZINE TRANQUILIZERS
(Chlorpromazine, Promazine,
Prochlorperazine, Etc.)

Minimal doses of the phenothiazine tranquilizers induce drowsiness and mild hypotension in as many as 50% of patients. Larger doses cause drowsiness, severe postural hypotension, tachycardia, dryness of the mouth, nausea, ataxia, anorexia, nasal congestion, fever, constipation, tremor, blurring of vision, stiffness of muscles, and coma. I. V. injection of solutions containing more than 25 mg./ml. of these drugs causes thrombophlebitis and cellulitis in a small number of patients.

Prolonged administration may cause leukopenia or agranulocytosis, jaundice, and generalized maculopapular eruptions; overdosage causes a syndrome similar to paralysis agitans, with spasmodic contractions of the face and neck muscles, extensor rigidity of the back muscles, carpopedal spasm, motor restlessness, salivation, and convulsions.

Phenothiazine compounds in urine acidified with dilute nitric acid can be detected by the addition of a few drops of tincture of ferric chloride. A violet color results.

The acute fatal dose for these compounds appears to be above 50 mg./Kg. Fatal poisoning from ingestion of approximately 75 mg./Kg. has been reported.

Treatment.

Remove overdose by gastric lavage or emesis. For severe hypotension, levarterenol may be necessary. Control convulsions with pentobarbital. Avoid other depressant drugs.

Give antiparkinsonism drugs. In the presence of fever, sore throat, pulmonary congestion, or other signs of infection, give penicillin, 1 million units daily, or a broad spectrum antibiotic in maximal doses until the infection is controlled.

No measures have been helpful for jaundice other than discontinuing the drug.

PHOSPHATE, ORGANIC
(Pesticide Sprays: Parathion, TEPP, HEPT, EPN, OMPA, Malathion, Thimet, Phosdrin, Systox)

Absorption of organic phosphate occurs by inhalation, skin absorption, or ingestion and results in marked depression of cholinesterase, causing continuous and excessive stimulation of the parasympathetic nervous system. Acute symptoms appear within hours after exposure and include headache, sweating, salivation, lacrimation, vomiting, diarrhea, muscular twitching, convulsions, and respiratory and visual difficulty. **Contracted pupils** with above symptoms and history of exposure in preceding 24 hours warrant therapy.

Treatment.

Counteract parasympathetic stimulation.
1. Atropine, 2 mg. ($\frac{1}{30}$ gr.) I. M. every 30 minutes until symptoms are relieved or signs of atropinization (dilated pupils, dry mouth) appear. Repeat as necessary to maintain complete atropinization. As much as 12 mg. ($\frac{1}{5}$ gr.) of atropine has been given safely in the first two hours.
2. If ingested, induce vomiting or wash stomach.
3. Sodium or magnesium sulfate, 30 Gm. in 200 ml. (one glass) water.
4. Oxygen, with positive pressure, if pulmonary edema or respiratory difficulty appear.
5. Prolonged artificial respiration may be necessary.
6. Take blood sample for r. b. c. cholinesterase levels. (This is of no practical value in immediate diagnosis or treatment of acute episode but aids in late confirmation of diagnosis and in follow-up therapy.)

PHOSPHORUS, INORGANIC
(Rat Paste, Fireworks, and Matches)

Phosphorus poisoning may result from contact, ingestion, or inhalation. Phosphorus is a local irritant and systemic toxin which acts on the liver, kidneys, muscles, bones, and cardiovascular system. Toxicity is manifested early by garlic taste, pain in the upper gastrointestinal tract, vomiting, and diarrhea. There is headache, pleuritis, extreme weakness, jaundice, oliguria, petechiae, prostration, and cardiovascular collapse.

Treatment.

Remove by catharsis and by aspiration of an inactivating agent following lavage. Give supportive treatment.

1. Lavage copiously with copper sulfate, 0.1%, (1 Gm. in 1 qt. water); repeat three to four times an hour for a total of 5 to 10 qt. of solution, or -
2. Lavage with potassium permanganate, 1:2000 (1 Gm. in 2 qt. water). Repeat three to four times.
3. Use tap water lavage or induce emesis if 1. and 2. are not available.
4. Sodium or magnesium sulfate, 30 Gm. (1 oz.), in 200 ml. (one glass) water; and mineral oil, 120 ml. (4 oz.). (No other oils may be used.)
5. Whites of eggs beaten in milk as demulcent.
6. Observe carefully over several days for appearance of jaundice and liver involvement (toxic hepatitis).
7. Symptomatic measures as indicated.

PSYCHOTOMIMETIC AGENTS

Psychotomimetic agents can be classified as follows: (1) LSD (lysergic acid diethylamide): Semisynthetic, from ergot. (2) DMT (dimethyltryptamine): Synthetic and from a South American plant (Piptadenia peregrina). (3) DET (diethyltryptamine): Synthetic. (4) "STP," DOM (2,5-dimethoxy-4-methylamphetamine): Synthetic. (5) Psilocybin and psilocin: Derivatives of 4-hydroxytryptamine. Synthetic; also from a mushroom (Psilocybe mexicana). (6) Bufotenine (dimethyl serotonin): Synthetic; also from Piptadenia peregrina, Amanita muscaria, and the skin of a toad (Bufo marinus). (7) Ibogaine: From the plant Tabernante iboga. (8) Harmine and harmaline: From plants (Peganum harmala and Banisteria caapi). (9) Ditran and phencyclidine (Sernyl®): Synthetic.

Manifestations requiring medical intervention are hyperexcitability, uncontrollability, ataxia, hypertension or hypotension, coma, and prolonged psychotic states. In addition,

LSD causes mydriasis, tremor, exaggerated reflexes, fever, psychopathic personality disorders, increased homicidal or suicidal risk, prolonged mental dissociation, and possible chromosome injury either in the user or in offspring.

Treatment.
1. Give chlorpromazine, 0.5 to 2 mg./Kg. I. M., to control the acute phase. (In STP poisoning, the combination is reported to be hazardous.)
2. Treat coma as for barbiturate poisoning.

SALICYLATES
(Aspirin, APC, PAC, Empirin®, Anacin®,
Bufferin®, Alka-Seltzer®, Sodium Salicylate, Oil
of Wintergreen)

Salicylate poisoning is most commonly caused by aspirin ingestion. Effects include acid-base disturbances, hypoprothrombinemia, and gastroenteritis. The acid-base disturbances are the most dangerous. Respiratory alkalosis appears first, followed by metabolic acidosis.

	CO_2 Content (Serum)	pH (Arterial)
Normal	25-28 mEq./L.	7.4
Respiratory alkalosis	↑	↑ or N
Metabolic acidosis	↓	↓

Salicylates stimulate the respiratory center, producing hyperpnea, CO_2 loss, a falling serum CO_2 content, and a normal or high arterial blood pH; this combination represents respiratory alkalosis. To compensate, the kidneys excrete increased amounts of bicarbonate, potassium, and sodium, but retain chloride. The chief dangers during this stage are hypokalemia and dehydration.

Salicylates interfere with carbohydrate metabolism in an unexplained manner, with resultant formation of fixed acids, probably ketones. This usually follows the alkalosis. Increased ketones and chloride, loss of base, and vomiting and diarrhea result in metabolic acidosis, characterized by low serum CO_2 content and low arterial pH. Acidosis occurs more commonly in children.

When the patient is first seen he may be in alkalosis, acidosis, or in a mixed stage. Accurate diagnosis and treatment are completely dependent upon the availability of determinations of serum CO_2 content, potassium, sodium and chloride, and arterial pH.

Salicylates are potent stimulators of metabolism, and hyperthermia may result.

The clinical picture includes a history of salicylate ingestion, hyperpnea, flushed face, hyperthermia, tinnitus, abdominal pain, vomiting, dehydration, spontaneous bleeding, twitching, convulsions, pulmonary edema, uremia, and coma. Salicylates may give a false-positive ketonuria and glycosuria, or true ketonuria and glycosuria may be present. The urine is unreliable as an indication of acidosis or alkalosis.

Treatment.

Remove poison; treat dehydration, shock, and electrolyte abnormalities; treat prothrombin deficiency.

1. Gastric lavage: Aspirate first without additional fluids, and then lavage with two to four quarts of warm tap water containing one heaping tablespoon of activated charcoal per 200 ml. (one glass).
2. Draw blood for initial blood CO_2, chloride, potassium, sodium, and arterial pH.
3. Perform Ecg. to evaluate potassium effect.
4. Treat dehydration and alkalosis with 0.9% saline and added potassium as indicated (see pp. 131 and 134).
5. Treat acidosis with Ringer's lactate (Hartmann's solution; see p. 430). This fluid is similar to normal extracellular fluid.
6. Appropriate adjustments of sodium and potassium in fluids should be based on serum sodium and potassium determinations. Serial Ecg.'s may be of value in controlling hypokalemia (see p. 426).
7. In most instances of acidosis, administration of large amounts of sodium bicarbonate or sodium lactate is unnecessary and unwarranted. However, if the blood pH falls below 7.15, these agents are probably indicated; $1/6$ molar sodium lactate, 20 ml. per Kg. I.V., or sodium bicarbonate, 0.4 Gm. per Kg. I.V. every two hours.
8. Attempts to rapidly raise a low CO_2 content to normal are contraindicated under any circumstances.
9. Vitamin K_1 (Mephyton®), 50 mg. ($3/4$ gr.), should be given I.V. once daily for hypoprothrombinemia.
10. Whole blood or platelet transfusion is recommended for thrombocytopenia.
11. Peritoneal dialysis or hemodialysis may be lifesaving for critically ill patients with a high serum salicylate concentration and/or renal insufficiency.

SILVER NITRATE

Silver nitrate poisoning is manifested by nausea, vomiting, diarrhea, bluish discoloration about the mouth, and shock.

Treatment.
Remove by lavage with a precipitating agent and by catharsis.
1. Gastric lavage with large quantities of salt solution to precipitate silver as a chloride.
2. Give sodium or magnesium sulfate, 30 Gm. in 200 ml. (one glass) water.
3. Whites of eggs beaten in milk as demulcent.
4. Symptomatic measures as indicated.

SNAKE AND LIZARD (GILA MONSTER) BITES

The venom of poisonous snakes and lizards may be neurotoxic or hemotoxic. Neurotoxins cause respiratory paralysis; hemotoxins cause hemolysis and destruction of endothelial lining of blood vessels. The manifestations of poisoning include local pain, thirst, profuse perspiration, nausea, vomiting, stimulation followed by depression, local redness, swelling, extravasation of blood, and shock.

Treatment.
The treatment of snake bite remains controversial because of the dearth of adequately controlled and documented studies on the subject. The following suggested measures must be individualized.
1. Immobilize the patient and the bitten part immediately. Do not allow walking, running, or use of alcoholic or stimulant beverages.
2. Apply tourniquet immediately above the wound and release every 10-15 minutes, progressing proximally above the area of advancing edema.
3. Depending upon the area, make superficial incisions approximately $1/8$ to $1/4$ inch deep and $1/4$ inch long over each fang mark.
4. After questioning the patient for history of allergy and testing him for serum hypersensitivity with 0.02 ml. of 1:100 dilution of antiserum in 0.9% saline, give specific antisera subcutaneously. I.V. administration may be necessary if the patient is in shock. (Follow the printed instructions of the serum manufacturer.)
5. Carry or otherwise transport patient to the nearest medical facility for further treatment as necessary.
6. Observe and treat for shock (see p. 12).

7. Corticosteroids may provide temporaty relief.
8. Give barbiturates or opiates as necessary for relief of apprehension or pain.

SPIDER BITES AND SCORPION STINGS

The toxins of the less venomous species of spiders and scorpions cause only local distress. The toxins of the more venomous species, including black widow spiders (Lactrodectus mactans), cause generalized muscular pains, convulsions, nausea and vomiting, variable C.N.S. involvement, and collapse.

Treatment.
1. Avoid local incision of wound, suction, and tourniquet. Immobilize the bitten part.
2. Keep patient recumbent and quiet. Transport by carrying if necessary. Do not let him walk.
3. Give specific antivenin if available to severely ill patients or those under 14 years of age.
4. Calcium gluconate, 10%, 10 ml. I.V., for relief of muscle pain, and repeat as necessary.
5. Warm baths to relieve pain and combat convulsions.
6. Sedation and supportive measures as indicated.

STRYCHNINE

Strychnine poisoning may result from ingestion or injection. Poisoning causes C.N.S. manifestations such as convulsions, opisthotonos, dyspnea, foaming at the mouth, coma, and asphyxia.

Treatment.
Prevent convulsions by deep sedation.
1. Keep patient quiet in a darkened room. Avoid stimuli.
2. Give amobarbital sodium (Sodium Amytal®), 0.5 Gm. (7½ gr.), or similar barbiturate in 10 to 20 ml. water slowly I.V. If convulsions continue, repeat in one-half hour. For mild cases or when parenteral barbiturate is not available, give up to five times hypnotic dose of oral barbiturate. **Do not use opiates.**
3. Ether or chloroform inhalation may be used if necessary to keep patient quiet.
4. Oxygen and artificial respiration during convulsions.
5. Lavage gently with potassium permanganate, 1:2000 (1 Gm. in 2 qt. water) before symptoms appear.
6. Symptomatic measures as indicated.

WASP, BEE, YELLOW JACKET, AND HORNET STINGS

Stings of these common insects, although locally painful, usually cause only transient, mild symptoms. Sensitive individuals may develop an acute allergic or even fatal anaphylactic response. Local cold compresses, applications of baking soda solution, and oral salicylates or antihistamines are sufficient treatment. Multiple stings may cause a shock-like reaction with hemoglobinuria.

Prevention.
Sensitive individuals should avoid unnecessary exposure to areas most apt to harbor these insects. Desensitization (**caution**) by graduated injections of mixed whole insect extract has been reported to be of value in preventing subsequent systemic reactions.

Treatment.
  A. Emergency Measures: Give epinephrine hydrochloride, 1:1000 solution, 0.2 to 0.5 ml. subcut. or I. M.; and then diphenhydramine hydrochloride (Benadryl®), 5 to 20 mg. slowly I. V. Treat shock.
  B. General Measures: Corticotropin (ACTH) or the corticosteroids may be necessary to support shock therapy.

31...
Drugs and Hormones

Determination of Drug Dosages for Children.

Young's Rule: $\dfrac{\text{Age of Child}}{\text{Age} + 12} \times \text{Adult Dose} = \text{Child's Dose}$

Clark's Rule: $\dfrac{\text{Weight of Child}}{150} \times \text{Adult Dose} = \text{Child's Dose}$

Although the above rules are useful guides, dosages for children cannot always be derived from adult dosages. For example, infants are relatively tolerant to epinephrine and belladonna alkaloids; and relatively more sensitive than adults to the effects of opiates and barbiturates.

CENTRAL NERVOUS SYSTEM DEPRESSANTS

INTRAVENOUS ANESTHETICS

Thiopental Sodium (Pentothal®).
Pentothal is widely used as a general anesthetic because it makes possible easy induction and maintenance of anesthesia in expert hands, and because recovery is rapid. It is available in 0.5, 1, 5, and 10 Gm. ampules ready to be made up into a 2.5% solution. For induction, inject 2 to 3 ml. I.V. in 10 to 15 seconds. Complete effect occurs in 35 seconds. If relaxation has not occurred, give an additional 2 to 3 ml. Increments of 0.5 to 1 ml. are given as indicated to maintain anesthesia, but the drug becomes long-acting if more than 1 Gm. is given.

Respiratory arrest and laryngospasm may occur during thiopental administration. The drug should be used only with adequate premedication by experienced personnel in circumstances where equipment is available to treat complications.

SEDATIVE-HYPNOTIC DRUGS

Any of the drugs listed in the table on p. 486 may cause drowsiness, mental confusion, headache, euphoria, excitement, tremor, and slurred speech. More severe toxicity is manifested by delirium, coma, slow and shallow respirations, and circulatory collapse. Side effects peculiar to individual drugs in the list are noted. These agents must be used with special care in combination with alcohol, tranquilizers, morphine, or other C.N.S. drugs.

PHENOTHIAZINES AND OTHER TRANQUILIZERS

These drugs are used for their antipsychotic, calming, and antiemetic effects. They may cause drowsiness, hypotension, a parkinsonism-like syndrome, muscle spasm, and anticholinergic effects. Jaundice and marrow depression occur rarely.

Agent	Dose (3-4 Times Daily)
Chlorpromazine (Thorazine®)*	25-50 mg.
Promazine (Sparine®)*	50-200 mg.
Promethazine (Phenergan®)*	25 mg.
Triflupromazine (Vesprin®)*	10-20 mg.
Prochlorperazine (Compazine®)*	5-10 mg.
Trifluoperazine (Stelazine®)	1 mg.
Perphenazine (Trilafon®)*	2-4 mg.
Fluphenazine (Permitil®, Prolixin®)	1 mg. (do not exceed 10 mg./day)
Thioridazine (Mellaril®)	10-25 mg.
Thiopropazate (Dartal®)	10 mg.
Trimeprazine (Temaril®)	2.5 mg.
Chlorprothixene (Taractan®)*	25 mg.
Chlordiazepoxide (Librium®)	5-20 mg. (oral or I.V.)

*Parenteral dose form for I.M. injection available. Use maximum of one oral dose.

ANTICONVULSANTS

See table, pp. 488-90.

ANALGESICS, ADDICTING
(Ask patient regarding idiosyncrasies.)

Codeine Sulfate or Codeine Phosphate.
Give orally or subcut. 15 to 60 mg. ($1/4$ to 1 gr.) every four to six hours as necessary; smaller doses can be given oftener.

SEDATIVE-HYPNOTIC DRUGS
(See p. 485.)

	Oral Dose		MLD†
	Hypnotic (Single Dose)	Sedative (3-4 Times a Day)	
Short-acting			
Pentobarbital*	100-200 mg.	30 mg.	1.5 Gm.
Secobarbital*	100-200 mg.	30 mg.	2 Gm.
Paraldehyde	12-16 ml.		50 Gm.
Hexobarbital (Sombulex®, Evipal®)	250-500 mg.		2 Gm.
Ethinamate (Valmid®)	0.5-2 Gm.		5 Gm.
Methyprylon (Noludar®)	200-400 mg.	50-100 mg.	5 Gm.
Ethchlorvynol (Placidyl®)	0.5-1 Gm.	100-200 mg.	15 Gm.
Chloral hydrate‡	0.5-1 Gm.		2 Gm.
Chlorobutanol (Chloretone®)	0.5-1 Gm.		
Intermediate-acting			
Amobarbital*	100-200 mg.	15-30 mg.	1.5 Gm.
Aprobarbital (Alurate®)	120 mg.	20-40 mg.	2 Gm.
Butabarbital (Butisol®)	100-200 mg.	8-60 mg.	2 Gm.
Vinbarbital (Delvinal®)	100-200 mg.	30 mg.	2 Gm.
Heptabarbital (Medomin®)	200-400 mg.	50-100 mg.	2 Gm.
Meprobamate (Miltown®, Equanil®)‡		400 mg.	16 Gm.
Glutethimide (Doriden®)	500 mg.		5 Gm.
Long-acting			
Phenobarbital*		15-30 mg.	1.5 Gm.
Mephobarbital (Mebaral®)		30-60 mg.	2 Gm.
Ectylurea (Nostyn®, Levanil®)		150-300 mg.	15 Gm.
Chlordiazepoxide (Librium®)‡		5-10 mg. §	
Diazepam (Valium®)‡		2-10 mg. §	
Phenaglycodol (Ultran®)		200 mg.	
Bromides‡	No longer prescribed, but still used in proprietary mixtures.		

*These barbiturates are also available as sodium salts for parenteral administration. Parenteral forms of other sedatives are available, but experience with their use is limited.

†Most of the drugs listed have been used in successful suicidal attempts or have been lethal after therapeutic accidents.

‡Specific toxicity reactions (see also p. 485):

Chloral hydrate: Gastric irritation.

Meprobamate: Purpura and other sensitivity reactions.

Chlordiazepoxide and diazepam: Long action leads to cumulative effects.

Bromides: Acneiform rash; increased oral, nasal, and lacrimal secretions; toxic psychosis.

§Do not exceed 50 mg./day.

Morphine Sulfate or Morphine Hydrochloride.
Oral: 8 to 20 mg. ($1/8$ to $1/3$ gr.) every three to six hours
as necessary.
Subcut. : Same as for oral, or smaller.
I. V. : (Emergency only.) 8 to 16 mg. ($1/8$ to $1/4$ gr.).

Meperidine Hydrochloride (Demerol®).
Give orally or I. M. , rarely given I. V. because of severe
side reactions. If I. V. route is employed the drug should be
well diluted and given over no less than a two-minute period.
Subcutaneous injection causes local irritation. Orally or I. M. ,
give 50 to 100 mg. every four hours as necessary.

Anileridine Hydrochloride (Leritine®).
Oral: 25 to 50 mg. every three to four hours as necessary.

Anileridine Phosphate (Leritine®).
Subcut. or I. M. : 25 to 50 mg. every four to six hours as
necessary.

Dihydromorphinone Hydrochloride (Dilaudid®).
Use about one-fourth the dose of morphine.
Oral or Subcut. : 2 to 4 mg. every four to six hours as
necessary.
Rectal: Can be given as a suppository.

Levorphanol Tartrate (Levo-Dromoran®).
Oral: 2 mg. every three hours as necessary.
Subcut. : 2 to 3 mg. every four hours as necessary.

Preoperative Medications According to Age

Age in Years	Weight in Pounds	Morphine Sulfate	Scopolamine Hydro-bromide or Atropine Sulfate
Under 1	7-20	None	0.05 mg. ($1/1200$ gr.)
1 to 2	21-30	1.5 mg. ($1/40$ gr.)	0.06 mg. ($1/1000$ gr.)
3 to 4	31-38	2 mg. ($1/30$ gr.)	0.08 mg. ($1/800$ gr.)
5 to 6	39-46	2.5 mg. ($1/24$ gr.)	0.10 mg. ($1/600$ gr.)
7 to 8	47-55	3 mg. ($1/20$ gr.)	0.12 mg. ($1/500$ gr.)
9 to 10	56-63	4 mg. ($1/15$ gr.)	0.15 mg. ($1/400$ gr.)
11 to 12	64-78	4.5 mg. ($1/14$ gr.)	0.18 mg. ($1/350$ gr.)
13 to 14	79-100	5 mg. ($1/12$ gr.)	0.20 mg. ($1/300$ gr.)
15 to 16	101-120	8 mg. ($1/8$ gr.)	0.25 mg. ($1/250$ gr.)
17 to 18	121-140	8 mg. ($1/8$ gr.)	0.30 mg. ($1/200$ gr.)
19 and older	Over 140	10 mg. ($1/6$ gr.)	0.40 mg. ($1/150$ gr.)

[Cont'd. on p. 491.]

ANTICONVULSANT DRUGS *

Drug	Indications	Average Daily Dose	Toxicity and Precautions	Remarks
Acetazolamide (Diamox®)	Grand mal	1-3 Gm. in divided doses (0.25 Gm. 3 times a day initially). Drowsiness and paresthesias may occur (reduce dose).		Drowsiness and paresthesias may occur (reduce dose).
Bromides (potassium bromide or sodium bromide)	All epilepsies, especially as adjuncts.	3-6 Gm. in divided doses	Psychoses, mental dullness, acneiform rash (stop drug; may resume at lower dose).	Rarely used now. Effective at times when all else fails.
Chlordiazepoxide (Librium®)	Mixed epilepsies	15-60 mg.	Drowsiness, ataxia.	Useful in patients with behavior disorders.
Diazepam (Valium®)	Mixed epilepsies	8-30 mg.	Drowsiness, ataxia.	Useful in patients with behavior disorders; also in status epilepticus (5-10 mg. I.V. infusion).
Diphenylhydantoin sodium (Dilantin®)	Grand mal, some cases of psychomotor epilepsy.	0.4-0.6 Gm. in divided doses	Gum hypertrophy (dental hygiene); nervousness, rash, ataxia, drowsiness, nystagmus (reduce dosage).	Safest for grand mal and psychomotor epilepsy. May accentuate petit mal.
Ethosuximide (Zarontin®)	Absence, akinetic, and myoclonic attacks.	750-1500 mg.	Drowsiness, nausea, vomiting.	Useful in minor attacks in children.
Ethotoin (Peganone®)	Grand mal	2-3 Gm.	Dizziness, fatigue, skin rash (decrease dose or discontinue).	

Mephenytoin (methyl-phenylethylhydantoin, Mesantoin®)	Grand mal, some psychomotor epilepsy. Effective when grand mal & petit mal coexist.	0.3-0.5 Gm. in divided doses	Nervousness, ataxia, nystagmus (reduce dose); pancytopenia [frequent blood counts); exfoliative dermatitis (stop drug if severe skin eruption develops).	Does not cause gum hypertrophy.
Mephobarbital (Mebaral®)	As phenobarbital	0.2-0.9 Gm. in divided doses	As for phenobarbital. Usually has no advantage over phenobarbital and must be used in twice dosage.	
Meprobamate (Equanil®, Miltown®)	Absence attacks, myoclonic seizures.	1200-2000 mg.	Drowsiness	
Metharbital (Gemonil®)	Grand mal	0.1-0.8 Gm. in divided doses	Drowsiness (decrease dose)	Especially effective in seizures associated with organic brain damage and infantile myoclonic epilepsy.
Methsuximide (Celontin®)	Petit mal, psychomotor epilepsy.	1.2 Gm. in divided doses	Ataxia, drowsiness (decrease dose or discontinue).	
Paramethadione (Paradione®)	Petit mal	0.3-2 Gm. in divided doses	As for trimethadione	Toxic reactions stated to be less than with trimethadione. Other remarks as for trimethadione.

*Reproduced, with permission, from Chusid and McDonald, Correlative Neuroanatomy & Functional Neurology, 14th Ed. Lange, 1970.

ANTICONVULSANT DRUGS (Cont'd.)

Drug	Indications	Average Daily Dose	Toxicity and Precautions	Remarks
Phenacemide (Phenurone®)	Psychomotor epilepsy	0.5-5 Gm. in divided doses	Hepatitis (liver function tests at onset; follow urinary urobilinogen at regular intervals); benign proteinuria (stop drug; may continue if patient is having marked relief); dermatitis (stop drug); headache and personality changes (stop drug if severe).	
Phenobarbital	All epilepsies, especially as adjunct.	0.1-0.4 Gm. in divided doses	Drowsiness (decrease dose); dermatitis (stop drug and resume later; if dermatitis recurs, stop drug entirely).	One of safest drugs. May sometimes aggravate psychomotor seizures. Toxic reactions rare.
Phensuximide (Milontin®)	Petit mal	0.5-2.5 Gm. in divided doses	Nausea, ataxia, dizziness (reduce dose or discontinue); hematuria (discontinue).	
Primidone (Mysoline®)	Grand mal	0.5-2 Gm.	Drowsiness (decrease dose); ataxia (decrease dose or stop drug).	Useful in conjunction with other anticonvulsants.
Trimethadione (Tridione®)	Drug of choice in petit mal	0.3-2 Gm. in divided doses	Bone marrow depression, pancytopenia, exfoliative dermatitis (as above); photophobia (usually disappears; dark glasses); nephrosis (frequent urinalysis; discontinue if renal lesion develops).	Do not use alone for grand mal; may aggravate this condition.

Methadone (Dolphine®).
Dosage of 5-10 mg. subcut. provides analgesia similar to morphine. Recently recommended in gradually reduced dosage for heroin or morphine addiction.

Phenazocine Hydrobromide (Prinadol®).
I.M.: 2 mg. every four to six hours as necessary.

NARCOTIC ANTAGONISTS
(See p. 474.)

These drugs are specific antagonists **only** for severe respiratory depression due to morphine and pharmacologically related drugs. They may be used by experienced physicians in detection of addiction.
Caution: Smaller doses must be used in addicts to avoid severe withdrawal reactions.

Nalorphine Hydrochloride (Nalline®).
I.V.: 5 to 10 mg. for nonaddicts. May repeat twice at 15-minute intervals.
Subcut.: 2 mg. for addicts. May repeat twice at 15-minute intervals.

Levallorphan (Lorfan®).
I.V.: 1 mg. for nonaddicts. Two additional doses of 0.5 mg. may be given at 15-minute intervals.
Subcut.: 0.5 mg. for addicts. Two additional doses of 0.5 mg. may be given at 15-minute intervals.

ANALGESICS AND ANTIPYRETICS, NONADDICTING
(See also Analgesics, Addicting, above.)

Aspirin.
Oral (preferred): 0.3 to 1 Gm. every three to four hours as necessary.
Rectal: Give in a thin starch paste.

Sodium Salicylate.
Same dosages as for aspirin (also enteric-coated).

Indomethacin (Indocin®).
Analgesic and anti-inflammatory agent; 50 to 200 mg. orally per day in divided doses. Untoward effects include headache, dizziness, light-headedness, tinnitus, rash, stomatitis, and gastrointestinal symptoms, including peptic ulceration.

Phenacetin.
Oral: 0.3 Gm. three to four times daily in case of salicylate intolerance.

Colchicine.

Anti-inflammatory agent. For gout, give orally, 0.5 mg. every hour until relief occurs or diarrhea begins, or until 12 to 15 doses have been taken. Toxic in high doses.

Pentazocine (Talwin®).

Dosage of 30 mg. subcut. I.M. or I.V. every three to four hours. Stated to be equivalent to 10 mg. of morphine. Has the advantage of requiring less record keeping since it is not a narcotic. As a newly marketed drug, its effectiveness and potential side effects must be proved by experience and study.

Propoxyphene Hydrochloride (Darvon®).

Used as a substitute for codeine but has less potent analgesic effect. Available also with APC (Darvon Compound®). Give orally, 65 mg. four times daily. (APC is aspirin, phenacetin, and caffeine.)

Oxyphenbutazone (Tandearil®).

Similar in indications, dosage, action, and side effects to phenylbutazone.

Phenylbutazone (Butazolidin®).

Used as an analgesic, antipyretic, and anti-inflammatory agent in the treatment of rheumatoid spondylitis and gout which fail to respond to less toxic drugs. Adverse effects occur in 40% of patients and include edema, nausea, rash, epigastric pain, vertigo, and stomatitis. Peptic ulcer activation with bleeding, hepatitis, hypertension, agranulocytosis, and purpura may also occur. Use with caution and only for short periods. Initially, give 50 to 100 mg. orally four times daily with meals or milk; maintain with 50 to 100 mg. orally every 12 hours.

CENTRAL NERVOUS SYSTEM STIMULANTS

Analeptics.

Picrotoxin and pentylenetetrazol are still sometimes used to combat profound coma due to overdosage with central depressants, although the evidence in favor of their effectiveness is questionable. **Caution:** These agents, if employed, are only an adjunct to other measures utilized to prevent respiratory failure and shock.

A. Picrotoxin: Give I.V., 9 mg. at intervals of 30 minutes, until a response to painful stimuli occurs or deep tendon reflexes return.

B. Pentylenetetrazol (Metrazol®): Give 100 mg. I. V. at intervals of 30 minutes (as for picrotoxin, above).

Direct Stimulants.

These drugs are used for the treatment of narcolepsy, as anorexiants, and as stimulants, especially with serious depression. Adverse effects include overstimulation, activation of peptic ulcer, and emotional dependence. Tolerance may develop.

A. Amphetamine Sulfate (Benzedrine®): Give orally, 5 to 10 mg. two or three times daily.

B. Dextroamphetamine Sulfate (Dexedrine®): Give orally, 2.5 to 5 mg. two or three times daily.

C. Methamphetamine Hydrochloride (Desoxyn®): Give orally, 2.5 to 5 mg. two or three times daily, to stimulate the C. N. S. and depress the appetite.

Antidepressants ("Mood Elevators").

These drugs are used as adjuncts in the treatment of psychogenic depression. They include the drugs related chemically to the phenothiazine tranquilizers and the less effective and more toxic monoamine oxidase inhibitors.

A. Drugs Related to Phenothiazines:
1. Imipramine (Tofranil®) - Orally 25 mg. three times daily, increasing every few days as necessary to a maximum of 250 mg. per day. Maintenance doses of about 150 mg. per day may be established after an effect is apparent.
2. Amitriptyline (Elavil®) - Dosages as for imipramine.

B. Monoamine Oxidase Inhibitors:
1. Nialamide (Niamid®).
2. Isocarboxazid (Marplan®).

AUTONOMIC NERVOUS SYSTEM DRUGS

PARASYMPATHOMIMETIC DRUGS

Physostigmine Salicylate.

Topical: 0.25 and 0.5% solution as miotic.

Neostigmine Methylsulfate (Prostigmin®).

Used parenterally in respiratory crises of myasthenia gravis and paralytic ileus. Contraindicated in asthma. Available for subcut. or I. M. injection in solutions containing 0.5 mg./ml. (1:2000) or 1 mg./ml. (1:1000).

A. Myasthenia Gravis Crises: 1 mg. every 20 minutes for two or three doses as necessary.

B. Paralytic Ileus: 0.5 to 1 mg. every four to six hours.

Neostigmine Bromide (Prostigmin®).
For oral administration. Give 45 to 150 mg. per day.

Pyridostigmin Bromide (Mestinon®).
Anticholinesterase effect in myasthenia gravis with fewer unpleasant side effects than neostigmine preparations. Contraindicated in patients with asthma. Give orally, one 60 mg. tablet every four hours during the day, increasing to 12 tablets daily as necessary for relief of symptoms.

Pilocarpine Hydrochloride.
Topical: 0.5, 1, and 2% solution as miotic.

SYMPATHOMIMETIC DRUGS

Epinephrine.
A. Epinephrine Solution, 1:1000: Give subcut., 0.2 to 0.5 ml.; repeat as necessary. (For children, give one-half the adult dose.)
B. Epinephrine Inhalation, 1:100: Use 0.5 ml. in nebulizer as necessary to abort or relieve bronchial spasm.
C. Epinephrine Suspension: Epinephrine in oil (0.2%) for prolonged effect. Give I. M., 0.75 to 1 ml. every 10 to 15 hours.

Levarterenol Bitartrate (Levophed®): See p. 580.

Metaraminol Bitartrate (Aramine Bitartrate®).
Potent vasopressor with prolonged duration of action. Also has an inotropic effect on the heart.
Subcut. or I. M.: 2 to 10 mg.
I. V.: 15 to 100 mg. as a continuous infusion in 500 ml. of isotonic saline or 5% dextrose in water at a rate adjusted to maintain pressure. Onset of action is slower and duration of action longer than those of levarterenol; at least ten minutes should elapse before dosage is increased.

Ephedrine Hydrochloride or Ephedrine Sulfate.
Oral or Subcut.: 15 to 50 mg.; repeat as necessary. Stimulant side effect.
Topical: 0.5 to 3% as drops or nasal spray.

Phenylephrine Hydrochloride (Neo-Synephrine®).
Oral: 10 mg.
Topical: 1/4 to 1% as drops or nasal spray.
I. M., 5 mg., or I. V., 0.5 mg., repeated in one hour as necessary to maintain blood pressure. May be given as slow I. V. infusion of 100 to 150 mg. in 1000 ml. of 5% glucose in water as a pressor agent. Has no appreciable inotropic effect.

Mephentermine Sulfate (Wyamine®).
Vasoconstricting agent of value for relief in congestion of nasal mucous membrane (topical). Valuable for temporary treatment of hypotension in shock (I. V. or I. M.). Has inotropic and vasopressor effects.

Topical: 0.5% as drops or nasal spray.

I. M.: 15 to 30 mg. repeated in one to four hours as necessary to maintain blood pressure.

I. V.: 5 to 30 mg. given at a rate of 1 mg. per minute by continuous infusion. Repeat in 30 to 60 minutes as necessary to maintain blood pressure. 30 mg. may be diluted with 100 ml. of 5% dextrose and administered as continuous I. V. drip to maintain pressure.

Methoxamine Hydrochloride (Vasoxyl®).
Valuable for temporary relief of hypotension in shock.

I. M.: 10 to 20 mg. repeated in 60 to 90 minutes as necessary to maintain blood pressure.

I. V.: (Emergency only.) Give no more than 10 mg. at a rate of 1 mg. per minute. May use 35 to 40 mg. in 250 to 500 ml. of 5% dextrose in water.

Isoproterenol Hydrochloride (Isuprel®).
Used as a bronchodilator in asthma and as a cardiac accelerator to prevent ventricular slowing or asystole in Stokes-Adams syndrome (chronotropic effect). Increasing use in shock with low cardiac output because of its capacity to stimulate force of heart muscle contraction (inotropic effect).

Sublingual: 10 to 15 mg. three or four times daily for asthma.

Oral Inhalation: 0.5 ml. of 1:200 solution in nebulizer for asthma.

I. V.: For frequent bouts of asystole or excessive slowing of ventricular rate, give a slow infusion of 2 mg. in 500 ml. of 5% dextrose in water to maintain a ventricular rate of 70.

Methoxyphenamine Hydrochloride (Orthoxine®).
Used in asthma. Give orally, 50 to 100 mg. every four hours as necessary. More effective in preventing than in treating acute asthma.

PARASYMPATHOLYTIC DRUGS

The following drugs are **contraindicated** in patients with glaucoma and should be used with care in patients with pyloric obstruction or prostatic hypertrophy.

Belladonna Tincture.
Give orally, 10 drops three times daily, to inhibit gastric acid secretion, and increase dosage by one drop daily to the point of dryness of mouth or blurring of vision (whichever comes first). Then fix the dose at three drops less than that at which toxicity appeared.

Atropine Sulfate.
Oral, Subcut., or I.V.: 0.3 to 1 mg. two to four times daily.
Topical: 0.5 to 1% solution as mydriatic.

Scopolamine Hydrobromide.
Oral or Parenteral: 0.3 mg.; repeat as necessary.
Topical: 0.1 to 0.2% solution as mydriatic.

Homatropine Hydrobromide or Homatropine Hydrochloride.
Topical: 1 to 2% solution as mydriatic.

Cyclopentolate Hydrochloride (Cyclogyl®).
Topical: 0.5%, 1%, and 2% ophthalmic solution as a mydriatic.

Methantheline Bromide (Banthine®).
Inhibits gastric acid secretion and relaxes smooth muscle. May cause dry mouth, blurred vision, urinary retention, and constipation. Used in treatment of peptic ulcer and dysuria. Give orally, 50 to 100 mg. three or four times daily.

Propantheline Bromide (Pro-Banthine®).
Same indications and side effects as methantheline bromide. Give orally, 15 to 30 mg. three or four times daily.

Methscopolamine Bromide (Pamine®).
Same indications and side reactions as methantheline bromide. Give orally, 2.5 mg. three or four times daily.

Oxyphencyclimine Hydrochloride (Daricon®).
Same indications and side effects as methantheline bromide. Give orally, 10 mg. every 12 hours.

Trihexyphenidyl Hydrochloride (Artane®).
For paralysis agitans. May produce blurred vision and dry mouth. Give orally, 1 to 5 mg. three times daily.

Dicyclomine Hydrochloride (Bentyl®).
Oral: 10 mg. three or four times daily as antispasmodic.

Benztropine Methanesulfonate (Cogentin®).
Most effective agent against rigidity and spasm in paralysis agitans when combined with trihexyphenidyl, cycrimine,

or dextroamphetamine sulfate. Give orally, 0.5 mg. once or twice daily, and increase as necessary up to 5 mg. daily.

Cycrimine Hydrochloride (Pagitane®).

For paralysis agitans when tolerance to trihexyphenidyl develops. Same side effects as trihexyphenidyl. Give orally, 0.04 to 5 mg. three or four times daily.

Rabellon® (Hyoscine Hydrobromide, 0.4507 mg.; Atropine Sulfate, 0.0372 mg.; and Scopolamine Hydrobromide, 0.0119 mg.).

For paralysis agitans. Same side effects as atropine. Give orally, 1/4, 1/2, or one tablet two to four times daily.

CARDIOVASCULAR DRUGS

DIGITALIS PREPARATIONS

See tables below and on p. 498.

Oral Administration of the Digitalis Drugs*

Urgency	Drug	Dosage
Moderate	Digitalis	0.4 Gm. (6 gr.) every 8 hours for 3 doses.
	Digitoxin	0.4 mg. every 8 hours for 3 doses.
	Digoxin	1 mg. every 8 hours for 3 doses.
Intermediate	Digitalis	0.2 Gm. (3 gr.) 3 times daily for 2 days, or 0.1 Gm. (1 1/2 gr.) 4 times daily for 3 days.
	Digitoxin	0.2 mg. 3 times daily for 2 days.
	Digoxin	0.5 mg. twice daily for 2 days, or 0.25-0.5 mg. 3 times daily for 3 days.
Least	Digitalis	0.1 Gm. (1 1/2 gr.) 3 times daily for 4-5 days.
	Digitoxin	0.1 mg. 3 times daily for 4-6 days.
	Digoxin	0.25-0.5 mg. twice daily for 4-6 days.

*Reproduced, with permission, from Sokolow, in Current Diagnosis & Treatment 1970. Krupp, Brainerd, Chatton, and Margen, Eds. Lange, 1970.

PARENTERAL ADMINISTRATION OF THE DIGITALIS DRUGS*

Glycoside and Preparations Available	Dose		Method of Administration	Speed of Maximum Action and Duration
	Digitalizing	Maintenance		
Ouabain, 1 ml. and 2 ml. ampules, 0.25 mg. ($^1/240$ gr.)	0.25-0.5 mg. ($^1/240$-$^1/120$ gr.)	Not used for maintenance	0.25-0.5 mg. diluted in 10 ml. saline slowly, I.V.; follow with another drug (see below).	$^1/_2$-1$^1/_2$ hours; duration, 2-4 days.
Deslanoside (Cedilanid-D®), 2 ml. and 4 ml. ampules, 0.4 and 0.8 mg.	1.6 mg.	0.2-0.4 mg.	1.2 mg. I.V. or I.M. and follow with 0.2-0.4 mg. I.V. or I.M. every 3-4 hours until effect is obtained.	1-2 hours; duration, 3-6 days.
Digitoxin (dilute before use), 1 ml. and 2 ml. ampules, 0.2 and 0.4 mg.	1.2 mg.	0.05-0.2 mg.	0.6 mg. I.V. or I.M. followed by 0.2-0.4 mg. every 4-6 hours until 1.2 mg. is given.	3-8 hours; duration, 14-21 days.
Digoxin (dilute before use), 1 ml. ampules, 0.5 mg.	1.5 mg.	0.25-0.75 mg.	1 mg. I.V. and 0.5 mg. in 3-4 hours; then 0.25 mg. every 3-4 hours until effect is obtained.	1-2 hours; duration, 3-6 days.

*Reproduced, with permission, from Sokolow, in Current Diagnosis & Treatment 1970. Krupp, Brainerd, Chatton, and Margen, Eds. Lange, 1970.

ANTIARRHYTHMIC AGENTS

These drugs are used for the prevention of symptomatic ectopic premature beats; paroxysmal atrial, nodal, or ventricular tachycardia; and paroxysmal or chronic atrial fibrillation. (For prevention or treatment of Stokes-Adams syndrome due to ventricular asystole or slowing of ventricular rate, see isoproterenol, p. 495.)

Quinidine Sulfate and Quinidine Gluconate.

Recommended doses have varied tremendously. Quinidine is available as quinidine sulfate, 0.2 Gm. tablets; and as quinidine gluconate in a 10 ml. ampule containing 0.8 Gm. The following are approximate doses:

A. Premature Beats: Quinidine sulfate, 0.2 to 0.4 Gm. orally three to four times daily.

B. Conversion: Never attempt conversion of atrial fibrillation with quinidine unless the patient is digitalized. It may produce a 1:1 flutter with a disastrously rapid ventricular rate.

   1. Oral - Quinidine sulfate, 0.4 Gm. every two hours for five doses or until conversion to sinus rhythm takes place. If conversion does not occur and if no significant toxic clinical or Ecg. manifestations develop, repeat the following day, using 0.6 Gm. in place of previous dose. The dose may be increased to 0.8 Gm. on the third day, but it is dangerous, and under these circumstances very careful clinical and Ecg. observations for toxicity must be made, preferably in a hospital.

   2. I. M. - Quinidine gluconate appears to be the preparation of choice. Maximum safe dose is approximately 0.4 Gm. every two hours for five doses in treatment of paroxysmal tachycardias as above.

C. Maintenance Dose: For prevention of further attacks, give quinidine sulfate, 0.2 to 0.6 Gm. three or four times daily. Begin with small doses and increase as necessary.

Procainamide Hydrochloride (Pronestyl®).

Oral: 0.5 to 1 Gm. every three to six hours.

I. M. (Parenteral Route of Choice): 1 Gm. followed by 0.5 to 1 Gm. every three to six hours depending on the urgency. With renal insufficiency, limit second and subsequent injections to 0.5 Gm.

I. V. (Emergency Only): Give 200 mg. (2 ml.) in two minutes. Wait four minutes. Repeat this procedure for a maximum of 1 to 1.5 Gm. or until the desired effect is achieved. Continuous Ecg. observation and repeated blood pressure readings are mandatory.

Lidocaine (Xylocaine®).

A remarkably effective, rapidly acting agent of special value for multiple ventricular premature beats or paroxysmal ventricular tachycardia. Duration of action is short.

I.V.: 50 to 100 mg.; may be repeated every 5 to 20 minutes.
I.V. drip: If arrhythmia recurs, use slow I.V. drip in 5% dextrose in water. Titrate the concentration as necessary. Do not exceed 3 Gm. in 24 hours.

Propranolol (Inderal®).

This new drug, developed as a beta-adrenergic blocking agent, also has quinidine-like properties. It is effective in prevention or treatment of ectopic (especially ventricular) arrhythmias when other methods fail. It appears to be of particular value in digitalis-induced arrhythmias. It is used in a manner similar to quinidine and procainamide.

Oral: 10 to 30 mg. t.i.d. before each meal and at bedtime.
I.V.: 1 mg./minute with continuous Ecg. and BP monitoring. The dose may be repeated every 3 to 5 minutes for a total of 3 to 5 mg.

Serious side effects include hypotension, heart block, and severe bronchospasm. Propranolol may induce heart failure in an undigitalized patient with limited cardiac reserve.

CORONARY DILATOR DRUGS

Glyceryl Trinitrate Tablets (Nitroglycerin).

The drug of choice in the treatment of the acute attack of angina pectoris. Also used in the treatment of acute biliary and renal colic. May produce headache, palpitation, flushing, dizziness, and hypotension. Tablets slowly deteriorate with exposure to air. Give sublingually, 0.3 to 0.4 mg. May be repeated one or two times. Two or three minutes are required before its action is manifested.

Erythrityl Tetranitrate (Erythrol®, Cardilate Sublingual®).

Oral: 15 to 60 mg. every four to six hours. Long-acting.
Sublingual: 5 to 15 mg. three or four times daily.

Pentaerythritol Tetranitrate (Peritrate®).

Oral: 10 mg. three or four times daily.

VASODILATORS AND VASOCONSTRICTORS

Papaverine Hydrochloride.

Oral, I.V., or Intra-arterial: For acute vasospasm, 30-65 mg.

Dioxyline Phosphate (Paveril®).
   Oral: 0.2 Gm. three times daily.   A papaverine analogue.

Ergotamine Tartrate (Gynergen®).
   For migraine most effective shortly after onset of headache.   To be avoided with diffuse liver disease.   Do not repeat more than once weekly.
   I. M. : 0.25 to 0.5 mg. (treatment of choice).
   Oral: 4 mg.; follow with 2 mg. hourly to a maximum of 10
   mg.

Ergotamine With Caffeine (Cafergot®).   (Ergotamine, 1 mg.,
         and caffeine, 100 mg.)
   Two tablets at onset of headache.   Follow with one tablet
every 30 minutes for not more than six tablets or until pain is
relieved.   Thereafter, give initial dose of as many tablets as
are required to relieve headache.   Give no oftener than twice
weekly.

Dihydroergotamine Methanesulfonate (Dihydroergotamine®).
   Give I. M., 1 mg. at onset of migraine.

Tolazoline Hydrochloride (Priscoline®).
   Peripheral vasodilator.   Give orally, 50 mg. three to
five times daily after meals.   Begin with 25 mg. twice daily
and increase slowly.   Gastric irritation is common.   May also
be given intra-arterially, 50 mg., in acute vasospastic states.

Methysergide Maleate (Sansert®).
   May be effective in preventing episodes of migraine.
Contraindicated in pregnancy and peripheral vascular disease.
The oral dose is 2 mg. two to four times daily, preferably
with meals.   May cause hazardous fibrotic disorders, involving primarily the retroperitoneal area (retroperitoneal
fibrosis), but also possibly other tissues.

DIURETICS

   The thiazide diuretics are the most effective diuretics for
oral administration.   The organic mercurial compounds are
the most effective for parenteral administration.

THIAZIDE DIURETICS

   Chlorothiazide, hydrochlorothiazide, and numerous substituted derivatives of these compounds are the most effective

oral diuretics now available. They also have an important role in the treatment of hypertension (see p. 507). These compounds are sulfonamide derivatives which appear to inhibit renal tubular reabsorption of sodium and chloride, resulting in increased water diuresis similar to the mercurials. They also cause an increased potassium and bicarbonate excretion somewhat similar to that caused by the carbonic anhydrase inhibitors. These drugs can be given continuously without the development of tolerance and with reasonable safety. In intractable heart failure, a strict low-sodium diet and parenteral administration of mercurial diuretics may also be necessary to prevent fluid retention.

The more potent derivatives of this group are not clearly more effective than the parent compounds in reducing potassium and bicarbonate diuresis. Hypokalemia, with increased sensitivity to digitalis, may occur; it is best prevented by rest periods of one to three days of each week. Potassium depletion, which may be dangerous, is most effectively prevented by a supplement of potassium chloride, 1 Gm. three or four times daily (or equivalent). Effective (but less reliable) is a diet high in potassium content: bananas, orange juice, nuts, meat, milk, eggs. Hyponatremia or hypochloremic alkalosis may also occur.

These drugs should not be given to patients with severe hepatic or renal disease; hepatic coma may occur with the former, severe acidosis with the latter. Other side effects which occasionally occur are anorexia, nausea, postural hypotension, weakness, muscle pain, skin rash, and headache. Hyperglycemia and, in susceptible individuals, precipitation of diabetes mellitus, may result from thiazide therapy. Acute gout is frequently precipitated in the presence of the chronic disease. Reversible hyperuricemia may be induced. Thrombocytopenia and agranulocytosis occur rarely.

The following are the recommended daily doses, to be divided into two doses orally:

Bendroflumethiazide (Naturetin®), 5 to 10 mg.

Benzthiazide (NaClex®), 25 to 100 mg.

Chlorothiazide (Diuril®), 0.25 to 1 Gm.

Cyclothiazide (Anhydron®), 1 to 2 mg.

Flumethiazide (Ademol®), 0.25 to 1 Gm.

Hydrochlorothiazide (Esidrix®, Hydro-Diuril®, Oretic®), 25 to 100 mg.

Hydroflumethiazide (Saluron®), 25 to 100 mg.

Methyclothiazide (Enduron®), 2.5 to 10 mg.

Trichlormethiazide (Naqua®, Metahydrin®), 2 to 8 mg.

CHLORTHALIDONE
(Hygroton®)

A sulfonamide that acts similarly to the thiazides. Oral dosage is 50 to 200 mg. daily, reducing dose to 50 to 100 mg. daily; or give as often as necessary to maintain dry weight.

MERCURIAL DIURETICS

The mercurials reduce distal tubular reabsorption of sodium and chloride with consequent diminished water reabsorption.

These agents are of value in the treatment of salt and water retention associated with heart failure, cirrhosis, and drug-induced edema. Mercurials are contraindicated in acute nephritis and must be used with caution in chronic renal disease. They are a valuable aid when rapid diuresis is necessary to differentiate between pulmonary disease and mild fluid retention due to heart failure.

Mercurials lose their effectiveness in the presence of hypochloremic alkalosis, marked hyponatremia, and advanced chronic renal disease.

Undesirable side effects are infrequent but may be serious. Sensitivity reactions include stomatitis, febrile reactions, rash, and gastrointestinal disturbances. Fatalities due to shock and cardiac arrhythmia after intravenous administration rarely occur. It is advisable to employ small doses intramuscularly initially. The urine should be examined periodically for evidence of renal damage due to mercury.

Hyponatremia may result from excessive sodium diuresis. Hypochloremic alkalosis may follow excessive chloride loss. Hypokalemia with digitalis intoxication may follow chronic potassium diuresis.

Ammonium chloride orally and aminophylline intravenously enhance the diuretic effect of the mercurials.

Meralluride Injection (Mercuhydrin®).
I. M. or I. V.: 1 to 2 ml.

Mercurophylline Injection (Mercuzanthin®).
I. M. or I. V.: 1 to 2 ml. as necessary (135 mg./ml.).

Mersalyl and Theophylline Injection (Salyrgan-Theophylline®).
I. M. or I. V.: 1 to 2 ml. as indicated.

Mercaptomerin Sodium, Sterile (Thiomerin®).
Subcut. or I. V.: 1 to 2 ml. as indicated.

ETHACRYNIC ACID (Edecrin®) AND
FUROSEMIDE (Lasix®)

A new, potent oral diuretic with onset of action in 30 to 60 minutes. It causes a significant sodium and potassium loss. Hypokalemia and hyponatremia may occur. Oral dosage is 25 to 50 mg. initially and 50 to 100 mg. thereafter if indicated, depending upon response.

Furosemide produces similar effects. The initial daily dosage is 20 to 40 mg. orally.

TRIAMTERENE
(Dyrenium®)

A new diuretic which does not cause potassium depletion. It may be used in conjunction with the thiazides or mercurial diuretics. Initial dose is 100 mg. twice daily orally after meals; maintenance dose is 50 to 100 mg. daily orally.

ACIDIFYING DIURETICS

Ammonium Chloride.
This drug is chiefly used to potentiate the action of mercurial diuretics, and to correct hypochloremic alkalosis. The mercurials will not exert a diuretic effect in the presence of hypochloremic alkalosis.

Ammonium chloride ceases to be effective after three to five days of administration. Therefore, a five-day rest period after five days of administration is indicated.

The ammonium ion is metabolized by the liver. The chloride ion contributes to increased plasma acidity. The drug may therefore produce hepatic coma in severe liver disease, or severe acidosis in renal insufficiency. Gastrointestinal side effects are fairly common.

Oral: 6 to 8 Gm. daily as enteric-coated tablets in divided doses for five-day periods. Mercurial diuretics are given after the first day as indicated.

XANTHINE DIURETICS

Aminophylline.
The chief value of this drug as a diuretic is to enhance the effectiveness of the mercurials. Aminophylline increases glomerular filtration rate; mercurials inhibit tubular reabsorption of sodium, chloride, and water.

This drug is also valuable for its bronchodilating effect in acute bronchial asthma, and for the relief of paroxysmal dyspnea associated with left ventricular failure.

Oral administration is of doubtful value.
I. V. : 0.5 to 1 Gm. **very slowly** exactly 45 minutes after a
mercurial diuretic has been given I. V. or I. M.

CARBONIC ANHYDRASE INHIBITOR

By inhibiting renal tubular carbonic anhydrase, acetazolamide produces transient diuresis with increased urinary
excretion of sodium and potassium bicarbonate. An alkaline
urine and mild metabolic acidosis results. The thiazide
drugs are more effective diuretics.

This drug is of value in the correction of metabolic alkalosis and in the short-term treatment of glaucoma.

Acetazolamide (Diamox®).
Oral: 250 mg. once daily or every other day.
I. V. : 250 mg. once daily or every other day when oral
medication cannot be taken.

SPIRONOLACTONE (Aldactone®)

Spironolactone is an antagonist to aldosterone, the adrenal steroid which controls renal tubular reabsorption of sodium. It therefore causes sodium diuresis without potassium
loss. It can be combined with a thiazide to neutralize the
potassium-wasting effect of the latter drug. The onset of effect may be delayed for five to seven days. The response of
patients with congestive failure and primary aldosteronism
has been variable. This drug may be a more promising supplementary drug in the resistant edema of cirrhosis and
nephrosis. It is expensive.

Give orally, 25 mg. four times daily for five to eight
days. Continuation depends on effectiveness.

URICOSURIC DRUGS

It is important to maintain a daily urinary output of 2000
ml. or more in order to minimize the precipitation of uric
acid in the urinary tract. This can be further prevented by
giving alkalinizing agents to maintain a urine pH of about 6.0.
If a significant uricosuric effect is not obtained in the presence of overt renal dysfunction, do not increase the dose of
the drug beyond the limits stated below. Avoid using salicylates with any other uricosuric drug, since they antagonize the
action of other uricosuric agents.

Probenecid (Benemid®).
    Begin with 0.5 Gm. daily and gradually increase to 1 to 2 Gm. daily.

Salicylates.
    Five to 6 Gm. daily.

Sulfinpyrazone (Anturane®).
    Start with 100 mg. daily and gradually increase to 200 to 400 mg. daily. In any case the maintenance dose is determined by observation of serum uric acid response or, preferably, the urinary uric acid response. Ideally, one attempts to maintain a normal serum urate level.
    Caution: The parent compound of sulfinpyrazone is phenylbutazone. When it is given over a protracted period, careful observation for prevention and treatment of similar adverse effects is warranted.

Allopurinol (Zyloprim®).
    An alternative to be used when the uricosuric agents listed above are not tolerated. It blocks the formation of uric acid from xanthine by inhibiting xanthine oxidase. Its effect is not blocked by salicylates. It is also used in instances of impaired renal function and recurrent uric acid lithiasis. Infrequently, it may precipitate gout. Dosage is 100 to 200 mg. two to four times daily orally, together with colchicine, 0.6 mg. one to three times daily, in order to achieve normal plasma uric acid level.

ANTIHYPERTENSIVE DRUGS

    The etiology of essential hypertension is not known. The objective of treatment is to delay or improve cardiac, renal, cerebral, and ocular complications by careful control of blood pressure. Correctable causes of hypertension must be ruled out (see p. 53).
    The antihypertensive drugs now available may produce mild or severe side effects which can be dangerous. They must not be given without clinical justification. Many patients with significant hypertension require no more than reassuring explanation, weight control, sedation, judicious guidance, and possibly a strict low-sodium diet.
    If antihypertensive drugs are given, careful supervision with adequate blood pressure readings (supine and standing) are necessary. The physician must be thoroughly familiar with the characteristics of the drugs used. They should be administered in a manner which will allow objective evalua-

tion of their effectiveness and side effects when used singly or in combination. Intelligent cooperation by the patient is essential.

RAUWOLFIA ALKALOIDS

Rauwolfia is a mild antihypertensive and sedative drug whose action and side effects are essentially due to the alkaloid reserpine. The primary value of this drug is to potentiate the action of the ganglionic blocking drugs and the newer sympatholytic agents. Even in this role it is being supplanted by the thiazide diuretics.

Undesirable side effects include drowsiness, nasal congestion with headache, nightmares, depression to the point of psychosis, parkinsonism, and gastric hyperacidity.

Reserpine.
   Oral: 0.1 to 0.25 mg. three times daily initially. Maintenance dose is 0.25 mg./day.
   I.M.: 2.5 mg. every eight to 12 hours, for temporary use with hypertensive crisis.

PHTHALAZINE DERIVATIVES

Hydralazine is a mild hypotensive agent which is occasionally effective when given alone but is more effective when combined with ganglionic blocking agents or the thiazides. It is a cardiac stimulant, i.e., it increases cardiac output and renal blood flow. For these reasons it may be of value as an adjunct to the ganglionic blocking agents. Undesirable side effects are common and include headache, tachycardia, and nausea and vomiting. A syndrome resembling lupus erythematosus may appear, with joint pains and swelling, skin rash, fever, and even L.E. cells in the blood. This disappears when the drug is withdrawn.

Hydralazine Hydrochloride (Apresoline®).
   Oral: 10 mg. four times daily. Gradually increase to 50 mg. four times daily if necessary.

THIAZIDE DIURETICS
(See also p. 501.)

Chlorothiazide, hydrochlorothiazide, and many new substituted derivatives of these drugs frequently have a mild hypotensive action when given alone. They may be somewhat more effective when used with reserpine. When used with ganglionic blocking or sympatholytic agents, the dosage of the latter may have to be reduced by 50% to prevent severe postural hypotension.

GANGLIONIC BLOCKING AGENTS

These drugs inhibit the transmission of nerve impulses through both sympathetic and parasympathetic ganglia. Sympathetic ganglion blockade produces vasodilatation with resulting lowering of blood pressure, chiefly in the standing position. Hypotension must be avoided, especially in patients with a history of coronary insufficiency or cerebral thrombosis.

Parasympathetic blockade produces side effects which must be controlled either by diminishing the dose or by the use of antidotes. Side effects include blurring of vision, dry mouth, nausea, vomiting, intractable constipation, urinary retention (especially with prostatic hypertrophy), and impotence. Constipation must be controlled with either mild cathartics daily or with neostigmine, 15 to 30 mg. daily by mouth. Sudden absorption of accumulated drug from the bowel may produce peripheral vascular collapse.

In addition to individual factors, other considerations also increase the hypotensive response. These include alcohol, excessive exercise, undue heat or fever, hemorrhage, pregnancy, and anesthesia. Hypotensive response **must** be determined by blood pressure determinations in the erect and supine positions. The patient should be taught to do this at home.

These drugs should be reserved for patients with severe hypertension who have not responded to milder drugs. If chlorothiazide or hydrochlorothiazide or any of their derivatives is added, the dose of the ganglionic blocking agent should be diminished by 50% and then readjusted according to pressure response.

Avoid abrupt termination of hypotensive therapy.

Mecamylamine Hydrochloride (Inversine®).

This drug is completely absorbed from the intestine. The effect of each dose lasts six to 12 hours. The initial dose is 2.5 mg. twice daily. Increase by increments of 2.5 mg. every other day as indicated. The average daily dose is 25 mg. in three divided doses, the morning dose being smaller than the others. Tolerance may develop. The maximal daily dose is 60 mg.

Pentolinium Tartrate (Ansolysen®).

This agent is especially valuable when given subcut. for rapid control of an acute hypertensive crisis.

Subcut.: The initial dose is 2 to 3 mg. every four to six
   hours. A response should be manifest in one-half hour,
   and the maximum effect is reached in two hours. Increase by increments of 0.5 to 1 mg. every four to six
   hours until the desired response is obtained. The effective single dose varies from 2 to 10 mg.

SYMPATHETIC BLOCKING AGENTS

These drugs act selectively on the post-ganglionic sympathetic nervous system, blocking adrenergic transmission.
The actions of circulating epinephrine and norepinephrine are
not antagonized. Undesirable side effects result partly from
unopposed parasympathetic activity and from excessive sympathetic suppression. Symptoms reported include abdominal
cramps, diarrhea, fatigue and muscle pain following excessive exercise, edema, marked morning orthostatic hypotension, and failure of ejaculation. Atropine controls the diarrhea; diuretics control the edema. Hot weather, fever, excessive exercise, salt loss, and alcohol necessitate lower
doses.

Guanethidine Sulfate (Ismelin®).
This drug has a prolonged action and is given once daily
by mouth. The initial dose is 10 mg. ($1/6$ gr.) daily. Increase by increments of 10 mg. every five days until a desirable effect is achieved. The average daily effective dose
is 60 mg. (1 gr.). Rarely, doses up to 400 mg. (6 gr.) per
day have been reported necessary.
   When given with the thiazide drugs, the dose of guanethidine must be reduced.

Methyldopa (Aldomet®).
This drug will control both supine and standing BP in
about two-thirds of patients with moderate hypertension; the
postural effects may predominate. Concomitant thiazide therapy is desirable, both to potentiate the hypotensive effects of
the drug and to counteract fluid retention. The latter and
drowsiness are its main side effects.
   Oral: An initial dose of 250 mg. two or three times daily is
      gradually increased at intervals of two to three days to a
      total daily dose (divided into two to four doses) of 0.75 to
      2.5 Gm.
         This drug should be given under careful supervision by
      the physician until a stable dosage schedule is established.

ANTIHISTAMINE DRUGS

The antihistamines are chiefly of value in seasonal hay fever, acute urticaria, and angioneurotic edema. They are also of definite value in the relief of atopic dermatitis, contact dermatitis, serum sickness, and drug reactions. Diphenhydramine or dimenhydrinate is effective in the control of motion sickness. This class of drugs has also proved effective in the management of the symptoms of labyrinthine disturbances, and for the relief of nausea and vomiting. In

Generic Name	Trade Name	Daily Oral Dose
Ethylenediamine Derivatives		
Antazoline hydro-chloride	Antistine®	100 mg., 2-4 times
Chlorcyclizine	Di-Paralene®, Perazil®	100 mg., 2-3 times
Chlorothen	Tagathen®	25 mg., 3-4 times
Methapheniline	Diatrine®	50 mg., 4 times
Methapyrilene	Histadyl®, Semikon®, Thenylene®	50-100 mg., 4 times
Promethazine	Phenergan®	25 mg. once daily at bedtime
Pyrilamine maleate	Neo-Antergan®, etc.	25-50 mg., 3-4 times
Thonzylamine	Neohetramine®, Thonzylamine®	50-100 mg., 3-4 times
Tripelennamine	Pyribenzamine®	50 mg., 3-4 times
Aminoalkyl Ethers		
Dimenhydrinate	Dramamine®	50-100 mg., 3-4 times
Diphenhydramine	Benadryl®	50 mg., 3-4 times
Doxylamine	Decapryn®	12.5-25 mg.; 4 times
Alkylamines		
Chlorpheniramine maleate*	Chlor-Trimeton®, Teldrin®	4 mg., 3-4 times
Pheniramine maleate	Trimeton®	25 mg., 3 times. Also available as elixir for children, 7.5 mg., 3 times

*Sedation infrequent.

combination with other drugs they have proved effective in the treatment of paralysis agitans.

About 20% of patients will have some type of side reaction, including lassitude, fatigue, drowsiness, euphoria, nervousness, insomnia, tremors, anorexia, nausea, vomiting, constipation, diarrhea, headache, tinnitus, and dizziness. Hypersensitivity reactions may occur, such as dermatitis from oral or topical administration, leukopenia, and agranulocytosis. The incidence of hypersensitivity reactions is extremely low.

RESPIRATORY DRUGS

EXPECTORANTS, SEDATIVE

Soothing effect only.

Sugar Lozenges (Cough Drops).
As desired. **Note:** ''Medicated'' proprietary lozenges have no advantage over ordinary fruit drops, hard candy, etc.

Syrupy Cough Mixtures (Commonly as a Vehicle With Codeine).
A. Terpin Hydrate Elixir: 4 to 12 ml. every three to four hours.
B. Hydriodic Acid Syrup: 4 to 8 ml. every three to four hours.
C. Lemon Juice, Honey, Whisky (Equal Parts): 4 to 8 ml. every three to four hours.

EXPECTORANTS, SPUTUM LIQUEFACTION

Steam Inhalation.
For 30 minutes four times daily. **Note:** Adding tincture of benzoin or other aromatic substances does not increase the efficiency of steam inhalations.

Ammonium Chloride.
Give 0.5 Gm. every four hours in liquid vehicle.

COUGH SUPPRESSANTS

These consist of the narcotic group of drugs used to partially suppress the exhaustive effects of unproductive cough. They are given in doses one-fourth to one-half the usual analgesic dose.

EXPECTORANTS, BRONCHODILATOR

For allergic bronchospasm, give antihistamines (see p. 510). For inflammatory bronchospasm, give sympathomimetic drugs: epinephrine, ephedrine, isoproterenol, phenylephrine, methoxyphenamine (see pp. 494-5).

GASTROINTESTINAL DRUGS

GASTRIC ANTACIDS

Many preparations of magnesium, aluminum, and calcium are available, singly or in combination, for use as antacids. The magnesium compounds tend to have a laxative effect and the aluminum and calcium compounds a constipating effect. Sodium bicarbonate may be used as an antacid but will cause alkalosis if used to excess.

Antacids are given orally between meals or alternating with milk and cream in ulcer diets. In acute peptic ulcer, it is often necessary to give antacids at frequent intervals during the waking hours.

ANTIDIARRHEAL AGENTS

Bismuth Subcarbonate.
   2 Gm. orally after each loose stool.

Kaolin.
   15 to 60 Gm. orally every three to four hours.

Bismuth Magma and Paregoric.
   ℞   Bismuth magma
          Paregoric, $\overline{aa}$ 4 ml. after each loose stool.

Paregoric.
   4 ml. orally after each loose stool.

Diphenoxylate Hydrochloride With Atropine Sulfate (Lomotil®).
   Oral: 2.5 mg. three or four times daily.

ANTINAUSEANT AGENTS

Chlorpromazine Hydrochloride (Thorazine®).
   (See also p. 485.) May produce jaundice and hypotension.

Prochlorperazine (Compazine®).
　Oral: 5 to 10 mg. three or four times daily.
　I. M.: 5 to 10 mg. every four hours, administered as noted
　　for Chlorpromazine, above.

Diphenhydramine Hydrochloride (Benadryl®).
　Oral: 50 mg. three or four times daily.

Dimenhydrinate (Dramamine®).
　　Give orally, 50 to 100 mg. three or four times daily.

Meclizine Hydrochloride (Bonine®).
　　Give orally, 50 mg. every six to 12 hours.

Cyclizine Hydrochloride (Marezine®).
　　Give orally, 50 mg. three times daily after meals.

Promazine Hydrochloride (Sparine®).
　Oral: 25 to 50 mg. three or four times daily.

CATHARTICS
(Laxatives, Bulking Agents, Lubricants, Wetting Agents)

Mild Cathartics.
　A. Aromatic Cascara Sagrada Fluidextract: Four to 8 ml.
　　in evening.

　B. Dioctyl Sodium Sulfosuccinate (Colace®, Doxinate®): 50
　　to 240 mg. daily with glass of water.

　C. Magnesia Magma (Milk of Magnesia): 15 ml. in evening.

　D. Petrolatum Liquid (Mineral Oil): 15 to 60 ml. in evening
　　or one-half dose each morning and evening.

　E. Psyllium Hydrophilic Mucilloid (Metamucil®): 4 to 7 Gm.
　　daily or three times daily. Follow with full glass of water.

Strong Cathartics.
　A. Castor Oil: 15 to 30 ml. taken in the morning. Neoloid®
　　is an emulsified castor oil preparation that has the ad-
　　vantage of being less unpleasant to the taste than plain
　　castor oil.

　B. Magnesium Citrate Solution: 200 ml. in morning.

　C. Magnesium Sulfate (Epsom Salt): 15 Gm. in morning.

ANTIANEMIC DRUGS

Megaloblastic Anemias.

A. Cyanocobalamin (Vitamin B_{12}): This is the crystalline factor required for normal maturation of erythrocytes, granulocytic leukocytes, and megakaryocytes in the bone marrow. It is also required for the functional integrity of the nervous system and for the health of the lingual and alimentary mucosa. It is identical with the extrinsic factor in food and requires the presence of gastric intrinsic factor to facilitate absorption. It is effective in the treatment of some macrocytic anemias with megaloblastic arrest in the bone marrow. These diseases include primary pernicious anemia, tropical sprue, and sometimes nutritional macrocytic anemia.

1. Uncomplicated cases -
    a. To institute remission - 15 mcg. I. M. one or two times weekly.
    b. Maintenance - 15 mcg. I. M. every other week.
2. Cases with neurologic complications -
    a. To institute remission - 15 to 30 mcg. I. M. one or two times weekly until maximal hematologic and neurologic response is achieved.
    b. Maintenance - 15 mcg. I. M. every other week.

B. Liver for injection is now standardized and labeled in terms of its vitamin B_{12} content. It may be substituted for cyanocobalamin (vitamin B_{12}).

C. Folic Acid: Effective in producing hematologic remission in diseases mentioned above. Folic acid is the drug of choice in nutritional macrocytic anemia, macrocytic anemia of pregnancy, and megaloblastic anemia of infancy. It may be effective in sprue syndromes. It is contraindicated as the sole treatment of addisonian pernicious anemia because neurologic manifestations encountered in this disease may progress in the face of hematologic remission. Give orally, 5 to 15 mg. daily.

Hypochromic Anemia. (Due to blood loss.)

Oral:

Ferrous sulfate - 0.2 to 0.4 Gm. three times daily after meals.

Ferrous gluconate - 0.3 Gm. three times daily after meals.

Ferrous carbonate - 0.5 to 1 Gm. three times daily after meals.

Ferric ammonium citrate - 1 to 2 Gm. four times daily after meals.

Ferric ammonium citrate solution (50%) - 4 ml. three times daily after meals.

Ferrous sulfate syrup (0.12 Gm./tsp.) - 4 to 8 ml. two or three times daily.

I. M.: Iron-dextran complex (Imferon®): This agent should
be restricted for use only in diagnosed cases of iron-
deficiency anemia. There is no mechanism for excreting
parenterally administered iron, and unwarranted use may
produce exogenous hemosiderosis. Iron-dextran complex is indicated only in those situations in which parenteral therapy is deemed preferable to oral therapy.
These situations include gastrointestinal intolerance and
the need for rapid replenishment of iron stores when oral
therapy is ineffective, as in massive gastrointestinal
bleeding.

Significant local or systemic reactions are infrequent.
Rarely, a combination of headache, fever, nausea and
vomiting, myalgia, and regional adenopathy may appear.

Dosage:
1. For adults - [normal value of hemoglobin (Gm./100
   ml.) − patient's hemoglobin level (Gm./100 ml.)] ×
   0.255 = Gm. of iron needed. On the first day administer 50 mg. (1 ml.). Thereafter, 100 to 250 mg.
   (2 to 5 ml.) may be given daily.
2. For children and small adults -
   a. Over 20 lbs. (and small adults), 100 mg. (2 ml.)
      daily.
   b. 8 to 20 lbs., 50 mg. (1 ml.) daily.
   c. Less than 8 lbs., 25 mg. (0.5 ml.) daily.
   Inject intragluteally with a long needle; retract
   subcutaneous tissue over the site of the injection to
   prevent leakage along the needle tract with resultant
   skin stain.

ANTICOAGULANT DRUGS

Heparin Sodium.
Inhibits coagulation of blood immediately after I. V. administration. Duration of action is short. The optimal dose
of heparin is that which prolongs the clotting time (Lee-White)
to 20 to 30 minutes for four hours after a single injection.
(1 mg. = 100 U.S.P. units.)
A. Mode of Administration:
   1. I. V. -
      a. Intermittent dose technic - 5000 to 7500 units (50 to
         75 mg.) every four hours. Check the Lee-White
         clotting time before each subsequent dose until the
         optimal level is reached.
      b. Continuous drip technic - 20,000 units (200 mg.)
         are added to one liter of physiologic saline or 5%

> dextrose in water and administered at the rate of
> approximately 1 ml./minute. Check the Lee-White
> clotting time in two hours, and thereafter as indi-
> cated.

2. I. M. - 20,000 units (200 mg.) administered through a
   25 gauge needle will usually be effective for eight to
   12 hours. Mild pain and hematoma may occasionally
   occur at the injection site. Check the Lee-White
   clotting time as indicated.

3. Subcut. - Slow administration of heparin, 20,000 units
   (200 mg.)/ml. through a 25 gauge needle into the subcutaneous fat one inch below the posterior iliac crest
   usually prolongs the clotting time to the desired degree for 12 to 16 hours with the following doses:
   a. 100 lb. patient - 20,000 units (200 mg.) daily.
   b. 150 lb. patient - 25,000 units (250 mg.) daily.
   c. 200 lb. patient - 30,000 units (300 mg.) daily.

B. Antidotes are rarely necessary because of the short action of the drug. Coagulation time of heparinized blood
   is rapidly returned to normal by I. V. injection of a 1%
   solution of protamine sulfate diluted in physiologic saline.
   Give a dose equal in milligrams to that of the administered heparin. Duration of action of protamine is two
   hours. Toluidine blue in a dose of 4 to 6 mg./Kg. administered slowly I. V. in physiologic saline is also effective. Toluidine acts more slowly than protamine, but
   its effect lasts many hours.

PROTHROMBIN DEPRESSANTS

The following drugs act by inhibiting the synthesis of
prothrombin in the liver, thereby producing hypoprothrombinemia. They do not affect already circulating prothrombin.
The Quick or Link-Shapiro methods of determining prothrombin concentration are the most accurate. The optimal prothrombin level required to inhibit intravascular clotting is 20
to 30% (35 to 27 seconds). Spontaneous hemorrhage may
occur with concentrations below 10% (60 seconds). Antidotes
in case of spontaneous hemorrhage are phytonadione (Mephy-
ton®), 50 to 150 mg. I. V. (usually 50 mg.), and fresh whole
blood transfusions.

Bishydroxycoumarin (Dicumarol®).

If prothrombin concentration is normal, 300 mg. of bishydroxycoumarin are given orally in one dose. Thereafter,
the prothrombin concentration must be determined daily and
bishydroxycoumarin given in doses designed to produce the
prothrombin level designated above. A given dose exerts its
effect only after a latent period of 12 to 24 hours, and the ef-

fect of a given dose should be measured by a prothrombin time done on the second day after the dose. Usually 200 mg. are given the second day and 50 to 200 mg. daily thereafter. Give no additional drug if the prothrombin level goes below 20% (35 seconds) on any given day.

Warfarin Sodium (Coumadin®, Panwarfin®).

With a normal prothrombin concentration, therapeutic hypoprothrombinemia is induced in adults by an initial dose of 75 mg. within 21 to 24 hours. This may be given orally or I.V., the latter resulting in slightly lower (5%) prothrombin concentration in a slightly shorter period of time (three to five hours). Since these initial doses may produce hypoprothrombinemia which persists for as long as five to six days, daily prothrombin determinations are imperative for the first week. The average daily oral maintenance dose varies from 5 to 20 mg. (average, 10 mg.). Although the incidence of hemorrhagic phenomena is slightly higher with this drug, it has the advantage of a uniform rate of absorption from the gastrointestinal tract and hence greater consistency of the levels achieved.

Phenindione (Hedulin®, Danilone®).

With normal prothrombin concentration, give an initial dose of 200 to 400 mg. orally divided into a morning and evening dose. The daily maintenance dose is 50 to 150 mg. in divided doses. Anticoagulant effects of this drug appear somewhat more uniform, more rapid in onset, and shorter in duration than those of bishydroxycoumarin.

DRUGS FOR PARASITIC INFECTIONS*

Toxic Effects.

The principal toxic and side effects of the drugs described in the following pages are indicated, but no attempt has been made to list all contraindications and precautions. The manufacturer's package insert should be consulted for additional details of toxicity and side effects, as well as for special technics required for some parenteral drugs (e.g., rate of administration, preliminary or test doses). In severe disease, consultation with a specialist in parasitic infections is desirable. A few drugs are gastrointestinal irritants; in general, it is advisable to give oral drugs with a full glass of water and, unless otherwise indicated, during or after meals.

Pregnancy and intestinal ulcers are contraindications to the use of most of these drugs.

Dosage.

In the table, dosage is oral unless otherwise stated. Dosage for infants and children is on a less secure basis than for adults; when not shown in mg./Kg. body weight, dosage should be taken as a fraction of the adult dose, as follows: Under 15 lb., give one-eighth of adult dose; 15 to 30 lb., give one-fourth of adult dose; 30 to 60 lb., give one-half of adult dose; over 60 lb., give approximately the adult dose.

Amodiaquine Hydrochloride (Camoquin®).

An alternative drug to chloroquine for suppression or treatment of malaria, but less frequently used. It is closely related to chloroquine chemically and pharmacologically; the side effects are similar; and cautions and contraindications are probably the same. Amodiaquine can cause yellow and blue-gray pigmentation of the skin as well as agranulocytosis. Not available for injection.

Antimony Potassium Tartrate (Tartar Emetic).

Drug of choice for Schistosoma japonicum. Available as a powder that should be freshly prepared as a 0.5% solution. Administer I.V. very slowly, taking great care to avoid leakage. Patients must be hospitalized and should remain recumbent for several hours after treatment. The drug is effective but highly toxic.

A. Side Effects: Mild side effects include vomiting, diarrhea, abdominal pain, syncope, paroxysmal coughing, and rashes. Severe untoward reactions include exfoliative

---

*By Robert S. Goldsmith, MD, MPH, DTM&H, Assistant Professor of Tropical Medicine and Epidemiology, University of California Medical Center, San Francisco.

dermatitis, toxic liver necrosis, toxic myocarditis, and pneumonia. Rapid administration causes severe coughing, vomiting, and collapse. Fatalities reported. Perivascular leakage may cause severe necrosis. **Caution:** Patients should be under continuous observation during treatment, with epinephrine immediately available.

B. Contraindications: Cardiac, renal, pulmonary, and hepatic insufficiency, except hepatic disease due to schistosomiasis.

Antimony Sodium Dimercaptosuccinate (Stibocaptate, Astiban®).

A drug of first choice for the treatment of Schistosoma haematobium and mansoni infections; it appears to be as effective as stibophen. Both drugs are given I.M. Their side effects appear to be the same, but antimony sodium dimercaptosuccinate has the advantage of being given over a shorter course.

The contraindications are the same as for stibophen.

Antimony Sodium Gluconate, Pentavalent (Pentostam®, Solustibostan®).

Drug of choice for cutaneous and visceral leishmaniasis. Available in sterile, aqueous solution, 1 ml. containing the equivalent of 100 mg. of pentavalent antimony. Pentamidine should be used for the initial treatment of cases from the Sudan, which are often resistant to antimony.

A. Side Effects: No appreciable local irritation. Temperature, headache, gastrointestinal symptoms, and cutaneous eruptions occasionally occur. Less common complications are agranulocytosis and cerebral hemorrhages. **Caution:** In individuals who react unfavorably to the initial injections, it may be advisable to administer the drug on alternate days.

B. Contraindications: Pulmonary or renal disease.

Aspidium Oleoresin (Extract of Male Fern).

Aspidium oleoresin was at one time the major drug for the treatment of tapeworm infections, but because of its toxicity it has been superseded by newer drugs. It should be used fresh in a solution containing 25% (w/w) of the active ingredient filicin. It is difficult to obtain in the U.S.A.

A. Side Effects: Highly toxic. Nausea, vomiting, diarrhea, colic, and headache are common. Variations in absorption or susceptibility may result in bloody diarrhea, jaundice, vertigo, convulsions, and optic neuritis. Permanent blindness and death have occurred. **Caution:** Hospitalization and a posttreatment purge plus bed rest are essential.

B. Contraindications: Ulcers of the gastrointestinal tract, marked anemia, and renal, hepatic, or cardiac disease.

Do not give to elderly or debilitated patients or to infants.

Bephenium Hydroxynaphthoate (Alcopara®).

A drug of choice for hookworm infections. Light infections can be managed without drugs. Supplied as granules in 5 Gm. packets (5 Gm. of salt contain the equivalent of 2.5 Gm. of bephenium base). The bitter granules are best suspended in a flavored syrup, and food should be withheld for 2 hours. The dosage for children weighing less than 22 kg. is 2.5 Gm. twice daily. Laxatives are not used.

A. Side Effects: Negligible toxicity. Vomiting is the only common symptom; mild dizziness, abdominal cramping pain, and diarrhea occur occasionally. **Caution:** Where drug-induced vomiting may be hazardous, the general condition of the patient should be improved before the drug is given.

B. Contraindications: None.

Bithionol (Bitin®).

Drug of choice for the treatment of Paragonimus westermani infections; may be effective for Fasciola hepatica infections.

A. Side Effects: Vomiting, diarrhea, headache, and skin rashes are frequent but generally mild and transient.

B. Contraindications: Not established.

Chloroquine Phosphate (Aralen®).

Used prophylactically to suppress symptoms of malaria but does not prevent infection. Clinical malaria may ensue after drug is stopped. It is also the drug of choice for terminating acute attacks of malaria, but radical cure only occurs for falciparum malaria. In falciparum malaria, if the patient does not show a prompt response to chloroquine, parasite resistance to this drug must be considered.

Chloroquine is one of the drugs of choice for extraintestinal amebiasis. May be tried for Clonorchis sinensis infections, but usually produces only temporary suppression of ova.

Available as tablets containing 125 or 250 mg. of the diphosphate. Chloroquine hydrochloride available for parenteral injection.

A. Side Effects: Chloroquine given in the usual chemosuppressive doses has essentially no toxic effects. Minor side effects occasionally encountered include headache, vertigo, malaise, anorexia, diarrhea, blurring of vision, pruritus, and urticaria. Prolonged suppressive use has not been associated with irreversible retinopathy. **Use with caution** in the presence of liver disease not due to amebiasis.

B. Contraindications: Severe gastrointestinal or neurologic disease, blood dyscrasias, and psoriasis.

Dehydroemetine Dihydrochloride.
Dehydroemetine has the same indications, side effects, and contraindications as emetine, but appears to be less toxic than emetine. Further comparative studies are needed to establish this.

Dichlorophen (Anthiphen®).
One of the alternative drugs of choice for Taenia saginata and for Diphyllobothrium latum infections. (Not available in the United States.)
A. Side Effects: Minimal.
B. Contraindications: Probably T. solium infections because worms are partially digested when passed, resulting in the release of ova into the gastrointestinal tract. Since the drug has no effect on ova, in T. solium infections there is a potential for cysticercosis.

Diethylcarbamazine Citrate (Hetrazan®, Banocide®).
Kills microfilaria, but death of adult Wuchereria bancrofti, Brugia malayi, and Loa loa may require several treatments over one to two years. Does not kill adult Onchocerca volvulus. Available as a syrup containing 24 mg./ml. and as a 50 mg. tablet. Take orally after meals.
A. Side Effects: Reactions are fairly frequent but not severe and usually disappear within a few days despite continuation of therapy. These include headache, malaise, arthralgia, nausea, and vomiting. Severe allergic reactions may result from disintegration of microfilaria (particularly with O. volvulus and Loa loa). Corticosteroids may be necessary to control these allergic reactions: fever, pruritus, edema of the skin, lymphadenitis, and rashes. **Caution:** In treating O. volvulus infections, particular care is needed. Start with small daily doses and increase slowly. If ocular lesions are pronounced, give corticosteroids in advance and concurrently with treatment.
B. Contraindications: None.

Diiodohydroxyquin (Diodoquin®, Lanodoxin®, Yodoxin®).
A drug of choice for intestinal amebiasis but not effective against extraintestinal infections. Supplied as 0.65 Gm. tablets. Iodine content 63%.
A. Side Effects: Infrequent. About 3% of patients may have nausea, vomiting, diarrhea, pruritus ani, or headache. Iodine sensitivity, manifested by fever, furunculosis, rashes, and swelling of salivary glands is rarely encountered. **Caution:** Discontinue if rashes occur or if diarrhea is severe or persistent.
B. Contraindications: Severe thyroid or hepatic disease or known iodine sensitivity.

Emetine Hydrochloride.

A drug of choice for curing extraintestinal amebiasis and for stopping (but not curing) acute amebic dysentery. Also drug of choice for Fasciola hepatica infections. Available in solution in ampules. Administered by deep subcutaneous or intramuscular injection. Patients should be hospitalized and confined to bed during treatment and after discharge should remain sedentary for several weeks.

A. Side Effects: Toxic manifestations are frequent and may appear at any dosage level, but usually after 3 to 4 days of treatment. They include pain and weakness at the injection site; vomiting and diarrhea; generalized weakness, aching, and tenderness of skeletal muscles; hypotension, precordial pain, tachycardia, dyspnea, and electrocardiographic abnormalities. **Caution:** Stop treatment in the event of precordial pain, tachycardia, hypotension, significant electrocardiographic changes, persistent gastrointestinal effects, or marked neuromuscular symptoms. Avoid inadvertent intravenous administration.

B. Contraindications: Aged or debilitated patients, young children, and patients with renal or cardiac disease or with marked hypertension.

Glycobiarsol (Amoebicon®, Milibis®, Wia®).

Glycobiarsol, a pentavalent arsenical, is used in conjunction with other drugs for the treatment of intestinal amebiasis. Controversy exists about whether the moderate effectiveness of the drug warrants the risk of its toxicity. Supplied in 250 and 500 mg. tablets.

A. Side Effects: Although infrequent, they include nausea, vomiting, diarrhea, and skin rashes. Rarely, arsenical toxicity may occur including exfoliative dermatitis, agranulocytosis, encephalitis, and hepatitis. Severe symptoms should be treated with dimercaprol (BAL). Glycobiarsol turns the stools black.

B. Contraindications: Hepatic disease (including amebic hepatitis), renal disease, and the presence of visual field abnormalities.

Hexylresorcinol (Caprokol®, Crystoids®).

Hexylresorcinol by retention enema is the drug of choice for the treatment of Trichuris trichiura infections, but it is only recommended for patients with gastrointestinal symptoms or anemia. A soapsuds enema should precede the retention enema.

Hexylresorcinol by mouth is an alternative drug for the treatment of roundworm, hookworm, and Hymenolepis nana infections. Avoid alcohol and fatty foods for 24 hours before and after treatment. The day before treatment, total diet should be reduced and the evening meal limited to soft foods.

Administer drug in the morning with water; no food is to be taken for the next five hours. Two hours after the dose, give a saline purge. Repeat course in three days. Drug is available as 0.1 and 0.2 Gm. gelatin-coated pills.

A. Side Effects: Nearly devoid of systemic toxicity, but irritating to the oral mucosa, perianal skin, and occasionally the gastric mucosa. **Caution:** Pills must be swallowed intact. When giving hexylresorcinol by enema, cover perianal area and buttocks with a coating of petrolatum to prevent superficial burns.

B. Contraindications: Peptic ulcer, intestinal obstruction or perforation, and colon ulcers.

Iodochlorhydroxyquin (Vioform®, Entero-Vioform®, Nioform®).

Closely related to diiodohydroxyquin. Similar indications, side effects, and contraindications. Available as enteric-coated tablets containing 0.25 Gm. of the drug. Daily dose is one tablet three times daily after meals for ten days. Mild diarrhea may occur on the second or third day, but it is usually transitory. Severe gastric distress is occasionally reported.

Lucanthone Hydrochloride (Miracil-D®, Nilodin®).

An alternative drug against Schistosoma haematobium and S. mansoni, available in 200 mg. tablets. Since it is given orally, it is valuable for mass treatment. Serious toxic manifestations occur more frequently in adults than in children. Therefore, it should be used only for children under age 16.

A. Side Effects: Nausea and vomiting in more than 20% of patients. Skin may become yellow during therapy but will clear subsequently. Sweating and circulatory disturbances occur occasionally. Significant C.N.S. toxicity may occur, including vertigo, tinnitus, tremors, headache, convulsions, and psychosis.

B. Contraindications: Cardiac and renal disease.

Melarsoprol (Mel B®).

Drug of choice for African trypanosomiasis with C.N.S. involvement. It is composed of an arsenical combined with its antagonist, dimercaprol (BAL).

A. Side Effects: Colic, neuritis, agranulocytosis, reactive encephalopathy, and hypertension, as well as myocardial, renal, and hepatic damage, are common. Fatalities have occurred. Symptoms seen during the first three-day course may not recur in subsequent courses, but hypersensitivity reactions may develop; these can be controlled by desensitization and corticosteroids. **Caution:** Hospitalize patient and inject the drug slowly I.V. In debilitated patients, begin with as little as 18 mg. and increase dose progressively.

B. Contraindications: None.

Metronidazole (Flagyl®).

An alternative drug for the treatment of Trichomonas vaginalis in females and the treatment of choice in males. Usually given orally, but topical application by insertion into the vagina, combined with oral therapy, is used for refractory cases (500 mg. intravaginally each day plus 250 mg. orally twice daily for 10 days). Male dosage is 250 mg. twice daily for 10 days. Available as an oral tablet containing 250 mg. and as a vaginal insert containing 500 mg.

When metronidazole is used at three times the normal dose, it appears to be an effective intestinal and extra-intestinal amebicide. Additional clinical trials to determine its efficacy and safety at these doses are needed.

A. Side Effects: Unpleasant taste, nausea, vomiting, diar-rhea, epigastric distress, vaginal or urethral burning, vertigo, headache, and a temporary decrease of WBC occasionally develop. Incoordination, paresthesias, urticaria, pruritus, and darkening of the urine are rare-ly reported. **Caution:** Since this drug is chemically sim-ilar to nitroimidazoles that have caused blood dyscrasias, it should probably be reserved for women who have not responded adequately to other topical drugs. It should be used for men only if the sexual partner has had a recur-rence after treatment. Total and differential counts should be performed, especially if a second course of therapy is necessary. Discontinue if C.N.S. symptoms appear.

B. Contraindications: Blood dyscrasias or active C.N.S. disease.

Niclosamide (Yomesan®).

The drug of choice for the treatment of tapeworm infec-tions except T. solium.

A. Side Effects: Uncommon. Mild nausea, vomiting, and intestinal colic reported infrequently.

B. Contraindications: T. solium infections for the same reasons as given for dichlorophen.

Niridazole (Ambilhar®).

A new and promising drug for the treatment of schisto-somiasis. Oral administration and low toxicity make it use-ful for mass treatment. High cure rates have been achieved for Schistosoma haematobium and S. mansoni with oral dos-ages of 25 mg./Kg. daily for five to seven days. Action against S. japonicum has not been sufficiently investigated.

A. Side Effects: Occasional nausea, vomiting, abdominal cramping pain, headaches, T-wave flattening or inver-sion, and transitory inhibition of spermatogenesis. Urine becomes deep brown during therapy. Some side effects do not appear until after three to four days of

treatment - rashes, confusion (rare), and convulsions
(very rare). **Caution:** Use cautiously in elderly or debilitated patients or in patients who have unusually high
serum transaminase levels or coronary artery disease.
B. Contraindications: Do not give concurrently with isoniazid.

Paromomycin (Humatin®).

An antibiotic with negligible gastrointestinal absorption
used as an alternative drug for the treatment of intestinal
amebiasis. Available as a capsule (250 mg.) or as a syrup
(125 mg./5 ml.).
A. Side Effects: Probably produces more untoward reactions
than diiodohydroxyquin. These include vomiting, diarrhea, skin eruptions, headache, vertigo, and generalized
abdominal pain. **Caution:** Watch for overgrowth of resistant organisms. Significant absorption followed by
nephrotoxicity is theoretically possible in patients having
extensive intestinal ulcerations.
B. Contraindications: None.

Pentamidine (Lomidine®).

A drug of choice for the prophylaxis and early treatment
of African trypanosomiasis and for the treatment of Pneumo-
cystis carinii infections. An alternative drug for visceral
leishmaniasis. It cannot be used for the late stages of trypanosomiasis because it does not reach the C. S. F. and cannot
be given intrathecally. Available as a powder that should be
stored in dry, cool place. Solutions should be used within 5
to 7 days after preparation and stored in the refrigerator.
Protect from light to avoid production of hepatotoxic compounds.
A. Side Effects: Minimal by I. M. injection; rarely, hypotension, tachycardia, nausea, and vomiting. Inadvertent
I. V. inoculation may reproduce the later symptoms plus
dyspnea and incontinence. **Caution:** Use cautiously in
patients with hypertension, diabetes mellitus, hepatic or
renal dysfunction.
B. Contraindications: None.

Piperazine Citrate (Antepar®, Multifuge Citrate®, Parazine®).

Drug of choice for Ascaris lumbricoides and Enterobius
vermicularis infections. There are no essential differences
in the therapeutic effectiveness of the various piperazine
salts. Piperazine citrate is available as a syrup which contains the equivalent of 100 mg. of piperazine hexahydrate per
ml. or as tablets each containing the equivalent of 250 or 500
mg. Give before or after meals. Cathartics are not used.
A. Side Effects: Low toxicity. Occasional nausea, vomiting,
mild diarrhea, abdominal cramps, and headache. Trans-

itory neurologic symptoms, rashes, and weakness are rare. **Caution:** The drug may be cumulative in the presence of impaired renal excretion.
B. Contraindications: None.

Primaquine Phosphate.

Drug of choice for the radical cure of Plasmodium vivax, P. ovale, and P. malariae since it is effective against the exo-erythrocytic forms. The routine use of primaquine to treat all individuals who have been in malarial endemic areas is questionable. Probability of exposure should determine its use. Available in tablets each containing 26.3 mg. of the phosphate salt, equivalent to 15 mg. of the base.
A. Side Effects: Mild headache, gastrointestinal symptoms, methemoglobinemia, and leukocytosis are infrequently observed. Leukopenia is rarely seen except in patients who have active collagen disorders. Hemolysis may occur in patients whose red blood cells are deficient in glucose-6-phosphate dehydrogenase. This deficiency is most likely in Negroes and in Caucasians from the Mediterranean area; a test for it is available. A severe hemolytic reaction generally occurs, however, only when the dosage exceeds 26 mg. per day for 14 days. **Caution:** Discontinue if there is a pronounced darkening of the urine, a drop in hemoglobin, or severe cyanosis.
B. Contraindications: Active collagen disorders or conditions requiring the concurrent use of quinacrine or bone-marrow depressants.

Pyrimethamine (Daraprim®, Malocide®).

The drug of choice in conjunction with trisulfapyrimidines for the treatment of toxoplasmosis. An alternative drug for the suppression (prophylaxis) of clinical malaria. It should not be used to treat acute attacks of malaria because of its slow action, and it cannot be used for radical cure of Plasmodium vivax. Available in tablets each containing 25 mg.
A. Side Effects: At the low dosages used for malarial suppression, there are no significant toxic symptoms. At the high dosages used for toxoplasmosis, the drug inhibits folic acid metabolism, which may result in vomiting, megaloblastic anemia, leukopenia, and thrombocytopenia. These can be alleviated by treatment with folinic acid (10 mg./day I.M.).
B. Contraindications: None.

Pyrvinium Pamoate (Povan®).

Drug of choice for Enterobius vermicularis and alternative drug for Strongyloides stercoralis. Available in tablets, each containing 50 mg., and as a pediatric suspension containing 10 mg./ml. No pretreatment or posttreatment purges are necessary.

A. Side Effects: Usually well tolerated, but may cause nausea, vomiting, or diarrhea in some patients. Posttreatment stools are frequently stained red. **Caution:** Tablets should be swallowed intact to avoid staining the teeth. Few reports are available on the use of the drug in children weighing under 22 lb.
B. Contraindications: None.

Quinacrine Hydrochloride (Mepacrine®, Atabrine®).

Treatment of choice for Giardia lamblia and Taenia solium infections. Alternative drug for other tapeworm infections. Available in 100 mg. tablets. Prescribe bland, semisolid, nonfat diet for 24 hours before therapy, saline purge the night before, fasting thereafter. Give drug with water in the morning, followed by saline purge one to two hours after the last dose. Save the expelled worm and examine for scolex.

A. Side Effects: Severe nausea and vomiting are common. Symptoms may be reduced by confining the patient to bed, and by preliminary use of chlorpromazine or phenobarbital. The drug should be administered by duodenal tube if the patient cannot tolerate it orally. Confusion or toxic psychosis is induced in some patients. **Use cautiously** in the elderly, in young children, and in patients with a history of psychosis.
B. Contraindications: Psoriasis, exfoliative dermatitis, and concurrent use of primaquine.

Quinine Sulfate.

Drug of choice for strains of Plasmodium falciparum resistant to chloroquine and an alternative parenteral drug for patients unable to take or retain oral drugs. It acts only against erythrocytic trophozoites and schizonts. Quinine alone will control an acute attack of resistant P. falciparum malaria, but in a substantial proportion of infections, particularly from Southeast Asia, it fails to prevent recurrence. Addition of pyrimethamine, with either sulfadiazine or dapsone, substantially lowers the recurrence.

Quinine sulfate is supplied as tablets containing 120, 200, and 300 mg. or as quinine hydrochloride for I.V. use.

A. Side Effects: Produces mild toxic effects in many patients, including slight deafness, tinnitus, vertigo, dizziness, palpitations, gastrointestinal symptoms, and visual disturbances. An occasional supersensitive patient may also develop dyspnea, hypotension, pruritus, purpura, asthma, delirium, and deafness. Deaths have occurred from small doses. Severe hemolysis and hemoglobinuria (black-water fever), followed by oliguria or anuria, may be initiated by quinine in rare instances, particularly if the blood smear shows heavy parasitemia or if the drug is given I.V. **Caution:** Patients receiving oral treatment

should rest in bed; their urine output should be measured.
I. V. use is hazardous. Oral treatment, by stomach tube
if necessary, should be started as soon as possible. I. V.
administration should be by slow drip accompanied by
frequent monitoring of blood pressure, pulse, and urinary
output. Hypotension, arrhythmia, or hemolysis may develop. Quinine toxicity develops rapidly in the presence
of oliguria.
  B. Contraindications: Known hypersensitivity, hemoglobin-
     uria, tinnitus, and optic neuritis.

Stibophen (Fuadin®, Neoantimosan®, Reprodral®).

Drug of choice for Schistosoma mansoni infections; alternative drug for S. haematobium and japonicum infections.
Supplied in 3.5 and 5 ml. ampules containing 8.5 mg. antimony per ml. Give I. M. May be used on an outpatient basis.
  A. Side Effects: Less toxic than antimony potassium tar-
     trate. Pain at injection site. Nausea, vomiting, myal-
     gia, arthralgia, and rashes may require modifying or
     interrupting therapy. **Caution:** Inadvertent I. V. admin-
     istration should be carefully avoided. The first dose
     should be small, 1.5 to 2 ml., to test the susceptibility
     of the patient. Discontinue in the event of recurrent
     vomiting, persistent joint pain, febrile reactions, pro-
     gressive proteinuria, or blood dyscrasias (test urine and
     blood weekly).
  B. Contraindications: Severe renal and cardiac insufficiency
     and hepatic disease not caused by schistosomiasis.

Suramin Sodium (Germanin®, Antrypol®).

Drug of choice (in combination with diethylcarbamazine)
in the treatment of Onchocerca volvulus infections. Also
used for the treatment of African trypanosomiasis. Supplied
as a dry powder. A 10% solution in distilled water should be
prepared no more than 30 minutes before use.
  A. Side Effects: Immediate reactions in a few patients in-
     clude vomiting, urticaria, unconsciousness, or shock.
     Late reactions include skin rashes, paresthesias, and
     hematuria. Agranulocytosis or hemolytic anemia are
     rare. Modify treatment if heavy proteinuria develops
     and discontinue if casts appear. **Caution:** Do not con-
     tinue therapy in patients who show intolerance to initial
     doses. Drug reactions are more pronounced in mal-
     nourished patients.
  B. Contraindications: Renal disease.

Tetrachloroethylene.

An alternative drug for the treatment of hookworm infections. Light infections can be managed without drugs. Generally available only as a veterinary preparation in liquid

form or in gelatin capsules each containing 0.2, 1, or 5 ml.,
but this preparation is safe and effective for man. Use fresh
drug. Avoid alcohol and fatty food for 24 hours before and for
four days after therapy. Patient should have a light meal the
night before and only water in the morning. Give drug orally
in the morning, followed by bed rest and no food for four hours.
Opinions vary on desirability of posttreatment purge at two
hours.

A. Side Effects: Nausea, vomiting, abdominal cramps, dizziness, vertigo, headache, and drowsiness. **Caution:**
   Use cautiously in the presence of severe anemia or in
   dehydrated or debilitated patients. If ascarids are present, they must be cleared first with piperazine or thia-
   bendazole. Tetrachloroethylene stimulates Ascaris to
   hyperactivity, which may result in bowel perforation or
   obstruction.

B. Contraindications: Pregnancy, hepatic disease, gastroenteritis, alcoholism, and severe constipation.

Thiabendazole (Mintezol®).

A new drug that has a broad spectrum of action against
roundworms. Particularly useful for the treatment of strongy-
loidiasis and cutaneous larva migrans. Under investigation
for treatment of Trichinella spiralis. Available as a white
suspension containing 100 mg. per ml. Give after meals.
Purges and dietary restrictions are not necessary.

A. Side Effects: Dizziness, nausea, and vomiting are frequent. Abdominal cramps, diarrhea, headache, drowsiness, and pruritus are less common. Rarely, tinnitus,
   paresthesias, bradycardia, visual disturbances, and
   allergic reactions. The drug imparts an odor to the
   urine of some patients. **Caution:** Since the drug may
   cause drowsiness or dizziness, it should not be used by
   those patients whose activities require mental alertness.

B. Contraindications: None.

Tryparsamide.

An alternative drug for African trypanosomiasis with
C.N.S. involvement. Supplied as a powder that should be
prepared as a 10% aqueous solution for I.V. use.

A. Side Effects: The drug is an arsenic compound. Toxic
   reactions are frequent, including dermatitis, gastrointestinal disturbances, jaundice, nephritis, and Herxheimer
   reactions. Optic neuritis occasionally occurs and may
   progress to blindness. **Caution:** Eyes should be checked
   frequently before and during treatment. Discontinue drug
   at earliest symptoms of optic neuritis (pain, photophobia,
   or lacrimation) or changes in results of tests for central
   vision or visual fields.

B. Contraindications: Optic atrophy.

DRUGS FOR PARASITIC INFECTIONS*

Infecting Organism	Drug of Choice	Adult Dose	Alternative Drugs	Adult Dose
		Roundworms (Nematodes)		
Ascaris lumbricoides (roundworm)	Piperazine citrate	75 mg./kg. (maximum 3.5 Gm.) daily for 2 days.	Thiabendazole	25 mg./kg. (maximum 1.5 Gm.) b.i.d. for 2 days.
Trichuris trichiura (whipworm)	Hexylresorcinol (0.1% solution)	500 ml. by rectal retention for 1 hour.	Thiabendazole†	25 mg./kg. (maximum 1.5 Gm.) b.i.d. for 2 days.
Necator americanus (hookworm)	Bephenium or Tetrachloroethylene	One 5-Gm. packet b.i.d. for 3 days. A single dose of 0.12 ml./kg. (maximum 5 ml.).	Thiabendazole	25 mg./kg. (maximum 1.5 Gm.) b.i.d. for 2 days.
Ancylostoma duodenale (hookworm)	Bephenium	One 5-Gm. packet b.i.d. for 1 day.	Tetrachloroethylene or Thiabendazole	A single dose of 0.12 ml./kg. (maximum 5 ml.). 25 mg./kg. (maximum 1.5 Gm.) b.i.d. for 2 days.
Strongyloides stercoralis	Thiabendazole	25 mg./kg. (maximum 1.5 Gm.) b.i.d. for 2 days.	Pyrvinium pamoate†	Effectiveness and dosage not established.
Enterobius (Oxyuris) vermicularis (pinworm)	Piperazine citrate or Pyrvinium pamoate	65 mg./kg. (maximum 2.5 Gm.) daily for 8 days. Single dose, 5 mg./kg. (maximum 250 mg.); repeat after 2 weeks.	Thiabendazole	25 mg./kg. (maximum 1.5 Gm.) b.i.d. for 1 day; repeat in 7 days.
Trichinella spiralis (trichinosis)	Thiabendazole† Corticosteroids for severe symptoms	25 mg./kg. (maximum 1.5 Gm.) b.i.d. for 2 to 4 days depending on response. 20 to 40 mg. (prednisone) daily, reduced after 3 to 5 days.	None	
Cutaneous larva migrans (creeping eruption) (dog and cat hookworm in man)	Thiabendazole	25 mg./kg. (maximum 1.5 Gm.) b.i.d. for 2 days, repeat in 2 days if necessary; or apply as topical ointment.	None	

Parasite	Drug	Dosage		Dosage
Visceral larva migrans (dog and cat roundworm in man)	No specific therapy; corticosteroids for severe symptoms.	20 to 40 mg. (prednisone) daily, reduced after 3 to 5 days.	Thiabendazole† or Diethylcarbamazine†	25 mg./kg. (maximum 1.5 Gm.) b.i.d. for 2 to 4 days. / 120 mg. t.i.d. for 30 days.
Filaria				
Wuchereria bancrofti W. (or Brugia) malayi Loa loa	Diethylcarbamazine	2 mg./kg. once for 1 day / 2 mg./kg. twice for 1 day / 2 mg./kg., t.i.d. for 20 days	None	
Onchocerca volvulus (river blindness)	Diethylcarbamazine **plus** Suramin‡	25 mg. daily for 3 days / 50 mg. daily for 3 days / 100 mg. daily for 3 days / 150 mg. daily for 12 days / 100 mg. (test dose) I.V., then 1 Gm. I.V. at weekly intervals for 5 weeks.	None	
Dracunculus medinensis (guinea worm)	Niridazole§	25 mg./kg. daily for 7 days.	None	
Tapeworms (Cestodes)				
Taenia saginata (beef tapeworm)	Niclosamide‡ **or** Quinacrine hydrochloride	4 tablets (2 Gm.) chewed thoroughly in a single dose after a light meal. / 4 doses of 200 mg., 10 minutes apart; 600 mg. sodium bicarbonate with each dose.	Aspidium oleoresin **or** Dichlorophen§	4 to 8 Gm. plus 8 Gm. acacia in water; one-half of dose taken early in a.m., the rest 1 hour later; or single dose of aspidium by duodenal tube to prevent vomiting. / 70 mg./kg. divided in 3 doses in 24 hours.
Diphyllobothrium latum (fish tapeworm)				
Taenia solium (pork tapeworm)	Quinacrine hydrochloride	4 doses of 200 mg., 10 minutes apart; 600 mg. sodium bicarbonate with each dose.	Aspidium oleoresin **or** Niclosamide‡	4 to 8 Gm. plus 8 Gm. acacia in water; one-half of dose taken early in a.m., the rest 1 hour later; or single dose of aspidium by duodenal tube to prevent vomiting. / 4 tablets (2 Gm.) chewed thoroughly in a single dose on an empty stomach followed by a severe purge in 2 hours.
-larval stage (cysticercosis)	None			

*Adapted in part with permission from Medical Letter on Drugs & Therapeutics 11(6):21-28, March 1969.

†Effectiveness not established or of low order.

‡In the United States, this drug is available from the Parasitic Disease Drug Service, Parasitic Diseases Branch, Epidemiology Program, National Communicable Disease Center, Atlanta, Georgia 30333.

§Not available for clinical use in the United States.

DRUGS FOR PARASITIC INFECTIONS (Cont'd.)

Infecting Organism	Drug of Choice	Adult Dose	Alternative Drugs	Adult Dose
Hymenolepis nana (dwarf tapeworm)	Niclosamide‡	4 tablets (2 Gm.) chewed thoroughly in a single dose each day for 5 to 7 days.	Quinacrine hydrochloride	Four doses of 200 mg. 10 minutes apart; 600 mg. sodium bicarbonate with each dose; repeat in 1 or 2 weeks if necessary.
Echinococcus granulosus (hydatid disease) E. multilocularis	None			
Flukes (Trematodes)				
Schistosoma haematobium	Niridazole§ or Antimony sodium dimercaptosuccinate‡	25 mg./kg. daily in divided doses for 5 to 7 days. Total dosage of 40 mg./kg. in 5 divided doses given I.M. once or twice a week.	Lucanthone§ (only for children under 16 because of toxicity in adults) or Stibophen (8.5 mg. antimony per ml.)	15 mg./kg. daily in 3 doses for 6 to 8 days. Test dose of 1.5 ml. Then 4 ml. daily I.M. 5 days per week to a total of 80 ml.
Schistosoma mansoni	Antimony sodium dimercaptosuccinate‡ or Stibophen (8.5 mg. antimony per ml.)	Total dosage of 40 mg./kg. in 5 divided doses given I.M. once or twice a week. Test dose of 1.5 ml., then 4 ml. daily I.M. 5 days/week to a total of 80 to 100 ml.	Lucanthone§ (only for children under 16 because of toxicity in adults) or Niridazole§	15 mg./kg. daily in 3 doses for 6 to 8 days. 25 mg./kg. daily in divided doses for 7 days.
Schistosoma japonicum	Antimony potassium tartrate (0.5% solution)	Intravenous doses of 8, 12, 16, 20, 24, and 28 ml. on alternate days, continuing at 28 ml. on alternate days until a total of 360 ml. has been given.	Stibophen (8.5 mg. antimony per ml.) or Antimony sodium dimercaptosuccinate‡	2, 4, and 6 ml. on days 1-3, followed by 8 ml. daily for 11 doses (a very toxic amount). Total dosage of 40 mg./kg. in 5 divided doses given I.M. once or twice a week.
Clonorchis sinensis (liver fluke) Opisthorchis Sp.	Chloroquine phosphate‡	250 mg. t.i.d. for 6 weeks.		
Paragonimus westermani (lung fluke)	Bithionol‡	30 to 50 mg./kg. on alternate days for 10 to 15 doses.	Chloroquine phosphate‡	250 mg. t.i.d. for 6 weeks.

Parasite	Drug	Dosage	Drug	Dosage
Fasciola hepatica (sheep liver fluke)	Emetine hydrochloride **or** Dehydroemetine dihydrochloride‡	1 mg./kg. (maximum 65 mg. daily) subcut. or I.M. for 7 to 10 days. / 1 mg./kg. daily I.M. or subcut. for 10 days (maximum total dose 1 Gm.).	Bithionol†‡	30 to 50 mg./kg. on alternate days for 10 to 15 doses.
Fasciolopsis buski (large intestinal fluke)	Hexylresorcinol	1 Gm.	Tetrachloroethylene	0.12 ml./kg. (maximum 5 ml.).
Heterophyes heterophyes Metagonimus yokogawai	Tetrachloroethylene	0.12 ml./kg. (maximum 5 ml.).	Hexylresorcinol	1 Gm.

Gastrointestinal and Genitourinary Protozoa

Parasite	Drug	Dosage	Drug	Dosage
Entamoeba histolytica (amebiasis)				
Asymptomatic	Diiodohydroxyquin	650 mg. t.i.d. for 21 days.	Paromomycin	500 mg. t.i.d. for 7 days.
Mild intestinal infection	Diiodohydroxyquin **plus** Chloroquine **followed by** Glycobiarsol	650 mg. t.i.d. for 21 days. / 250 mg. (salt) b.i.d. for 21 days. / 500 mg. t.i.d. for 7 days.	Paromomycin **plus** Chloroquine **followed by** Glycobiarsol	500 mg. t.i.d. for 21 days. / 250 mg. (salt) b.i.d. for 21 days. / 500 mg. t.i.d. for 7 days.
Dysentery or severe diarrhea	Emetine **or** Dehydroemetine dihydrochloride‡ **plus** Oxytetracycline (with either emetine or dehydroemetine) **followed by** Course of treatment for mild intestinal infection	1 mg./kg. (max. 65 mg.) I.M. or subcut. daily for the least number of days necessary to control symptoms (usually 4-6 days; max. 10 days). / 1 to 1.5 mg./kg. I.M. or subcut. daily up to 10 days (maximum total dose 1 Gm.). / 500 mg. every 6 hours for 7 days.	Metronidazole	800 mg. t.i.d. for 10 days (3 times the dose recommended for other conditions; effectiveness still under investigation).

†Effectiveness not established or of low order.
‡In the United States, this drug is available from the Parasitic Disease Drug Service, Parasitic Diseases Branch, Epidemiology Program, National Communicable Disease Center, Atlanta, Georgia 30333.
§Not available for clinical use in the United States.

DRUGS FOR PARASITIC INFECTIONS (Cont'd.)

Infecting Organism	Drug of Choice	Adult Dose	Alternative Drugs	Adult Dose
Entamoeba histolytica (amebiasis), Cont'd.				
Hepatic abscess	Emetine **or** Dehydroemetine dihydrochloride† **followed by** Chloroquine **plus** Diiodohydroxyquin	1 mg./kg. (max. 65 mg.) I.M. or subcut. daily for 10 days. 1 to 1.5 mg./kg. daily I.M. or subcut. for 10 days (max. total dose 1 Gm.). 250 mg. (salt) twice daily for 28 days. 650 mg. t.i.d. for 21 days.	Metronidazole	800 mg. t.i.d. for 10 days (3 times the dose recommended for other conditions; effectiveness still under investigation).
Dientamoeba fragilis	Diiodohydroxyquin	650 mg. t.i.d. for 10 days.	A tetracycline	250 mg. q.i.d. for 7 days.
Giardia lamblia	Quinacrine hydrochloride	100 mg. t.i.d. for 5 to 7 days.	Metronidazole	250 mg. t.i.d. for 10 days.
Trichomonas vaginalis	Topical agents		Metronidazole	250 mg. t.i.d. for 10 days.
Balantidium coli	Oxytetracycline	500 mg. q.i.d. for 10 days.	Diiodohydroxyquin†	650 mg. t.i.d. for 21 days.
Blood and Tissue Parasites: Plasmodia				
Plasmodium falciparum, vivax, malariae, and ovale (malaria)				
All plasmodia except resistant strains of P. falciparum				
Suppression of disease while in endemic area (prophylaxis) and eradication of infection after departure	Chloroquine phosphate **plus** Primaquine phosphate	500 mg. (300 mg. base) once weekly and continued for 8 weeks after last exposure in endemic area. 26.3 mg. (15 mg. base) daily for 14 days but starting after last exposure in endemic area.	Amodiaquine dihydrochloride **plus** Primaquine phosphate	520 mg. (400 mg. base) once weekly and continued for 8 weeks after last exposure in endemic area. 26.3 mg. (15 mg. base) daily for 14 days but starting after last exposure in endemic area.
Oral treatment of malarial attacks	Chloroquine phosphate	1 Gm. (600 mg. base), then 0.5 Gm. in 6 hours, then 0.5 Gm. daily for 2 days.	Amodiaquine dihydrochloride	780 mg. (600 mg. base) first day, then 520 mg. (400 mg. base) daily for 2 days.
Parenteral treatment of severe illness	Chloroquine hydrochloride	250 mg. (200 mg. base) I.M. every 6 hours (max. 1 Gm. daily) until oral therapy is possible.	Quinine dihydrochloride	600 mg. in 300 ml. normal saline I.V. over at least 30 minutes; repeat in 6 to 8 hours until oral therapy is possible.

Condition	Drug	Dosage	Alternative drug	Alternative dosage
For eradication of infection (radical cure) following clinical cure with chloroquine.	Primaquine phosphate	26.3 mg. (15 mg. base) daily for 14 days.	None	
(Chloroquine alone is curative for P. falciparum except for resistant strains.)				
Resistant strains of P. falciparum				
Oral treatment of attacks	Quinine sulfate **plus plus either**	650 mg. t.i.d. for 14 days.	None	
	Pyrimethamine	25 mg. b.i.d. for 3 days.		
	Sulfadiazine **or**	500 mg. q.i.d. for 5 days.		
	Dapsone	25 mg. daily for 28 days.		
Parenteral treatment of severe illness	Quinine dihydrochloride	600 mg. in 300 ml. normal saline I.V. over at least 30 minutes; repeat in 6 to 8 hours until oral therapy is possible. (Maximum/24 hours is 2 Gm.)	None	
Blood and Tissue Parasites: Leishmania				
L. donovani (kala azar, visceral leishmaniasis)	Antimony sodium gluconate‡	600 mg. I.M. or I.V. daily for 6-10 days; course may be repeated for resistant cases.	Pentamidine isethionate‡	2 to 4 mg./kg. I.M. daily for up to 15 doses.
L. tropica (oriental sore, cutaneous leishmaniasis)	Antimony sodium gluconate‡	600 mg. I.M. or I.V. daily for 6 to 10 days.	Topical or local treatment such as carbon dioxide snow, infrared therapy, or radiotherapy.	
L. braziliensis (American muco-cutaneous leishmaniasis)	Antimony sodium gluconate†‡	Not certain, probably same as for other Leishmania infections.	Amphotericin B† **or** Cycloguanil pamoate†,§	0.25 to 1 mg./kg. by slow infusion daily or every 2 days up to 8 weeks. A single I.M. injection of 350 mg. base.
Blood and Tissue Parasites: Trypanosomes				
T. cruzi (South American trypanosomiasis, Chagas' disease)	None			

†Effectiveness not established or of low order.
‡In the United States, this drug is available from the Parasitic Disease Drug Service, Parasitic Diseases Branch, Epidemiology Program, National Communicable Disease Center, Atlanta, Georgia 30333.
§Not available for clinical use in the United States.

DRUGS FOR PARASITIC INFECTIONS (Cont'd.)

Infecting Organism	Drug of Choice	Adult Dose	Alternative Drugs	Adult Dose
Blood and Tissue Parasites: Trypanosomes (Cont'd.)				
T. gambiense (African trypanosomiasis, sleeping sickness) —early disease (hemo-lymphatic stage)	Pentamidine isethionate‡	4 mg./kg. I.M. daily for 10 days.	Suramin‡	100 mg. (test dose) I.V., then 1 Gm. I.V. on days 1, 3, 7, 14, and 21.
T. rhodesiense (African trypanosomiasis, sleeping sickness) —early disease (hemo-lymphatic stage)	Suramin‡	100 mg. (test dose) I.V., then 1 Gm. I.V. on days 1, 3, 7, 14, and 21.	Pentamidine isethionate‡	4 mg./kg. I.M. daily for 10 days.
T. gambiense or T. rhodesiense —late disease with C.N.S. involvement	Melarsoprol‡	2 to 3.6 mg./kg. I.V. daily for 3 doses; after 1 week 3.6 mg./kg. I.V. daily for 3 doses; may be repeated again after 10 to 21 days.	Tryparsamide§ plus Suramin‡	One injection of 30 mg./kg. I.V. every 5 days to a total of 12 injections; may be repeated after 1 month. One injection of 10 mg./kg. I.V. every 5 days to a total of 12 injections; may be repeated after 1 month.
—chemoprophylaxis	Pentamidine isethionate‡	4 mg./kg. I.M. every 3 to 6 months.	Suramin‡	100 mg. (test dose) I.V., then 0.3 to 0.7 Gm. I.V. every 2 to 3 months.
Other Protozoan Parasites of the Tissues				
Toxoplasma gondii (toxoplasmosis)	Pyrimethamine plus Trisulfapyrimidines	25 to 50 mg. daily for 1 month. 0.5 to 1.5 Gm. q.i.d. for 1 month.	None	
Pneumocystis carinii	Pentamidine isethionate‡	4 mg./kg. I.M. daily for 12 to 14 days.	Pyrimethamine† plus Sulfadiazine	25 mg. daily in divided doses for 12 to 14 days. 2 Gm. daily in divided doses for 12 to 14 days.

†Effectiveness not established or of low order.
‡In the United States, this drug is available from the Parasitic Disease Drug Service, Parasitic Diseases Branch, Epidemiology Program, National Communicable Disease Center, Atlanta, Georgia 30333.
§Not available for clinical use in the United States.

ANTI-INFECTIVE CHEMOTHERAPEUTIC AND ANTIBIOTIC AGENTS

Some Rules for Antimicrobial Therapy.

Antimicrobial drugs properly used give striking therapeutic results. They can also give rise to serious complications and should therefore be administered only upon proper indication. The following steps merit consideration in each patient.

A. Etiologic Diagnosis: Formulate an etiologic diagnosis based on clinical observations. Microbial infections are best treated early. Therefore, the physician must attempt to decide on clinical grounds (1) whether the patient has a microbial infection that can probably be influenced by antimicrobial drugs, and (2) the most probable kind of microorganisms causing this type of infection.

B. "Best Guess": Based on a "best guess" about the probable cause of the patient's infection, the physician should choose a drug that is likely, on the basis of experience, to be effective against the suspected microorganism.

C. Laboratory Control: Before beginning antimicrobial drug treatment, obtain meaningful specimens for laboratory examination to determine the causative infectious organism and, if desirable, its susceptibility to antimicrobial drugs.

D. Clinical Response: Based on the clinical response of the patient, evaluate the laboratory reports and consider the desirability of changing the antimicrobial drug regimen. Laboratory results should not automatically overrule clinical judgment. The isolation of an organism that reinforces the initial clinical impression is a useful confirmation. Conversely, laboratory results may contradict the initial clinical impression and may force its reconsideration. If the specimen was obtained from a site which is normally devoid of bacterial flora and not exposed to the external environment (e.g., blood, CSF, pleural fluid, joint fluid), the recovery of a microorganism is a significant finding even if the organism recovered is different from the clinically suspected etiologic agent and may force a change in antimicrobial treatment. On the other hand, the isolation of unexpected microorganisms from the respiratory tract, gut, or surface lesions (sites that have a complex flora) must be critically evaluated before drugs are abandoned which were judiciously selected on the basis of an initial "best guess."

E. Drug Sensitivity Tests: Some microorganisms are fairly uniformly susceptible to certain drugs; if such organisms are isolated from the patient, they need not be tested for drug susceptibility. For example, pneumococci, group A hemolytic streptococci, and clostridia respond pre-

Blood Levels of Antibiotics Frequently Obtained With Commonly Used Doses

Drug	Daily Dose	Route	Expected Avg. Concentration/ml. Blood
Penicillin G	1 million units	I.M.	0.3-1 unit
	1 million units	Orally	0.03-0.3 unit
Streptomycin	2 Gm.	I.M.	15-25 μg.
Chloramphenicol	2 Gm.	Orally	15-25 μg.
Tetracycline	2 Gm.	Orally	10-20 μg.
Erythromycin	2 Gm.	Orally	2-5 μg.
Novobiocin	2 Gm.	Orally	1-5 μg.
Kanamycin	1 Gm.	I.M.	1-5 μg.
Gentamicin	3 mg./Kg.	I.M.	2-5 μg.
Polymyxin B	150 mg.	I.M.	1-2 μg.
Colistimethate sodium	300 mg.	I.M.	2-4 μg.
Vancomycin	2 Gm.	I.V.	1-10 μg.
Methicillin	8-10 Gm.	I.M. or I.V.	2-10 μg.
Oxacillin, cloxacillin, dicloxacillin	6 Gm.	Orally	1-5 μg.
Cephalothin	8-10 Gm.	I.M. or I.V.	2-10 μg.
Cephaloridine	4 Gm.		5-20 μg.
Ampicillin	4-6 Gm.	Orally	1-5 μg.
	6 Gm.	I.M. or I.V.	4-20 μg.

dictably to penicillin. On the other hand, some kinds of microorganisms (e.g., coliform gram-negative rods) are sufficiently variable in their response to warrant drug susceptibility testing whenever they are isolated from a significant specimen.

Antimicrobial drug susceptibility tests (commonly called "disk tests") usually give valuable results. Occasionally there is a marked discrepancy between the results of the test and the clinical response of the patient. The following possible explanations (among others) of such discrepancies may have to be considered:

1. Failure to drain a collection of pus or to remove a foreign body.
2. Failure of a poorly diffusing drug to reach the site of infection (e.g., joint cavity, pleural space) or to reach intracellular phagocytized bacteria.
3. Superinfection in the course of prolonged chemotherapy. After suppression of the original infection or of normal flora, a second type of microorganism may establish itself against which the originally selected drug is ineffective.

4. Emergence of drug-resistant mutants from a large microbial population.

5. Participation of two or more microorganisms in the infectious process of which only one was originally detected and used for drug selection.

F. Adequate Dosage: To determine whether the proper drug is being used in adequate dosage, a serum assay can be performed as follows: Blood is drawn from the patient receiving antimicrobial therapy. Serum is separated and two-fold dilutions prepared in broth. Each tube, and suitable controls, are inoculated with a culture of the microorganism previously isolated from the patient, properly diluted to give pre-incubation concentrations of 10^4 bacteria per ml. After incubation for 24 hours at 37° C., clear tubes (where bacterial growth was inhibited) are subcultured on blood agar plates. Twenty-four hours later that dilution of serum is reported which is both completely inhibitory and bactericidal for the infecting organism.

In general, serum should be bactericidal in a dilution of 1:10 or greater to effect reliable cure of bacterial endocarditis, sepsis in a debilitated host, etc. In infections limited to the urinary tract, the antibacterial activity of urine can be similarly estimated.

G. Adverse Reactions: The administration of antimicrobial drugs is commonly associated with untoward reactions. These fall into several groups. (1) Hypersensitivity: The most common hypersensitivity reactions are fever and skin rashes. Hematologic or hepatic disorders and anaphylaxis are rare. (2) Direct toxicity: Most common are nausea, vomiting, and diarrhea. More serious toxic reactions are impairment of renal, hepatic, or hematopoietic functions or damage to the eighth nerve. (3) Suppression of normal microbial flora and "superinfection" by drug-resistant microorganisms, or continued infection with the initial pathogen through the emergence of drug-resistant mutants.

In each case, the physician must evaluate the desirability of continuing a given drug regimen against the risk of discontinuing it. He must evaluate the severity and prognosis of each untoward reaction and choose between continuing a probably offending drug and discontinuing the drug but risking uncontrolled infection. An effective antimicrobial drug regimen which evokes hypersensitivity reactions can sometimes be continued with the simultaneous use of corticosteroids. In the presence of impaired renal function, toxic accumulation of drugs is likely. Therefore, reduction in dosage or frequency of medication is often necessary in renal failure.

H. Discontinue Treatment: If the patient is responding favorably to the administration of antimicrobial drugs as judged

DRUG SELECTIONS, 1969-70

Suspected or Proved Etiologic Agent	Drug(s) of First Choice	Alternative Drug(s)
Gram-negative cocci		
Gonococcus	Penicillin (1)	Erythromycin (2), cephalo-sporin (3), tetracycline (4)
Meningococcus		
Other neisseriae		
Gram-positive cocci		
Pneumococcus	Penicillin (1)	Cephalosporin, erythromy-cin, lincomycin
Staphylococcus, nonpenicillinase-producing		
Streptococcus viridans		
Streptococcus, hemo-lytic		
Staphylococcus, peni-cillinase-producing	Penicillinase-resist-ant penicillin (5)	Cephalosporin, vancomycin, erythromycin, lincomycin
Streptococcus faecal-is (enterococcus)	Penicillin plus strep-tomycin	Penicillin plus kanamycin, ampicillin plus streptomycin
Gram-negative rods		
Aerobacter (Entero-bacter)	Kanamycin	Tetracycline, gentamicin, chloramphenicol
Bacteroides	Tetracycline	Penicillin
Brucella	Tetracycline plus streptomycin	Streptomycin plus sulfona-mide (6)
Escherichia		
E. coli sepsis	Kanamycin	Cephalothin, ampicillin
E. coli urinary tract infection (first attack)	Sulfonamide (7)	Ampicillin
Hemophilus (menin-gitis, respiratory infections)	Ampicillin	Chloramphenicol
Klebsiella	Cephalosporin plus ampicillin	Tetracycline plus streptomy-cin
Mima-Herellea	Kanamycin	Tetracycline, gentamicin
Pasteurella (plague, tularemia)	Streptomycin plus tetracycline	Sulfonamide (6)
Proteus		
P. mirabilis	Penicillin, ampicillin	Kanamycin, gentamicin
P. vulgaris and other species	Kanamycin	Chloramphenicol, genta-micin
Pseudomonas		
Ps. aeruginosa	Polymyxin	Gentamicin
Ps. pseudomallei (melioidosis)	Chloramphenicol	
Ps. mallei (glan-ders)	Streptomycin plus tetracycline	
Salmonella	Chloramphenicol, ampicillin	Cephalosporins
Serratia	Gentamicin	Kanamycin
Shigella	Ampicillin	Tetracycline
Vibrio (cholera)	Tetracycline	Chloramphenicol
Gram-positive rods		
Actinomyces	Penicillin (1)	Tetracycline, sulfonamide
Bacillus (eg., anthrax)	Penicillin (1)	Erythromycin
Clostridium (eg., gas gangrene, tetanus)	Penicillin (1)	Tetracycline, erythromycin
Corynebacterium	Penicillin (1)	Erythromycin, cephalosporin
Listeria	Tetracyclines	Penicillin (1)
Nocardia	Sulfonamide (6)	Tetracycline

DRUG SELECTIONS, 1969-70 (Cont'd.)

Suspected or Proved Etiologic Agent	Drug(s) of First Choice	Alternative Drug(s)
Acid-fast rods		
Actinomyces	Penicillin (1)	Tetracycline, sulfonamide
Mycobacterium tuberculosis	INH plus PAS plus streptomycin	Other antituberculosis drugs
Myco. leprae	Dapsone or sulfetrone	Other sulfones
Nocardia	Sulfonamide (6)	Tetracycline, cycloserine
Spirochetes		
Borrelia (relapsing fever)	Tetracycline	Penicillin
Leptospira	Penicillin	Tetracycline
Treponema (syphilis, yaws)	Penicillin	Erythromycin, tetracycline
Mycoplasma	Tetracycline	Erythromycin
Psittacosis-lymphogranuloma-trachoma agents	Tetracycline, sulfonamide (6)	Erythromycin, chloramphenicol
Rickettsiae	Tetracycline	Chloramphenicol

(1) Penicillin G is preferred for parenteral injection; penicillin G (buffered) or penicillin V for oral administration. Only highly sensitive microorganisms should be treated with oral penicillin.

(2) Erythromycin estolate and triacetyloleandomycin are oral forms, which give highest levels. Lower levels achieved with base or stearate.

(3) Cephalothin and cephaloridine are the best accepted cephalosporins.

(4) All tetracyclines have the same activity against microorganisms and all have comparable therapeutic activity and toxicity. Dosage is determined by the rates of absorption and excretion of different preparations.

(5) Parenteral methicillin, nafcillin, or oxacillin. Oral dicloxacillin or other isoxazolylpenicillin.

(6) Trisulfapyrimidines have the advantage of greater solubility in urine over sulfadiazine for oral administration; sodium sulfadiazine is suitable for intravenous injection in severely ill persons.

(7) For previously untreated urinary tract infection, a highly soluble sulfonamide such as sulfisoxazole or trisulfapyrimidines is the first choice.

by appropriate clinical or laboratory findings, treatment should be discontinued as soon as possible to minimize untoward drug reactions.

Penicillins.

All penicillins share a common chemical nucleus (aminopenicillanic acid) and a common mode of antibacterial action - the inhibition of cell wall mucopeptide (peptidoglycan) synthesis. The penicillins can be arranged according to several major criteria:

(1) Susceptibility to destruction by penicillinase (i. e. , hydrolysis by the β-lactamase of bacteria).

(2) Susceptibility to destruction by acid pH (i. e. , relative stability to gastric acid).

(3) Relative efficacy against gram-positive versus gram-negative bacteria.

A. Antimicrobial Activity: All penicillins specifically inhibit the synthesis of rigid bacterial cell walls which contain a complex mucopeptide. Most penicillins are much more active against gram-positive than against gram-negative bacteria, probably because of chemical differences in cell wall structure. Penicillins are inactive against bacteria which are not multiplying and thus form no new cell walls ("persisters").

One million units of penicillin G equal 0.6 Gm. Other penicillins are prescribed in grams. A blood serum level of 0.01 to 1 μg./ml. penicillin G or ampicillin is lethal for a majority of susceptible microorganisms; methicillin and isoxazolylpenicillins are $1/5$ to $1/50$ as active.

B. Resistance: Resistance to penicillins falls into four different categories:

1. Certain bacteria (e. g. , some staphylococci, gram-negative bacteria) produce enzymes (penicillinases, β-lactamases) which destroy penicillin G, ampicillin, and other penicillins. Clinical penicillin resistance of staphylococci falls largely into this category.

2. Certain bacteria (e. g. ; coliform organisms) produce an enzyme (amidase) which can split off the side chain from the penicillin nucleus and thus destroy biologic activity.

3. Certain bacteria are resistant to some penicillins although they do not produce enzymes destroying the drug. Clinical methicillin resistance falls into this category.

4. Metabolically inactive organisms which make no new cell wall mucopeptide are temporarily resistant to penicillins. They can act as "persisters" and perpetuate infection during and after penicillin treatment. L-forms are in this category.

C. Absorption, Distribution, and Excretions: After parenteral administration, absorption of most penicillins is complete and rapid. Because of the irritation and consequent local pain produced by the I. M. injection of large doses, administration by the I. V. route (continuous infusion, or intermittent addition to a continuous drip) is often preferred. After oral administration, only a portion of the dose is absorbed - from $1/3$ to $1/20$, depending upon acid stability, binding to foods, and the presence of buffers. In order to minimize binding to foods, oral penicillins should not be preceded or followed by food for at least one hour.

After absorption, penicillins are widely distributed in body fluids and tissues. This varies to some extent with the degree of protein binding exhibited by different penicillins. Penicillin G, methicillin, and ampicillin are moderately protein bound (depending upon the method of measurement, 30 to 60%), whereas the isoxazolylpenicillins are highly protein bound (85 to 95%). It is probable that intensive protein binding diminishes the amount of drug available for antibacterial action in vivo. With parenteral doses of 3 to 6 Gm. (5 to 10 million units) of penicillin G, injected by continuous infusion or divided I. M. injections, average serum levels of the drug reach 1 to 10 units (0.6 to 6 μg.)/ml. A rough relationship of 6 Gm. given parenterally per day, yielding serum levels of 1 to 6 μg./ml., also applies to other penicillins. Naturally, the highly serum bound isoxazolylpenicillins yield, on the average, lower levels of free drug than less strongly bound penicillins.

Special dosage forms of penicillin have been designed for delayed absorption to yield low blood and tissue levels for long periods. The outstanding example is benzathine penicillin G. After a single I. M. injection of 1.5 Gm. (2.4 million units), serum levels in excess of 0.03 unit/ml. are maintained for ten days and levels in excess of 0.005 unit/ml. for three weeks. The latter is sufficient to protect against beta-hemolytic streptococcal infection; the former to treat an established infection with these organisms. Procaine penicillin also has delayed absorption, yielding levels for 24 hours.

In many tissues, penicillin concentrations are equal to those in serum. Much lower levels are found in the joints, eyes, and CNS. However, with active inflammation of the meninges, as in bacterial meningitis, penicillin levels in the CSF exceed 0.2 μg./ml. with a daily parenteral dose of 12 Gm. Thus, pneumococcal and meningococcal meningitis may be treated with systemic penicillin and there is no need for intrathecal injection.

Most of the absorbed penicillin is rapidly excreted by the kidneys into the urine. About 10% of renal excretion is by glomerular filtration and 90% by tubular excretion, to a maximum of about 2 Gm./hour in an adult. Tubular excretion can be partially blocked by probenecid (Benemid®) to achieve higher systemic levels. Individuals with impaired renal function tend to maintain higher penicillin levels longer.

Renal excretion of penicillin results in very high levels in the urine. Thus, systemic daily doses of 6 Gm. of penicillin may yield urine levels of 500 to 3000 μg./ml. Penicillin is also excreted into sputum and milk to levels of 3 to 15% of those present in the serum. This is the case in both man and cattle. The presence of penicillin in the milk of cows treated for mastitis presents a problem in allergy.

D. Indications, Dosages, and Routes of Administration: The penicillins are by far the most effective and the most widely used antimicrobial drugs, and one or another member of the group is the drug of choice in a wide variety of infections.

   1. Penicillin G - This is the drug of choice for infections caused by gonococci, pneumococci, streptococci, men-

ingococci, non-β-lactamase producing staphylococci, Treponema pallidum and many other spirochetes, Bacillus anthracis and other gram-positive rods, clostridia, Listeria, and Bacteroides.

a. I. M. or I. V. - Most of the above-mentioned infections respond to aqueous penicillin G in daily doses of 0.6 to 5 million units (0.36 to 3 Gm.) administered by intermittent I. M. injection every four to six hours. Much larger amounts (6 to 120 Gm. daily) can be given by continuous I. V. infusion in serious or complicated infections due to these organisms. Sites for such I. V. administration are subject to thrombophlebitis and superinfection and must be rotated every two days and kept scrupulously aseptic. In enterococcus endocarditis, kanamycin or streptomycin is given simultaneously with large doses of penicillin.

b. Oral - Buffered penicillin G (or penicillin V) is indicated only in minor infections (e. g. , of the respiratory tract or its associated structures) in daily doses of 1 to 4 Gm. (1.6 to 6.4 million units). About one-fifth of the oral dose is absorbed, but oral administration is subject to so many variables that it should not be relied upon in seriously ill patients.

c. Intrathecal - With high serum levels of penicillin, adequate concentrations reach the CNS and CSF for the treatment of meningitis. Therefore, and because of the danger of injection into the subdural space of more than 10,000 units of penicillin G (which can give rise to convulsions), intrathecal injection has been virtually abandoned.

d. Topical - Penicillins have been applied to skin, wounds, and mucous membranes by compress, ointment, and aerosol. These applications are highly sensitizing and rarely warranted. (An exception is the use of penicillin ointment placed into the eye of the newborn to prevent gonococcal ophthalmia.) Rarely, solutions of penicillin (e. g. , 100,000 units/ ml.) are instilled into joint or pleural space infected with susceptible organisms.

2. Benzathine penicillin G - This penicillin is a salt of very low water solubility. It is injected I. M. to establish a depot which yields low but prolonged drug levels. A single injection of 2.4 million units I. M. is satisfactory for treatment of beta-hemolytic streptococcal pharyngitis and perhaps for early syphilis. An injection of 1.2 to 2.4 million units I. M. every three to four weeks provides satisfactory prophylaxis for rheumatics against reinfection with group A streptococci. There is no indication for using this drug by mouth. Procaine penicillin G is another repository form for main-

taining drug levels for up to 24 hours. For highly susceptible infections, 300 to 600 thousand units I. M. are
usually given once daily.

3. Ampicillin, carbenicillin - These drugs differ from
penicillin G in having greater activity against gram-
negative bacteria, but, like penicillin G, they are
destroyed by penicillinases.

Ampicillin is the drug of current choice for bacterial meningitis in small children, especially meningitis due to H. influenzae; 150 mg./Kg./day are injected
I. V. Ampicillin can be given orally in divided doses,
3 to 6 Gm. daily to treat urinary tract infections with
coliform bacteria, enterococci, or Proteus mirabilis.
It is ineffective against Enterobacter and Pseudomonas.
In Salmonella infections, ampicillin, 6 to 12 Gm. daily
orally, can be effective in suppressing clinical disease
(second choice to chloramphenicol in acute typhoid or
paratyphoid) and may eliminate salmonellae from some
chronic carriers. Ampicillin is somewhat more effective than penicillin G against enterococci and may be
used in such infections in combination with kanamycin
or streptomycin. Carbenicillin is more active against
Proteus and Pseudomonas.

4. Penicillinase-resistant penicillins - Methicillin, oxacillin, cloxacillin, dicloxacillin, nafcillin, and others
are relatively resistant to destruction by β-lactamase.
The only indication for the use of these drugs is infection by β-lactamase producing staphylococci.

a. Oral - Oxacillin, cloxacillin, dicloxacillin (the isoxazolylpenicillins), or nafcillin may be given in doses
of 0.25 to 0.5 Gm. every four to six hours in mild
or localized staphylococcal infections (50 to 100
mg./Kg./day for children). Food must not be given
in proximity to these doses because it will seriously
interfere with absorption.

b. I. V. - For serious systemic staphylococcal infections, methicillin, 8 to 16 Gm., or nafcillin, 6 to
12 Gm., is administered I. V., usually by injecting
1 to 2 Gm. during 20 to 30 minutes every two hours
into a continuous infusion of 5% dextrose in water or
physiologic salt solution. The dose for children is
methicillin, 100 to 300 mg./Kg./day, or nafcillin,
50 to 100 mg./Kg./day.

E. Adverse Effects: The penicillins undoubtedly possess
less direct toxicity than any other antibiotics. Most of
the serious side effects are due to hypersensitivity.

1. Allergy - All penicillins are cross-sensitizing and
cross-reacting. Any preparation containing penicillin
may induce sensitization, including foods or cosmetics.
In general, sensitization occurs in direct proportion to
the duration and total dose of penicillin received in the

past. The responsible antigenic determinants appear
to be degradation products of penicillins, particularly
penicilloic acid and products of alkaline hydrolysis
bound to host protein. Skin tests with penicilloyl-
polylysine, with alkaline hydrolysis products, and with
undegraded penicillin will identify some hypersensitive
individuals. Among positive reactors to skin tests,
the incidence of subsequent penicillin reactions is high.
Although many persons develop antibodies to antigenic
determinants of penicillin, the presence of such antibodies does not appear to be correlated with allergic
reactivity (except rare hemolytic anemia), and serologic tests have little predictive value. A history of a
penicillin reaction in the past is not always reliable;
however, if there is a possible history of reaction to
penicillin, the drug should be administered with caution.

Allergic reactions may occur as typical anaphylactic shock, typical serum sickness type reactions (urticaria, fever, joint swelling, angioneurotic edema, intense pruritus, and respiratory embarrassment occurring seven to 12 days after exposure), and a variety of
skin rashes, oral lesions, fever, renal abnormalities,
eosinophilia, hemolytic anemia, other hematologic
disturbances, and vasculitis. LE cells are sometimes
found. The incidence of hypersensitivity to penicillin
is estimated to be 5 to 10% among adults in the U.S.A.,
but is negligible in small children.

Individuals known to be hypersensitive to penicillin
can at times tolerate the drug during corticosteroid
administration. "Desensitization" with gradually increasing doses of penicillin is also occasionally
attempted but is not without hazard.

2. Toxicity - The toxic effects of penicillin G are due to
   the direct irritation caused by I.M. or I.V. injection
   of exceedingly high concentrations (e.g., 1 Gm./ml.).
   Such concentrations may cause local pain, induration,
   thrombophlebitis, or degeneration of an accidentally
   injected nerve. All penicillins are irritating to the
   CNS. There is little indication for intrathecal administration at present. In rare cases a patient receiving
   more than 50 Gm. of penicillin G daily parenterally
   has exhibited signs of cerebrocortical irritation, presumably as a result of the passage of unusually large
   amounts of penicillin into the CNS. With doses of this
   magnitude, direct cation toxicity (Na^+, K^+) can also
   occur. Potassium penicillin G contains 1.7 mEq. of
   K^+ per million units (2.8 mEq./Gm.), and potassium
   may accumulate in the presence of renal failure.

   Large doses of penicillins given orally may lead to
   gastrointestinal upset, particularly nausea and diarrhea.

Oral therapy may also be accompanied by luxuriant
overgrowth of staphylococci, Pseudomonas, Proteus,
or yeasts, which may occasionally cause enteritis.
Superinfections in other organ systems may occur with
penicillins as with any antibiotic therapy. Methicillin
and isoxazolylpenicillins have occasionally caused
granulocytopenia, especially in children.

Cephalosporins.

Cephalosporins are a group of compounds closely related
to the penicillins. The mode of action is the same as that of
penicillins, there is some (limited) cross-allergenicity, and
they are resistant to destruction by β-lactamase.

A. Antimicrobial Activity: Cephalosporins inhibit the synthesis of bacterial cell wall mucopeptide in somewhat the
same way as do the penicillins. They are resistant to
destruction by β-lactamase, but they can be hydrolyzed
by a cephalosporinase produced by certain microorganisms. The cephalosporins are bactericidal in vitro in
concentrations of 1 to 20 μg./ml. against most gram-
positive microorganisms, except Streptococcus faecalis,
and in concentrations of 5 to 30 μg./ml. against many
gram-negative bacteria, except Pseudomonas, Herellea,
Proteus, and Enterobacter. There is at least partial
cross-resistance between cephalosporins and β-lactamase-
resistant penicillins. Thus, methicillin-resistant staphylococci are also resistant to cephalosporins.

B. Absorption, Distribution, and Excretion: Cephalothin and
cephaloridine are not significantly absorbed from the gut.
After parenteral injection, they are distributed widely,
and 50 to 70% of the drug in serum is protein-bound. Concentrations in synovial fluid, CNS, and CSF are low after
parenteral injection. Thus, cephalothin is not a drug of
choice in meningitis. Excretion of cephalosporins is primarily by tubular secretion into the urine.

Urine levels may reach 200 to 1000 μg./ml. In the
presence of impaired renal function, very high blood and
tissue levels of cephalosporins may accumulate and exert
toxic effects.

Cephaloglycine and cephalexin are somewhat better absorbed from the gut, and therapeutic urine levels are
reached after oral doses.

C. Indications, Dosages, and Routes of Administration:
1. Oral - Cephaloglycine or cephalexin, 0.5 Gm. four
times daily orally, yields urine concentrations of 50 to
500 μg./ml. - sufficient for treatment of urinary tract
infections due to coliform organisms.
2. I. V. - Cephalothin (Keflin®), 8 to 16 Gm. daily (for
children, 50 to 100 mg./Kg./day) by continuous drip,
gives serum concentrations of 5 to 20 μg./ml. This is
adequate for the treatment of gram-negative bactere-

mia or staphylococcal sepsis, or as a substitute for
penicillin in serious infections caused by susceptible
organisms in persons allergic to penicillin (although
some cross-hypersensitivity exists). Cephaloridine
(Keflordin®, Loridine®), 4 Gm. daily (for children, up
to 100 mg./Kg./day) I. V., gives serum levels of 10 to
25 µg./ml. It is used for the same indications.

3. I. M. - Cephaloridine, 0.5 to 1 Gm. I. M. every six
hours, is used for the same indications as above in
less severely ill patients. Cephalothin is too painful
when injected I. M.

D. Adverse Effects:

1. Allergy - Cephalosporins are sensitizing, and a variety of hypersensitivity reactions occur, including anaphylaxis, fever, skin rashes, granulocytopenia, and
hemolytic anemia. Cross-allergy also exists with penicillins and can produce the same hypersensitivity
reactions. Perhaps 10 to 30% of penicillin-allergic
persons are also hypersensitive to cephalosporins.

2. Toxicity - Local pain after I. M. injection, thrombophlebitis after I. V. injection. Renal damage with tubular necrosis and uremia has been reported for cephaloridine but not for cephalothin.

Erythromycin Group (Macrolides).

The erythromycins are a group of closely related compounds. They inhibit protein synthesis and are active against
gram-positive organisms - especially pneumococci, streptococci, staphylococci, and corynebacteria - in concentrations
of 0.02 to 2 µg./ml. Neisseriae and mycoplasmas are also susceptible. Activity is enhanced at alkaline pH. Resistant mutants occur in most microbial populations and tend to emerge
during prolonged treatment. There is complete cross-resistance among all members of the erythromycin group. The pro-
pionyl ester of erythromycin (erythromycin estolate) and the
triacetyl ester of oleandomycin are among the best absorbed
oral preparations. Oral doses of 2 Gm./day result in blood
levels of up to 2 µg./ml., and there is wide distribution of the
drug in all tissues except the CNS. Erythromycins are excreted largely in bile; only 5% of the dose is excreted into the urine.

Erythromycins are the drugs of choice in corynebacterial
infections (diphtheroid sepsis, erythrasma) and in mycoplasmal pneumonia. They are most useful as substitutes for penicillin in persons with streptococcal and pneumococcal infections who are allergic to penicillin.

A. Dosages:

1. Oral - Erythromycin estolate or triacetyloleandomycin,
0.5 Gm. every six hours (for children, 40 mg./Kg./
day). Erythromycin base or stearate yields 25 to 35%
lower tissue levels.

2. I. V. - Erythromycin lactobionate or glucoheptonate,

0.5 Gm. every 12 hours.

B. Adverse Effects: Nausea, vomiting, and diarrhea may
   occur after oral intake. Erythromycin estolate or triacetyloleandomycin can produce acute cholestatic hepatitis
   (fever, jaundice, impaired liver function). Most patients
   recover completely. Upon readministration, the hepatitis
   promptly recurs. It is probably a hypersensitivity reaction. The base or stearate does not cause liver toxicity.

Tetracycline Group.

The tetracyclines are a large group of drugs with common
basic chemical structures, antimicrobial activity, and pharmacologic properties. Microorganisms resistant to this group
show complete cross-resistance to all tetracyclines.

A. Antimicrobial Activity: Tetracyclines are inhibitors of
   protein synthesis and are bacteriostatic for many gram-
   positive and gram-negative bacteria, including anaerobes,
   and are strongly inhibitory for the growth of mycoplasmas,
   rickettsiae, chlamydiae (psittacosis-LGV-trachoma
   agents), and some protozoa (e.g., amebas). Equal concentrations of all tetracyclines in blood or tissue have
   approximately equal antimicrobial activity. Such differences in activity as may be claimed for individual tetracycline drugs are of no practical importance. However,
   there are great differences in the susceptibility of different strains of a given species, and laboratory tests are
   important. Because of the emergence of resistant
   strains, tetracyclines have lost some of their former
   usefulness. Proteus and Pseudomonas are regularly resistant; among the coliform bacteria, pneumococci, and
   streptococci, resistant strains are increasingly common.

B. Absorption, Distribution, and Excretion: Tetracyclines
   are absorbed somewhat irregularly from the gut. Absorption is limited by the low solubility of the drugs and by
   chelation with divalent cations, e.g., Ca^{++}. This produces binding by food, milk, antacids. A large proportion of orally administered tetracycline remains in the
   gut lumen, modifies intestinal flora, and is excreted in
   feces. Of the absorbed drug, 20 to 50% is protein bound
   in the blood. With full systemic doses (2 Gm./day),
   levels of active drug in serum reach 2 to 10 μg./ml. The
   drugs are widely distributed in tissues and body fluids,
   but the levels in CNS, CSF, and joint fluids are only 3 to
   10% of serum levels. Tetracyclines are specifically deposited in growing bones and teeth.

   Absorbed tetracyclines are excreted mainly in bile and
   urine. Up to 20% of oral doses may appear in the urine
   after glomerular filtration. Urine levels may be 5 to 50
   μg./ml. or more. With renal failure, doses of tetracyclines must be reduced or intervals between doses increased. Up to 80% of an oral dose appears in the feces.

Demethylchlortetracycline, methacycline, and doxycycline are well absorbed from the gut but are excreted much more slowly than others, leading to accumulation and prolonged blood levels. Specially formulated buffered tetracycline solutions can be injected parenterally.

C. Indications, Dosages, and Routes of Administration: At present, tetracyclines are the drugs of choice in cholera, mycoplasmal pneumonia, infections with chlamydiae (psittacosis-LGV-trachoma), and infections with some rickettsiae. They may be used in various bacterial infections provided the organism is susceptible, and in amebiasis.

1. Oral - Tetracycline hydrochloride, oxytetracycline, and chlortetracycline are dispensed in 250 mg. capsules. Give 0.25 to 0.5 Gm. orally every six hours (for children, 20 to 40 mg./Kg./day). In acne vulgaris, 0.25 Gm. once or twice daily for many months is prescribed by dermatologists.

The "long-acting drugs" - demethylchlortetracycline, methacycline, and doxycycline - are dispensed in 50 or 150 mg. capsules. Give 0.15 to 0.3 Gm. orally every six hours (for children, 12 to 20 mg./Kg./day).

2. I.M. or I.V. - Several tetracyclines are formulated for I.M. or I.V. injection. Give 0.1 to 0.5 Gm. every six to 12 hours in individuals unable to take oral medication (for children, 10 to 15 mg./Kg./day).

3. Topical - Tetracycline, 1% in ointments, can be applied to conjunctival infections.

D. Adverse Effects:

1. Allergy - Hypersensitivity reactions with fever or skin rashes are uncommon.

2. Gastrointestinal side effects - Gastrointestinal side effects, especially diarrhea, nausea, and anorexia, are common. These can be diminished by reducing the dose or by administering tetracyclines with food or carboxymethylcellulose, but sometimes they force discontinuance of the drug. After a few days of oral use, the gut flora is modified so that drug-resistant bacteria and yeasts become prominent. This may cause functional gut disturbances, anal pruritus, and even enterocolitis with shock and death.

3. Bones and teeth - Tetracyclines are bound to calcium deposited in growing bones and teeth, causing fluorescence, discoloration, enamel dysplasia, deformity, or growth inhibition. Therefore, tetracyclines should not be given to pregnant women or small children.

4. Liver damage - Tetracyclines can impair hepatic function or even cause liver necrosis, particularly during pregnancy, in the presence of preexisting liver damage, or with doses of more than 3 Gm. I.V.

5. Kidney damage - Outdated tetracycline preparations

have been implicated in renal tubular acidosis and
other forms of renal damage.
6. Other - Tetracyclines, principally demethylchlortetracycline, may induce photosensitization, especially in
blonds. I.V. injection may cause thrombophlebitis,
and I.M. injection local inflammation with pain.

Chloramphenicol.

Chloramphenicol is a synthetic drug which inhibits the
growth of many bacteria, rickettsiae, and chlamydiae in concentrations of 0.5 to 10 μg./ml. There is no cross-resistance
with other drugs.

After oral administration, chloramphenicol is rapidly and
completely absorbed. Administration of 2 Gm./day orally to
adults results in blood levels of 20 μg./ml. In children, chloramphenicol palmitate, 50 mg./Kg./day orally, is hydrolyzed
in the gut to yield free chloramphenicol and give a blood level
of 10 μg./ml. Chloramphenicol succinate, 25 to 50 mg./Kg./
day I.M. or I.V., yields free chloramphenicol by hydrolysis,
giving blood levels slightly lower than those achieved by oral
administration. After absorption, chloramphenicol is widely
distributed to all tissues, including the CNS and CSF. It penetrates cells readily. Ten percent of active drug is excreted
by glomerular filtration into the urine.

The remainder is metabolized or excreted by glucuronide
conjugation in the liver.

Because of its potential toxicity, chloramphenicol is at
present a possible drug of choice only in the following cases:
(1) symptomatic Salmonella infection, e.g., typhoid fever;
(2) Hemophilus influenzae meningitis, laryngotracheitis, or
pneumonia that does not respond to ampicillin; (3) occasional
gram-negative bacteremia; and (4) severe rickettsial infection,
e.g., Rocky Mountain spotted fever. It is occasionally used
topically in ophthalmology.

In serious systemic infection, the dose is 0.5 Gm. orally
every four to six hours (for children, 30 to 50 mg./Kg./day)
for seven to 21 days. Similar amounts are given I.V.

Adverse Effects: Nausea, vomiting, and diarrhea occur
infrequently. The most serious adverse effects pertain to the
hematopoietic system. Adults taking chloramphenicol in excess of 50 mg./Kg./day regularly exhibit disturbances in red
cell maturation after one to two weeks of blood levels above
25 μg./ml. There is anemia, rise in serum iron concentration, reticulocytopenia, and vacuolated nucleated red cells in
the bone marrow. These changes regress when the drug is
stopped and are not related to the rare aplastic anemia.

Serious aplastic anemia is a rare consequence of chloramphenicol administration and represents a specific, probably genetically determined individual defect. It is seen more
frequently with either prolonged or repeated use. It tends to
be irreversible and fatal. Fatal aplastic anemia occurs 13

times more frequently after the use of chloramphenicol than as a spontaneous occurrence. Hypoplastic anemia may be followed by the development of leukemia.

Chloramphenicol is specifically toxic for newborns, producing the highly fatal "gray syndrome" with vomiting, flaccidity, hypothermia, and collapse. Chloramphenicol should only rarely be used in infants, and the dose must be limited to less than 50 mg./Kg./day in full-term infants and less than 30 mg./Kg./day in prematures.

Aminoglycosides.

Aminoglycosides are a group of drugs with similar chemical, antimicrobial, pharmacologic, ototoxic, and nephrotoxic characteristics. Important members are streptomycin, kanamycin, neomycin, and gentamicin.

1. Streptomycins.

Streptomycin is a product of Streptomyces griseus. Dihydrostreptomycin was derived from it by chemical reduction, but it is no longer used because of serious ototoxicity. Streptomycin can be bactericidal for gram-positive and gram-negative bacteria and for Mycobacterium tuberculosis. Its antituberculosis activity is described below.

In all bacterial strains there are mutants which are 10 to 1000 times more resistant to streptomycin than the remainder of the microbial population. These are selected out rapidly in the presence of streptomycin. Treatment with streptomycin for four to five days thus results either in eradication of the infecting agent or the emergence of resistant infection which is intractable by the drug. For this reason, streptomycin is usually employed in combination with another drug to delay the emergence of resistance. Streptomycin may enhance the bactericidal action of penicillins, particularly against Streptococcus faecalis.

Streptomycin is not significantly absorbed from the gut. After I. M. injection, it is rapidly absorbed and widely distributed in body fluids and tissues except the CNS and CSF. Streptomycin does not penetrate well into living cells. Thus it is only slightly active against intracellular phagocytized bacteria and fails to eradicate those chronic infections in which most organisms are intracellular. With 2 Gm. given I. M. daily, serum levels reach 20 μg./ml.

Streptomycin is excreted mainly by glomerular filtration into the urine, where the concentration may be five to 50 times higher than in serum. In renal failure, excretion of streptomycin is impaired and accumulation to toxic levels occurs unless the dose is greatly reduced and the intervals between injections are lengthened.

A. Indications and Dosages: The principal indications for streptomycin at present are (1) serious active tuberculosis; (2) plague, tularemia, or occasional gram-negative sepsis; (3) Klebsiella pneumonia and acute brucellosis (used in conjunction with tetracycline); (4) bacterial endocarditis caused by Streptococcus faecalis or Streptococcus viridans (used in conjunction with penicillin); and (5) rare acute urinary tract infections caused by susceptible organisms. Activity is enhanced in alkaline urine.

The dose in the nontuberculous infections is 0.5 to 1 Gm. I. M. every eight to 12 hours (for children, 20 to 40 mg./Kg./day), depending on severity of the disease.

B. Adverse Effects: Allergic reactions, including skin rashes and fever, may occur upon prolonged contact with streptomycin, e. g. , in personnel preparing solutions. The principal side effects are nephrotoxicity and ototoxicity. Renal damage with nitrogen retention occurs mainly after prolonged high doses or in persons with preexisting impairment of renal function. Damage to the eighth nerve manifests itself mainly by tinnitus, vertigo, ataxia, loss of balance, and occasionally loss of hearing. Chronic vestibular dysfunction is most common after prolonged use of streptomycin. Streptomycin, 2 to 3 Gm./day for four weeks, has been used to purposely damage semicircular canal function in the treatment of Ménière's disease.

Streptomycin should not be used concurrently with other aminoglycosides, and great caution is necessary in persons with impaired renal function.

2. Kanamycin (Kantrex®).

Kanamycin is the most prominent aminoglycoside for systemic use in gram-negative sepsis. Kanamycin is bactericidal for many gram-positive (except enterococci) and gram-negative bacteria in concentrations of 1 to 10 μg./ml. Activity is enhanced at alkaline pH. Some strains of Proteus are susceptible, but Pseudomonas and Serratia are often resistant. In susceptible bacterial populations, resistant mutants are rare. Kanamycin exhibits complete cross-resistance with neomycin but not with gentamicin.

Kanamycin is not significantly absorbed from the gut. After I. M. injection (0.5 Gm. every six to 12 hours), serum levels may reach 5 to 10 μg./ml. The drug is distributed widely in tissues but does not reach significant concentrations in the CSF, joints, or pleural fluid unless injected locally. Excretion is mainly by glomerular filtration into the urine, where levels of 10 to 50 μg./ml. are reached, and into the bile. In the presence of renal insufficiency, the drug may accumulate rapidly and reach toxic levels.

A. Indications and Dosages: The principal indication for systemic kanamycin is bacteremia caused by gram-negative enteric organisms or, occasionally, serious urinary tract infection with Enterobacter, Proteus, or other "difficult" organisms. The I. M. dose is 0.5 Gm. every six to 12 hours (15 mg./Kg./day). In renal failure, the dose is reduced. For example, if the serum creatinine is 6 mg./ 100 ml., kanamycin, 7 mg./Kg. I. M., is followed by 3.5 mg./Kg. I. M. every 18 hours.

B. Adverse Effects: Like all aminoglycosides, kanamycin is ototoxic and nephrotoxic. Kanamycin is probably less toxic than neomycin. Proteinuria and nitrogen retention occur commonly during treatment. This must be monitored and the dose or frequency of injection adjusted when creatinine clearance falls. In general, these nephrotoxic effects are reversible upon discontinuance of the drug. The auditory portion of the eighth nerve can be selectively and irreversibly damaged by kanamycin. The development of deafness is proportionate to the level of drug and the time of its administration, but it can occur unpredictably even after a short course of treatment. Loss of perception of high frequencies in audiograms may be a warning sign. Ototoxicity is a particular risk in patients with impaired kidney function. The sudden absorption of large amounts of kanamycin (or any other aminoglycoside) can lead to respiratory arrest. This has occurred after the instillation of 3 to 5 Gm. of kanamycin (or neomycin) into the peritoneal cavity following bowel surgery. Neostigmine is a specific antidote.

3. Neomycin.

Neomycin is analogous in all pharmacologic and antibacterial characteristics to kanamycin. However, it is believed at present to be somewhat more toxic when given parenterally and is therefore used mainly for topical application and for oral administration.

A. Indications, Dosages, and Routes of Administration: After oral intake, only a minute portion of neomycin is absorbed. Most of the drug remains in the gut lumen and alters intestinal flora. For preoperative reduction of the gut flora, give neomycin, 1 Gm. orally every four to six hours for two to three days before surgery. In hepatic coma, ammonia intoxication can be reduced by suppressing the coliform flora of the gut with neomycin, 1 Gm. orally every six to eight hours, and limiting the protein intake. Oral neomycin, 50 to 100 mg./Kg./day, is effective against enteropathic Escherichia coli. To control surface infections of the skin (pyoderma), ointments containing neomycin, 1 to 5 mg./Gm., are applied several times daily. Solutions containing 10 mg./ml. of neomycin can be instilled (up to a total of 0.5 Gm./day) into infected joints, pleura, or tissue spaces. Paromomycin (Humatin®), a close relative of neomycin, is given in a dosage of 1 Gm. orally every six hours for the treatment of intestinal amebiasis.

B. Adverse Effects: All topically administered forms of neomycin may produce sensitization. Hypersensitivity reactions occur particularly in the eye and skin after repeated
use of neomycin ointments. Topical or oral neomycin
rarely produces systemic toxicity. However, oral neomycin alters the intestinal flora and thus predisposes to
superinfection. Staphylococcal enterocolitis, occasionally fatal, has followed the use of neomycin for preoperative
''bowel sterilization.''

4. Gentamicin (Garamycin®).

Gentamicin is an aminoglycoside antibiotic which shares
many properties with kanamycin but differs in its antimicrobial activity. In concentrations of 0.5 to 5 μg./ml., gentamicin is bactericidal not only for staphylococci and coliform organisms but also for many strains of Pseudomonas, Proteus,
and Serratia. Gentamicin is not significantly absorbed after
oral intake. After I.M. injection, gentamicin is rapidly absorbed and widely distributed (except into the CNS). Thirty
per cent of the drug in serum is protein-bound. With full
doses (3 mg./Kg./day), serum levels reach 3 to 5 μg./ml. In
the presence of renal failure, there is marked accumulation
of the drug to toxic levels. Gentamicin is excreted by glomerular filtration into the urine, where levels are 10 to 100 times
higher than in the serum.

A. Indications, Dosages, and Routes of Administration:
Gentamicin is used in severe infections caused by gram-
negative bacteria which are likely to be resistant to other,
less toxic drugs. Included are sepsis, infected burns,
pneumonia and other serious infections due to coliform
organisms, Klebsiella-Enterobacter, Proteus, Pseudomonas, and Serratia. The dosage is 2 to 3 mg./Kg./day
I.M. in three equal doses for seven to ten days. In life-
threatening infections, up to 5 mg./Kg./day have been
given. In urinary tract infections caused by these organisms, 0.8 to 1.2 mg./Kg./day is given I.M. for ten days
or longer.

For infected burns or skin lesions, creams containing
0.1% gentamicin are used.

Renal function must be monitored by repeated creatinine clearance tests, although nephrotoxicity is said to be
infrequent with recommended doses and in the absence of
preexisting renal damage. About 2 to 3% of patients develop vestibular dysfunction (perhaps because of destruction of hair cells), and occasional cases of loss of hearing
have been reported.

Polymyxins.

The polymyxins are a group of basic polypeptides bactericidal for most gram-negative bacteria except Proteus and

especially useful against Pseudomonas. Only two drugs are used: polymyxin B sulfate and colistin (polymyxin E) methane-sulfonate.

Polymyxins are not absorbed from the gut. After parenteral injection they are distributed in some tissues but do not reach the CNS, CSF, joints, or ocular tissues unless injected locally. Blood levels usually do not exceed 1 to 2 μg./ml. Polymyxins are excreted into the urine (colistin more rapidly than polymyxin B), where concentrations of 25 to 300 μg./ml. may be reached. Excretion is impaired in renal insufficiency, so that accumulation to toxic levels can occur.

A. Indications, Dosages, and Routes of Administration: Polymyxins are indicated in serious infections due to Pseudomonas and other gram-negative bacteria which are resistant to other antimicrobial drugs.

1. I. M. - The injection of polymyxin B is painful. Therefore, colistimethate, which contains a local anesthetic and is more rapidly excreted in the urine, is given I. M., 2.5 mg./Kg./day, for urinary tract infection.

2. I. V. - In Pseudomonas sepsis, polymyxin B sulfate, 2.5 mg./Kg./day, is injected by continuous I. V. infusion.

3. Intrathecal - In Pseudomonas meningitis, give polymyxin B sulfate, 2 to 10 mg. once daily for two to three days and then every other day for two to three weeks. (Colistimethate must not be given intrathecally.)

4. Topical - Solutions of polymyxin B sulfate, 1 mg./ml., can be applied to infected surfaces, injected into joint spaces, intrapleurally or subconjunctivally, or inhaled as aerosols. Ointments containing 0.5 mg./Gm. of polymyxin B sulfate in a mixture with neomycin or bacitracin are often applied to infected skin lesions. Solutions containing polymyxin B, 20 mg./L., and neomycin, 40 mg./L., can be used for continuous irrigation of the bladder with an indwelling catheter and a closed drainage system.

B. Adverse Effects: The toxicities of polymyxin B and colistimethate are similar. With the usual blood levels, there are paresthesias, dizziness, flushing, and incoordination. These disappear when the drug has been excreted. With unusually high levels, respiratory arrest and paralysis can occur. Depending upon the dose, all polymyxins are nephrotoxic, producing tubular injury. Proteinuria, hematuria, and cylindruria tend to be reversible, but nitrogen retention may force reduction in dose or discontinuance of the drug. In individuals with preexisting renal insufficiency, kidney function must be monitored (preferably by creatinine clearance) and the dose reduced or the interval between injections increased.

Antituberculosis Drugs.

Singular problems exist in the treatment of tuberculosis and other mycobacterial infections. They tend to be exceedingly chronic but may give rise to hyperacute lethal complications. The organisms are frequently intracellular, have long periods of metabolic inactivity, and tend to develop resistance to any one drug. Combined drug therapy is often employed to delay the emergence of this resistance. "First line" drugs, often employed together in tuberculous meningitis, miliary dissemination, or severe pulmonary disease, are streptomycin, isoniazid, and aminosalicylic acid. A series of "second line" drugs will be mentioned only briefly.

1. Streptomycin.

The general pharmacologic features and toxicity of streptomycin are described above. Streptomycin, 1 to 10 μg./ml., is inhibitory and bactericidal for most tubercle bacilli, whereas most "atypical" mycobacteria are resistant. All large populations of tubercle bacilli contain some streptomycin-resistant mutants, which tend to emerge during prolonged treatment with streptomycin alone and result in "treatment resistance" within two to four months. Therefore, streptomycin is usually employed in combination with another antituberculosis drug. Streptomycin penetrates poorly into cells and exerts its action mainly on extracellular tubercle bacilli.

For combination therapy in tuberculous meningitis, miliary dissemination, and severe organ tuberculosis, streptomycin is given I. M., 1 Gm. daily (30 mg./Kg./day for children) for weeks or months. This is followed by streptomycin, 1 Gm. I. M. two to three times a week for months or years. In tuberculous meningitis, intrathecal injections (1 to 2 mg./Kg./day) are sometimes given in addition.

The vestibular dysfunction resulting from prolonged streptomycin treatment results in inability to maintain equilibrium. However, some compensation usually occurs so that patients can function fairly well.

2. Isoniazid (INH).

Isoniazid is the most active antituberculosis drug. It inhibits most tubercle bacilli in a concentration of 0.2 μg./ml. or less. However, most "atypical" mycobacteria are resistant. In susceptible large populations of Mycobacterium tuberculosis, isoniazid-resistant mutants occur. Their emergence is delayed in the presence of a second drug. There is no cross-resistance between isoniazid, streptomycin, aminosalicylic acid, or ethambutol.

Isoniazid is well absorbed from the gut and diffuses readily into all tissues, including the CNS, and into living cells. A dose of 8 mg./Kg./day results in blood levels of 2 μg./ml. or more. The inactivation of isoniazid - particularly its acetylation - is under genetic control. In "rapid inactivators," plasma levels are 0.2 μg./ml. or less six hours after ingestion of 4 mg./Kg. of isoniazid, whereas in "slow inactivators" plasma levels at that time are 0.8 μg./ml. or more. Isoniazid and its conjugates are excreted mainly in the urine.

Isoniazid is the most widely used drug in tuberculosis. In active, clinically manifest disease, it is given in conjunction with streptomycin and aminosalicylic acid or ethambutol. The initial dose is 8 to 10 mg./Kg./day orally (up to 20 mg./Kg./day in small children); later, the dosage is reduced to 5 to 7 mg./Kg./day.

Children (or young adults) converting from a tuberculin-negative to tuberculin-positive skin test may be given 10 mg./Kg./day (maximum: 300 mg./day) for one year as prophylaxis against the 5 to 15% risk of meningitis or miliary dissemination. For this "prophylaxis," isoniazid is given as the sole drug.

Toxic reactions to isoniazid include insomnia, restlessness, dysuria, hyperreflexia, and even convulsions and psychotic episodes. Many of these are attributable to a relative pyridoxine deficiency and peripheral neuritis and can be prevented by the administration of pyridoxine, 100 mg./day.

3. Aminosalicylic acid (PAS).

p-Aminosalicylic acid, closely related to p-aminobenzoic acid, inhibits most tubercle bacilli in concentrations of 1 to 5 μg./ml. but has no effect on other bacteria. Resistant Mycobacterium tuberculosis emerges rapidly unless another antituberculosis drug is present.

p-Aminosalicylic acid is readily absorbed from the gut. Doses of 8 to 12 Gm./day orally give blood levels of 10 μg./ml. The drug is widely distributed in tissues (except the CNS) and rapidly excreted into the urine. To avoid crystalluria, the urine should be kept alkaline.

Common side effects include anorexia, nausea, diarrhea, and epigastric pain. These may be diminished by taking p-aminosalicylic acid with meals and with antacids, but peptic ulceration may occur. Sodium p-aminosalicylic acid may be given parenterally. Hypersensitivity reactions include fever, skin rashes, granulocytopenia, lymphadenopathy, and arthralgias.

4. Alternative Drugs in Tuberculosis Treatment.

The drugs listed alphabetically below are usually considered only in cases of drug resistance (clinical or laboratory) to "first line" drugs and when expert guidance is available to deal with toxic side effects.

Capreomycin 0.5 to 1.5 Gm./day I.M., can perhaps substitute for streptomycin in combined therapy. It is not commercially available. It is nephrotoxic and ototoxic.

Cycloserine (Seromycin®), 0.5 to 1 Gm./day orally, has been used alone or with isoniazid. It can induce a variety of CNS dysfunctions and psychotic reactions. In smaller doses (15 to 20 mg./Kg./day) it has been used in urinary tract infections.

Ethambutol (Myambutol®) is sometimes considered a "first line" drug to substitute for p-aminosalicylic acid in combined therapy. It is effective in doses of 15 to 25 mg./Kg./ day orally. It is better tolerated than p-aminosalicylic acid. The most serious toxic effect is retrobulbar neuritis and partial loss of vision.

Ethionamide (Trecator®), 0.5-1 Gm./day orally, has been used in combination therapy but produces marked gastric irritation.

Pyrazinamide (PZA, Aldinamide®), 2 to 3 Gm./day orally, has been used in combination therapy but may produce serious liver damage.

Rifampin, 0.45 to 0.9 Gm./day orally, may be used in combination with ethambutol. It is also active against various bacteria and chlamydiae. Its toxic effects are not yet known.

Viomycin (Vinactane®, Viocin®), 2 Gm. I. M. every three days, can occasionally substitute for streptomycin in combination therapy. It is nephrotoxic and ototoxic.

SULFONAMIDES AND SULFONES

Sulfonamides.

More than 150 different sulfonamides have been used at some time, the modifications being designed principally to achieve greater antibacterial activity, a wider antibacterial spectrum, greater solubility, or more prolonged action. Because of their low cost and their relative efficacy in some common bacterial infections, sulfonamides are still used widely in many parts of the world. However, the increasing emergence of sulfonamide resistance (e. g., among streptococci, meningococci, and shigellae) and the higher efficacy of other antimicrobial drugs have drastically curtailed the number of specific indications for sulfonamides as drugs of choice. The present indications for the use of these drugs can be summarized as follows:

(1) First (previously untreated) infection of the urinary tract: Many coliform organisms, which are the most common causes of urinary infections, are still susceptible to sulfonamides.

(2) Chlamydial infections of the trachoma-inclusion conjunctivitis-LGV group: Sulfonamides are often as effective as tetracyclines in suppressing clinical activity, and they may be curative in acute infections. However, they often fail to eradicate chronic infection.

(3) Parasitic and fungal diseases: In combination with pyrimethamine, sulfonamides are used in toxoplasmosis. In combination with trimethoprim, sulfonamides are sometimes effective in falciparum malaria. Alone or in combination with cycloserine, sulfonamides may be active in nocardiosis.

(4) Bacterial infections: In underdeveloped parts of the world, sulfonamides, because of their availability and low cost, may still be useful for the treatment of pneumococcal or staphylococcal infections; bacterial sinusitis, bronchitis, or otitis media; bacillary (shigella) dysentery; and meningococcal infections. In most developed countries, however, sulfonamides are not the drugs of choice for any of these conditions, and sulfonamide resistance of the respective etiologic organisms is widespread.

(5) Leprosy: Certain sulfones are the drugs of choice in leprosy.

A. Antimicrobial Activity: The action of sulfonamides is bacteriostatic and is reversible upon removal of the drug or in the presence of an excess of p-aminobenzoic acid (PABA). Susceptible microorganisms require extracellular PABA in order to synthesize folic acid, an essential step in the formation of purines. Sulfonamides are structural analogues of PABA, can enter into the reaction in place of PABA competing for the enzyme involved, and can form nonfunctional analogues of folic acid. As a result, further growth of the microorganisms is inhibited. Animal cells and some sulfonamide-resistant microorganisms are unable to synthesize folic acid from PABA but depend on exogenous sources of preformed folic acid. Other microorganisms may be sulfonamide-resistant because they produce a large excess of PABA.

B. Pharmacologic Properties: The soluble sulfonamides are readily absorbed from the gut, distributed widely in tissues and body fluids, and excreted primarily by glomerular filtration into the urine. Enough active drug remains in the urine to permit effective treatment of urinary tract infections (usually 10 to 20 times the concentration present in the blood). In order to be therapeutically effective for systemic therapy, a sulfonamide must achieve a concentration of 8 to 12 mg./ml. of blood. This is accomplished by full systemic doses listed below.

"Long-acting" sulfonamides (e. g., sulfamethoxypyridazine, sulfadimethoxine, sulfameter) are readily absorbed after oral intake, but urinary excretion is very slow, resulting in prolonged blood levels. "Intermediate-acting" sulfonamides (e. g., sulfamethoxazole) are also excreted relatively slowly. All of these compounds may have a convenience factor but cause a higher incidence of severe toxic reactions.

"Insoluble" sulfonamides (e. g. , succinylsulfathiazole) are absorbed only slightly after oral administration and are largely excreted in the feces. Their action is mainly a temporary suppression of the intestinal flora.

For parenteral (usually intravenous) administration, sodium salts of sulfonamides are used because of their greater solubility. Their distribution and excretion are similar to those of the orally administered, absorbed sulfonamides.

C. Dosages and Routes of Administration:

1. Topical - The application of sulfonamides to skin, wounds, or mucous membranes is undesirable because of the high risk of allergic sensitization or reaction and the low antimicrobial activity. An exception is the use of sodium sulfacetamide solution (30%) or ointment (10%) to the conjunctivas.

2. Oral - For systemic disease, the soluble, rapidly excreted sulfonamides (e. g. , sulfadiazine, sulfisoxazole) are given in an initial dose of 2 to 4 Gm. (40 mg./Kg.) followed by a maintenance dose of 0.5 to 1 Gm. (20 mg./Kg.) every four to six hours. Trisulfapyrimidines USP may be given in the same total doses. Urine must be kept alkaline.

For urinary tract infections (first attack, not previously treated), trisulfapyrimidines, sulfisoxazole, or another sulfonamide with equally high solubility in urine are given in the same (or somewhat lower) doses as shown above. Following one course of sulfonamides, resistant organisms usually prevail.

For "intestinal surgery prophylaxis," insoluble sulfonamides (e. g. , succinylsulfathiazole, phthalylsulfathiazole), 8 to 15 Gm./day, are given for five to seven days before operations on the bowel. Salicylazosulfapyridine, 6 Gm./day, has been given in ulcerative colitis, but there is little evidence of its efficacy.

"Long-acting" and "intermediate-acting" sulfonamides (e. g. , sulfamethoxypyridazine, sulfadimethoxine, sulfamethoxazole) can be used in doses of 0.5 to 1 Gm./day (10 mg./Kg.) for prolonged maintenance therapy (e. g. , trachoma) or for the treatment of minor infections. These drugs have a significantly higher rate of toxic effects than the "short-acting" sulfonamides.

3. I. V. - Sodium sulfadiazine and other sodium salts can be injected I. V. in 0.5% concentration in 5% dextrose in water, physiologic salt solution, or other diluent in a total dose of 6 to 8 Gm./day (120 mg./Kg./day). This is reserved for comatose individuals or those unable to take oral medication.

D. Adverse Effects: Sulfonamides produce a wide variety of side effects - due partly to hypersensitivity, partly to

direct toxicity - which must be considered whenever unexplained symptoms or signs occur in a patient who may
have received these drugs. Except in the mildest reactions, fluids should be forced, and - if symptoms and
signs progressively increase - the drugs should be discontinued. Precautions to prevent complications (below) are
important.

1. Systemic side effects - Fever, skin rashes, urticaria;
   nausea, vomiting, or diarrhea; stomatitis, conjunctivitis, arthritis, exfoliative dermatitis; hematopoietic
   disturbances, including thrombocytopenia, hemolytic
   (in G6PD deficiency) or aplastic anemia, granulocytopenia, leukemoid reactions; hepatitis, polyarteritis
   nodosa, vasculitis, Stevens-Johnson syndrome; psychosis; and many others.

2. Urinary tract disturbances - Sulfonamides may precipitate in urine, especially at neutral or acid pH, producing hematuria, crystalluria, or even obstruction.
   They have also been implicated in various types of
   nephritis and nephrosis.

E. Precautions in the Use of Sulfonamides:

1. There is cross-allergenicity among all sulfonamides.
   Obtain a history of past administration or reaction.
   Observe for possible allergic responses.

2. Keep the urine volume above 1500 mg./day by forcing
   fluids. Check urine pH - it should be 7.5 or higher.
   Give alkali by mouth (sodium bicarbonate or equivalent,
   5 to 15 Gm./day). Examine fresh urine for crystals
   and red cells every two to four days.

3. Check hemoglobin, white blood cell count, and differential count every three to five days to detect possible
   disturbances early.

Sulfones Used in the Treatment of Leprosy.

Several drugs closely related to the sulfonamides have
been used effectively in the long-term treatment of leprosy.
The clinical manifestations of both lepromatous and tubercu-
loid leprosy can often be suppressed by treatment extending
over several years.

A. Absorption, Metabolism, and Excretion: All sulfones are
   well absorbed from the intestinal tract, are distributed
   widely in all tissues, and tend to be retained in skin, muscle, liver, and kidney. Skin involved by leprosy contains
   ten times more drug than normal skin. Sulfones are excreted into the bile and reabsorbed by the intestine. Consequently, blood levels are prolonged. Excretion into the
   urine is variable.

B. Adverse Effects: The sulfones may cause any of the side
   effects listed above for sulfonamides. Anorexia, nausea,
   and vomiting are common. Hemolysis or methemoglobinemia may occur.

C. Dosages and Routes of Administration:
   1. Diaminodiphenylsulfone (DDS, dapsone, Avlosulfon®)
      is the most widely used and least expensive drug. It
      is given orally, beginning with a dosage of 25 mg.
      twice weekly and gradually increasing to 100 mg. three
      to four times weekly and eventually to 300 mg. twice
      weekly.
   2. Sulfoxone sodium (Diasone®) is given orally in corre-
      sponding dosage.
   3. Solapsone (Sulphetrone®), a complex substituted deriva-
      tive of DDS, is given initially in a dosage of 0.5 Gm.
      three times daily orally. The dose is then gradually
      increased until a total daily dose of 6 to 10 Gm. is
      reached.
   4. Other classes of drugs are used uncommonly. An
      ethyl mercaptan (Ditophal®) may be applied to the skin.
      Thiosemicarbazones (e. g. , amithiozone, Tibione®)
      permit the rapid emergence of resistance if used alone.
      Therefore, if administered, they are given with a sul-
      fone.

SPECIALIZED DRUGS AGAINST
GRAM-POSITIVE BACTERIA

Bacitracin.

This polypeptide antibiotic is selectively active against
gram-positive bacteria, including penicillinase-producing
staphylococci, in concentrations of 0.1 to 20 units/ml. Bacitracin is very little absorbed from gut, skin, wounds, or mucous membranes. Topical application results in local effects
without significant toxicity. Bacitracin, 500 units/Gm. in
ointment base, is often combined with polymyxin or neomycin
for the suppression of mixed bacterial flora in surface lesions.
Systemic administration of bacitracin has been abandoned because of its severe nephrotoxicity.

Lincomycin (Lincocin®).

This drug resembles erythromycin and is active against
gram-positive organisms (except enterococci) in concentrations of 0.5 to 5 µg./ml. Lincomycin, 0.5 Gm. orally every
six hours (30 to 60 mg./Kg./day for children), yields serum
concentrations of 2 to 5 µg./ml. The drug is widely distributed in tissues, and it is claimed that it has a special affinity
for bones. Excretion is through bile and urine. Lincomycin,
0.6 Gm. , can also be injected I. M. or I. V. every eight to 12
hours. The drug appears to be an alternative to erythromycin
as a substitute for penicillin. Success in bone infections has
been reported.

Common side effects are diarrhea and nausea. Impaired liver function and neutropenia have been noted. If 3 to 4 Gm. are given rapidly I. V., cardiorespiratory arrest may occur.

Novobiocin.

Many gram-positive cocci are inhibited by novobiocin, 1 to 5 μg./ml., but resistant variants tend to emerge during treatment. Novobiocin, 0.5 Gm. orally every six hours, yields serum concentrations of 2 to 5 μg./ml. It is widely distributed in tissues and excreted in urine and feces. It can also be given I. M. or I. V. In the past, a possible indication for novobiocin was infection caused by penicillinase-producing staphylococci. However, many better drugs are now available, so that no clear indication for novobiocin exists.

Skin rashes, drug fever, and granulocytopenia are common side effects.

Ristocetin.

Ristocetin has been abandoned because of its toxicity and low efficacy.

Vancomycin (Vancocin®).

This drug is bactericidal for most gram-positive organisms, particularly staphylococci and enterococci, in concentrations of 0.5 to 5 μg./ml. Resistant mutants are rare, and there is no cross-resistance with other antimicrobial drugs. Vancomycin is not absorbed from the gut. It is given orally (3 to 4 Gm./day) only for the treatment of staphylococcal enterocolitis. For systemic effect the drug must be administered I. V. After I. V. injection of 0.5 Gm. over a period of 20 minutes, blood levels of 10 μg./ml. are maintained for one to two hours. Vancomycin is largely excreted into the urine. In the presence of renal insufficiency, marked accumulation may occur and have toxic consequences.

The only indications for vancomycin are serious staphylococcal infection or enterococcal endocarditis that cannot be managed with penicillins. Vancomycin, 0.5 Gm., is injected I. V. over a 20-minute period every six to eight hours (for children, 20 to 40 mg./Kg./day). It can also be given by continuous I. V. infusion.

Vancomycin is intensely irritating to tissues. I. M. injection or extravasation from I. V. injection sites is very painful. Chills, fever, and thrombophlebitis commonly follow I. V. injection. The drug is both nephrotoxic and ototoxic, and renal function must be monitored.

URINARY ANTISEPTICS

These drugs exert antimicrobial activity in the urine but have little or no systemic antibacterial effect. Their usefulness is limited to urinary tract infections.

Nitrofurantoin (Furadantin®).

Nitrofurantoin is bacteriostatic and bactericidal for both gram-positive and gram-negative bacteria in concentrations of 10 to 500 μg./ml. The activity of nitrofurantoin is greatly enhanced at pH 6.5 or lower.

Nitrofurantoin is rapidly absorbed from the gut. The drug is bound so completely to serum protein that no antibacterial effect occurs in the blood. Nitrofurantoin has no systemic antibacterial activity. In kidney tubules, the drug is separated from carrier protein and excreted in urine, where concentrations may be 200 to 400 μg./ml.

The average daily dose in urinary tract infections is 100 mg. orally four times daily (for children, 5 to 10 mg./Kg./day), taken with food. If oral medication is not feasible, nitrofurantoin can be given by continuous I. V. infusion, 180 to 360 mg./day.

Oral nitrofurantoin often causes nausea and vomiting. Hemolytic anemia occurs in G6PD deficiency. Hypersensitivity may produce skin rashes and pulmonary infiltration.

Nalidixic Acid (NegGram®).

This synthetic urinary antiseptic inhibits many gram-negative bacteria in concentrations of 1 to 50 μg./ml. but has no effect on Pseudomonas. In susceptible bacterial populations, resistant mutants emerge fairly rapidly.

Nalidixic acid is readily absorbed from the gut. In the blood, virtually all drug is firmly bound to protein. Thus there is no systemic antibacterial action. About 20% of the absorbed drug is excreted in the urine in active form to give urine levels of 10 to 150 μg./ml.

The dose in urinary tract infections is 1 Gm. orally four times daily (for children, 55 mg./Kg./day). Adverse reactions include nausea, vomiting, skin rashes, drowsiness, visual disturbances, and rarely, convulsions.

Methenamine Mandelate.

This is a salt of methenamine and mandelic acid. The action of the drug depends on the liberation of formaldehyde and of acid in the urine. The urinary pH must be below 5.5, and sulfonamides must not be given at the same time. The drug inhibits a variety of different microorganisms except those (e. g. , Proteus) which liberate ammonia from urea and produce strongly alkaline urine. The dosage is 3 to 6 Gm. orally daily.

Acidifying Agents.

Urine with a pH below 5.5 tends to be antibacterial. Many substances can acidify urine and thus produce antibacterial activity. Ammonium chloride, methionine, and mandelic acid are sometimes used. The dose has to be established for each patient by testing the urine for acid pH with test paper at frequent intervals.

SYSTEMICALLY ACTIVE DRUGS IN
URINARY TRACT INFECTIONS

Many antimicrobial drugs are excreted in the urine in very high concentration. For this reason, low and relatively nontoxic amounts of aminoglycosides, polymyxins, and cycloserine (see Antituberculosis Drugs) can produce effective urine levels. Many penicillins and cephalosporins can reach very high urine levels and can thus be effective in urinary tract infections.

ANTIFUNGAL DRUGS

Most antibacterial substances have no effect on pathogenic fungi. Only a few drugs are known to be therapeutically useful in mycotic infections. Penicillins and sulfonamides are used to treat actinomycosis; sulfonamides and cycloserine have been employed in nocardiosis.

Amphotericin B (Fungizone®).

Amphotericin B, 0.1 μg./ml., inhibits in vitro several organisms producing systemic mycotic disease in man, including Histoplasma, Cryptococcus, Coccidioides, Candida, Blastomyces, Sporotrichum, and others. Amphotericin B, 100 Gm. I. V., results in average blood and tissue levels of 1 to 2 μg./ml. and thus can be used for treatment of these systemic fungal infections. Intrathecal administration is necessary for the treatment of meningitis.

Amphotericin B solutions, 0.1 mg./ml. in 5% dextrose in water, are given I. V. by slow infusion. The initial dose is 1 to 5 mg./day, increasing daily by 5 mg. increments until a final dosage of 1 to 1.5 mg./Kg./day is reached. This is usually continued for many weeks. In fungal meningitis, amphotericin B, 0.5 mg., is injected intrathecally three times weekly; continuous treatment (many weeks) with an Ommaya reservoir is sometimes employed.

The I. V. administration of amphotericin B usually produces chills, fever, vomiting, and headache. Tolerance may be enhanced by temporary lowering of the dose or administration of corticosteroids. Therapeutically active amounts of

amphotericin B commonly impair kidney and liver function
and produce anemia. Electrolyte disturbances, shock, and a
variety of neurologic symptoms also occur.

Griseofulvin (Fulvicin®, Grifulvin®).

Griseofulvin is an antibiotic that can inhibit the growth of
some dermatophytes but has no effect on bacteria or on the
fungi that cause deep mycoses. Absorption of microsized
griseofulvin, 1 Gm./day, gives blood levels of 0.5 to 1.5 µg./
ml. The absorbed drug has an affinity for skin and is deposited there, bound to keratin. Thus, it makes keratin resistant
to fungal growth, and the new growth of hair or nails is first
freed of infection. As keratinized structures are shed, they
are replaced by uninfected ones. The bulk of ingested griseofulvin is excreted in the feces. Topical application of griseofulvin has little effect.

Oral doses of 0.5 to 1 Gm./day (for children, 15 mg./Kg./
day) must be given for six weeks if only the skin is involved
and for three to six months or longer if the hair and nails are
involved. Griseofulvin is most successful in severe dermato-
phytosis, particularly if caused by Trichophyton or Micro-
sporon.

Side effects include headache, nausea, diarrhea, photo-
sensitivity, fever, skin rashes, and disturbances of the nervous and hematopoietic systems.

Nystatin (Mycostatin®).

Nystatin inhibits Candida species upon direct contact.
The drug is not absorbed from mucous membranes or gut.
Nystatin in ointments, suspensions, etc. can be applied to
buccal or vaginal mucous membranes to suppress a local Candida infection. After oral intake of nystatin, Candida in the
gut is suppressed while the drug is excreted in feces. However, there is no good indication for the use of nystatin orally
because increase in gut Candida is rarely associated with disease.

ANTIVIRAL CHEMOTHERAPY

Several compounds are now available which can influence
viral replication and the development of viral disease.

Amantadine hydrochloride (Symmetrel®), 200 mg. orally
daily for two to three days before and six to seven days after
influenza A infection, reduces the incidence and severity of
symptoms. The most marked untoward effects are insomnia,
dizziness, and ataxia.

Idoxuridine (Herplex®, Stoxil®), 0.1% solution or 0.5%
ointment, can be applied topically every two hours to acute
dendritic herpetic keratitis to enhance healing. It is also

used, in conjunction with corticosteroids, for stromal disci-
form lesions of the cornea to reduce the chance of acute epithelial herpes. It may have some toxic effects on the cornea
and should probably not be used for more than two to three
weeks. I.V. injection of idoxuridine (40 to 80 mg./Kg./day)
has been proposed for herpetic encephalitis.

Methisazone (Marboran®) can inhibit the growth of smallpox virus in man if administered to exposed persons within
one to two days after exposure. Methisazone, 2 to 4 Gm.
daily orally (for children, 100 mg./Kg./day), gives striking
protection against the development of clinical smallpox and
permits an asymptomatic, immunizing infection. Methisazone
can also inhibit the growth of vaccinia virus and is used for
the treatment of complications of smallpox vaccination (e. g. ,
progressive vaccinia). The most pronounced toxic effect is
profuse vomiting.

VITAMINS

WATER-SOLUBLE VITAMINS

Vitamin C.
A. Prophylactic: Adult maintenance is 70 mg./day.
B. Therapeutic: Saturation of tissues requires 3 to 4 Gm.
   This may be given orally in doses of 0.3 to 1 Gm. daily
   for 4 to 10 days. (15 oz. of fresh orange juice repre-
   sents about 250 mg. of ascorbic acid.)

Vitamin B_1 (Thiamine).
A. Prophylactic: Adult maintenance is 0.8 to 1.2 mg./day.
B. Therapeutic: The severely ill patient or one with a gastrointestinal disorder which prevents absorption may require 30 to 60 mg. of thiamine hydrochloride I.V. or
   I.M. twice daily. Oral administration, where practical,
   should be substituted as soon as response to parenteral
   therapy has begun, the dosage tapering to 10 mg. daily
   by mouth.

Vitamin B_2 (Riboflavin).
A. Prophylactic: Daily portions of milk, lean meat, leafy
   green vegetables, and occasional servings of organ meats
   will maintain adequate tissue levels. Adult maintenance
   is 1.2 to 1.7 mg./day.
B. Therapeutic: Oral administration of 5 to 15 mg. of riboflavin daily will cause disappearance of symptoms within
   4 to 6 days.

Nicotinic Acid (PP Factor).
A. Prophylactic: A diet ample in protein will supply most of the required nicotinic acid (converted from tryptophan in the body). Adult maintenance is 13 to 19 mg./day.
B. Therapeutic: Nicotinamide, 50 to 300 mg. I.M., I.V., or by mouth, given daily with a high-calorie, high-protein diet and supplementary supplies of thiamine, riboflavin, and pyridoxine. Dried yeast, 30 Gm. two or three times daily, serves as maintenance therapy.

Vitamin B$_6$ (Pyridoxine).
A. Prophylactic: Estimated at 2 to 5 mg./day for adults; 10 mg./day for pregnant women; 0.26 mg./liter of formula for infants.
B. Therapeutic: 25 mg. orally or parenterally per day.

Folic Acid (Pteroylglutamic Acid).
A. 0.4 mg. of folic acid daily by mouth will not effect a response in vitamin B$_{12}$ deficiency and therefore will not obscure its presence. No more than this may be used "prophylactically."
B. Therapeutic: For macrocytic anemia of pregnancy, megaloblastic anemia of infancy, nutritional macrocytic anemia, and sprue, 5-15 mg. per day orally or I.M.

Vitamin B$_{12}$ (Cyanocobalamin).
A. Prophylactic: 0.6 to 2.8 μg. daily.
B. Therapeutic: Parenteral therapy is necessary. Fifteen to 30 μg. of vitamin B$_{12}$ I.M. daily for 5 to 7 days, then 30 to 50 μg. per month to maintain remission. Maintenance of remission requires at least 1 μg. per day.

FAT-SOLUBLE VITAMINS

Vitamin A.
A. Prophylactic: Adult maintenance is 5000 I.U./day.
B. Therapeutic: Give 5000 to 25,000 I.U. of vitamin A or an equivalent amount of carotene daily for six weeks or until skin lesions have cleared. If fat absorption is impaired, a water-dispersible preparation, additional bile salts, or an intramuscular preparation must be used.

Vitamin D$_2$ and Vitamin D$_3$.
A. Prophylactic: Maintenance dose in children is 400 I.U./day.
B. Therapeutic: In rickets, 4000 to 5000 I.U. of vitamin D orally per day plus adequate milk intake. Similar dosages are required for treatment of osteomalacia in adults.

Resistant rickets may require huge doses of vitamin D (150,000 to 1.5 million units daily for 1 or 2 months).

Vitamin K.
  A. Prophylactic: There is no generally accepted human requirement.
  B. Therapeutic: Use water-soluble vitamins (menadione sodium bisulfite). In the jaundiced patient one may give 50 mg. vitamin K_1 I.V. repeatedly on successive days. If hepatocellular damage is present, response may be poor.

  In hypoprothrombinemia caused by bishydroxycoumarin or salicylates, give phytonadione (vitamin K_1), 5 mg. orally. For major bleeding, give 10 to 15 mg. I.V. slowly at a rate not to exceed 10 mg. per minute. When reduced coagulability must be maintained, interval heparin may be used until subsequent doses of a coumarin or indandione again are effective.

HORMONES AND HORMONE-LIKE AGENTS

Hormones may be used therapeutically in two distinct ways:
  A. Specific Therapy:
    1. As a substitute for a hormone which is lacking in the patient's internal environment, e.g., the use of thyroid in hypothyroidism, posterior pituitary substance in diabetes insipidus, testosterone or estrogen in hypogonadism, adrenocortical preparations in Addison's disease, and insulin in diabetes mellitus.
    2. To suppress undesirable hormone production in the patient, e.g., the use of adrenocortical steroids to suppress ACTH secretion in adrenogenital syndrome; the use of thyroid to suppress TSH stimulation of certain forms of goiter.
  B. Nonspecific Therapy: For stimulation or suppression of certain reactions within the body, e.g., the use of testosterone in patients with inanition; the use of the sex steroids in patients with carcinoma of the breast and prostate; the use of corticotropin and corticosteroids in the arthritic, allergic, and collagen diseases.

Precautions in Use of Hormones.
  Hormones given to a normal individual suppress (at least temporarily) the activity of the gland producing that hormone (e.g., thyroid, adrenal cortex). Protein hormones may give

rise to allergic reactions and antihormone production when injected. Prolonged administration of excessive corticotropin (ACTH) and cortisone may cause all of the deleterious effects of Cushing's disease; estrogens in excess damage spermatogenesis in the male; continued complete thyroid replacement therapy may impair future thyroid function; and insulin in excess may result in irreversible changes in the brain. With the above exceptions, hormones may be given indefinitely as long as the need exists.

ANTERIOR PITUITARY

Chorionic Gonadotropin and PMS.
Preparations from urine of pregnant women or pregnant mares (chorionic gonadotropin) have a principal action similar to that of luteinizing hormone (e. g. , Antuitrin-S®, A. P. L.®, Pregnyl®); and preparations from serum of pregnant mares (PMS) and anterior pituitary glands of sheep and hogs have a principal action similar to that of follicle-stimulating hormone (e. g. , Gonadogen®).

A. Hypogonadotrophic Hypopituitarism: As a therapeutic test for diagnosis, give 5000 I.U. of chorionic gonadotropin three times per week, I. M. , for 4 to 6 weeks. Return of gonadal function confirms the diagnosis.

B. Cryptorchism: Test using chorionic gonadotropin to determine (usually at age eight) whether descent of testes will occur at puberty. Failure of either of the following schedules to cause descent of testicles implies mechanical obstruction.
1. Total dose 6000 I.U. ; give 100 I.U. twice weekly, increasing 100 units per week up to 500 I.U. twice weekly, I. M. , without rest periods until total is given.
2. 500 to 1000 I.U. three times a week, I. M. , for 6 weeks, with repetition if necessary after 6 weeks' rest.

C. Infertility Due to Anovulatory Cycles: As a rarely successful last resort, 500 I.U. daily of PMS or pregnant mare serum gonadotropin (e. g. , Gonadogen®) may be given I. M. from the fifth to 14th days of the cycle, followed by 500 I. U. of chorionic gonadotropin daily, I. M. , from the 15th to 24th days. Antihormones to pregnant mare serum form rapidly.

Human menopausal gonadotropin (HMG, Pergonal®) has become widely used in the treatment of anovulatory cycles. It is more effective than PMS but is not yet widely available.

Corticotropin (ACTH).
Available preparations include an aqueous form, a lyophilized powder, and longer-acting corticotropin-gel. A re-

cently synthesized 24-amino acid human ACTH (Synacthen®) has recently become commercially available.

A. Treatment: For miscellaneous collagen diseases, such as rheumatoid arthritis, rheumatic fever, and lupus erythematosus; in allergic states; in some disorders of skin, blood, and liver; and for overwhelming infections (with antibiotics) (see also Cortisone, p. 578) -

1. Repository corticotropin injection (corticotropin gel), 40 units I. M. once daily until therapeutic effect is achieved; maintain on 10 to 20 units once daily.

2. Corticotropin injection, 20 units in 5% dextrose in water by continuous I. V. drip over 8 hours.

B. As Test for Adrenal Insufficiency: See p. 243.

C. Hydrocortisone replacement therapy should be used for hypopituitary patients undergoing surgery. ACTH is not used.

Thyrotropic Hormone.
A. Carcinoma of the Thyroid: To increase therapeutic ^{131}I uptake, give 10 mg. Thytropar® in aqueous solution I. M. daily for 1 to 8 days.

B. Pituitary Myxedema (Diagnostic Test): See p. 230.

POSTERIOR PITUITARY

Posterior Pituitary Extracts and ADH (Vasopressin).
A. Diabetes Insipidus: (For diagnostic test, see p. 224.)

1. Posterior pituitary (powdered extract) may be used in doses of 15 to 40 mg., inhaled as snuff or sprayed into the nose as powder every 3 to 10 hours as necessary; may be irritating to the mucous membranes.

2. Vasopressin injection (20 units/ml.), 0.5 to 1 ml., I. M. or subcut., every 4 to 8 hours.

3. Vasopressin tannate (in oil, 5 units/ml.) - Initially, 0.3 to 1 ml. I. M., every 24 to 48 hours until polyuria and polydipsia are controlled; maintain on minimum dose. **Caution:** Warm and shake vial before injection.

B. Obstetric Use: To secure uterine contraction in induction of labor or in postpartum hemorrhage.

1. Posterior pituitary injection (obstetric strength), 0.5 to 1 ml. subcut. or I. M.

2. Oxytocin injection, 1 ml. diluted to 500 to 1000 ml. in slow intravenous infusion to induce labor or for treatment of uterine inertia during labor; 0.5 to 1 ml., I. M., to control postpartum bleeding. (The intramuscular administration of posterior pituitary extract in labor should be withheld until the cervix is fully dilated.)

C. Intestinal Action: In gassy intestinal distention, for control of abdominal distention, for dispelling gas shadows during x-ray procedures.

1. Posterior pituitary injection (surgical strength), 0.5 to
   1 ml. subcut. or I. M.
2. Vasopressin, 0.5 to 1 ml. subcut. or I. M.

THYROID

Thyroid Hormone.

The preparation most commonly used is thyroid (desiccated thyroid gland). Thyroxine, one of the purified thyroid
hormones, is about 600 to 1000 times more potent by weight
than desiccated thyroid. Sodium liothyronine (T_3, Cytomel®)
may be given orally or parenterally in a ratio of 0.025 mg.
T_3 to 60 mg. thyroid. The average maintenance dose is 0.05
to 0.1 mg. daily in divided doses. It is almost as active orally
as parenterally and may decrease protein-bound iodine level.
Sodium levothyroxine (T_4, Synthroid®) is given orally for thyroid replacement. Maintenance dose is 0.15 to 0.4 mg. daily.

A. Hypothyroidism, Myxedema, Juvenile Myxedema, Cretinism: In adults, treatment may begin with dose of 6 to
   15 mg. of thyroid per day (or equivalent dose of T_3 or
   T_4), increasing at weekly or biweekly intervals to a total
   of 120 to 180 mg. per day orally; very rarely is more required. In presence of cardiovascular disease, in panhypopituitarism, and in patients over 40 years old, increase dosage very slowly. Infants and children are
   treated with smaller doses, but only a dose close to the
   toxic level is effective in cretinism or juvenile myxedema.
   In myxedema coma, large doses of T_3 (100-200 μg.) given
   intravenously plus large doses of cortisol are required.
B. Hyperfunctioning Adenomas or Simple Goiters: To reduce
   size of goiter by suppression of TSH, increase thyroid
   dosage gradually to maintenance level of 180 to 360 mg. of
   thyroid per day orally over 3- to 6-month period.
C. Sterility, Habitual Abortion, Amenorrhea: As adjuvant
   therapy, give 120 to 180 mg. thyroid per day, orally, in
   addition to other therapy.
D. Hyperexophthalmic Graves' Disease: As treatment to
   prevent further exophthalmos, give 100 to 200 mg. thyroid orally daily, while hyperthyroidism is brought under
   control by gradual means.

Antithyroid Agents (Hyperthyroidism).

Iodine is now used principally in preparing a patient for
surgery. The thiourea derivatives offer the smallest incidence of cure and the longest treatment time but are available
and inexpensive, and are often used in preparing the patient
for radioiodine therapy or surgery, or by themselves in mild
disease. Radioiodine is the treatment of choice for most
moderately severe cases and in the elderly, those in poor

condition, and those who refuse surgery. Medical treatment causes fewer complications and disturbs the patient less than surgery, but thyroidectomy is quicker and removes the goiter and, with it, the potentialities of pressure and cancer. Commonly used antithyroid drugs are:

A. Saturated solution of potassium iodide or strong iodine solution (Lugol's solution), 5 to 10 drops three times a day in water.

B. Propylthiouracil: When used alone, treatment time is 6 months to 2 years. The gland becomes larger and more vascular. Leukopenia, drug rashes, and, very rarely, agranulocytosis may occur; the recurrence rate is 50%. In preparation of a patient for surgery, treat patient until euthyroid, adding iodine therapy for 10 to 14 days prior to operation. Oral dose is 200 to 300 mg. daily in evenly spaced doses every 4 to 8 hours.

C. Methimazole (Tapazole®): Oral dose is 5 to 15 mg. daily, slowly increased to 40 to 80 mg. daily.

D. Iothiouracil Sodium (Itrumil®): Oral dose is 50 to 100 mg. daily. Observe precautions as for propylthiouracil.

E. Sodium radioiodide (^{131}I), given in single or divided oral dose which is determined from the estimated weight of thyroid gland; initial dose for hyperplastic gland is usually 120 to 200 μc of radioiodine per gram of thyroid tissue; nodular glands require higher doses. May follow in 48 hours with antithyroid drugs. Patient may be retreated if necessary 3 to 6 months later. Maximum effect appears in 1 to 5 months. Relapse rate is 3 to 5%. Hypothyroidism is produced in 5 to 40% of cases. Other ill effects are not known, but therapeutic radioiodine is usually avoided in patients under 40 years of age, or in pregnancy.

PARATHYROID

Parathyroid Hormone.

Used only in acute states, as tolerance soon occurs (usually within a week). Parathyroid hormone is rarely used, if at all.

A. Acute Hypoparathyroidism: Parathyroid injection, 100 to 200 U.S.P. units I.V., in doses of 25 to 50 units every 6 to 12 hours during acute phase, with calcium and vitamin D.

B. Diagnostic Test of Reactivity to Parathyroid Hormone (Ellsworth-Howard Test): See p. 234.

Parathormone-like Agents.

A. Calcium:
   1. Hypoparathyroidism, acute (tetany) - 10 ml. of 10% solution of calcium gluconate or calcium chloride, or

500 ml. of a 0.2% solution of either given over a 1-hour
period gives an immediate but transient effect lasting
8 to 12 hours.

2. Hypoparathyroidism, chronic - Calcium chloride, 10
ml. of 30% solution well diluted, sometimes with lico-
rice syrup, orally thrice daily after meals. Calcium
gluconate, 15 Gm. daily, or calcium lactate, 8 Gm.
daily in divided doses with each meal, may also be
used. Vitamin D and aluminum hydroxide may be
given at the same time to increase the absorption of
calcium and reduce the absorption of phosphorus from
the intestine.

B. Vitamin D: In chronic hypoparathyroidism, vitamin D or
D_2 alone, in 50,000 unit capsules, one to three capsules
daily as need is determined by urinary Sulkowitch test
and blood calcium level, is usually effective. A low phosphate diet and aluminum hydroxide are useful adjuncts.
Because it is less expensive and causes fewer side reactions, vitamin D is preferred to dihydrotachysterol.

C. Dihydrotachysterol (Hytakerol®): For chronic hypoparathyroidism (chronic low-calcium tetany), potent dihydrotachysterol, 1 to 3 ml. of the oily solution (2 to 6 capsules), may be given three times daily by mouth until
normal serum calcium level is obtained; dosage is then
gradually reduced to 0.25 to 1 ml. daily as need is determined by urinary Sulkowitch test (see p. 118). This
preparation is moderately expensive.

PANCREAS

Insulin.

For diabetes mellitus, insulin is usually injected subcut.
or I. M. (or I. V. in emergency) in amounts sufficient to maintain the patient's blood sugar at desirable levels. The dose
may vary from three to 1000 units daily of the insulin form
having the desired duration of action. Thus quick-acting regular insulin is used in diabetic acidosis and during infections
or surgical stress, whereas the continued control of the patient usually requires a long-acting insulin given alone or in
combination with regular insulin to secure an intermediate
effect. (See table on p. 576.)

Oral Hypoglycemic Agents.

Oral hypoglycemic agents are not appropriate for the diabetic patient who can be controlled by diet alone, and should
not be used as the sole medication in juvenile-onset diabetes
or unstable adult-onset diabetes. Careful control of the patient and the diet are still essential. Sulfonylurea treatment
should usually be considered in maturity-onset diabetes, in

Types of Insulin

Insulin	Form	Action in Hours	
		Maximum	Duration
Regular	Amorphous or crystalline zinc	4	10
Protamine zinc	Turbid suspension with excess of protamine, which, in mixtures, converts added regular insulin to protamine-bound insulin and lengthens its action.	14	< 40
Isophane (NPH)	Neutral suspension of crystalline insulin with protamine; none of protamine is unbound so that added regular insulin acts unaltered.	12	30
Globin insulin	Insulin bound to globin.	10	24
Lente insulin	Zinc insulin crystals in acetate buffer, insoluble at body pH.	12	30
Ultra-lente	Crystals only.	16	40
Semi-lente	Ground-up crystals.	14	48

patients who have had no history of ketosis, and in those whose insulin requirement is less than 40 units.

Suitability for oral therapy may be determined by a response test (see below) or by a trial of therapy. The trial should be discontinued if ketonuria appears when insulin is discontinued.

The criteria of success should include a fasting blood sugar and a 3-hour postprandial blood sugar of less than 110 mg./100 ml. (Somogyi), and a urine loss of less than 2 Gm. of glucose per 24 hours.

A. Sulfonylureas: Tolbutamide (Orinase®), acetohexamide (Dymelor®), and chlorpropamide (Diabinese®) apparently increase production of insulin by the pancreas, which must be capable of producing insulin. They are **not insulin substitutes.** These agents may be used for older, obese patients with mild diabetes beginning late in life which cannot be controlled by diet alone. They are **not useful** in childhood diabetes, ketosis (past or present), for preoperative or postoperative management, or in emergency.
1. Half-life - Tolbutamide, 5 hours; acetohexamide, 24 hours; chlorpropamide, 35 hours.
2. Dosage - Tolbutamide, 1 to 2 Gm. daily in divided doses; acetohexamide, 0.5 to 1.5 Gm. daily; chlorpropamide, 200 to 500 mg. daily.

3. Toxicity -
    a. Tolbutamide - 1% of subjects develop rashes, bone marrow depression, and mild gastrointestinal symptoms. Cholangiolytic block with jaundice occasionally occurs but does not cause severe damage.
    b. Acetohexamide - Side effects similar to those of tolbutamide.
    c. Chlorpropamide - Allergic rashes and jaundice are slightly more frequent than with tolbutamide.
B. Biguanides: Phenformin hydrochloride (DBI®) is useful in all ages, but particularly in children and older unstable diabetics. The biguanides are best used in severe, brittle diabetes to lessen the need for large insulin doses.
    1. Dosage - 100 to 200 mg. daily in two to four doses.
    2. Toxicity - Early in treatment there may be intolerable anorexia, nausea, and vomiting if the daily dose exceeds 150 mg. After 1 to 4 months of therapy, treatment may have to be discontinued because of lethargy, weight loss, and fatigue. Lactic acidosis is a serious hazard in any diabetic, particularly in the presence of renal or hepatic disease (in which phenformin is contraindicated).

Response Tests for Sulfonylurea Effectiveness.

The patient takes no insulin for 2 days while continuing on his regular diet. Tolbutamide sensitivity is indicated by a blood sugar fall to 110 mg./100 ml. 4 hours after a 3 Gm. dose. Chlorpropamide sensitivity is indicated by a 3-hour postprandial blood sugar of 110 mg./100 ml. 7 hours after a dose of 1 Gm.

Glucagon.

Glucagon is a polypeptide extracted from the pancreas which in small doses produces prompt elevation of blood sugar by mobilizing hepatic glycogen (0.5 to 1 mg. subcut.). The action of glucagon is brief, and it should not be substituted for I.V. dextrose in emergency situations.

ADRENAL CORTEX

Warning: During treatment with corticosteroids, corticotropin, or desoxycorticosterone acetate, watch closely for acute symptoms of hypokalemia, hypernatremia, edema, and hypertension. All but desoxycorticosterone acetate may also be associated with manifest or insidious osteoporosis, gastroduodenal ulceration, and psychosis, and may mask infections, particularly latent tuberculosis. Careful selection of patients and administration of a high-protein, low-salt diet with additional potassium (usually KCl, 3 to 4 Gm./day orally), and antacids and anti-secretory drugs directed at the stomach, may minimize these recognized hazards in patients taking large doses of cortisol. Mineral metabolism is less affected by synthetic corticosteroids; if "large" doses are needed for prolonged periods, they should be used rather than cortisol. Unless the steroids are withdrawn gradually, withdrawal symptoms may appear during the subsequent temporary adrenal insufficiency.

Hydrocortisone and Cortisone.

A. Acute Adrenal Insufficiency (Primary or Secondary):
1. Hydrocortisone sodium succinate (Solu-Cortef®) (134 mg. = 100 mg. free hydrocortisone), 100 mg. in 2 to 10 ml. water or saline I. V. or I. M. over 2 minutes followed by 50 to 100 mg. in one liter of 5% glucose in saline every 6 hours.
2. Hydrocortisone phosphate, 100 mg. I. V. or I. M., and repeat 50 to 100 mg. every 6 hours.

B. Prevention of Adrenal Crisis Following Adrenalectomy or Hypophysectomy:
1. After the incision is made for adrenalectomy, give 100 mg. of hydrocortisone sodium succinate or phosphate I. M. followed by 50 mg. every 6 hours for three doses; then every 8 hours for six doses. Then give oral therapy.
2. Cortisone acetate, 50 mg. I. M. every 4 hours for 24 hours prior to and 75 to 100 mg. I. M. immediately before surgery.
    After bilateral adrenalectomy: 75 to 100 mg., I. M., every 4 to 6 hours with I. V. dextrose and saline for 48 hours; thereafter oral hydrocortisone. After hypophysectomy: 50 mg., I. M., every 6 to 8 hours with I. V. dextrose and saline for 48 hours; thereafter orally.

C. Chronic Adrenal Insufficiency: The amounts of cortisone and hydrocortisone required to ensure adequate metabolism of carbohydrate, protein, and fat are too small to assure normal electrolyte and water balance. For this reason, up to 15 Gm. of sodium chloride per day and fludrocortisone (9α-fluorohydrocortisone), 0.1 to 0.25 mg. every 1 or 2 days, may be required. The estimated daily secretion of the adrenal cortex is equivalent to 20 mg. of cortisol per day. This amount does not seem to cause the spread of coexistent active tuberculosis.
1. Hydrocortisone, 10 to 20 mg. orally daily in divided doses.
2. Cortisone acetate, 12.5 to 50 mg. orally per day, usually given in divided doses at 8:00 a. m. and 4:00 p. m.

D. Rheumatoid arthritis, rheumatic fever, lupus erythematosus disseminatus and other collagen diseases, gout, allergic states, overwhelming infections, inflammatory disease of eye and bowel, pulmonary fibrosis, sarcoidosis, edema of nephrotic syndrome, and some disorders of skin, blood, and liver. Give synthetic glucocorticoids in large doses initially and decrease to the lowest level capable of producing a therapeutic effect; divided doses are used with gradual reduction to avoid withdrawal symptoms or exacerbations of disease.

Fludrocortisone Acetate (9α-Fluorohydrocortisone).

Systemic use is limited by exceedingly powerful salt- and water-retaining and gluconeogenic effects (20-50 times those of hydrocortisone). Fludrocortisone is used in chronic adrenocortical insufficiency to supplement cortisone or hydrocortisone and in the treatment of the salt-losing adrenocortical syndrome. Fludrocortisone ointment is an effective agent in certain skin diseases. It is occasionally useful in autonomic insufficiency in controlling postural hypotension.

Other Corticosteroids.

These steroids are powerful glucocorticoids with virtually no sodium-retaining activity. Average daily dosages are given, with relative potency compared with hydrocortisone in parentheses.
  A. Dexamethasone (Decadron®, Deronil®): 1.5 to 3 mg. (25 ×).
  B. Methylprednisolone (Medrol®): 8 to 16 mg. (5 ×).
  C. Triamcinolone (Aristocort®, Kenacort®): 8 to 16 mg. (5 ×).
  D. Betamethasone (Celestone®): 1.2 to 2.4 mg. (25 ×).
  E. Paramethasone (Haldrone®): 4 to 8 mg. (10 ×).
  F. Fluprednisolone (Alphadrol®): 3 to 6 mg. (10 ×).
  G. Prednisone: 5 to 20 mg. (3.5 ×).
  H. Prednisolone: 5 to 15 mg. (4 ×).

ADRENOCORTICAL INHIBITORS

A number of compounds have been used experimentally as inhibitors for the purposes of testing and in the treatment of adrenocortical hyperplasia and cancer. Amphenone, a very toxic drug, inhibits all of the secretions of the adrenal cortex. Metyrapone (Metopirone®), derived from amphenone, is effective by mouth and is nontoxic in the dosages usually given; it selectively inhibits 11-beta-hydroxylation to form cortisol.

Aldosterone excess may be counteracted by adrenal suppression with metyrapone (Metopirone®), 500 mg. every 4 hours, combined with ACTH suppression by means of corticoids; or by blocking aldosterone effect upon the kidney with spironolactone (Aldactone®), 25 mg. four times daily orally.

ADRENAL MEDULLA

Epinephrine.
- A. Sympathomimetic Effect: In acute bronchial spasm, urticaria, angioneurotic edema, supraventricular tachycardia, or cardiac standstill, give epinephrine injection
(1:1000), subcut. or intracardially, 0.1 to 1 ml.
- B. Hemostatic, Vasoconstrictor Effect: For topical application to control hemorrhage or reduce the congestion of the
nasal mucosa, use epinephrine hydrochloride, 5 to 6 drops
of freshly-prepared solution (1:2000 to 1:50,000).

Levarterenol Bitartrate (ʟ-Norepinephrine).
In the correction of hypotension associated with shock
(e. g. , after myocardial infarction), 4 mg. may be added to
one liter of I. V. infusion fluid (up to 12 mg. may be added if
a rapid flow is needed). Give initially at a rate of 20 to 40
drops per minute and later as necessary to maintain blood
pressure at ideal level (85 mm. systolic). Frequent blood
pressure readings are mandatory. Average maintenance dose
ranges from 8 to 15 drops I. V. per minute. Adequate urine
volume must be constantly maintained. Premature withdrawal
of drug may result in rapid fall in blood pressure. Too much
drug may produce dangerously high blood pressure levels.
Perivenous infiltration will result in widespread sloughing,
which may be minimized by the prompt infiltration of the area
with 1 to 2 ml. of phentolamine methanesulfonate (Regitine®).
Whole blood or plasma, if indicated, should be administered
at another site.
After initial improvement, 0.5 to 1 mg. may be given
I. M. every 2 to 6 hours as indicated to maintain blood pressure.

OVARIES (FOLLICLE)

Estrogens.
- A. Hypogonadism (primary, surgical, or x-ray), menopause, atrophic vaginitis, panhypopituitarism, osteoporosis, Paget's disease, acromegaly, and gigantism (after
epiphyses are closed):
  1. Synthetics -
     a. Diethylstilbestrol, 0.5 to 2 mg./day, orally at bed-
time.
     b. Dienestrol, 0.5 to 1 mg./day, orally at bedtime.
     c. Hexestrol, 1 to 3 mg./day, orally at bedtime.
  2. Estradiol dipropionate (in oil), 1 ml. once or twice a
week I. M. An aqueous suspension of microcrystals
may be used in oil-sensitive allergic patients.
  3. Conjugated estrogenic substances (Premarin®), 0.625
to 5 mg./day orally.

    4. Ethinyl estradiol, 0.05 to 0.2 mg./day orally.

    5. Estradiol cyclopentylpropionate (Depo-Estradiol®), 1 to 3 ml. every 3 weeks I. M.

    6. Estradiol valerate (Delestrogen®), 1 to 3 ml. every 3 weeks I. M.

    7. Chlorotrianisene (Tace®), 24 mg./day for several days to saturate fat; weak estrogenic effect continues for 3 to 6 weeks thereafter.

B. Cancer of the Prostate: Diethylstilbestrol, 1 to 5 mg. (or even much larger amounts) orally daily.

C. Metastatic cancer of the breast (estrogen-dependent type), particularly in remaining breast tissue and soft tissues such as pleura and lung; especially when the patient is 5 years past the menopause.

    1. Diethylstilbestrol, 2 to 50 mg. orally daily in two or three doses. Comparable doses of other estrogens may also be given.

    2. Ethinyl estradiol, 2 to 3 mg. orally per day. (0.05 mg. of ethinyl estradiol corresponds roughly to 1 mg. of stilbestrol in action.)

D. Threatened Abortion: Diethylstilbestrol, 25 mg. orally every half hour until cramps stop or for a total of six doses; thereafter, 25 mg. three to four times daily.

E. Amenorrhea: Diethylstilbestrol or other estrogen in comparable dosage to provide cyclic, constant, or increasing stimulation of the uterine endometrium over 3 to 6 weeks. If bleeding develops, withdraw the drug for 1 week and then repeat.

F. Menorrhagia and Functional Uterine Bleeding: Diethylstilbestrol, 2 to 5 mg. daily orally, or other estrogens in comparable dosage.

G. Dysmenorrhea: Diethylstilbestrol, 1 to 5 mg. orally per day from first to twelfth days of cycle, to inhibit ovulation. Repeat with each cycle.

H. To Relieve Postpartum Breast Engorgement: Diethylstilbestrol, 5 mg. orally per day for 3 to 4 weeks; withdraw slowly.

I. Postmenopausal osteoporosis:

    1. Estrogens (in women) -

        a. Given for 40 days in continued cycles, interrupted by 10 days' rest. Diethylstilbestrol, 0.5 to 1 mg. daily.

        b. Ethinyl estradiol, 0.5 mg. daily.

        c. Conjugated estrogenic substances, 2.5 mg. orally daily.

    2. Androgens (in men) - Methyltestosterone, 10 to 40 mg. sublingually daily for 6 to 12 months.

J. To Limit Growth of Tall Girls (Before Menarche):

    1. Diethylstilbestrol, 5 mg. orally daily for 3 to 9 months during observation.

ORAL CONTRACEPTIVES AVAILABLE IN THE UNITED STATES

Combination Products

Trade Name	(mg.)	Estrogen	(mg.)	Progestogen
Enovid®	0.075	Mestranol	5	Norethynodrel
	0.1	Mestranol	2.5	Norethynodrel (Enovid-E®)
	0.15	Mestranol	9.85	Norethynodrel
Norinyl®	0.05	Mestranol	1	Norethindrone
	0.1	Mestranol	2	Norethindrone
Norlestrin®	0.05	Ethinyl estradiol	1	Norethindrone acetate
	0.05	Ethinyl estradiol	2.5	Norethindrone acetate
Ortho-Novum®	0.05	Mestranol	1	Norethindrone
	0.06	Mestranol	10	Norethindrone
	0.1	Mestranol	2	Norethindrone
Ovulen® and Ovulen-21®	0.1	Mestranol	1	Ethynodiol diacetate
Provest®	0.05	Ethinyl estradiol	10	Medroxyprogesterone acetate
Noriday®	0.05	Mestranol	1	Norethindrone

Sequential Products

Trade Name	(mg.)	Estrogen	(mg.)	Progestogen
C-Quens®	0.08	Mestranol	2	Chlormadinone acetate
Oracon®	0.1	Ethinyl estradiol	25	Dimethisterone
Ortho-Novum SQ®	0.08	Mestranol	2	Norethindrone
Norquen®	0.008	Mestranol	2	Norethindrone

2. Conjugated estrogenic substances, 2.5 to 10 mg. daily; start with lower dose and increase if menstrual bleeding occurs.

OVARIES (CORPUS LUTEUM)

Progesterone and Ethisterone.

A. Menorrhagia and Functional Uterine Bleeding:
   1. Progesterone (in oil), 10 mg. I. M. daily for 3 to 5 days; sometimes combined with testosterone.
   2. Hydroxyprogesterone caproate (Delalutin®), 250 to 350 mg., I. M., 125 mg./ml. in oil; effect lasts 7 days; bleeding follows injection by 14 to 19 days.

B. Contraception: Norethindrone (Norlutin®) and norethynodrel with mestranol (Enovid®) have similar actions. Five to 20 mg. per day orally of either preparation for 14 to 21 days initiates withdrawal bleeding in amenorrhea; 10 mg. daily for 7 days will control anovulatory uterine bleeding; and 5 to 10 mg. from the fifth to the 25th days of the menstrual cycle will prevent conception. Either compound given continuously may produce pseudomalignant endometriosis; and administration during pregnancy may masculinize the female fetus. (See also table, p. 582.)

   Norethindrone acetate (Norlutate®) is about twice as potent as Norlutin®.

   Norethindrone with mestranol (Ortho-Novum®) is another agent which has recently been introduced for this purpose. Give daily beginning on the fifth day after onset of menses and continue for 20 days; then resume on the fifth day of the cycle, etc. If break-through bleeding occurs, the dose may have to be increased to 10 mg. or more.

C. Premenstrual Tension: Ethisterone, 5 to 10 mg. orally daily for 12 days before next expected period.

D. Threatened Abortion: Medroxyprogesterone acetate (Provera®), 10 to 20 mg. per day, increased as necessary to control bleeding and then reduced to maintenance dose during first trimester; or norethindrone or Enovid®, 20 to 60 mg. per day orally in divided doses until bleeding is controlled. Hydroxyprogesterone caproate (Delalutin®), 125 to 150 mg. I. M. every 2 weeks, may also be used.

E. Therapeutic test to determine presence of endogenous estrogen production: See p. 252.

TESTIS

Testosterone and Methyltestosterone.

Testosterone is ineffective when swallowed and increases 17-ketosteroid excretion. Methyltestosterone is effective orally, causes an increase in creatinuria, and depresses 17-ketosteroid output; it is much more active sublingually or buccally (avoiding inactivation of steroids by the liver) and has caused jaundice. Virilization may occur in women receiving more than 300 mg. of testosterone per month. Testosterone accelerates the growth of cancer of the prostate.

A. Male hypogonadism, either primary or secondary to panhypopituitarism; male climacteric; hypogonadal dwarfism; delayed puberal growth and development; Addison's disease; senile osteoporosis:
   1. Methyltestosterone orally (or methyltestosterone buccal tablets), 10 mg. daily.
   2. Testosterone propionate injection (in oil), 25 mg. I. M. three times weekly.
   3. Testosterone pellets, 75 to 300 mg. implanted under skin every 4 to 6 months.
   4. Testosterone cyclopentylpropionate (Depo-Testosterone®) (in oil), 100 to 300 mg. I. M. every 10 to 30 days.
   5. Testosterone enanthate (Delatestryl®), 100 to 300 mg. I. M. every 10 to 30 days.
   6. Fluoxymesterone (Halotestin®, Ora-Testryl®, Ultandren®), a fluoro derivative of methyltestosterone and five times as potent. The dosage is 2 to 10 mg. daily by mouth. This may be the best androgen to promote growth. Masculinization is minimal.

B. Menorrhagia: Testosterone propionate injection (in oil), 100 to 300 mg. I. M., for 1 to 5 days.

C. Endometriosis:
   1. Testosterone propionate injection (in oil), 50 to 500 mg. I. M. daily.
   2. 19-Nor-steroids - Norlutin®, Norlutate®, or Enovid® (see p. 583), 5 to 20 mg. orally per day, increasing to 10 to 40 mg. per day.

D. Menopause, Premenstrual Tension, Mastodynia: Methyltestosterone, 10 mg. buccally daily for 12 days before expected menstrual period.

E. Oligospermia and Infertility: Testosterone therapy in substitution dosage (as above for hypogonadism) occasionally causes atrophy of testicular elements within 1 to 3 months followed by return to normal testicular structure and increased sperm production 1 to 6 months after treatment is discontinued.

F. Metastatic carcinoma of the breast, especially during menstrual life, or with bony metastases (may develop fluid retention, masculinization, and marked hypercalcemia, which may be followed by Sulkowitch tests on the urine; see p. 118):

1. Testosterone propionate injection (in oil), 50 mg. I. M. three times weekly. Doses of 50 to 500 mg. have been given I. M. daily.
2. Testosterone cyclopentylpropionate (Depo-Testoster-one®) (in oil), 300 mg. I. M. every 3 weeks.
3. Methyltestosterone, 40 mg. daily, sublingually or buccally.
4. Fluoxymesterone (Halotestin®, Ultandren®), 10 to 40 mg. daily by mouth.

Anabolic Hormones.

The following relatively new drugs are claimed to have greater anabolic effects than the testosterone preparations listed above. These claims have yet to be fully evaluated. Most of these drugs appear to induce BSP retention, and they may have other as yet unrecognized side effects.

A. Norethandrolone (Nilevar®): 30 to 50 mg. daily orally.
B. Stanolone (Neodrol®): 50 to 150 mg. I. M. once or twice a week.
C. Methandrostenolone (Dianabol®): 5 mg. per day orally.
D. Nandrolone phenylpropionate (Durabolin®): 25 mg. per week or 50 to 100 mg. I. M. or subcut. every 2 weeks.
E. Oxymetholone (Anadrol®, Androyd®): 2.5 mg. orally three times daily.
F. Stanozolol (Winstrol®): 1 to 2 mg. three times daily orally.

32...

Medical Genetics

Genetic factors have been revealed to play central roles in morphologic and physiologic abnormalities which characterize disease entities. New technics of chromosomal analysis and nuclear sex determination have revealed correlations with abnormal sex differentiation, mongolism, mental retardation, somatic defects, infertility, and metabolic disorders. Recent biochemical studies have demonstrated specific enzyme deficiencies and protein alterations in a wide variety of hereditary disorders, providing tests not only for diagnosis but for identification of inapparent defects in relatives of the propositus. The recognition of latent heterozygote carriers of genetic abnormalities may be of great value in directing prophylactic measures (special dietary controls, use of appropriate medication, avoidance of aggravating drugs and environmental factors) and in marriage counselling. It is now possible to estimate the possibility of occurrence of many hereditary diseases; unfortunately, however, most diseases known or likely to be genetically determined cannot be accurately predicted at present.

BASIC CONCEPTS OF MEDICAL GENETICS

The nucleus of the normal human cell contains 46 chromosomes. Two of these are sex chromosomes. The remainder can be classified on the basis of physical appearance and segregated into 22 pairs. With modern technics it is possible to discern alterations of form and number of chromosomes in cells obtained from blood, bone marrow, skin, mucosa, and other tissues of specific interest.

The sperm and the ovum normally each contain one of each of the pairs of autosomal chromosomes and one sex chromosome, i.e., 23 unpaired (haploid) chromosomes. Upon fertilization, the full number of 46 diploid chromosomes is reconstituted. In the normal state the chromosomal pattern (karyotype) of all somatic cells is identical. Abnormal numbers of chromosomes (aneuploidy) may result from either addition or loss of chromosomes.

Each chromosome is composed of thousands of units (genes) arranged in regular order. The corresponding genes (alleles) on a chromosome may carry identical gene instruc-

586

tions (homozygous) or dissimilar instructions (heterozygous). If heterozygous, one gene may be expressed as a bodily characteristic (dominant) while the other is overtly unexpressed (recessive). At fertilization, the reassortment of chromosomes is purely by chance, so that either of the pairs of chromosomes from one parent has an equal chance of combining with either of the corresponding pairs from the other parent. Normal as well as abnormal characteristics are inherited in the same way, either as autosomal dominant or autosomal recessive or sex-linked. The term **genotype** refers to the hereditary constitution or combination of genes which characterizes a given individual or group of genetically identical organisms. The genotype may not always be manifest. The term **phenotype** refers to the recognizable morphologic or functional characteristics expressed by a genetic trait.

Genes may undergo transformations (mutation) which may produce new characteristics somatic or functional in nature. Such mutations may be inapparent, but in many circumstances can be correlated with the sudden appearance of heritable disease. Another type of mutation consists of rearrangement, breakage, and junction of chromosome.

GENETIC ABNORMALITIES

Classification of Genetic Disorders.
  A. Chromosomal (Cytogenetic) Abnormalities: Abnormal chromosome numbers.
    1. Sex chromosome abnormalities (e.g., Turner's syndrome, Klinefelter's syndrome).
    2. Autosomal trisomy syndromes (e.g., 21-trisomy or Down's syndrome; "13-15" or "16-18" trisomy syndromes).
  B. Autosomal dominant hereditary disorders (e.g., osteogenesis imperfecta, retinoblastoma).
  C. Autosomal recessive hereditary disorders (e.g., phenylketonuria, galactosemia).
  D. Sex-linked (X-linked) hereditary disorders (e.g., hemophilia, color blindness).
  E. Incompletely understood disorders with a possible genetic basis (e.g., hypertension, atherosclerosis, neoplastic diseases).

Diagnosis.
    The recognition of genetic disease is above all dependent upon an awareness of the possibility. Clinical manifestations which should suggest the possibility of genetic disorders include sterility, menstrual irregularities, abnormal body size and configuration, abnormal development of the sexual organs, absence of normal secondary sex characteristics, mental re-

KARYOTYPES

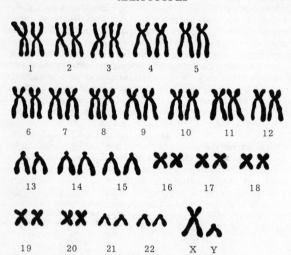

Normal Male

Down's Syndrome, Showing Trisomy for Chromosome Number 21

tardation, multiple congenital anomalies, glycosuria, anemia, and significant metabolic disturbances. In addition to a careful clinical evaluation, biochemical or chromosomal studies - often of an elaborate nature - may be required to establish the existence of a genetic effect. All possible measures should be taken to distinguish between acquired congenital defects (e.g., infection or drug toxicity during pregnancy) and hereditary disorders. The physician must obtain as complete a family pedigree as possible. Information regarding the incidence of family defects and consanguinity is often difficult to obtain, either because of ignorance, misunderstanding, or feelings of shame on the part of the patient or his family. It may be necessary to evaluate the genetic makeup of other family members, to determine whether they are similarly affected, normal, or carriers. The carrier can only be recognized by laboratory procedures.

SEX CHROMOSOME ABNORMALITIES

Number of Nuclear Chromatin Bodies	Number of Chromosomes	Sex Chromosomes (Karyotype)	Physical Appearance (Phenotype)	Diagnosis
None	45	XO (or X)	Female. No significant secondary sex characteristics.	Turner's syndrome
	46	XY	Female. Secondary female characteristics. Normal external female genitalia.	Testicular feminization. Gonads are testes. Sterile. Amenorrhea.
	46	XY	Male	Normal male
	47	XYY	Male	"Normal" male with potentially mentally defective offspring
One	46	XX	Female	Normal female
	47	XXY	Male	Klinefelter's syndrome
Two*	47	XXX	Female	Often normal. May have mental retardation, sterility, abnormal menses.
	48	XXYY	Male	Klinefelter's syndrome with severe mental retardation
	48	XXXY	Male	
	49	XXXYY	Male	
Three	49	XXXXY	Male	

*The XXYY male usually has a single chromatin body.

GLOSSARY OF GENETIC TERMS

Abiotrophic disease: Genetically determined disease which is not evident at birth but which becomes manifest later in life.

Acquired: Not hereditary; contracted after birth or in utero (cp. Hereditary).

Alleles: See Allelic genes.

Allelic genes: Paired genes or partner genes; genes occupying the same locus on homologous (paired) chromosomes and which, therefore, normally segregate from each other during the reduction-division of mitosis.

Allelomorphic genes: See Allelic genes.

Analogous: Similar in structure but not of the same origin.

Aneuploidy: An irregular number of chromosomes, as is found in various abnormal states.

Autosomes: The chromosomes (22 pairs of autosomes in man) other than the sex chromosomes (cp. Sex chromosome).

Barr body: See Chromatin body. A sex chromatin mass occurring in cells from females, considered to be X chromosome chromatin.

Chimera: An individual demonstrating mosaicism (q. v.).

Chromatin body: A special stainable body in the nucleus of body cells, apparently related to the staining characteristics of the X chromosome.

Chromosome: A small thread-like or rod-like structure into which the nuclear chromatin divides during mitosis. The number of chromosomes is constant for any given species (23 pairs in man: 22 pairs of autosomes and one pair of sex chromosomes). Each chromosome is composed of a linear arrangement of small bodies called genes, each of which occupies a specific locus on its chromosome.

Cistron: A gene specified as a hereditary unit of function.

Congenital: Existing at or before birth; not necessarily hereditary (cp. Familial).

Crossover: An exchange of homologous segments of paired chromosomes. Genes linked in a single chromosome may interchange with their alleles in homologous partner chromosomes.

Deletion: Loss of a small segment of a chromosome.

Diploid: Having 2 sets of chromosomes, as normally occurs in the somatic cell; having 2 full sets of homologous chromosomes.

Dominant: Designating a gene whose phenotypic effect largely or entirely obscures that of its allele (cp. Recessive).

Drumstick: A variant of sex chromatin. An accessory lobe on the nucleus of neutrophilic polymorphonuclear leukocytes of females. Absent in cells from the male. It consists of a fine stainable thread and a round stainable head which occur in a small percentage of neutrophils from females.

Duplication: Repetition of a small segment of a chromosome.

Eugenics: The science dealing with factors which improve the hereditary qualities of future generations, especially the human race.

Familial: Pertaining to traits, either hereditary or acquired, which tend to occur in families.

Gamete (germ cell): A cell which is capable of uniting with another cell in sexual reproduction (i.e., the ovum and spermatozoon).

Gene: A unit of heredity which occupies a specific locus in the chromosome which, either alone or in combination, produces a single characteristic. It is usually a single molecule which is capable of self-duplication or mutation.

Genetic carrier state: A condition wherein a given hereditary characteristic is not manifest in one individual but may be genetically transmitted to the offspring of that individual.

Genetics: The science concerned with the phenomena of inheritance and biologic variation.

Genome: The complete set of hereditary factors as contained in the haploid assortment of chromosomes (i.e., in a gamete).

Genotype: The hereditary constitution, or combination of genes, which characterizes a given individual or a group of genetically identical organisms (cp. Phenotype).

Germ cells (gametes): Cells capable of uniting with other cells sexually in reproducing the organism, spermatozoa in the male and ova in the female (cp. Somatic cells).

Haploid: Having a single set of chromosomes, as normally carried by a gamete.

Hereditary: Transmitted from ancestor to offspring through the germ plasm (cp. Acquired).

Heterozygotic (Dizygotic or Fraternal) Twins: Twins derived from 2 distinct fertilized ova (cp. Homozygotic Twins).

Heterozygous: Having 2 members of a given hereditary factor pair which are dissimilar, i.e., the 2 genes of an allelic pair are not the same (cp. Homozygous).

Homologous chromosomes: Paired or sister chromosomes resulting from normal miosis.

Homozygotic (Monozygotic or Identical) Twins: Twins derived by division of one fertilized ovum into 2 at an early stage of development (cp. Heterozygotic Twins).

Homozygous: Having 2 members of a given hereditary factor pair which are similar, i.e., the 2 genes of an allelic pair are identical.

Idiogram: A diagrammatic representation of a chromosome complement based on measurement of the chromosomes of a number of cells.

Index case: See Proband.

Karyotype: The chromosomal constitution of a cell, individual or species.

Locus: The specific site of a gene in a chromosome.

Meiosis: A special type of cell division occurring during the maturation of sex cells, by which the normal diploid set of chromosomes is reduced to a single (haploid) set, 2 successive nuclear divisions occurring, while the chromosomes divide only once.

Mosaic, Mosaicism: A different constitution in adjacent tissues of an animal resulting from a mutation or from embryonic incorporation of tissue from a nonidentical (genotypically different) twin. No intolerance for such tissue is evident. Human blood type and sex mosaics have been identified.

Mutation: A transformation of a gene, often sudden and dramatic, with or without known cause, into a different gene occupying the same locus as the original gene on a particular chromosome; the new gene is allelic to the normal gene from which it has arisen.

Nondisjunction: Failure of a sister pair of chromosomes to separate properly at cell division.

Pedigree: A table or diagram illustrating ancestral lineage; a genealogy.

Penetrance: The likelihood or probability that a gene will become morphologically (phenotypically) expressed. The degree of penetrance may depend upon acquired as well as genetic factors.

Phenotype: The visible characteristics of an individual or those which are common to a group of apparently identical individuals (cp. Genotype).

Polyploid: Having more than 2 full sets of homologous chromosomes (cp. Diploid).

Proband: An individual demonstrating a given hereditary trait or characteristic who is detected independently of the other members of the family. The first proband detected is referred to as the "index case" or "propositus."

Propositus: See Proband.

Recessive: Designating a gene whose phenotypic effect is largely or entirely obscured by the effect of its allele (cp. Dominant).

Reduction-division: A division involving the separation of members of a homologous pair of chromosomes; a reduction to the haploid state.

Segregation: The separation of 2 genes of a pair in the process of maturation so that only one goes to each germ cell.

Sex chromatin: See Chromatin body.

Sex chromosome: The chromosome or pair of chromosomes which determines the sex of the individual (cp. Autosomes). (In the human female, the sex chromosome pair is homologous, XX; in the male, nonhomologous, XY. Unusual combinations of sex chromosomes that have been found are as follows: XO, XXX, XXY, XXXY, XXXX, and XXXXY. These variations result in alterations of normal sex characteristics, physical abnormalities, and mental retardation.)

Sex linkage: The influence of sex on transmission of hereditary traits. There are 2 main types of sex-linked inheritance depending upon whether the sex-linked genes are located in the X or the Y chromosome. Sex linkage may be absolute or incomplete.

Sibship: Children of the same parents. (Also sometimes used to signify all blood relations.)

Somatic cells: Cells incapable of reproducing the organism (cp. Germ cells).

Translocation: The attachment of extra chromosomal material to another chromosome, probably resulting from an unequal exchange of chromosomal substance between 2 different chromosomes during cell division.

Trisomy: The existence of 3 chromosomes of one variety, rather than the normal pair of chromosomes.

Zygote: The cell formed by the union of 2 gametes in sexual reproduction.

33...

Selected Diagnostic and Therapeutic Procedures

This chapter consists of selected diagnostic and therapeutic procedures which are frequently employed or are of current general interest. Other clinical and laboratory procedures are included elsewhere in this Handbook.

The importance of adequate training and experience by the physician before the performance of any of these procedures must be emphasized. An emergency tray should be readily available in case untoward reactions or complications occur. In appropriate circumstances the patient or his legal guardian should be requested to sign a release form just as for a surgical procedure.

INTRAMUSCULAR INJECTIONS

Indications.

For the parenteral administration of certain drugs which are specifically adapted to intramuscular use, either because the drugs are ineffective, poorly tolerated, or unsafe when administered by other routes.

Precautions.

The drug manufacturer's recommendations must be followed carefully. Large volumes of drugs or the more irritating drugs should be injected into the larger muscles with needles long enough to deposit the medication well within the muscle. If soreness of the injected muscle is anticipated, try to avoid using muscle areas which may significantly interfere with the patient's work or other activities. Avoid even slight depression of the plunger of the syringe during needle insertion. The plunger should be retracted slightly when the needle is in the desired portion of the muscle to make certain that it is not in a blood vessel. Injections should not be given through contaminated or infected skin.

Method. (See p. 595.)
A. Gluteal Area: The upper outer quadrant of the gluteal area - not to be confused with the buttock, i.e., the fleshy lower ("cheek") portion of the gluteal area - is commonly employed since it is farthest from vulnerable

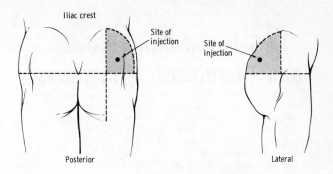

Sites of Gluteal Muscle Injection

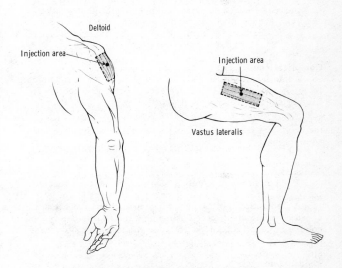

**Sites of Deltoid and Vastus Lateralis
Muscle Injection**

nerves and blood vessels. The prone position with the
toes turned in is preferable. The skin should be cleansed
thoroughly with an appropriate antiseptic solution. The
sterile needle is introduced quickly into the muscle at a
90° angle to the surface of the skin. Avoid even the
slightest depression of the plunger of the syringe during
needle insertion. The plunger should be retracted when
the needle is in the desired portion of the muscle to make
certain that the needle is not in a blood vessel. The drug
should then be injected and the needle rapidly withdrawn.
Massaging the site of injection may help to speed absorption of the medication and reduce soreness.

B. Lateral Aspect of Thigh (Vastus Lateralis): This area is
preferred by some because of the alleged lower incidence
of neurovascular complications.

C. Deltoid Area: This area has the advantage of convenience
because it is readily accessible without undressing, but
the muscle area is small and only small quantities of
fluid can be injected. Avoid injection into the middle and
lower thirds of the arm. If the patient is right-handed,
use the left arm for the injection.

Complications.
    Aside from local soreness, complications are uncommon.
Infection, hematoma, "cold abscess," arterial embolism,
inadvertent intravenous administration of drugs unsuited for
I. V. use, and nerve injury may occur.

VENIPUNCTURE AND INTRAVENOUS THERAPY

Indications.
    For collection of samples of venous blood for diagnostic
purposes or for the certain or rapid administration of systemic medication. Intravenous therapy may be indicated when
speed of administration is required, when expansion of blood
volume is required, and when other routes of drug administration are ineffective, impossible, or hazardous.

Precautions.
    Take time to find a suitable vein. Avoid using veins which
are immediately adjacent to vulnerable nerves and arteries.
Employ the smallest needle consistent with the intended purpose. Use only drugs which are specifically adapted to intravenous use, and follow the manufacturer's recommendations
carefully - especially in such matters as proper dilution of
the drug and rate of administration. If there is any evidence
that a needle or catheter is no longer within the lumen of the
vein (local pain, swelling, or extravasation of blood), withdraw the needle immediately and select another vein. Take

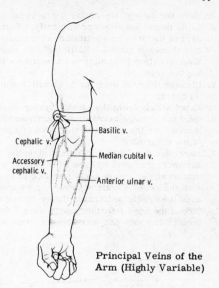

Cephalic v.

Accessory
cephalic v.

- Basilic v.

- Median cubital v.

- Anterior ulnar v.

**Principal Veins of the
Arm (Highly Variable)**

extreme care to avoid accidental intra-arterial injection.
Always question the patient beforehand regarding drug sensitivity.

Method.

Superficial veins are available in many parts of the extremities. Although there is considerable individual variation
in the anatomy of the veins, there is generally little difficulty
in selecting a suitable vein either for blood withdrawal or drug
injection. The veins in the antecubital space and forearm are
most frequently employed for routine intravenous procedures
(see above).

A. Venipuncture:

1. Select a superficial large vein which is not only easy
to see and feel but which has adequate supporting connective tissue so that the needle can be inserted easily
and left in place if necessary. If repeated venipunc-
tures are contemplated, begin distally in the forearm
veins and move up to more proximal veins with subsequent injections.

2. Apply a tourniquet snugly above the injection site, sufficiently tight to obstruct venous return but not so
tight that arterial flow is obstructed.

3. Have the patient clench his fist several times if the veins do not stand out prominently. Patting of the skin of the area or application of hot compresses is sometimes required. "Milking" the vein in the cephalad direction is sometimes useful as a means of filling the vein.

4. Cleanse the skin over the area with a suitable antiseptic agent.

5. Expel all air from the sterile syringe and needle.

6. Hold the syringe between the thumb and fingers and immobilize the vein with the index and middle fingers of the other hand.

7. Force the needle in a proximal direction through the skin with the bevel up (see illustration) with a firm motion at the lowest angle possible (almost parallel) with the vein. Continue to exert forward pressure until the needle penetrates the vein, and then gently thread the needle farther up the vein. Avoid passing through the vein and piercing the other side.

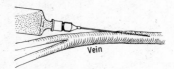

Vein

Needle Placement in Vein

B. Withdrawal of Blood: Pull back gently on the plunger of the syringe until the desired quantity of blood is obtained. Remove the tourniquet and withdraw the needle with a rapid, smooth motion while exerting pressure over the wound with a gauze pad or cotton pledget soaked in antiseptic solution. Discharge the sample promptly but gently into an appropriate container.

C. Intravenous Therapy:

1. Single injections of drugs - When it is certain that the needle is well within the vein, remove the tourniquet and draw back the plunger slightly; if blood freely enters the syringe, administer the drug at the recommended rate. Withdraw the needle and compress the puncture site.

2. Intravenous infusion - When prolonged intravenous infusion is necessary, an indwelling needle or catheter is employed. Large veins away from joints are most satisfactory for this purpose. If large veins cannot be found (e.g., obese patients or those in shock), it may

be necessary to perform a venous cutdown. Venous catheterization has been greatly simplified by the use of sterile, packaged complete venous catheterization sets (e.g., Intracath®, Jelco® [modified Rochester®], Medicut®) which have disposable needles and silicone-treated catheters. When the venous catheterization set is employed, venipuncture is made in the usual manner and the relatively comfortable and soft in-dwelling catheter can be used for prolonged infusions without arm restraints. Thrombophlebitis may occur after 10-12 hours depending upon the size of the vein, the nature of the administered solution, and variable individual factors. Catheter breakage and embolism to the heart may occur.

Complications.

Hematoma, local tissue sloughing, untoward drug reactions (including anaphylaxis), thrombophlebitis, and local or systemic infection (including viral hepatitis) may occur.

URINARY BLADDER CATHETERIZATION

Indications.

Urinary catheters are used for diagnostic purposes to explore the urethra for evidence of obstruction; to obtain "sterile" urine specimens from patients who are unable to void; to recover residual urine in the bladder after voiding; and to introduce contrast media into the bladder (for x-ray diagnosis). They are used therapeutically to relieve urinary retention.

Precautions.

Catheterization should not be performed by inexperienced personnel. Aseptic technic should be observed throughout the procedure. Because of the presence of bacteria in the urethra, it is impossible to pass a catheter in a completely sterile manner; secondary cystitis rarely occurs, however, unless there is residual urine in the bladder. Rubber catheters are preferably autoclaved before use, but they may be cleansed and sterilized in antiseptic solutions (e.g., quaternary ammonium chloride) or by boiling in each instance for 20 to 30 minutes.

The urethra must be adequately lubricated with a water-soluble lubricant (not with oils). Topical urethral anesthesia with a safe agent may be advisable. It is important to warn the patient beforehand about the discomfort that may be expected. Sedation may be helpful. Catheters must be of the right size for the patient and should be inserted carefully and gently.

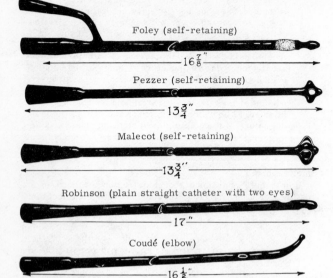

Types of Catheters. (Reproduced, with permission, from
Smith: General Urology, 6th Ed., Lange, 1969.)

Equipment.
1. Sterile soft rubber catheters (see above), usually
   sizes 8 to 12 F. (French) for children; 14 to 18 F. for
   women; and 16 to 20 F. for men. A self-retaining
   (Foley) catheter can be used if constant drainage is
   indicated.
2. Sterile short metal catheter, 14 to 16 F. (for women).
3. Surgical clamp, sterile.
4. Sterile blunt-tipped glass syringe with rubber bulb.
5. Sterile water-soluble lubricant.
6. Liquid soap or benzalkonium chloride (Zephiran®),
   1:1000 aqueous solution.
7. Mercuric oxycyanide solution, 0.1%.
8. Lidocaine (Xylocaine®), 2%, or procaine, 2%.
9. Sponges.
10. Sterile gloves.

Method. (See pp. 601-2.)
A. Men: A mild sedative may be given one-half hour before
   the procedure. The patient should be lying in a comfort-

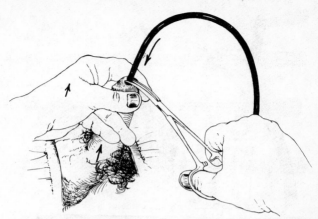

Technic of Catheterization. A sterile water-soluble lubricant is first instilled into the urethra by means of a bulb syringe. The penis is drawn taut with one hand. The catheter, held near its tip with a sterile clamp, is introduced into the urethra; the other end of the catheter is held between the fourth and fifth fingers of the hand holding the clamp. The clamp is then moved up on the catheter and the catheter introduced farther into the urethra. (Reproduced, with permission, from Smith: General Urology, 6th Ed., Lange, 1969.)

able, supine position with the legs extended. The glans penis should be washed well with soap and water or antiseptic solution (e.g., benzalkonium chloride [Zephiran®], 1:1000 aqueous solution, or 0.1% mercuric oxycyanide solution). Topical instillation of 5 to 10 ml. of sterile 2% lidocaine (Xylocaine®) or 2% procaine solution into the urethra may be advisable three to five minutes before the procedure. Lubricate the urethra thoroughly by instilling approximately 10 to 15 ml. of sterile water-soluble lubricant (e.g., K-Y Jelly®) with a blunt-tipped glass syringe. Select a soft rubber catheter of adequate size and body (16 to 20 F.) to prevent coiling up at the external sphincter. The catheter can be manipulated with a sterile gloved hand. It is often simpler, however, to grasp the catheter near its tip with a sterile clamp and to hold the other end of the catheter between the fourth and fifth fingers of the same hand. The catheter tip is then inserted into the urethra and advanced farther into the urethra by progressively moving the clamp up on the catheter (see illustrations). The urine should flow freely when the bladder is entered; and is collected in suitable

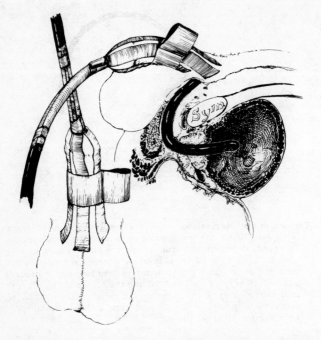

Taping the Plain Catheter in Place in the Male. Four strips
of half-inch adhesive tape are placed on the penis and
catheter. They are bound to the catheter by two pieces of
half-inch tape just distal to the glans and at the point where
they terminate on the catheter. A piece of one-inch tape is
placed about the midpenis in such manner that a loop is
formed which will separate if erection occurs. (Modified
and reproduced, with permission, from Smith: General
Urology, 6th Ed., Lange, 1969.)

    sterile containers for diagnostic studies as indicated. If
prolonged catheter drainage is planned, a closed system
collecting bag should be used to help prevent retrograde
infection. If it is necessary to provide constant drainage
with a plain catheter, tape the catheter to the penis as
shown above.

B. Women: The patient should be lying on the bed or examining table in the lithotomy position, with legs spread widely apart. The vulva must be cleansed well with soap and
water or sponged thoroughly with an antiseptic solution.

There must be adequate illumination for the ready identification of the urethral meatus. The labia are held apart
and the catheter (after being dipped into sterile lubricant)
is then introduced into the urethra. A short metal catheter (14 to 16 F.) is considered to be most satisfactory,
but a soft rubber catheter may serve perfectly well. It
may be advisable to anesthetize the urinary meatus for
three to five minutes before the procedure with a cotton
pledget soaked in 2% lidocaine or procaine. A plain
catheter can be used for constant drainage by taping it to
the shaved labia majora. Collect urine specimens in
suitable sterile containers if indicated.

Complications.

If bladder catheterization is performed properly, complications should be infrequent. Infection, hemorrhage, injury
to the urethral mucosa, systemic reaction to the local anesthetic, or embolism (from lubricants) may occur.

LUMBAR PUNCTURE

Indications.

For the withdrawal of C.S.F. for diagnostic examination,
particularly for evidence of symptomatic or asymptomatic infection or of hemorrhage of the C.N.S. The determination
of spinal fluid pressure may be of value in the diagnosis of
C.N.S. tumors or obstructions. Spinal puncture or drainage
is also used for therapeutic purposes. Spinal fluid specimens
may be used for microbiologic, serologic, cytologic, or
chemical analysis.

Precautions and Contraindications.

Lumbar puncture should be performed only by physicians
and surgeons trained in the technic. The patient must either
be cooperative or physically unable to struggle during the procedure. Sterile technic must be observed during the entire
procedure. Lumbar puncture should be performed very cautiously if intracranial pressure is significantly increased,
especially if due to infratentorial tumors. (There is danger
of compressing the medulla and injuring its vital centers, or
of damaging the cerebellum.) Always check for papilledema
before attempting lumbar puncture. Do not draw more spinal
fluid than is required.

Equipment (Sterile Tray).
1. Two lumbar puncture needles (19 and 22 gauge).
2. Hypodermic syringe, 2 ml., with two one-inch needles
   (24 gauge).
3. Three-way stopcock.

4. Glass manometer.
5. Procaine solution, 1%.
6. Tincture of iodine, 2% (weak tincture), or providone-iodine (Betadine®).
7. Alcohol, 70%.
8. Four stoppered test tubes.
9. Sponge forceps.
10. Sponges and towels.

Position of Patient. (See below.)

A. Lying Position: The patient lies on his side with his head supported by a pillow, well immobilized, and his knees drawn up so that forehead and knees are brought together. The entire spine should be in the horizontal plane.

B. Sitting Position: The patient straddles the back of a straight-backed chair with his head resting on his arms, which are folded on the back of the chair.

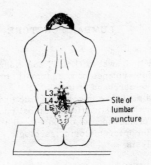

Seated Position for Lumbar Puncture

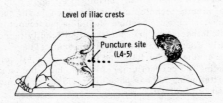

Lying Position for Lumbar Puncture

Explanation to Patient.

Reassure the patient about how much pain he may expect. Do not mention possible after-effects unless specifically asked by the patient. Tell the patient what is being done in the course of the procedure. This will prevent sudden changes of position. Stress the necessity of maintaining a flexed position.

Technic.

Puncture is best performed between the fourth and fifth or the third and fourth lumbar vertebrae. Feel for the "soft spot" in the midline between the spinous processes of the selected vertebrae, and mark the site with the end of an applicator stick. Disinfect the skin and wear sterile rubber gloves. Make a skin wheal with 1% procaine and then deeply infiltrate with the anesthetic. Select a 19 or 20 gauge spinal needle unless suppurative meningitis is suspected, in which case use a larger, 15 gauge needle. With the thumb and two fingers of both hands firmly holding the hub and shaft of the spinal needle, insert the needle (with stylet held in place with thumb) in the midline with a sustained pressure until the needle has penetrated both skin and muscles. Then push gently and slowly with the needle directed slightly (10 to 15° angle) toward the head of the patient. If bone is encountered, the direction of the needle must be changed. There is a sensation of sudden "give" when the needle penetrates the dura. Remove the stylet from time to time to see if the needle is in the subarachnoid space. If gross blood is obtained, withdraw the needle and repeat puncture with another needle. When spinal fluid appears, make the necessary pressure measurements before fluid escapes and then collect specimens in sterile containers as indicated.

A. Manometric Reading: When fluid appears, promptly connect three-way stopcock and manometer.
    1. Record normal pressure and effect of respiration and of straining.
    2. Queckenstedt sign - Pressure on either jugular vein should produce a marked rise in C. S. F. pressure unless an arachnoid or intraspinal block is present. When jugular pressure is released, the manometer reading should fall promptly to its original level. Record initial, highest, and final pressure.

B. "Bloody Tap": If fluid is bloody, leave the needle in place and permit 1 to 2 ml. to drain into a test tube. If bleeding is due to puncture, fluid will often clear rapidly, and subsequent tubes can be satisfactory for examination. If fluid containing fresh blood continues to come from the needle, the puncture is unsatisfactory and must be repeated at another time. However, bloody fluids can be used for some examinations, particularly bacteriologic cultures and animal inoculations.

C. Collection of Specimens: Always obtain at least three sterile specimens, each about 2 to 3 ml., in separate tubes. For special examinations, additional tubes or larger amounts may be necessary. Tubes should be taken to laboratories promptly. Essential examinations are as follows:

Tube 1: Protein, glucose.
Tube 2: Serology for syphilis, colloidal gold curve.
Tube 3: Cell count, differential count, culture,
stained smear for bacteria (e.g., acid-fast),
animal inoculation.

D. Completion of Lumbar Puncture: After specimens are collected, withdraw the needle rapidly and apply a small sterile dressing, or cover the puncture hole with collodion.

Complications.

When lumbar puncture is performed competently and with due caution, complications are rare. The commonest spinal puncture reactions are headache, dizziness, weakness, and anxiety. These are best avoided by not focusing the patient's attention on their possibility, by reassurance, and by keeping patients known to develop reactions flat in bed for one or two days. Most other individuals develop little if any headache if ambulatory immediately after puncture. Headache, if it develops, is best controlled by keeping the patient flat in bed and administering salicylates or codeine.

More serious complications include infection and herniation of the medulla or the cerebellum into the foramen magnum, causing damage to vital centers or even death.

ABDOMINAL PARACENTESIS

Indications.

For the removal of abnormal accumulations of fluid from the peritoneal cavity for diagnostic or therapeutic purposes. The specimen may be used for microbiologic, cytologic, or chemical analysis.

Precautions.

Abdominal paracentesis must be done only by physicians and surgeons trained in the technic. Sterile technic must be observed during the entire procedure. The needle insertion site should be selected to avoid possible damage to blood vessels of the anterior abdominal wall or to the viscera (see below). The urinary bladder must be emptied before the procedure. Avoid too rapid withdrawal of fluid because of possible syncope.

Equipment (Sterile Tray).
1. Procaine solution, 1%.
2. Sterile syringe with hypodermic and intramuscular needles.
3. Scalpel (sharp-pointed).
4. Trocar (with obturator).
5. Anticoagulant.
6. Sterile containers for specimens.
7. Epinephrine and morphine for emergency use.
8. Fifty cm. of sterile rubber tubing.

Method.
Request the patient to empty his bladder or, in case of retention, catheterize just before the procedure. The patient should be seated upright in a chair or on the edge of a table. The site chosen for puncture is usually just to the left of the rectus abdominis or in the midline, halfway between the umbilicus and the symphysis pubis (see below). Mark the site with the end of an applicator stick, and cleanse the skin with suitable antiseptic. Infiltrate with 1% procaine solution down to the peritoneum. Incise the skin with a scalpel and push the trocar carefully through the abdominal wall; a sudden giving sensation indicates that the peritoneal cavity has been entered. Withdraw the obturator and let fluid flow into appropriate containers. If fluid fails to flow freely, reinsert the stylet and gently rotate and move the trocar back and forth in case the omentum or intestine is obstructing the end of the trocar. After fluid has been withdrawn and collected in citrated con-

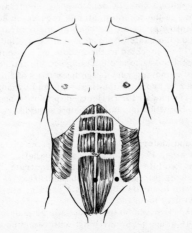

Preferred Sites for Abdominal Paracentesis

tainers, remove the trocar and apply a sterile dressing with a tight abdominal binder.

Diagnostic Paracentesis.

In instances of questionable diagnosis of a surgical abdomen, the character of small amounts of free peritoneal fluid can be important.

By inserting a small plastic catheter of the Intracath®, Jelco®, or Medicut® type following local anesthesia, small amounts of fluid can be aspirated for examination.

This is done in the supine position with aspiration attempted as indicated in the left or right lower quadrant.

Complications.

Hemorrhage, infection, intestinal perforation (especially in patients with tuberculous peritonitis), syncope, and shock may occur.

THORACENTESIS (THORACIC PARACENTESIS)

Indications.

For the removal of abnormal accumulations of fluid from the pleural space for diagnostic or therapeutic purposes. The specimens may be used for microbiologic, cytologic, or chemical analysis.

Precautions.

Thoracentesis must be done only by physicians and surgeons trained in the technic. Sterile technic must be observed during the entire procedure. The site for aspiration of fluid is selected on the basis of physical and x-ray findings. The needle should be inserted at the middle or lower margin of the intercostal space to avoid damage to the intercostal vessels. Avoid removing very large quantities of fluid at one time in order to avoid mediastinal shift and syncope. Fluid should be withdrawn with airtight equipment to prevent pneumothorax. Epinephrine and morphine should be available for emergency treatment of shock and pain.

Equipment and Materials.

1. Procaine, 1%, or other local anesthetic. As anticoagulant, sterile solutions of sodium citrate, 2.5% (1 ml./ 10 ml. fluid); heparin, 10,000 units/ml. (0.3 ml./100 ml. fluid); or disodium EDTA, 10% (1 ml./100 ml. fluid) may be used.
2. Syringes, 5 and 50 ml.; needles, 22 gauge, 26 gauge, and 16 gauge (7.5 cm. long) with round bevel; three-way stopcock with attached rubber tubing; surgical clamp (mosquito). Other aspiration apparatus may be used.

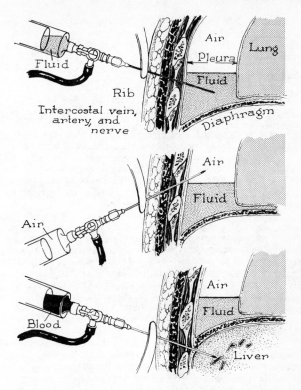

Thoracentesis. Top: A successful tap with fluid obtained.
Note the position of the needle with relation to the intercostal bundle, and the use of the clamp to steady the needle
at skin level. Center: Air is obtained as the needle is
shifted upward. Bottom: A bloody tap results from an ex-
cessively low position of the needle with puncture of the
liver. (Redrawn and reproduced, with permission, from
G. E. Lindskog and A. E. Liebow, Thoracic Surgery and
Related Pathology. Appleton-Century-Crofts, 1953.)

3. Two sterile test tubes for culture and chemical tests; bottle for specific gravity determination, cell count, cytology, and cell button; sterile 500 ml. bottle for guinea pig inoculation.

Standard Method.

Observe strict sterile technic.

A. Adults: Have the patient sit upright in a comfortable position, leaning slightly forward with his elevated arms resting on a bedside stand padded with pillows. The usual aspiration point for large effusions is at the eighth intercostal space at the posterior axillary line or at the angle of the scapula. If the fluid is loculated or if the first tap is dry, it may be necessary to use a fluoroscope.

1. Using sterile technic, infiltrate the skin, subcutaneous tissue, and pleura with 5 to 10 ml. of 1% procaine solution through a 22 gauge needle.

2. Connect 50 ml. syringe, stopcock, and 16 gauge needle. Insert the needle slowly at the lower margin of the intercostal space (except when making a tap on the anterior chest wall, in which case the needle is passed through the center of the interspace) until fluid can be aspirated easily. Grasp the needle with the surgical clamp as close to the skin as possible to steady the needle at the chest wall.

3. Aspirate fluid to 50 ml. mark; turn the stopcock and discharge fluid into the container via tubing. The volume of fluid removed at one sitting depends upon circumstances. As much as 2 L. can often be gradually evacuated at one sitting from a large effusion. If untoward symptoms of any sort develop, slow the rate of aspiration or discontinue until another occasion.

B. Infants: Thoracentesis may be indicated if a pneumonia patient fails to improve in the expected time and if there is dyspnea due to pressure on the mediastinum (as indicated by shifting of apex impulse). Perform an intradermal tuberculin test. Obtain a chest film to determine the presence of fluid. Prepare the skin and introduce the needle as for adults, but remove only small amounts of fluid at a time to avoid the danger of mediastinal shift. (The mediastinum becomes relatively fixed at three weeks.) Drainage may be repeated as necessary. If fluid is too thick to drain, surgical intervention may be necessary to effect closed or open drainage.

Alternate Method.

A 14 gauge intravenous Intracath® can be used instead of the rigid 16 gauge needle. It has two very obvious advantages: (1) It is less traumatic to lung and pleura; and (2) the long Intracath® can be threaded toward the base of the pleural cavity and more fluid thus aspirated.

Complications.

Syncope, respiratory symptoms, pneumothorax, infection, hemorrhage, and shock may occur.

PERICARDIAL PARACENTESIS

Indications.

For the removal of abnormal accumulations of pericardial fluid for diagnostic or therapeutic purposes. The specimen may be used for microbiologic, cytologic, or chemical analysis.

Precautions.

Pericardial paracentesis should be performed only by physicians and surgeons trained in the technic and must always be done in a hospital. Sterile conditions must be observed during the entire procedure. Anteroposterior and lateral chest x-rays should be obtained whenever possible. The internal mammary artery may be avoided by inserting the needle either as close to the sternum as possible or 3 to 4 cm. to the left of the sternum. The needle should be inserted in the middle of the selected intercostal space in order to avoid bleeding from the intercostal vessels. Vigorous rhythmic movement of the needle indicates that the needle is within the cardiac muscle, in which case it should be rapidly retracted until there is no further needle motion. Some clinicians utilize an Ecg. lead (unipolar precordial lead) attached to the needle to help determine whether or not the needle has reached the epicardium. When the ECG shows a pattern of injury (sudden rise in ST-T segment) the epicardium has been reached. If purulent fluid is suspected, it usually is advisable to insert the needle close to the sternum in order to avoid pleural contamination.

Equipment.

As for thoracic paracentesis. Some prefer an 18 gauge instead of a 16 gauge needle.

Method.

Observe strict sterile technic. The patient should be placed in a semi-recumbent position (about 60°) supported by bed elevation and pillows. The puncture site is usually anterior, just within the area of cardiac dullness as localized by palpation, percussion, and x-ray findings. The fifth or sixth intercostal spaces are usually selected, below the left nipple. In massive effusions the puncture may be performed posteriorly below the tip of the scapula. The site should be marked with the end of an applicator stick. The skin should be cleansed and antiseptic applied. Infiltrate the skin and subcutaneous tissues with procaine. Connect the 50 ml. syringe,

stopcock, and 18 gauge needle. Insert the needle slowly
through the middle of the intercostal space at an angle directed slightly upward and toward the spine. Further introduce
the needle with constant suction. When fluid is aspirated with
ease, a surgical clamp should be attached to the needle next
to the skin to prevent further entry of the needle. Aspirate,
and then turn the stopcock to discharge fluid via the rubber
tubing into sterile containers for further diagnostic study.

Complications.
    Pericardial paracentesis is more difficult and hazardous
than thoracic or abdominal paracentesis. Complications include intercostal artery hemorrhage, internal mammary
artery hemorrhage, cardiac puncture, cardiac arrhythmias,
pneumothorax, infections (pleural, pericardial, or systemic),
and shock.

PERCUTANEOUS NEEDLE BIOPSY OF LIVER

Indications.
    Biopsy provides information regarding the cause, nature,
activity, severity, and prognosis of liver disease. Tissue
may also be used for microbiologic or chemical analyses.

Contraindications.
    Bleeding tendencies, patient noncooperation, local (or,
in some cases, systemic) infection, inability to detect liver
dullness, and physical prostration.

Precautions.
    Liver biopsies must be done only by physicians and sur-
geons trained in the technic who have a thorough understanding of primary and secondary hepatic disorders. The biopsy
must always be done in a hospital, although preliminary
studies may be performed on an outpatient basis. Bleeding
time, clotting time, prothrombin time, and platelet count
should be determined; if a bleeding tendency is noted, it must
be corrected before biopsy is attempted. Avoid introducing
the needle more than 2 cm. below the surface of the liver.

Method.
    The patient is given a mild sedative about one-half hour
before biopsy. The procedure is explained to the patient, and
the patient is placed in a supine position. Intercostal or sub-
costal biopsy sites may be selected, depending upon the degree
of hepatic enlargement. In the absence of hepatomegaly, the
intercostal approach is both safe and satisfactory. The ninth
or tenth intercostal space is used depending upon the area of
greatest dullness on hepatic percussion. The needle is inserted in the middle of the selected interspace in the mid-
axillary or axillary line. The patient must not inhale while

Vim-Silverman Technic of Liver Biopsy

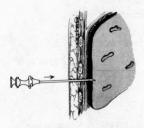

(1) The outer needle, with stylet in place, is advanced to just within the liver surface.

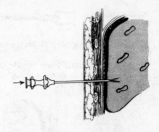

(2) The stylet is removed and the inner needle is inserted to its full length through the outer needle.

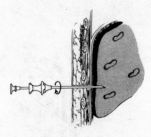

(3) The outer needle is advanced with slight rotation over the inner needle and plug.

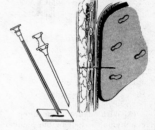

(4) Both needles are withdrawn. Tissue biopsy is removed for placement in fixative.

the intercostal biopsy is performed. If the liver is enlarged considerably, the abdominal approach may be preferred and the biopsy performed in the area of the midclavicular line.

Sterile technic must be observed throughout the entire procedure. Anesthetize the skin and pericapsular tissue. Insert the Vim-Silverman or other coring type of needle (or Menghini suction type needle with syringe) just inside the liver capsule. Have the patient breathe gently or hold his breath. Insert the needle farther into the desired depth of the liver, obtain specimens, and rapidly but gently withdraw the needle. Place a clean, sterile dressing over the wound.

Complications.

Hemorrhage, pain, shock, damage to adjacent organs, bile peritonitis, and infection may occur.

614

Menghini Technic of Liver Biopsy

(Longitudinal Section of Menghini Needle)

(1) With a small-bore needle (No. 24), infiltrate the area selected for insertion of the biopsy needle.

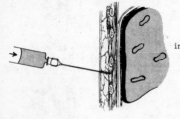

(2) Insert Menghini needle in mid-intercostal space.

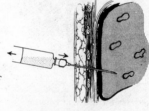

(3) With needle in the liver parenchyma, withdraw the plunger and aspirate cellular material.

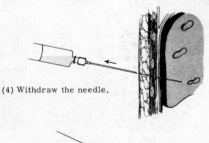

(4) Withdraw the needle.

(5) Place cellular material in a flat-bottomed dish containing fixative.

TRACHEOSTOMY

Markedly diminished pulmonary reserve or excessive secretions which cannot be adequately removed by tracheal aspiration may be an indication for tracheostomy. Positive-pressure breathing through a tracheostomy may be life-saving and should be instituted promptly when oxygenation is inadequate in spite of other measures.

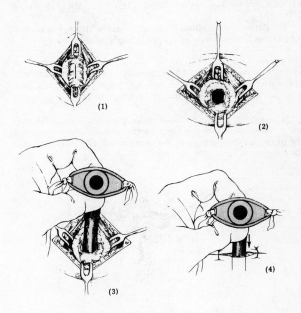

(1)

(2)

(3)

(4)

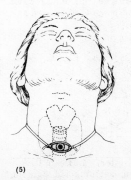

(5)

Technic of Tracheostomy.
  (1) Surgical approach in children. Third and fourth tracheal rings split in midline. No cartilage removed.
  (2) Surgical approach in adults. Anterior section of third tracheal ring removed.
  (3) Insertion of tracheostomy tube.
  (4) Loose suturing of both ends of wound.
  (5) Tube tied in place.

SIGMOIDOSCOPY

The patient must be relaxed and the physician must be very gentle and reassuring. The patient may be examined in several positions:

(1) Routine office patients or very ill patients - Left lateral (Sims') position.

(2) Bed patients - Prone position with thighs and legs well elevated by sandbags or firm pillows, or knee-chest position.

(3) Patients examined in proctologist's office - Inverted or head down position (use a special invertable table).

Procedure.

(1) The well-lubricated sigmoidoscope, with obturator held in place by the thumb of the right hand, is inserted into the anus, directed toward the patient's umbilicus.

(2) As soon as the sphincters have been passed, the obturator is removed by the right hand and the sigmoidoscope is held in the left. Passage of the instrument is thereafter done under direct vision.

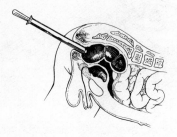

(3) Under direct vision, the scope is now directed toward the sacrum and slowly advanced, its course being altered as necessary to follow the lumen.

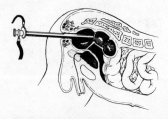

Redrawn from illustrations by Frank Netter, M.D., in R.A. Hopping: Common disorders of anus, rectum, and sigmoid,

(4) Sigmoidoscope at the rectosigmoid junction. It is now almost in alignment with the long axis of the body.

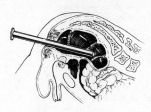

(5) Sigmoidoscope in the sigmoid colon, the tip directed somewhat to the left. Obstructing mucosal folds may be passed by elevating them with the tip of the scope or suction, or by gentle inflation.

BUCCAL AND VAGINAL SMEARS FOR SEX CHROMATIN ANALYSIS

Indications.

To determine the chromosomal sex of an individual by demonstration of sex chromatin bodies in somatic cells to assist in the study of hypogonadal and hermaphroditism syndromes. The number of chromatin bodies in a cell is one less than the number of X chromosomes in that cell. Since sex chromatin analysis is easily obtained and relatively inexpensive, the method is of practical clinical value in determining chromosomal sex.

Method.

   Epithelial cells from the buccal or vaginal mucous membranes can be used for sex chromatin determination. Buccal
cells may be obtained by scraping the inner side of the cheek
with a spatula; and vaginal cells can be obtained by aspiration
or with a spatula or cut tongue depressor (see pp. 394-5).
Prepare smears by placing a small pool of epithelial cells on
a microscope slide, press another slide over it, and gently
draw the slides apart. Fix smears immediately in 95% ethyl
alcohol without allowing them to dry. Smears may be stored
in the fixative but should preferably be stained within 48
hours. The actual staining of the smears should be performed
by persons skilled in the technic since improperly prepared
slides may lead to errors in interpretation.

   The sex chromatin (Barr) body is a solid planoconvex
mass approximately 1 micron in diameter, usually located
near or at the inner surface of the nuclear membrane. The
sex chromatin body represents the heterochromatic X chromosome. The number of nuclei containing the sex chromatin
is counted under oil immersion, a total of 100 cells being
examined.

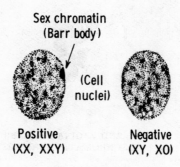

Normal Sex Chromatin Pattern

Interpretation.

   Normal females have sex chromatin bodies in 40 to 60%
of cells counted and are "chromatin positive." Normal males
do not possess these chromatin bodies, and are "chromatin
negative." The presence or absence of chromatin bodies,
therefore, may be of value in differentiating those conditions
in which the gonads are of one sex but contradictions exist in
the chromosomal sex or the morphologic expression of sex.
Sex chromatin bodies are diminished in number in the immediate postnatal period and during treatment with corticosteroids, ACTH, and estrogens.

TONOMETRY

Indications.

Tonometer readings should be taken on all patients over 25 years of age having routine eye examinations or general medical examinations and on any patient in whom increased intraocular pressure (glaucoma) is suspected.

Contraindications and Precautions.

Tonometry should not be done on any person with an infected eye, as the infection could be spread to other patients by the tonometer. It is extremely important to clean the tonometer before and after each use by carefully wiping the footplate with a moist sterile cotton swab. A local anesthetic solution must be instilled in each eye before the reading. The examination should not be performed without proper instruction in the technic. The tonometer must be well-calibrated and properly applied to the cornea. Serial readings may be necessary over a period of hours or days and other eye examinations may be necessary. The examination may be without value, or even hazardous, in uncooperative patients.

Equipment.

1. Tonometer (Schiotz) with weights.
2. Proparacaine (Ophthaine®, Ophthetic®), 0.5% solution, or benoxinate (Dorsacaine®), 0.4% solution.
3. Sterile cotton swabs moistened with sterile saline.
4. Tonometer chart.

Method.

Instill 1 drop of ophthalmic local anesthetic solution into each eye. Have the patient lie on his back and ask him to fix his gaze on a spot on the ceiling with both eyes. The tonometer is then placed gently on the corneal surface of each eye and the scale reading is taken from the tonometer. The intraocular tension is determined by referring to a chart which converts the scale reading to mm. Hg. Readings normally range from 12 to 20 mm. Hg (Schiotz), and readings of 20 to 25 mm. Hg or more require further evaluation. Tonometer readings may have to be repeated several times at different hours of the day or on different days.

Schiotz
Tonometer

Complications.

If tonometry is properly performed, complications are rare. Infection or trauma may occur.

Appendix

STAINING METHODS

In the various methods given, it is usual first to fix the smears of unknown material on the slide. Drying of the stained preparations is best done by exposure to air. Blotting paper is sometimes used. Warming over a flame may cause distortion if too much heat is used, so it is wise to hold the slide with one's fingers (to prevent overheating).

Acid-fast Stain.
A. Ziehl-Neelsen: Fix smear by heat. Cover with carbolfuchsin, steam gently for five minutes over direct flame (or for 20 minutes over water bath). Wash with water. Decolorize in acid-alcohol until only a faint pink color remains. Wash with water. Counterstain 10 to 30 seconds with Löffler's methylene blue. Wash with water and let dry.
B. Kinyoun Carbolfuchsin Acid-fast Stain (Am. J. Pub. Health 5:867, 1915): (Formula: Basic fuchsin, 4 Gm.; phenol crystals, 8 Gm.; 95% alcohol, 20 ml.; distilled water, 100 ml.) Stain fixed smear for three minutes (no heat necessary) and continue as with Ziehl-Neelsen stain.

Aniline Dyes.
Stain for 30 to 60 seconds and wash in water. The aniline dyes include gentian violet, methylene blue, safranin, toluidin blue, acid fuchsin, and methyl blue.

Carbolfuchsin. (Tilden's method to study mouth organisms.)
To a drop of sputum (or blood or culture) add an equal amount of 10% formalin and let stand five minutes. Spread thin on slide and let dry in air. Stain with carbolfuchsin for 10 to 20 seconds. Wash with water and let dry.

Eosin and Methylene Blue (Alcohol-soluble).
Stain for one minute in 1% alcohol-soluble eosin. Rinse with water for one minute. Place in 1% methylene blue (aqueous) for one minute (or as found necessary). Rinse with water and let dry. Decolorize with absolute alcohol or acetone.

Giemsa's Stain for Blood.   (Purchase stain ready made.)
Immerse the slide in stain diluted 1:50 for 30 to 45 minutes. Rinse gently in distilled water for three to five minutes.
Dry in air and examine. Do not blot.

Gram's Stain (Hucker Modification).
Cover with crystal violet for one minute. Wash with
water. Do not blot. Cover with Gram's iodine for one minute.
Wash in water. Do not blot. Decolorize for 30 seconds with
gentle agitation in acetone-alcohol (acetone 30 ml. and 95%
alcohol 70 ml.). Wash in water. Do not blot. Cover for 10
to 20 seconds with safranin (2.5% solution in 95% alcohol).
Wash with water and let dry.

Methylene Blue (Löffler's Alkaline Methylene Blue).
Cover smear with stain for 30 seconds. (Cover for five
minutes in diphtheria or in Vincent's angina.) Wash with water
and let dry.

Peroxidase Stain (Goodpasture).
Only cells of the myeloid series will show the peroxidase
reaction: sharply outlined, deep-blue granules.
Use dried blood smear. Cover with measured amount of
stain for one minute. Add equal quantity of water, which
should contain one drop of hydrogen peroxide per 8 ml. Let
stand four minutes. Rinse in water and let dry.

Wright's Stain.
See p. 628.

COMPOSITIONS OF SOLUTIONS, STAINS, AND REAGENTS

Distilled water should be used in making reagent and stain
solutions.

A.C.D. Solution:

Trisodium citrate	13.2
Citric acid	4.8
Dextrose	14.7
Water	1000.0

Use 120 ml. for 500 ml. blood.

Acetic Acid Solutions: (A few drops of 5% copper sulfate added
to 15 ml. of dilute acid prevents growth of molds.) Prepare
3% acetic acid by adding 7 drops of glacial acetic acid to 100
ml. water. Prepare 6% acetic acid by adding 14 drops of
glacial acetic acid to 15 ml. distilled water or 6 ml. of
glacial acetic acid to distilled water to make 100 ml.

Alcohol, Acid:
1. One part HCl; 99 parts of 95% alcohol; or
2. Five parts nitric acid; 95 parts of 95% alcohol.

Alkaline Copper Tartrate Solution: To 40 Gm. anhydrous
sodium carbonate in 400 ml. of distilled water add 7.4 Gm.
tartaric acid, dissolve, and add 4.5 Gm. copper sulfate.
Dilute to 1 L.

Benedict's Qualitative Solution: 173 Gm. sodium citrate;
17.3 Gm. copper sulfate; 100 Gm. sodium carbonate;
distilled water to make 1000 ml. Use heat to dissolve sodium citrate and carbonate in 800 ml. water. Pour through
folded filter paper into a glass graduate and make up to 850
ml. Dissolve copper sulfate in 100 ml. water. Pour the
citrate-carbonate solution into a large beaker and add the
copper sulfate solution slowly, with constant stirring, and
make up to 1000 ml. This solution does not deteriorate on
standing.

Benedict's Quantitative Sugar Reagent: 200 Gm. of crystalline sodium carbonate (or 100 Gm. of the anhydrous salt);
200 Gm. of sodium or potassium citrate; 125 Gm. potassium
thiocyanate; 18 Gm. crystalline copper sulfate; 100 ml. of
5% solution of potassium ferrocyanide; distilled water to
make 1000 ml. Use heat to dissolve the citrate, carbonate,
and thiocyanate in 800 ml. water; filter if necessary.
Dissolve copper sulfate separately in 100 ml. water, add
slowly to other solution, stirring constantly. Add ferrocyanide solution, cool, and dilute to exactly 1 L. The
only reagent requiring exact weighing is the copper sulfate.
25 ml. of above reagent is reduced by 50 mg. glucose.

Benzidine Solution: Dissolve 1 Gm. pure benzidine dihydrochloride in 20 ml. glacial acetic acid; add 30 ml. distilled
water and 50 ml. 90% ethyl alcohol. Store in dark bottle.

Boas' Reagent: Dissolve 5 Gm. resublimed resorcinol and 3
Gm. cane sugar in 100 ml. 95% alcohol.

Buffer Solution for Wright's Stain: Mix 6.63 Gm. monobasic
potassium phosphate and 2.56 Gm. dibasic sodium phosphate
with 1000 ml. distilled water. Buffered distilled water can
be prepared to the proper pH for Wright's stain (6.4 to 6.7)
by adding a tablet of phosphate buffer. (Certified Buffer
tablets, pH Coleman Company, Maywood, Ill.) Similar tablets can be obtained to adjust the pH of water used for
Giemsa's stain to 6.4.

Carbolfuchsin Stain:
1. Stain for tubercle bacilli - Add 10 ml. filtered saturated alcoholic solution (3%) of basic fuchsin to 100 ml.
   of 5% aqueous solution of carbolic acid.
2. Dilute carbolfuchsin - Add 5 ml. of above stain (for
   tubercle bacilli) to 95 ml. distilled water.

Cleaning Solutions, for Glassware:
1. Bichromate - Slowly add 250 ml. of commercial sulfuric acid to 750 ml. of water. Dissolve 100 Gm. of
   sodium dichromate in hot water and add this to the
   diluted acid solution.

2. Alkaline - Commercial alkaline detergent solutions are available.
3. Use in hood - Add 100 ml. nitric acid to 900 ml. concentrated sulfuric acid. This solution fumes. While cold it removes grease; when hot it oxidizes organic materials.

Crystal Violet Stain:
1. Solution A - 10 Gm. crystal violet (gentian violet) in 100 ml. 95% alcohol.
2. Solution B - 10 Gm. ammonium oxalate in 1000 ml. water.
3. Final Stain - 100 ml. of solution A and 800 ml. solution B.

Darrow's Solution (KNL): 4 Gm. sodium chloride, 6 Gm. sodium lactate, and 2.7 Gm. potassium chloride per liter of water.

Dawson's Solution: Mix 8 Gm. sodium chloride and 5 Gm. sodium bicarbonate in 1000 ml. distilled water.

Distilled Water, Buffered: See Buffered distilled water under Buffer.

Double Oxalate Solution (Potassium and Ammonium Oxalate): Double oxalate for sedimentation rate and hematocrit: Potassium oxalate, 2 Gm.; ammonium oxalate, 3 Gm.; water to make 100 ml. 0.2 ml. of solution is sufficient to provide anticoagulant for 5 ml. of blood. Place required amount in test tube and evaporate to dryness at room temperature or at low heat so as not to destroy the anticoagulant.

Ehrlich's Reagent: Add 2.7 Gm. of paradimethylaminobenzaldehyde to 20 ml. concentrated hydrochloric acid and 80 ml. water.

Ehrlich's Diazo Reagent:
1. Solution A - 1 Gm. sulfanilic acid; 10 ml. concentrated hydrochloric acid; distilled water to make 200 ml.
2. Solution B - 0.5 Gm. sodium nitrite in 100 ml. distilled water.
3. Final solution - Immediately before using add 0.1 ml. of solution B to 10 ml. of solution A.

Esbach's Reagent: Dissolve 20 Gm. of citric acid and 10 Gm. of picric acid in one liter of water.

Fouchet's Reagent: 25 Gm. of trichloroacetic acid and 0.9 Gm. ferric chloride (9 ml. of 10% ferric chloride solution) and distilled water to make 100 ml.

Gentian Violet (Crystal Violet) Stain: Grind 2.5 Gm. gentian violet and 10 ml. 95% alcohol in mortar; while grinding add 2 ml. aniline oil and 88 ml. distilled water. Let stand a few days and filter. To test for deterioration, let a drop of stain fall in a beaker of water; if precipitate forms, stain cannot be used.

Gentian Violet Stain With Glycerin: Mix 20 ml. of gentian violet with 80 ml. of 30% glycerin. Use 15 ml. of 3% crystal violet in 95% alcohol; mix this with 85 ml. of 30% glycerin.

Giemsa's Stain for Blood: 0.5 Gm. of powdered Giemsa's stain (National Aniline Co.) is dissolved in 33 ml. of glycerin at 131°F. (55°C.) for two hours. It is then mixed with 33 ml. of absolute methyl alcohol, filtered, and kept in a stock bottle. For staining, one drop of stain is mixed in a small container with 15 drops of water buffered to pH of 6.4.

Goodpasture's Stain:
1. Dissolve 0.05 Gm. sodium nitroprusside in 1 or 2 ml. of water, mix with 100 ml. alcohol, and add 0.05 Gm. benzidine (CP), 0.05 to 0.1 Gm. basic fuchsin.
2. Use 1:200 dilution hydrogen peroxide for diluting stain (2 drops to 15 ml. water). Cover with Goodpasture's stain one minute; add equal amount hydrogen peroxide for three to four minutes. Rinse well in water, and dry by blotting.

Gower's Solution for RBC: Add 12.5 Gm. sodium sulfate and 33.3 ml. of glacial acetic acid to 200 ml. distilled water.

Gram's Iodine Stain: Add 6 Gm. potassium iodide and 3 Gm. of iodine crystals to 900 ml. of distilled water.

Hartmann's Solution (Ringer's Lactate): Isotonic for human blood. Contains 3 Gm. sodium lactate, 6 Gm. sodium chloride, 0.3 Gm. potassium chloride, 0.2 Gm. calcium chloride, and water to make 1000 ml.

Hayem's Fluid for RBC: Add 2.5 Gm. mercuric chloride, 25 Gm. sodium sulfate, 5 Gm. sodium chloride, to 1000 ml. distilled water.

Hydrochloric Acid (HCl):
1. Concentrated HCl = 36.5% by weight. This is a 12N solution.
2. Dilute HCl = 10% by weight. Prepare by mixing 100 ml. of concentrated hydrochloric acid with 219 ml. water.
3. N/10 HCl (e.g., for hemoglobin) = 11.5 ml. concentrated hydrochloric acid to 1000 ml. water. This has a pH of 1.0.

Iodine Disinfectant Solution: (As skin antiseptic, etc.) Contains 10 Gm. iodine crystals, 5 Gm. potassium iodide, 10 ml. water, and 90 ml. of 95% alcohol.

Iodine Solution for Examining Protozoa: Grind 1 Gm. of potassium iodide and 1 Gm. of iodine together in mortar with 5 ml. water, and then make up to 100 ml. with water. Transfer, with any excess iodine, to a glass-stoppered dark glass bottle. Filter before using. May also use Lugol's solution.

Isotonic Solutions: (For mammals; approximately 300 mOsm./L.)
1. 0.9% sodium chloride
2. 1.3% sodium bicarbonate

3. 2.5% sodium citrate

4. 5% dextrose

Jenner's Stain: Obtain Jenner's eosinate of methylene blue as a powder or tablet. Dissolve 0.5 Gm. of the dye in 100 ml. absolute methyl alcohol (neutral). Keep tightly stoppered in dark bottle.

Leukocyte Diluting Fluid (for WBC): Filter if not clear.
1. For blood WBC - 15 ml. glacial acetic acid and 475 ml. water. (Add 5 ml. of 1% gentian violet to distinguish from RBC solution.)
2. For spinal fluid WBC - 0.2 Gm. crystal violet, 10 ml. glacial acetic, 90 ml. water.

Locke's Solution: Isotonic for mammals; pH = 7.5. Contains 9 Gm. sodium chloride, 0.42 Gm. potassium chloride, 0.18 Gm. anhydrous calcium chloride, 0.15 Gm. sodium bicarbonate, 1 Gm. dextrose, and water to make 1000 ml. Dissolve sodium bicarbonate before adding calcium chloride.

Löffler's Alkaline Methylene Blue Stain: Add 30 ml. of filtered saturated alcoholic solution (3%) of methylene blue to 100 ml. water, and add 2 drops of a 10% solution of potassium hydroxide.

Lugol's Solution: Dissolve 10 Gm. of potassium iodide and 5 Gm. of iodine in 100 ml. of distilled water.

May-Grünwald Stain: See Jenner's stain.

Molybdate Phosphate Solution: Add 35 Gm. molybdic acid to 5 Gm. of sodium tungstate and dissolve in 200 ml. of water. Add 200 ml. of 10% sodium hydroxide and boil vigorously until ammonia is no longer liberated. Cool, dilute to 350 ml. and add 125 ml. of concentrated phosphoric acid.

Normal Saline: Common name for physiological salt solution, q.v.

Normal Solutions: A normal solution is one which contains one equivalent weight of an acid or base per liter. The "absolute reference" is replaceable hydrogen. One equivalent weight of any acid is the amount of that acid which contains 1 Gm. of replaceable hydrogen. One equivalent weight of a base is the amount of that base which will exactly neutralize one equivalent weight of an acid.

Some examples are:

Normal solution of HCl = 36.5 Gm. HCl/L. (molecular wt.).

Normal solution of H_2SO_4 = 49 Gm. H_2SO_4/L. ($1/2$ of the molecular wt.).

Normal solution of NaOH = 40 Gm. NaOH/L. (molecular wt.).

N/10 Solutions are made by accurate dilutions of the normal solutions. See also hydrochloric acid and sodium hydroxide. N/10 HCl = pH 1.0; N/10 NaOH = 13.2.

Obermayer's Reagent: Add 4 Gm. ferric chloride to 1000 ml. concentrated HCl (sp. gr. 1.16 to 1.19).

Pandy's Reagent: Add 10 Gm. phenol crystals to 100 ml. water; keep in incubator several days, shaking frequently; use clear supernatant fluid (is saturated solution).

Peroxidase Stain (Osgood and Ashworth):

1. Solution A - In 99 ml. ethyl alcohol (95%), dissolve 0.3 Gm. benzidine base. Add 1 ml. of a saturated aqueous solution of sodium nitroprusside. Good for 8-10 months.
2. Solution B - To 25 ml. distilled water add 0.3 ml. fresh 3% hydrogen peroxide. Make just before use.

Physiological Salt Solution ("Normal Saline"): Isotonic for mammals: 8.5 to 9.0 Gm. NaCl in 1000 ml. water.

Platelet Counting Solution (Rees-Ecker): 3.8 Gm. sodium citrate; 0.2 ml. neutral 40% solution of formaldehyde; 0.05 Gm. brilliant cresyl blue; water to make 100 ml.

Polychrome Methylene Blue: Mix according to directions on bottle.

0.2% Potassium Chloride Solution: 2 Gm. potassium chloride per liter of water.

Potassium Ferricyanide Solution: Dissolve 1 Gm. potassium ferricyanide in 250 ml. of distilled water. Store in a brown bottle.

Prothrombin Time Solutions:

1. Sodium oxalate - Dissolve 1.34 Gm. of pure anhydrous sodium oxalate in 100 ml. distilled water.
2. Calcium chloride - Dissolve 1.11 Gm. of pure anhydrous calcium chloride in 100 ml. distilled water.
3. Thromboplastin solution - Excellent thromboplastin is available commercially.

Randolph Solutions (for eosinophil counts):

1. Solution I - 50 ml. 0.1% methylene blue in propylene glycol and 50 ml. distilled water.
2. Solution II - 50 ml. 0.1% phloxine in propylene glycol and 50 ml. distilled water.
3. Working solution - Stable for only four hours. Mix equal amounts of I and II. May have to vary these proportions slightly as solutions age.

Ringer's Lactate: See Hartmann's solution.

Ringer's Solution: 8.6 Gm. sodium chloride, 0.3 Gm. potassium chloride, 0.33 Gm. calcium chloride per liter of water.

Ringer-Locke Solution: Locke's solution without dextrose.

Robert's Reagent: Mix 500 ml. saturated solution magnesium sulfate and 100 ml. concentrated nitric acid.

Safranin Stain: Dissolve 1 Gm. of safranin in 100 ml. water and add 35 ml. glycerol.

Scarlet Red Stain (Sudan IV): Add scarlet red in excess to mixture of 50 ml. of 70% alcohol and 50 ml. acetone, and filter.

Schaudinn's Solution: See p. 340.

Sodium Hydroxide (NaOH): Saturated solution is 50% by weight; is 19N solution. To make normal sodium hydroxide, mix 100 Gm. sodium hydroxide (CP) and 100 ml. water; let stand 24 hours. Take 57 ml. of clear supernatant fluid and dilute to 1000 ml. with water. This is 1N NaOH. Rapid method of making approximately normal sodium hydroxide is to dissolve 42 Gm. of sodium hydroxide in 1000 ml. water. It is necessary to check normality: Add methyl red and bromthymol blue, titrate to a yellow color with normal oxalic acid (see Normal Solutions). Normal oxalic acid is a 6.3% solution in distilled water.

Sodium Lactate, M/6: 18.7 Gm. sodium lactate per liter of water.

Sodium Nitroprusside Reagent: Add 10 Gm. of sodium nitroprusside crystals and 2 ml. of concentrated sulfuric acid to 100 ml. water. Keep in brown glass bottle.

Sudan III Stain: Make saturated solution in 70% alcohol and filter.

Sulfate-Tungstate Solution for Micro Blood Sugar: Place 10 Gm. of anhydrous sodium sulfate and 15 ml. of 10% sodium tungstate solution in a 500 ml. volumetric flask. Fill flask half full with water and shake until sulfate dissolves. Dilute to volume. Place 4 ml. of this solution in each of a number of clean dry centrifuge tubes, rubber-stoppered, and set away upright. Put 0.1 ml. of blood into such a tube.

Sulfuric Acid-Sulfate Solution: In 12 ml. of 2/3 normal sulfuric acid dissolve 2 Gm. anhydrous sodium sulfate and dilute to 100 ml.

Sulkowitch Reagent: 2.5 Gm. oxalic acid; 2.5 Gm. ammonium oxalate; 5 ml. glacial acetic acid; water to make 150 ml.

Tannic Acid: Prepare fresh a 5% aqueous solution.

Tincture of Iodine (skin antiseptic): Dissolve 50 Gm. of potassium iodide and 70 Gm. of iodine in 50 ml. of water. Dilute to make 1000 ml. with 95% alcohol.

Trichrome Stain: Dissolve in 100 ml. distilled water 0.6 Gm. chromotrope 2R, 0.15 Gm. light green SF, 0.15 Gm. fast green FCF, 0.7 Gm. phosphotungstic acid, and 1 ml. acetic acid.

Tsuchiya's Reagent: Add 1.5 Gm. crystals of phosphotungstic acid and 5 ml. concentrated hydrochloric acid to 93.5 ml. of 95% alcohol.

Tyrode's Solution (pH = 8.0): Contains 8 Gm. sodium chloride, 0.2 Gm. potassium chloride, 0.1 Gm. anhydrous calcium chloride, 1 Gm. sodium bicarbonate, 0.1 Gm. magnesium chloride, 0.05 Gm. acid sodium phosphate (NaH_2PO_4), 1 Gm. dextrose, and water to make 1000 ml. Dissolve the sodium bicarbonate before adding calcium chloride.

Washburn Stain (for platelets or for peroxidase stain): Dissolve 0.3 Gm. of benzidine and then an equal amount of basic fuchsin in 100 ml. of 95% alcohol. Add 1 ml. of a saturated aqueous solution of sodium nitroprusside. This stain will keep eight months. Disregard a slight precipitate which may form.

Water, Buffered, Distilled: See Buffered distilled water.

WBC Diluting Fluid: See Leukocyte diluting fluid.

Wright's Stain for Blood: Grind 0.1 Gm. of certified powdered stain in mortar, adding small amounts of absolute methyl alcohol (acetone-free). Add total of 60 ml. alcohol. Evaporation of alcohol will cause precipitate to form on slides; if this occurs, add 2 ml. of methyl alcohol per 10 ml. of staining solution.

Zenker's Fixative Solution: Requires 5 Gm. of corrosive mercuric chloride, 2.5 Gm. of potassium bichromate, 1 Gm. of sodium sulfate, and water to make 100 ml. of solution.

Zinc Sulfate Solution for Parasite Examinations: Add 331 Gm. of zinc sulfate (technical grade) to water to make 1000 ml. The sp. gr. is 1.180.

STAINING FOR EOSINOPHILS IN NASAL SECRETIONS AND SPUTUM

Prepare thin smears. Air dry.

Fix with absolute methyl alcohol 2 to 3 minutes.

Mix equal parts Jenner's (May-Grünwald) stain (see p. 625) and distilled water and flood slide. Stain 5 minutes. (May counterstain with 1% aqueous solution methylene blue 30 seconds.)

Rinse and air dry.

Enumerate eosinophils per 100 leukocytes.

Under oil immersion, enumerate eosinophils per 100 leukocytes.

DRUGS INTERFERING DIRECTLY WITH CHEMICAL TESTS*

Many drugs and metabolites react with ferric chloride and affect tests for ketone bodies, phenylpyruvic acid, homogentisic acid, and melanogen. Dyes (e.g., methylene blue, phenazopyridine, BSP, phenosulfonphthalein, indigo-carmine, indocyanine green, azure A) color plasma and urine; they affect most colorimetric procedures. Some drugs act as indicators (e.g., phenol-phthalein, vegetable laxatives) and affect tests carried out at a particular pH.

Test	Drug	Effect†	Cause
Bilirubin	Caffeine, theophylline	−	Color reaction depressed
BSP	Dyes (e.g., phenazo-pyridine)	+	Interfering color
Calcium	Edathamil (EDTA)	−	Interferes with dye-binding methods; no effect on flame methods.
Chloride	Bromide	+	Reacts like chloride
Cholesterol	Bromide	+	Enhances color when iron reagent used
	Metandienone	+	Interferes with Zimmer-man reaction
Glucose	Dextran	+	Copper complex in cop-per reduction methods
Iron	Intravenous iron-dextran	+	Total iron increased
Iron-binding capacity (unsaturated)	Intravenous iron-dextran	−	Available transferrin saturated
Protein	Dextran	−	Hemodilution
Quinidine	Triamterene	+	Interfering fluorescence
Uric acid	Ascorbic acid, theophylline	+	Phosphotungstic acid reduced
Urine			
Catechola-mines	Erythromycin, methyldopa, tetracyclines, quinine, quinidine, salicylates, hydralazine, B vitamins (high dose)	+	Interfering fluorescence
Chloride	Bromide	+	Reacts like chloride
Creatinine	Nitrofuran derivatives	+	React with color reagent
Glucose	Some vaginal powders	+	Contain glucose: urine contaminated
(Benedict's test)	Drugs excreted as glu-curonates	+	Reduce Benedict's reagent
	Salicylates	+	Excreted as salicyluric acid
	Ascorbic acid (high doses)	+	Reduces Benedict's reagent
	Chloral hydrate	+	Metabolites reduce
	Nitrofuran derivatives	+	Metabolites reduce
	Cephalothin	+	Black-brown color
5-HIAA	Phenothiazines	−	Inhibit color reaction
	Mephenesin, methocarbamol	+	Similar color reaction
17-OH steroids, 17-Ketogenic steroids 17-Keto-steroids	Meprobamate, phenothia-zines, spironolactone, penicillin G	+	Similar color reactions
	Cortisone	+	Mainly 17-OH and 17-KGS

*Reproduced, with permission, from Lubran, M.: The effects of drugs on laboratory values. M. Clin. North America **53**:211-22, 1969.

†+ Indicates a false-positive or enhanced effect; − a false-negative or dimin-ished effect.

DRUGS INTERFERING DIRECTLY WITH CHEMICAL TESTS (Cont'd.)

Test	Drug	Effect†	Cause
Urine (Cont'd.)			
Pregnanediol	Mandelamine	+	Unknown
Protein	Tolbutamide	+	Metabolite precipitated by salicylsulfonic acid and by heat and acetic acid
Phenolsulfon- phthalein	Dyes and BSP	+	Interfering colors
Uric acid	Theophylline, ascorbic acid	+	Phosphotungstic acid reduced
Vanillylman- delic acid	Mandelamine	+	Similar color

†+ Indicates a false-positive or enhanced effect; − a false-negative or diminished effect.

DRUGS AFFECTING PROTHROMBIN TIME (QUICK ONE-STAGE TEST) OF PATIENTS ON ANTICOAGULANT THERAPY WITH COUMARIN OR PHENINDIONE DERIVATIVES*

Prothrombin Time Increased By	Prothrombin Time Decreased By
Heparin	Vitamin K (in polyvitamin preparations and some diets)
Salicylates (in excess of 1 Gm./day)	
Phenylbutazone, oxyphenbutazone	Corticosteroids
Oral sulfonamides	Mineral oil
Broad-spectrum antibiotics (e. g., tetracyclines)	Barbiturates
	Antihistamines
Hydroxyzine	Chloral hydrate
Clofibrate	Diuretics
Diphenylhydantoin	Digitalis (in cardiac failure)
D-Thyroxine	Griseofulvin
Thyroid hormones	Glutethimide
Anabolic steroids (e. g., norethandrolone)	Oral contraceptives
	Xanthines (e. g., caffeine)
Metandienone	
Cholestyramine	
Indomethacin	
Quinine, quinidine	
Methylthiouracil, propylthiouracil	
Phenyramidol	
Amidopyrine	
Benziodarone	
ACTH	
Alcohol (in large amounts)	
Para-aminosalicylic acid	
Mefenamic acid	

*Reproduced, with permission, from Lubran, M.: The effects of drugs on laboratory values. M. Clin. North America 53:211-22, 1969.

CONVERSION TABLES

CENTIGRADE TO FAHRENHEIT TEMPERATURES
(1°C = 1.8°F.; 1°F. = 0.54°C.)

C°	F°	C°	F°	C°	F°	C°	F°
0 = 32	35.5 = 95.9	40 = 104	60 = 140
5 = 41	36 = 96.8	40.5 = 104.9	65 = 149
10 = 50	36.5 = 97.7	41 = 105.8	70 = 158
15 = 59	37 = 98.6	41.5 = 106.7	75 = 167
20 = 68	37.5 = 99.5	42 = 107.6	80 = 176
25 = 77	38 = 100.4	43 = 109.4	85 = 185
30 = 86	38.5 = 101.3	45 = 113	90 = 194
32 = 89.6	39 = 102.2	50 = 122	95 = 203
35 = 95	39.5 = 103.1	55 = 131	100 = 212

POUNDS TO KILOGRAMS
(1 Kg. = 2.2 lb.; 1 lb. = 0.4536 Kg.)

lb.	Kilo.	lb.	Kilo.	lb.	Kilo.	lb.	Kilo.
5	2.3	60	27.2	115	52.2	170	77.1
10	4.5	65	29.5	120	54.4	175	79.4
15	6.8	70	31.7	125	56.7	180	81.6
20	9.1	75	34.0	130	58.9	185	83.9
25	11.3	80	36.3	135	61.2	190	86.2
30	13.6	85	38.6	140	63.5	195	88.5
35	15.9	90	40.8	145	65.8	200	90.7
40	18.1	95	43.1	150	68.0	205	93.0
45	20.4	100	45.4	155	70.3	210	95.3
50	22.7	105	47.6	160	72.6	215	97.5
55	25.0	110	49.9	165	74.8	220	99.8

FEET AND INCHES TO CENTIMETERS
(1 cm. = 0.39 in.; 1 in. = 2.54 cm.)

ft.	in.	cm.	ft.	in.	cm.	ft.	in.	cm.	ft.	in.	cm.
0	6	15.2	2	7	78.7	3	10	116.8	5	1	154.9
1	0	30.5	2	8	81.2	3	11	119.3	5	2	157.5
1	6	45.7	2	9	83.8	4	0	121.9	5	3	160.0
1	7	48.3	2	10	86.3	4	1	124.4	5	4	162.6
1	8	50.8	2	11	88.8	4	2	127.0	5	5	165.1
1	9	53.3	3	0	91.4	4	3	129.5	5	6	167.6
1	10	55.9	3	1	93.9	4	4	132.0	5	7	170.2
1	11	58.4	3	2	96.4	4	5	134.6	5	8	172.7
2	0	61.0	3	3	99.0	4	6	137.1	5	9	175.3
2	1	63.5	3	4	101.6	4	7	139.6	5	10	177.8
2	2	66.0	3	5	104.1	4	8	142.2	5	11	180.3
2	3	68.6	3	6	106.6	4	9	144.7	6	0	182.9
2	4	71.1	3	7	109.2	4	10	147.3	6	1	185.4
2	5	73.6	3	8	111.7	4	11	149.8	6	2	188.0
2	6	76.1	3	9	114.2	5	0	152.4	6	3	190.5

ELEMENTS AND ATOMIC WEIGHTS

Name	Symbol	Atomic Number	Atomic Weight	Valence	Sp. Gr.
Aluminum	Al	13	26.97	3	2.7
Antimony (stibium)	Sb	51	121.76	3, 5	6.6
Arsenic	As	33	74.91	3, 5	5.7
Barium	Ba	56	137.36	2	3.8
Bismuth	Bi	83	209.00	3, 5	9.7
Bromine	Br	35	79.916	1	3.1
Calcium	Ca	20	40.08	2	1.5
Carbon	C	6	12.01	2, 4	3.5
Chlorine	Cl	17	35.457	1	1.5
Chromium	Cr	24	52.01	2, 3, 6	6.9
Cobalt	Co	27	58.94	2, 3	8.7
Copper	Cu	29	63.57	1, 2	8.3
Fluorine	F	9	19.00	1	1.1
Gold (aurum)	Au	79	197.2	1, 3	19.3
Helium (liquid)	He	2	4.003	0	0.15
Hydrogen (liquid)	H	1	1.008	1	0.07
Iodine	I	53	126.932	1	4.9
Iron (ferrum)	Fe	26	55.85	2, 3	7.8
Lead (plumbum)	Pb	82	207.21	2, 4	11.3
Lithium	Li	3	6.940	1	0.53
Magnesium	Mg	12	24.32	2	1.7
Manganese	Mn	25	54.93	2, 4, 6, 7	7.4
Mercury (hydrargyrum)	Hg	80	200.61	1, 2	13.6
Molybdenum	Mo	42	96.95	3, 4, 6	9.0
Nickel	Ni	28	58.69	2, 3	8.6
Nitrogen (liquid)	N	7	14.008	3, 5	0.81
Oxygen (liquid)	O	8	16.0000	2, 3, 4, 8	1.1
Palladium	Pd	46	106.7	2, 4	12.1
Phosphorus	P	15	31.02	3, 5	1.8+
Platinum	Pt	78	195.23	2, 4	21.4
Potassium (kalium)	K	19	39.10	1	0.87
Radium	Rd or Ra	88	226.05	2	...
Radon (niton)	Rn	86	222.	0	...
Selenium	Se	34	78.96	2, 4, 6	4.3
Silicon	Si	14	28.06	4	2.4
Silver (argentum)	Ag	47	107.880	1	10.5
Sodium (natrium)	Na	11	22.997	1	0.97
Strontium	Sr	38	87.63	2	2.5
Sulfur	S	16	32.06	2, 4, 6	2.0
Tin (stannum)	Sn	50	118.70	2, 4	7.3
Tungsten (wolframium)	W	74	184.0	6	18.6
Uranium	U	92	238.07	4, 6	18.7
Vanadium	V	23	50.95	3, 5	5.7
Zinc	Zn	40	91.22	4	7.0

DESIRABLE WEIGHT TABLES (IN POUNDS)

This table was derived primarily from data of the Build and Blood Pressure Study, 1959, Society of Actuaries.

Men (Age 25 and Over)

Height* Feet Inches		Small Frame	Medium Frame	Large Frame
5	2	112-120	118-129	126-141
5	3	115-123	121-133	129-144
5	4	118-126	124-136	132-148
5	5	121-129	127-139	135-152
5	6	124-133	130-143	138-156
5	7	128-137	134-147	142-161
5	8	132-141	138-152	147-166
5	9	136-145	142-156	151-170
5	10	140-150	146-160	155-174
5	11	144-154	150-165	159-179
6	0	148-158	154-170	164-184
6	1	152-162	158-175	168-189
6	2	156-167	162-180	173-194
6	3	160-171	167-185	178-199
6	4	164-175	172-190	182-204

*With shoes with one-inch heels.

Women† (Age 25 and Over)

Height‡ Feet Inches		Small Frame	Medium Frame	Large Frame
4	10	92-98	96-107	104-119
4	11	94-101	98-110	106-122
5	0	96-104	101-113	109-125
5	1	99-107	104-116	112-128
5	2	102-110	107-119	115-131
5	3	105-113	110-122	118-134
5	4	108-116	113-126	121-138
5	5	111-119	116-130	125-142
5	6	114-123	120-135	129-146
5	7	118-127	124-139	133-150
5	8	121-131	128-143	137-154
5	9	126-135	132-147	141-158
5	10	130-140	136-151	145-163
5	11	134-144	140-155	149-168
6	0	138-148	144-159	153-173

†For girls between 18-25, subtract 1 pound for each year under 25. ‡With shoes with two-inch heels.

AVERAGE HEIGHT AND WEIGHT FOR CHILDREN

Age Years	BOYS					GIRLS				
	Height			Weight		Height			Weight	
	ft.	in.	cm.	lb.	Kg.	ft.	in.	cm.	lb.	Kg.
Birth	1	8	45.7	7½	3.4	1	8	50.8	7½	3.4
½	2	2	66.0	17	7.7	2	2	66.0	16	7.2
1	2	5	73.6	21	9.5	2	5	73.6	20	9.1
2	2	9	83.8	26	11.8	2	9	83.8	25	11.3
3	3	0	91.4	31	14.0	3	0	91.4	30	13.6
4	3	3	99.0	34	15.4	3	3	99.0	33	15.0
5	3	6	106.6	39	17.7	3	5	104.1	38	17.2
6	3	9	114.2	46	20.9	3	8	111.7	45	20.4
7	3	11	119.3	51	23.1	3	11	119.3	49	22.2
8	4	2	127.0	57	25.9	4	2	127.0	56	25.4
9	4	4	132.0	63	28.6	4	4	132.0	62	28.1
10	4	6	137.1	69	31.3	4	6	137.1	69	31.3
11	4	8	142.2	77	34.9	4	8	142.2	77	34.9
12	4	10	147.3	83	37.7	4	10	147.3	86	39.0
13	5	0	152.4	92	41.7	5	0	152.4	98	45.5
14	5	2	157.5	107	48.5	5	2	157.5	107	48.5

634

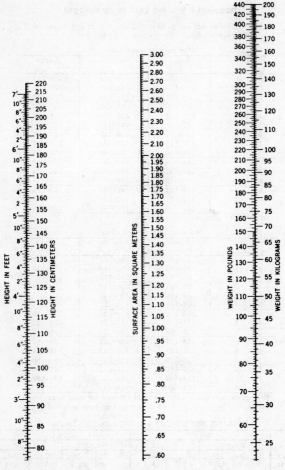

Nomogram for the Determination of Body Surface Area of
Children and Adults. (Reproduced, with permission, from
W. M. Boothby and R. B. Sandiford, Boston M. & S. J. **185:**
337, 1921.)

Formula for Calculating Approximate Surface Area in Children.

Surface Area (sq. m.) = $\frac{4 W + 7}{W + 90}$, where W is weight in Kg.

Index